NEW ENGLAND REDWARE PITCHER

EARLY NEW ENGLAND POTTERS AND THEIR WARES

Lura Woodside Watkins

HARVARD UNIVERSITY PRESS · CAMBRIDGE

1950

Distributed in Great Britain by
Geoffrey Cumberlege, Oxford University Press, London

Printed in the United States of America

TO MALCOLM, my son
whose sympathetic understanding
has been an inspiration

Preface

This book is the result of more than fifteen years of research. The study has been carried on, partly in libraries and town records, partly by conferences with descendants of potters and others familiar with their history, and partly by actual digging on the sites of potteries. The excavation method has proved most successful in showing what our New England potters were making at an early period now almost unrepresented by surviving specimens.

Over all these years I have had the willing assistance of many persons, whom I here wish to thank publicly. Two of them have been of immeasurable help in forwarding the publication of the book: Mr. Curt H. Reisinger and Mr. David McCord. To Mr. Reisinger I owe a boundless debt of gratitude for his very practical aid and to Mr. McCord my devoted thanks for the time he has spent and the moral support he has given when the end was uncertain.

Some friends have coöperated by research in records or by the gift of documentary material or notes which they themselves have made. Among these are Miss Margaret H. Jewell, of Portland, Maine; Prof. Frederick H. Norton, of the Massachusetts Institute of Technology; Mr. Arthur W. Clement, of Brooklyn, New York; Miss Edna M. Hoxie, of Berkley, Massachusetts; Mrs. H. H. Buxton, of Peabody, Massachusetts; Mr. Albert N. Peterson, of Providence, Rhode Island; Mr. Austin G. Packard, of Ashfield, Massachusetts; and Mrs. Mabel M. Swan, of Scituate, Massachusetts. In this field the historical societies have also been most helpful. I am especially grateful to Mr. Fred W. Bushby, of the Peabody Historical Society, for the loan of a large collection of notes, to Mr. F. W. Hutt, of the Old Colony Historical Society at Taunton, and to Mr. Elmer M. Hunt, of the New Hampshire Historical Society.

For information freely given and for aid in locating sites I am indebted to Mrs. Helen F. Adams, Mr. Horace Bardwell, Mrs. Harriet E. Brown, Mrs. Carrie B. Carpenter, Mrs. Ada Hunt Chase, Miss Mary Persis Crafts, Mrs. W. J. Craig, Mrs. Elizabeth Davis, Mrs. Kelsey Flower, Miss Helen Holley, Miss Annie Stilphen, Miss Daisy Waterhouse, and Miss Grace Wheeler. Mr. John Norton Brooks and Mr. George A. Risley, both descendants of potters, have contributed much by the loan of original account books and the gift of photographs.

Especial thanks are due those patient people who have cheerfully allowed us to dig up their lawns and yards. For this I am particularly under obligation to Miss Louise Hanson and to Mr. and Mrs. Chester T. Cutler and their young son, Thomas Allen, who recovered at Danvers the earliest slip-decorated shard that can be attributed to any known potter and place in America. The trustees of Ravenswood Park in Gloucester were also most kind in permitting excavation on their land.

A few devotees have done the hard work

of digging. First and foremost among them is my husband, Charles Hadley Watkins, whose enthusiasm has been almost as great as my own. Others who have put their backs into it are our nephew Thomas P. Watkins and our good friends Charles S. Livingstone and Richard H. Marchant. My gratitude to them all!

And lastly I would like to thank Russell B. Harding, my photographer, who has put untold hours and energy into the making of fine illustrations for the book, and to Forrest Orr, who has subordinated a great artistic talent to the business of making the line drawings in Chapter XXIX.

Lura Woodside Watkins

Winchester, Massachusetts
May 1949

Contents

Introduction

I Techniques 5

II Seventeenth-Century Potters 13

III James Kettle's Shard Pile 21

IV The Provincial Potters of Charlestown 24

V A Potter's Daybook 30

VI A Woman Introduces Stoneware 34

VII Redware Potting from Boston to the Cape 39

VIII Excavations on the Bayley Sites of 1723–1799 48

IX The Osborns of Danvers and Other Essex County Potters 62

X The Quaker Potters of Bristol County 74

XI Stoneware Potting in Eastern Massachusetts 80

XII Some Potteries of Central and Western Massachusetts 92

XIII The Whately and Ashfield Group 101

XIV Pioneer Craftsmen of New Hampshire 110

XV The Clarks of Lyndeboro and Concord 120

XVI North of Concord 130

XVII Redware Potters of Vermont 136

CONTENTS

XVIII Vermont Stoneware Potteries 141

XIX Early Maine Potteries 155

XX The Maine Industry After 1800 160

XXI Early Connecticut Redware and the Goshen Group 171

XXII The States Family of Greenwich and Stonington 178

XXIII Potters of New London County 184

XXIV Hartford and New Haven Potteries 192

XXV Pots and Dishes of Norwalk 198

XXVI Rhode Island 207

XXVII Bennington and Kindred Developments 211

XXVIII The Art Potteries 222

XXIX Redware Forms 234

APPENDICES

I Documents Relating to the Parkers of Charlestown 245

II Check List of New England Potters 249

III Bibliography 271

LIST OF ILLUSTRATIONS 277

INDEX 281

PLATES 293

EARLY NEW ENGLAND POTTERS AND THEIR WARES

Introduction

New England pottery falls into four categories: first, common red earthenware fashioned from native clay; second, stoneware, made of materials brought from outside the New England states; third, wares of buff or white body cast in molds for mass production, typified by Fenton's Bennington output; fourth, decorative pottery designed by trained artists. This book is primarily concerned with the first two classifications — the work of the traditional potters. For the sake of completeness, however, chapters on the later developments have been added.

Since redware was the only type of pottery generally made here before the Revolution, it presents an unusual degree of interest to the historian and the artist. Its manufacture (in the old sense of handcraft) has been so far forgotten that in the next generation such knowledge as I have here assembled would have been lost forever. And yet, it is one of the very few folk arts that have been practiced by Anglo-Saxons on this side of the Atlantic.

The growth of this craft in New England was subjected to far different influences than was that of the Pennsylvania-German potters. When the Germans came to Pennsylvania, the country had been occupied for more than one hundred years. They brought with them a fully developed traditional art which they were free to express here as they had in their home land. In New England, potters arrived with the first contingents of the pioneer settlers and had to work under the most adverse conditions. Of necessity, their time was occupied in making utilitarian vessels. Although they had doubtless learned in England the arts and refinements of decoration, they had little opportunity to practice them here. The need for useful objects was greater than the urge to elaborate them. Thus, after two or three generations in the harsh life of the pioneer community, they lost the ability for conscious artistic expression in this medium. There is little play of fancy in the early decorated wares, such as they were, but rather an insistence upon the geometrical that is akin to contemporary Indian art.

Simple though New England redware may be, it is nevertheless sturdy and vigorous in form and it has a charm that is difficult to define. Lustrous glazes, soft colors, and shapes of good proportion combine to make a virile, handsome ware. Earthy by its very nature, with its suggestion of soil, leaves, and trees, it captures the essence of the early potter's environment. That its beauty is largely accidental makes it no less lovable: its variations are like the changes of Nature herself, never ending, ever yielding fresh enjoyment. It is truly an expression of simple people — men almost without conscious thought of art. Like them their pottery is strong, direct, stripped of pretense and foolish ornamentation. It was created to fill a demand, and, incidentally, to please those who came to buy.

Red earthenware is one of the least durable ceramic types. Porous and brittle, easily cracked and chipped, it has not survived in quantity sufficient to give more than the slightest hint of its once widespread use in New England. Unlike the finer English earthenware and porcelain owned by the

colonists, it was intended for the humbler domestic purposes. It was a pottery for the kitchen and the dairy and, far more frequently than is supposed, for the table. The myth of the colonists having nothing but wood and pewter for tableware must be discounted. The wood and pewter have survived; the redware, except for shards in potters' dumps, has not. Its cheapness and fragility contributed to its disappearance from the household effects that were so carefully handed on from one generation to another. Today there are to be found only occasional rare pieces from the eighteenth century and, except in fragmentary form, virtually none from earlier pioneer days. In fact, redware of any period is so little known that many persons have never become conscious of its existence. Neither the potters nor their wares hold a position in history commensurate with their one-time importance.

The list of New England potters is such a long one that it is little less than amazing to find almost no mention of them in historical records. Grist mills, saw mills, blacksmiths' and shoemakers' shops are noted over and over, but potteries almost never. Neither have our writers on American ceramics given us any appreciation of the extent of the potting industry. When one glances at the appended check list and sees the roster of two hundred and fifty or more potters who were working in New England before 1800 and of more than five hundred who were engaged in this craft in a small way before 1850, one comes to a realization that they have been neglected. Perhaps because the later craftsmen sold their wares from peddlers' carts, a snobbish attitude towards them arose. Nevertheless, the earlier men frequently entered this trade from the finest and most respected families and they themselves often had positions of responsibility in their communities.

Clay, however, was a humble material, found in abundance, and the products of clay could be bought for a few pence. The potter's workshop was often only a shed and his tools cost comparatively little. In a country where big business and expansion was the goal even in those earliest days of shipping fish across the ocean, it is no wonder that these small craftsmen were doomed to oblivion.

In colonial days a potter's shop was to be found in nearly every town of any consequence. The artisan worked in the native glacial clay, which in New England could be dug almost anywhere near the seacoast or bodies of water. Often the potter turned his ware in some convenient shelter on his own homestead — a shed or the end of the barn would serve his purpose — and frequently he eked out a living by farming or fishing. A good workman could make enough pottery to supply a fair-sized village and still have time for husbandry. Potting was a seasonal occupation. Clay was dug in the fall, dried through the winter, and the wares, made whenever occasion offered, were burned in the warm weather.

Potshops were usually manned by three or four persons. The owner or master potter did most of the work of "throwing" or turning the ware. For assistants he perhaps had one or two boys and a man to take charge of the kiln and the burning. The apprentice system was in vogue, and lads of fourteen were indentured to master workmen for a period of seven years. This long course of training insured that the young men would eventually attain a high degree of skill, that they would be able to turn out ware in the exact proportions required and with the utmost speed. Frequently the master's own children were trained in their father's craft. While sons and apprentices did not always practice their art after they reached the age of twenty-one, many of them did remain in

the trade, and it is not unusual to find potteries carried on by one family through four or five generations and for one hundred years or more. Occasionally a number of families, united in the craft, worked together, bringing the making of pottery to something like an industry, but it was never conducted on the large scale of a factory. Potting of this order was unknown before the nineteenth century.

The colonial redware potter may truly be called a "folk" artisan. Each craftsman handed on to his sons or apprentices whatever knowledge he had acquired. Techniques, forms, and decorations were wholly traditional, with little variation before 1800. These potters as a class were uninfluenced by any developments in the commercial potteries of England — a fact that is equally true of the common clay workers of that country. They pursued their own course, knowing that their customers would be satisfied with the wares so long familiar to them. Until changing conditions in the nineteenth century brought about a revolution in the manufacture of kitchen utensils, both potters and buyers knew what to expect of one another. Certain pots and pans for cooking, certain dishes for the table, certain jars for preserves or butter were the household requirements. Now and then a potter somewhat timidly attempted embellishment of one sort or another. His apprentices were likely to copy his mannerisms, with the result that some distinguishing features may point to certain origins. Otherwise, unless some identifying decoration was employed, the redware pottery reveals nothing of its source. It is rarely marked — never until a late period — and it remains a mystery for the enjoyment of those who like a thing for what it is rather than for a name impressed upon it.

The New England pottery tradition had its roots in the soil of England and Europe, but it grew in this country along lines of its own, dictated by the needs of a pioneer environment. From such traditional handcraft, creating beauty as a by-product of necessity, the folk art develops. That New England folk potters never attained the richness of expression shown by their contemporaries in Europe is easily understood. Simple living, with simple wants, and the Puritan dislike of ostentation restrained any exuberance they might have displayed during the early period, while the rapid changes of the Revolution and the subsequent trend towards industrialism destroyed the later practice of traditional handcraft. This American ware did, however, achieve a considerable degree of beauty which should be properly evaluated before it entirely disappears from our culture.

Bernard Rackham and Herbert Read in their invaluable work *English Pottery* have laid down a few criteria for judging ceramic design that could hardly be better expressed. I venture to quote a few passages:

> The form of an earthenware vessel should in the first place be strictly appropriate to its use. It may be unfailingly demonstrated that all departures from utilitarian form, *when the intention is utilitarian*, weakens the aesthetic appeal. We do not mean to imply, however, that purely decorative forms are not appropriate to earthenware technique; but in that case a different canon of aesthetic criticism must be applied. . .
>
> In addition to symmetry and balance, a good vessel possesses *vitality*, a quality due to the instinct of the potter. Symmetry and balance do not necessarily imply vitality, which is a less obvious characteristic, due to the suggestibility of the lines and mass of a vessel. The eye registers and the mind experiences in the contemplation of energetic lines and masses a sense of movement, rhythm, or harmony which may indeed be the prime cause of all aesthetic pleasure.

The same authors, in common with many others, believe that the best decoration on pottery is abstract, "conforming to the abstract nature of the ceramic art." It should emphasize rather than oppose the form and mass of a vessel; "a 'leaf-fringed legend' about its shape is likely to detract attention from the essential properties of that shape. Any such 'legend' should never interfere with the *repose* of the vessel; the vessel should be completely satisfactory from *one and any* point of view."

Judged by these standards of balance, vitality, and suitable decoration, much of our early New England redware falls into the category of fine art. Its symmetry is not the mechanical perfection of the modern factory product; its decoration often represents the difficult attempt at variation of surface made under the most restricted limitations of materials; but it does have vitality. And, most important of all, it is successful as a useful ware. In addition to that, it pleases the eye, especially in surroundings similar to those for which it was originally intended. Its preeminent qualities are sturdiness and repose.

CHAPTER ONE

Techniques

Until the latter part of the eighteenth century New England potters made redware only, since the local glacial clay was suitable for no other purpose. It was the same material from which common bricks were made. At first, the potters found this clay sufficient for their every need; later, when they wished to meet the ever-increasing demand for stoneware, they were obliged to transport clays from New York, New Jersey, or Pennsylvania.

The essential equipment of an early pottery was a clay mill for washing and breaking up the clay, a smaller mill for grinding glaze, one or more wheels for turning ware, shelves for drying it, and a kiln for burning. In addition there would be an assortment of kettles, sieves, crocks, and tubs used in preparing the ingredients.

Clay for coarser objects was not cleaned with a great deal of care, although it was washed and the pebbles picked out by hand. Mixed with water, it was put through the clay or "pug" mill. Eighteenth-century mills were made of stones similar to those of a grist mill, laboriously chipped into shape by hand. I have found numerous references to these early stones (see Chapter XV). They were superseded in the early nineteenth century by a tub or half hogshead in which blades attached to a central shaft were revolved by a horse hitched to a capstan bar. In this simple apparatus the clay was broken and churned about, allowing stones and other extraneous matter to sink to the bottom, while the cleaned clay and water ran off. After being washed, the wet clay was made into balls and stored away until needed. Before it could be used on the wheel, however, the prepared lumps had to be kneaded, in order to eliminate air bubbles and to make them of an even consistency. Finally the clay was divided into sections of the approximate size desired for various articles. In later practice the amounts were determined by weighing, but it is probable that more haphazard methods prevailed in colonial days.

Early redware was made almost entirely by "throwing" upon the potter's wheel. In southwestern Connecticut alone do we find any evidence of the use of molds, and then only for pie plates and platters or trays. Molds belong to the era of mass production. In the later period they were adopted by some of the larger potteries, which thus strayed away from the traditions of the craft. The small men still kept to the wheel. The old "kick" wheel was operated by foot power. It was constructed with a heavy fly-

wheel on the lower part, which was connected by a vertical shaft to a disc of heavy wood (usually lignum vitae) or iron above. The lower wheel, in the most primitive apparatus, was turned by direct pressure from the potter's foot, or, in another type, by means of a treadle connected to the shaft. Upon the "head," or plate, the potter placed his lump of clay, which took shape under his skillful hands, while the wheel revolved slowly or rapidly, as he desired. After the vessel was formed, it was carefully detached from the wheel, sometimes by running a wire under it, and transferred to a board placed near the workman's seat. The process was repeated until the board was filled with a dozen or more pieces, when it was carried away and replaced with another. In summer these boards, pots and all, were set out in the sun for the ware to dry; in winter, they could be left in a warm place near the kiln. Large wooden pegs driven into the wall of the shop provided a resting place for them when they were not in use elsewhere. After a few days the ware was ready for glazing.

Lead is the principal ingredient in the glaze on redware. Powdered galena (lead sulfide) was employed in England; red lead or litharge in this country. There are records of importations of lead from England in the early seventeenth century. In New England the powdered lead was mixed with a quantity of sand or fine loam screened through a horsehair sieve, water was added, and the whole ground to a creamy consistency in the glaze mill. In some potteries ground glass was added to the glaze compound in the effort to produce a hard brilliant surface.

A glaze mill apparatus was formed of two small mill stones, the lower having a trough or spout by which the liquid mixture could run into a pot or other container. In grinding glaze, the upper stone was turned laboriously by hand. Such a mill, from the pottery of Hervey Brooks in Goshen, Connecticut, is illustrated in Fig. 4. It is described by the potter's grandson, John Norton Brooks, as follows:

> This machine, for it could have been so called one hundred and twenty-five years ago, when it was probably in use, is made out of a solid piece of native granite, chiseled roughly on the outside edge and tooled on the upper surface of the rim. The revolving grinding disc is apparently made from the same piece of granite, and the stone mason's work is so perfect that there is a full sized grinding area in the whole interior. The revolving piece has mounted in it a wrought iron forging with a hole in the center which engages a pin in the center of the base. The wooden pin is about seven inches long.
>
> The mode of operation was to pour the pigment to be ground together with the required amount of water in the center hole, then the wooden pin was placed in the drilled hole of the upper member, and with this pin the disc was revolved, grinding the pigment in the water until it had worked its way across the stone and run out of the outlet. The apparatus is still in working order and the grinding disc can be easily removed.

Almost all pots except flower pots or water coolers were given a glaze either on one surface or on both. If the object to be glazed was an ordinary cooking utensil or pan, the potter poured some of the mixture into the vessel, washed it around a bit, and drained off the surplus. He then wiped the edge of the piece and set it aside to dry. If the ware was to be glazed both inside and outside, the workman held it by the base and dipped it in the glaze tub, taking care that the glaze should not run down on the base when the piece was set upright. The compound of lead and silica formed a glassy and brilliant surface on the ware when it was burned. After firing, it had a transparent yellowish color, according to the basic hue of the clay. That is, the color is in the body and not in the glaze. Red clay, while sometimes fine and

smooth, generally contains numerous impurities, as did also the glaze materials. When the pottery was burned, these imperfections produced charming and doubtless unexpected colorings. Mottlings and streakings of orange, green, brown, and red made pleasing variations on the surface of the ware, adding to its decorative quality. Irregularities in the temperature of the kiln during burning also caused similar changes of color.

There were only one or two ways by which a potter could intentionally change the color of his ware. One method was to make a brown or black glaze by the addition of manganese. A small quantity of this inexpensive material would produce brown in shades from light tan to deepest chocolate; a greater proportion — about one part of manganese to nine of lead — gave black. The black glaze, often extremely brilliant, was used principally for mugs, jugs, pitchers, and teapots. Some potters made an excellent green by calcining brass or copper filings and incorporating a small quantity of the resulting oxides with the glaze. Since this was a more difficult and costly process, green was reserved mostly for decoration, and it is only rarely that we find a jug or a jar wholly glazed with a true green.

That the early potter was not unconscious of the decorative possibilities of color is certain; but he was limited in his choice of materials and in the colors he could produce on red clay. Cobalt blue, for instance, when added to clear lead glaze and applied to a redware body, produces black. Within the range of color possible with a clear glaze or those stained with manganese or ferrous oxides, the potter got an astonishing number of effects. Plain red or brown surfaces were frequently daubed with brown or black splashes applied with the fingers or with a brush. In the course of burning, the darker color blended into the background or flowed softly down the sides of the vessel. This method of splashing was perhaps derived from the Dutch potters. Ware so treated is to be seen in pictures of Dutch interiors painted by seventeenth-century artists. An interesting example occurs in Adriaen Brouwer's "Pancake Turner" (Johnson Collection, Philadelphia Museum). This type of work appears more frequently in Connecticut, where continental European influence was pronounced, than in northern New England. Fragments found at Danvers and Newburyport show, however, that it was a general practice. Occasionally small spots of dark glaze were spattered on or made to flow down in fine streakings. The jar in Fig. 50 is an example of such intentional effort at decoration. Bands of brown were brushed on the edges of bowls with similar results. Other variations within the color range of the New England potter were grayish tones produced by the addition of a small quantity of white slip to the glaze mixture, spatterings of green on lighter green or grayish grounds, and mixtures of white and green glazes applied with a brush.

A few potters, especially in the early period, made attempts at simple decoration by incising or tooling lines on the body of the ware before it was glazed. This was accomplished by holding a pointed instrument against the vessel while it was slowly turned around on the wheel. Wavy bands of apparent complexity were tooled with a small metal comb having four or more points. This style is found particularly in Essex County, Massachusetts. Incising on redware was not altogether successful, because the lead glaze flowed into the toolings, partly obscuring them. Bold ridges in bands, like those on the Bayley mugs (Fig. 18), are more effective.

Slip decoration was generally practiced throughout New England before 1800 and to a lesser degree until 1860. Ware so ornamented turns up more frequently in Connecticut than elsewhere, because it was made

later there, but the method was not limited to Connecticut potteries. We unearthed quantities of slip-decorated ware at the site of the Bayley pottery in Newburyport, Massachusetts, and have found occasional fragments in such widely-separated places as Dorset, Vermont, and Danvers, Whately, and Weston, Massachusetts. Accordingly, we may attribute this type of decoration to early potteries in general, realizing that the bulk of plain earthenware extant today was made at a relatively late period. A slip-decorated pan dated 1830 (Fig. 55) was made as a christening gift for a child in East Kingston, New Hampshire, only five miles from Exeter, where it undoubtedly originated.

In decorating with slip a liquid white or "pipe" clay was trailed on the body of the ware before it was glazed. The process was carried out by the use of a clay cup with one or more quills inserted in it, through which the slip might be poured in much the same way as a cook ices a birthday cake. By dexterous twists of the hand the potter was able to get a number of interesting effects, although he usually limited his efforts to a series of fine lines, zigzags, or irregular scrolls. Connecticut potters, who were responsible for most of the pie plates with notched edges, frequently trailed names or other lettering upon them. Such inscriptions as "Mince Pie," "Lemon Pie," or "Sarah's Dish" are not uncommon. They, too, sometimes used a multiple quill cup, as did the Pennsylvania potters, while a single quill was the rule in northern New England. In early specimens, tiny dots of green were spattered over the trailed lines. Plates were sometimes brushed with green and light-colored slips before being decorated. The application of slip with a brush is uncommon, but the results are bold and striking. Specimens so treated are generally very early.

Another use of white slip, found in the Bayley pottery and on pieces from other sources, may have been suggested by the practice of Dutch Delft potters, who were accustomed to spread a coating of white over a darker body. The Dutch used tin enamel glaze over a buff body; our New England potters put white clay over the red body of their vessels and then washed them with a clear lead glaze. When finished, the pottery was light yellow in color wherever the slip was applied. I have seen this process employed on pans, jars, bowls, and washbowls. The bowls were glazed black on the exterior, but the other pieces show the common red body outside. The washbowls were further decorated with spongings of brown. The example illustrated (Fig. 29) is twelve and one-half inches in diameter. Large parts of another bowl found in the Bayley pottery place the type as of the eighteenth century. It is probable that American potters in making light-colored wares were trying to approximate the appearance of the English country earthenware from Staffordshire and Bristol. Having a buff clay for body, the English reversed the color process in slip decoration. Their ground was yellow and their slip for decorating was stained brown with manganese. Yellow dishes and mugs, striped or dotted with brown, or sometimes beautifully combed, were a common English type in the seventeenth and eighteenth centuries.

Notched-edge plates and oval or rectangular platters with elaborate trailings and combings of black, white, and green slips on a dark ground are found in Massachusetts and Connecticut. I have several of these colorful pieces. One shows a certain regularity of design; another is a crude attempt at marbling. Such work is also found on mugs, porringers, jars, chambers, and other objects. After questioning many people and seeing numerous collections, I have come to the conclusion that ware of this type was made outside of New England, especially as

I have never found the slightest evidence in the form of shards of its manufacture here.

After being decorated and glazed, the ware was again allowed to dry for a time and was then stacked in the kiln. In early times redware kilns were simple structures designed to burn wood and were built with bricks made from the same clay used for the ware itself. Kiln bricks were somewhat larger than ordinary house bricks, measuring approximately nine by four by two and one-half inches. In every early site where I have uncovered the remains of a kiln I have found this to be true. These dimensions were, in fact, so generally adhered to that I discovered Daniel Bayley's 1750 pottery by this means alone.

Frederick H. Norton has studied and measured the wood-burning kilns at Exeter and Gonic, New Hampshire. The one at Exeter is typical. Rectangular in form, with a sprung arch crown or ceiling, it had three fire arches for the fuel. Just above them was the floor of the kiln, in which were holes for the escape of gases. Holes in the crown permitted the smoke to pass out and up through trap doors in the roof of the kiln house. A door at one end gave entrance to the interior of the structure. This was bricked up at each burning, although a peek hole above it allowed the potter to watch the temperature of the ware inside. Experience enabled him to judge when it was hot enough and when it was time to open the kiln. Although trial pieces were inserted for testing, the whole operation was a bit similar to the ways of old-fashioned housewives with their cooking: the results were usually successful, but not invariably so. Since the structure would bear no greater heat than the earthenware within it, the brickwork of the kiln was bound around with iron bands to prevent its collapse in case of too high a temperature. The highest temperature reached in firing was about 1800°.

In stacking or "setting" the kiln no saggers were used. The ware was placed directly upon the floor and then piled up closely, one piece upon another. Potters knew many ingenious tricks for burning the greatest possible number of vessels at one time. Large pots were placed upside down with smaller objects underneath them. Jugs or pitchers were set between the pots. Milk pans or plates were stood on edge, one inside the other, in rows the length of the kiln. Every available inch was occupied. Clay fashioned by hand into various shapes prevented contact between the pieces. Setting tiles, or flat slabs of clay, were perhaps the most common type of support. Laid on top of a tier of pots, they provided a resting place for the next row above. Bowls were set one inside the other with three-pointed cockspurs or stilts of clay to separate them. Such tripods of burned clay (Fig. 6) are to be found in all early pottery dumps. They were hastily squeezed into shape by hand and often bear the potter's finger prints. In some later potteries, strips of clay molded in triangular form were cut to the required lengths and put together to make cockspurs — a slight advance over the hand method. Rings made of thin strips of clay were also used as supports.

The burning took from thirty to thirty-six hours, occupying rather less time than in English potteries where coal was used. The ware had to be burned at a comparatively moderate temperature, because too great heat made it collapse. It was impossible to regulate the wood fires to a nicety and many a kilnful of ware must have been destroyed by the carelessness or inattention of workmen who watched the kiln overnight. The temperature was brought to its highest point during the second half of burning. The fires were then allowed to die down and the furnace and its contents to cool. A. Aikins, in a lecture on the manufacture of pottery before the Royal Institution in London, 1833,

said: "If the air has been still during the burning, and due care has been observed, the articles in every part of the kiln will be properly baked; but a high wind always renders the heat very unequal, so that the ware in the windward part of the kiln will not be baked enough, while that in the leeward part will be over-burnt, and run to a slag." Many pieces of redware, darker on one side than on the other, show evidence of these irregularities.

Redware was rarely marked, except when made for presentation. Then the name or date was sometimes incised. At least two examples have the date *1808* within an incised wreath; one, a straight-sided jar bearing the initials *L M*; the other, a jug marked *J G*. The latter may be seen in the museum at Old Sturbridge Village, Massachusetts. The source of these pieces has not been ascertained. The name *Edward Towle* has been seen scratched in a similar manner on the cover of a small jar. During the later period of redware making, a few potters used hand stamps to identify their products. A small greenish-yellow jar owned by Mrs. Earle E. Andrews is stamped *John M. Safford/ Stew Pot.* Safford was working in Monmouth, Maine, in 1855. Thomas Crafts of Whately, Massachusetts, used the mark *T. Crafts & Co.* on milk pans, while Hervey Brooks of Goshen, Connecticut, had a similar stamp: *H. Brooks.* The Brooks mark I have seen on lard pots and stove tubes.

Stoneware is a hard pottery, burned at a high temperature and glazed with common salt or with a wash of dark brown clay known as "Albany slip." Its compact body makes it a perfect container for liquids, and it is impervious to the action of acids. In this respect it is greatly superior to the wares made from red-burning clays. New England clays cannot be burned successfully at a temperature high enough to produce such a dense and vitreous ware. The only New England clay that could possibly be used for the purpose is found on Martha's Vineyard, but it has been proved unsuitable without an admixture of other material. This lack of stoneware clay explains why the first potters were limited to the production of earthenware and why no stoneware was made during the first one hundred years. The potters of New York, New Jersey, and Philadelphia, having a plentiful supply of proper material near at hand, were turning out stoneware at a much earlier date. It was only after the colonies had been settled for some time and transportation had become less difficult that clay was brought from New Jersey and the manufacture of this superior pottery begun.

Aikins' 1833 account of stoneware making in England, where the methods were probably quite similar to those employed here, says that for an article of great compactness the clay was used either alone or mixed with a small quantity of sand. For very large vessels, refuse stoneware, ground to a fine powder, was added; while, in superior wares, ground flint was a component. By these means an extremely firm body could be made. New England stoneware was not always as good as the best English product. It was frequently porous to the point of absorbing water, either from insufficient firing or from the practice of adding a portion of red clay. New Jersey clay was expensive, while the native red clay cost virtually nothing. It was, therefore, a matter of economy for the potters to make their imported material go as far as possible.

Whatever the mixture, it was put through a pug mill with water and prepared as usual for the potter's wheel. Nearly all early stoneware articles were turned, although mid-nineteenth-century pottery was sometimes shaped in molds. When formed, the vessels had to be carefully dried and were then arranged in the kiln. Wads of clay mixed with sand were squeezed into convenient shapes for separat-

ing the pots so they would not stick together. Bars and slabs were cut for setting tiles, and not infrequently discs or doughnut-shaped pieces were placed between jugs and jars as they were piled one above another. Quantities of the peculiar devices of this kind are scattered about stoneware shard piles (Fig. 8).

In order to give the pots a fine brown color, it was customary in England to dip the tops and bottoms of the vessels in a slip stained with red ocher. This practice, especially in the earlier potteries, was not unknown in New England. Pieces marked *Boston* or *Boston/ 1804* were so treated, and Charlestown stoneware was sometimes given an all-over brown stain. As a rule, however, New England stoneware is a light gray or buff. According to Solon, German potters obtained a brown color on their wares by bringing the kiln temperature to an extremely high point and then dropping it suddenly. This produced the so-called "tiger" ware upon which the salt glaze appears in brown globules. Their method of doing this was a trade secret, not copied, intentionally, at least, in this country. Occasional specimens of New England stoneware do, nevertheless, have a "tiger" surface, which was doubtless occasioned by some accident in firing.

During the first half of firing the ware was burned at a low temperature. It was then brought to its highest point — about 2300° — and the glaze was added by the simple expedient of shoveling hot common salt through the openings in the top of the kiln. In the heat of the oven, the salt volatilized, settling on the surface of the pottery and becoming united with it in a thin but perfect glaze. When the stoneware was finished, its surface was slightly pitted like that of an orange. One may recognize this type of pottery by the texture.

The action of the salt affected only those portions of the vessels that were exposed to its vapor. Since they were nearly all upside down or covered by other pots standing upon them, the salt glaze did not reach their interior parts. A lining glaze was not really needed, because the ware was hard and not easily penetrated by liquids; hence, none was used to protect the interior surface of the first stoneware. As early as 1800, "Albany slip," a clay that fused to a natural glaze when burned, was found suitable for the purpose. The action of salt was not required for this glaze. Accordingly, pieces so treated could be placed under crocks or jars in the kiln, thereby saving space. Slip glaze was usually brown in color, ranging from a light tan to almost black. After the eighteenth century, it was universally applied on the inner surfaces of New England stoneware, and its absence indicates either a very early product or one of foreign manufacture. In the later period many articles were given a dark brown hue by a complete wash of this Albany slip. Large pitchers, batter jugs, kitchen bowls, and measures were turned out in this ugly dark color. Their bases alone show the buff or gray of the natural body. Stoneware of this type remained in favor during the Civil War period and later, when a great deal of pottery was made in molds rather than by hand turning.

The New England stoneware makers decorated their pots by incising lines or patterns upon them or by brushing or trailing on designs in blue or brown slip. Both methods show the influence of the Dutch and German potters. Incised decoration is more likely to be found on stoneware dating before 1825, while slip decoration appears even on very late examples. Incised ships, animals, fish, flowers, or figures, without color, are seen on early ware. Occasionally swashes of blue were brushed across the design, and it was a custom to use such touches of color around the handles. More rarely the incised motif

was filled in with color between the lines, as in early German pottery. Small stampled eagles, hearts, tassels, or other symbols were sometimes used as repeats.

Stoneware decorated with cobalt-blue slip was made in all parts of New England. The best of it was produced in the period from 1840 to 1860. At that time rounded jugs and jars had been replaced by those having straight sides, and the feeling for good form had been supplanted by an urge for ornamentation. In an effort to overcome the prosaic shapes of the pots, and partly, also, because the plane surfaces offered a tempting background for decoration, the potters did not hesitate to utilize bold and striking design. A flower resembling the day lily was a rather common motif. It was applied with a brush and seems to have been used in many potteries. Other naturalistic motifs, such as birds, deer, vines, houses, and various flowers, all reflecting the familiar suroundings of the craftsman, made nineteenth-century stoneware a true expression of native feeling. Some early pieces were patterned with simple combinations of lines and dots poured from a slip cup, but the brush was used in embellishing the greater number of stoneware vessels: with this implement the potter was able to attain the broadest and freest expression of his ideas. Brown slip, notably on the Norton jugs made at Bennington, was sometimes substituted for the more ordinary cobalt blue. When the body color of the ware was buff, the contrasting tones of brown were extremely pleasing.

In a few rare instances stoneware was ornamented with molded and applied figures. Water coolers made by Franklin Wight at St. Johnsbury and Ashfield bear a bas-relief of Diana or a full-length figure of Washington (Fig. 102). Work of this kind was often done by potters of German descent in Pennsylvania and Ohio, but it is not at all common in the New England states. There is no denying the effectiveness of molded decoration on stoneware, which depends on form more than color for its beauty.

CHAPTER TWO

Seventeenth-Century Potters

The scarcity of surviving specimens of early redware has led to the assumption that only pewter and wooden vessels were used by the pioneers in New England, and the rare mention of potters in historical records has contributed to this belief. Nevertheless, a careful study of land and probate records shows that there were in fact potters among the first arrivals here and that they plied their trade over long periods.

Earthenware is mentioned in Essex County, Massachusetts, probate inventories as early as 1644. Joanna Cummings of Salem, who died in June of that year, owned "glasses, trayes & earth weare & other old lumber"; the inventory of Jane Gaines, Lynn, dated November 1644, lists "an earthen pott"; "2 earthern potts & yarn" were included in the estate of Margery Wathin of Salem, who died before July 1644. Earthen pans were owned by Francis Lightfoot of Lynn (1646), by Emme Mason, Salem (1646), and Giles Badger, Newbury (1647), while milk pans are noted in the inventory of John Hardy, Salem (1652). "Pots with butter" bequeathed by Mary Hersome of Wenham (1646) point to a use of earthenware long customary in Staffordshire. "Earthen dishes, wooden dishes & bowles" were owned by Henry Birdsall of Salem (1651); and "an earthen platter" was among the utensils of Henry Somerby. "Juggs" are frequently mentioned. These were probably of German or Flemish stoneware, which was brought to this country by way of England. In other inventories of this period reference is made to drinking pots, stone bottles, gallipots, stone pots, and Holland jugs.

The mention of earthenware in these early inventories is not, of course, positive indication of a local product. Rarely are the descriptions full enough to give complete information. Rather by the fact that, as the years went on, earthenware to the value of four or five shillings was to be found in nearly every home are we led to the conclusion that common pottery of little value was generally owned. Much of this was undoubtedly native redware made by local potters whose names we now know.

The inventory of Theodore Price of Salem, dated April 10, 1672, lists "earth wt. ware and

redware, 10 s." White earthenware was the Delft of Holland — a prized possession, treasured for its decorative qualities and infrequently used. Delft is also indicated by the terms "Holland ware" and perhaps is also meant when "painted dishes" are noted, although redware potters applied the word "painting" to slip decoration. The term "earthenware" I believe is usually intended to designate the common red pottery, because the items are listed among things of lesser value, such as wooden dishes or the coarser kitchen and dairy utensils.

The Essex County probate records reveal that before 1675 earthen basins, porringers, and salt cellars were in use and they name such other articles as "poter's ware," earthen chambers, honey with the pots (perhaps English ware), "old pottage pots," and a pitcher. One inventory of 1674 lists "som whight earthen ware, 10 s." and "pailes, pigines & earthen wares, 6 s." About one-third of the inhabitants of Essex County who died between 1665 and 1675 had earthenware of sufficient worth to pass on to their descendants, while the proportion of the living who numbered it among their utilities must have been vastly greater.

In the records from 1675 to 1681 earthenware is mentioned sixty-three times, earthen pots, fourteen times, and earthen dishes, twelve times. Earthen jugs, pans, porringers, and platters are listed, besides milk pans, pudding pans, jars, pitchers, and other forms that were in all probability of the same material.

By this time pottery was being sold in the shops. The list of such ware in the house and warehouse of George Corwin, a Salem merchant who died in 1684, is illuminating: "In the Shop, Erthen ware & wooden ware, 3 s.; In the Lower Warehouse, 35 doz. Erthen ware, 3 li.; In the two Closets Adjoyning (the red chamber) 10 doz. Erth. ware, 3 Erthen pots; In the Closet, Erthen ware & a Glase botle, 5 s.; In the Pewter Rome, 4 boles, 1 Tray & Erth. Ware, 10 s.; Erthen Ware, 18d.; In the Kitchin, Erthen ware, 6 s.; In the Seller Under the House, 24 qt. Jugs, 4 s., 4 Jares, 4 s., 1 Erth. Pot, 1 s.; In the Closet of Kitchin Chamber, 43 pls. [parcels] Erthen ware at 2 s. per doz., 7 s. 2d., 10 pls. Erthen ware, 2s. 6d."

More evidential than the above records are the numerous fragments dug out by Sidney L. Strickland at Kingston, Massachusetts, on the site of the first Howland house, which was burned with its contents about 1690. Among remnants of English buff earthenware and German blue and gray stoneware, Mr. Strickland found two redware milk pans, two lard pots, and a slip-decorated pan or platter of undoubted American origin. Other decorated plates and pans identical in character to those made by very early Massachusetts potters, as proved by a study of their shard piles, have also been recovered under the lean-to floor of the old Jabez Howland house in Plymouth.

It may easily be understood that the earliest potteries were established along the seacoast, for at first the waterways provided almost the only means of travel and communication. In the Massachusetts Bay Colony, Salem, Gloucester, Ipswich, Charlestown, and Boston had potteries in the 1600's. No record of a seventeenth-century pottery in Plymouth has come to light, although Bristol, Rhode Island, in Plymouth Colony, boasted a potter among its first settlers. It is probable that some of the Connecticut towns along the coast and up the Connecticut River had potters among their craftsmen in the first half of the century, but there is no known record of their presence, even in those places where earthenware was later extensively produced. Edward E. Atwater, in his *History of the Colony of New Haven*, says that he found documentary evidence that almost every trade, including pottery making, was carried on in the first ten years of the settlement of

New Haven. As late as 1750, however, native pottery was shipped from Charlestown to Norwich, Stonington, and Killingworth, Connecticut, and even later was sent overland to Connecticut in exchange for produce. The Connecticut colonists for many years bought their household redware from sloops that plied along the coast from Massachusetts and New York. Not until 1750 is there record of a Connecticut potter, and he was a stoneware man.

In New Hampshire a redware potter was established as early as 1720, and several others followed in the early part of the century. But, for the most part, comparatively late dates must be assigned to the pioneers of the industry in Vermont, New Hampshire, and Maine. With but few exceptions, the potteries in those states did not begin until after the Revolution. However in northern New England this traditional craft continued to be practiced to a much later period than elsewhere.

The manufacture of bricks and of earthenware go hand in hand. For this reason the earliest potteries are found in those places where brickmaking was first carried on. What was probably the first brick kiln in New England was built in Salem. Rev. Francis Higginson, writing in July 1629, says: "It is thought here is good clay to make Bricke, and Tyles and Earthen pots, as need to be. At this instant, we are setting a brick-kill on worke to make Brickes and Tyles for the building of our houses." There was, indeed, good clay in Salem — a bed seventy feet deep, which proved to be an inexhaustible supply, furnishing material for one of the great centers of the potting industry. The clay beds along the Mystic River were also utilized at a very early period by the founders of Medford and Charlestown. In Boston there is record of brickmaking as early as 1635, when Thomas Mount, on October 26, was given leave by the selectmen to fence a piece of marsh before his house for making brick. Again, in October 1644, Jasper Rawlines was granted liberty to use a rod of upland for the same purpose. A watchhouse constructed at Plymouth in 1643 is thought to have been made of local brick supplied by one Grimes at eleven shillings per thousand; and it is said that Scituate had a brickyard at the same period.

Brickmaking was carefully regulated in the seventeenth century to insure correct preparation of the clay and uniform size of the finished product. The General Court of Massachusetts Bay Colony ordered, June 10, 1679, that all bricks when made should measure nine by two and one-quarter by four and one-half inches, and that the molds used should be "well shod with iron." It was stipulated that the clay be dug before November first and turned over in the following February or March, one month before it was to be used. The addition of salt or brackish water to temper the bricks was forbidden. Another regulation, dated November 10, 1711, gives the size of bricks as nine by two and one-half by four and one-half inches.

There is little remaining evidence of the early use of tiles for roofing, but there is no doubt that they were actually made, for I have unearthed them in a pottery dump in Danvers (see Chapter III). Since architects have expressed some skepticism about them, because no house now standing is so equipped, I have taken pains to gather a few notes about their manufacture. In 1646 the General Court passed an order that "Tyle Earth to make sale ware shall be digged before the first of the 9 mo, & turned over in the last of 1st month ensuing a month before it be wrought." A later marginal note says "Tile Earth for House covering." Edward Johnson, in his *Wonder-Working Providence*, mentions lime, brick, and tile making about 1647, and tilers were among the tradesmen whose wages were regulated by a statute of

the General Court in the 1640's. They were to receive not more than two shillings per day when boarding themselves or fourteen pence per day "with dyett." Another bit of evidence appears in the mention of tilers' hammers for sale in the stock of George Corwin, a Salem merchant who died in 1684. A more conclusive reference occurs in a description of Boston written about 1657. It says that the town had "large, spacious houses, some fairly set forth with brick, tile, slate, and stone." Furthermore, on October 25, 1692, the Massachusetts Bay Colony passed a law requiring fireproof construction of Boston buildings. It reads in part:

(Sect. I) That henceforth no dwelling-house, shop, warehouse, barn, stable, or any other housing of more than eight feet in length or breadth, and seven feet in height, shall be erected and set up in Boston, but of stone or brick, and covered with slate or tyle, unless in particular cases where necessity requires, — being so judged and signified in writing under the hands of the justices and selectmen of the said town, or major part of both, — the governour, with the advice and consent of council, shall see cause to grant license unto any person to build with timber or cover with shingle. . .

(Sect. III) That every owner of such house or buildings so set up contrary to said law, shall cause the same to be covered with slate or tyle; or otherwise such houses or buildings shall be deemed a common nusance, and the owner thereof proceeded against accordingly.

This old law was reënacted after the disastrous Boston fire of 1760, with the same provision that buildings over seven feet in height should be covered with slate or tiles.

It is the considered opinion of E. Stanley Wires, who has spent a life-time in the tile business, that redware tiles for roofing were tried from time to time, but that the New England climate, with its alternate periods of freezing and thawing, proved them unsuitable for the purpose.

The first New England potter of whom we have any record is Philip Drinker, who, with his wife Elizabeth and two boys, Edward and John, came to Charlestown, Massachusetts, on the ship *Abigail* in 1635. He was then thirty-nine years of age and an experienced potter. In 1638 he owned a "Dwelling with a garden platt" at the east end of the common lands (now Sullivan Square), where the Mystic River bridge of today connects Charlestown and Everett. For a number of years he was the ferryman over the river. In this location he worked with the assistance of his son Edward and an apprentice, John Goldsmith. Drinker must have prospered, for after a time he built another house, which is mentioned in his will as the "House I now live in with the Kiln and garden, with the piece of marsh meddow adioyning." This property became Edward's upon his father's death in 1647, "with all the lead, wood and fagotts I had of brother *James*,* with all the tooles belonging to my trade." Edward continued to practice his trade in Charlestown and then in Boston until 1700. Goldsmith completed his apprenticeship with the son, as directed in Philip Drinker's will: "My will is that *John Gouldsmith* serve the rest of his tyme with my son *Edward*, he to fulfill the Indenture; only instead of 12s there mentioned, my son *Edward* shall give him 5s when his tyme is expired."

In 1635, also, two other potters arrived in New England. One of them, William Vincent (called Vinson), is known to have been in Salem in that year and was perhaps the William Vincent of Bromfield, Essex, England, who is recorded in the Suffolk Deeds, August 25,1636, as giving bond for Abraham Page of Great Baddow, Essex. The name Vincent is common in the Low Countries, and it is probable that he came from one of

* Probably James Green, his next neighbor, who may have been his wife's brother. There is no record of a James Drinker.

the numerous Lowland families that migrated to Essex County, England, around 1600. This theory is strengthened by the fact that he called himself "pot-baker" — a Dutch term. In 1641 Vinson had a house in Potter's Field. The exact location of his kiln is known, for it was accidentally unearthed some years ago. Unfortunately, no one was sufficiently interested to gather and preserve the pottery fragments that must have been buried there. This kiln was under the center of Bridge Street, where Planter's Street (formerly Potter's Lane) crosses it. William Vinson lived on the north side of the lane.

Vinson's stay in Salem did not last more than ten years altogether, for in 1645 he had moved to Gloucester. Whether he was succeeded by another potter I have been unable to learn. The district afterwards became famous for its potteries, but only indirectly as a result of this first shop. Vinson lived until 1690. In Gloucester he ran a tavern and a mill in addition to his regular calling. That he kept on with his pottery making is proved by an item in the Essex Quarterly Court records dated November 15, 1670, when he brought suit against John Tode (Todd) of Rowley to recover a debt of twelve pounds, twelve shillings for thirty-two earthen pots. Vinson is memorialized in the names of the cove and street that still bear his name. His house stood between Main Street and the harbor front. He also owned Five Pound Island, which has recently been incorporated in the state fish pier.

John Pride, the other early Salem potter, was granted twenty acres of land in 1636. His home was at Winter Harbor, an inlet not far from Salem Willows. In a mortgage deed it is described as being "near Mr. Holgrave's stage." Winter Harbor was settled by fishermen who lived on the inner side of the peninsula that forms the little bays, and a "stage" was one of their platforms for drying fish. Some accounts say that Pride lived at Juniper Point near by. All this area is now built over, so that the exact location of his kiln will probably never be determined. That he actually made pottery is certain. In 1644 he went before the Court with a petition concerning delivery of "50 doz of earthenware to Mr. Ruck," a Boston trader. When he died three years later, his inventory mentioned "37 doz. of earthenware," valued at £4, 12s, 6d. At that time he owned a dwelling house, barn, and workhouse.

After the departure of Vinson and the death of Pride, there is little further reference to the potter's trade in Salem for many years. The following note occurs in a list of debtors to the estate of Samuel Archer, who owned and operated lighters for carrying goods aboard ship or about the harbor: "28: 9: 1663, for the french potter, 6s." The "french potter" may have been William Vinson, who perhaps sent shipments on Archer's boats from Gloucester to Salem. On the other hand, a passage in the *Diary of William Bentley*, dated January 30, 1798, points to the existence of still another seventeenth-century pottery in the town. The Castle Hill to which he refers was an elevation south of the settlement that was virtually surrounded by water at high tide and, in consequence, a delightful summer resort for the Silsbee family. The entry reads:

> This evening in company with the family of Silsbee, I went up to *Castle Hill* to spend the evening with the family of Easties, lately connected by marriage. Mr. Easties showed me two places, where evidently had been cellars, north of the hill & one below the other, easterly. I also saw a place on the south side, in a valley formed on the south side of the hills, where formerly was a Potter's kiln. The iron funnel was found under the roots of a black cherry tree & is now the iron of a mantle in a chimney of the farm house. The houses on the Cellar must have been early as they were not recollected by the father of the last Judge Lynde as early as 1680.

Vinson, through his grandson Joseph Gardner and perhaps other apprentices, became the godfather of all Essex County potters. Gardner started a business of his own when he was twenty-one years old. He had bought a small piece of land on the outskirts of Gloucester, on the road to Eastern Point. It is described as being at the "easterly end of Peter Mud's Neck," now the junction of Eastern and Rocky Neck Avenues. In "the house then erected to make earthenware in" Joseph Gardner worked in his dual capacity of potter and fisherman. Although little more is known about his career, he was still called "potter" in 1749, the year of his death. A clay bed and evidences of a clay pit near by are the only indications of his activities there during nearly sixty years. In 1721 Gardner appealed to the town for assistance in defraying doctors' and nurses' bills incurred while his mother-in-law was sick. Aid of this kind was customarily given in early communities, and his applying for it does not signify a lack of enterprise on Gardner's part.

Another potter who must have learned his trade with William Vinson was Jacob Davis. Born in Gloucester in 1662, he labored as a young man running a sawmill with his father near the head of Little River in West Gloucester. Just when he first began to make redware is uncertain. In 1699, two years after his marriage to Mary Haskell, when he bought a house and land on the river road in Ipswich, he was styled "potter." Fragmentary evidence of his sojourn in the town may still be found in an Ipswich garden where Davis's house used to stand. After remaining in that location until 1710, he sold the house and returned to Gloucester. In 1715 and 1717 he is mentioned as a potter in Gloucester deeds. He seems to have owned and operated the mill in his native town continuously after 1685. Just before his death he built a new dwelling house and barn on the west side of Little River. This, with an orchard and twenty acres of land, constituted his homestead. Authorities have disagreed as to whether the house was the one later known as the Freeman house. Quantities of redware were unearthed when a garden was laid out on the Freeman grounds a few years ago, but, as the building was long used for a tavern, the presence of shards has little significance. An inventory of Davis's household possessions includes these items: 105 lb. of lead, Li 1: 6: 3; 8 milk pans, 5s: 4d; 12 earthen vessels, 6s: 6d; jugs and mortar, 6s: 6d; and more earthen ware, 2s.

Other late seventeenth-century potters in Essex County were James Kettle (Kettell), who worked in Beverly and Danvers from about 1685 to 1710, and Jonathan Hayward, his brother-in-law, who began potting in Beverly about 1695. An account of Kettle and our discoveries at the site of his pottery appears in the following chapter.

Jonathan Hayward lived near the Danvers line in Beverly on what is now Conant Street. He was born there May 6, 1673, and no doubt acquired the potter's art from Kettle, who had married Hayward's sister Elizabeth. In 1703, soon after his marriage to Mary Flint, he bought land on the south side of the Country Road (Conant Street) at the foot of Leech's Hill, but there is no indication of his building a house or potshop on the lot. His wife having died, he was married a second time, November 30, 1715, to Abigail Fuller. She lived but a few months. The record says that she died at her father's house in Salem Village. October 28, 1717/18, Hayward purchased one and one-half acres of land from William Dodge on the southeast corner of the Country Road and the road to Beverly. In 1733 he owned a dwelling house and barn on this lot "near new precinct meeting house." This was presumably his homestead and the location of his pottery. An ancient house now stands on the lot, but whether any part of it was erected by Hayward I

have not ascertained. Some crisis, illness perhaps, must have occurred at this time, for Hayward and his wife "Elizabeth," on September 19, 1733, conveyed their house near the church and six acres of land to their son Jonathan, a physician of Woburn. They were then living in Connecticut. Two later conveyances (1740) are mortgages of land on the Country Road. I have found no record of Hayward's death. As this potter was working in Beverly from 1694 to 1733, a more thorough attempt should be made to learn his history and to locate his pottery.

While the few scattered potters of Essex County were making their small contribution towards what was later to become an important craft in that region, Edward Drinker and his successors were laying the foundations for a further development of potting in Charlestown. When Drinker's father died in 1647, Edward was twenty-five. He continued to carry on the family trade in the location where his father had worked before him. As sole potter for Charlestown and Boston he made a good living. In 1655 he purchased a warehouse building "in a place called Wapping Roe" (now Wapping Street), close by the Charles River ferry landing. This was a more convenient shipping point than his dock on the Mystic River.

Drinker would probably have spent his days peacefully on his father's acres had he not got entangled in a religious controversy that raged furiously in Charlestown for a time. He was one of eight strong-minded persons who dared oppose infant baptism and the theory of infant damnation. Thomas Gould, the leader of these radicals, was twice admonished by the General Court, but continued to advertise his opinions. In 1663 meetings were held at his house, and two years later a church was formed. This was a breach of the law. After a public debate between the Anabaptists and six elders of the established church, Gould and two of his associates, in spite of a petition from many of the Charlestown people, were sent to prison for a year. Drinker, meanwhile, after a brief detention in jail, had escaped to Boston. Already he had made purchases of land in the city. In 1663 he bought a house and shop on Elm Street from William Cotton. Seven years later he acquired another house and land on Purchase Street (then called Belcher's Lane), northwest of William Brown's ropewalk. This estate near Fort Hill was approximately where Pearl and Purchase Streets cross today. At that time it was on the waterfront, and Drinker's land ran down to the sea. This was the site of his Boston pottery. In his will Drinker mentions "my Land lying below the ropewalk to the Seaward, commonly cal'd the Workhouse yard."

Edward Drinker's career in Boston was eminently successful. The tax list of 1687 shows that he then owned twelve houses, mills, and wharves, a horse, and twenty cows. Moreover, he persisted in his Anabaptist proclivities, even when the Court closed the new church and nailed up its doors. He lived to see it permanently established. Drinker was a potter until 1700, when he died without issue, leaving his property to his third wife and to her niece. For more than thirty-five years he had supplied Boston with its pots and pans. He seems to have had no competitor, except for a brief period — and his rival (if he was one) moved away.

This second Boston potter, John Wilkins, first appears in Boston records June 25, 1670, when he bought a house and land next the famous Hutchinson mansion in Dock Square on the street leading to the town dock. During the ten years of his residence there, three little Wilkinses were born to the potter and his wife, the former Anstis Gold-Bissell. Waters, in his *Genealogical Gleanings in England*, says that Wilkins came from Wiltshire and that he was a glassmaker, having been trained in a London glasshouse. His

wife, bereft of her first husband's family by the plague, was an adventurous spirit and did not hesitate to share Wilkins's fortunes in a new country. It is said that she even returned to England in order to secure some materials for her husband's business. This story must be taken for what it is worth. Wilkins is invariably called a potter in Boston deeds. In 1680 he became one of the first proprietors of Bristol, Rhode Island, "within the Colony of New Plimouth." Shortly thereafter he mortgaged his Boston property and, in 1693, sold it.

After Drinker's removal from Charlestown, the potting business was carried on there by the Kettell family.* Samuel, the first of the name to practice the craft, was a son of Richard Kettell, and, it is thought, a cousin of James Kettle of Salem Village, previously mentioned. He was born November 19, 1642, and must have learned his trade in the Drinker shop, succeeding Drinker's apprentice, John Goldsmith, who had turned to chocolate grinding as a means of earning a living. Samuel Kettell probably built his own shop shortly before his marriage to Mercy Hayden in 1665 (there is no record of his having taken over the Drinker kiln). He and his nephews, John, William, and Richard, each the son of a different brother, carried on the earthenware industry in Charlestown for about one hundred years.

Samuel died in 1694. His nephew John had already succumbed to smallpox at the age of thirty, William was but a lad of fourteen or fifteen, and Richard a mere infant. His stepson, Benjamin Frothingham, whose mother Kettell had married shortly before his decease, was also too young to run the pottery, although he worked at the trade after 1700. For this reason, the Kettell house, land, and workshop were willed to a daughter, Mercy Badger, whose son Stephen later improved the inheritance for some fifty years as one of Charlestown's leading potters. This property stood on the corner of Bow Street and Ropemaker's Lane (now Arrow Street). To his wife Kettell bequeathed half a house and the income of his Negro "Robbin" for five years. This is the earliest mention of a Negro slave among the Charlestown potters.

* Originally Kettle.

CHAPTER THREE

James Kettle's Shard Pile

If it were possible to excavate all the earlier pottery sites, we would get a clearer picture of the clay craft in New England. Unfortunately the many changes wrought in three hundred years have made nearly all such spots unavailable for digging. It was therefore extremely gratifying to locate one site where a seventeenth-century potter had worked and to find the owner willing to cooperate by allowing us to dig over his yard.

James Kettle (or Kettell, as later generations have called themselves) was working in Salem Village, now Danvers, as early as 1687. As Essex County is still partly rural, with much open land, I went through his land records carefully, hoping that I might find Kettle's pottery in an accessible location. At first the search was rather confusing, since Beverly and Danvers were both originally parts of Salem and the boundary line between them was twice changed. After a church had been built in the section now known as Danvers, the parish was called Salem Village to distinguish it from Salem proper. In that parish James Kettle and several other potters lived. A reference in a deed to Frostfish River, now Frostfish Brook, was the one clue that led me to the discovery of Kettle's land on the very edge of Salem Village. At this point the brook still bubbles its way merrily into Porter's River, a tidewater creek.

On September 14, 1704, James Kettle sold to Captain John Putnam and others a small lot of marsh land at the head of the river. The boundaries of the piece began at a walnut tree in the northwest corner, ran south into the river channel, and thence down stream to a stake "where James Kettle's house now stands." The lot contained only sixteen poles, or 1452 square feet. Whatever its shape, it could not have extended more than one hundred feet from the head of the river. With these dimensions in mind, we explored the marsh and then the higher ground, with the result that at exactly the estimated point we found pottery fragments in garden ground between two houses facing on Conant Street (the old "country road"). Further investigation revealed a quantity of shards behind the garage of Number 73, the home of Warren Pennell.* On this spot we were soon able to secure unique information about earthenware of the early period.

James Kettle was the son of John of Manchester and Gloucester, for whom Kettle Cove was named. John was perhaps the brother of William Kettell (Kettle), the founder of the Charlestown family of that

* Now owned by Chester T. Cutler.

name. This theory is strengthened by the fact that James spent his last years in Charlestown. James was born in Gloucester, March 20, 1664/65, just before his father sold his house there. Either at that time or later the family moved to Salem, where the father died in 1685. Within three years, the widow married Samuel Corning of Beverly and was dismissed from the Gloucester church. The records leave us in doubt as to whether James spent his apprentice years in Gloucester. He could have been trained there by William Vinson, but, if not, he probably worked from about 1678 to 1685 with Samuel Kettell in Charlestown.

Sidney Perley in a paper entitled "Rial Side: Port of Salem in 1700" * says that Kettle bought land in Salem Village of Jacob Barney, April 21, 1687, and that he built thereon the dwelling later known as his "mansion" house. Perley's map of the village and Kettle's land records place this lot and house in the location where we found the fragments.

Kettle married Elizabeth Hayward of Beverly, whose brother Jonathan also became a potter. They had five children who were baptized in the Beverly church. Before 1695 both had transferred their membership to the church in Salem Village. This was the parish of the witchcraft delusion. Besides the house at Frostfish River, Kettle owned another with an acre of land that he purchased in 1700 from Samuel Wolcott. In 1702 he acquired in addition thirteen acres at the easterly end of Leech's Hill, later known as "Brown's Folly," where the Danvers reservoir is now located. In 1709/10 James Kettle moved to Charlestown, buying still a third house there and establishing a pottery. He lived but two years thereafter, dying November 24, 1712.

One third of the Danvers property went to Kettle's widow, the rest to his son James and daughter Elizabeth. The property was owned by the heirs until 1724, when James, Jr., and Jonathan disposed of the estate to John Batchelder and his son. At that time James, Jr., was living in Charlestown. He had been trained to be his father's successor, but he took up the trade of leather dressing. The records show, therefore, that our findings may be dated from 1687, when Kettle built his home, to 1709/10, when he went to Charlestown.

Upon first consideration our most striking discovery seemed to be about a dozen extremely crude and badly potted jars, unglazed, and squatty in shape (Fig. 10). Their walls, sloping outward from neck to base, were nearly three-quarters of an inch thick and their bases rather thin. Their curious form made us wonder what their purpose could have been and whether they represented all their maker's skill or his lack of it. They might almost have been practice pieces made by boy apprentices, except that smearings of glaze and circular scars indicate that they had been used as supports for other objects in the kiln.

These vessels and fragments of jars with an inside glaze (the type later known as lard pots) were our first finds. They seemed to point to rather crude work. But the discovery of a few thin shards encouraged me to believe that James Kettle was capable of better things and that he and our other earliest potters were more skillful than their successors. This opinion was confirmed when we unearthed a handful of small reddish fragments decorated with delicate lines of yellow slip. Mere bits as these pieces are, they are large enough to show a greater refinement in technique than appears in similar shards from later potteries. They seem to be parts of deep dishes glazed on the inside only and of bowls glazed both within and without and slip decorated on the inner or upper surface. The bowl rims curve outward and over. One or two pieces show

* *Essex Institute Historical Collections*, vol. IV, no. 1.

slip trailing on both sides. As far as I have been able to learn, no object thus decorated is now in existence.

In a later digging in 1945 we found the fragment of a fifteen-inch pan illustrated in Fig. 11. For the first time we were able to study a piece large enough to give an idea of the design. The slip decorating is very neatly done. Its original yellow color stood out against a light tan background and was sprinkled with fine dots of green.

With seventeenth-century forms in mind, I expected to find parts of jugs or pitchers with straight necks and bulbous bodies, and my expectations were realized. Unfortunately not enough rim fragments were found to indicate whether the jugs had spouts. Their general contour suggests the true jug or drinking pot. Since working at the Kettle pottery, I have purchased a vessel of similar type of about two-quart capacity (Fig. 12). It is undoubtedly of American origin and perhaps of the same period. All pieces of the Kettle jugs have a peculiar dark brown glaze suggestive of gun metal and not at all like the high lead glaze of the jars and pans. In color and texture they somewhat resemble our late stoneware glazed with Albany slip. It is not always possible to determine from damaged fragments just what was the potter's intention as to glaze, and these shards may have been merely overfired. But, since this glaze is almost wholly confined to Kettle's drinking jugs, intended for table use, he may have burned them at a higher temperature to make them waterproof. They were vessels of considerable delicacy to be made from such coarse materials and exhibit the potter's skill in shaping thin rims.

Kettle's baking dishes and milk pans are so much like those made in country potteries even as late as 1850 that they could in no wise be distinguished from them. They are, if anything, "slicker" in appearance than some later products and do not exhibit the signs of "primitive" finish one might expect to find in such early work. There are no ridges made by fingers held against the outside of pans while they were being turned; James used a stick or rib to smooth his pieces. Perhaps finish was a matter of temperament. Early potters, like those of today, may have tolerated or detested crudities according to their feeling. Lack of smoothing off could approximate decoration; more often it represented simply hasty work — still decorative, but unintentional. A conscientious potter, striving to avoid such irregularities, achieved a more symmetrical vessel, but one less pleasing to the eye.

One of the most surprising finds in this shard pile was the presence of a number of roof tiles. They measure seven by ten inches, are about one half an inch thick, and have two holes punched at one end for the nails. None were perfect examples, as they had been discarded because they were warped or rough, and they had evidently been put to use in kiln-setting. As noted in the previous chapter, roof tiles were a feature of New England architecture in the seventeenth century, but, proving unsuitable, were superseded by wooden shingles.

CHAPTER FOUR

The Provincial Potters of Charlestown

During the Provincial period Charlestown, more than any other place in the Massachusetts Bay Colony, was a center for artists and craftsmen. Cabinetmakers, pewterers, goldsmiths, silversmiths, and potters worked there side by side. Directly across the Charles River from Boston and only a few minutes away by ferry, the little town stood in a somewhat isolated position on a peninsula almost entirely surrounded by marshes and water. On the north, the Mystic River separated it from Malden and Medford, although a neck at the northwestern extremity connected it with Cambridge. In the center of the peninsula rose Breed's Hill where the Battle of Bunker Hill was to be fought and where the famous monument now stands; to the north and west was Bunker Hill itself. Between the northerly slopes of these eminences and the Mystic River were huge clay pits that supplied potters and brickmakers for many years, until much of the land had been dug away. The church and village, clustered about an open square and running along the waterfront, were in the southwestern part of the settlement. A town dock for the accommodation of boats was early cut far into the marshy shore. Around this inlet or canal, known as "Wapping Dock," or merely "Wappin'," many of the pothouses were built. It was the heart of the earthenware trade. About halfway up the dock was a swing bridge, built to save steps in crossing from one side to the other. At least one potter advertised his shop as being near this landmark. Close by was Joiners Street, where the cabinetmakers worked.

Before its destruction by the British in 1775, Charlestown must have had a distinctly English flavor. The names of its streets suggested old England rather than a new pioneer community. Wapping was reminiscent of London; High and Market Streets of the small English towns; while Middlegate was a purely English term for Middle Street.

The eighteenth-century potters who worked in the town, shipping their wares from their own docks, numbered nearly forty. Approximately half of them owned their own kilns, and in 1750 eight or nine shops were in operation simultaneously. This unusual activity explains why Boston had no successful pottery during this century. The earthenware became known as "Charlestown

ware" and is so mentioned in a claim for loss after the Boston fire of 1760.

Thanks to the monumental *Genealogies and Estates of Charlestown*, compiled by Thomas Bellows Wyman in 1879, it has been possible to unearth a good bit of information about the lives and interrelations of these early craftsmen, while a potter's account book kept from 1747 to 1757 throws much light on their products. That so little of their ware has survived (I have never seen a specimen that I could attribute directly to an early Charlestown pottery) is due to the burning of the town during the Revolution, with the consequent destruction of the potteries and of nearly all the houses and their contents. However, the wide distribution of the earthenware makes it certain that a great deal of pottery found in New England originated in Charlestown.

At the close of the seventeenth century the Kettell pottery was the only one in operation. We may assume that Samuel Kettell's nephew William and his stepson Benjamin Frothingham, who were only young boys at the time of his death, managed to complete their training, perhaps in Boston, and to use the kiln until such time as they were old enough to have their own establishments. Frothingham seems to have had a distaste for clay, and an inheritance made it possible for him to become a tavern keeper. In 1709/10 he sold to James Kettle (Kettell), newly arrived from Salem Village, a piece of property between Main Street and the river. That Kettle set up a pottery there is indicated by an inventory taken after his death two years later, which mentions "The Dwelling house and Land adjoining, Work Houses, Stone and three Wheeles, new Earthen Ware, and 700 li. led." William Kettell worked as an independent potter until he passed away in February 1718/19. At that time, and probably much earlier, he owned a workshop noted in the inventory of his estate.

Richard Kettell lived in a double house with his brother until that part of the dwelling was sold to settle the estate. In 1724 he bought a house of Katharine Cutler and plied his trade for many years thereafter — as nearly as can be reckoned, for well over half a century. He had a family of twelve children and apparently was not too prosperous. In 1757 he received a share of the "Thanksgiving" money given out by the town.

The old Samuel Kettell pottery was deeded to Stephen Badger by his father in 1726. He was then thirty years of age and had been twice married. He, too, had a long career. By 1767 he had retired and had moved to Natick to spend his remaining years. The house on Bow Street he sold in 1770. Rev. Stephen Badger, well known in Natick history, was his son.

Another potter who probably worked at first for the Kettells was Philip Cutler. He is recorded as a man with a family soon after 1700. His first purchase of property was in 1714, when he acquired the house on Back Street that he sold eight years later to James Kettell, Jr. Cutler then moved to Boston and started a pottery on Sea Street, which he ran in conjunction with a tavern for a number of years. The workhouse on his Charlestown lot was converted by young Kettell, a leather worker, to the purposes of a smokehouse.

In 1714 Isaac Parker, a young man of twenty-two, set up in business for himself. The land survey of that year mentions his "new kill house" on Graves Street (approximately where the Navy Young Men's Christian Association stands today). Parker and his family occupy an important place in potting history. An account of their activities will be found in Chapters V and VI.

One of the most prominent Charlestown potters, and a merchant as well, was Thomas Symmes. He began his career in partnership with John Webber. In 1726 they bought a house and wharf on Wapping Street, which

they occupied together. There they built the necessary workhouses and carried on the earthenware trade for eight years. Their association was concluded by a sad accident. During a celebration in honor of the crown princess at Fort William, Webber was killed by the explosion of a cannon. The catastrophe is mentioned in the *Boston News-Letter* of May 16, 1734. Webber left a wife and five children. Symmes, whose wife had died the previous year, married the widow, bought the other half of the property, and continued as before. A Negro, Cesar, became his by this transfer. Later he bought another slave for ninety-three pounds and he also owned a Negro woman, Symbo, valued at two hundred pounds. Thomas Symmes is sometimes called "potter," sometimes "gentleman." His business transactions were many and he acquired a considerable estate for his time. Soon after marrying Ruth Hall Webber, he built a new house on land between Wapping Street and the river, establishing his home and shop in a most convenient location on the very edge of the town dock. A further account of Symmes is given in the chapters that follow.

Other potters who were working in Charlestown before 1725 were Nathaniel Lord, a brother-in-law of Richard Kettell, John Pierce, and Eliphalet Newell. Lord's career was brief. He was born in 1701 and died in 1729. In 1723 he bought land from Richard Kettell and he probably worked with him. Pierce went to live in Boston about 1735, but cannot be traced after that. Newell was a son-in-law of James Kettell, having married his daughter Abigail. He owned land on Bow Street, but there is no record of his having had a kiln. His son James, after him, was a potter, but does not seem to have made much of a success of his trade, for in later years his taxes were twice abated for poverty.

By the middle of the century Charlestown ware was known far and wide, and many more men were apprenticed to the trade in the numerous flourishing potteries. The smoke of the wood-burning kilns in the peaceful town was beginning to be a nuisance. There was also a constant danger of fire should sparks fall on the wooden houses. The General Court on April 20, 1741, passed an act "Relating to Common Nusances," which reads as follows:

> For preventing of desolation by fire, that may happen by erecting of potters' kilns & houses near to dwelling-houses and other buildings & the inconvenience and mischief that may accrue to the neighborhood by the offensive and unwholesome smoak & stench proceeding from the kilns when on fire,
>
> Be it enacted
>
> If any person set up potters' kiln or kiln house in any place within either of the seaport or market towns in this province, other than such place heretofore used for the purpose, or as selectmen with two or more Justices of the peace shall design or approve, shall pay 31 pounds — one third to his majesty, one third to poor of town, one third to informer.

The period from 1740 to 1775 was the heyday of pottery making in Charlestown. At least a dozen master potters appear during this time. The locations of all the kilns are not known, but others can be determined from the land records. Some passed from one potter to another. With the exception of the Kettell, or Badger, shop on Bow Street and the Parker kiln, later owned by Josiah Harris, all of the pothouses were near the town dock. There the clay workers lived in close company and perhaps in equally close competition. At this time in our history, however, there was work enough for all, and few competent potters left town. The earthenware was sent by boat along the seacoast as far north as Casco Bay and around Cape Cod as far south as the Connecticut River. This method of selling by water was the only one possible in an era when roads were bad and

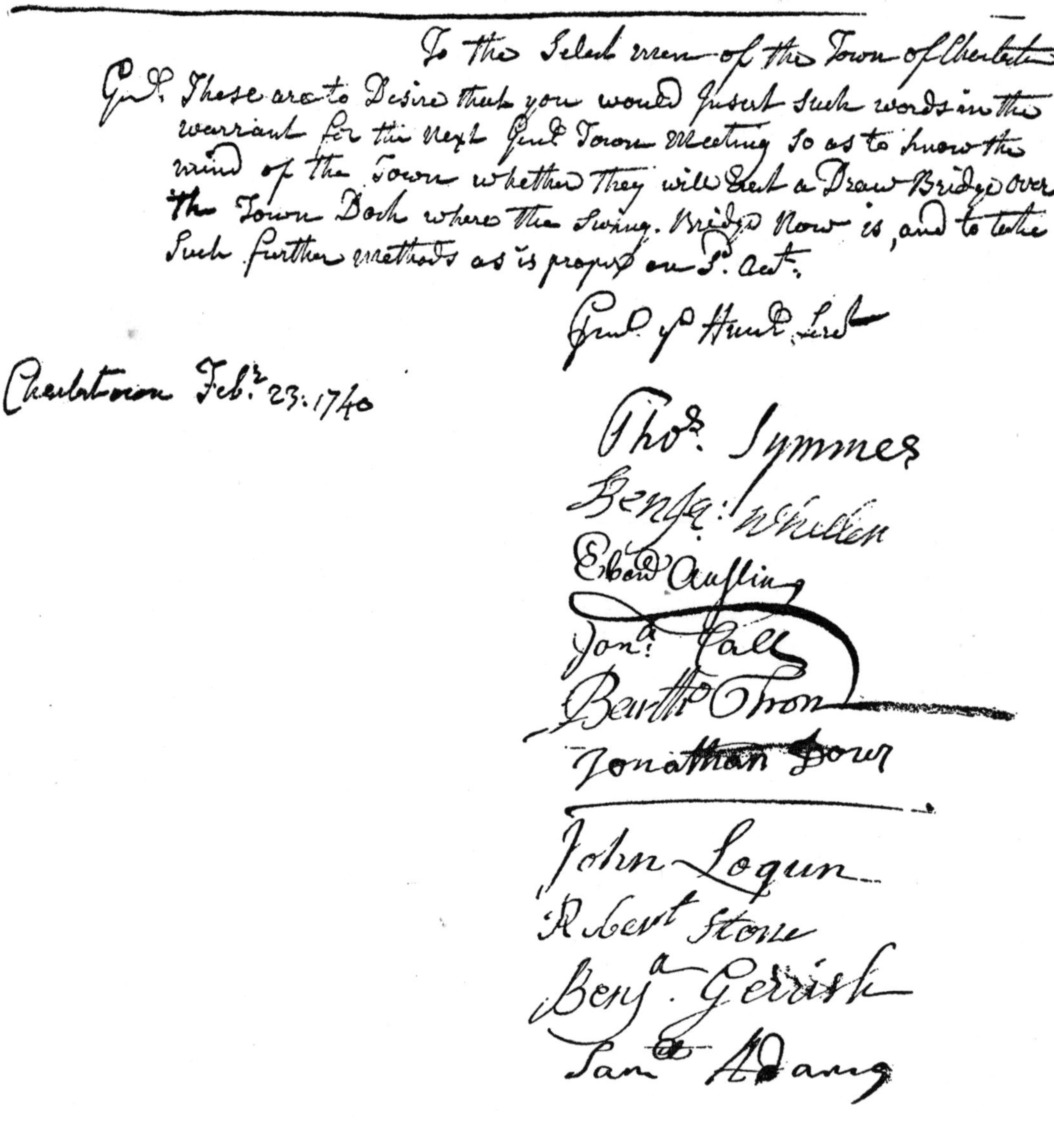

To the Select men of the Town of Charlestown

Gent. These are to Desire that you would Insert such words in the warrant for the Next Genl Town Meeting so as to know the mind of the Town whether They will Sett a Draw Bridge over the Town Dock where the Swing Bridge Now is, and to take such further methods as is proper on sd. Act.

Genl. yr Humle. Servt.

Charlestown Feby. 23: 1740

Thos. Symmes
Benja: Whitten
Edwd Aufling
Jona. Call
Bartho Thron
Jonathan Dowr
John Logun
Robert Stone
Benja. Gerrish
Saml Adams

Petition concerning a new bridge over the town dock, Charlestown, Mass., with signature of Thomas Symmes.

inland towns scattered, and when the larger markets were in the seacoast settlements.

Two of the earlier earthenware makers were Daniel Edes and his son Daniel. They owned land and a wharf east of the swing bridge, next to Thomas Symmes. Here, near what is now the entrance to the Charlestown Navy Yard, they worked from 1726 until the death of the father in 1764. The younger Daniel, meanwhile, had moved to Lexington. The Mannings, William and Daniel, both born in Cambridge, were potters in Charlestown, beginning in the 1730's. Daniel lived only a few years, but William survived until the Revolution, training his son Daniel in the potter's trade. William Manning was the ferryman in 1748 and presumably lived not far from the dock. At the time of his death, he owned land north of Wapping Street. His property was entirely destroyed by the British; and his claim for loss, presented to the town, mentions "Two dwelling Houses, Work House & Kiln House & Out House belonging to me and wife — 266£s., 10s., 4d."

John Harris is another prominent name in the annals of Charlestown potters. His career as an independent potter began in 1746 (he was then twenty-eight), when he bought a house, shop, and kiln at auction from Michael Brigden and Grace Parker, Isaac's widow. This outfit had previously belonged to James Ingalls, Parker's nephew, who had built a kiln upon it in 1741. It lay between Wapping Street and the head of the town dock and extended down the easterly side of the thoroughfare leading to the dock. Ingalls had mortgaged this property to Mrs. Parker, who, in order to finance a new business, put the land and buildings up for sale. In addition to this pottery, Harris, after the death of Thomas Symmes in 1755, acquired the latter's buildings on the waterfront. In 1767 he disposed of the Ingalls kiln and houses to Jonathan Penney and Daniel Manning (William's son), who organized as Jonathan Penney & Co. and manufactured earthenware until the fire of 1775 destroyed their equipment. This pottery, which cost the owners ninety-three pounds, was valued by them eight years later at £293. A large proportion of the valuation was for ware. The complete inventory reads:

	£. s. d.
To a workhouse	100– 0–0
To a kilnhouse and Shed	20– 0–0
To Claymill and Stone	5–10–0
To horse taken in Concord fight	6–18–0
To 20 Cord of wood	13– 6–8
To a small boat	2– 3–4
To 2 thousand Boards, ¼ thousand plank	7– 4–0
To 3 potters wheels	2– 8–0
To the potters tools	2–16–0
To Earthen ware	166–13–4
To 6 load of Clay and glaising	2– 8–0
To 1 wheel Barrow and two Small Anchors	1– 8–0
To 1 hundred and half Lead	2–14–0

Manning died two years after this claim was made, and his partner was his administrator. Penney evidently rebuilt the pottery and continued to operate it after the Revolution, for a deed dated 1789 * mentions the "street to Wapping at Penny's corner, where is now a pot-house." This was the year of Penney's death. A few years later the buildings were sold to a house carpenter, who presumably used them for other purposes.

John Harris also made a claim after the fire, estimating his loss at £893. The inventory of his property includes "a Dubbel house; a house; a barn 20 x 30; three-story warehouse, 18 x 40; 2 do., 14 x 40; mill; two work-houses, 18 x 40, and one 20 x 30; a 'Cill' house, 24 x 30; and cooper's shop. 14 x 16." Harris's establishment was probably

* From Henley to Hall and Putnam.

better equipped than any in town. He ran it until his death in 1780.

Another Harris, Josiah, worked from about 1745 to 1786. He lived in and owned half of the double "mansion" first occupied by Isaac Parker and his family on the corner of Bow Street and Graves Lane. After Parker's death, a married daughter lived on one side, while the widow and her son John retained the other. Harris bought the daughter's half in 1758. Five years later he acquired from Parker's granddaughter land farther down the street towards the river — a purchase that included the kiln and workhouse built by Isaac Parker. The street survey of 1767 notes that Pratt's Lane, off Graves Street, "leads through between Josiah Harris's Work House & Kiln House." Harris lived until 1786, but went out of business after the war. He had lost buildings worth £200 in the fire. An attachment on his property in 1782 mentions his house, a cellar, remains of a potter's kiln, and a wharf.

John Harris, son of John the potter, bought Josiah Harris's holdings in 1783. In a ledger kept by Rea & Johnson, painters, which is filed in the library of the Harvard School of Business Administration, appears a bill to "John Harris, potter of Charlestown," dated April 15, 1786. This would seem to indicate that the younger Harris was a potter. However, there is no evidence to this effect, although brickmaking was one of his numerous and varied activities. The bill was probably contracted during his father's lifetime.

During this period Robert Standly, Joseph Larkin, and Battery Powers were operating kilns, and the names of several other potters are known. Powers was one of the few who were able to continue in business after the disaster of the fire. He was a potter as early as 1758, but just when he first had an establishment of his own is uncertain. In 1775 he made the following claim for loss:

	£. s. d.
To my Pot house	60– 0–0
To Kiln house	50– 0–0
To mill for Grinding Clay & Stone	5– 0–0
To 3 wheels for making ware	3– 0–0
To Sundry working tools	1–14–0
To ½ thousand bords	1– 4–0
To Earthen ware	20– 0–0
To 6 Cords of wood	6– 0–0
	242– 3–0

Powers' buildings were near the town dock, east of Joiners Street and near the Penney pottery. He was still called "potter" in 1795, when he sold part of his land. He died in Boston in 1807.

The only one of the early redware potters of Charlestown to carry on into the nineteenth century was John Runey. In 1788 he bought land of Nathaniel Newhall on the "old Main street leading to the Battery." This location, not far from the swing bridge, seems to have been the site of his shop. Newhall, also a potter, was probably his assistant. In 1803 he purchased land outside the town on the way to Medford. This farm, which stood on a road known as Three-Pole Lane on Rangeway 4, was thereafter the Runey homestead. When Runey died in 1829, he left it to his son John, who continued the business begun by his father. In 1842 the second John and his son, John, Jr., were listed in the Charlestown Directory, with a house in Three-Pole Lane. Five years later their works was on Vine Street in Cambridge, and the firm was known as Runey & Co. The son James S. was now included. In 1856 John and James Runey were back at the earlier location, which, by that time, was a part of Somerville.

CHAPTER FIVE

A Potter's Daybook

Little documentary evidence concerning our early potters has been found. When such material comes to light, as it so rarely does, it is of the greatest value. By some fortunate circumstance the account book of John Parker of Charlestown, which he kept for ten years, is preserved in the library of the Harvard School of Business Administration.

Parker was the son of Isaac, who has been noted as having a house and kiln on Graves Street. When his father died in 1742, John was but seventeen years of age. For a few years he worked for his mother and Thomas Symmes (see Chapter VI). In 1748 he rented his workhouse to Dr. Isaac Rand. Thereafter, while still running his own business, he did odd jobs for other potters, turning ware, setting kilns, grinding lead — doing a day's work wherever it was needed.

The account book begins in 1747, one year before his marriage to Abigail Center. He was then working for Samuel Bodge, setting his kiln or making trips to Boston, and receiving his payment from Mrs. Bodge's store in such commodities as sugar, candles, chocolate, tea, or vinegar. On his own account he made a substantial sum of money by furnishing "sugar drips" or molds to the Boston confectioners at four and five shillings a dozen. Now and then he made mugs, pots, or pitchers for Charlestown citizens, and he sent shipments of earthenware to all parts of New England. In November 1749 he provided the potter Daniel Edes with earthenware worth £28, 18s. His sales to his own customers were fewer after 1749, when his time seems to have been taken by Joseph Larkin, John Harris, Josiah Harris, Robert Standly, and Samuel Bodge.

The list of Parker's activities while he was in the employ of Joseph Larkin during September and October 1753 illustrates the procedure in a pottery of that day. More important, it gives decided proof that the early redware maker was not limited in his output to coarse jugs, pots, and pans for the kitchen, but was accustomed to furnish all the smaller and more delicate articles that were for use on the table. It has hitherto been supposed that small wares were introduced at the time of the Revolution as a substitute for things ordinarily imported. It is, however, a fact that such forms were made in the colonies from the earliest times. Only the extreme fragility of the ware has prevented our having examples of these once familiar objects, which in their day were as common as pewter, brass, or iron.

The account with Joseph Larkin follows:

Sept. 1753	To Setting Kiln	1 – 10 – 0
Oct. 1st	To making 4 Doz pudn pans @ 2/4	9 – 4
the 2d	" " " " Boles @ 2/	8 – 0
the 2d	" " 8 " porringers @ 1/6 To 4 Doz Qut pitchers @ 2/8	19 – 8
the 3d	Made 2 Doz platers @ 1/8 & time spent	5 – 0
the 4	to Making 5 Doz S. platers 4 Doz L pudn pans 1 Doz S ditto	19 – 0
the 5th	to Making 3 Doz pudn pans @ 20d 1 Doz qut muggs @ 2/4 12 Doz pt Do @ 1/8 ½ Doz pots @ 1/8	1 – 8 – 2
the 6th	to Making 4 Doz Platers @ 2/4	9 – 4
the 8th	To Making 3 Doz Do @ 2/4	7 – 0
the 9th	To Drawing Kiln going to Boston ec	1 – 5 – 0
the 12th	To Making 2 Doz Milk pans @ 3/6 & 2 Doz platers @ 2/4	11 – 8
the 15th	To Making 4 Doz pudn pans @ 2/4	9 – 4
16	" " 5 " platers @ & 3 Doz Boles @ 2/	17 – 8
the 20th	To making 1 Doz Chamber pots 2/ & 4 Doz Boles 8/	10 – 0
the 22	To Making 8 Doz Boles @ 2/ 3 Doz pudn pans @ 2/4	1 – 3 – 0
the 23	To Drawing Kiln picking out ware Writing and going to Boston	15 – 0
	To Making 3½ Doz pudn pans	8 – 0
24	" " 2 " qut pitchers 3 Doz L plates, 1 Doz pots @ 1/8	10 – 0
1754	July the 12th To 1 Days Work	1 – 5 – 0
23	To Setting Kiln 30/ Setting up 15/	2 – 5 – 0
	August the 8th To setting your Kiln	1 – 10 – 0
	To Writing 1 Day	1 – 2 – 6

[Other similar entries]

The credit side of this account shows that Parker received in payment several commodities, including ten and one-half dozen mugs at four shillings and ten dozen mugs at two-and-six.

Immediately following the Larkin account is one with Bodge and Larkin, who had a joint order to be filled. Parker was paid partly with finished earthenware and partly with food. In the summer of 1754 he was at work making bowls, pans, pitchers, pots, mugs, platters, chamber pots, and twenty dozen gallipots for John Harris. He also notes:

August	28	To Setting Kiln 30/	4–0–0
	31	To Helping Down the Kiln 1 Day 17/6	2–4–0
Sept	4	To Picking Ware Writing & going to Boston	2–4–0
	7	To grinding Mill of Clay 10/	1–4–0
		To Drawing Kiln 10/	1–4–0

For this work he was paid with earthenware and other things, including a "child's chair of Mr. Sam'l Larkin."

Parker worked for Josiah Harris in 1754, 1755, and 1756. In the summer he turned ware; in winter, he made occasional trips to Boston, perhaps to deliver pottery, or he labored at the harder tasks of digging clay or splitting wood. He did "writing" for all who employed him, for he was a well-educated young man.

Once (in 1755) Parker rendered an account to Standly & Bodge for setting their kiln three times. Among the "sundrys" received of Mrs. Bodge for this service were several "pitchers of flip." April 1, 1756, he charged Joseph Larkin two pounds for the rental of his wheel for two years; May 15, he sold him the wheel for four pounds, ten shillings. During that year he set the kilns for John and Josiah Harris, as well as for Larkin.

An examination of the items in Parker's account book reveals that he and other potters of his day were making the following forms in redware: milk pans, pudding pans, bread pans, pots, large and small, basins and small basins, jugs, quart and pint mugs, quart pitchers, "little" pitchers, large and small bowls, porringers, cups, large plates, platters, small, large, and "great," sugar drips, and "jegers."

There is no mention in the book of "painting" the ware (the potter's term for slip decoration), nor is any purchase of white clay noted. Parker apparently never did the glazing or finishing: he was employed as a thrower and in doing general labor for the other potters. Hence, if any of the objects turned by him were subsequently decorated, either with slip or in any other way, he would have had no occasion to make note of it. Nevertheless, the Charlestown potters, like others whose refuse piles I have investigated, undoubtedly decorated their pans, plates, platters, and perhaps their bowls in this manner. Thomas Symmes, Parker's uncle, advertised his "red and yellow Ware of divers Sorts" in 1744. It is virtually certain that mid-eighteenth-century potters everywhere practiced slip decoration.

There is good reason to believe that glazing and decorating were done by women in the early potteries, even as today. William Kettell had a woman apprentice, Ann Mackdugle, whose death in Charlestown is recorded, May 24, 1712. An advertisement in the *Boston News-Letter* of June 18, 1716, gives notice of the arrival of Irish servants on the ship *Globe*, Captain Nicholas Cursell. Among the passengers were women trained to different trades: milliners, ribbon and lace weavers, a butter maker, and an "Earthen Ware Potter Maker." We do not hear much about these women potters. Since women in the trades were indentured for a period of years, they were given the status of servants, and so do not appear in colonial records in

any other capacity. I have come across only one instance where a woman actually ran a pottery, and she was the mother of this same John Parker.

Parker's daybook shows how widespread was the distribution of the ware. It was sent by boat all along the seacoast to purchasers in many New England towns. The list of Parker's customers represents the patronage of only one man, a minor potter: it is suggestive of the greater extent of business done by his contemporaries. He rendered accounts to the following:

Joseph Malin and Joseph Williams, Norwich
George Boyd, Samuel Marshall, Mrs. Eleanor Marshall, widow, and Tobias Lear, Piscataqua (Portsmouth)
Joshua Freeman, Casco Bay
Benjamin Griffith and Daniel Gray, Killingworth, Connecticut
Clement Minor, Stonington, Connecticut
Thomas Rand, Cape Ann
Deborah Brewster, Duxbury
James Lewes, Barnstable
John Smith and Heman Stone, Harwich
Daniel Mann, Wrentham
Joseph Adams, Roxbury
John Smith, Milford
Mary Flagg, Boston
Daniel Newhall, Malden

Aside from its importance as a potter's record, the Parker book is full of interest as a human document. It contains the dates of the births of Parker's children and the times when they had measles or smallpox, or when the younger children were inoculated against the dread disease. It notes that on July 23, 1749, Parker's house was burned and that ten years later he moved into a new home "in Middlegate." When the ledger had served its usefulness, it was turned over to the Parker children. One page has an original poem in childish handwriting, possibly that of little Nancy. Its title is "Honer to the Hill," and it is filled with that deep sense of God's omnipresence and of the wondrousness of nature that pervades literature of the period.

CHAPTER SIX

A Woman Introduces Stoneware

A third member of the Parker family — the mother, Grace — is the only woman known to have run an early New England pottery in her own name. She was the central figure in a most astounding drama. Her desperate attempt to introduce an innovation in the manufacture of pottery places her among the memorable women of her day. Her story is revealed in a number of petitions and other documents in the Massachusetts State Archives. These are reproduced in their entirety in Appendix I for those who wish to consult them, although all the essential facts are told in this chapter.

Grace Parker was the daughter of Stephen Hall, a weaver and painter, and apparently a man of culture. She was born in Cambridge June 17, 1697, and married Isaac Parker when he was twenty-three years old and she but eighteen. Only the year before, he had built the kiln on the corner of Graves Street and Pratt's Lane where he was to carry on his business for many years. His house, the double "mansion" purchased by Josiah Harris after Parker's death, stood on the corner of Graves Street and Austin (Bow) Street. It must have indeed have been a mansion to have accommodated the family of eleven children that the Parkers proceeded to bring into the world, besides providing quarters for the Negro man, Acton, the Negro boy, Jack, and presumably a woman servant.

There is every evidence that Parker was a successful potter, well able to support this large household. The inventories of the Parkers' belongings indicate that they lived more than comfortably, owning many things that were considered luxuries in their day. Among their pieces of furniture were two joint stools, six leather chairs, three great chairs, seven black chairs and twelve others, a couch, a large black walnut table, and a looking glass worth fifteen pounds. At the time of Isaac's death, they possessed thirty-one pictures and 182 pounds of pewter. Mrs. Parker's inventory mentions Delft and china bowls, mugs, and plates, besides two sets of china and many small things of glass and brass. She also had twenty bound books, a Bible, and fifty-eight pamphlets. The family became prominent in Charlestown and Boston affairs. A son Daniel was a goldsmith in Boston, and a grandson Isaac, Harvard grad-

uate, became representative to Congress and Chief Justice of the Commonwealth.

Until the late 1730's, Isaac Parker was contented with his trade of redware potter. However, being perhaps rather better informed than some of his contemporaries, he was conscious of the defects of red earthenware, and, realizing the need of a safer and more durable type of pottery, he was seized with the desire to produce it himself. No doubt he was also activated by an ambition to increase his income, as he might well do, were he given a monopoly on making a better product. In short, he wanted to make stoneware.

In Parker's day no stoneware had been manufactured in Massachusetts Bay Colony, or, as far as I have been able to learn, elsewhere in New England. We have his own statement that a great deal of it was used in the province, but, he says, it was all brought from New York, Philadelphia, and Virginia, where the potters held closely guarded the secret of its manufacture. A number of business men with whom Parker discussed his plans encouraged him in the project. They saw that it would be a great advantage for the people of the province to be able to buy stoneware made at home, rather than to spend money outside the colony.

Parker's greatest difficulty was to learn the "mystery" of making the ware. For this purpose he took a trip to New York to investigate the potteries there, but the tradespeople were so wary he was unable to obtain the slightest information. As a last resort, he sent to Philadelphia for a man who had been trained there in the stoneware potter's art. The new employee with his wife and child arrived in Boston July 14, 1742, on the brigantine *Mary*. Variously recorded as Duchee, Deshee, and Deusha, he was, in fact, James Duché, son of Anthony Duché, a potter of Philadelphia. The family were French Huguenots who had come to Philadelphia in 1700; the father and mother (Anniet Doz) were married there in the First Presbyterian Church five years later. James was born in 1715. His brother Andrew is of note for his attempts to make porcelain in Georgia — a tale which has been ably related by Rudolph P. Hommel in *The Chronicle* (November 1934, January 1935) of the Early American Industries Association. Mr. Hommel has also recently established the fact that Anthony Duché and his older sons were making stoneware in Philadelphia before 1730, when they applied unsuccessfully for a subsidy and a monopoly on the manufacture. James and his wife, the former Hannah Preston, had been married but five years when they came to Boston, and were very poor indeed. Upon arriving in Charlestown, they were added to the already large responsibilities of the Parkers and were supported by them.

James Duché was perhaps skilled enough as a potter, but he was lacking in knowledge of the properties of New England clay. The stoneware makers of New York and Philadelphia had never had any trouble on this score, because they had suitable clay nearby. But Duché was unaware, as were several others after him, that New England clays cannot be burned at the high temperature necessary for producing perfect stoneware. Parker had heard of Martha's Vineyard clay being used for the purpose, and, fearing that the cost of transporting clay from New York or Philadelphia would eat up the greater part of any profit he might make, he decided to make a trial of the material nearer at hand.

Considerable money had now been spent on the journey to New York and on Duché's transportation and board. Parker was ready to begin, but it was imperative that he should have some financial backing. In September 1742 he presented a petition to the General Court, stating that he had for several years past been endeavoring at great expense to find out the art of making stone-

ware, that he had now done so, and had employed a man to assist him. He explained why it would be of advantage for Massachusetts to have the business carried on, but said he was unable to provide the funds to do so. Therefore he asked for a loan of £125 and the sole privilege of manufacturing the ware for whatever time the Court should see fit.

The petition was granted on Parker's terms. He was advanced £125 in bills of the new emission (five hundred pounds old tenor), for which he was to give land security worth two hundred pounds. This loan was to be payable without interest on or before the last day of December 1746, provided the money was ûsed for the intended purpose; but, in case it was not so used, the whole sum was to be paid within one year. Parker mortgaged six lots of land to William Foye, Treasurer of the Province, and the money was paid him October 14, 1742. Three weeks later he died.

Not much imagination is needed to picture the difficult situation of his wife, left with such a large family, most of whom were too young to work, and with the added burden of the Duchés. Mrs. Parker was not long in making up her mind how to proceed. After consulting with her friends, she decided to carry on the project herself. This was the more feasible, because Thomas Symmes, her brother-in-law, was ready and willing to go into the business with her. Symmes, successful as potter and merchant, was well able to guide the financial end of the enterprise. Mrs. Parker turned over to him one half the money appropriated to her husband, taking in exchange a mortgage on his two houses. As it was then unusual for a woman to do business in her own name, the partnership was called Thomas Symmes & Company. Mrs. Parker, however, seems to have directed the project, and her name appears first, or alone, in the state documents. On December first, the new firm, including James Duché as a copartner, petitioned the General Court for the monopoly previously granted to Isaac Parker. They received a favorable response and were allowed the sole privilege of making stoneware for a period of fifteen years. Severe penalties were imposed upon any person who should build a stoneware kiln or use a kiln already built for that purpose.

The town records show that Symmes in 1742 was granted by the selectmen and two justices of the peace "liberty to erect a potter's kiln on his own land near his dwelling house." He also went to the expense of putting up new buildings and securing new equipment. Duché built the furnace of Vineyard clay, and a large quantity of ware was made and burned. The result was that the stoneware was ruined, and, even worse, the kiln itself, having shrunk with the heat, fell to pieces. Duché imputed this disaster to the newness of the structure. Hopefully they repaired the damage and made a second "parcel" of ware, which turned out as badly as the first. This time he thought the wood for firing was unsuitable. They made still a third attempt, but with no better success. It was by now perfectly evident that the clay itself was at fault. A whole year was thus wasted, and during that time Symmes & Company expended twice the sum lent them by the province, as well as part of Mrs. Parker's estate, without having anything to show for their time and labor.

Grace Parker must have had an uncommon amount of perseverance and of faith in her ultimate success. A load of clay was brought from New York and the work begun all over again. Duché built another small kiln in which some stoneware was burned with excellent results. Encouraged by having made good stoneware at last, Mrs. Parker resolved to go on with the enterprise, which she considered of public benefit, in the hope that eventually she would find suitable clay

nearer home. Meantime, at an expense of three hundred pounds, she sent Duché to Philadelphia for more clay. Just why it was necessary for him to get it from such a distance cannot be explained, unless for the reason that he was accustomed to the clay from that region or could perhaps obtain it in Philadelphia at less cost. During 1743 and 1744 the partners produced stoneware without mishap, although they saw that there would be no profit in the business while they were obliged to transport their clay from so great a distance. A sloop load landed at their wharf cost between eight and nine hundred pounds.

That the manufacture was more than a mere abortive attempt at making a new commodity is proved by the advertisement of the company in the *Boston Gazette*, April 16, 1745: "Made and sold reasonably by Thomas Symmes & Co. at Charlestown near the Swing-Bridge, blue and white stone ware of forty different sorts; also red and yellow Ware of divers Sorts, either by Wholesale or Retail." The "red and yellow" ware was undoubtedly redware decorated with white slip, similar to the pottery made by James Kettle and a number of other eighteenth-century potters whose refuse piles I have investigated. Both Symmes and the Parkers were continuing their red earthenware business, as they had previously done. The term "blue and white stone ware" was applied at the period both to the English scratched blue salt glaze and to the common light-gray ware with blue decoration introduced to this country by Flemish and German potters. Pennsylvania potters and Connecticut merchants advertised "blue and white stoneware" butter pots, jars, and chamber pots. It is safe to assume that Symmes & Company were not attempting to imitate the finer English wares and that they had no more ambitious scheme than to supply the public with ordinary serviceable stone vessels.

In spite of all obstacles, Grace Parker and Symmes might have been successful, had the war with the French and Indians not checked all business for a time. Like a heroine of Greek tragedy, poor courageous Mrs. Parker was beset by one misfortune after another. In March 1745, her young daughter Anne died; in November, her oldest son was killed in the Cape Breton expedition, leaving a wife and child partially dependent upon his mother. The health of her son John and her "kinsman" (probably her nephew James Ingalls) was becoming so seriously affected as a result of working in the stoneware pottery that they were no longer able to support themselves by making earthenware. Furthermore, she had lost so much money, she was obliged to sell some of her property.

Mrs. Parker's name appears at this time in a newspaper notice in connection with a vendue or auction. Several years before his death her husband had taken with Michael Brigden a mortgage on James Ingalls' land and buildings. Since Ingalls had just built in 1741 the kiln that was put up for sale three years later, it seems likely that he went into the stoneware venture with his aunt. November 1, 1744, the *Boston News-Letter* advertised: "Charlestown Earthenware — To be sold on reasonable Terms, A dwelling House and Land in Charlestown, near the Swing-Bridge, with a House and Kiln for the making Earthen Ware; as also a Warehouse and other Convenience necessary for that Business. Inquire of the Printer." This was the Ingalls pottery, which he conveyed to his aunt and Michael Brigden the following year and which they announced for sale in December 1746. A notice in the *Boston Gazette*, dated December 9, reads: "Charlestown Earthenware — To be sold by publick Vendue on Tuesday the 16th Currant, two o'clock Afternoon, at the Three Crane Tavern at Charlestown a Dwelling House, Potter's Kiln House and Kiln in Wapping

Street In Charlestown aforesaid, any Person minding to purchase the same before said time may inquire of Michael Brigden or Grace Parker." It has already been noted that John Harris purchased the property, thereby supplying Mrs. Parker with additional funds, of which she was sadly in need.

The war was the insuperable obstacle to the furtherance of her plans. All business was seriously affected, and it was a matter of danger as well as of expense to transport the clay to New England. Although search was made for suitable clay nearer at hand, none could be found. For a time the manufacture of stoneware was suspended. James Duché went back to Philadelphia, probably in 1746. He was taxed in Charlestown during 1745 and 1746, but thereafter his name does not appear on the list of citizens. The date for the payment of the loan to Isaac Parker was fast approaching, and Grace Parker was unable to raise the needed sum. In October 1747 she petitioned the Court for an extension of time, asking that she might be permitted to make five annual payments. In the petition she recounted the story of her trials, saying, however, that she and her partner were not "yet altogether discouraged, altho' the Purchase of Clay & Wood is likely to be so expensive (even when the War is over), that any advantage they may ever receive by it is very uncertain & precarious." She said that she could not without the utmost difficulty repay the money within the time set.

The General Court allowed Mrs. Parker an extension of the time until December 1751, permitting her to make three yearly payments. Whether she made any further attempt to manufacture stoneware is uncertain. From John Parker's notebook, it is clear that he, at least, continued the business of making redware. In 1748 he charged to his mother's account eight shillings for mending her mill and three pounds for "repairing the Kiln at Sundry times." The next year, also, he made similar charges, indicating that her pottery was in operation. In a petition drawn up after their mother's death, John and his brother Daniel mention smallpox as having put a stop to the stoneware business, but do not say when this happened. Two of John's children were afflicted by the disease in 1752, and James Ingalls died the same year, perhaps from the same cause. It is quite possible that Symmes & Company were still struggling along after 1750. Mrs. Parker had managed by selling part of her estate to pay two hundred pounds out of the five hundred owed the province. Altogether she had lost "at least Two Thousand pounds old tenor by the abovementioned Scheme laid at first for the good of this Province."

It is perhaps more than a coincidence that Grace Parker died only five months after the passing of her partner in July 1754. Symmes' death must have been the hardest blow in her series of misfortunes, removing, as it did, all hope of carrying her plans to completion. Mrs. Parker's ventures had failed, but *she* had not failed. She had succeeded in bringing to public notice the need for a ware which after her time entirely supplanted common redware. In the words of her second petition, her disappointments were "no other than what have usually attended such as have enterprized things new & uncommon, how beneficial soever they may in time have prov'd to the Publick, or gainfull to the after-undertakers."

CHAPTER SEVEN

Redware Potting From Boston to the Cape

The earthenware industry in Boston, which was begun by Edward Drinker from Charlestown about 1663 and which was carried on briefly by John Wilkins from 1670 to 1680, came to a standstill after Drinker's death in 1700. His heirs sold his property to Joseph and John Breed of Lynn, mariner and farmer, and there is no evidence that anyone succeeded to Drinker's business. For the next twenty years the records do not mention any potter. In 1720, however, Philip Cutler of Charlestown moved to Boston and bought a tenement and land on Sea Street in the south end of the town. The bounds of the property show that his house was on the westerly side of the road, while, across the way, he owned beach and flats running to low-water mark. Three years later the selectmen gave him permission to "Erect a Timber Dwelling on his land in Boston near Windmill Point." He was then a potter, but combined his trade with other activities in order to eke out a living. In 1727 his petition for a license as alehouse keeper was approved, and he is mentioned as a retailer in 1729. Cutler died four years later, leaving real estate worth £530. Nothing is known about his pottery.

Throughout the eighteenth century the names of only two or three other potters appear in Boston records. The few sporadic attempts in competition with the Charlestown trade failed of their objective. With one exception, there was no successful potter in Boston.

A court record of 1735 speaks of Curtis Chamlett (also spelled Chamlet, Chamblet, Camlet) as a potter. He appears to have been the son of Henry Chamlett, born in Boston before 1700. He married Mary Adams April 28, 1726, and went the following year to Charlestown with his wife and child. It is probable that he worked with Philip Cutler, for his departure from Boston coincides with the opening of Cutler's tavern and possibly with the close of the pottery.

The will of one Curtice Champnoine of Boston, potter, is recorded April 26, 1738. He left property to his wife and children; otherwise, nothing is known about him.

The name of David Symonds appears with an advertisement in the *Boston Gazette*, June 18, 1751. It reads: "*Earthen Ware* made and sold by Wholesale or Retail, by *David Simons* at *New Boston*, Potter, on the North

side of Doctor *Mayhew's* Meeting-House." Symonds, for so his name is recorded in deeds, in the spring of 1750 had bought land and buildings on Chambers Street from Stephen De Blois, who took a mortgage on them. The buildings had formerly been used for a snuff mill, but were converted by Symonds to the purposes of a potshop. "Doctor Mayhew's Meeting-House" was the old West Church on Lynde Street, which ran parallel to Chambers. The pottery must have stood to the northwest of the church in the block now bounded by Chambers, Cambridge, and Lynde Streets, and just back of the Harrison Gray Otis house.

Symonds was working at his trade as early as 1748.* He occupied his Lynde Street place until December 1766, when he was dispossessed of his shop in a suit brought by Samuel Parkman. Symonds lived in Boston and held town offices until 1783. His widow, dying in 1795, left her house and land on Lynde Street to the church.

Advertisements published in the *Boston Evening Post* in May and October 1769, mentioning tortoise-shell plates and other ware of superior quality, have given rise to much speculation. They have led some writers to the assumption that earthenware of the English Whieldon type was actually made in Boston. The facts are far different. Investigation proves that the 1769 pottery made nothing more sophisticated than had its predecessors. The first notice, appearing in the issues of May 2, reads:

> Wanted, Samples of different clays and fine white Sand. Any Person or Persons that will send about 5 pounds of Clay and a Pint of fine white Sand to Leigh's Intelligence Office, in Merchant's Row, Boston, if it is the sort wanted the Proprietors will have the advantage of Proposals made to them to supply a quantity.—Twenty Dollars per Month with Victuals Drink Washing and Lodging given to any persons Skill'd in Making Glazing and Burning common Earthen Ware who can be well recommended. Enquire of the Printer.

* Suffolk County Court Record.

The owner of the intelligence office, whose name appears in the above paragraph, was one Benjamin Leigh, a Boston business man who was agent for a Delft pottery in London. In company with John Allman, a potter, he had conceived the idea of making superior earthenware of the kind then imported from England. Their first step was to advertise for clay and workmen. It may be only a coincidence, but eight days later "Mr. Richardson a Potter" arrived in town from Connecticut on the sloop *Polly*. It is possible that he came in response to the information that a pottery was about to start in Boston. The advertisement must also have brought the desired samples of clay and sand, for on May 31 Leigh and Allman, armed with specimens, presented a petition to the General Court asking for financial encouragement. In it they said:

> That y^r Petitioners have at their great expence found Clays that will answer to make all kinds of Potters ware, samples of which we now present to y^r Excellency and Honours view. They are such as we import from Europe at a great expence and for which large sums of money are continually remitting.
>
> Your Petitioners are desirous of carrying on this Factory in an extensive manner so as not only to supply this Province with that article but our Neighbouring Colonys besides there being at this Time not one of this business in North America but your Petitioners. And your Petitioners are notwithstanding labour is so excessively high determined to sell their ware cheaper than it can be imported in order to stop the Importation of the same. Another advantage your Petitioners would point out to your Excellency and Honours will arise by this Factory the employing a Number of Poor Children which are now at the Expence of the Publick.
>
> Your Petitioners are fully sensible of the great Spirit this Honble Court have always shewen,

to Encourage New manufactorys; the good effects of which has in many instances appear'd. Your Petitioners humbly acquaint this Honble Court that their stock in Trade, is too small to carry on their business to any advantage, to themselves or the Publick. Therefore Prays the assistance of this Honble Court in a Sum of Mony; to encourage them to carry their good designs into Execution. The favour granted shall be repaid again with a most gratefull acknowledgment of y[r] Petitioners — etc.

The Court granted the partners two hundred pounds. Almost immediately they found a suitable location with a house and other buildings in the westerly part of Boston. The property was on the west side of Leverett Street, which was a continuation of Lynde Street, and hence not far from the shop where Symonds had worked. A second notice concerning the pottery appeared in the *Post*, October 30, 1769:

Wanted immediately at the new Factory in New Boston, four boys for Apprentices to learn the Art of making Tortoise-shell Cream and Green Colour Plates, Dishes, Coffee and Tea Pots, Cups and Saucers and other Articles in the Potter's Business, equal to any imported from England. Any Persons inclined to Bind out such Lads to the aforesaid Business is desired to apply immediately at the said Factory or at Leigh's Intelligence Office.

However ambitious their intentions, as indicated by this announcement, Leigh and Allman were doomed to failure. They might have been saved the disappointment, financial and otherwise, of their abortive attempt to make tableware, had they been better acquainted with the properties of New England clays. In exactly one year from the time of their purchase they conveyed their pottery and land to Joseph Warren, and the venture came to an end.

Forty years elapsed before another attempt was made to produce fine ware. The name of the Boston Porcelain and Glass Company is familiar to students of glass history, for its furnace was the nucleus of the great New England Glass Company, which lasted seventy years. Its porcelain department was not so successful. The company was incorporated February 14, 1814, by Jesse Putnam, Thomas Curtis, and George Blake, with a capital of $200,000. It was an ambitious undertaking in a period when money was scarce, but the hope of making porcelain in America was keen. The firm erected buildings at Lechmere Point in East Cambridge, just across the Charles River from Boston. Deming Jarves, author of *Reminiscences of Glass-Making* (1854), is almost the sole source of information about this concern. He says that the "china department under the direction of a Mr. Bruitan proved an entire failure for lack of proper materials." Again the unsuitability of New England clay prevented the manufacture of anything better than ordinary earthenware. That the company produced pottery of some kind is proved by deeds of sale to the New England Glass Company, in which "earthenware" remaining in the buildings is mentioned, with permission for its former owners to dispose of it in the period before the glass company took possession.

Although so few potteries persisted in Boston, a number flourished in the outlying communities. As early as 1733 the Hall brothers, Joseph, Jr., Peletiah, and David, were established potters in Dorchester, on the country road from Milton to Boston. Sons of Joseph and Silence Hall of Charlestown, they were undoubtedly trained in one of the shops in that area. Joseph, the eldest, was born in 1701; Peletiah, three years later; David, in 1711. Peletiah's potting activities extended over a span of fifty years and he is called "potter" in deeds as late as 1777. He outlived his brothers by many years, since both died before 1762. In the numerous transfers of property from one member of this family to another, there is no mention of a pottery shop.

Each owned land near the Dorchester-Roxbury line, but their homes were in the village. In 1740 Joseph sold four acres bounded by the burying place, a town road, and the road leading to Dorchester Neck. Peletiah and David shared a dwelling house, orchard, and pasture land on the easterly side of the country road. The long continuation of their enterprise is proof of its success.

Two other Halls, father and son, are found in Medford, and later in Roxbury. They appear in Charlestown records, although they actually lived on the other side of the Mystic River. The elder, known as Jonathan, Jr., was born in Charlestown, October 12, 1706, and married twice into local families. His first wife was Elizabeth Tufts, whose brother James of Medford, a brickmaker, owned the yards near the river where bricks are still burned. Brooks, in his *History of Medford*, says that James Tufts and his son carried on the pottery business as well for many years. Shortly before his death in 1753, Hall bought five acres of land north of Tufts' property. The son Jonathan, then twenty years of age, did not long remain in Medford. Within three years he had moved to Roxbury, where, in January 1756, he bought half an acre of land and buildings on the "great Country Road." Two newspaper items in the *Boston Gazette* concerning this second Jonathan have been noted by George Francis Dow. One, dated January 31, 1763, says that "an incendiary attempted to set fire to his Work-house" near his dwelling house. A reward of one hundred pounds was offered for information leading to the conviction of the "Inventor of said Villany." That Hall had a determined enemy would appear from the announcement on October 24 of the same year that he had "lost his Shop by fire together with its contents of a considerable value." The young potter was apparently unable to rise above so great a calamity. Four years after this event he gave up his shop and, on June 2, 1767, he sold his holdings in Roxbury.

The Halls of Roxbury and Dorchester were followed by two young men, Ebenezer Baker and William Seaver, Jr., who bought a house and began business together, October 31, 1769, in what was then Braintree, but now part of Dorchester. Their partnership lasted but a short time, as Seaver moved to Taunton to initiate the manufacture of stoneware. Baker remained in Dorchester and was called "potter" as late as 1778, but in 1785 "gentleman." His pottery is said to have stood exactly where Baker's chocolate factory, until recently owned by Ebenezer's descendants, may be seen today.

The trade in that district then passed to Enoch Fenno, a native of Dorchester, who was perhaps an apprentice of Baker's. He married Mary Holden of Dorchester in 1780 and settled in the section of Milton now Mattapan. He bought one hundred and four acres adjoining the estate once owned by Rev. Peter Thacher and he occupied the Thacher house until it was burned in 1798. The potshop was in the V between Thacher and Mattapan Streets. Fenno converted this building into a dwelling after the loss of his other house. He lived and worked there for many years. The cellar holes of the Thacher house and of Fenno's later habitation were plainly visible near Pine-Tree Brook in 1887. They are now hidden under a group of modern dwellings. A small pond where the potter had dug clay could also be seen sixty years ago. When this pottery was in operation, the site was a favorable one for trade, as the travel to Dedham passed the door.

A small earthenware shop was in existence in Dorchester in the 1840's. It is mentioned in Haskel & Smith's *Gazetteer* (1843) and in Hayward's *Gazetteer of Massachusetts* (1846). The *Massachusetts Statistics of Industry* for 1845 show that it was run by a single potter with a meager output worth but $150 a year.

Clayworkers, wandering from place to place, remained for short periods in a number of the Boston suburbs. Some went from Charlestown to points a little more remote from the city. Daniel Edes was in Watertown from 1761 to 1764 and in Lexington the following two years. Ezra Porter of Danvers also worked in Watertown in the middle of the century. Samuel Bodge was a potter in Newton in 1787.

The *Boston News-Letter* of May 15, 1760 has the following reference to a pottery in Cambridge: "Friday night at X o'clock, a Potter's Work-House at Cambridge, belonging to Mr. Prentiss, was entirely consumed by Fire, together with a large Quantity of wood Therein." This was probably the shop of Deacon Henry Prentiss (or Prentice), a well-known brickmaker, whose grandson Samuel became a potter in Gorham, Maine. Brickyards and redware potteries were often run in close conjunction. This is but another instance of a man in a brickmaking family adopting the potter's calling.

Daniel Felton from Danvers settled in a part of Dedham now Needham at the time of his marriage in 1765. In deeds he is styled "potter." He was born in the Essex County town in 1743 and went back there to die in 1828. In 1778 he bought land with a house and barn on the road from Dedham to Medfield and practiced his craft in that location.

Far more important than these minor potteries was the one founded by Abraham Hews of Weston in 1765. The Hews pottery is still running in Cambridge and is the only one of all the early redware shops to grow into a big business. The first Abraham was twenty-four years old when he began to make earthenware in Weston. The beautiful house that he later built and occupied is standing even today on the main street of the town, just east of the Baptist church. The workshop stood a short distance east of the house. For one hundred years the successive generations of the family carried on their trade in this building. About the time of the Civil War a new shop was built on the other side of the Post Road, where it joins the present highway. In 1871 this shop in turn was abandoned, and the whole manufacture moved to its present site in North Cambridge. The firm name A. H. Hews was then adopted.

The founder of the business called himself "potter" in the land records until 1796; thereafter he retired to farming. His son Abraham, born in 1766, then took over the management. He, in time, was succeeded by his sons, Abraham and Horatio. The latter was the father of Albert Horatio Hews, the last of the name to head the concern. The Hews family were true executives, better suited than the average craftsman to build up an industry. In 1814 the second Abraham is noted in deeds as "gentleman," meaning that he was a director or manager rather than an actual workman. When the manufactory was transferred to its larger buildings in Cambridge, it employed fifteen men and produced annually eight hundred thousand pieces of ware, principally flowerpots. By 1889 the force had grown to eighty-five or one hundred men and the yearly output to seven million pieces. In prosperous seasons the Hews pottery, in addition to other ornamental wares, has made as many as twenty million flowerpots. Its growth must, of course, be attributed to machine methods that make possible such a large output. Although several potters still work there at the wheel, the restrictions of mass production preclude any vigorous self-expression.

A superficial examination of the early Hews site revealed little of interest: the flowerpot industry had begun before the first shop was abandoned. Because the ground has since been cultivated for a garden, only occasional fragments of the earlier redware could be found. Among them were two pieces of slip-decorated dishes, evidence that the first

Abraham Hews, like others of his time, ornamented his wares by this method. The only important relic that we discovered was a glaze-mill stone, which now lies before the side doorway of the old Hews house, occupied by Allen T. Wheeler. In the house itself, purchased by Mr. Wheeler with part of its contents, were several unusual articles of redware, shown in Fig. 65. The jug, formerly owned in Weston, is pleasing in color and has a characteristic straight neck. A discussion of the wares made at the Hews pottery in the seventies and eighties will be found in Chapter XXVIII.

While not strictly included in the category suggested by the heading of this chapter, some small potteries in Concord and Westford may be noted here. One was owned by Seth Ross (Rose), who ran a potshop for about fifteen years in the rear of the Wright Tavern in Concord, where he was innkeeper. After his death it was offered for sale at auction. A notice of the sale appeared in the *Boston Gazette*, February 11, 1765: "Potter's House, with the Works & Cooper's Shop, Warehouse, Mansion House, Barn & Lands adjoining just by Concord Meeting House (a good seat for Trade) will be sold by Public Vendue, March 6 next, it being the estate of *Seth Rose*, Innholder, late of Concord, deceased." The buildings described are presumably those depicted in Amos Doolittle's famous "View of the Town of Concord." They stand between the tavern and the church on the edge of a small mill pond.

Romance rather than statistics compounds the story of another Concord pottery. Nevertheless, I have verified the tale by finding fragments of earthenware, which speak louder than facts or figures. No less a reporter than Henry Thoreau is my source of information. In *Walden* he says:

> Farther in the woods than any of these, where the road approaches nearest to the pond, Wyman the potter squatted, and furnished his townsmen with earthenware, and left descendants to succeed him. Neither were they rich in worldly goods, holding the land by sufferance while they lived; and there often the sheriff came in vain to collect the taxes, and "attached a chip," for form's sake, as I have read in his accounts, there being nothing else he could lay his hands on. One day in midsummer when I was hoeing, a man who was carrying a load of pottery to market stopped his horse against my field and inquired concerning Wyman the younger. He had long ago bought a potter's wheel of him, and wished to know what had become of him. I had read of potter's clay and wheel in Scripture, but it had never occurred to me that the pots we use were not such as had come down unbroken from those days, or grown on trees like gourds, and I was pleased to hear that so fictile an art was ever practised in my neighborhood.

Thoreau then goes on to say that Wyman's "tenement" was later occupied by an Irishman, Hugh Quoil, after whose death it was torn down. Thoreau was at Walden in 1845. At that time only traces of the cellar remained.

Walden Pond is now governed by the Metropolitan Park Commission and its shores used as a pleasure ground. The spot where the "road approaches nearest to the pond" was familiar to me. At that point a steep slope runs down to the water. Where heavy rains had gullied the embankment, I picked up enough pottery wasters to assure the location of Wyman's workshop, and at the top of the slope, near the road, I discovered numbers of very large bricks from his kiln. A cellar hole across the road marks the site of a good-sized house, which is indicated on the 1830 plan of Concord as belonging to Thomas Wyman. Whether this Thomas was actually the son in question, or a more recent descendant, come to greater prosperity, I was unable to ascertain. The shards included pieces of pans, pots, and mugs, with the usual brown and black glazes.

Another obscure pottery was operated in Westford, north of Concord, in the early

nineteenth century, by one James Burn or Bourne. He is said to have lived on the farm owned in the seventies by Samuel N. Burbeck and to have died there at a very advanced age. Contrary to custom, his potshop was in another locality. It stood in the rear of the John W. Abbot estate and the residence of Nathan S. Hamblin in the center of town. Burn dug his clay for a time on the north side of Prospect Hill. Except that fragments were found years ago on the site of his shop, little else is known about him.

Some of the finest earthenware has been collected in the region between Quincy and Cape Cod. Whether this was produced in a few potteries near the coast — perhaps Abington or Kingston — or whether it is really part of the tremendous Charlestown output that was sold along the bay will never be determined. In trying to attribute pottery found in this area, a possible Charlestown origin must always be considered. The names of customers in Wrentham, Duxbury, Barnstable, and Harwich who bought Charlestown ware occur in John Parker's 1750 day book, and a further reference to it is found in the reminiscences of Seth Sprague of Duxbury, written about 1775.* The writer says: "Our furniture consisted of six *second handed* old fashioned chairs, one white pine table, three or four pewter plates, two wooden plates, and a small quantity of brown earthen ware, made at Charlestown, and a small quantity of hollow ware, and our house was as well furnished as was those of young beginners at that day, in country towns generally."

Almost every authority on American ceramics has stated as a fact that pottery was made in the German colony at Quincy known as Germantown. Their reason for believing this to be so was that Judge Cranch, a descendant of Richard Cranch, one of the proprietors of the glassworks and other manufactures there, had picked up fragments of stoneware near the site of the enterprise. This I have done, also, and I have found shards of slip-decorated redware near the shore. I cannot, however, obtain any real proof that pottery making was one of the Germantown industries. There is a list of the male members of the community in 1757 which I have used in the attempt to discover through their land records whether any of them were potters, but the search was fruitless, as was an examination of documents in the state archives. It seems likely that Judge Cranch's finds were merely household breakage, particularly in view of the fact that stoneware could not be made of the local clay.

In 1765 a potter described as either Dutch or German arrived in Abington, a little way below Quincy. He is said to have come directly from across the seas, but there is a possibility that he was one of the immigrants to Germantown. By 1765 the projects there had proved unsuccessful, and the craftsmen were obliged to seek employment elsewhere. John Henry Benner, therefore, may have settled in this village not far from Germantown to establish himself anew. His story is illuminated by the existence of several authenticated pieces of his craftsmanship. The teapot and pitcher shown in Figs. 30 and 31 may be seen in the historical museum of the Dyer Memorial Library of Abington.

Benner's house and shop were on the land of a prominent citizen, Woodbridge Brown, and were situated close by the clay pits. Whether Brown, and later his son Samuel, leased the property to Benner, or whether they had a financial interest in the pottery, is unknown. At present the land, more recently known as the Dyer estate, is owned by Homans the florist, and is about one-half mile south of Abington Center on the road to Whitman.

Back of the ploughed portion of this open land, I found in 1942 a small section of Ben-

* William Bradford Weston, *Hon. Seth Sprague of Duxbury, Plymouth Co.*

ner's waste pile on the very edge of a small clay pit filled with water. The shards recovered were for the most part similar to the Bayley pieces (see Chapter VIII) and showed no marked dissimilarity to the work of our potters of English descent. The one notable exception was a fragment of a bowl or jar with slip stripings trailed horizontally on the *outside*. Much of the ware is of a brilliant red-orange color treated with splashings and dribblings of dark glaze. The rims are turned with great precision. On the whole, one would say that Benner was a superior potter. This opinion is confirmed by examination of the charming little teapot, which was obtained from a descendant of Benner for the Public Library collection. It is the only complete redware teapot made by an eighteenth-century American potter that I have seen. Any question as to its provenance may be answered by the fact that it has a flat base — a characteristic feature of American turned pieces in contrast to the ringed feet of imported ones.

Benner died January 16, 1796, at the age of sixty-eight. He left a wife, Margaret, and two children, but the pottery seems to have come to an end with his passing.

In nearby Braintree, Peter Clark was running a pottery as early as 1763. He came from a Danvers family that moved to Braintree before he was born. He kept up his Danvers associations and was probably trained there. He even went back to Danvers in 1772 for clay. In 1768 he was selling his wares in Hingham and elsewhere in that vicinity. His story is told in detail in Chapter XVI in connection with his later career in New Hampshire.

The origin of an earthenware shop in Kingston, formerly a part of Plymouth, is uncertain. It was run by the Bradfords, descendants of Plymouth's early governor, but where they learned their trade is a bit of a mystery. The first member of the family to engage in clay work was John, son of Robert. He is called "yeoman and brickmaker" in Kingston records. John was born in 1732 and was running his brickyard on Jones River soon after the middle of the century. His land lay on Wapping Road (the old highway to Bridgewater) about one and one-half miles west of the present Kingston village, and it ran north to the river. John Bradford's sons, Noah and Stephen, both became potters. The fact that Noah is said to have learned his craft in Kingston leads to the belief that his father may have been something of a redware potter as well as a brickmaker.

Stephen Bradford remained on the home farm. On June 12, 1798, his father conveyed to him a small lot of land on the northeast corner of his house lot. By successive purchases from Ellis and Nathaniel Bradford and from Pelham Holmes in 1800 and 1801, Stephen acquired other property near his father's land and the river. Soon after the turn of the century, he built a sizeable home. This is still standing and occupied. It is a large square building of brick, well constructed, but evincing early New England thrift in the use of bricks of odd sizes for its back wall. It is known that another dwelling once stood in the field to the west, and this was doubtless the John Bradford house. Beyond this, a cartway, called by the Bradfords "Brickiln Road," leads north through the woods to the clay pits and brickyard. In 1945, directed by E. B. Verney of Kingston, we visited the Bradford site. The early workshop was apparently west of the Stephen Bradford house, for we found quantities of shards in that part of the garden.

Stephen Bradford was three times married. By his first wife, the former Polly Tupper, he had a son Stephen, who grew up to follow his father's trade and to carry on the pottery after his father's death in 1837. The first Stephen lived to the age of sixty-five. The earthenware business continued until the early fifties; at least, Stephen, Jr., was running the pottery in 1851, but not in 1855.

The few fragments recovered on the site

show a style slightly different from that of Danvers pottery. Pots glazed on the inside only were a common item, as elsewhere, but were peculiar in having an impressed decoration effected by a cogglewheel a little distance below the rim. The Bradfords made a great variety of flowerpots, plain and fancy, some with a green glaze.

It has been stated that Noah Bradford of Kingston (born May 29, 1761) was the same Noah Bradford who worked in West Barnstable from 1819 to about 1830. I believe the Cape Cod potter was the Kingston man's son. The granddaughters of the West Barnstable Bradford, Mrs. Fred B. Livesley and Miss Elfleda J. Bradford, were living in 1939. It seems rather unlikely that their grandfather should have been born 178 years before that time. Moreover, a Noah Bradford, whose age was given as eighty-two, died in the almshouse at Kingston, Dec. 20, 1841, while the Barnstable man must have passed away before 1832. He is referred to in that year by his successor as the "late" Noah Bradford.

My interpretation of the story is that the elder Noah left Kingston in his youth — his marriage is not recorded there — to settle on Cape Cod. His son, the Barnstable potter, went to that town from Hyannis. In 1819 he bought of Prince Nye "a piece of land with a potter's shop thereon" in West Barnstable. Whether this was the property of some predecessor or his own shop built on leased land does not appear. Bradford ran the pottery until failing health forced him to sell it.

The next owner was Daniel Parker, Jr., who informed the public by an advertisement in *The Patriot*, July 18, 1832, that he had taken the stand of the late Noah Bradford and would "supply Cape towns with earthenware made from the hands of the Potter who for years superintended the establishment." Parker carried on the pottery alone and apparently without much success. In the *Executive Documents Relative to the Manufactures in the United States* is his report that the total value of his tools and stock was but three hundred dollars and that he made only five hundred dollars' worth of earthenware in a year. In March 1833, both land and shop were advertised for sale at public vendue.

In the mid-nineteenth century the Barnstable pottery was run by Benjamin Parker, whose name appears in the *New England Mercantile Union Directory* in 1849 and in the *Massachusetts State Directory* in 1851. According to an elderly neighbor, Mr. Eldredge, who remembered the pottery as it was in his youth, it was operated at a later period by the Wrights of Taunton. I have been unable to amplify this statement except to connect Parker with the Wrights by the fact that he was working in Taunton in 1866. He lived near the Wrights and was presumably employed by them as theirs was the only pottery in town.

The West Barnstable pottery stood on land now owned by the Dutra family at a turn of the main road west of the village. Shards have been found back of the house and scattered about the grounds, and a few complete specimens are in collections. Inasmuch as all pieces with a fine green glaze found in southeastern Massachusetts are invariably accredited to the Barnstable pottery, I must say that the attribution seems to me unfounded. The examples of green glaze with a positive Barnstable history which give the basis for this theory are dull in tone and quite similar to the green flowerpots made in Kingston and elsewhere about one hundred years ago. It must be remembered that a green color was not the monopoly of any one pottery: it was used in Portland, Maine, in Essex County, Massachusetts, and in other places. It seems far more probable that the brilliant green jugs, jars, and pitchers that do, in fact, appear in the southeastern part of the state are the products of the numerous Berkley-Somerset group or of the early Charlestown potters who sold their wares to the Cape Cod towns.

CHAPTER EIGHT

Excavations on the Bayley Sites of 1723-1799

The most reliable information about eighteenth-century redware derives from the fragments of discarded objects that were invariably left in potters' dumps. Many such waste piles must be awaiting the excavator's shovel. Others are buried beyond recall beneath buildings. In 1934 my husband and I, by chance, had opportunity to do some rather extensive digging at Newburyport, where, from 1764 to 1799, two generations of the Bayley family had worked as potters. The construction of a bypass under High Street had occasioned the removal of many dwelling houses and shops, including the whole block bounded by Summer, High, and Winter Streets. When we arrived upon the scene, a steam shovel had already ploughed the area, scooping away tons of earth to a depth of twenty-five feet or more. On both sides of the cut, at the cellar level of the demolished buildings, the ground was still undisturbed. Running parallel with Summer Street, the shelf thus formed was ten or twelve feet wide; on the opposite side, six or eight. Below cellar level, the loosened earth sloped at a steep angle to the bottom of the cut.

The Bayley house and shop had stood close to the junction of High and Summer Streets. All that remained of the pottery dump when we began our work was a small segment of shelf running back about fifty feet from High Street. By stepping over the edge of the slope, we could dig in under the surface, which we were not allowed to disturb. As this point, we were about eight feet below the level of the street. The quantity of earthenware that we managed to uncover in the short time at our disposal before the construction work was finished convinced us that an even larger amount had been removed by the steam shovel. In fact, the operator of the machine told us that he had been digging through pottery for two days. This material had been dumped elsewhere on the road for fill. Nevertheless, our findings are, we believe, a distinct contribution to the history of native ceramics.

Since our discovery at Newburyport, we have also obtained a small supply of fragments from the shard pile of a still earlier Bayley at Rowley. The Bayley story, therefore, really begins at Rowley, although, in

order to elucidate the earlier data, the record of results is here first set down from the Newburyport angle.

The potting Bayleys were descended from James Bayley, one of the first settlers of Rowley. In 1668 the pioneer's son John married Mary Mighill and set up housekeeping in a tiny house on Wethersfield Street near the corner of Kiln Lane, a narrow way that took its name, not from the pottery, but from Deacon Mighill's lime kiln. The dwelling was enlarged in the next generation by Nathaniel Bayley. It continued to be the home of the Bayley family until 1902, when it was torn down.

Joseph Bayley, potter, one of Nathaniel's children, was the son in his generation who owned and occupied the house. Born October 17, 1701, Joseph was nearly twenty-one at the time of his father's death. When he came of age, his uncles, Jonathan, Thomas, and James Bayley, who had an interest in the homestead, assigned their rights to him, and he was thenceforth the head of the family.

Joseph Bayley married Sarah Jewett June 12, 1725. For more than two years he had been plying his trade. He is first called "potter" in a deed dated January 18, 1723. It is possible that he had been apprenticed to one of the master potters in Charlestown, but rather more likely that he had learned his craft nearer home. According to present information, there were only two men operating potteries in Essex County during Bayley's apprentice years — Jonathan Hayward, whom I have mentioned as living on the Country Road from Beverly to Salem Village, and Joseph Gardner, Vinson's grandson, in Gloucester. Since the Bayleys are known to have had friends and business dealings in Gloucester, it is probable that Joseph spent his seven years of training there.

In 1735 Bayley and his wife were dismissed from the Rowley church and were admitted to membership in the third parish of Newbury. Four children were born to them in Rowley and two more in their new home. The family settled in that part of Newbury that was later set off as Newburyport. Their house stood on Bartlett's Lane (Winter Street), opposite the present site of the Newburyport railroad station. The location is determined by a description of the land in a mortgage deed from Bayley to Benjamin George, dated February 22, 1737/38, and in another from Josiah Bartlett to Samuel Swett. Unfortunately their "ten rods of land" were entirely removed during the cutting of the bypass. Later it transpired that several other potters also lived and worked on Bartlett's Lane. Joseph Bayley carried on his pottery there until 1761, the administration on his estate being dated June 8 of that year. An inventory of his possessions shows that they were few and simple — he was perhaps keeping house alone. It reads:

One Bed and Bedstead 74/
One timepiece 24/ apparel 26/ 8 Books 18/ pewter 12 pound 12/2 2 iron pots 6/8 Scales and weights 8/ Steelyard 1/6 Box iron 1/8 a Shovel and tongs 3/ 3 tramels 5/4 a warming pan 6/ a frying pan 4/ 4 old tables 8/ three Chests 8/8 2 Desks 7/4 Some old Chairs 4/8 a looking glass 2/4 Earthen and Glassware 4/ wooden ware 3/ a Saw 5/4 a Gun 6/ a lamp and skimmer 2/4 a Sieve and Candlestick 1/1 9 lb of flax 6/ old Iron 8/6 a Mortar 2/ three wheels 6/8 three presses and a plate 10/8 A stone 13/4 half a Kilnhouse and kiln utensils 9/ two Jars 1/6 a House

At this time Joseph Bayley's son Daniel, who succeeded him, was doubtless the owner of the other half of the pottery. A third workman is indicated by the number of wheels. Daniel was born June 27, 1729, in Rowley. He was only six years old when the family moved to Newbury, but no doubt was able to turn ware by the time he was sixteen. In 1763, the year when Newburyport was set off as an independent town, Daniel

Bayley bought of Moses Ordway for a little more than twelve pounds a lot of land on the corner of High Street and Summer (then Ordway's Lane). The lot had a frontage of thirty-six feet and a length of sixty-four feet. St. Paul's Church and churchyard were on the other side of the lane. Here Daniel proceeded to erect a dwelling house and workshop. In a mortgage deed to Daniel Farnham, dated March 26, 1764, the property is described thus: "One certain Dwelling House and Potter's Shop and Kiln adjoining and the Stone and Floor for grinding the Clay the Wheels Irons and Utensils to the Potters' business belonging and in said Shop together with about Ten Rods of Land on which the House Shop &c are Erected and Situated near Saint Paul's Church in Newburyport aforesaid."

The story of Daniel Bayley is one of unusual interest. He was more than a routine craftsman and had to his credit other accomplishments besides potting. An attendant at St. Paul's he became the church organist and choir leader, and for many years officiated in this capacity at the old organ brought from King's Chapel, Boston. His love of music turned his attention to the publication of psalm tunes. Finding the existing collections scanty and difficult to read, he proceeded to collate old favorites and new songs. These he printed himself and sold from his house.

In this connection the name of Daniel Bayley is not unknown to bibliophiles. There has been some disagreement among them as to whether Bayley actually did his own presswork or had it done for him by a Boston printer. It is true that the first two collections were little more than reprints, "printed and sold by Bulkeley Emerson and Daniel Bayley," but Bayley's assurance that *The American Harmony*, published in 1769, was "printed and sold by the Author" may be accepted as fact. The inventory of his estate mentions "1 Printing press and Roll" and "Bookbinder's Tools" — evidence that printing was indeed one of his avocations. Thus Isaiah Thomas's claim to have made the first book printed in Newburyport seems to be refuted.*

It has been said that Daniel Bayley was also a coppersmith. I have found no proof of this theory. Lumps of copper unearthed at the pottery site were probably material for coloring glaze. The inventory mentions ten pounds of old copper, twenty-seven pounds of leaden weights, and seventy-seven pounds of pewter, besides the household garnish weighing thirty-two pounds. While Bayley may have dabbled in metalwork, it is more likely that he took these materials in exchange for earthenware and later disposed of them, perhaps to the local pewterer Edward Rand.

Judging by the inventory, Daniel was a man of taste in dress and in the furnishings of his home. He was the owner of four "Jacketts" of black velvet, broadcloth, linen, and fustian, of three coats, broadcloth, fustian, and "wooling," three pairs of breeches, a waistcoat, four caps, two hats, two wigs in a box, and a walking stick. His wife had such clothing as cloaks of silk and broadcloth, dresses of light and dark chintz, a "taffity" gown, a "harebine" gown, a "bussel" petticoat, bonnets, caps, and a lawn apron. It is easy to picture the couple after a hard week in shop and house, setting forth on Sunday in their gala attire.

The inventory notes the following items relating to the pottery: "½ Potter's kiln and house, 5Li; 1 Stone and muffler, 3/; † ½ of the clay knives, 6/; Potter's shop and half loose boards, 9Li; clay and raw ware, 3/; 1 horse cart, 3Li; empty casks and tubs, 1Li, 4/."

* A list of Bayley's publications will be found in the author's article, "The Bayleys: Essex County Potters," *Antiques* (November 1938).

† A muffler is a small kiln, sometimes used for glazing.

KNOW all men by these Presents, That I Daniel Bayley of Newbury port in the County of Essex and Commonwealth of Massachusetts Potter

in consideration of the Sum of Two pounds ten Shillings

Lawful money, of the Commonwealth of Massachusetts already paid me by John Pilsbury of Newbury port in the Same County of Essex Mariner

the receipt whereof I do hereby acknowledge, have Given, Granted, Bargained, Sold, Conveyed and Confirmed, and by these presents, do Give, Grant, Bargain, Sell, Convey and Confirm unto him the said John Pilsbury and his Heirs and Assigns for ever:

A Certain Piece of Land Situate in Newbury port aforesaid Containing one Rod & one ninth part of a rod. Bounded as follows Viz - Northwesterly on Sun Street So Called, three feet & nine inches, Southwesterly on my own Land, four Rods & three Quarters, Southeasterly on Land Belonging to the Heir of Joshua Pilsbury Decd four feet - Northeasterly on Said John Pilsbury's Land, four Rods & three Quarters to the Street before mentioned

To HAVE and to HOLD the above bargained Premises, with all their Privileges and Appurtenances, to him the said John Pilsbury and his Heirs and Assigns, to the sole use of him the said John Pilsbury and his Heirs and Assigns for ever. And I the said Daniel Bayley do for my self my Heirs Executors and Administrators, covenant and engage to and with the said John and his Heirs, Executors, Administrators and Assigns, that at the time of the delivery hereof I am lawfully Seized in Fee simple of the above bargained Premises, that the same are free of all Incumbrances, that I have good right, full power, and lawful authority to Grant, Bargain Sell and Convey the same to him the said John and his Heirs and Assigns to have and to hold the same in manner, and for the use aforesaid; and that I and my Heirs will Warrant, Secure and Defend the above-bargained Premises to him the said John Pilsbury and his Heirs and Assigns for ever, against the lawful Claims of all persons.

In witness whereof I the said Daniel Bayley

have hereunto set my Hand and Seal this fifteenth day of May in the year of our Lord, one thousand seven hundred and Eighty nine

Signed, Sealed and Delivered
in presence of

Joseph Somerby

Paul Noyes

Daniel Bayley

Essex ss May 19th 1789 The above-named Daniel Bayley

personally acknowledged the foregoing instrument by him Signed, to be his Deed,

Before Dudley Atkins Just. Pacis.

Signature of Daniel Bayley of Newburyport, Mass., on a deed dated May 15, 1789.

At the age of twenty-one, Daniel was in Gloucester. His marriage intentions to Elizabeth Dennen were published there April 21, 1750, and a week later at Newbury, shortly before the event. A child born in Gloucester the following year was named Daniel. This infant must have suffered the fate of so many colonial babies, for a second son, also named Daniel, was born to the couple in Newbury four years later. The young potter lived in Gloucester but a short time, for he was back in Newbury in 1753.

Here I must digress to tell one of the strange coincidences of research. In Ravenswood Park, Gloucester, a tract maintained as a public forest, there is a row of cellar holes on what was formerly the "Pest House Road," which ran parallel to the "Old Salem Path." At one of these sites I found unusually large bricks. They were five by nine by two and one-half inches, as compared with the ordinary house brick measuring four by seven (or eight) by two. In the opinion of Professor F. H. Norton of the Department of Ceramics at the Massachusetts Institute of Technology, they were kiln bricks.

On the basis of this slight clue, we secured permission from the park trustees to do some digging. Near the cellar we found pottery fragments and similar bricks in an area the size of a large room. They were not more than a foot below the surface and were pretty thoroughly disintegrated. With them were a few pieces of salt glaze, Delft, and early type English cream ware, but no fragment or object likely to have been made after 1760. Since we recovered rim parts of at least fifty different objects, we continued to work in the hope that positive proof would be forthcoming of the existence of a pottery on the site. The needed evidence at last came to light in the form of a spur — one of the triangular supports or stilts of clay used for stacking bowls in a kiln.

The question of the ownership of the little pottery in the woods now arose. Neither recorded history nor the knowledge of the best-informed persons now living gave the slightest clue. A study of county records, however, revealed the names of several landowners in the vicinity of the sparsely settled Salem Path. One of them was Daniel Bayley's elder brother Nathaniel, who, as early as 1747, occupied a log house in Freshwater Cove, where he raised a family, and in 1760 died of smallpox. Sudden recollection of Daniel's Gloucester marriage supplied a key to the mystery. Members of the Dennen family had owned land on the north side of the Salem road. Furthermore, Bayley's second wife, Sarah (Thomas) Stone, the widow of John Stone, was also a Gloucester woman. In 1751 she was living in the same neighborhood. Various other names and Daniel Bayley's own signature on deeds and mortgages added more links to the chain connecting him with this romantic spot.

It is not difficult to reconstruct the story. In 1749 Gloucester's veteran potter, Joseph Gardner, who for more than fifty years had supplied the town with earthenware, passed on. Quite probably, the young Daniel, learning of the event while visiting his brother's home, seized the occasion to strike out for himself in a new and favorable location. Either at the home of Elizabeth Dennen's parents or in a place of his own, he set up a kiln. Clay was plentiful nearby at Dolliver's Neck; wood was abundant in the forest; and a market was not far away. The future looked bright. Then the smallpox horror descended upon Gloucester and created the wildest panic. Business was at a standstill. This misfortune, coupled with the loss of his child, perhaps from the dreaded epidemic, must have prompted Daniel to retreat to his former home in Newbury.

In Newburyport, Daniel presumably went into business with his father, Joseph. His daughter Elizabeth was born there April 2,

1753, and Daniel, his second namesake, July 15, 1755. In June 1765, only a year after he had built the High Street pottery, his wife died. Two weeks later Daniel announced his marriage intentions to Sarah Stone. Reading between the lines, one may perhaps find a reason for this seemingly indecent haste. In 1760 he had lost his brother; in 1761, his father. Now his wife was gone, leaving him in a new home with two small children to care for. What more suitable than his marriage to a widow, already the mother of three children, whom he had known in his youth at Gloucester? With Sarah, Daniel lived out his days. Four other children came to swell the household: William, born May 9, 1766; Anna Thomas, January 6, 1769; Nathaniel, June 16, 1771; and Mary, August 6, 1775.

Sarah Bayley died in 1792. A fortnight later her husband was laid beside her in St. Paul's churchyard. Today one may see the gravestones of the couple less than two feet from the southeast wall of the present church. As I stood at the spot one warm spring day, the music of the organ rumbled through the open window above; the ground shook, and with it, the bones of Daniel Bayley. I thought he would have been pleased to have it so.

Daniel's namesake and his half brothers, William and Nathaniel, all became potters. Daniel and William worked with their father until his death, when the property was divided between the two young men. So exact was the partition that an imaginary line was drawn through the center of the house door to a stake in the land behind. William was given the half of the house on Summer Street, with "the privilege to bake in the Oven in the North-west end of said house as long as the said chimney shall stand." Daniel inherited the other half, with a larger portion of the land, and the pottery buildings. The other brothers and sisters, after some family disagreements, were each paid one hundred dollars from the estate. Nathaniel married Abigail Pilsbury of Newbury March 2, 1793, and had one child born in 1794. Three years later he bought land of Lydia Knap on Back Street, southwest of the potter Ebenezer Morrison. There is no indication that he had a pottery of his own, and he probably worked for Morrison. In 1829 he was the sexton of St. Paul's Church, his name appearing in this connection in the probate records of Edward Rand of Newburyport. Nathaniel Bayley died of consumption in Newburyport at the age of seventy-eight.

It is, of course, impossible to distinguish the work of the elder Daniel from that of his sons in the pieces recovered from the Bayley pottery. The enterprise must be judged as a family affair. Apparently the father was the moving spirit, for the business was discontinued shortly after his death. June 25, 1796, Daniel, Jr., mortgaged his share of the property, including the pottery buildings, to Caleb Stickney. Three years later, February 22, 1799, he died. William followed him in May of the same year.

The inventory of the older brother's estate lists "the kiln house and kiln, \$20; 1 mill to grind clay, \$3.33; about 200 feet shelve boards, \$1.33; one kiln and one Quarter of Raw Ware, \$12.50; Potter's Shop, \$33.33; Two Wheels, \$3.33"; and a few tools and implements. There is no evidence that any of the children of either brother followed their father's trade.

Thus, before 1800, an industry that had flourished for eighty years, through three generations, passed out of existence. That it came to a sudden conclusion is one of the helpful circumstances in studying the wares recovered. *All the shards excavated at Newburyport fall into the period from 1764 to 1799.*

So little pottery dating from the eighteenth century is in existence today that we were surprised by the variety of forms revealed by our Newburyport discoveries. The

following list of articles that we found complete, or in fragments of sufficient quantity or size to show dimensions, is only partly representative of the things made in this one pottery. The measurements are given in inches, the width by the height.

- Pudding pans — 8¼ x 5½ or 5¾; 8 x 6½; 7 x 4; 4 x 3
- Lard pots — 6 x 7½; 7 x 8; 8½ x 11
- Deep dishes — of all diameters from the size of a saucer 5 x 1⅜ to large pans
- Milk or bread pans — of various sizes, the largest 18½ x 4½
- Bowls — 4 x 1½; 4¼ x 2; 6 x 2; 6 x 2¾; 6¾ x 3¼; 7 x 3¼
- Bowls with rolled rim — 4 x 2
- Pitchers (body only) — 6 x 7; 3 x 4¼; 2¾ x 3½
- Straight mugs — 3 x 4; 3¾ x 5¾; 3¾ x 6¼; 4 x 6½
- A curved mug — 3¾ x 5¼
- A porringer — 5¾ x 2¾
- A washbowl — about 14 x 4½
- Chamber pots — from 6½ x 5½ to 8 x 6¼
- Jugs — one measuring 6 x 8½
- Teapots
- Beakers
- Baking dishes with steep sides

The greater proportion of utensils made in the Bayley pottery were undecorated and purely utilitarian. Lard pots, pudding pots, and deep baking dishes predominated. Bayley's lard pots were sometimes lined with a coffee-colored glaze, or, quite as often, with greenish-black or mottled dark brown. It would be impossible to distinguish them from similar jars made in any one of a hundred New England potteries.

The deep pudding pots, somewhat slope-sided, like a flowerpot, were also unglazed outside, but covered on the interior with a coffee-colored or greenish glaze. In one instance we found fragments of this form in a true and brilliant green. Our best specimen was recovered from the dump without chip or scratch, although its unglazed surface, as in all other examples, is sand-colored from long exposure to the earth. A break in the body of any piece that has been buried will, however, show its basic red color.

Pudding dishes, broader, but not so deep, were common. We have no specimen in its entirety, but the shards give clear evidence of their size and shape.

As in all potteries, there were huge pans for setting milk or raising dough. Ordinarily milk pans are coated inside with a perfectly plain glaze, giving a reddish-brown color. The artistic soul of Daniel Bayley must have revolted against the dreariness of such objects. He varied the coloring with happy results. One large pan of which we have a part is gray-green with fine dark spatterings of smooth color; another, smaller, is greenish or yellowish with rosy mottling; and the largest of all, eighteen and one-half inches in diameter, is a mahogany color, with areas of plain and streaked glaze. The smaller slope-sided pans, which are the "platters" advertised by eighteenth-century potters, were numerous. Their great variety within the small range of Bayley's colors suggests that they were intended to emerge from the fireplace to the dining table. No doubt they were used for pastries or meat pies, or for the deep-dish apple pie still baked in the country. All milk pans and smaller dishes of the same shape were unglazed outside. The Newburyport specimens were not finished too smoothly, but show clearly the parallel marks left by the potter's fingers in turning.

Many fragments of ware without glaze were in the waste pile. They were parts of jars or pots whose purpose is uncertain: even when washed on one surface, redware does not always hold liquids without oozing; unglazed objects could not be used in cooking. Parts of the rims and bases of very large

jars indicate that water coolers were made in this way. The clay in the specimens found is, however, so extremely coarse, that I have hesitated to include water jars as a Bayley product.

On the Winter Street side of the excavation, on the corner of High Street, we found jars similar in shape to a lard pot, but slightly elaborated by tooled bands. They were peculiar in being glazed on the *exterior* of the base only (Fig. 20). I believe them to be earlier than our other finds, for an example of this type appears among the Rowley fragments. They are probably the work of Joseph Bayley or his Bartlett Lane contemporaries.

With one exception, the remaining objects to be described are glazed on both inner and outer surfaces. The bases were left plain. In this category, but without decoration, are jugs, mugs, bowls, and pitchers.

Jug fragments were so few in the Newburyport excavation that one might almost conclude that the Bayleys made none. Since jugs were probably the commonest article of pottery manufacture, it is more reasonable to assume that in the tons of material carried away by the steam shovel, there were many such fragments. The pieces illustrated bear the closest resemblance to Bayley's other work. We found one jug that was virtually complete. It was found in a cistern-like cavity in the embankment, whence came some of the most interesting shards recovered. The color is a mahogany brown with fine streakings. It may be observed that the handle of the jug in Fig. 20 rises from the shoulder, while the handle of our complete specimen springs from the neck. Whether this variation in practice is significant of period or only of the potter's whim is difficult to determine.

The mugs made by Bayley and his sons are handsome affairs. Their height places them at once in the century of tall ale tankards. Compared with these fine drinking vessels, the cans of later days are stolid, squatty, and insignificant. In color, the Newburyport mugs range from a brownish black through browns, plain and mottled, to delightful shades of orange with fine streakings of brown. Occasionally a greenish hue is also present. The black mugs are severely plain, with only a slight tooling at the base. They were doubtless ordinary tavern ware. One of them is a departure from the straight cylindrical form (Fig. 18*d*). In the specimens with lighter glaze we see the hand of the artist. These pieces are turned with very thin walls and are decorated around the body with a broad band of six tooled ridges. There is good reason to believe that the more ornate types are of earlier origin. Joseph Bayley tooled his mugs at Rowley before 1735. The small example, minus handle, is from a technical standpoint the finest piece of redware potting I have seen. It is exceedingly thin, not only at the rim, but also near the base, which is sharply defined inside. Only a highly skilled potter could so manipulate the rather coarse-grained and crumbly native clay.

A man who could make such fine mugs would have no difficulty in turning the delicate bowls and cups shown in Fig. 19. These are by far our most important finds at Newburyport. All of them are restorations, but even a great deal of patching cannot rob them of their charm. Several correspond in size to the larger English teacups of the period. For this reason, and because a matching saucer was found, there can be no question that they were intended for serving tea or coffee. The saucer, however, was not one of a country potter's regular forms. It seems to have appeared about the time of the Revolution, when lack of importations led even the humblest craftsman to try his hand at making tea bowls. Bayley's cups were the "small bowls" of the eighteenth-century men. They were used without saucers for

either coffee or tea. An old print reproduced in A. S. Turberville's *English Men and Manners in the Eighteenth Century* (1926) shows the interior of a coffee house, where each man sitting at the table has just such a bowl before him, while many others are ranged upon a counter ready for use.

The mottled and dripped effects in the small greenish-brown bowls can neither be adequately described nor illustrated. They are ever different and ever pleasing. A true black was evidently the intention for some of them. The larger bowl in Fig. 19 has a mahogany glaze on the exterior, while the inside is of an orange hue. The interesting streakings on this and other examples may have been caused by the dripping of glaze from pieces higher up in the kiln. (These bowls were stacked one inside the other for burning, with a three-pointed cockspur between. Three spur marks scar the glaze on the upper surface of each one.)

One bowl form has a ledge inside the rim, suggesting that a cover was intended to rest upon it. It was probably a tiny sugar bowl, scaled to the proportions of teapots and pitchers of the colonial era. In the same illustration may be seen the base of a tumbler or beaker and a low small bowl of graceful contour.

We found numerous fragments of reddish-orange bowls or cups edged with a narrow line of light slip in the style of Astbury in England. As befitted ware for the table, they are finished in a superior manner. In fact, the quality of the Newburyport ware was so excellent that, in spite of the redware body, the question of its native origin was raised. Doubts were allayed by examination of bases. All are flat, like the bottom of a common jug; in no case does a ring appear as on English cups, saucers, or pitchers.

Although the number of pitcher fragments was not large, we obtained enough examples to illustrate several sizes and forms. A small cream pitcher is about the size of an English Jackfield creamer and was probably inspired by some such prototype. In spite of the loss of its spout and its spottiness where the glaze has flaked away, this little jug still retains its pristine charm. A half-pint pitcher is notable not so much for beauty of form as for its light green hue — shading into rose where the glaze is thin — and the attempt at decoration with incised lines. Only two other instances of incised decoration came to light. A fragment in Fig. 20, which displays both straight and wavy lines, is part of a straight-sided crock. It is almost red in color, with brown spots. The other, unglazed, was apparently an experimental piece. Quart pitchers, black or brown, must have been a common product. In shape they correspond to the example in Fig. 41. I have succeeded in putting together the lower half of a somewhat smaller type with straight sides, but was unable to find either rim or lip. Another shape (Fig. 20), thick and heavy, was either a pitcher or a teapot. It obviously had a handle, but its complete outline must be left to the imagination.

Half a cover and sections of black teapots showing the strainer perforations were found. Both resemble in size and shape a type of redware teapot made long after the close of the Bayley pottery, but there can be no question that they are parts of pottery discards and therefore products of the eighteenth century.

Judging by our discoveries, slip decoration was practiced at Newburyport upon only three classes of articles — deep dishes, chamber pots, and porringers. The fragments of chamber vessels far outnumbered the remainders of dishes, and only one recognizable porringer was found. Strangely enough, the Bayley family seems to have exerted its ingenuity upon the humble and intimate toilet utensils rather than upon objects of more public utility. Or, perhaps, our perspective

was warped by finding an undue number of the objects: we may have struck a discarded kilnful of them. At any rate, the collection is amazing and unique, showing, as it does, a variety of necessities not usually handed on to posterity.

The restored mug in Fig. 25 is an excellent specimen of free brushwork. The piece is unusual in color: a mottled yellowish green with light yellow decoration. Another is a finely streaked brown. In this instance, the trailed slip had a little manganese in its composition, for it is dotted with brown. The effect may have been unintentional and the reason for the piece having been discarded. The simple crossing of wavy lines on a third was carried out on a light ground with green dots and mottlings. Many fragments reveal a rosy red with strong yellow lines; others, a deep red or brown background. Several are glazed in dull light or dark green, which in some cases is pleasantly shot through with yellow or rose tones. Two mugs are lettered in a flowing script. Unfortunately, the key pieces are missing and one can distinguish only the word *betwixt*. The other is marked with a name — apparently *Mary* (Daniel Bayley's daughter). This gift pottery probably came from the hand of the young William Bayley, who presumably expressed his youthful spirits in such capers. Other chamber vessels without decoration were recovered almost in their original state. One mug was unearthed intact except for a few rim chips. It is a rich brown outside and a brownish green within. Black glaze was used both inside and out on many specimens and upon others as an exterior coating only, with a green or brown lining. All the variations of glaze color possible with the materials available were exhausted on these common objects.

Slip-decorated dishes were the poor man's china in the eighteenth century. The ingenuity expended in obtaining simple but effective designs indicates that they were not merely cooking dishes, although they could be used in the oven. In their day, they were doubtless accepted without any appreciation of their artistic value. It is amusing to observe that similar wares from Mexico find a ready sale today among those who tire of mechanical perfection.

All the Bayley dishes are flat in the middle and have sloping rims. The decoration was generally applied to the center of the dish and around the slanting circumference. It often took the form of straight or wavy lines, or, occasionally, a definite motif used as a repeat. Both brush and quill work were employed. The pan or "platter" in Fig. 22 is one of our important finds. It bears the initials *W B* brushed on — doubtless the work of William Bayley. The background color, now somewhat iridescent, is a greenish yellow with rosy tints where the glaze is thin. The yellow of the painted bands is dotted with green, which has flowed into the glaze here and there. Even in its wrecked state, it is a beautiful object. Other examples range from chocolate brown through rosy tans to a real yellow. Specklings of green throughout the decorated portions frequently appear. A rim fragment in deep olive brown — the only one in that color — has the peculiarity of flaring back instead of curving straight up.

One of our first discoveries was a shattered porringer. Unfortunately, its fragments were collected before we suspected the possibility of restorations, and portions were lost. The remainder is shown in Fig. 23. It closely resembles a porringer shown in *Staffordshire Pots and Potters*, by Rhead and Rhead, page 102. The English example is slightly deeper in proportion to its diameter, but the decoration is similar. Our porringer is light yellowish brown in color, brushed with yellow slip.

An unusual employment of white slip to cover the entire background is shown in the

fragments of a washbowl on Fig. 20b, bottom row. This process resembles the Delft technique, the intention being to produce a lighter colored ware than would the natural glazed clay. The plain surface of the piece is varied by spongings of dark brown glaze.

It would be tedious to discuss these and other fragments at greater length. Some have incising or peculiar coloring; others, oddity of form. There are rims of various jars, straight-sided or bulbous, and portions of many a pitcher, mug, and bowl. Careful study of thousands of these shards makes it possible to determine with reasonable accuracy the objects of which they were a part.

The knowledge acquired through examining so great a quantity of wasters from the Daniel Bayley pottery enabled us to interpret the smaller findings at Rowley and Gloucester.

We guessed the approximate site at Rowley, because we knew that Joseph Bayley lived in the family homestead and presumably worked in his shed or barn. Unfortunately, the ground near the house has been cultivated and recultivated, and the spot where the barn stood is now concealed under a garage and cement walk. Although bits of pottery were strewn about the present yard and lawn, digging here and there yielded nothing. The pieces we found were scattered over an acre of land east of the pottery site and two feet below its level, where they had washed downhill from the dump. A recent ploughing made possible the recovery of these fragments, which would otherwise still be hidden under the turf.

Looking back to 1720, we must realize that virtually nothing is known about folk earthenware of that period in America and relatively little in England. Bearing this fact in mind, one must place a greater value on the bits dug up at Rowley. That they are really pottery discards and not merely broken shards thrown away by housewives is evident from the imperfections of firing, form, and glaze.

The most striking thing about Joseph Bayley's ware is its close resemblance to the work of his son and grandsons. Tradition, not fashion, determined the shapes and styles of the folk potters.

Among the Rowley fragments is a black piece with design delicately trailed in light slip (Fig. 17). It is apparenthly the *interior* of a small bowl. As noted above, but one example of dark glaze with decoration turned up at Newburyport. Parts of little bowls and other small forms difficult to identify reveal that the early eighteenth-century potters made articles on the same diminutive scale as the china of the period. There is one piece, jet-black, which seems to be part of a tiny teapot. Black teapots were not unknown thus early: they were imported to America in 1715. Accordingly, there is no reason why a skilled native potter should not have tried his hand at making them. Parts of ordinary milk pans, pots, jugs, and jars, make up the greater number of fragments. Tooled mugs, very much like those in Fig. 18 appear.

There is little to say about Daniel Bayley's 1750 product, except that it shows the transition from Joseph Bayley's style to the freer experimentation of his son's later period. Among the Gloucester potsherds are pieces of dark bowls decorated on the inside with light slip; there are mugs that might have been, and perhaps were, tooled with the same implements used by Joseph; there are fragments of dishes with a tracing of slip decoration, finer, but less freely executed, than that of the Newburyport examples; there are thin cups rimmed with yellow slip. The glaze colors are more generally dark, with little spattering or mottling, and green does not appear at all. As a rule, however, except for slight variations of form, the work remained virtually unaltered throughout three generations, from 1720 to 1799.

THE BAYLEY SITES

The Bayleys were not the first or only men to carry on the potter's trade in Newbury. They were preceded many years earlier by Abraham Annis, who was living there at least as early as March 1708, when his son Abraham was born. At a later time, the Annises lived side by side on the Bradford road. September 29, 1737, they sold their property to Joshua Bayley and moved to Haverhill. The son was then running the pottery. The father's deed mentions "My House barn & all my now Dwelling" and about twenty-nine acres. Abraham, Jr., sold "My house wherein I now dwelleth in Newbury, together with my Potter's Shop with my Mill for Grinding Clay with all the Materials for Potting with all other privileges & profits belonging to my House & Shop and also ½ acre where my House standeth." Abraham had married Abigail Sawyer only two years before and was still young enough to make a fresh start. This he did in Haverhill, where he worked at potting and farming until after 1767.

During the sixty years when Joseph Bayley and his son and grandsons were supplying Newburyport with pots and dishes, several other clayworkers ran potshops in the neighborhood. Apprentices were trained, and new craftsmen carried on when the older ones deserted the wheel. On the northwest side of Bartlett's Lane, near the home of Joseph Bayley, lived the potter Stephen Kent and his wife Hannah. Kent's history is unknown, except that he died in March 1747/48, and his estate, administered by his son Clement, was divided between his wife, his sons Clement and William, and his three married daughters. Part of the real estate was divided, while the remaining property, by the mother's request, was settled on Clement. It included a dwelling house, work house, and land worth some two hundred pounds, and such items of personal estate as earthenware and glasses to the value of fifty-five pounds or more, and a "riding chair." * Although Kent was an old Newbury name, neither Stephen nor his son are recorded as having been born there. Clement Kent was married and the father of six children before Daniel Bayley started his pottery by St. Paul's church. He continued the business he had inherited until 1773. In August and September of that year he disposed of much of his land together with his pot house. This was sold to Abraham Gallishaw. Kent died before January 25 of the following year.

Meanwhile he had trained a nephew in the art of pot making. Young Ebenezer Morrison, son of Kent's sister Emma (Emme, Ammi) and Spindelow Morrison, was apprenticed to his uncle at the age of thirteen years. At this time the boy was a town charge, and it was by decision of the selectmen that he was fated to become a potter. The original indenture between Clement Kent and Ebenezer Morrison is on file at the Essex Institute in Salem. It is one of the most interesting documents in the history of potting. By this agreement, dated November 26, 1754, the selectmen "Put and Bound one Ebenezer Morrison one of this Town's Poor To be an Apprentice to Clement Kent of Newbury aforesd Potter, to learn his Art, Trade, or Mystery, and with the said Clement Kent & Sarah his Wife after the Manner of an Apprentice, to serve from the Date hereof for and during the Term of Seaven Years & Six months to be compleat and ended." It was stipulated that Morrison should serve his master and mistress, keep their secrets, obey their commands, do no damage to their property and to report if he saw others doing so, not to waste their goods, not to commit fornication nor to contract matrimony within the said term, "at cards, Dice, or any other unlawful Game he shall

* Charles Messer Stow, by means of a discussion in the *New York Sun*, has established that a riding chair was a two-wheeled chaise.

not play," should not absent himself by day or night without their leave, nor haunt taverns, alehouses, or playhouses. On the other hand, he was to be taught the art of being a potter; they were to find for him "good and sufficient Apparel, Meat Drink washing & lodging in sickness and in health." At expiration of his time he was to be given two suits "of apparel for all parts of his body. . . one of them to be new & Decent fit for Lord's Day, & the other fit for Working Days," and they should teach him to read and write English well and "to Cypher as far as the Rule of three or so as to Keep a Tradesman's Book."

It is pleasant to record that Morrison fulfilled the contract, that he married Sarah Nowell of Newbury as soon as his apprenticeship was ended, and that he settled down nearby to a successful career as a potter. In fact, he prospered so well that in time he acquired, by successive releases from the heirs, rights in the estate of his former master. In 1797 he bought eighteen rods of land with buildings on the southerly side of High Street, almost opposite Bartlett's Lane. The lot was situated on a little way that ran through from High to Back Street, which bounded it on the rear.

As early as 1775 Morrison had built a kiln southeast of his house and at some distance from it. The town fathers voted, March 15, "to grant Ebenezer Morrison liberty to set up a Potter's Kiln at or near the North West Side of Burying Hill to be under the Direction of the Selectmen for the time being." This site was in the vicinity of the western entrance to the old burying ground south of High Street. At the time when the underpass was under construction, a new wall was provided for the cemetery. In the trench made for it we discovered quantities of fragments, plain and slip decorated, all quite similar to the Bayley shards. The cut for a connecting road from High Street to the underpass exposed other wasters on the edge of Morrison's Back Street property.

The right of Ebenezer Morrison "to Dig Clay near the Burying Ground" was questioned at a meeting of the selectmen, August 11, 1784, and was referred to a committee for investigation. They recommended, March 16, 1785, that "no person whatever be suffered to dig any clay or gravel upon the town's land near the burying ground." This regulation could not have interfered seriously with the potter's getting clay, as all the land in the area seems to be one vast clay bed.

Sarah Ann Emery, in her *Reminiscences of a Nonagenarian*, written in 1879, recalls Morrison's pottery in the following passage: "In my childhood Frog pond was the center of a tangled wilderness of alder and other bushes, and at the upper end there was a frightful ravine. Near this gully stood the gun house, where the cannon belonging to the artillery company was kept. Back on the heights stood an ancient windmill. . . Back of the pond was located quite an extensive pottery for the manufacture of brown glazed earthenware."

In April 1803, Morrison was put to rest in Old Burying Hill near the spot where he had worked so long. The appraisal of his pottery effects was modest. The shop was valued at ten dollars, the wheels at two dollars, and the clay mill and lead mill at two dollars each. The one item of consequence was "Blacking for ware say 500 lbs.," worth seven dollars. This, of course, was manganese.

The name of another Newburyport potter, John Thomas, appears in a Suffolk County Inferior Court record of the early 1780's. Neither his birth nor his death occurred in Newburyport, but such records concerning him as are found in the vital statistics of the town suggest that he may have been a nephew of Daniel Bayley's wife, Sarah Thomas Stone. If so, he was the son

of her brother William and was baptized in Gloucester in 1757. He was three times married in Newburyport: first, to Sarah Larry, November 23, 1777; second, to Elisabeth Morrill, November 30, 1779; and third, to Sarah Foss, in 1787. The court files record a suit brought by Thomas against Joseph Wilson, potter, of Providence. By this it would appear that Thomas worked for Wilson and was trying to recover wages. It is probable that he also was employed by Daniel Bayley. He may have been the John Thomas of Gloucester birth who started a pottery in Yarmouth, Maine, in 1791.

CHAPTER NINE

The Osborns of Danvers and Other Essex County Potters

For two centuries the name of Danvers has been associated with pottery making. At least one hundred natives of the town were clayworkers, and their shops and kilns lined the streets. They were perhaps most numerous in the Revolutionary period: twenty-two young potters marched away in Captain Eppes' company to the battle of Lexington, and in Captain Foster's company there were twelve from Central Street alone. Five Danvers potters gave up their lives in this battle. During the next quarter century, the business was at its height. In 1798 some twenty master potters had their own potshops and kilns in the south parish of the town, now Peabody, and somewhat later there were no less than thirty-three separate establishments. These men worked side by side, not apparently in cutthroat competition, but in a communal effort that was stimulated by a constant demand for their wares. Among them were the Osborns and Cooks on Central Street, the Goldthwaites, Southwicks, and others on Lowell Street, and several related workmen on Main and Washington Streets.

Contrary to the general impression, Joseph Osborn did not originate the earthenware business in Danvers — James Kettle antedated him by many years — and Osborn was not even the first in his own parish. As early as 1731, several years before Osborn is mentioned in records as a potter, Kettle's son Jonathan, who called himself "Kettell," had built a pottery on the lot now 31 Andover Street. Family tradition, however, gives the same date for the founding of the Osborn pottery. The Osborns exerted an influence on New England potting that is amazing when considered in relation to the industry as a whole. From the parent tree in Danvers the branches extended throughout Massachusetts, New Hampshire, Maine, and Rhode Island, and even into New York State, spreading the old traditions and techniques to the frontier. It is not mere coincidence that potters of this name appear in Exeter,

Dover, Loudon, and Gonic, New Hampshire, or that descendants were connected with potteries in Wiscasset, Newcastle, and Biddeford, Maine.

Joseph Osborn and his brother Paul were grandsons of the Quaker, William Osborn, who is noted as having been surveyor for the glasshouse that was started in Salem in 1642. It has been said that William was likewise a potter, but there is no foundation for the statement. Joseph was born October 26, 1702; Paul, a few years later. Where they served their apprenticeship we do not know, but it seems probable that they were pupils of Jonathan Hayward, whose Beverly pottery was only a few miles away. At his shop they may have met Jonathan Kettell, Hayward's nephew, who married a Beverly girl in 1725. We know that Joseph and Jonathan were friends, for later they owned land jointly in the Northfield, where there were clay pits. Joseph Osborn began his career as a joiner and is so called in a deed of 1738. Not until the following year is he designated "potter." Nevertheless, there is an entry dated June 1736 in the account book of Nathan Felton, charging Joseph Osborn, potter, for carting "four lodes of clay," and giving him credit for ware. In August 1739, Felton bought a "die pot" for five shillings, and other earthenware. At about the time when Joseph Osborn embraced his chosen occupation, Paul, having married into the Shove family of Dighton, removed to Assonet Neck in the section of that town now known as Berkley. Among the Quakers in that little colony he founded a pottery tradition that was hardly less influential than that of Danvers.

The fact that the Osborns were Quakers, and therefore not permitted to marry outside their own sect, may account for the large number of the family, so closely related, who remained in the same trade for generations. More than thirty of the name, most of them Joseph Osborn's descendants, were potters in Peabody. Four of his sons — Joseph, Jr., Israel, Abel, and Aaron, worked with him and after him; five of the sons of Joseph, Jr. — Joseph 3d., Jonathan, John 3d., Daniel, Jr., and Amos — were potters; and two of the sons of Aaron — Caleb and John Proctor — followed in their father's footsteps. At least seven in the next generation are recorded as potters, while numerous later descendants and members of collateral branches swell the roster.

It may be of interest to trace the fortunes of the two most important Osborn potteries — the original Joseph Osborn shop at 88 Central Street and the Amos Osborn pottery at 102. The first pothouse was built where the Peabody-Foster house now stands. This became the property of Joseph, Jr., and then of his son John 3d. The kiln was in the rear, and the pug mill, turned by a horse, was operated between the workshop and the house of Joseph, Jr. next door. A granddaughter of John 3d., Mrs. Eliza S. (Cheever) Osborn, wife of Lewis Osborn, has written her recollections of the old pottery. She says that her greatest joy as a child was to ride around on the horse's back or on the arm of the mill. Frequently her grandfather or her Uncle Kendall made toy pieces for her or allowed her to model the clay for herself. This uncle was the Kendall Osborn who, it is said, on his wedding day in 1824, presented each of his brothers with a jug. Mrs. Osborn relates:

> The front of the shop turned down on hinges, making a shelf to dry the ware on, — I used to watch them bring out long boards covered with pots and pans to dry in the sun. He [Grandfather] had men working for him that we didn't know, and we were little children. The men would yell at any child that hardly dared to walk on the sidewalk, for fear they would stumble over them. Once I got up when grandfather did, at three o'clock in the morning, and went over

with him to the kiln. He went round with a little ladder and a pair of tongs, and took out a brick here and there to peek in and see if the kiln was red hot all through, for he could tell when [the pots] were sufficiently burned and never entrusted this care to anyone. The ovens were built up about once a fortnight, just as they burn bricks now, then pulled down when done and built up again with a new lot.

The busy life of John Osborn 3d. ended in 1845. His sons, Miles and Henry, carried on the business until 1853, when Henry turned storekeeper.

The Amos Osborn shop (Amos was a younger brother of John 3d.) is still in use. It is now known as the Paige pottery. Until a few years ago it was operated continuously in the same old way — the wares thrown on the wheel and fired in a wood-burning kiln. The kiln has been replaced by a more modern device, but otherwise the building has remained much the same. The old kiln stood where the packing room is today, next to the Cowdrey house, and its original walls are still in place. It had no chimney, the smoke issuing from an opening in the roof. There were shutters for the purpose of closing this vent. The turning room, with its six wheels, was back of the kiln, and in the rear was the usual clay mill. Amos Osborn dug clay from his own pits near the John Clary house on what is now Pulaski Street.

Amos lived at 106 Central Street in a house that later became the barn on the Moses B. Paige estate; his sons, Amos and Philip, lived across the street in No. 93, an old house torn down about 1900. After their father's death in 1836, the two sons deserted the family calling, and eventually the pottery was leased to Joseph Reed, who bought it in 1866. Reed was a grandson of Joseph Whittemore, also a potter, who in 1778 had purchased Jonathan Kettell's house and land and had continued with the aid of his son Daniel to run the Kettell shop. Reed had spent his early married life in Andover, but returned to Peabody in 1850, still, however, in the capacity of a potter. He leased the works to Rufus Lamson of Exeter, New Hampshire, and later to C. F. Worthen, whose name is sometimes seen on stoneware crocks. These containers are not of Peabody manufacture, but were made for Worthen and stamped with his name. No stoneware was produced in Peabody. In 1872 Moses B. Paige came from Winthrop, Maine, to get employment in this pottery, and four years later bought it.

There are many local anecdotes about the men who worked at 102 Central Street in this later period, when the old domestic wares were gradually superseded by articles less useful, though still of red clay. Among the apprentices in Joseph Reed's day were Charles A. Lawrence, who later on started a potworks in Beverly, Benjamin Stevens, and Amos P. Bodge. In the seventies Jacob Steinbrecher was a turner there; he afterwards had a pottery of his own in Lynn.

Perhaps the most famous craftsman employed at the Paige pottery was John Donovan, who was born in Exeter in 1851 and died in 1932. He was a turner for nearly sixty years, having become a skilled potter at the age of fifteen. I once watched John Donovan at work making kitchen bowls. He was able to complete one in from two to three minutes. One by one they would be laid on the drying board. Donovan meantime chatting quietly with his visitors; the board would be carried away, and he would begin another round. Speed was an important consideration in producing utilitarian vessels, but it took phenomenal skill to make them of uniform shape at the same time. During Donovan's day the Paige pottery sold commercially little herb pots with covers and a lip, almost identical to those made in the early days of potting. They were not made

as reproductions, but in the ordinary course of events.

Edwin A. Rich, a Vermonter, worked in the pottery about 1880, and James Crawford Porter, an extremely able turner, was one of the later employees. Upon the death of John Donovan, the old tradition, too, passed away. Two Italians, Ermano and Luigi Paolucci, attempted to throw pots and to run the kiln, but they had not enough skill to do excellent hand work and they found machine methods unprofitable in competition with the great modern factories. They nevertheless turned out a number of interesting things in Italian style. These were principally pitchers and large deep dishes, tin-enameled, and painted in gay floral designs. They also succeeded in producing some colored glazes, such as a soft rose color, on a redware body.

While the Osborns are the most famous in Danvers potting annals, there were several other families that operated kilns for generation after generation. One of the earliest was Daniel Purinton, who is mentioned as "potter" in a deed dated March 2, 1738. At other times he is called "glazier." It is thought that he was the son of James Purinton of Salisbury, but there is no record of his birth. He married Joseph Osborn's sister Sarah. Their son Clark joined the Quaker colony at Dighton and was engaged in the pottery business on the Taunton River as early as 1753. Daniel Purinton's first home was on the north side of Boston Street (the way from Peabody to Salem), east of Watson Street.

Not the least important among these South Danvers craftsmen are the Southwicks, also of Quaker descent. They stemmed from the famous Lawrence Southwick, who, on account of his religion, was banished from Salem in the dead of winter. Joseph and William of the fifth generation were both potters and both lived on Lowell Street; Joseph at No. 151, where his kiln and shop stood in 1786, and William at No. 161, now the home of Mrs. Perley King, a direct descendant. Joseph was blessed with four daughters, but William, born in 1715, had a son William who became a potter, and he in turn had three sons, William, Jedediah Kilbourn, and James Chapman, who followed the family calling.

As there has always been a curious tradition that the Southwicks were noted principally for a black glaze, I once made a visit to 161 Lowell Street, seeking to verify the story by the discovery of fragments. This expedition met with success. Far back on the land, near the brook, I unearthed a quantity of shards from this pottery. I was not surprised to find glazes of all the usual colors, including a tan with brown smudges. The black was in about the same proportion that would be expected in any redware dump. It should be emphasized that redware from different potteries cannot be distinguished by any peculiarity of glaze, for all potters followed the same procedure, turning out shades of brown, black, and even green, in addition to the redder tones produced by a clear glaze over the natural body. Black, especially, was one of the commonest glazes, and, judging by examples I have found in many shard piles, it was often deep and brilliant.

The Wilsons also were a prominent family of artisans. Their homestead included the land near 141 Andover Street and eastward where Route 128 now crosses it. The first two potting Wilsons were sons of Robert, a farmer. They were Robert, known as Robert, Jr., who remained in Danvers, and Joseph, who went to Dedham and thence to Providence, Rhode Island. When Robert, Jr., died in 1782, he left property worth £627, including six lots of land, his house, barn, potter's shop, and cornhouse, a riding chair, and a large personal estate. He seems to have done well in his trade. His son Robert, known as Robert 3d., and a younger son Job

were potters. By an order of the court, Robert 3d., as administrator of his father's estate, was obliged to sell a large part of the elder Robert's property to pay certain debts. This was not done until April 9, 1793, when two-thirds of the land and buildings, and an interest in the business was acquired by Isaac Wilson 3d. He, too, was a craftsman in clay. The three Wilsons ran the shop together for a time, but Robert 3d. and Job both passed away before 1800, while Robert's son Robert, who had worked but a short time as a potter, died three years later at the age of twenty-seven. Upon Isaac's decease in 1809, this early pottery must have come to an end.

Another family of potters who settled early in the town were the Goldthwaites. The first of the name was Thomas, born in Voluntown (Petersham), Massachusetts, in 1738. He worked in Danvers for a few years, but in 1765 was of Springfield. His brother William, seven years younger, was apprenticed to Daniel Purinton. Later he lived on the corner of Main and Holten Streets, where the brick "Patterson" house now stands. An inventory of his estate taken in 1809 reveals that he owned two shops and a barn in addition to his dwelling.

Thomas's son Samuel remained in Peabody and was in the earthenware business with Peter Twiss and Robert Stone in 1798 at the westerly end of Lowell Street, in the neighborhood known as "The Kingdom." Several other Goldthwaites, whose relationships are uncertain, also worked on Lowell Street: John and his son Daniel at No. 40 and Nathaniel at No. 54 (the Floyd house). Daniel was later established at 88 Washington Street.

It would be tedious to enumerate all of these men, especially in view of the fact that so little of their prodigious output has survived. A few pieces of Danvers pottery may be seen in the rooms of the Peabody Historical Society on Washington Street, while a considerable collection of Essex County ware is on view at the Essex Institute in Salem. These examples cannot be identified as the work of individual craftsmen, but may be considered as partially representative of the industry that once flourished in the locality. It will be noted that no example with slip decoration is in either collection, and, indeed, ware so ornamented seems to be unknown in present-day Peabody. This does not mean that such a technique was never practiced in this particular district. We know that James Kettle made decorated earthenware, and undoubtedly his son followed his example. The absence of such types may be explained by the fact that very little pottery made before 1800 has been preserved, and further for the reason that the Danvers men became almost mass producers of common ware and may sooner have lost the urge to create decorative articles. In the 1800's the Peabody potters made thousands of strictly utilitarian pots that were not even intended for household purposes. The *Executive Documents Relative to the Manufactures in the United States*, based on the 1830 census, show that they were then supplying ten thousand corroding pots annually for the lead works in Salem. They therefore turned rather early from the fashioning of wares that delight a collector's heart, and we may be sure that their best day was over more than one hundred years ago.

Although the South Danvers potters were so active and the manufacture at Newburyport successful, the earthenware business flourished at one time or another in nearly every township of Essex County. The excellence and abundance of clay, the proximity of home markets, and the ready means for shipping the wares encouraged many craftsmen to enter the trade.

Soon after the establishment of the Danvers industry by Osborn and Jonathan Kettell, Nathaniel Symonds, son of Thomas Sy-

monds, a joiner, started a family enterprise in the Northfield section of Salem. This district, midway between Salem and Danversport, was the site of the clay beds. Symonds acquired land and a homestead there by gift and inheritance, and the family worked in that location for nearly one hundred years. Nathaniel's sons, William and Nathaniel, served in the Revolutionary War and then returned to the pottery. In 1781, ten years before his death, the father deeded his estate to William. The sons survived only to middle age and were succeeded by a third Nathaniel, William's son, who carried on the business during his early life, but in 1837 was called "cordwainer." John Symonds was the last to run this works in Northfield. His shop stood on the corner of Osborn and North Streets.

Nearby, where the Prince School stands today, was the shop of William Butterfield, started about 1831. Butterfield died of consumption ten years later, after having sold his establishment to Daniel Goldthwaite of Peabody.

Contemporary with the first Nathaniel Symonds was Enoch Goodell, or Goodale. His father, a resident of Salisbury, conveyed to him land and buildings in Salem at the time of his marriage in 1746 to Elizabeth Buxton. He lived in Salem and pursued his trade there throughout the century, dying after 1807. Although the name Goodale appears elsewhere in potting annals, I have been unable to trace a connection with this family. Enoch Goodale's sons were not potters.

As noted in the account of Newburyport, Abraham Annis ran a pottery in the first half of the eighteenth century in Haverhill. He and his father had moved up the Merrimac in 1737 and are mentioned in a deed of 1741. Annis is called "potter" in a conveyance dated January 2, 1749, by which he received from his father sixty-two acres of land, "partly in the District of Haverhill and partly in the Town of Haverhill." In 1754 he was styled "yeoman."

Across the river in Bradford, John West was established as early as 1767, the year when his first child was born. He had married Elizabeth Bartlett of Newburyport. His shop stood on the bank of the Merrimac a short distance east of where the bridge now connects Bradford with Haverhill. An inventory of his possessions, taken May 7, 1781, shortly after his death, includes the following items:

	£.	s.	d.
Homestead and buildings	240.	0.	0
40 acres in Methuen	120.	0.	0
Salt meadow in Newbury	7.	0.	0
A stone to grind clay	1.	10.	0
3 turning wheels	1.	7.	0
2 seives		6.	0
earthen ware in the pot house		60.	0
earthen in "yeuse"		10.	0
510 lb of "Baar Lead"	10.	12.	0

Horse, 2 cows, 15 sheep, 2 swine, horse cart, two old "sleys"

West also owned a watch, silver shoe and knee buckles, and a brooch. He was evidently a successful potter in fairly comfortable circumstances.

A later pottery in Bradford was brought to my attention when a friend found a mug with a Bradford history. Its uninspired shape and quite ordinary color did not suggest eighteenth-century workmanship, and I could not believe that it came from the hand of John West. Accordingly, I was not surprised to read in J. D. Kingsbury's *Memorial History of Bradford, Massachusetts*, "There is a tradition of a pottery established on Bradford Highlands, where brown earthen ware was made for a time." The much larger mug shown with this example in Fig. 59 was purchased in the same locality. Since it duplicates the smaller one in every least detail of form, proportion, and finish, we may assume that it was made by the same man.

The early history of the earthenware in-

dustry in Gloucester has been told in preceding chapters. It will be recalled that William Vinson, one of New England's earliest potters, lived and worked in Gloucester from 1645 to 1690, and that his grandson Joseph Gardner carried on the business of potting until 1749. Jacob Davis also plied his craft in the town for some years before 1717.

After the death of Gardner in 1749 and Daniel Bayley's brief sojourn shortly thereafter, Gloucester was without a potter until the arrival of Joseph Procter about 1766. An energetic young man of twenty-three, Joseph came from the Danvers section of Salem. He was descended from the ill-fated John Procter, who had been executed as a wizard in the previous century. Joseph's story is so full of human interest, even though none of his ware has been identified, that it is worth recording. It gives an unusual picture of "big business" in the eighteenth century; for Procter was not merely another little craftsman sitting at his wheel: he was an organizer, an executive, with his finger in many pies.

An account of this man's career was written in 1868 by his great-grandson Charles Procter on the occasion of a family gathering to celebrate the one-hundredth anniversary of Joseph's wedding day. From this record and from the potter's account books, kept from 1783 to 1806, I have drawn the substance of the story.

Upon arriving in Gloucester, Procter bought a tract of land fronting on Canal Street (now Western Avenue) and running east along the waterfront nearly to Washington Street. This was in the section of town near the "Cut" or canal where the waters of the Annisquam run into the harbor. After his marriage to Elizabeth Epes in 1768, Procter lived for a short time on Granite Street, where the eldest of his nine children was born. Soon, however, the family moved into a new house that he built facing the harbor. This was Procter's homestead throughout his lifetime.

Joseph Procter's ambitions were higher than those of the ordinary craftsman of his day, and it is probable that he was supplied by inheritance or marriage with the necessary funds to further them. A mill, erected a short distance back of his home, was the center of his various operations. The bed of the old millpond that he created by damming a stream lies under the present Mansfield Street. The dam was located at the point where the street ends, a little east of the old dwelling known as the James Cogswell house. One of Procter's huge millstones may still be seen on the Cogswell lawn, on the very spot where the mill must have stood.

Procter's mill was considered a triumph of mechanical engineering in its day. Within it were two sets of stones, one for corn, and one for wheat, a winnowing machine, and an apparatus for boiling chocolate. In other buildings were a coopering shop, where the necessary hogsheads and barrels were made, and a smithy for light forging and repair work. As the business increased, Procter added building after building and bought wharves and warehouses. He was soon actively engaged in shipping. His products were sent far and wide by sea. For this purpose he built and outfitted his own schooners. Some of these boats were fishermen: Procter dried their catches in his own fish yards; others were coasters or traders. His account book shows that he shipped earthenware and chocolate to southern ports, especially to Virginia, and it is said that he sent fish and pottery to the West Indies in exchange for cocoa and other merchandise. From time to time, also, he erected dwelling houses.

An inventory of Procter's estate taken in August 1805 lists the family dwelling house with barn and outbuildings, the "long house" and barn, the "new house," a "flake yard with the fish house thereon standing," the

mill, mill pond, and potato patch between the mill and the dam, the dwelling house west of the mill, a share in a wharf and store, and one-third of Pew No. 34 in the First Parish Meeting House. At least three of these buildings are still standing. The "long house" is the structure with a grocery store in one end at the corner of Pond Street and Western Avenue. The dwelling next to it is another of Procter's, probably the "new house." The house "west of the mill" is the old Cogswell place. The tools and machinery for all his enterprises had surprisingly little money value. His glaze mill and potter's wheels were worth only $1.50, while twenty-nine dozen chocolate pans were listed at $3.48.

Joseph Procter was a man of hale and hearty personality, well endowed by nature to carry on his numerous ventures. It is recorded that he was extremely genial and sociable, that he loved children, and was kind to the poor. He was somewhat of a musician and played the violin in an amateur band that used to meet for practice in the mill. There, of an evening, above the sound of rushing water, might be heard the strains of the flute, clarinet, and strings. Procter loved a joke. In order to keep the curious away from his fast-moving mechanisms, he may have originated the story that there was a ghost, Uncle Suts, in the mill.

The many entries in Procter's account book disclose that earthenware was sold or consigned to nearly sixty different persons. Specific items, with one or two exceptions, are not mentioned. This is a disappointment to the student. One Joseph Locke was charged, June 14, 1788, for "earthenware delivered to the Cape"; and, February 10, 1789, for "earthenware dld to Newmarket." A sale to Abraham Somes in "Mount Desart" is entered. At least five ship captains were given ware to carry or send to Virginia. Pitchers that were sold for six pence, seven pence, and one shilling each are noted, and, in one bill, "mugs for the fishermen." To Dr. I. Babbit, Procter sold a "Doctor's Jug." The only items of interest or importance are "4 Green Paint[d]" (pitchers) at three shillings each, sold to Daniel Rogers, and two others of the same kind that went to Captain Isaac Wharf. The unusually high price of these pieces would indicate that a good deal of work had been expended upon them. That they were decorated or "painted" with green slip cannot be doubted. We surmise that these pitchers were special orders.

Joseph Procter died in 1805 as the result of fatigue and exposure incurred while helping get afloat a ship that had gone ashore on Coffin's Beach. The last entry in his ledger of a shipment of earthenware is dated 1799. While he may have turned pottery in his later years, it is more likely that he was occupied after 1800 with his more lucrative mercantile enterprises.

Other potters supplied the town with pots and pans during the nineteenth century. In the late period of redware, a young man named Lewis Mason established a small business in Pigeon Cove, Rockport, building his shop back from the street on the land now numbered 168 Granite Street. He had previously spent some time in Connecticut, returning to Rockport a few years before his marriage to Elizabeth Moody in 1879. As Mason's death occurred six years later, the pottery was of brief duration, although its memory still lingers with older residents, who recall the ware being sold from a peddler's cart.

The little town of Merrimacport, or West Amesbury, as it used to be called, was the location of one of the best known and longest-lived potteries in Essex County. On the shore of the Merrimac River, in a community that once had some commercial importance, the industry begun in Amesbury before 1775 by Benjamin Bodge was carried on for almost a century. I have been unable to learn any-

thing of the birth or ancestry of this man. It seems highly probable that he was Benjamin, nephew of the potter Samuel Bodge, Sr., of Charlestown, who was baptized there January 18, 1746/47 and who thereafter disappears from Charlestown records. Bodge is first found in Haverhill and Amesbury records when he married Susanna Pecker in Haverhill, September 27, 1770. He was then a potter. Two years later his son John was born. John grew up to be a potter also; he migrated to Fayette in Maine, where he and his son later owned a potworks. At some time before the birth of his daughter Susanna, May 6, 1775, Benjamin Bodge moved to Amesbury. His wife having died at that time, or shortly thereafter, he was married again in the following October to Sarah Sargent of Amesbury. In 1781 his third marriage, to Mehitabel Sheppard of Haverhill, is recorded.

Although Benjamin Bodge was undoubtedly working at his trade during these years, he is first mentioned as potter in deeds when he bought a holding of Enoch Rogers, April 4, 1782. This is described as a "persel" of land west of the "town burying place near the middle of the town upon the main road that runs through the town," and north of the highway. On the west the lot abutted on Bodge's own land, which he must have acquired at some previous time. With this purchase Bodge was assured of "all privileges and appurtenances excepting that of keeping fowls such as turkies or hens or any other fowls that cannot with proper care be kept upon the highway."

William Pecker, brother of the first Mrs. Bodge, must have come to Amesbury about 1780. Born in Haverhill, October 10, 1758, the young man, it is said, was apprenticed to one Goodhue, a potter from Essex. Goodhue's name does not appear in any of the Essex, Haverhill, or Amesbury statistics: this family tradition may be taken for what it is worth. In 1784 Pecker and his brothers sold their grandfather's house in Haverhill. At that time he was a potter of Amesbury and was perhaps working for Bodge.

The Bodge pottery continued until the latter part of 1791, when it's owner, who was then living in Poplin, New Hampshire, sold it (December 5) to Timothy Gordon, a blacksmith. Up to this time there is no record of Pecker's having been a landowner, but in the following year he purchased a lot of some eleven acres on Red Oak Hill in West Amesbury. Three years later he acquired from Micajah Pillsbury seventeen acres and a dwelling house with another lot of thirty-six acres. His house lot, bordering on the estate of Enoch Rogers, was doubtless in the vicinity.

Pecker worked at the pottery trade for many years and turned out beautiful pieces similar to the jugs in Fig. 40. These have delightful rosy tones accented by brushings of dark glaze. The one without a handle was purchased in Merrimacport from a direct descendant of the potter. William Pecker suffered a tragic death in 1820, being crushed in the collapse of one of his kilns. The inventory of his estate shows that he had not been greatly successful in a financial way and that he was doing some farming to help along. He had disposed of the greater part of his land, leaving an acre or so with his house, barn, and buildings, and a large lot between the river road ("the new highway") and the river. The only reference to the pottery is the mention of a small quantity of "potter's weare."

Already for four years William Pecker's nephew, James Chase, had been working in the port, and he took over the business. Chase, the son of Pecker's sister Hannah and Edmund Chase, was born in West Amesbury April 9, 1779. At the age of thirty-two he married Olive Lucas of Charlestown. He was at that time living in Andover. Once established in Merrimacport, James Chase was

eminently successful, carrying on his earthenware factory until death took him in 1849. In 1840 his output was worth one thousand dollars a year and he employed two men.

During Chase's lifetime the pottery stood south of the village road on land running down to the river, where it was banked up with a retaining wall. Here was his house, his workshop and kilnhouse, his woodhouse and barn. The dwelling was probably the "old house" noted in Chase's inventory, which, with other buildings, was valued at eighteen hundred dollars. He also owned a house occupied by his son Phineas and another in which his daughter Olive and her husband Erastus Hutchins lived. Altogether his real estate was appraised at $4398. The items relating to the pottery are: "Clay mill, $5.00; 2 turning wheels, $5.00; Lead mill, $1.00; Sundries in kiln house, $.75; and Horse, $50.00." The tools of the potter were surely few and simple. Chase was otherwise distinguished by his ownership of a church organ, which his wife as administratrix rented. Five years after his death, several of the heirs relinquished their rights in the Chase property to their brothers, William and Phineas, and their sister Olive. The deed specifies the potter's shop, barn, and other buildings on one lot and a dwelling house on the other.

Phineas Chase succeeded his father in the Merrimacport pottery, and it continued to be a going concern. At some time before 1863 he moved the works to his own land at the top of the hill on the road leading up from the river. Not very much is known about his activities, except that pieces of Chase pottery from this later period are frequently encountered about the country. In 1856 the *New England Business Directory* lists the firm of Chase and Kendrick, indicating a partner.* Although Phineas Chase died before 1864, the pottery was running in the next year, turning out ware to the value of $1550 annually. Richard Chase was working there within the memory of John Donovan of Peabody, who recalled his producing a green glaze. The building on the hill where the later Chases worked is still standing on the Tuckwell estate. It is now used as a machine tool shop, the only evidence of its former purpose being the huge handmade pegs in the walls where the drying shelves rested. The Tuckwells informed me that the clay for the pottery was brought from Plaistow, New Hampshire.

Such examples of Chase ware as I have seen have been generally of a quite utilitarian nature. A collection of unused ware inherited by Frank Winn of Merrimacport, a great-great-grandson of William Pecker, includes a bean pot and numerous other dishes and vases glazed only on the inside. The deep pan in Fig. *76b* is the typical baking dish made by country potters from time immemorial.

The name of Smith Sargent may also be noted in connection with Merrimacport. He was a potter there in 1825.

William Tarbell, a potter from Danvers, lived in the central part of Beverly. As a boy he was apprenticed to a master craftsman in his native town. At the age of twenty-four he was married to Anna Venn. Four years later, in 1782, he bought land in Beverly and presumably began his potting business there at that time. Anna died in 1796, and her husband took a second wife, Abigail Carter. Tarbell now purchased a piece of land whose bounds give a clue to the location of his pottery. Beginning at the end of a stone wall near Tarbell's house, the line of the lot ran northerly by the highway leading from the Essex Bridge to the Beverly Cotton Manufactory, thence southerly to land of William Woodberry, and easterly by the Woodberry heirs and Tarbell's land to the first point. The

* A recently discovered bill of sale, dated November 10, 1852, reveals the association of "Kendrick & Mann" under the style "West Amesbury Pottery."

Tarbell pottery continued for many years, William's son and namesake becoming his assistant and partner. The elder Tarbell died in 1815, the younger only four years later.

There is no mention of any other potter in Beverly records until Robert Herrick of Wenham arrived in town at the time of his marriage. I have been unable to learn whether Herrick worked in the town.

The Lawrence pottery in Beverly is still remembered by older persons. Founded in 1866 by Charles A. Lawrence, a Portuguese, whose real name was Solares, it was manned by a group of skilled workmen who had been apprentices or employees of Joseph Reed at the Osborn-Paige pottery in Peabody. Among these men were Benjamin Stevens and Amos P. Bodge. Edwin A. Rich, who had come to the Paige pottery after working in Keene, New Hampshire, and various places in the west, went to work for Charles Lawrence in 1887, remaining with him as one of his most skillful turners until Lawrence's death and the close of the enterprise in 1906. Thomas Pitman of Marblehead was employed at Beverly as a decorator.

During the sixties Lawrence produced the familiar types of redware. The pitcher in Fig. 57 is an example of his output that looks much older in style than it really is. It is brushed with white and green slips, which contrast agreeably with the brownish-red background. A decade later the concern was making terra cotta and decorated wares in the taste of the period. Vases of classic design were turned for home embellishment. It is said that Rich's talent for creating beautiful forms led to much experimentation and to the commercial expansion of the pottery. At one time the company produced as many as 183,500 pieces annually. After 1900 they advertised flowerpots, antique pottery, and roasting pans, and were wholesale dealers in stoneware, Rockingham, and yellow wares, glassware, and drain pipe.

Potteries may have been in existence in Lynn at an early period, but the only one of which I have a record was in a section of the present town of Saugus known as Cliftondale. It was started by one William Jackson, from Manchester, England. He had bought a farm in Cliftondale (then part of Lynn) in 1808, and, finding a deposit of clay on his land, he came to the conclusion that it would be possible to make from it a fine kind of earthenware, similar to English importations. In this hope, he put up a suitable plant, consisting of a large building and two smaller ones, and procured the best equipment and workmen he could find. Production was begun in 1811 and kept up for four years, but Jackson was doomed to disappointment, financial and otherwise, for the clay proved to be the usual variety from which only common redware could be made.

Jackson advertised his wares in glowing terms in the *Boston Gazette* of December 16, 1811. It is evident from the list of forms that they did not differ greatly from those turned out by New England potters, although there was perhaps a greater variety. The advertisement reads:

LYNN EARTHEN WARE

The Subscriber informs the public that he has commenced the manufacture of useful EARTHEN WARE, at his residence, five miles from Malden Bridge, on the old road to Salem. The Clay which he works is of *late discovery*, and has been tried in the Potteries in England, and pronounced to be "*of uncommon fine texture, and in quality superior to any of the kind yet found in England.*" From the reception and approbation his Ware has already gained he hopes to meet with patronage; and for the accomodation of Boston Customers he has engaged the *Long Rooms* over Messrs. JOSEPH CALLENDER & Co's Grocery Store, *Marlboro'-street* — where he will have for sale, every Monday, Tuesday, and Saturday, a very large assortment of

LYNN EARTHEN WARE

by wholesale — The following articles with many others, are ready for sale, viz.

Pitchers, from ½ pint to 2 gallons — pint, quart, and 2 quart Jugs, *warranted* equal to any Stone Ware, and much handsomer — Pudding Pans and Boilers — Bread Pans — Pie do. — Bean Pots — Pickle do. one to six gallons, warranted to hold Vinegar — Cake Potts, with covers — preserve do. with do. — Tamarind do. Flower do., all sizes — a few very handsome Flower Urns — Herb Teas, Medicine and Stew Pots, with covers, which will bear any fire — Butter and Lard Pots, of superior quality.

Country Traders are respectfully informed that early in the Spring there will be a large assortment of the above Ware, together with Milk Pans, ready for sale at the LYNN POTTERY

WM. JACKSON

Another list published in the same paper, August 4, 1814, mentions still other articles and is a valuable record of a potter's output in the early years of the century. In fact, it is the only such record of this period that I have found.

LYNN WARE.

For sale by DEXTER DANA, No. 15, Exchange-street, at the factory prices,

— VIZ —

Pitchers from pint to 3 galls.
Mugs, quart and pint,
Bowls " "
Bowls, wash,
Sugar bowls,
Tumblers,
Salts,
Stew Pots and Covers, qt. and pint,
Plates of all sizes,
Dishes do. do.
Platters do. do.
Pudding Pans do. do.
Pots do. do.
Bake Pans do. do.
Preserve Pots,
Flower Pots, all sizes,
Coolers,
Butter Pots and Covers,
Butter Boxes and Covers,
Butter Tubs and Covers,
Pickles Pots and Covers,
Cake Pots,
Gali-Pots,
Stool Pans,
Bed Pans,
Chambers, 3 sizes,
Blacking Jugs, pint and half pint,
Essence Spruce do.
Jugs from qt. to 3 galls.

Jackson's earthenware was also sold by Wainwright & Jackson in their store on Exchange Street. Thomas Jackson of this firm was connected with the Boston Porcelain and Glass Company. The two may have been related.

The home of William Jackson is remembered by residents of Cliftondale. It stood in the rectangle bounded by Central Street, Lincoln Avenue, Foss Court, and Jackson Street. The meadow where the clay was dug is on Central Street, west of Jackson.

CHAPTER TEN

The Quaker Potters of Bristol County

The importance that may attach to a few bits of old paper is exemplified by my discovery of some crude accounts kept by Preserved Peirce of Swansea, trader. Preserved owned a sloop called the *Rosemary*, in which he sailed up and down Mt. Hope Bay and along the coast of Rhode Island and Connecticut selling wooden ware, pewter, pottery, and such articles as tea kettles, hats, and shoe buckles, or bartering his stock for flour or flax, lead and manganese for the potters, or brass and copper for the metalworkers. In this way he purveyed along the waterways the merchandise which at a later period would have been sent out on peddlers' wagons.

One sheet reads: "Preserved Peirce Sailed from Swanzey September the 14, 1786 For Connecticut/ To Road Island the same day the wind Norwest and today the same way / 15

Fortunately, Peirce itemized the earthenware, which he carried in considerable quantity, and he noted the names of several potters who supplied him with it. This 1786 list is priced, the first column of figures representing the cost per article in pence.

60 L Milk pans	12	3. 0. 0
40 S Milk pans	9	1.10. 0
20 Platters	7	0.11. 8
160 L plates	3½	2. 6. 8
44 S plates	2½	0. 9. 2
35 L Basons	4	0.11. 6
16 S Basons	3	0. 4. 0
14 L pots	12	0.14. 0
10 M pots	9	0. 7. 6
16 S pots	7	0. 9. 4
16 Bread pans	9	0.12. 0
7 Red Chambr pots	7	0. 4. 0
70 Chambr pots	12	3.10. 0
27 Jugs & Pitchers	12	1. 7. 0
80 quart Mugs	6	2. 0. 0
50 pint Mugs	4½	0.18. 9
80 S Mugs	3½	1. 0. 0
42 L Bowles	9	1.11. 6
180 pint Boles	4½	3. 7. 6
60 S Bowles	3½	0.15. 0
60 L Porngers	5	1.05. 0
34 S Porngers	3½	0. 9.11
2 Churns	22	0. 3. 8
1 Gallon Jug	1/10	0. 1.10
		Ls 27.10. 3
		2.18. 6
		30. 8. 6

A briefer list made out for a previous voyage in 1782 mentions pint "pottingers" at six pence and creamers at four pence. At the earlier date all prices were relatively higher.

The potters named in the account are Asa and Azariah Shove, whose bill of earthenware came to more than forty-two pounds; George Shove, with a bill of thirty-six pounds, one shilling; and Clark Purinton, to whom Peirce brought lead. With this information I hastened to the Bristol County Registry of Deeds, where I soon found myself floundering in a bewildering mass of data about the Shove family and others who constituted the largest and most enduring group of pottery workers in southern Massachusetts. It was not long before I came across the name of Paul Osborn, brother of Joseph, who I had long known had gone to Dighton from Danvers at an early period. Thence, by gradual steps, and with the aid of Miss Edna M. Hoxie, a direct descendant of the Shove and Boyce families, I worked out the interrelationships of this most interesting colony, all of whom were Quakers.

The Shoves were among the first settlers of Taunton in the part later set off as Dighton and then as Berkley. They built their homestead at the northerly end of Assonet Neck. In the early 1700's Edward Shove was the owner of the estate. As time passed his descendants acquired property all along the road to the neck. This thoroughfare remains much the same today and is still the only way down this peninsula, long famous as the location of Dighton Rock.

It is a curious circumstance that not only did Paul Osborn marry into the Shove family, but his two sisters also found mates among the sons of Edward Shove. This is partially explained by the fact that Quakers were not allowed to marry outside the faith. Paul married Elizabeth, daughter of Edward Shove, about 1730; Philadelphia Osborn married Theophilus Shove in 1736; and Phebe became the wife of Edward Shove three years later. Osborn's sister Eleanor and her husband Edward Upton from Danvers, parents of the potters Isaac and Samuel Upton of East Greenwich fame, were also part of the Berkley community for a time, while Clark Purinton, son of Paul's sister Sarah, and William Boyce, his sister Elizabeth's son, sought their fortunes in Dighton at a somewhat later date. The numerous intermarriages of these families with each other and with the Chaces of Somerset made complicated relationships.

Inasmuch as Paul Osborn, who was born about 1704, was considerably older than any potting member of the Shove clan, he was probably the founder of the old-time craft in Berkley and the teacher of his brothers-in-law. When Osborn married Elizabeth Shove, her brother Edward was only fourteen years of age, while her youngest brother, Nathaniel, born in 1723, was nearly twenty years younger than Osborn. There is no indication that they got their training outside of Berkley.

Just before young Edward Shove's marriage, when he had already become a master potter, Paul Osborn made his first purchase of land at Assonet Neck; the following year (1740) he and Edward bought of Edward, Sr., twenty acres on which "our pottery shop" was already standing. This was on the west side of the road to the neck. Osborn and Edward Shove carried on their pottery and made their home in this location for about twenty years. In 1748 a division of the estate, including the house and barn, was recorded — Edward to have the east side and Paul the west.

In this Osborn-Shove pottery were trained the young Nathaniel, Edward's sons Samuel and Asa, and some of the nephews. Osborn had no children, unless Paul of Danvers, born there in 1731, was his son. In any event, the Danvers Paul did not become a potter. Isaac

Upton, who was a lad in his early teens when his family lived in Berkley, was no doubt one of the first apprentices. George Shove, son of Edward's brother George, must also have learned the trade with his uncles. In due time he married Sarah Upton, sister of Isaac and Samuel. Paul's nephew, William Boyce, went to Berkley in 1754, when he was twenty-seven years old. He had therefore already acquired his training in Danvers, but he was closely associated with Osborn and Shove and eventually bought the pottery. The nephew Clark Purinton, mentioned in Peirce's accounts, settled across and down the river in that part of Swansea now Somerset. Clark, too, had learned the art of potting in Danvers, where his father Daniel ran a potworks as early as 1736. William Boyce and Clark Purinton wedded Lydia and Sarah Shove, the sisters of George Shove the potter. Azariah and Theophilus Shove, Jr., both nephews of Edward Shove, also went into the earthenware business, but, as they lived in Swansea, Theophilus at least was probably apprenticed to Clark Purinton, whose daughter Lydia he married.

Thus it will be seen how the Osborn tradition, with its familiar forms and ways of making them, was transplanted to these Quaker communities, and why it is that so great a similarity prevails almost everywhere in the Massachusetts potters' art. From 1739 or earlier until after 1880, pottery was made at Assonet Neck, and at an even later date the descendants of Clark Purinton were carrying on this business in "Pottersville" across the river. The originator of this industry eventually forsook Berkley for New York State. In 1755 Osborn sold to Nathaniel Shove part of a house that he had acquired from Theophilus Shove and to Edward his westerly half of the dwelling where both were then living. In 1764 both he and Edward Shove were in Beekman, Dukes County, New York. In the following year Osborn sold to William Boyce his part of the homestead formerly owned by Edward Shove, Sr., including one acre on the westerly side of the highway to the neck, with dwelling house, pottery house, kiln house, and hog house thereon. He was then of Albany.

Edward Shove returned to Berkley. His will, drawn up in 1778, bequeathed to his son Asa (Samuel had died at the age of twenty-three) all land and buildings except a legacy to his daughters, with his "husbandry, potter's, currier's carpenter's tools, all my cooper's ware, and a large iron pot," livestock, etc. Asa Shove lived until 1826, but gave up potting for farming at some time after 1786, the year of the Peirce accounts. Azariah Shove also depended upon farming after reaching middle age.

The pottery business at Assonet Neck was carried on by William Boyce and his descendants until a late period. When William died shortly before 1799, his heirs released their shares in his property to their brother John, who was running the pottery at that time. John was then nearly forty years old. March 25, 1805, he sold to his brother Enoch, who was thirteen years younger than he, one half of the kiln, kiln house, and potter's shop, and the north end of the house that had belonged to their father, together with the privilege of grinding clay in the south part of the cellar and of passing to the well to draw water. John lived until 1839; Enoch until 1859. By this time, the pottery, which had also provided a living for their two sons, each named after his father, was being run on a comparatively small scale. It is probably the one mentioned in Haskel & Smith's *Gazetteer* of 1843 as being in Freetown, since Assonet Neck is close to the Freetown line. The second John and Enoch worked together until the death of Enoch in 1876. John Boyce survived until 1893. In his later years he devoted only part time to the pottery, which closed some years before his death. People

now living, however, can remember the large milk pans and deep plates made by Enoch and John Boyce.

Although there is a local tradition that potting was carried on in Somerset (formerly Swansea) as early as 1705, I can find no documentary evidence to substantiate the story. Clark Purinton was called a potter of Swansea, February 6, 1753, when he bought his first lot of land from Obadiah Baker. This is the first actual record of the earthenware trade in Somerset that I have discovered. Afterwards, by successive purchases, largely from the daughters of Ebenezer and Obadiah Baker, he acquired some thirty-five acres on "Taunton Great River." Succeeding Clark Purinton,* at least three other generations of the name have been makers of earthenware in Somerset, where they, with the Chaces and others, created such a flourishing industry that the central part of the town was called "Pottersville." Clark himself worked at his trade throughout his days.

At the time of the Revolution, Purinton, George Shove, and William Boyce owned a sloop, the *Warren*, which they used for selling their wares down the river. This vessel, the first from their town to be a casualty of the war, was captured by the British just off Newport, as she was sailing there with a load of earthenware. She was used by the enemy for two months as a despatch boat and was then stripped of her rigging and beached. With unusual courtesy, the English sent a message to the owners, telling them where they could find the sloop. To their surprise, the earthenware was still in the hold, although rather badly damaged. Because the potters were all Quakers, and therefore supposed to be noncombatants, they put in a claim for eighteen pounds, ten shillings, to the British Commissioner appointed to inquire into losses of American loyalists. Unfortunately for their case, Clark Purinton had enlisted in the Revolutionary forces, a fact that may have reached the commissioner's ear, for the claim was never paid.

Upon his passing in 1786, Purinton left to his sons Clark and Edward his farming and pottery implements. The inventory of materials and apparatus in his pottery lists twelve tons of clay, $15; seven hundred pounds of lead, $35; manganese; and the wheels, specifying that they had "pine bottoms and lignum [vitae] tops."

Clark, Jr., had already associated himself with Asa Chace in an arrangement not uncommon in this closely related group. In 1781 they had purchased together several acres of land from the Ebenezer Baker estate. On November 4 of the following year, they agreed upon a division by which Asa Chace was to have one half of the land and one half of a dwelling house they had built upon it, while Clark Purinton had the other, including one half of the well. The latter, however, released his rights in the land, excepting a convenient landing on the north side of the lot and a driftway by the river with liberty to pass and repass to his side of the cellar. Asa Chace had his own pottery shop north of the Purinton kiln. This arrangement seems to have been a lasting one. The lot is still in the hands of a direct descendant of the Purintons — Fernald L. Hanson, great-great-grandson of Clark, Jr. The well used jointly by the two potters is still there, although the house has long since disappeared.

The second Clark Purinton lived until 1817. His will directed that his farming, "pottering," and shoemaker's tools should be left to his four sons. Of these, George was the one to continue the family trade. By a division of his father's property in 1835, he was given land adjacent to Clark Chace, Asa's son, with a wharf, kiln house, kiln, and shop.

Family history reveals that the Purinton

* This spelling was changed by some of Clark's descendants to "Purrington," but the original orthography presents the actual pronunciation.

kiln stood near a great ledge of pudding stone close by the river. In 1945, with the assistance of Miss Louise Hanson, we found a small section of the early dump under the lawn of the Hanson house near this rock. This was something of an accomplishment, as the land had been frequently changed and filled along the waterfront, and the business of finding early fragments was confused by the presence of stoneware from the neighboring Somerset Pottery and by later redware shards. The fragments were badly disintegrated by the action of salt water, but, even so, they were evidential. We learned from them that the Essex County tradition prevailed at Somerset in every least detail. There were the same bits of tooled mugs, the same bowl rims, the same brilliant black, dotted brown, and orange colorings, and the same type of deep plates with green-dotted slip decoration that we had found at the Bayley pottery in Newburyport (Fig. 27). Indeed, the resemblance is so uncannily close, it suggests the possibility that Daniel Purinton, who is said to have been born in Salisbury, acquired the exacting skill of turning from Joseph Bayley in Rowley. Bayley's activities in Rowley were coincident with the time when Daniel Purinton was in his teens. If this be hazarding a bad guess, then the ability of potters everywhere to learn the precision of throwing according to type becomes ever more astonishing. From these fragments also we ascertained that plates with notched edges — the Connecticut pie-plate form — were unknown to Bristol County potters, even as to their contemporaries farther north.

The theory that the Chaces founded the potting industry in Somerset is not borne out by the records. Asa Chace's ancestors for three generations were farmers, as was the father of his wife, Esther Buffinton. Since Asa was only nine years of age when Clark Purinton came to town, it is reasonable to suppose that he became an apprentice in the Purinton pottery and then quite naturally drifted into the partnership with Purinton's son. He first appears in Swansea land records as a potter in 1768, when he bought seven acres of Ebenezer Chace. When Asa and the younger Clark Purinton made division of their property, Asa was thirty-eight years old. His death occurred in August 1812. In the settlement of his estate, four fifths went to his sons Stephen, Clark, and Joseph, and one fifth to his daughters. The inventory notes two acres of land with buildings, worth $1600; another small lot, $65; a kiln of earthenware, $100; and three tons of clay, $5.25. Although they had been trained as potters, Stephen and Joseph promptly sold the pottery land and buildings to their brother Clark, who thereafter was the sole proprietor of the future "Somerset Pottery."

Several other members of the family were connected with the Chace pottery or had shops of their own. Asa's nephew, Enoch Boyce Chace, son of his brother Stephen and Lydia Boyce (daughter of William the potter) worked at the trade until his untimely death in 1825. Stephen, son of Asa's brother William, became an independent potter. At the time of his death in 1843, he owned a homestead, thirteen acres of meadow land, two houses, and outbuildings, including an "Earthern Pottery" worth $2900. Among the materials in the shop was "Venetian red" to the value of forty dollars.

Chace was indirectly responsible for the first steps in the career of a famous man when, on January 28, 1791, Elijah Cornell was apprenticed to him. This young man's mother, Sarah (Miller) Cornell, had made a second marriage with Asa's cousin, Benjamin Chace, and Elijah was no doubt familiar with the pottery from earliest childhood. Born in Swansea in 1771, he had got what schooling he could there and had done a little teaching, but he evidently had a bent for the potter's craft. After his apprenticeship was ended, he

worked as a journeyman potter. For an ambitious youth, this was not enough. In 1805 he sold out his holdings in Swansea and went to Westchester Landing in New York. Cornell's subsequent history is one of many moves and much hardship, but gains interest because he was the father of Ezra Cornell, founder of Cornell University. Little Ezra gained the fortitude that was his while working in his father's redware pottery. In 1819 the family settled in De Ruyter, New York, where, after a period of teaching, Elijah again established a pottery, which Ezra helped to build. In 1943 we visited this site and were rewarded by the discovery of a small collection of fragments. Elijah had evidently advanced somewhat beyond the rather restrained technique of the Massachusetts potters, for in De Ruyter he decorated a good deal of his ware with slip of two colors, black and white, either marbled or applied in bold wavy lines against backgrounds of contrasting hue.

During the lifetime of Clark Chace nothing but redware was made in the Somerset potteries. A short time after the business had passed to his sons in 1836, there were seven different shops in the town, each with its own little output. The three Chace brothers saw that there was more money to be made in the manufacture of stoneware. To this end they remodeled their plant and incorporated as the Somerset Potters' Works. Under their management the pottery enjoyed a high degree of prosperity for many years. The fortunes of this concern are told in Chapter XI.

The methods and equipment of the Somerset redware potters were no different from those of dozens of others in the trade. Each man had his own workshop and kiln, and one or two wheels. The clay was procured locally. According to William A. Hart, Somerset's historian, the kilns were either round or square, from ten to twelve feet in diameter, and eight or nine feet high at the center. Most of them had four arches, a few six. None were provided with chimneys as in the large stoneware kilns of the Somerset pottery, and all were updraft until a very late period. Wood was the fuel used — oak at the beginning of firing and then pine, when it was time to increase the temperature. It was no unusual sight to see a thousand cords of wood at one time stacked about the town. During the early days the earthenware was sold by boat along the coast. After land travel became easier, the Somerset potters loaded peddlers' wagons and went out on the road to sell their products.

As it is still possible in the small town of Somerset to locate some of the pottery dumps, it may not be amiss to mention the potters who ran the little shops. The last descendant of the Purinton family to practice the potter's art was George S., son of George. He lived in a house formerly owned by one Samuel Purinton that originally stood on Assonet Neck, but was moved down the river over the ice to Pottersville. The building was placed on a site west of the spot where the Hanson house now stands and probably about where the Chace-Purinton house had stood before. Mr. Hanson remembers this home of his grandparents. George Purinton's kiln was on the waterfront. Another Purinton, Samuel, had a shop on a lane near Wood Street, between Riverside Avenue and the water. He was succeeded there by his son David P. Purinton (Purrington), who, in turn, was followed by Samuel B. Collins. Numerous fragments from their kiln may be found along the river's edge. They are principally parts of glazed flowerpots — some of a pleasant green color. Another potter, George Brown, was located at the foot of Cusick's Lane on the site afterwards occupied by the "Harrington's Switch" turnout of the street railway. Charles E. Hathaway, an apprentice of Samuel Purinton, turned to stoneware potting, as did the Synan brothers. Their work is described in the following chapter.

CHAPTER ELEVEN

Stoneware Potting in Eastern Massachusetts

During the Provincial period there was little incentive to manufacture stoneware, because bulky articles, taxed on the value rather than on the weight, could be imported at exceedingly low prices. A good deal of such heavy pottery was shipped from Liverpool — hence the term "Liverpool ware." After the Revolution, when freights had to be paid according to measure, articles of the kind became more costly and, in consequence, really scarce.

Manufacturers were becoming increasingly conscious of the defects of earthenware and the need of a better and safer pottery for household utensils. Public-spirited writers occasionally presented their views on the subject in the hope of stimulating the potters' interest in making a superior ware. The following excerpt from an article in the *Pennsylvania Mercury*, February 4, 1785, describes vividly the dangers of lead glazing and urges the manufacture of pottery glazed with salt:

> The best of Lead-glazing is esteemed unwholesome, by observing people. The Mischievous effects of it fall chiefly on the country people, and the poor everywhere. Even when it is firm enough, so as not to scale off, it is yet imperceptibly eaten away by every acid matter: and mixing with the drinks and meats of the people, becomes a slow but sure poison, chiefly affecting the nerves, that enfeeble the constitution, and produce paleness, tremors, gripes, palsies, &c, sometimes to whole families.
>
> It is wished the Legislature would consider of means for discountenancing the use of Lead in glazing Earthen-Ware, and encourage the application of the most perfect and wholesome glazing, produced only from Sand and Salts: materials, these, everywhere to be collected within these states. A small bounty or exemption, on this, might be sufficient to the end. But, what if public encouragement was to be given on home-made Stone-Ware, rather than on Earthen-Ware?
>
> Stone-Ware is now scarce and dear amongst us, as the housewife knows. This is owing to its great bulk and low value, that scarcely affords to pay the freight on measure. . . It is this circumstance that renders the manufacturing these wares an object to our enterprising people, peculiarly promising of profit and permanent advantage.

Another factor that helped to bring about the introduction of stoneware manufacture was the overproduction of redware during the Revolutionary period, resulting in the

failure of many such potteries; on account of the scarcity of imported earthenware, many new redware shops had been added to the long list of those already in operation. Lord Sheffield, in his *Observations on the Commerce of the United States*,* noted that the supply of common pottery exceeded the demand. He says:

> Manufactures of glass, of earthenware, and of stone, mixed with clay, are all in an infant state. From the quantity and variety of the materials which must have been deposited by nature in so extensive a region as the United States, from the abundance of fuel which they contain, from the expense of importation, and loss by fracture, which falls on glass and earthenwares, from the simplicity of many of these manufactures, and from the great consumption of them, and a firm persuasion that they will receive the early attention of foreign or American capitalists, are at once produced. Coarse tiles and bricks of an excellent quality, potter's wares, *all in quantities beyond the home consumption* [italics mine], a few ordinary vessels of stone mixed with clay, some mustard and snuff bottles, a few flasks or flagons, a small quantity of sheet-glass and of vessels for family use, generally of the inferior kinds, are all that are now made.

With competition so keen, it was inevitable that many changes should take place. In Charlestown, where so many potteries had once flourished, only two or three were carried on after the Revolution. The Danvers industry, at its height around 1800, was at last almost wholly confined to the shops of the Osborn and Southwick families, while the sons of other formerly successful potters sought a living in the mountains of New Hampshire or the wilds of Maine. The redware potter either succumbed to competition or removed to the frontier.

Several New England potters attempted to make stoneware before the Revolution. With the exception of Grace Parker of Charlestown, all of them lived in Connecticut. An account of the industry in that state appears in later chapters. In Massachusetts the first successful stoneware potter was William Seaver of Taunton. Tradition dates the beginning of his manufacture of the ware at 1772 or earlier, but the correct date may be nearer 1790. Samuel Hopkins Emery, in his *History of Taunton*, is authority for the statement that Seaver was engaged in the stoneware business with Ebenezer Baker in Dorchester previous to 1772. Records show that the partnership was a fact. It probably began when the two young men, on October 31, 1769, bought a dwelling house and five acres of land in Braintree, "lying near Milton Bridge." Whether Emery is correct in his assumption that they were actually making stoneware at that time is less easily proved. He says that Seaver moved to Taunton in order to secure his clay by boat up the Taunton River, thereby saving half the distance. This sounds reasonable and may be the explanation of the brief duration of their enterprise. They doubtless succumbed to the same obstacles that prevented the success of Grace Parker's Charlestown pottery: the expense of transporting materials around Cape Cod from New Jersey, or even from Martha's Vineyard, would more than offset any profit. No example from this early Dorchester pottery is known, although some pieces may have survived. They would not be recognizable, because it was not customary in New England to mark stoneware with firm or place names until around 1800.

The partnership lasted only three years, Seaver moving to Taunton, while Baker remained in Dorchester. There is no reason to believe that Baker afterwards made anything other than redware.

An account book kept by William Seaver, which dates from 1786 to 1812, together with

* Published by Matthew Carey in successive numbers of the *American Museum* and collected in a volume printed in Philadelphia in 1791.

numerous personal articles owned by him or connected with his career as a major in the Revolution, may be seen at the Old Colony Historical Society in Taunton. In a paper read before this society, George Bosworth says that Seaver went to Albany for a short time before settling in Taunton. This is a significant fact, because stoneware manufacture was established at an early date in and near Albany. It is quite possible that Seaver went there to learn the proper methods and the sources of necessary materials.

In 1772 he built a kiln opposite his house on the easterly side of Crooked Lane, now Ingell Street, where it crosses High. This was on the water side of High Street, on what was called the "No. 2 Landing Place of Taunton Great River." Emery says this was a stoneware kiln, where the first stoneware in Bristol County was produced, and also the first American crucible, made before 1793. However, Seaver also made earthenware throughout his career, and his account book shows that his business was largely in that material, as well as in the manufacture of "stick" (wooden) heels. The earliest mention of stoneware as such in Seaver's accounts is dated June 6, 1791, and records the sale of a gallon stone jug for two shillings to Nathan Carver. All items in the 1780's, including such objects as pots, pans for milk, bread, or pudding, cups, mugs, bowls, porringers, plates, platters, chambers, flowerpots, and milk pails are obviously redware. There is also an entry of three dozen "Galley potts" at one shilling per dozen, sold to Daniel Brewer. The stoneware seems to have been limited for the most part to pots and jugs. It may be noted that Seaver charged two shillings, eight pence, for a three-gallon jug or a two-gallon pot, while a gallon pot was worth one and eight. He occasionally mentions "paint" pots. These were probably not receptacles for paint, but were ornamented with slip — a process known to potters as "painting" — and were no doubt the familiar gray ware bedecked with cobalt blue. Another early entry notes a stone butter pot, one shilling, eight pence. Seaver also made stone chambers and ink stands.

It is said that the Major owned a small vessel, the *Sam Adams*, which was used to bring clay from New Jersey and from Gay Head, unloading it at his own landing. Emery, quoting from Atwood's *Reminiscences of Taunton*, says that the Gay Head Indians brought clay up the river in their canoes. There seems to be no doubt that Seaver mixed his more expensive New Jersey clay with the nearby marl from Martha's Vineyard — a custom practiced by other early stoneware potters. His accounts show that he bought clay at Amboy, paying twelve dollars for one load and thirty-seven dollars for another, besides the expense of freighting. For a quantity of white clay purchased of Samuel Leonard he paid two dollars. This was doubtless used for slip decoration on plates and platters.

That this early Bristol County pottery did a fair business is evident from the fact that the wares were shipped to New London and New York. Seaver's son John soon became his father's partner, and later, a younger son, William, was connected with the Seaver business. He, however, seems to have conducted the stick-heel manufactory, for an account book kept by him after the Major's death, makes no reference to pottery. The Major died July 28, 1815, but the pottery, it is said, continued for a number of years, being abandoned, however, before 1830. A small part of the original building was still standing in 1893 and was then in possession of the Seaver family. A picture by a primitive artist depicts a view of the Seaver house and buildings, which were torn down in 1871.

The second attempt at establishing the much-needed manufacture of stoneware took place in Boston in 1794. Thomas Pem-

berton, in his *Description of Boston*, written in that year, says: "At the Stone Pottery lately set up in Lynn street by Mr. Fenton from New Haven, all kinds of stone vessels are made after the manner of the imported Liverpool ware and sold at a lower rate. The clay for this manufacture is brought from Perth Amboy in New Jersey."

The new potter was none other than Jonathan Fenton, father of Richard and Christopher Webber Fenton of Bennington fame. His stay in Boston was brief. Apparently he encountered the same difficulties as had his predecessors in the matter of expense for transporting clay. Although his name appears neither in the Boston directories nor in the land records, two of his children were born in the city — Sally, September 1794, and Melyndia, January 1796. His pottery ran for only two years, for in January 1797 he was in Walpole, New Hampshire. In 1801 he started a pottery in Dorset, Vermont.

Some exceedingly handsome early stoneware with the Boston mark is found near the city. Most of it is colored brown by an ocher stain, and a number of pieces have interesting decoration. Jugs and jars with the mark *Boston 1804* are also discovered from time to time. Until recently I had supposed that all this ware emanated from the same pottery, but after studying many examples, I have come to the conclusion that they come from two different places. The mark on undated ware usually has letters of the same size, but, when the word *Boston* appears with the 1804 date, the letter B is larger than the other letters. This latter mark is sometimes found, too, without the date.

The identity of "Boston 1804" is one of the mysteries of potting history that has so far defied research. The problem seemed on the way to solution when I acquired the beautifully incised jar shown in Fig. 90. In addition to its elaborate decoration, it has on the reverse the signature in script *Marshall Timson.* Just below the word *Boston,* scratched under the design, is the name *Lydia Osborn.* The ornamentation of this piece was evidently a matter of trial and error, for the plain side shows clearly that an unsatisfactory embellishment had been smoothed out, leaving traces of the young lady's name and the word *Charlestown.* At first sight, it looked like an easy matter to put Timson in his place and to prove that he was responsible for the Boston pieces. But it has been impossible to get the least trace of this man or his ancestry, in spite of an exhaustive search of available records and documents.

My present opinion (subject to change without notice) is that stoneware marked *Boston* with *even-sized* letters was made in the pottery of Jonathan Fenton, or perhaps some unknown successor — even Marshall Timson. The 1804 pieces have a somewhat different style. They were either made in a Boston works of brief duration or were the work of a Charlestown potter. There is evidence for this second theory.

Frederick Carpenter, a stoneware potter, was born November 13, 1771, in Lebanon, Connecticut, not far from Jonathan Fenton's native town. He was in Boston at the time of his marriage to Diana Heath, December 1796, and subsequently, when his first child was born, October 17, 1797. The conclusion is obvious that he was working for Fenton, especially as he soon moved back to New Haven, where he had no doubt learned his trade in the Fentons' pottery. His second child was born there in September 1799. It is well known that Jonathan Fenton's brother Jacob was running a stoneware kiln in New Haven at this time and that he went from the Connecticut city to Burlington, New York, in 1801. In this same year, which marked the closing of the New Haven pottery, Carpenter returned to Massachusetts and settled in Charlestown — a fact verified by the birth

of a third child in March. In 1803 he purchased land in the town.

Carpenter was by all accounts a stoneware maker, and yet there is no record of an organized stoneware business in Charlestown before 1812, when the Edmands pottery was founded with Carpenter as its master workman. We may well ask what he was doing in the intervening time. There are some extremely fine stoneware jars with the Charlestown mark that are generally assumed to have been made by Edmands, but which could be the work of Frederick Carpenter in the period from 1801 to 1812 (Fig. 95). Another supposition is that he may have put a Boston mark on some of his ware for sales purposes. There is a strong resemblance between the early Boston and Charlestown pieces. The forms are quite similar; ocher stain was used in both places to obtain a rich brown tone; and incised decoration of unconventional type appears on a Charlestown jar (Fig. 94) as well as on the Timson pot.

In any event, we may consider that much early Charlestown stoneware was made by Frederick Carpenter. When Barnabas Edmands and his brother-in-law, William Burroughs, established their potworks, neither one was a potter. Edmands had been a brass founder, and it is unlikely that at the age of thirty-four he ever became a skilled potter, although he was so called in deeds after 1812. Burroughs was a resident of Boston, and his interest in the business was a financial one. Carpenter, in fact, is mentioned as having been Edmands' "partner" in the early days. The pottery stood on Austin Street near the present site of the State Prison. The land was purchased February 12, 1812, and the buildings erected soon thereafter. Edmands lived nearby on Richmond Street (now Rutherford Avenue).

After the death of Carpenter in 1827, Charles Collier became the foreman and master craftsman of the works. In 1831 the pottery was still comparatively small. Only five men were employed. They received $1.25 a day for their services — good pay indeed for those times. The annual output was estimated at $3700. Clay was brought from New York and New Jersey, and wood, the largest item of expense, was the only fuel.

In 1839 Edmands exhibited a very large stone jug at the second annual fair of the Massachusetts Charitable Mechanics' Association. It was described as "an excellent specimen of so large an article of stone ware" and was said to have been turned on the wheel by an expert workman. Again, two years later, they again succeeded in obtaining awards at the Mechanics' Fair — one, a diploma for Charles Collier, the other, for the company. Since they were the only entrants in the field, we cannot judge the quality of their exhibits by the fact that they won prizes. The commentary from the catalogue of the fair is worth quoting in full:

> The Committee have but a limited field on which to construct a Report, as they find but two articles of Stone Ware offered for exhibition — one, a large Fifteen Gallon Water Pitcher, made by Mr. C. Collier; the other, a Water Jar, of nearly equal capacity, from the manufactory of Barnabas Edmands & Co., of Charlestown. The Committee find the material of these two articles of a very superior quality and the workmanship of a higher character than any that they have ever before met with of this country's manufacture. They show an advance in the article, highly creditable to the makers, and give promise that the hitherto almost untrodden field of the finer quality of Stone Ware manufactures may soon be occupied by the skill and taste of our countrymen. The Committee, however, could not but notice, that a general fault in all articles made of Stone Ware, applied, (at least in one of the specimens) to those now exhibited. They found that the covers to the articles were not made with that care and fitness which they deem highly necessary; and they felt surprised that articles showing such a high state

of improvement in the art, should not have met with a greater share of attention in this respect.

In 1840 several of Edmands' relatives, including his sons, William B., Edward Townsend, and Thomas Russell Burroughs, and his brother Benjamin, were working in the pottery. Two years later, one had turned to carpentry and another to painting. Barnabas and William then carried on with the assistance of Sanford P. Lundy and Charles Collier. Later changes in the personnel would be of little interest. In 1845 fourteen men were employed at the works, which at that time turned out eighteen thousand dollars worth of stoneware annually. At some time before the middle of the century, the plant was removed to the easterly end of Medford Street on the Mystic River, where there were better wharfing facilities. Barnabas Edmands, who was seventy-two years old in 1850, then decided to retire and to sell the business to his sons Edward Townsend and Thomas Russell Burroughs. In partnership with Charles Collier, they ran the pottery as Edmands & Company. During this decade the firm bought jugs by the dozen from Sidney Risley's pottery in Norwich, Connecticut.* Their exhibition at the Mechanics' Fair of 1856 was a display of drain pipe, fire brick, and tomato jars. The drain pipe was produced by means of machinery invented and patented by Charles Collier. This branch of stoneware making was later abandoned, as it was found unprofitable in competition with western manufacture.

The firm name was Powers & Edmands in 1868, and another change occurred when it became Edmands & Hooper. The latter style was retained until the pottery closed in 1905, although the business was then owned by John B. Edmands. The buildings were razed in 1927. Barnabas Edmands lived for twenty-two years after his retirement, highly respected as one of Charlestown's oldest and most influential citizens.

Examples of Charlestown stoneware, especially those marked *Edmands & Co.*, are frequently found. The earliest pieces are marked simply *Charlestown*; those of the next period bear the name *Barnabas* (or *B*) *Edmands* (*Edmunds*)/*Charlestown*, and somewhat later *Barnabas* (or *B*) *Edmands & Co./ Charlestown*. Jars bearing the Charlestown mark only are usually undecorated, except for tiny impressed motives, such as hearts, eagles, or tassels, which appear in threes. The Edmands & Company stoneware, made in the period of freest decorative expression, is remarkable for elaborate and often striking design. Straight-sided crocks and pots that would otherwise be completely uninteresting are so charmingly enlivened by their ornamentation that in spirit, if not in date, they fall into the category of folk pottery.

Encouraged perhaps by the success of the Edmands family, a potter who was also of Charlestown parentage and possibly a former apprentice in the Austin Street pottery, started a works in Chelsea. The Winnisimmet Company was selling lots and developing property there, and, June 27, 1836, "Loammi Kendall, potter" bought three thousand feet of land with ferry privileges on the northwest side of the Salem Turnpike (now Broadway). Kendall paid down three hundred dollars, securing at the same time a mortgage of one thousand dollars from the company. The pottery he erected stood just southwest of Fifth Street, near the present Chelsea Square.

In 1837 Kendall exhibited at the first fair of the Massachusetts Charitable Mechanics' Association and received praise for his work. He had made three urn-shaped flowerpots, which were said to be fair in quality and exceedingly good in form and proportions. He seems not to have been immediately suc-

* Account book of Sidney Risley.

cessful and he got into trouble with the land company over a breach in the condition of his mortgage. The company took possession of his premises in April 1843. Nevertheless, he came to same arrangement with them and was given another mortgage, which he paid off in 1845.

Thenceforth Kendall continued to run his establishment without interruption, making stoneware and, it is said, earthenware. Stone jugs marked *Chelsea* or *Loammi Kendle* [*sic*] represent the potter's output. His later crocks are sometimes decorated with a robin-like bird. In 1870 the pottery was moved to a V-shaped piece of land between Park and Pearl Streets, south of the square. One Zephaniah Bassett held a mortgage on the land and buildings. I have talked with one of his descendants, who could recall the Kendall pottery. As a boy of fifteen he was accustomed to drive across Chelsea Bridge from East Boston, where his father was a baker, in order to buy bean pots and other earthenware. There was a great deal of breakage in the business and he made frequent trips.

There was little other competition with the Edmands pottery in the Boston area. For a brief period T. Sables & Company made pottery in Medford in connection with the Lawrence rum distillery. I have seen only one piece of stoneware bearing their firm mark — a nicely shaped low jar. A poorly potted jug marked simply *Medford* gives evidence that their wares were not always of the same quality.

Sables & Company was composed of two brothers, Thomas and John, and Job Clapp, all of Medford, and all potters. October 24, 1838, they acquired a large plot of land east of Medford Square, between Mystic Avenue (then Ship Street) and the Mystic River. A dwelling house and other buildings were standing on the lot, and these they probably converted to pottery uses. They shared the dock with Fitch & Lawrence, last of Medford's many distillers to remain in business. Oakman Joyce of Medford held a mortgage on the premises. It is a measure of their lack of success that he foreclosed it in 1844. Haskel & Smith's *Gazetteer* (1843) mentions one pottery in the town in 1840. This was undoubtedly the Sables company, which seems to have been the only one to operate in Medford after colonial days.

In the mid-nineteenth century stoneware manufacture in eastern Massachusetts was confined to the potteries in Charlestown, Chelsea, Taunton, and Somerset. Judging by the wide distribution of the wares, the industry was competitive to a degree unknown in former times. And Bristol County had come to the front as a factor.

There is evidence that the Seaver pottery in Taunton was continued by some other firm. In 1837 ten thousand dollars' worth of stoneware was turned out annually by a concern that employed six men. The existence of a pottery in 1840 and of a stoneware manufactory in 1845 has been verified and indicates a continuous business. Stoneware marked *Wm. H. Ingell*, *J. W. Ingell*, or *M. G. Ingell*, with the place name *Taunton/ Mass.*, belongs to this period. The second mark stands for Jonathan W. Ingell, who for a time eluded research, because he was invariably called "manufacturer" or "trader" in deeds, without reference to his actual occupation. He and his brother William H. owned brickyards in the Weir Bridge district of Taunton, where they produced fire brick and apparently some stoneware. Upon the settlement of the estate of George A. Ingell, the heirs, Jonathan, William, Mary O. (widow of Benjamin), and Mary A. Ingell (by guardian), sold at auction, June 1, 1850, one-fifth part of the "Pottery lot" with the buildings thereon to Elias E. and Alexander Standish for the meager sum of $162. This property was northwest of the point where the New Bed-

ford and Taunton Railroad crosses Ingell Street and not more than a quarter of a mile from the old Seaver pottery.

Alexander Standish was already running a stoneware pottery on Bow Street (now Presbrey's Court), almost opposite the end of Second Street and a short distance from the Ingell land. He appears to have bought out the Ingells in order to stifle competition, for he sold their pottery lot the following February with the express condition that the premises were "not to be used as or for a pottery without permission of the grantors."

Standish, who came from Plympton, was in business with Franklin T. Wright, a resident of nearby Dighton. Just when their pottery was built is not known, but it was probably as early as 1846, when Standish bought a house lot on Second Street. The partnership continued until about 1855: Standish's name is not listed in the city directory of 1857. Meantime, at some period of the pottery's existence — perhaps at its beginning — Standish ran the business alone. The mark *A. Standish/ Taunton, Mass.* was then used. The firm name *Standish & Wright* next appears, and this was followed by *F. T. Wright & Co./ Stoneware/ Taunton, Mass.* as late as 1866. Two years later Wright's son had joined the firm, and the same mark with the word *Son* instead of *Co.* is found on their jugs. Neither Wright nor Standish is called "potter" in deeds, although they are noted in directories as "stoneware manufacturers." During the fifties and sixties they kept five employees busy and at one time produced ware worth fifteen thousand dollars yearly. The workmen's names are in the directories and other records: Marcus P. Chase, in 1848 and until 1857; Asher Applegate, from 1850 to 1859; Peter Dunbar and Thomas Levins, 1850; Alfred W. Letts, in 1857; George E. Wyman, Benjamin Parker, and R. C. Dalton, in 1866.

I have been told by a resident of Barnstable that the Wrights of Taunton ran the Barnstable pottery in the late period. This being so, Benjamin Parker was either the former owner of the Barnstable shop, which was running in 1851, or his son.

Taunton stoneware is by no means uncommon. Such examples as I have seen with the Wright mark have been uninspired in style. An Ingell jug and small crock decorated with floral sprays are of more interest.

At Pottersville, the Chace brothers, Leonard, Benjamin G., and Clark Chace, added stoneware manufacture to redware potting in the 1840's. Before 1847 they put up a new building with suitable equipment for the purpose. In that year they incorporated as the Somerset Potters' Works. Leonard and Benjamin conveyed to the corporation for the sum of $8669 land with part of a dwelling house, two stoneware kilns, one brick kiln, a cement mill, three clay mills, and a wharf. This land lay along the east side of the new highway to "Egypt," being bounded on the north by their own land, running to the river on the east, thence at a tangent southerly by the land of George Purinton, and then northwesterly through his dwelling house. This was without doubt the old mansion originally occupied by Asa Chace and Clark Purinton.

Today this industry would be considered a small one, but in the mid-nineteenth century the stoneware pottery and the earthenware shops played a vital part in the economy of the town. In 1857 six men were employed in the stoneware factory and five in the other shops. The yearly output of stoneware was valued at nine thousand dollars. This was but little more than half the quantity produced at that time in Charlestown, but it was sufficient to supply the needs of southeastern Massachusetts.

In 1882 the Chaces were getting along in years and their plant was becoming old and dilapidated. They therefore found it expe-

dient to sell out. The new company reorganized the business, rejuvenated the old buildings, and erected new ones with more modern kilns. Following these improvements, affairs at the Somerset pottery were run on a larger scale. The turning room, in a building one hundred by thirty-seven feet, had wheels for thirteen workmen. There were four kilns, three of them for stoneware and one for earthenware. During the next ten years they continued to manufacture various kinds of utensils, principally such things as snuff jars and other commercial containers. Among their specialties were huge crocks, up to sixty gallons in capacity. Except for the very largest vessels, hand methods still prevailed.

An 1886 advertisement of the Somerset Potters' Works in the *Boston Directory* announced that they were "Manufacturers of and Wholesale Dealers in White, Decorated, Rockingham, Yellow, Stone and Earthen Ware," with headquarters at 39 and 40 Commercial Wharf, Boston. In this decade the old-time production was gradually superseded by the manufacture of fire brick and stove linings. In 1891 the company was merged with another fire brick concern. All manufacture ceased there in 1909 and the buildings were razed. The remains of one of the kilns, some seventy feet long, and a heap of shards are now the only evidence of a once flourishing industry. A small square building at 3046 Riverside Avenue, which stood at the former entrance to the plant, was the company office. A still smaller structure nearby was the old Pottersville post office. The expansion and increased number of employees during the eighties and nineties is no doubt one cause of the great local pride in the Pottersville industry. Greater credit is due, however, to those early craftsmen, like Asa Chace and Clark Purinton, who produced wares that were not only useful but truly beautiful as well.

The clay for the Somerset Potters' Works was at first brought from Gardner's Island at the western end of Long Island Sound. It was used with an admixture of clay from Gay Head on Martha's Vineyard. The resulting product was often buff rather than gray. The Gay Head Indians made a business of coming to Pottersville from time to time with a four- or five-ton load, which they would sell or barter for other necessities. The superior clay from South Amboy, New Jersey, was also used. The great cost of transportation finally made it impossible for the Somerset works to compete with manufactories nearer the source of supply, and that was one of the reasons why the business failed in Pottersville.

Some of the stoneware made by the Chaces is quite handsome, with well-executed blue decoration. The marks *L. & B. G. Chace/ Somerset* and *Somerset Potters' Works* appear on the pieces. The chronology is uncertain. The *New England Business Directory* of 1856 lists "Somerset Pottery (B. G & C. Chace)" and also "Somerset Potters' Works —Leonard Chace, agt."

There were two smaller offshoots of the Chace pottery. After its demise, Charles E. Hathaway, who had been superintendent at the stoneware factory, went into business for himself. His shop stood north of Brightman's Lane (now Luther Avenue), between Riverside Avenue and County Streets, in front of the present High School. He made stoneware, specializing in colanders and large-sized crocks.

Well remembered by persons now living was the shop of Patrick and William Synan on the south side of Center Street, which leads west opposite the old post office. Both brothers had learned their trade in the Somerset pottery. After its closing, they started their own little business in 1893, continuing for about twenty years. Patrick Synan had been noted for his ability to turn

large vessels, but in his own pottery he engaged in the making of stoneware bean pots. The brothers became famous for these utensils and for their "jewelers' baskets," for which they found a market in Providence, Attleboro, New York, and elsewhere. The bean pots were sold in the Woolworth stores. It is said that each of the Synans could turn out twenty-five dozen of these useful receptacles in one day. They were at last obliged to close their pottery, although large orders were at hand, because the business had ceased to show a profit.

The Hathaway pottery closed in 1912, the other a year later. The last shipment of clay to Somerset was consigned to the Synan brothers and to Hathaway. The shutting down of these potteries spelled finis for the Somerset industry. During the sesquicentennial celebration of the incorporation of the town, William Hathaway, a brother of Charles, demonstrated the use of the potter's wheel in memory of the days when the word "Pottersville" signified an important industry.

The men of Taunton and Somerset soon had competitors in Worcester, where Frank B. Norton and Frederick Hancock from Bennington, Vermont, started a pottery in 1858. Norton was a grandson of the famous founder of the Bennington works and had had excellent training in his craft. He had married Jane, daughter of Richard L. Fenton. His partner, it is thought, was the same Hancock who had been with Leander W. Fenton in St. Johnsbury. Hancock remained in Worcester only a few years. In 1865 Norton was running the business alone. Three years later his sons were members of the firm, which was then known as F. B. Norton & Company.

Worcester stoneware is encountered in New England perhaps more generally than any other. In fact, Hayward's *Gazetteer* of 1858 gives the value of their annual output as eighteen thousand dollars, a sum not exceeded elsewhere in Massachusetts, except at Charlestown. By 1865, however, this total had declined to but little more than half the former amount. The ware was the usual assortment of crocks and jars that emanated from late stoneware potteries. A great deal of it, especially in the form of crocks, was made and marked for retailers of food products. I have seen one of these labeled *James Brothers/ Danielsonville, Conn.* and another with the mark *C. F. Worthen/ Peabody, Mass.* Worthen was running the Osborn pottery and presumably took on a line of stoneware goods to sell. All such jars may be identified by a characteristic large design in cobalt blue. Garden equipment similar to naturalistic objects made at West Sterling was also a part of the later Worcester output. William J. Walley was the modeler of their tree-stump seats topped with cushions. It is rumored that F. B. Norton insured that these seats would be form-fitting by sitting on the moist clay to give the proper impression. This was in the 1870's.

After 1875 the pottery works was on Water Street. The making of emery wheels, invented by a Swedish potter, Sven Polson, had been added to the manufacture as early as 1873. In 1885 the Norton Emery Wheel Company, which is still running, was incorporated, and the craftsmanship of the old-time artisans was succeeded by this more prosaic business.

Stoneware was made by Joseph O. Bullard and Alexander F. Scott as early as 1870 in a pottery at 14 Western Avenue, Allston (the Brighton area of Boston). The ware was marked *Bullard & Scott/ Cambridgeport, Mass.*, but this style does not indicate any change of address. Directories show that the concern was always located on Western Avenue and was doing business there in Scott's name in 1895. Bullard alone appears as late as 1909. Although this is a comparatively recent pottery, little is known about

it. Edwin A. Rich, of Peabody and Beverly note, worked there from August 1873 to October 1874. The jugs and jars are often nicely decorated with a bird.

Another little-known stoneware pottery was operated in the 1880's in the industrial village of Ballardvale, part of Andover. Such information as I have been able to get about it was obtained by visiting the site, talking with men who remembered the works, and by consulting the Andover Town Valuation Books.

The buildings stood a short distance northeast of the railroad crossing at the end of a lane that was passable ten years ago, but is now quite overgrown. We were first directed to this spot by Mr. Clemens, the crossing tender, whose brother, Edward H. Darrah, of Kingston, New Hampshire, used to work in the pottery grinding clay. In 1935 we found the storehouse still standing on the easterly side of the lane, while the ruins of the building where the clay was prepared and the shop where the ware was made and dried were on the westerly side. These remains and the kiln, constructed of fire brick, are still plainly in evidence (1943); the storehouse has been torn down. The shard pile is at the end of the former roadway, where the debris had been thrown down into a ravine.

This rather extensive plant in the 1880's was the property of George W. Simmons of Oak Hall, Boston, and later of his heirs, and was evidently leased by him to the men who ran it as a pottery. The "Stone shop and other Bldgs in the Yard" were at first given a valuation of twenty-nine thousand dollars (this entry is annotated "Pottery"). Before 1890, however, the assessment was lowered to five thousand dollars for the buildings and twenty-three hundred dollars for the land. The firm name at one time was Weston & Willard; later, Willard & Sullivan. Among the shards we found pieces marked *L. Willard & Sons/Ballardvale* or merely with the word *Ballardvale*. These were decorated with a late type of stenciled design. I have also seen the mark *Ballardvale Stoneware Manufacturing Company* on a jar with hand-painted blue decoration. As yet I am unable to throw any further light on Willard or his sons and partners.

James Oldroyd, who could remember the Ballardvale pottery as it looked when he was fifteen (in 1890), and his brother, ten years his senior, who had worked there, supplied us with the information that only common jugs and crocks of stoneware and earthen flowerpots were produced. Wood was the only fuel. The wares were shipped away by the railroad, which bounds the land on the west. About twelve men were employed — among them John and Martin Doherty of Andover.

Upon our second visit to the Ballardvale site in 1943, we found numerous fragments with well-executed motives applied by hand (Fig. 113), showing how late this traditional method of beautifying the wares was practiced. Among the pieces, too, was a churn cover — indication that the usual line of stoneware articles was made there. This company sometimes made jars for manufacturers or storekeepers. Such containers with the Ballardvale mark were made for Pearson's snuff mill in Byfield and appropriately inscribed with the firm name painted on in blue.

From 1878 until the close of the century or later an extensive manufactory in East Boston, known as the Boston Pottery Company, was engaged in the production of stoneware and other wares. It stood on Border Street near Condor Street. In the *Boston Directory* of 1893 an advertisement described it as follows: "Boston Pottery Co./ Manufacturers of every description of/ Stoneware/ Rockingham and Yellow Wares/ Earthen Ware Etc./ Representing capacity of 2500

cars per annum/ Largest Stone Ware Works in the United States/ Most Complete Stock Quality unsurpassed/ 11 and 12 Commercial Wharf/ Between Commercial Street and Atlantic Avenue, Boston." The extravagant claims of this notice indicate a large financial backing. The concern was, in fact, a local branch of a western company.

The Dorchester Pottery Works at 165 Victory Road, formerly Preston Street, is still in operation. It is the one company in New England that employs old-time methods of production. Although it manufactures stoneware commercially, it maintains the high standards of workmanship that characterized the potteries of an earlier day. Its large three-story building is the original factory started by George H. Henderson in the 1880's. Henderson came from a North Cambridge family and had previously been running the S. L. Pewtress pottery in New Haven under the style Henderson & O'Halloran. The Dorchester Pottery was the last concern to make salt-glazed ware. In 1897 the company advertised in the *Boston Directory*: "Dorchester Pottery Works/ Geo. Henderson, Proprietor/ Manu'r of/ Dip Baskets, Butter Pots, Jugs, Jars and Flower Pots/ Clay Specialties and Large Pots/ Promptly made to order/ 9 and 11 Preston Street, Dorchester, Mass."

This announcement would serve almost as well today, for the pottery is still making many of the old forms. Instead of being glazed with salt, however, they are coated with slips of brown, white, or light blue.

C. W. Henderson is the present owner of the pottery, while his wife, Ethel Hill Henderson, is its superintendent and manager. Mrs. Henderson actually served an apprenticeship in the works soon after her marriage, and she is thoroughly conversant with every process in the designing, making, burning, and glazing of ware, in the chemistry of its composition, and in the stacking and operation of the kiln. The work of turning is accomplished by two elderly Italian potters.

The huge circular kiln, twenty-five feet or more in diameter, holds enough ware at one time to fill one and one-half freight cars. It is downdraft, the gases passing down through the floor of the kiln into a flue that leads to a chimney in the corner of the kiln room. The fires are stoked at first with coal and then, for more intense heat, with wood. Burning takes about fifty hours, the cooling-off period about five days.

Some of the ware is decorated by an extremely able artist, Knesseth Dennisons, who carries on an independent business, buying his blanks from the Hendersons. A student of design, he has been able to revive in the ornamentation of mugs, bowls, and pitchers the same feeling that inspired the early decorators of stoneware. Painting with blue slip on white grounds or incising patterns on dark brown surfaces, he has an inexhaustible range of ideas. This pottery deserves a visit from all who have an affection for old-time craftsmanship.

CHAPTER TWELVE

Some Potteries of Central and Western Massachusetts

Redware potters in any given period turned out articles closely resembling those made by their contemporaries and usually indistinguishable from them. One might, therefore, see little point in relating the stories of their small establishments. However, by means of a record of pottery sites, earthenware owned for several generations in a small town may often be given an attribution with a fair degree of certainty, and, aside from its historical importance, the detailed account of locations presents a great deal of human interest. Accordingly, in this chapter are included notes about a number of places where redware was made, even though the data about them may be negligible.

One of the first potters to work in Worcester County was Charles Bailey. He was born in Amesbury, August 27, 1744, moved to Harvard, Massachusetts, in 1767, and thence to Brookfield. It seems likely that his shop was in North Brookfield, for the business was continued in that locality by one Elisha Drake as soon as Bailey had departed. Drake was then a young man, but he carried on his trade in Brookfield until after 1823. In 1815 he was joined by Samuel Stevens, who worked in Brookfield until 1837, removing thence to North Adams, Michigan. Stevens in 1816 had married Lucy Johnson of Woodstock, Connecticut, where he may have worked in the Bugbee pottery.

Considerably later the potting business was pursued with varying fortunes in East Brookfield. The first shop was built by James Smith at some time after his departure from the firm at West Sterling in 1868. It stood a short distance east of the farm now known as Drake's Garden on the road to North Brookfield. Francis H. Drake, present owner of the farm, says that his father, Arthur Howard Drake, applied for work in this pottery, but was refused because he had no knowledge of turning on the wheel. Determined to acquire the art, he set up a wheel in his own barn, where he practiced until his work was acceptable. The small building now used for a produce stand was at one time his workshop. From Arthur Drake his son learned that Smith & Brown were not particularly successful. When one night the young man saw them stoking the kiln with the pottery shelving, he suspected that they were trying to set fire to the building. They

did, in fact, burn it down. This must have occurred just before the establishment of another works in 1879.

The new pottery was run by Richard Linley, a businessman, and Abner S. Wight, whose career may be traced in the potting annals of Marlborough and Keene, New Hampshire, and West Sterling, Massachusetts. He was already a white-haired man, known to his workmen as "Uncle" Abner, when he came to East Brookfield, and he left the general management of the business to his son Edward Marcellus. Their factory was located in the Stevens Block, between South and Quabaug Ponds. The site lies about five hundred feet south of Route 9 and east of a spur track of the railroad that crosses the highway. A going business was maintained here until 1888. John Donovan, who spent so many years in the Peabody pottery, worked at East Brookfield from 1880 to 1884. He is authority for the statement that the company employed four turners and two apprentices. A photograph of the pottery hands taken at this time shows that there were numerous other employees and that the manufacture was conducted on no small scale.

Francis Drake in his boyhood found work there molding and painting flowerpots. He says that Linley & Wight produced a general line of redware, such as bean pots and crocks, besides a number of novelties. Among the latter he recalls slippers pressed in molds and banks shaped like apples, pears, and other fruit. He still owns a peculiar covered crock with handles and a pouring spout and a cylindrical unglazed vase decorated with applied handmade roses, an example of his father's craftsmanship. There is also in my collection a bank in the form of a house which is attributed to this pottery.

Linley & Wight were succeeded by Watson & Howlen, who later moved the plant to Southbridge, where they manufactured chimney tops and flue linings.

The neighboring town of Brimfield is said to have had its local potter as early as 1780. There is some question about his name, but information obtained by Rev. Randolph Hill from Miss Anna Tarbell, who owned a pitcher made in Brimfield, seems to verify the fact that the maker was David Bugbee. If so, he was perhaps the son of Daniel Bugbee of Woodstock, Connecticut, a one-time resident of Brimfield, as there is no record of a David Bugbee being born in the town. Miss Tarbell learned that the potter's shop was at East Hill and that his clay pits were near Sherman Pond.

There is more certainty about the history of James Moore, who is mentioned in the *History of Brimfield*, by Rev. Charles M. Hyde, as having owned a shop on the hillside back of the house later occupied by Mrs. Alfred Pierce. I investigated this site in 1940 and found a few fragments. The location appears to be the same as that of the Bugbee pottery. James Morgan Moore, son of James, was born in Woodstock, August 18, 1808. It is improbable that James the father was the potter, as all but one of his twelve children were born in Woodstock. The younger James married Rebecca Adams of Southbridge in 1834 and must have begun to work in Brimfield at about that time. Other potters may have carried on this small shop in the interim between Bugbee's death or departure and Moore's arrival.

The Shakers at Shirley made redware pipes and probably other things before 1800. In the *Diary of William Bentley*, under date of July 19, 1795, we find: "We were invited to smoak, & some pipes of their own casting were brought. They were of clay, & the stems called stails, were of osier. . . For a dozen of their pipes they would receive nothing."

In numerous instances it has been possible

to connect the potters trained in Danvers with shops in western Massachusetts or New Hampshire. Less frequently does one encounter such records concerning the men of Charlestown. The name of Joseph Thorp, appearing in an advertisement in the *Massachusetts Spy or Worcester Gazette*, December 9, 1784, is an exception. The paragraph reads:

> To Be Sold
>
> The Pot-House and Works formerly occupied by Joseph Thorp and lately by Jonathan Nash, situated in Worcester, about two miles and a half from the Meeting House, on the great road leading to Springfield,—There is a convenient Dwelling-House adjoining the Potter's Works which will be sold with them; also a Shoemaker's shop and an acre and an half of good land, an excellent garden spot, and will well accomodate a Tanner or Currier.
>
> The Premises may be entered on immediately by the Purchaser, to whom the terms of payment will be made easy.
>
> For further Particulars enquire at said Potter's Works of
>
> Jonathan Nash,
>
> Worcester, Dec. 3d, 1784

Joseph Thorp was the son of John of Dedham, where he was baptized September 15, 1745, and where he remained until he was twenty-one and presumably a full-fledged potter. In 1766 he went to Charlestown. He made his home there with the potter John Harris until after 1769. In 1773 he was in Worcester. His son Reuben was born there in that year, and a daughter arrived two years later. After this date, there is no record to show when Thorp sold out to Nash, nor do we know what became of Nash himself. The site of this pottery is in the thickly settled part of Worcester. Reuben Thorp is almost surely the potter who was working in Turner Centre, Maine, in 1803.

A Danvers man, Thomas Goldthwaite, appeared in Springfield in 1763. On January 5 he bought land on the west side of "Town Street." Goldthwaite was a potter in this location until he entered the service of his country in the Revolutionary War. He died soon after his return and his property was sold. The deed of sale mentions potter's works then standing on the land.

Another early Worcester County pottery existed in Fitchburg, although there is but little information to amplify the fact. I have in my collection a barrel-shaped, pint-sized, black ale mug, quite thin and beautifully turned, which, judging by its appearance, must have been made before 1775 (Fig. 36). Attached to it is a torn paper that says: "clay dug and made in Fitchburg. . . given to T. Marshall by his cousin Jon. . ." Whether Jonathan, the cousin of T. Marshall, was the potter whose hand fashioned the mug I shall perhaps never know, and, in any event, the rest of the name has been lost.

Beyond Fitchburg, as one goes over the road to Greenfield, is the town of Orange. Emma Fitts Bradford, a resident, wrote in the November 1936 issue of the *Early American Industries Chronicle* an account of the potteries that were once operated in the northern section of the town. She ascertained that there had been three distinct shops and determined the sites of two of them. The first was that of Abijah Marble; the second was owned by John Goddard, who lived on what is now the Adin Taylor farm; the third was run by Charles Goddard on the Amos Goddard place. Mrs. Bradford found some interesting examples of North Orange earthenware, including a deep pan, jugs, pots, a covered jar, and a slip-decorated salt, which she presented to the North Orange Historical Society. From several sources she learned that the ware was peddled about the neighboring towns by Joseph ("Joe") Southwick. Joe worked in one of the potteries during the summer and

traveled about the country with his horse and cart the rest of the year.

To this information it may be added that John Goddard was the youngest son of David, one of the first settlers of Orange. He was the father of Solomon Goddard, born in 1796, who had a pottery in Troy, New Hampshire, and who is said to have learned his trade in his father's shop. Solomon had sons John, Charles, and Amos, all of Orange. There is a possibility that this second John was the potter of Orange, and it is almost a certainty that Charles was the proprietor of the third shop mentioned by Mrs. Bradford. The Goddard pottery was a family affair lasting through several generations. The names Marble and Southwick are familiar ones among the Peabody craftsmen. Without doubt they had gone west from that community to earn a living in the country.

There is record of a late eighteenth-century pottery in Petersham, which is said to have been operated by two former Hessian soldiers, George Hatstat and Peter Hart. Their kiln, mentioned in the *Athol Transcript* (April 3, 1883), stood on the property known as Deer Farm, now the home of Mr. and Mrs. J. Robert Moore.

Perhaps the best-known pottery in Worcester County is the one at West Sterling. It stood in the shadow of Mount Wachusett, from which it took its name. The letterheads of the Wachusett Pottery indicate that it was founded in 1820. Edwin H. Coolidge, whose interesting article, "The Pottery Business in Sterling," appeared in *Old-Time New England*, July 1932, says that he was unable to find any record of the works before a purchase of land by Henry Tolman, a potter of Troy, New Hampshire, in 1837, although he believes it was in operation before that date. The pottery was situated on the easterly bank of a beautiful running stream in the village of West Sterling, where the foundations of the buildings may still be seen. Clay was brought from a pit one and one-half miles away. This concern was at first about the size of the average country pottery, making twenty-five hundred dollars worth of redware per annum and employing only three men. Even in 1855, statistics show that it had not progressed beyond this status, but in 1865 its output had doubled.

Henry Tolman was assisted and then succeeded by his son Henry, who in 1849 was running the works under the style H. Tolman Jr. & Co. The father had evidently retired, and he died two years later. The firm is also listed in the *New England Directory* of 1849 as Tolman & Wight. It is possible that Abner S. Wight, son of John Wight of Dublin, New Hampshire, already had an interest in the Sterling pottery, although, by all accounts, he did not purchase it until about 1860. A bill of ware headed *W. D. Sime & Co.* and dated July 2, 1853, is receipted by J. D. (Jonas Dustin) Wight, Abner's brother, who was the company clerk. As Mr. Coolidge does not mention Sime, he may have been merely an agent for the pottery. In 1856 the firm name was Wight & Willard (later A. S. Wight & Company), Tolman having withdrawn from the partnership. Abner Wight and his associate carried on a thriving business until after the close of the Civil War. The pottery's affairs were then taken over by Marcus L. Snow, James Smith, and Marcellus Wight, Abner's son, as Snow, Smith & Company. Several other changes in management occurred. In 1869 it was in the hands of Snow and a new partner, Henry Coolidge, who ran the works successfully as Snow & Coolidge until the death of the latter in 1881. During this period the business was so increased that fifteen or twenty men were employed, and the earthenware was sold throughout New England, New York, and even as far west as Indiana. The village in consequence became prosperous, for the turners at the pottery were earning three or

four dollars a day and laborers two dollars — comparatively high wages at the time.

In the early seventies a large storehouse was built and in 1876 a new kiln. Unfortunately a disastrous fire in August of that year destroyed the entire group of buildings, with the exception of the new storehouse. Six months later the Wachusett Pottery, with a larger and better plant, was again in operation. Eventually Snow, acquiring control of the works, began to manufacture emery wheels along with the flowerpots and other wares. He sold the business in 1887 to a corporation known as the Sterling Emery Wheel Company, who abandoned the making of redware and moved soon afterward to Ohio. This, briefly, is the business history of the pottery.

About its products I have been able to learn a great deal, partly from two sales bills owned by Frederick H. Norton and partly from actual excavation on the site of the pottery and storehouse, which has been undisturbed for many years. The earliest record of the wares is the Sime bill abovementioned. This is headed "All Kinds of Earthen Ware, Fancy Pressed Ware with Rockingham Glaze of the best Quality." With visions of mottled Rockingham ware à la Bennington, we attacked the West Sterling dump, but, after many hours of digging, where shards were so plentiful as merely to require turning over, we recovered nothing of this description except two cuspidors, which could hardly be considered evidential. There were, however, innumerable flowerpots and other objects with a plain dark brown glaze on a redware body. Some of them were "pressed" ware made in molds of plaster of Paris, which we also found in the waste pile. Obviously this small country pottery, trying to satisfy the inexplicable demand for brown-colored earthenware, was advertising as Rockingham the usual redware with a manganese glaze. The general understanding of "Rockingham" in the forties was a ware — usually buff stone or earthenware — with a plain dark glaze. The first Rockingham at Bennington was of this kind; so there was perhaps an excuse for applying the term to simple brown-glazed redware. In any event, we found no mottled Rockingham except the spittoons: certainly not any of the fluted cake dishes or "feet" warmers or soap dishes mentioned in the sales list. It is probable that Sime was getting these more sophisticated products from other sources.

The list of earthenware in the 1853 bill comprises cake, cream, lard, and bean pots, milk, bake, and pudding pans, boilers, stove tubes, kneading bowls, fancy glazed flowerpots, flowerpots with saucers attached, others glazed or for hot beds, pipkins, soft soap dishes, shaving mugs, jugs, preserve pots, and wash bowls. The Rockingham articles were spittoons, fancy glazed flower vases (thirteen to eighteen inches), cake pots, nappies, pitchers, wash bowls, fancy fluted cake dishes, pie plates, round or "oblong square" soap dishes, foot warmers, and blancmange coolers.

A bill dated September 14, 1866, is headed "Snow, Smith & Co. (Successors to A. S. Wight & Co.) — Earthen Ware with Rockingham glaze." In addition to the articles listed on the earlier sheet, we find seed pans, glazed hanging vases, milk bowls, cake cups, hard soap dishes, and toy jugs and pitchers.

We unearthed large sections of many of these objects, together with a number of other things of the late redware period. A few vessels appeared entirely unglazed, while others of the same form were glazed inside. The secret of West Sterling Rockingham may indeed have been two firings. Among these forms are common lard pots, crocks with handles, and low curved jars with rounded rims. Bean pots and cuspidors of ordinary redware, glazed within, are numerous. The material could not have been very

durable for objects requiring such hard usage.

By far the greater proportion of fragments are parts of flowerpots, which seem to have been produced in countless styles (Figs. 79, 80). First, there are the hand-turned flowerpots with separate saucers. Except for the largest sizes, these have no collars. Flowerpots of this type were no longer made by hand in redware potteries after the introduction of machinery, which turned them out with such regularity that they could be more easily stacked for merchandising. The hanging flowerpot was in its heyday for twenty years or more after the Civil War; many of us can remember the jar of ivy or wandering Jew in our grandmother's window. At Sterling we found them plain or with ruffled edges, glazed and unglazed. Some have saucers attached, while others are designed with an ornamental pendant on the base. The saucers often have a good and simple motive molded underneath, where it can be observed when hanging. The glazed pots are dark brown or black in color and are frequently embellished with sprays of flowers painted over the glaze in colors and gold. Others of bowl shape, in many sizes, have merely a green band painted below the rim. Another method of decoration practiced in many potteries of the period was to color the whole pot with bright blue, red, rose, or green touched with gold, or perhaps to outline its molded pattern with these colors. We unearthed a section of one very large jar or flowerpot molded in really good design, indicating that the mold makers, whoever they were, were familiar with classic art.

The designers were less successful when they tried to make jars, boxes, and garden seats imitating the form and color of a tree trunk and its branches. These are said to have been the creations of an English journeyman potter named Morris, who made a brief sojourn at the pottery in the seventies. His work, requiring so much time for hand modeling, proved too expensive. When he disappeared one day, no one was concerned as to his whereabouts, and, although he finally asked permission to return, his letter remained unanswered. A Danish modeler, who said that he had studied sculpture under Thorwaldsen, was employed in the pottery at a later time. His work was excellent, but also too costly for a firm that was interested in mass production rather than art.

Of far greater importance than West Sterling, especially to the student of eighteenth-century ceramics, is the pottery of Jonathan Hall and his successors. Hall first settled in South Hadley and then removed to Northampton. He was living in South Hadley in 1769 and making earthenware in that year or even earlier. Putting two and two together, it is reasonable to conclude that he was the Jonathan Hall of Roxbury, who has been mentioned in connection with the burning of his pothouse in 1763. He sold out his Roxbury shop in 1767. The assumption, although it has not been proved, is that he went westward to this new location.

A great deal of data bearing on the materials and methods employed in pot making in early Northampton is to be found in the valuable manuscript notes collated by Sylvester Judd and now available in the Forbes Library of that town. From the Judd manuscript and from Judd's *History of Hadley* I have been able to piece together this unusually detailed account.

In 1770 Hall leased land from the town of Hadley at the south or lower end of the "street." This site may have been the location of a clay pit, for it is said that his pottery shop was in Hatfield. Judd secured this information from a Col. Porter, who had only a slight remembrance of the pottery and could well have been mistaken, or have confused the shop with that of another potter in Hatfield. Three years later Hall gave up his lease, paid his back debts, and removed to Northampton.

The only light shed on the potter's activities in Hadley comes from the account of Lt. Enos Smith with "Mr. Hall the Potter." In 1770 Smith carted to the pottery twenty-six loads of clay at two or three shillings a load, and during the next two years he kept Hall supplied with clay, cordwood, and timber. Even after the potter's removal to Northampton, Smith continued to furnish him with these necessities. Once he went to Boston for Hall and was gone eight days. The entire expense of the journey was but seven dollars — three shillings a day for himself, forty shillings for horses, and twenty-two shillings for cash charges. Hall paid for Smith's services, sometimes in cash, and sometimes by such recompense as several thousand shingles or clapboards, or, in one instance, with forty pounds of flax. A man named Pierce, who brought him a load of split pine, was paid in earthenware. Thus business was carried on largely by barter and with the minimum of cash transactions.

Isaac Sheldon of Northampton, born in 1774, was able in 1848 to remember Hall's pottery, but not its owner. He recalled watching the workmen turning ware. He said the potter lived next door to Thomas Lyman (now 301 Bridge Street) and his shop was in back of his other buildings. In Sheldon's day this property was owned by Mrs. Charles Lyman; today it is occupied by a gasoline station, and Glenwood Avenue crosses it. There are traditions of shards from the pottery dump in the meadow back of the pottery having been found by a school boy some seventy-five years ago. This site may still be worth investigating. In Northampton, Hall was able to reduce expenses by getting clay on or near his own land. He is said to have dug it on the river bank both above and below the old ferry. His term in Northampton was brief, for he died there in November 1776 after a long and expensive illness. He was then known as Captain Hall.

Within three years potting was again undertaken, under the management of Deacon Ebenezer Hunt. This works was presumably on the same site and must have been the pottery remembered by Sheldon. It was a more ambitious enterprise than Hall's, involving the hiring of several men and the construction of three kilns. Hunt himself was probably not a potter. His master craftsman was Ebenezer Gibbs, who came to him from Chatham.* With him or under him worked William Welch and a boy, Patrick. (Hall's wife, Mercy Welch, was a sister of John Welch, who married a daughter of the potter Isaac Parker of Charlestown. It is possible that William was her nephew and grandson of Parker.) Welch was paid at the rate of three shillings per day, while the boy received one and six.

Hunt's account of expenses for the "Pot House or Pottery" begins in January 1779 and is here reproduced as copied in part by Judd: †

Expenses by E. Hunt began on this Jany 1779

Jan. 21	Paid Samuel Parsons for the tools	104. 0. 0
May	Lead 171 lbs. @ 7/6 lb.	64. 2. 6
	freight from Boston	11. 17.
		75 19. 6
June	Work by Joiner 50/ day Clay 3/ load 4/	
	6 lbs. Lead @ 10/6 cw 100 lbs. White Clay	28. 0. 0
	Freight of Lead & Clay 39£	
	Horse to Boston to buy Lead 13£ 15s 10 lb. Litharge	
	@ 30/ lb. Antimony	

* Chatham, New Jersey, was the site of a redware pottery where the Norwalk potters were trained.

† Judd Mss., Northampton, Mass., "Prices and Account Books," p. 105.

July	Expenses to Springfield for sand 27£	
	Pecking the stones 24/	
	Iron pot — (?), ladle, ec of Pomeroy 30£	
	4 days & horse grinding clay 10£ 16/	
	Brick 15. 12. 0 Labor at various prices wood of Lynn and Clark 37. 6. 8	
Augt.	Labor calcining lead 64/ a day Glass, Hooks, & Staples	
Sept.	5 Loads clay for 2 & 3 kiln @ 42/ load	
	Horse and man grinding clay 56/ per day	
	Glass 20£ Labor at 2 kiln 22£ 10. 0	
Oct.	Magnesia £7. 4. 0 400 lbs. Lead @ 10/ Clay	19. 4. 0
	Labor 27. 12. 0 Freight 31. 14. 0	
Nov.	4 loads wood 24£ Brick, Wood 49. 4. 0	
Dec.	Rum Welch's labor 64. 16. 0	
	all to end of 1779	1256. 0. 2
1780	Wood & Labor to April 145. 10	1401. 10. 2
	[After this some entries are in legal currency]	
	Lead 90. Cwt White Clay 24/ Cwt Wood 6/ Lead, &c	
	[Expenses from April 1780 to April 1781 are only 28£ in this currency]	
1780	[Depressed currency]	
April	Lead 2. 3. 2 I Cwt White Clay 100£	
	60 for 1 Freight and expense of purchasing	
June	Flint glass, repairs, work at clay mill, logs for clay mill, freight for white clay 463£	
Aug	Cash for sand 13. 16. 0 Boards 39£ More wood, rum, lead	
Nov	Freight 111£ Glass & freight 11£ 2s	
Dec	Wood &c	
1780	all expenses	2081. 14. 0
1781	Silver money	
Feb 10	8 cwt bar lead @ 72/ 600 bricks @ 3/6 cwt	
April	Glass, wine, clay, wood, & cutting, linseed oil, horse	
May	to grind, Sand 1 load 25/8	
June	all of the acct for 1781	£ 38. 11. 9 as silver
1782	paper money	
Feb	Freight of Lead 195£ sieve 15/ Tin dipper	£7. 4. 0
to	Horse to Boston 105£ Antimony 24. 6. 0	
May	repairing Kiln 102£ horse, grinding, carting, broken brick, wood cutting, 2 Cords wood 52. 10 Getting sand £10. 10	
	all in this currency	£ 626. 19. 0

Income of Pot House
(by sale of ware)

1779	By Cash (continental money) from July to Dec.	2043. 19. 6
1780	By Cash to June (60 for 1) & Hard Money	1778. 8. 0
	By Cash in Silver & at silver prices from July, 1780 to July, 1781	£74. 0. 0
	By Cash in paper from July 1780 to June 1781	£3267. 5. 0

This is the only record I have found of operating costs in an early pottery and as such it is important. The currency, it will be noted, was inflated at this time. The cost of materials was considerable in proportion to the total outlay, since all lead, litharge, white clay, and antimony were freighted from Boston. Such items as "pecking the stones" and "calcining lead" show how laborious even the preparations for running a pothouse must have been. Stones were used for both clay mills and glaze mills in the eighteenth century, and they had to be chipped into shape by hand from the native granite.

The regular purchase of glass, which Judd says was "pounded" by the boy Patrick, brings a new element into the picture of pottery making. It was evidently a component of the glaze, although I have not learned of the ingredient being used in any other New England pottery. Certainly the Danvers potters of a later day did not include it in their formula. The addition of pounded glass would make a superior glaze. Its use was perhaps a customary practice among the New Jersey potters where Gibbs was trained. The white clay that was brought from such a distance was an English importation.

The Northampton pottery must have continued in operation for at least twenty years. As late as 1798 Gibbs was selling the wares in South Hadley to Stebbins & Snow. In November 1794 they purchased "Milkpans @ 7/6 doz; Chamberpots @ 7/6 doz; 2 qt. Juggs @ 7/6; 1 qt. Jugg @ 4/6; Large pots @ 7/6; smaller pots @ 4/6; Pitchers @ 7/6; Pudding Dishes 5/6 and 3/6; Large platters @ 4/6." In 1798 they bought "at the store" (presumably Hunt's store in Northampton) "Milk Pans 10/ doz; platters 8/ and 6/; Pots 10/ and 8/; Chambers 9/; Porringers 5/; Pudding Pans 10/ and 8/." For this earthenware Stebbins & Snow paid in goods. Two years later their account was charged for similar articles.

The Northampton potteries were succeeded in the nineteenth century by the numerous establishments in Whately, which are treated in a separate chapter.

There are hints of earthenware manufacture in the far western part of the state. In Field's *History of Berkshire County*, published in 1829, we read: "There is in the south part of the town [Lee] a bed of potter's clay of great abundance. A pottery has been established in the vicinity at which more or less earthen ware is made every year."

Field also mentions a pottery in "Williamson" (it can be no other than Williamstown) in the early 1800's. This may have been started at a considerably earlier date. John Norton, en route from Goshen, Connecticut, to Bennington, Vermont, in 1784, stopped over for some months in Williamstown. Since he was already supporting a family, the inference is that he was working in some pottery there.

A pottery existed in Great Barrington before the Revolution. In 1770 the town fathers voted to allow Dr. William Whiting to erect "works for the manufacture of earthenware within the limits of the highway opposite his dwelling house." Dr. Whiting was, of course, not a potter, and he hired a craftsman named Gray to carry on the establishment. Born in Bozrah, Connecticut, in 1730, Whiting had studied medicine and had then practiced for a time in Hartford. He went to Great Barrington early in 1765 to take the place of a doctor who had died and to live in his house. The dwelling stood on land more recently owned by the late Dr. C. T. Collins. The pottery site was therefore across the street from the Collins house. The project was probably not of long duration, but there is no doubt of its having been undertaken. Books kept by Dr. Whiting show that a great deal of earthenware was made and that in 1770, at least, he had an extensive trade.

CHAPTER THIRTEEN

The Whately and Ashfield Group

The potters of the Whately area were so numerous and their story so well documented that they merit a separate chapter. Whately, it may be said, is about ten miles north of Northampton. The motorist who turns off the state road to visit the little town, dreaming on its hillside above the Deerfield Valley tobacco farms, sees but slight evidence of the many industries that flourished there one hundred years ago. Only a few shops and sheds remain as relics of former activity: this barn was a pottery, that two-story building a wallet factory. One must have an inquiring spirit and an observing eye to visualize the town as it was, to see the busy workmen in their aprons, to hear the buzz of sawmills and the whir of machinery.

In the old days there were ironworks and brickyards, a fulling mill, and a satinet factory. Broom making, distilling, wood turning, carriage making, and the manufacture of combs, pocketbooks, and buttons gave occupation to many men. The pottery trade was carried on from 1778 or earlier to 1861. Twenty-one native-born potters who worked in Whately are known. Of this number, ten were members of the Crafts family.

The first potworks in this vicinity was operated as early as 1778 by Jonathan Pierce, who is called an Englishman, although he came from Wethersfield, Connecticut.* His shop stood just over the town line in Hatfield. In this location also, Stephen Orcutt was running a kiln in 1797. It was the site on the east side of West Brook known in 1899 as the Lemuel Waite place. At first Orcutt made only common earthenware, but, after entering into a partnership with Luke and Obediah ("Obed") Wait, he began to manufacture stoneware. For this purpose he erected a new kiln south of what was later the McLellan place, on land then owned by Samuel Wilder. At this time the partners showed their ingenuity by conducting water to the clay mill by means of a homemade aqueduct of board troughs about fifteen inches in diameter, elevated on a trestle. A pot from this period marked *Orcutt & Wait/Whately* may be seen in the Deerfield Memorial collection.

The Waits succeeded to the business, which was never very successful. In the 1820's Luke Wait moved to Chicopee, and

* He could have been the brother of John Pierce of Litchfield. Both were born in Wethersfield.

his brother afterwards followed him. The family, however, were said to be running the pottery in the next decade. Orcutt's two sons, Eleazer and Walter, born in 1796 and 1799, were trained in their father's craft, which Eleazer practiced in Troy, Albany, and other places in New York State, in Portland, Maine, and in Ashfield, Massachusetts.

When Thomas Crafts, the master potter of Whately, began pot-making, the Wait kiln was the only one in operation. His first shop was in "the Lane" (the old name for the road that now leads from Route 5 to the village). In 1806 he moved to a part of Whately known as Claverack, a settlement southeast of the town, sprawling along the Greenfield highway. He already owned a fifteen-acre farm with house and barns in that neighborhood. His first kiln and shop there were on the east side of the road; later he worked in the barn back of his large house (Fig. 62). In the surrounding land there are evidences of several kilns and dumps.

Until 1821 Thomas was engaged in making ordinary redware. Potting was then but one of his many interests, which included wagon making, blacksmithing, and farming. Just before that time, Sanford S. Perry, a Troy potter, had come to Whately and had introduced the manufacture of black teapots. Commercially, his venture was a failure. Competition with the enterprising Crafts may have been too keen, for, a year later, Thomas, too, was making teapots as good or better. In 1823 Perry & Company left town. Crafts was now embarked upon a remunerative undertaking that he carried on for more than ten years. In the meantime he built kilns for burning stoneware. His stoneware business, begun in 1833, was highly successful and lasted under his management until 1848. His son James M. Crafts then took it over, producing earthen drain tile as well, and employing ten or a dozen men. By this time pottery making had become an industry rather than an art and was subject to competition with the many other concerns that were operating on a large scale. After 1852, others attempted to keep the business going, but they were obliged to give it up entirely about 1861.

Whately stoneware bears the marks of several members of the family. Some account of the Crafts potters in Whately and elsewhere may therefore be helpful in dating pieces.

Although Thomas Crafts was the moving spirit of the group, there were two brothers, three sons, and other relatives who worked with him at one time or another. Crafts himself was born in 1781, his brother Rufus six years later, and Caleb in 1800. Thomas was energetic and independent, both in his own affairs and in those of a public nature. He held numerous town offices, was a justice of the peace, and twice state representative. As there is no record of his having lived outside of Whately, he must have been trained by Stephen Orcutt. In any event, it was Thomas who instructed his younger brothers, sons, and nephews in the art of making pots and pans.

The brother Rufus, except for a short period when he worked in the Wait pottery, was with Thomas until 1830. He then ran a redware kiln alone in the center of Whately. His pottery is mentioned by name in the *Executive Documents Relative to the Manufactures in the United States*, prepared for publication in 1832. The figures say that he produced and sold in Franklin County one thousand dollars worth of earthenware annually. His lead for glazing was procured in Salem, Massachusetts. Rufus Crafts employed two men at one dollar per day. The only one of his ten children to follow the family calling was Ralph Erskine Crafts. In 1830 he was making flowerpots in a shop on his father's land. This building was burned in 1843, the year of the father's death. After one more trial in a shop that he built on Mill Hill, Ralph

Erskine Crafts gave up potting to become a farmer.

The other brother, Caleb, spent his first and last years in Whately. In young manhood he went to Troy, remaining there until 1837. He afterwards made stoneware in Portland, Maine, and in Nashua, New Hampshire. From 1845 to the time of his death in 1854, Caleb Crafts worked in Whately. The jugs marked *C. Crafts & Co.* were undoubtedly produced during this last period. His son Edward Alonzo began his pottery career in 1849 at the age of nineteen in association with David D. and Isaac N. Wells. The firm, called Wells, Crafts, and Wells, utilized the old Thomas Crafts pottery. Fragments with their mark are to be found in the waste pile back of the great barn. In 1851 young Edward went to St. Johnsbury, Vermont, with his cousin Martin, and finally to Chicago.

Thomas Crafts' oldest son Martin was born in 1807 and worked with his father until 1834. After running potteries in Portland and Nashua, Martin, in the 1850's, was a wholesale stoneware merchant in Boston. In 1857 he returned to Whately and operated the Thomas Crafts pottery until its close. He used the marks *M. Crafts/ Whately* and *Martin: Crafts: Whately*.

James M. Crafts, although trained to be a potter, resembled his father in having many other interests, and his connection with the business in Whately and Nashua was rather in the capacity of manager or executive than as an actual artisan. It was he who wrote a history of Whately and compiled a genealogy of the family. Ten years younger than Martin, he went to Nashua shortly after his marriage, returning to Whately in 1842 to take charge of his father's pottery. Between 1849 and 1852 he was again in Nashua. In the ensuing years he manufactured redware water pipes and drainpipes, which at that time were being used to replace the old wooden conduits. The remains of his kiln, with short lengths of pipe adhering to the walls, may still be seen in the woods east of the railroad track, about a quarter of a mile from the old Crafts estate. Close by is a pit filled with water, where the family used to dig clay.

Another brother, Elbridge Gerry Crafts, had an interest in the tile works, for his name appears with that of James M. in 1861, when they were taxed for two hundred dollars. There is no evidence that Elbridge Gerry ever made pottery: he was a farmer. Because his name appears on a grotesque pitcher made in 1833 (he was then nineteen), it has been assumed that he modeled the piece. More probably the jug represents a portrait of the boy made in jest by one of his older brothers. A glance at the family pictures in the *History of Whately* shows the reason for this opinion. The date *1833* stands for the year when the stoneware pottery was started — a circumstance that explains also the sentiment: "United We Stand: Divided We Fall"; for at that time all three sons were at home with their father.

Thomas Spencer Crafts, a fourth son, was a potter, but remained in Whately only until he was twenty-five. He worked for a brief period at Nashua and then went to California during the gold rush.

Contemporary with Thomas Crafts were Justus and Justin, the twin sons of Graves Crafts, born in 1791. Trained by Thomas, Justus spent the greater part of his life in Whately potting and farming. It is said that both brothers went to Berlin, Vermont, for ten years or so when they were twenty-five years old. While this is possible, the land records of that town mention Justin only and show that he was there between 1823 and 1834. Justin returned to Whately for a few years and then went to Illinois. Justus Crafts was a redware potter. At first he used Rufus Crafts' old shop; after the Vermont venture, he built a house in Claverack north of the farm later known as the Allen Belden place,

using one end of it for his pottery. According to James M. Crafts, he was "a pleasant man, and loved to joke in some rhyme made up in the spur of the moment." He may have been the jokester who was responsible for the Elbridge Gerry pitcher.

Other Whately men who earned a living by working in clay were Quartus Graves, who owned a pottery in the Lane in the 1820's; Heman Swift, the last occupant of a shop built by an unknown predecessor on the Quinn land; and David Belden (Belding), who married Thomas Crafts' daughter Triphena. Thus we are able to account for eighteen of the twenty-one native potters who pursued this trade from time to time in the town.

Although Whately pottery is by no means plentiful today, the latest of it being more than eighty-five years old, it is still possible to find specimens. Some pieces, notably those bearing the mark *T. Crafts & Co.* are of excellent form; others are interesting for the decoration trailed or brushed on with cobalt slip. Little is known about the redware that was Thomas Crafts' first product. Virtually all parts of his land where bits of earthenware are still to be found have been leveled and the surface removed. In a small section that had escaped the shovel, we discovered numerous fragments of black-glazed teapots. Although redware teapots were not among the regular articles listed in the account books of early potters, they had in fact been made for decades, and even by some of the eighteenth-century men. The Crafts pots are particularly interesting, because they mark the transition from wares of the country workshop type to styles that were standard the world over. They were of common redware with a remarkably brilliant, almost metallic glaze. The round forms were turned on the wheel; those of oblong or rectangular shape were molded. Noses and handles were likewise molded and then attached to the bodies. The pieces were burned in saggers. We found many of these broken boxes with the rings of clay used for supporting the pots still adhering to their interiors. It is possible that two firings were required in order to obtain a firm body and hard glaze. A few shards of teapots in the biscuit stage suggest that such a dual process was employed.

A number of surviving teapots correspond to fragments unearthed. Of the eight in the Deerfield Memorial collection and one in my own (Fig. 63), no two are exactly alike or of the same measure. Those that were thrown on the wheel must have been made without a guide. I have never seen a complete specimen of rectangular or ovoid shape. They were apparently designed after familiar Staffordshire forms. For the most part, all the pots are severely plain. A few noses and the oval covers have shallow fluting. These American teapots may be distinguished from the English Jackfield types which they so closely resemble by the fact that they have no foot ring, as do all English examples.

It is interesting to note that Crafts' teapots were marketed in New York and Philadelphia; they were not sold locally to any extent. In 1832 Crafts reported that he was making 2,080 dozen yearly, selling them at wholesale for one dollar a dozen. At that time he was hiring only one man and two boys.

The fragments of glazed redware in the same waste pile and scattered about on the old farm are parts of ordinary kitchen utensils. Milk pans and jars were made until a late date. At least one pan with the impressed mark *T. Crafts* has come to light and is now in the collection of George S. McKearin. One piece of slip-decorated ware with a straight notched edge, found among the teapot shards, raised the question of its local origin. The elderly owner of the pottery site examined it and said that his mother used plates like it when he was a boy. Rectangular dishes of similar type, with others round or oval, fill

a cabinet in the Deerfield Memorial Museum, which houses principally the relics formerly owned by local families. It is safe to assume that Thomas Crafts' first redware was decorated in the same manner as was the ware of his early teachers and predecessors. There is, however, a possibility that the Deerfield Museum pieces may be the work of the Northampton potters, or may even have been brought up country from Norwalk. Only men trained in the New Jersey tradition made platters of that shape in New England.

The Crafts stoneware dump is on the slope of a deep ravine behind the barn on the old Crafts farm. We found there, as one would expect, an assortment of broken jugs, crocks, butter pots, bottles, flasks, and water coolers. Some of the pieces were embellished with designs of the usual nondescript floral style in cobalt blue. Judging by the size of the shard pile, the stoneware output must have been considerable, and the Crafts family strong competitors of the Bennington potters. The Whately stoneware was of sound workmanship, with now and then a flash of something more.

Students of our early industries will be interested in the curious sections of earthenware pipe made in Whately. Warped by a fire that destroyed the kiln, they still give an approximate idea of the dimensions as estimated by Howard G. Hubbard, formerly of the Skinner Museum in South Hadley, where the pipes now repose. He thinks the intended length of all sections was one foot. The diameter of the largest pipe is five inches, of the medium one, four and one-half, and of the small one, two and one-half. The walls are approximately one-half an inch thick. It will be noted that the small-sized pipes were set inside the larger for economy of space in setting the kiln. All have flat bases.

Closely allied to the Whately potteries was a small venture that lasted only eight years in South Ashfield. Although of brief duration, the Ashfield works turned out some of the handsomest stoneware ever made in New England. Its history is therefore worth recording at some length.

In the decade between 1840 and 1850 Ashfield was a town of about fifteen hundred inhabitants. Situated halfway between Shelburne Falls and South Deerfield, it embraced several communities. Its central village, then known as Ashfield Plains, stood on high land near the mill pond. Another settlement of nearly equal importance — South Ashfield, locally called "Tin-Pot" — lay a mile and a half to the south of the Plains.

The appellation "Tin-Pot" had been given to the village because it was a center of small industries and a starting point for peddlers' tours. Here were a tinware factory and the pottery. Ashfield Plains boasted a mill for turning wooden wares, and the whole township was noted for its production of essences distilled from native plants. Its manufacture of peppermint oil alone, which was carried on in several places, at one time yielded no less than forty thousand dollars a year. Combs for peddlers' outfits were made locally in a small way and in his own house by one Richard Cook, while the creation of palm-leaf hats and shirt bosoms provided pin money for many a housewife. Every season hundreds of young men took to the road, driving peddlers' carts or traveling by stage and afoot with tin trunks filled with Ashfield products. Nathaniel Hawthorne in *Passages from the American Notebooks* describes such a peddler, whom he saw when he was journeying by stage through the Berkshires. Thus, in the year 1848, when pottery was added to the list of merchandise sent out from the little town, Ashfield was a well-established manufacturing and trading post.

It is more than a coincidence that the making of stoneware was undertaken in Ashfield just as it was declining in Whately. The town was chosen for another attempt, because its

location was more favorable for distributing the product. The pottery building was erected by Walter Orcutt, son of Stephen of Whately, on land owned by the Guilford family. The unpretentious pothouses were placed on the east side of the road to Ashfield, a short distance above the South Ashfield four corners and just south of the Mill Pond brook, which crosses the road at that point and then winds southward back of the pottery land. Today the spot may be located diagonally across from the South Ashfield post office and a little north of a deserted blacksmith's shop with some tumbledown sheds in the meadow behind it. The upper part of one of these sheds is all that remains of the pottery.

John Luther Guilford, nephew and partner of Walter Orcutt, although he does not appear to have been himself a potter, retained a one-third interest in the business throughout its duration. Eleazer Orcutt, Walter's brother, who had previously been employed in Portland and Troy, worked in the pottery and may also have been a member of the firm, which was first known as Orcutt, Guilford & Company. Pitkin in his *Early American Folk Pottery* says that some of the ware is marked *W. & E. Orcutt & Co.*, but I have found no firm of the name in the town records, nor have I seen a piece of stoneware so labeled. According to Pitkin, Eleazer Orcutt attended to the firing of the kiln.

Little is known concerning the other workmen who were associated with the Orcutt family, except for David Belding, another Whately man, who became their successor. A brother of Guilford, William Frank, sold the ware from a peddler's cart, traveling the country over. That the ware was distributed both in this manner and by local sales is indicated by the marks *Orcutt, Belding & Co.* and *Walter Orcutt & Co.*, which appear on occasional examples. Although there are no less than five firm names to be found on Ashfield stoneware, only three successive organizations actually operated the pottery. In 1849 Orcutt, Belding & Company was taxed for three horses and stock in trade, worth $375. This was obviously a peddling outfit, distinct from the pottery concern, but allied with it. In 1850 Walter Orcutt & Company was assessed for a house, barn, store, one-half acre of land, and stock in trade. Orcutt, who lived in nearby Conway, was running the general store and post office in South Ashfield at that time. These marks, therefore, indicate the names of the distributors rather than those of the makers.

In 1850 Walter Orcutt sold his share of the "stone-ware factory" to Wellington Hastings and David Belding, while John Luther Guilford still retained his one-third interest. Belding was already connected with the pottery.* David, born in Whately March 7, 1813, was brought up among the potters there and was doubtless an apprentice of Thomas Crafts, whose daughter Triphena he married November 10, 1842. Five years previously he had bought a piece of land in South Ashfield, but probably did not settle there until the pottery was started. In the meantime, his young bride died only six weeks after their marriage. On October 12, 1845, Belding took a second wife — Sybil Maria (Hastings) Stanley, a widow with two children. His partner, Wellington Hastings, was Mrs. Stanley's brother, who came to Ashfield from Wilmington, Vermont. This partnership lasted for four years, and the majority of jugs, crocks, and churns found about Ashfield bear the Hastings & Belding mark.

It has been possible to learn more about the pottery in this period than at its beginning or its end. In 1908 Albert H. Pitkin went to Ashfield, where he gleaned some valuable bits

* His daughter and others of the family have always spelled the name "Belden," but the original Whately family was Belding; the potter so stamped his name on his jugs.

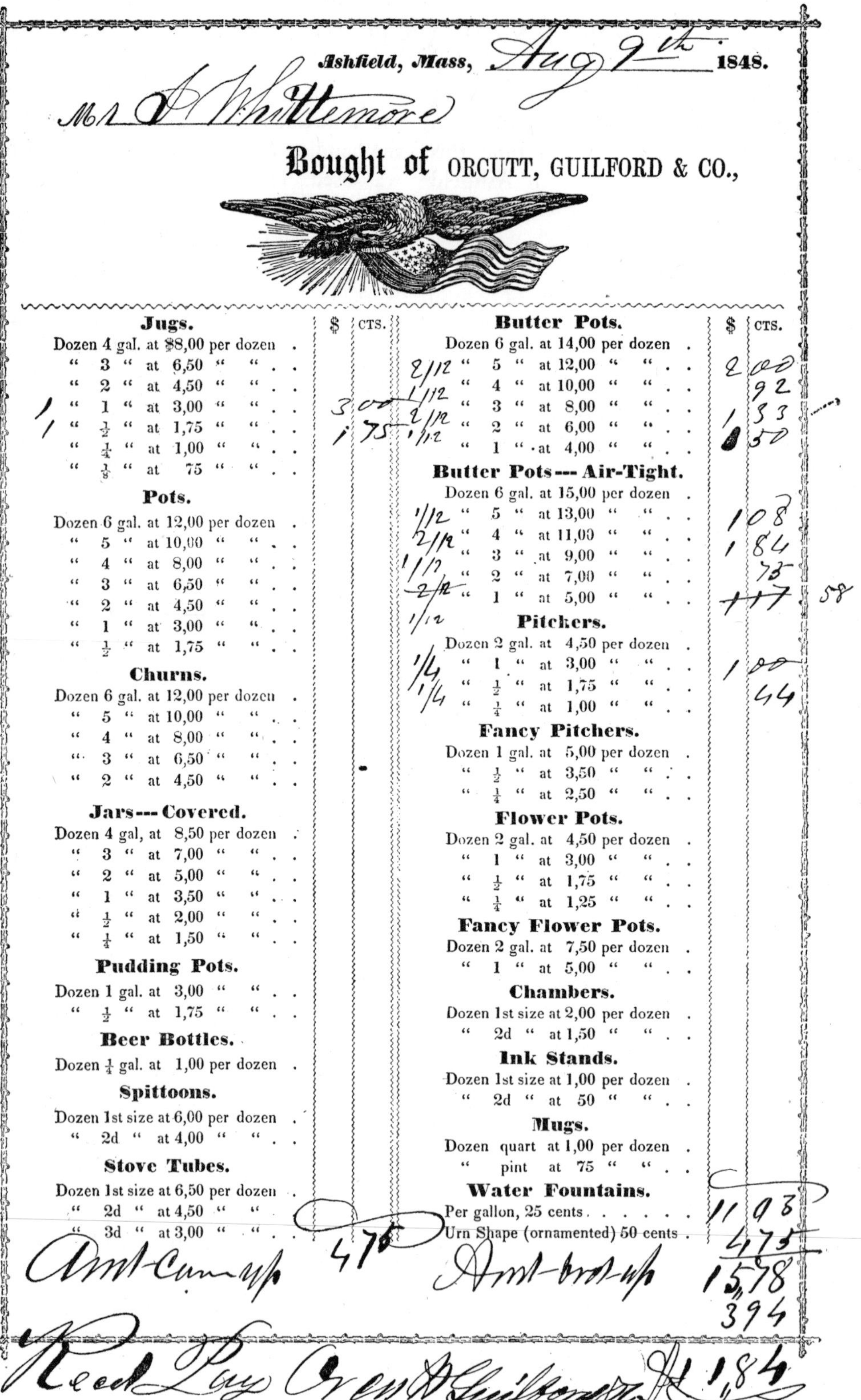

Ashfield, Mass, *Aug 9th* 1848.

Mr A Whittemore

Bought of ORCUTT, GUILFORD & CO.,

	Jugs.	$	CTS.
	Dozen 4 gal. at $8,00 per dozen .		
	" 3 " at 6,50 " " . .		
	" 2 " at 4,50 " " . .		
1	" 1 " at 3,00 " " . .	*3*	*00*
1	" ½ " at 1,75 " " . .	*1*	*75*
	" ¼ " at 1,00 " " . .		
	" ⅛ " at 75 " " . .		
	Pots.		
	Dozen 6 gal. at 12,00 per dozen .		
	" 5 " at 10,00 " " . .		
	" 4 " at 8,00 " " . .		
	" 3 " at 6,50 " " . .		
	" 2 " at 4,50 " " . .		
	" 1 " at 3,00 " " . .		
	" ½ " at 1,75 " " . .		
	Churns.		
	Dozen 6 gal. at 12,00 per dozen .		
	" 5 " at 10,00 " " . .		
	" 4 " at 8,00 " " . .		
	" 3 " at 6,50 " " . .		
	" 2 " at 4,50 " " . .		
	Jars---Covered.		
	Dozen 4 gal, at 8,50 per dozen .		
	" 3 " at 7,00 " " . .		
	" 2 " at 5,00 " " . .		
	" 1 " at 3,50 " " . .		
	" ½ " at 2,00 " " . .		
	" ¼ " at 1,50 " " . .		
	Pudding Pots.		
	Dozen 1 gal. at 3,00 " " . .		
	" ½ " at 1,75 " " . .		
	Beer Bottles.		
	Dozen ¼ gal. at 1,00 per dozen .		
	Spittoons.		
	Dozen 1st size at 6,00 per dozen .		
	" 2d " at 4,00 " " . .		
	Stove Tubes.		
	Dozen 1st size at 6,50 per dozen .		
	" 2d " at 4,50 " "		
	" 3d " at 3,00 " " .		
	Amt carried up	*4*	*75*

	Butter Pots.	$	CTS.
	Dozen 6 gal. at 14,00 per dozen .		
2/12	" 5 " at 12,00 " " . .	*2*	*00*
1/12	" 4 " at 10,00 " " . .		*92*
2/12	" 3 " at 8,00 " " . .	*1*	*33*
1/12	" 2 " at 6,00 " " . .		*50*
	" 1 " at 4,00 " " . .		
	Butter Pots---Air-Tight.		
	Dozen 6 gal. at 15,00 per dozen .		
1/12	" 5 " at 13,00 " " . .	*1*	*08*
2/12	" 4 " at 11,00 " " . .	*1*	*84*
1/12	" 3 " at 9,00 " " . .		*75*
~~*2/12*~~ *1/12*	" 2 " at 7,00 " " . .		
	" 1 " at 5,00 " " . .	~~*1*~~	~~*17*~~ *58*
	Pitchers.		
	Dozen 2 gal. at 4,50 per dozen .		
1/4	" 1 " at 3,00 " " . .	*1*	*00*
1/4	" ½ " at 1,75 " " . .		*44*
	" ¼ " at 1,00 " " . .		
	Fancy Pitchers.		
	Dozen 1 gal. at 5,00 per dozen .		
	" ½ " at 3,50 " " . .		
	" ¼ " at 2,50 " " . .		
	Flower Pots.		
	Dozen 2 gal. at 4,50 per dozen .		
	" 1 " at 3,00 " " . .		
	" ½ " at 1,75 " " . .		
	" ¼ " at 1,25 " " . .		
	Fancy Flower Pots.		
	Dozen 2 gal. at 7,50 per dozen .		
	" 1 " at 5,00 " " . .		
	Chambers.		
	Dozen 1st size at 2,00 per dozen .		
	" 2d " at 1,50 " " . .		
	Ink Stands.		
	Dozen 1st size at 1,00 per dozen .		
	" 2d " at 50 " " . .		
	Mugs.		
	Dozen quart at 1,00 per dozen .		
	" pint at 75 " " . .		
	Water Fountains.		
	Per gallon, 25 cents	*11*	*98*
	Urn Shape (ornamented) 50 cents .	*4*	*75*
	Amt brot up	*15*	*78*
		3	*94*

Recd Pay Orcutt & Guilford & Co $11,84

Bill of Orcutt, Guilford & Co., Ashfield, Mass., August 9, 1848.

of information from the stepdaughter of David Belding. These I have since confirmed with the aid of the family. At the time, this stepdaughter was living in South Ashfield and was the wife of John Luther Guilford. She was thus doubly connected with the firm. From the Guilfords Pitkin learned that the pottery employed seven men, of whom three worked at the wheel, and that it had only one kiln. He was told that a turner named Wight was exceedingly skillful in making offhand pieces and was considered the best workman. Another was Staats Van Loon, who first appeared in the Ashfield tax list in 1851 and who remained to become a member of the third firm. Ashfield tradition says that some of the potters came from Pennsylvania. It seems likely that Van Loon, at least, had migrated from the Pennsylvania region or from New York State.

In 1854 the Hastings & Belding company went into receivership. Thereupon, the business was taken over by Van Loon and George Washington Boyden of Conway, with Guilford still holding his one-third share. The pair struggled for two years without success, and in 1856 the undertaking was abandoned. But few pieces bearing their mark have been discovered.

The wares made by the three successive firms cannot be distinguished one from the other by any points of difference. They are all stoneware of rather ordinary quality, made of clay brought from Perth Amboy, New Jersey. Some pieces have a dense gray body; others — and they are in the majority — have a buff or light brown body of porous consistency. The former were well burned at a high temperature; the latter either were not fired to a proper degree of hardness or they may have contained an admixture of native clay. Between the two extremes are various gradations of color and quality. The ware was salt glazed in the usual manner and almost always decorated with a spray or other design in cobalt blue, with a blue swash over the impressed mark and sometimes around the handles. Less frequently a dash of brown was used. The interiors of pots and crocks were lined with Albany slip glaze, black, dark reddish brown, or light brown in color.

In addition to their blue-decorated stoneware, the Ashfield potters produced a good deal of ware covered with a dark slip glaze inside and out. A pitcher in Fig. 105, marked *Orcutt, Guilford & Co.*, is an example of this type. The bowl with ear handles and the jelly mold belonged to Mrs. John Luther Guilford and may also have been made during the first period.

All Ashfield pottery chips easily, especially when it has been allowed to stand in a damp place. This is a serious defect and in itself affords sufficient explanation for the failure of the works and its inability to compete with the hard, durable products of Bennington.

In September 1933 I discovered the pottery waste pile near the bank of the brook. On the surface of the ground, where they had been thrown eighty-five years before, lay fragments of all types. Among the shards was half a crock cover, warped in the marking and discarded. Its upper face was embossed by molding in a conventional leaf pattern. These recovered fragments, although their number was limited, proved of great assistance in studying the wares. Most of the pottery dump was buried by a minor catastrophe many years ago. In 1878 the Mill Pond dam at Ashfield Plains, during a freshet after heavy snows and a sudden thaw, burst, flooding the valley below and the village of South Ashfield. The old pottery building, then in use as a blacksmith's shop, was swept away, leaving only part of a shed at some distance from its original location, while tons of sand and debris were washed into the meadow on the pottery land. This flood effectively removed much of the evidence that might be so instructive today.

Enough of the old factory handiwork has been saved in Ashfield homes to give an adequate idea of its character. There are the usual common articles, such as egg and butter crocks, churns, pickle and preserve jars of different sizes, molasses jugs up to four-gallon capacity, one- and two-gallon cider pitchers, bean pots, and bowls. One of the largest utilitarian pieces is a five-gallon churn with the Hastings & Belding mark, formerly owned by Miss Alice Turnbull and presented by her to the South Ashfield Public Library.

In addition to these useful pots I have seen a number of offhand things that are far more interesting. In the latter category is a dog fashioned by Staats Van Loon for one of Belding's children. It was obviously made in a mold devised from one of those bisected iron dogs that were used to embellish the side rails of parlor stoves or were mounted on marble plinths to serve as door stops. The stoneware canine is entirely covered on the outer surface with a rich cobalt blue.*

The potter Wight made, as a gift for Belding's stepdaughter, a toy bank with the inscription, running twice across it, *Harriet Sophia Stanley, 1850. Aug. 17th.* This was presented on the child's tenth birthday. A miniature churn made by Wight for the same little girl was bought by Pitkin and may now be seen in his collection in the Wadsworth Atheneum, Hartford, Connecticut (Fig. 104). A perfect copy of the larger churns, even to the mark — *Hastings & Belding/ Ashfield, Mass.* — it is inscribed with the date *August, 1852* in blue. A moustache cup and a sand shaker from the Ashfield pottery are other offhand pieces recalled by descendants of the Belding family.

More important from a ceramic point of view than any of these trifling objects is the water cooler illustrated in Fig. 103. Not only is this a beautiful piece of potting, of graceful shape and fine proportions, but it is also elaborated in an unusual way with ornamental handles and a figure of Diana in relief. That it is an Ashfield product there can be no doubt, as it bears the Hastings & Belding mark. Even without the initials *F W*, which may be faintly discerned on the band under the figure, it would be safely ascribed to the same Wight who delighted in making presentation pieces. Examination of the Ashfield town records reveals the fact that Franklin Wight paid a poll tax in 1852 and 1853. I have since learned that he was a son of John Wight of Dublin and West Sterling and brother of Abner S. Wight. For a time, probably after his stay in Ashfield, he was employed at the Fenton pottery in St. Johnsbury, Vermont. While there, he doubtless made the cooler marked *L. W. Fenton/ St. Johnsbury, Vt.*, which serves as a frontispiece in John Spargo's *Early American Pottery and China.* A comparison of the two will show the very close similarity of form and decoration. Still a third Ashfield cooler (Fig. 102), of barrel shape with a relief figure of Washington, may be another example of Wight's handiwork. With the possible exception of some of the early jars from Charlestown and Boston, I do not know of any New England stoneware vessels that show such high quality of craftsmanship.

* See "The Stoneware of South Ashfield, Massachusetts," *Antiques* (September 1934).

CHAPTER FOURTEEN

Pioneer Craftsmen of New Hampshire

The earliest potters in New Hampshire lived in the towns along the seacoast. Just when the first of them built a kiln cannot be determined, but it is known that Henry Moulton of Hampton and Samuel Marshall of Portsmouth were plying their trade in the 1720's. Neither one was the son of a potter — a fact that suggests the presence of still earlier craftsmen in their vicinity.

Henry Moulton was born in Hampton March 1, 1698. His family lived on the Landing Road. In 1722 he married Mary Garland and in time became the father of six children. All but one of these little ones died in an epidemic in 1736. Overcome by this tragedy, he left Hampton with his bereaved wife and remaining child and went with others to found the new settlement of Sandown, in what was then a part of Kingston. Moulton apparently prospered in the new location, where he remained until his death in the summer of 1763. At that time he was still a potter. His estate comprised sixty-five acres of land, with a small house, barn, and shop, valued in the inflated currency of the day at twenty-five hundred pounds.

The handled strainer pictured in Fig. 75 was purchased by its former owner from an elderly man whose ancestors were early settlers in Sandown and who said that it had been owned by them in the town. Strainers of this shape were commonly used in the seventeenth century, as we learn from old Dutch paintings, but are virtually unique today. An early origin is therefore indicated for it. The piece may well be the work of Henry Moulton.

Samuel Marshall of Portsmouth was the son of George Marshall, a sailmaker. He is first noted as potter in a deed, May 23, 1729, when he signed away his interest in some family land. Not until 1736 is there any record that he was a property owner. In November of that year he bought from Joseph Jackson land and a wharf on "Canoo or Swinge Bridge Creek." This was a narrow lot bounded on the east by Horse Lane, the road from Joseph Moulton's to the water. The next year Marshall purchased an adjoining piece of land. Upon the northerly end of these holdings, facing on Joses Lane, he built a dwelling house. At the time of his death in

1749, Marshall also owned a warehouse. His inventory makes no mention of a shop, but notes his "Potters Working Geer or Tools," worth seventeen pounds, a "Parcel of Earthen Ware," and an old gundelow (barge). That the Marshalls were accustomed to some of the refinements of life is indicated by their possession of a set of "Chinea" cups and saucers and some porcelain bowls. There is evidence to show that Marshall was a wholesale dealer in pottery and perhaps did a shipping business, sending out consignments along the coast. In 1749 he bought earthenware from the Charlestown potter, John Parker. This business was carried on by his widow, who, according to Parker's account book, continued to order Charlestown ware.

During this same period, Nathaniel Libby, who attained his majority in 1731, was also making redware in Portsmouth and possibly working with Marshall. Libby went to Exeter in 1742/43, where he was a potter and storekeeper. His estate there is described as being on the "north side of the highway from Exeter Meeting House to Newmarket." Libby died in 1752. Two years later the younger Daniel Edes of Charlestown was in Exeter. It seems likely that he made an attempt to take Libby's place as the town potter, but his stay was brief.

Whether any other person tried to run a pottery in Exeter between this date and the time when Jabez (Jabesh) Dodge set up a new shop is uncertain. Jabez was the son of Benjamin Dodge, a chairmaker of North Beverly, Massachusetts, and he probably acquired his craft in Essex County. He was born in 1746/47. As he married Lydia Philbrick of Exeter in 1771, it is safe to assume that the Dodge pottery began at about that time.

Dodge's four sons were all trained to be potters. The eldest, Benjamin, born in 1774, departed for Portland to start a new business when he was twenty-five years old. The second son, Joseph, who was two years younger, was living in Portsmouth in 1804 and spent the rest of his life there as a clayworker. Joseph's house is still standing on Dearborn Street near the Piscataqua River. The site may be reached by following Vaughan Street from the railroad station until it becomes North Street west of the bridge; Dearborn crosses at this point. In 1830 Joseph Dodge was employing three men and turning out some twelve hundred dollars worth of redware each year. He is listed in the Portsmouth directory of 1839–1840, with a house at 3 Dearborn Street, corner of North, and a shop in the rear. His two sons, Jabez and Samuel, were here given their training in the family craft. Jabez is called "potter and cordwainer" in the directory for 1851. Samuel moved to Exeter, where he undoubtedly worked in his grandfather's pottery.

The third son of Jabez Dodge — Samuel, born in Exeter in 1783 — remained with his father and is said, on the authority of Frank Lamson, to have built the Exeter Pottery Works in 1819. Part of this large shop is standing and in use at 84 Main Street, west of the railroad crossing, but a section has been taken down and removed to the Edison Institute of Technology at Dearborn, Michigan, to house its former equipment, which was purchased by Henry Ford. In this display may be seen the wheels, wedging table, clay and glaze mills, iron kettle, and various smaller utensils, exactly as they were used in the pottery.

In 1932 Frederick H. Norton of the Massachusetts Institute of Technology made a thorough study of the methods employed at Exeter and of the kilns and their construction. This investigation he very ably presented in the magazine *Antiques* (July 1932). Professor Norton learned that the clay, obtained from several local sources, was considered the best in New England for throwing on the wheel. The lead glaze at Exeter

was mixed with loam instead of sand and was screened through a fine horsehair sieve. The glaze materials were compounded in the proportion of ten pounds of red lead to three pounds of loam. This latter ingredient is said to increase the viscosity of glaze and to prevent its flowing off the ware. A small quantity of flour paste was also added as a binder. The methods of firing and stacking the kilns at Exeter are discussed in the chapter on techniques.

Closely allied to the Dodges by marriage and partnership was the Lamson family. Asa Brown Lamson, born 1818, seems to have become the junior associate of Samuel Dodge, who, in 1849, was still managing the pottery. Lamson's second son, Frank Hudson, was associated with his father, carrying on the works to its close in 1895. Frank's sister Mary married Charles S. Dodge, a great-grandson of Jabez. It may therefore be said that the pottery was operated continuously by one family for four generations and over a period of about one hundred and twenty-five years.

Rufus Lamson, an older son of Asa Brown, ran the Osborn-Paige pottery in Peabody for a short time after 1868 and then went into the business in Portland.

Samuel Philbrick, whose sister Lydia was the wife of Jabez Dodge, was another Exeter potter. Three of his sons are known to have pursued this trade. Samuel, the oldest, born in 1785, and Joseph, eight years his junior, migrated to Skowhegan, Maine, in the early 1800's, establishing the potting business there. William, the youngest, worked in Exeter and was connected with the Dodge pottery for many years.

Many potters went to Exeter to serve their apprenticeship or to make a brief stay on their way to setting up their own establishments on the frontier. It is noteworthy that a number of the Maine potteries were started by men from Exeter. Joseph Osborn, grandson of the founder of the South Danvers pottery, settled in the town soon after his marriage in 1783. Some Peabody historians have thought that he originated the pottery there, but Jabez Dodge should be credited with the undertaking, as he had been working and raising a family in Exeter before Osborn's arrival. A John Osborn from Peabody was another of the Quaker family to migrate to Exeter. Oliver Osborn of a later generation was probably descended from one of these men. He manufactured portable earthenware furnaces in Exeter quite successfully for many years. Samuel Leavitt, member of an old Exeter family, worked for the Lamsons. In 1872 he was running a shop of his own on the Kingston road at the edge of town. John Donovan, one of the last and one of the most skillful of New England potters, was born in Exeter and was taught the art of turning by the Lamsons.

According to the Haskel & Smith *Gazetteer* (1843) there were three potteries in 1840. It is quite likely that the Dodges and Lamsons had separate shops at that time, with Philbrick, also, carrying on an independent business. I have been told, too, that there was once a tile factory in back of the jail, which could be one of the potteries noted.

During the Dodge ownership the Exeter pottery turned out the usual articles made in early shops. The earthenware was a light red in color, with glazes often pleasingly varied or mottled. The Lamsons produced large quantities of strictly utilitarian ware, such as jugs, milk pans, lard pots, bean pots, pudding pots and pans, and other cooking dishes, toilet articles, cuspidors, and chimney safes. These objects were given a glaze of uniform coloring. In the seventies and eighties, vases and fancy jars and jugs were made. Flowerpots of various kinds were the principal output in the closing years, the first style being the kind with an integral saucer; these were superseded about 1890 by the familiar straight

tapered pot without glaze. The skill of John Donovan proved that these could be made on the wheel with sufficient uniformity to be nested, thereby facilitating kiln setting and packing. They were, however, soon outmoded by mechanically formed flowerpots. The Lamson redware was sold from carts to hardware and general stores in the surrounding cities and towns. A great deal of it went east to Newburyport, Hampton, Portsmouth, and Rochester, or to Derry and other points west.

As the pioneer settlers moved into the interior, potters soon followed. In the 1790's they had arrived in a number of places in southern and southwestern New Hampshire. There is a record that Isaiah and Josiah Kidder were running a pottery in 1792 on their farm in New Ipswich. The Kidder brothers were engaged in a variety of industrial pursuits and it is possible that they were not themselves potters. A young native of the town who had acquired the art may have been hired by them to carry on their business. He was Isaac Brown Farrar, born in 1771, and destined to become the ancestor of many of the potting Farrars of Vermont. It is curious that local tradition in New Ipswich says that the Kidder pottery made stoneware. It is a bit difficult to see how they could do it. However, Isaac Farrar made a visit to Boston in the 1790's, where he no doubt heard of or saw Jonathan Fenton's newly established stoneware kiln. He may have learned from Fenton the secret of New Jersey clay and of the method of salt glazing. If any such attempt was made in New Ipswich, it could not have been successful. In 1798 Farrar left town to settle near Fairfax, Vermont, where he certainly did make stoneware.

From Danvers records we learn that Jedediah Felton, an apprentice of Joseph Whittemore of Andover Street, Peabody, went to Mason, adjacent to New Ipswich, in 1793. It is said that he owned a pottery "in the vicinity" for many years. His residence in Mason is confirmed by the birth of one of his children there in 1798. A potter, Ruel Richardson, is said to have worked in Mason for a long time before his death in 1814. Whether the two men were partners or whether Richardson succeeded Felton I have been unable to learn. History shows that Felton did not long remain in the town. Mason in the eighteenth century included large tracts of land and several of the present neighboring townships. Accordingly, while still remaining "in the vicinity," Jedediah could have been the "Felton from Danvers" who was one of the first men to establish the potter's business in Chesham or Pottersville.

It must be explained that Chesham is the new name and Pottersville the old for a settlement, once part of Harrisville, that lies between Marlborough and Dublin. Pottersville was the most important community of clay workers in southwestern New Hampshire, and earthenware was sent out from its kilns far and wide through New Hampshire, Vermont, and western Massachusetts. Clay of excellent quality was dug from an inexhaustible bed a short distance south of the schoolhouse. The industry was at its height just after the War of 1812, when eight or ten shops were operating in the district. The business then suffered a gradual decline, partly because English white crockery had come into use, and partly on account of the low price of tin ware. Eventually the potters were obliged to manufacture large ware and flowerpots only. In the early days, redware in this section of the state was a kind of currency that could always be exchanged for grain or other products.

David Thurston is said to have been in Pottersville in 1795 and Nathaniel Furber at an equally early period. It is known that Furber's shop was in the easterly part of Lot 16, Range 9 — a piece of property called the "Herrick Farm," which was owned by Mer-

rill Mason in 1881. Another South Danvers potter, Jedediah Kilburn Southwick, son of William, arrived in Pottersville to take over the Thurston shop in 1809. In 1820 he built a fine residence in the center of the village, which was his home until he died in 1843. Constructed of local brick, this house has survived to the present day. Jedediah's second son and namesake carried on the Southwick pottery to a later time.

Others who had small establishments were William Greenwood, who started a pottery about 1813 on the farm later owned by Milton White; Chauncy Metcalf, whose shop stood on the hill a little west of the house where Luke Knowlton lived in 1881; and Josiah Fitch, who succeeded Metcalf, removing his buildings to Lowellville and running a pottery there for a time. Daniel Greenwood practiced the potter's trade on his own farm. Aaron Smith and his son Aaron, Jr., ran a shop together. The father must have begun about 1820; the son, after the death of his father twenty years later. Aaron Jr.'s homestead was on Road 32.

In the spring of 1845 "Captain" John D. Wight, long a potter in Dublin, built what has since been known as the "Old Pottery" on the road to Dublin. His son Abner S. succeeded him before 1849, when Abner's name appears as a potter in the *New England Directory*. Local history says that he carried on the Dublin pottery until about 1860, or shortly before that time, when he went to West Sterling. The buildings were sold in 1866 to James A. White, who removed them to be reconstructed as dwelling houses.

At the same period, Eben Russell, with his son Osgood N., was carrying on what he called the "Dublin Earthen Ware Manufactory." This works was in Pottersville and was the first building on the north side of the southerly approach to the town from Harrisville. It stood at the top of the hill near the "junction of the ancient road with the present highway." Osgood N. Russell's house was directly opposite the pottery, and his father's home was the next to the west. Since the Russell pottery continued in operation longer than some of the others, it is better known.

Several bills of sale put out by the Russells and now in the possession of F. H. Norton show that they were still running in 1858, although they gave up the management of the pottery before 1860. These bills are of the greatest importance in showing what the redware potters were making just before the Civil War. A bill dated November 18, 1850, is headed "Eben Russell & Son/ Manufacturers of Brown Earthen Ware" and is receipted by O. N. Russell. The articles listed are pots with ears, pots and covers, pots for lard or butter, "O bean pots," bread and bake pans, jugs, preserve pots, stove tubes, shaving mugs, scalloped and plain glazed flowerpots, pitchers, stew pitchers and covers, pudding boilers, milk pans, wash bowls, quart and pint bowls, chamber pots, and pie plates. The "O" bean pot is presumably the old-fashioned open variety, in contrast to the newer covered bean pot for use in stoves. From a bill dated October 1861 we learn that the Dublin Earthen Ware Manufactory was then in the hands of Hart & Clark.

In 1854 Edwin Greenwood, son of William, and one Sargeant ran a pottery called the "Marlboro' Earthen Ware Factory." Its existence was probably brief, as by 1857 the Russell shop was the only one left in Pottersville, and only four men of the many who had been employed there were still at work. Sargeant & Greenwood's list of merchandise, in a bill dated January 6, 1854, comprises pots with ears, others with covers, common pots, bean pots and stove bean pots, pans for milk or bread, flat pans, chambers and wash bowls, fancy glazed flowerpots with saucers attached, others scalloped and glazed, common glazed and nest flowerpots, jugs, preserve and

butter pots, pitchers, stove tubes, pudding boilers, bowls, shaving mugs, and plates.

From the Pottersville district many craftsmen whose names are familiar elsewhere went out to improve their fortunes. Among them were Abner S. Wight and Edwin Greenwood, who went to West Sterling and afterwards to Keene, and Franklin Wight, Abner's brother, who worked in Ashfield and St. Johnsbury, Vermont.

John Wight, in his youth, figured in an early attempt to make white ware, which was not the success that some writers have supposed. Wight was born in Dublin in 1791. In 1813 he went to Jaffrey to work for the so-called "Crockery Ware Corporation." This concern represented an ambitious venture undertaken by some of the substantial citizens of Jaffrey at the instigation of Samuel Dakin from Mason. The company was incorporated and authorized to purchase and hold mines of white clay to the value of six thousand dollars and personal estate in the factory to ten thousand dollars. As the hope of making white ware was at its highest during the war year of 1813, the company was exempted from taxation. There is no question that the Crockery Ware Corporation actually got into operation and that it essayed to make white earthenware. Persons in Jaffrey are still familiar with the term "Moncton Yard" applied to the lot where the white clay from Moncton, Vermont, was dumped.

Less than four months after the incorporation of the firm, the company advertised in the *New Hampshire Sentinel*, October 2, 1813, that "one or two ingenious young men may find constant employment and generous wages at the business of turning in the Crockery Ware Factory at Jaffrey." The "ingenious" youths who answered this appeal were John Wight and Jonathan B. French of Troy. In the following spring they were assessed a poll tax as citizens of the town.

The *Sentinel* in May 1814 again printed a paragraph, inserted by the company, headed "notice to Wood Choppers" and saying, "One or two hundred cords of sound hemlock, spruce, or white pine wood, well split and dry, will be wanted at the Crockery Ware Factory in Jaffrey in the course of the following summer and winter. Apply to superintendent at Factory."

In spite of the masses of white clay in the Moncton Yard, the crockery ware concern was a failure. That Moncton clay is unsuitable when used alone has since been proved. Furthermore, the men who had undertaken to experiment with it at Jaffrey were entirely unskilled in the production of the finer kinds of earthenware. When we consider that Wight was only twenty-two and French still at the beginning of his career, and that neither of them had had any further training than they could have obtained in country redware potteries, it is no wonder that the affair was not a success. Dakin, it is true, was a Dartmouth graduate, and he may have studied the subject from a theoretical angle, but that was not enough.

The pottery was in existence about three years. In order to avert financial loss, it seems to have turned to the production of common redware: several specimens owned locally are red earthenware and not white crockery. In an attempt to get some light on this enterprise, I visited Jaffrey in the spring of 1941. In the location described a few years ago by John W. Poole 2d. as the spot where he had picked up shards when a boy (about ten rods southwest of the carpenter's shop of B. F. Cann), the sole remaining evidence was a large section of a redware pot imbedded in a stone wall. If a shard pile ever existed at this point, it is now buried beneath a roadway.

After the failure of the company, Wight moved back to Dublin. He sued the company in September 1816 for pay due him for one hundred and ninety-eight days' labor at

$1.34 a day, covering the period from May to December, 1814. For some reason Wight failed to recover in this suit, and a second litigation proved equally fruitless.

Jonathan French returned to Troy, where he went into partnership with Solomon Goddard. These two young men leased a potshop that had been built about 1812 by Daniel E. Farrar. It stood near the home owned in 1897 by Mrs. Gilbert Bemis, at the fork in the road leading north to Jaffrey from the brick church. After some three years together in this location, the pair separated, Goddard to build a pottery of his own and French to run a store.

Solomon Goddard, born May 2, 1796, was the son of John Goddard, a potter of Orange, Massachusetts, and was the second of fourteen children. He served his apprenticeship in his father's shop. While working with French he had acquired a house and two acres of land from Joshua Harrington, Jr. On this property he put up a potworks, making earthenware there until 1843, when he sold out to Eri J. Spaulding and went into the wooden ware business. Goddard's buildings were on the land later owned by Hiram W. Hutt. The *Executive Documents Relative to the Manufactures in the United States* say of Goddard that in 1831 he was making eight hundred dollars' worth of pottery annually. This was peddled partly in Massachusetts and partly in New Hampshire and Vermont. As he employed only one man at the meager sum of sixty-three cents per day, it is obvious that his factory was a small affair.

Another obscure Troy pottery was built by Constant Weaver in 1821 and operated by him and his son, but without success. Their shop stood back of the garden of the old hotel that still faces the green and which Weaver managed at the time.

The *History of Troy*, by M. T. Stone, M. D., says that there was once a pottery "on the brow of the hill just beyond the residence of John McCarley." It stood on the place that originally belonged to Rev. Ezekiel Rich and afterwards to Elisha H. Tolman. The writer says that the potter was unknown. The name Tolman, however, is the needed clue to his identity, for he was the same Henry Tolman who later appeared at West Sterling. A native of Troy, born in 1783, he was concerned in various activities. For three years he was a brickmaker in the yard of Thomas Wright and for three other years he worked in Derry, Vermont. Tolman also ran a tavern. He lived for at least sixteen years in a house later occupied by Sampson Wheeler. In 1831 he is mentioned by name in the *Executive Documents* previously quoted (his name, however, being misspelled "Solman." At that time he was producing one thousand dollars' worth of redware each year and employing two men at one dollar each per day. Half of this ware he sold in Vermont and half in Massachusetts and New Hampshire. Both Tolman and Goddard used New Orleans lead, which they procured in Boston.

Elderly residents of Troy can remember two later concerns that were devoted to the manufacture of decorated flowerpots. The first of these was started about 1875 by Charles Adelbert Farrar. He owned a brick shop diagonally across the road to the south from the railroad station. Flowerpots and jugs were the principal output. At first Farrar hired a man to do the decorating, which no doubt was accomplished by applying paint in the style of the period. Later he learned to do that part of the work himself. The second pottery was carried on by C. M. Silsby & Company in the old Whitcomb & Forristall pail shop at the north end of town. A year or two after its establishment, the managers were W. G. and R. M. Silsby, who were soon succeeded by Frank A. Aldrich and then by Henry McCormac. It is said that McCormac was a practical potter; the

Silsbys were not. These potteries did not find the business profitable; their buildings fell into decay, and the manufacture was wholly abandoned before 1885.

Farther west, in southern New Hampshire, potters were evidently at work at an early time. In 1819 the *New Hampshire Patriot and State Gazetteer*, published in Concord, advertised a pottery for sale in Alstead, mentioning "clay of an excellent quality for the manufacturing of earthen ware with building and apparatus for that purpose." How long this pottery had been running or what became of it I have been unable to ascertain. At Westmoreland, also, in far western New Hampshire, there was a modest pottery in 1830, where a man with a half-time helper turned out some two hundred dollars' worth of "brown ware" each year. He obtained lead from Philadelphia, but otherwise nothing is known about him.

The Hampshire Pottery of Keene is well known in New England, and its vases are still to be found in many homes. As a commercial enterprise, it was New Hampshire's most successful works. Less is known about the earlier small country potteries in Keene that furnished utilitarian wares to a busy community. As early as 1787 a potter was at work in a shop "northeast of Brown's store." Brown's is described as being opposite Foster's, a small building still standing in 1904 on the west side of Main Street, a few rods north of Clark's Tavern and west of the mill-pond. In this neighborhood were sawmills and gristmills and a blacksmith's shop. There was a pottery in Keene in 1830, but whether it was this same one or another I have been unable to learn. It employed two men and produced one thousand dollars' worth of ware annually. The Haskel & Smith *Gazetteer* mentions the presence of a potworks in 1840; this, at least, was probably the same.

The Hampshire Pottery began its existence as a redware factory. It was started in 1871 by James Scholly Taft and his uncle James Burnap. Taft, an industrious young man, had gone to work at the age of sixteen cutting wood for a woolen mill in Harrisville. He was then living with his parents, Asa and Nancy Burnap Taft, in his native village of Nelson. He soon got a job in the mill, but left it to work in a chair factory in Keene. He was able to purchase a small shop that his sisters were running in the town and presumably accumulated some capital.

On July 6, 1871, Taft and Burnap bought the Mile Stone Mill, which had been making clothespins and other wooden ware, and converted it into a pottery. Surrounded by land rich in clay, the building stood on the bank of the Ashuelot River. During that summer the potters whom they had engaged prepared a kiln of flowerpots, but, before these could be burned, the building caught fire and was destroyed with a loss of nearly four thousand dollars. By the following winter they had replaced the mill with a better structure and were again at work. The local paper noted: "Messrs. J. S. Taft & Co. have completed their new pottery and recommenced the manufacture of earthenware. The interruption of their business by fire which destroyed their old building was only 6 weeks duration. Their new building is 160 ft. long and two stories high and has been very thoroughly and substantially built."

Another Keene pottery was also erected in 1871 by the firm of Starkey & Howard. It was about the same size as the Taft shop and stood south of Water Street, just across the meadows from the other works. The Keene *Sentinel* says of it:

> Messrs. Starkey & Howard of this town have engaged in the manufacture of stone and earthenware, and propose to do a large business in both branches the coming season. They have erected a building south of Water St. 140 ft. long by 36 ft. wide, 2½ stories high, where they

will employ about 40 hands in the making of common earthenware and stoneware, together with drain tile and water pipe. The difficulty of procuring kaolin from New Jersey will prevent their making the stone ware until spring. Then our farmers can have their jars and jugs made to any pattern they desire. The works are under the charge of Mr. A. S. Wright, a practical potter of many years experience, who will take pleasure in explaining the several processes to visitors.

This "Wright" was Abner S. Wight, one of the founders of the pottery at West Sterling, Massachusetts, and son of John D. Wight of Marlborough. Starkey & Howard soon washed their hands of the pottery business. In June 1872, they sold the works to W. P. Chamberlain and E. C. Baker. Under this style, the firm continued for nearly two years, until, in March 1874, it was acquired by Taft. The building was burned in 1875, but was still in use the following year as a redware pottery, while Taft carried on the manufacture of stoneware in the Main Street works. Eventually the Myrtle Street factory was converted into a tenement house.

Taft's stoneware, decorated with motives in cobalt blue, was fashioned into the usual sturdy vessels and containers. A bill headed "Main Street Works / Keene Stone & Earthenware Manufactory" shows that in 1876 this branch of the output was no different from that of other makers of this ordinary ware. It itemizes jugs and molasses jugs, butter and cake pots, covered preserve jars, pitchers, churns, water kegs and spittoons. Under the heading "Myrtle Street Works / Earthen Ware," is a list of vases and flowerpots, as follows:

Hanging Vases
Vases — Band
Burnap Hanger
Bracket Pots
Grecian Medallion
Closed Saucer Pot
The Rustic
Saucer Pots — Band
" " — Decorated
" " — Unglazed
XL Cuspadore
The Centennial Cuspadore
Florists' Ware
Bean Pots
Handled and covered
Rockingham Teapots

Here again, as at West Sterling, the word "Rockingham" probably denotes a brown glaze on red earthenware.

The *New Hampshire Gazetteer* of 1872 gives the value of redware and stoneware made in the Keene potteries as thirty-five thousand dollars annually. In the eighties and nineties the Hampshire Pottery created several other types of ware, which are discussed in the chapter on art potteries.

Although not a pioneer pottery in the sense of belonging to an early settler, the stoneware manufactory of Martin Crafts at Nashua was the first of its kind in New Hampshire. Indeed, with the exception of the one just mentioned at Keene, it was the only stoneware concern in the state. Both local history and the data compiled by James M. Crafts give the year of its establishment as 1838.

This Crafts pottery was an offshoot of the stoneware business begun by Thomas Crafts in Whately in 1833. His son James M. was the first manager of the Nashua works when he was only twenty-one years of age, and while Martin, his brother, was still running a stoneware pottery in Portland, Maine. Martin went to Nashua in 1839 and bought out the business two years later. For ten years the Nashua shop was operated by Martin Crafts, and it is known as his pottery. In 1843 his uncle, Caleb Crafts, who had tried to make a success of the Portland business after Martin had abandoned it, was also in Nashua. His name appears in 1843 and 1845

directories. He then returned to Whately, leaving Martin in charge of the works. In 1849 James M. Crafts was again in Nashua, and he was soon followed by another brother, Thomas Spencer Crafts. Martin left the management to them in 1851, while he went to Boston to conduct a wholesale stoneware agency for the sale of their products. The pottery closed in 1852, James going back to Whately to take up farming, while the younger brother set out for California.

The factory stood on the east side of Main Street, north of what was then the Acton railroad. Martin and his relatives lived in a cottage nearby on Kinsley Street. They are said to have brought their clay from Boston by boat through the Middlesex Canal and up the Merrimac River. This was an easier course for a barge than the open ocean route to Portland and probably less expensive.

The Nashua *Directory* of 1850 contains this notice: "Stoneware Factory/ Commenced 1838/ Martin Crafts, Proprietor/ Amount of business annually $16,000/ Employed 9 hands." F. H. Norton, who quotes this item in his article "The Crafts Pottery in Nashua, New Hampshire," which appeared in *Antiques* (April 1931), estimates that, with an average price of thirty cents per piece, the pottery must have turned out fifty-three thousand pieces in a year. It was therefore no small enterprise.

A price list of the 1840's in my file enumerates the following articles in various sizes: jugs, water jugs, butter pots (straight), with covers, airtight butter pots, butter boxes, preserve or pickle pots, with covers, cream pots, with and without covers, churns, pitchers, flowerpots, bean pots, pudding pans, mugs, beer bottles, spittoons, kegs, and ice jars with covers.

Few of these containers seem to have survived. Professor Norton found straight-sided jugs and a jar and noted several marks. The earliest ware bore the name *T, Crafts & Co./ Nashua.* Later the mark *Martin Crafts/ Nashua* or *Martin Crafts/ Nashua, N. H.* was used. Other jugs bearing Thomas Crafts' Whately mark (*T. Crafts & Co./ Whately*) are stamped with the firm names of retailers in Nashua. Professor Norton deduced from this fact that Crafts had a going business with Nashua concerns before he started a pottery there and that the jugs in question are earlier than 1838. The straight shape, however, is not in favor of this theory, but is rather an indication of later manufacture. A jug with Thomas Crafts' Nashua mark (used before 1841) is potbellied in shape.

CHAPTER FIFTEEN

The Clarks of Lyndeboro and Concord

For more than a century the redware industry of a large area in southern New Hampshire was dominated by Peter Clark and his descendants and apprentices. Clark has been mentioned briefly in connection with Braintree, Massachusetts, the town of his birth and the location of his first pottery. He and his wife, the former Hannah Epps, stemmed from Danvers families. His father and grandfather, both Peter Clarks, were born in the Essex County town, as were the parents of Hannah Epps. Peter was born February 4, 1743, and married at the age of twenty.

A diary that Clark kept for more than thirty years was at one time owned by Mrs. Joseph N. Robinson of Malden, Massachusetts. Short quotations from it in an article by Leonard F. Burbank in *Antiques* (February 1928), indicate that he kept up his Danvers connections. He records going to Danvers for clay. This was doubtless white clay for slip decorating, as redware clay was abundant near Braintree. Clark was selling his own wares in Hingham as early as 1768. In other references to his potting activities, he mentions when he "sot" or "drawed" his kiln or "made ware."

The family's removal to New Hampshire took place in 1775. On January 25 he notes that they "sot out for Lyndeboro." The journey was apparently uneventful and he records their arrival two days later. The spring and summer he devoted to building and planting, but, by October, Peter Clark had begun to make pottery in the new site. The following February he moved into his house. He had but a short time to get established before enlisting in the Revolutionary forces. In August 1777 he "set out for Bennington," where he took part four days later in the famous battle. Clark attained the rank of major after this action. His sword, in the museum of the Bennington Battle Monument and Historical Association, preserves the memory of his war exploits. Returning safely from these momentous events, Clark practiced his craft until 1819 or later. Throughout the years the potter was identified with the public affairs of the little town. At times he was selectman or town clerk and he sometimes officiated as town moderator. In 1783

he was made a deacon in the Congregational Church, a position that he held for life. He was, in fact, a solid and conservative citizen, who prefered his title "Deacon" to the higher-sounding one of "Major." In dress he never deviated from the early style of a long-tailed wig, knee breeches, and long stockings, with knee and shoe buckles. His death occurred in 1826.

When Clark moved to Lyndeboro, he already had four little boys under thirteen years of age. They were all brought up to the potter's trade in time-honored fashion. When they grew up, the eldest son, Peter, worked in Lyndeboro, Concord, and Brownington, Vermont; the second son, William, and his family, carried on a pottery at North Lyndeboro Four Corners; the third son, Daniel, founded the well-known Millville pottery in Concord, where Benjamin also lived for a time before moving to Lebanon, New Hampshire.

The Clark pottery and several others associated with it were in North Lyndeboro, which was then on the edge of the wilderness and which even now is in sparsely settled country. Since this group was one of the pioneer potting communities in New Hampshire, it seemed worthy of investigation. We first paid a visit to Lyndeboro in 1940. We found the little village where the Clarks carried on their business reduced to a mere road crossing. The Stearns house in the southeast angle and another not far from the northeast corner were the only remaining buildings of the once busy neighborhood. The Goodrich house, mentioned in the town history as being opposite the pottery, had disappeared, although we found its cellar hole in the southwest corner lot. In a field directly across the highway and all along the roadside towards Francestown were quantities of pottery shards. This locality may be found where the Lyndeboro road crosses the main thoroughfare from Mont Vernon to Francestown.

Peter Clark's homestead is on a parallel roadway — the older turnpike between Francestown and Mont Vernon. The site is reached from the four corners described by following the Lyndeboro road to the first crossing and turning right; after passing a house on the right, one goes around a bend to a clearing on the left, where the cellar hole is plainly seen. This is known as the old Holden place. Besides the foundation of the large house with its huge central chimney there are signs of several smaller buildings and two wells. Down over a slope behind the cellar hole is a running brook. The only evidences of earthenware that we could discover were a number of setting tiles and a few fragments in a fill of rubble bricked up around the core of the house chimney. These, with gravel and sand, must have been cleared from the land for this purpose. A few more pieces of pottery — one a brilliant green — made the sum total of our findings. At a later time we learned that a potshop had stood in a clearing on the other side of the road. Local historians are quite at variance concerning the Lyndeboro pottery sites and their owners, but I feel rather certain that this was the original pottery of Peter Clark. We found there among other things some very thin pieces, quite akin to the eighteenth-century work of Daniel Bayley, as evidence of early manufacture.

As nearly as I can piece together the Clark family history from local records and from Daniel Clark's diary, I believe that Peter the father always lived on the Holden place, although he later built a pottery in another location. His oldest son, when he was almost thirty, helped his brother Daniel to establish himself in Concord and then, in 1796, struck out for the frontier as one of the first settlers of Brownington (Barton), in far northern Vermont. He remained there until after 1809,

returning then to his native place and resuming his trade. He built a pottery, it is said, that did more business than any other in town. This seems to have been the shop, or one of the shops, owned by the Clarks at the four corners.

William Clark, after working for a time with his Uncle Benjamin Epps in Gilmanton, New Hampshire, was a potter in Lyndeboro as long as he lived. Aided by his sons, Peter and Benjamin, he was running a business in 1826 and thereafter. Whether this was in the same building put up by his brother or in another is not known. Peter died in 1851; William, four years later. The Peter Clark shop was destroyed by fire in 1855, and the industry then came to an end. Peter of the third generation (son of William) was a potter by trade, but turned to farming, while his brother Benjamin forsook the business to become a minister.

Meantime a pottery is said to have been started by one Peter Clark in nearby Francestown as early as 1800. By a process of elimination, it can be determined that it was founded by Major Peter himself, for his son Peter was in Brownington in 1800 and his three grandsons of the name were then too young to have done it. The reason for this move was the difficulty of finding proper clay. Not much is known about the Francestown shop, except that it was running successfully in 1817, but failed eventually on account of the poor quality of the clay. This pottery was in the section still called Clark Village, not more than a mile from Clark's homestead. It stood on the south side of the road from Francestown where a lane runs in from the Sargent mills bridge to the old B. F. Clark pail factory. We visited this spot in 1942. Guided by Miss Annie Clark, a local resident, and one of Peter's descendants, we discovered the site about two rods from the main road, between the land and the river. The few fragments recovered did not indicate any great degree of skill in potting. A predominating yellowish glaze was their only distinctive feature.

Daniel Clark records in his diary under date of June 15, 1819, that there was an upset in Lyndeboro and that the Clarks had failed. He does not enlarge upon this simple statement, except to say that he had made many trips from Concord in the effort to stave off the collapse. It is quite unlikely that the whole family was involved. The father was then seventy-six years old. The younger Peter probably built his shop at the four corners after this failure. There he solved the family problem by bringing his clay the nearly fifteen miles from Amherst in order to insure a good product.

Such examples of the Clark earthenware as I have seen were rather thick and clumsy and lacking in the refinement so often exhibited in the work of Massachusetts potters. Turning pots in a remote country village, where only the merest necessities were in demand, must have been a humdrum business. Specimens of the handiwork of Peter and his descendants are pictured with Mr. Burbank's article in *Antiques*. Comparison of the jar (his Fig. 3) with that in our Fig. 16 leaves no doubt that Clark also made the one in my collection. This attribution is strengthened by the fact that its former owner is rather sure that she found it in Hingham, where Clark sold ware from his Braintree pottery. Its dimensions are virtually the same, and its combed bands in the same relation to each other and of the same number. The rounded base is another indication of identical workmanship. The Lyndeboro jar is one of a pair, made perhaps to hold flowers. It is greenish in color, blended with yellow and brown. My vase is decidedly yellow in tone with deep brown markings.

Several other Essex County families figure in the potting history of this small village. One of the earliest arrivals was Samuel

Whittemore, of Danvers birth, son of Samuel and Eleanor (Osborn) Whittemore. His father made the first permanent clearing north of the mountain. Samuel built his house on the hill east of the Whittemore farm buildings. He carried on his trade in Lyndeboro until 1798, then moved to Concord.

Ebenezer Hutchinson ran a shop nearly opposite the Goodrich place before 1815. Although the town history makes no mention of his pottery, its existence is established by the following notice in the *Farmer's Cabinet*, printed at Amherst, New Hampshire, under date of September 8, 1815:

> The subscriber having removed his pottery from Lyndeboro, to Vermont, acquaints those indebted to him that he will be at his father's house in Lyndeboro the 15th to the 20th day of September next, when he requests they will call upon him and make payment, or they may expect costs.
>
> *Ebenezer Hutchinson, April 8, 1815*

This young man was the son of Ebenezer Hutchinson, one of the pioneers of Lyndeboro. His father had built a log house on what was later the Goodrich farm. Ten of his eleven children were born in this modest dwelling. In 1853 the elder Hutchinson moved to Hancock and thence to end his days in St. Johnsbury, Vermont. Mr. Spargo notes a William Hutchinson who started a redware pottery in St. Johnsbury in 1815. This person was either Ebenezer Hutchinson or else his brother William. He had a brother of that name and the two may have founded the St. Johnsbury pottery.

In the spring of 1815, John Southwick, coming from Danvers with his bride, bought the Hutchinson shop and began to make pottery there. Later he was engaged in driving a six-horse hitch from Francestown to Boston, carrying country produce and returning with dry goods for the local stores. In 1841 he went back to Danvers.

Midway between Lyndeboro and Concord, a craftsman who may have been trained in the Clark group produced a great deal of pottery in North Weare. Several men of the town made bricks, and David Dow used the same clay bank. The exact date of his enterprise is not known, but its owner could have been David, son of Winthrop Dow, who was born September 19, 1802, and died November 13, 1874.

The story of Daniel Clark stands out more vividly than that of any other New England potter, save possibly Hervey Brooks, for he kept a diary of events from the time he was twenty-one almost until his death at the age of sixty. This line-a-day record has been preserved in the library of the New Hampshire Historical Society in Concord. It outlines the course of the potter's career, his ways and habits, and something of his external life, but tells little about personalities or his inner thoughts. Further record of the Millville pottery is to be found in surviving examples of the ware and from memories of the enterprise in its later stages.

The diary begins in 1789, when Daniel notes that he has burned his first kiln of ware at Lyndeboro. Later, in August, he says that he has made eight kilns of ware during the year and burned two. He had a one-half interest in the proceeds. A "kiln of ware" means enough pieces for one firing. It might be turned at any time. Apparently a careful list of the articles was kept as they were thrown, so they could be burned in the proper rotation. For instance, in March 1790, Daniel burned the third kiln made in the previous year. In 1791 he completed seven kilns of ware, but turned only three.

November 25, 1790, was the date of young Daniel's marriage to Mary Whitmarsh of Lyndeboro. He writes briefly on December 5, "Began to keep house." Late in the following year Daniel "went to Concord with Benjn [his brother] to look out for clay,"

and again on December 30, after taking a load of ware to Major Caleb Stark at Dunbarton, he visited Concord. He was already making plans to settle near a large town. That he found a home and shop is certain. The next March he moved from Lyndeboro to the western part of Concord on the Hopkinton road. By April the family was settled and went to meeting for the first time.

The exact location of Clark's first house in Concord is unknown. William W. Flint, who wrote an excellent brief summary of the Clark diary in *Old-Time New England*, (January 1927), thinks it may have been a mile or so west of the section later called Millville which was near the present site of St. Paul's School. Clark makes no mention of building either a house, kiln, or shop. He speaks, however, of a partnership in connection with his first burning of ware in Concord. This association may have been with his brother Peter, who came and went frequently between Lyndeboro and Concord, usually when the kiln was being fired. An indication that he was working in an old building is the note, November 1792, "Burnt the 6th and Last kl^{n} for this year, in the old durty shop."

The "durty shop" was soon to be replaced. A few days after the year's work was ended, Clark began to cut timber for a new potshop and to dig the cellar for a house. The latter was raised in April 1793, and he tells how the "joyners" came to do their part and how the masons finished the chimney in three days. During the first ten days of May, workmen hewed timber for the shop, which was completed on the twenty-seventh of June. The structure measured thirty feet by fifty, and the account says that fourteen thousand shingles were required to roof it. With some satisfaction, no doubt, the potter records on the third of the month that he had ground the first mill of clay in his new workhouse. A new kiln was built in July.

In 1802 Daniel Clark began to erect another house, which is thought to be the story-and-a-half dwelling still standing at 297 Pleasant Street (the Hopkinton road), and occupied by Arthur Estes Clark, the potter's great-great-grandson. This house was finished in 1804. A barn and shed were also built, but nothing is said about a shop or kiln. The potworks of the later Clarks stood just east of the dwelling.

As Clark progressed in business, his thoughts turned towards an even finer homestead. Its first cellar stone was laid in June 1808, almost directly across the way from the earlier house. During all of 1809 and 1810 masons and "plaisterers" were busy in the construction of the substantial mansion that is still in use as a home. On December 13 the family moved in, and Clark began to count the cost. He notes: "B. Swain finished his job of joiner work on the house $245 — plaistering 40 — $285." This was the principal expense for a house that today would cost not less than twelve thousand dollars. The place has a significance of local historical interest, because from its doorway Clark's daughter Mary stepped to present a bouquet to General Lafayette as he passed along the highway on his tour of New Hampshire.

From the brief daily entries in the diary it is possible to piece out the picture of life in a country pottery. Clay was always the first consideration. All the Millville potters dug their clay in the low lands east of Dimond Hill and south of the road. Daniel Clark first speaks of it, May 15, 1792: "Beg^{n} to dig clay M^{r}. Dimonds." After this day's work he writes: "Laid by work, ager in my head." The following week he dug clay — "good clay" — at Mr. Bradley's. He then proceeded to the business of grinding and began to turn ware. The next two days he notes: "fine weather for w^{r}," and we may be sure his newly fashioned pots and pans were out drying in the spring sunshine. In June Clark

paid seventy-five pounds for half of "Master Dimonds Land."

Meantime he had made trips to Lyndeboro for ware that must have been left behind in the moving and he began to travel about selling it. Under date of July 25, Clark records that he began to "cart ware" in Concord. This is the earliest reference I have found to peddling earthenware over the road. The potter made a three-weeks journey to Saratoga Springs, but whether in the way of trade he does not say. Later in the season he burned brick for Bradley and for Dimond. He never again mentions brickmaking. It seems likely that the establishment he first acquired in Concord was a yard for this purpose.

Daniel frequently notes the comings and goings of his brothers, Peter and Benjamin. The latter was working at the potter's trade. Newly married this year, he "sot of for Lyndeb° for his wife" in November and came to Millville to live. During the winter of 1793 he went back to Lyndeboro to burn ware. Two years later Benjamin settled in Concord on the Abner Flanders place. Each of the sons helped their father and each other at busy times. Daniel writes on January 7, 1794: "burnt Kiln wʳ for Benjn — he sick Peter helped." Another brother, William, who was working with his uncle Benjamin Epes (Epps) in Gilmanton, paid a visit to Daniel in 1793.

By the next year Clark had established enough of a business to sell pottery at wholesale. In February James Punchard bought three sleigh loads of ware for £9, 4s., 3d. During the next two years he is mentioned frequently. Oliver Flanders and John Dimond peddled earthenware, too, as did Peter Clark at times. Daniel himself made trips to Salisbury, Warner, Newport, Epsom, and Northwood with ware, besides doing an extraordinary amount of traveling to Lyndeboro and elsewhere. Considering the few and poor roads through the country in the eighteenth century, Clark must have been an intrepid traveler. In the midst of the winter of 1796, he made a three-days' journey to Hampton for fish.

One of the potter's principal concerns was for his lead supply. Scarcity of materials that had to be bought must have been a major obstacle for the country potter. Clark got his first lead from Major Stark. This was in bars, costing forty-five shillings per hundred weight. From Stark also he got hay for his horse in exchange for ware. In February 1795, he went to Amherst, New Hampshire, for his lead supply, buying enough to glaze two kilns of ware. Bar lead at that time cost fifty-four shillings and red lead fifty. In 1799 he purchased enough for four kilns, but at a cost of eleven dollars per hundred weight. Later purchases he made at Salem, Portsmouth, and Boston. The price of this commodity rose during the war years to twenty-four dollars a hundred pounds. In 1814 bar lead could not be obtained at any price, and the Clarks used lead ore from New Hampton. A purchase of litharge for glazing was made by Daniel's son Daniel in 1825.

Clark's diary establishes the fact that early potters used millstones for grinding their clay. Under date of July 11, 1806, he records: "Mr. Wood finished stone clay mill — cost $70.00," and, the following day: "first ground clay on stone mill." The use of millstones instead of a tub mill has been a moot question. The tub is evidently a later invention, adopted by Daniel Clark himself in 1817, when he notes briefly: "Set up tub to grind Clay."

The references to other potters in this account help to give a picture of the Millville industry as a whole. In the beginning years Daniel and his brothers, Peter and Benjamin, got along without help, except for the men who sold the ware. James Punchard, Oliver Flanders, John Dimond, Moses Flanders, and

others were among those who went out to peddle it. In 1796 a note is made of Peter's going to Lake Magog (Memphremagog) near the Canada line. Mr. Flint has assumed that he made this journey to sell earthenware. This seems unlikely, for a roadway of sorts had been slashed through the primeval forest to Derby only the year before: it would hardly have been passable in May and June for a peddler's cart. Peter Clark was prospecting for a home site on the frontier. He returned from this trip a month later, perhaps after building a cabin for his family, and is not mentioned as being in Concord thereafter. He was the first settler of Brownington, then part of Barton, Vermont, in 1796. In 1803 Daniel and his wife "Polly" paid Peter a visit. The journey of four days must have been a tedious and difficult one, and its being undertaken at all is proof of the strong attachment that existed between the brothers. Peter remained in Brownington until some time after June 1809, when Daniel again went to see him, but he later returned to Lyndeboro to carry on the potter's trade.

Benjamin Clark moved back to Lyndeboro from Concord in 1798. Daniel was then obliged to find a helper outside the family. Samuel Whittemore of Lyndeboro, a man some twenty years older than Daniel, had first worked for him in 1795. June 27, 1796, Daniel notes that Whittemore burned ware for him. July 6, he says: "John Whit^{e} here S W^{e} went home." During the following year Samuel Whittemore journeyed back and forth to take charge of burning. In 1798 he moved to Millville. After two years he went to live about a mile up the road in the district strangely named "Fush Market" or "The Market." A pottery dump on the Rhodes' land is thought to mark the site. Whittemore built a shop of his own, although for years he worked in the Clark pottery at critical times. On the other hand, Daniel Clark aided Whittemore in the processes of turning and burning. For many years he held a mortgage on Whittemore's property, which he foreclosed in April 1809. The entry on May 10: "Mr S. Whit very sick" may indicate either the result or the cause. Whatever the reason, Daniel Clark, Jr. moved into the Whittemore house the next spring. Samuel Whittemore died six years later at the age of seventy-eight. His son Peter, although he called himself a farmer in deeds, worked for Clark in various capacities. Entries such as "Peter went to P W^{s} turning w^{r}" or "Peter turned ware for P. Whitt^{e}" show that he was in charge of the family enterprise in its closing years.

The first apprentice in the Clark shop was Peter Flanders, son of Oliver, who went to live with the family and to learn his trade in 1795, when he was eleven years old. He remained with Clark until he was twenty-one, then went to Lyndeboro to work for a time. In 1807 he was back in Concord and was soon in business for himself. An entry in the diary, November 8, says: "Peter Flanders lost kiln w^{r} which fell down in burning." This was no unusual calamity for an inexperienced potter; it had happened to Clark himself. Flanders, after a period of driving the stage between Concord and Plymouth, sold his Millville property to Richard Flanders, Jr., and removed to Plymouth to start a pottery business there. In a deed dated March 3, 1813, he conveyed to Richard nearly three acres of land "with dwelling house, barn, and potter's shop thereon."

Previously, in 1805, Richard Flanders had come to the Clark pottery in Peter's place and had stayed with Clark for six months. He succeeded to the Flanders business the year before his marriage. In 1813 also he bought a clay bed of Reuben Dimond and he made a further purchase of land in 1819. His home and potshop were on the north side of the Hopkinton road at Millville and were situated where the Mercer house stood

in 1927, at the northwest corner of Fisk Road and the main highway. The lot is now vacant and has been filled with ashes, thus effectually concealing any evidences of pottery making. In 1829 Richard Flanders, Jr. gave a quitclaim deed for $25 to William Bodwell, a Concord potter, of a small piece of land and a "Potters shop standing on Joseph Stickney's land westerly of said land." Whether this points to the conclusion of the Flanders pottery is uncertain.

A third family, the Hazeltines, ran a redware shop of some importance about half a mile west of the Clark pottery. Joseph Hazeltine, its founder, was a native of Concord. He worked for the Clarks at times, but carried on an independent business until about 1880. His shop stood on the north side of the Hopkinton road, east of Miss Alice Moulton's land, and near the line where an iron fence now stands close by a barn on the next estate. The kiln was behind the shop. Hazeltine operated four wheels and must have had a number of men in his employ. Several pieces of his earthenware have survived. His grandson, Joseph Hazeltine, postmaster at Contoocook, cherishes a shaving mug, and the museum of the New Hampshire Antiquarian Society at Hopkinton has preserved a stew pot with handle made by Hazeltine in 1845.

Two members of the Dimond family followed the potter's trade, settling in Warner about fifteen miles west of Millville. Israel Dimond, who was one of Clark's earliest friends in Concord, lived on the estate there still known as Dimond Hill. In the early years of the century he established a pottery on the main road through Warner, about four miles east of the village at the corner of the old "Joppa" road. Later the neighborhood was called "Dimond's Corner." Israel Dimond built a large two-story shop and the store that was afterwards run by his son Col. Hiram. In 1828 he had retired and called himself "gentleman." Deeds of this year reveal that he conveyed property on both sides of the road to Hiram and to Timothy K. Dimond, who was likewise a potter. Timothy had previously acquired two acres with buildings from Francis M. Morrill, but he was no doubt carrying on the Dimond earthenware business in the original shop. Daniel Clark mentions Israel Dimond casually several times, once in 1810, when he bought a shed frame of him for forty dollars, and again in 1813, when they "swapped" horses. He also speaks of the boys going to Israel Dimond's.

Other names weave like threads through the fabric of Clark's story. Brief entries, such as "Jotham Reed came here" (January 29, 1806) and "Jotham Reed went off" (March 28), suggest that an apprentice was tried out and found wanting. On April 15 Keyes Powell arrived. He began by peddling ware, but in August started to work in the shop. He remained with Clark at least four years.

Clark's boys, Daniel and Peter, born in 1793 and 1794, were able to help in the pottery at an early age. Daniel was often sick. His symptoms of colic or "rheumatism in stomack" were possibly the result of that common potter's malady — lead poisoning. On several occasions he was incapacitated for months on end. At such times, as in October 1803, he notes: "boys finished Whittemores w^{r} turning." By "boys" he means Peter Flanders and perhaps another unnamed helper, or else his own children. By the time he was seventeen, Daniel, Jr. was entrusted with the business of buying lead in Salem. There could have been little opportunity for school or lessons in a young potter's life, and yet these craftsmen were far from illiterate. The father, who grew up in the backwoods at Lyndeboro, wrote an acceptable hand and his spelling was neither better nor worse than that of more highly educated men in his day. Many mistakes he corrected as the years went by. His daughter was a notably intellectual spinster in Concord.

The only other person who is mentioned as an employee at the pottery is one John Libbey. In March 1822 Clark writes: "Hired John Libbey to begin the first April for 1 year. agreed to give him $11.00 per month in ware & give in the house rent and pauster his cow summer season." The following January he sold Libbey a kiln of ware for fifty dollars. He is not mentioned thereafter.

As the years went on, the sons assumed more and more responsibility and were thus able to take over the management of the pottery after their father's death in 1828.

The only clues to the character of this industrious man occur in the accounts of his activities and not through any expression of his thought. Over and over he writes with seeming satisfaction, "finished" this or that. He was no doubt a driver of himself as well as of others. The backbreaking labor of digging clay and carting it, of cutting many cords of wood for the kiln, or even of working on the highway, and his frequent long journeys were perhaps too arduous for a man who was not constitutionally too rugged. Every year also he tried to turn out more and more ware. In 1804 he turned twenty kilns; in 1807, twenty-two; in 1810, "Burnt 26th and last kiln made in 1808." By that time he had established the most successful pottery business in New Hampshire.

The sons carried on this legacy together for a time. In New Hampshire business directories of 1849 and 1850, the name of Daniel Clark alone appears. When the second Daniel died in 1863, his son John Farmer Clark succeeded him. Many people can remember the Millville pottery of his day, which did not cease operations until his passing in 1885 left it without a master potter.

Numerous examples of redware made by the three generations of Clarks may be seen in the Harrison Gray Otis House, Boston, and in the museum of the New Hampshire Historical Society at Concord. The Boston pieces include a hand-modeled log cabin, a creamer and sugar bowl, jugs, and an assortment of late unglazed vessels made by John Farmer Clark. The unglazed ware comprises vases of pleasing form, bean pots, a candlestick, feeding cup, and mustard pot. Some classic forms with painted decoration executed by John Clark show a good sense of design. There is also in this collection a tall teapot of great refinement banded with incised straight and wavy lines, which is shown as an example of the early work of Daniel Clark. The fact that it is redware may easily have led to a confusion in the family tradition. A careful examination of the piece will convince any student that it is English earthenware of the type produced by Astbury and others about 1760. If further proof be needed, the base on a raised foot and the fine texture of the body, so superior to all of Clark's ware, are sufficient. *I have never seen a piece of early New England redware that did not have a flat base.*

The most significant example made at Millville is in the Concord collection. It is a large deep plate with dark brown glaze. The rim is ornamented with incised straight and wavy lines, and on the base is incised the inscription *Concord September th 12—1807*. This piece may possibly be the work of Peter Flanders, who started his Millville pottery in that year.

During the middle years of the last century a favorite "show-off" piece was the barrel form closed at both ends with a hole in the side to accommodate a cork. Several such kegs in different sizes are in the Concord museum. They are yellowish brown in color. One has a date—*1859*—scratched under the glaze. Barrel-shaped mugs were a popular form during presidential campaigns. Examples appear with a rough brown glaze incised *Hayes & Wheeler* or *Cleveland & Hendricks*. The New Hampshire Historical

Society also owns some unglazed jugs incised "Clay dug on site of St. Paul's school," with date *1876*. Like all unglazed ware from Millville, these are yellowish red.

Some bills of sale dated, respectively, 1830, 1838, 1840, and 1844, are preserved with Clark's diary. These, of course, represent the output of his son Daniel. The first mentions milk pans, large pots, bread pans, platters in two sizes, bean pots, and jugs; the second includes pudding pans, flat pans, and chambers; the third lists flowerpots and pitchers; and the fourth has an unusual item — "Low bean pots." This refers to the bean pot as we know it today — a new invention in 1844. All the evidence points to an exceedingly practical type of production. There is no indication either in the diary or in the earthenware that the Clarks practiced slip decorating as it was known to early New England potters, and few gift pieces from this pottery are known. We must conclude that only the plainest vessels were in demand in New Hampshire a century ago.

CHAPTER SIXTEEN

North of Concord

The most important potteries north of Concord were those at Boscawen and Plymouth. The Plymouth shops were manned by potters from Concord and Boscawen; the Boscawen industry was a branching out from Loudon. Even before 1800 the Osbornes were at work in Loudon. Their early history is shrouded in the mists of uncertainty. Mrs. Durgin of Boscawen, born in 1842, told me that her grandfather John Osborne, son of Jacob, was trained in Loudon to be a potter and that he had two uncles who were also potters. I have been unable to learn their names. It is probable that one of them was John, the father of Elijah Osborne of Loudon and Pittsfield, who, according to the *Biographical Review of Strafford and Belknap Counties*, was descended from the Danvers Osborns. Frederick H. Norton has written an account of the family's activities in Gonic, but he was unable to establish this connection.

Elijah is mentioned in deeds as a potter in 1830. About this time he married Margaret Green of Loudon and they had three sons, James L., Green, and John C. James was born in Loudon in 1831. When he was eight years old, the family moved to Gonic, near Rochester. Elijah started a pottery there, which he carried on with the aid of James and John throughout his lifetime. The son Green remained in Loudon, or returned there, to work at the potter's trade for a time. Eventually he became a farmer in Pittsfield. After Elijah Osborne's death, his sons continued in the business, carrying on the shop as partners until about 1875. John then withdrew from the concern, leaving James and his son William to manage the Gonic works until its close ten years later. The pottery building was still standing in 1930, when Professor Norton interviewed William A. Osborne and obtained from him some specimens of redware.

Gonic ware is characterized by mottled effects that were sometimes produced by dipping the fingers in a dark-colored glaze and dabbing it over a clear glaze. The ware was distributed in the usual way from peddler's carts among the surrounding towns. Milk pans sold for twenty cents, cups for ten, and large jars for forty-five or fifty cents.

It may here be noted that a Jacob Osborn, whose name appears in the *New England Business Directory* of 1856 was running a pottery at that time in Dover. It seems likely that he was a member of the Loudon family and was perhaps Jacob, Jr., brother of the John Osborne who went to Boscawen.

The Boscawen potters, and especially

Jeremiah Burpee, have been mentioned in other accounts of American ceramics. It has been supposed that Burpee made a choice type of stoneware, but actually he was just another redware potter. He went to Boscawen from Epping as a boy of eleven years, when his father, a brickmaker, settled there in 1792. He seems to have served his apprenticeship in Loudon, for he married Nancy Wells of that town in 1804. In that year also he began the brickmaking and pottery business in which he was engaged until his death in 1862.

The Burpee pottery site lies near the junction of the Andover road and the first road to the left as one goes north from Boscawen. The shard pile, which contains plentiful evidence of his product, is on a steep slope just west of the main road and south of this corner. The clay pit was below the slope in a hollow now leveled by highway construction. Across the main road was Burpee's house. This district, on account of the deep ravine, was known as the "Gulf." Burpee's first wife was killed there in 1817, when a frightened horse threw her sleigh over the Gulf bridge. Her husband, left with seven little ones, married within a few months Sally D. Gill. This second union was blessed with eleven children, so that the Burpee family, with its eighteen boys and girls, was indeed a large one. Several of the sons were trained in their father's shop, but James G. Burpee, born in 1830, was the one who succeeded to the business. The first son, Joshua, was probably a potter (in Meredith, see below).

When we visited Boscawen in 1937, some of the older residents still retained memories of the old pothouse. One of them (Mr. Flint) recalled being taken to the shop when he was five years old. His father's house had burned, and his parents went to buy a new stock of earthenware. He was able to describe the lard pots that his mother used for straining fat or for holding lye during the process of making soap. Mr. Flint said that the regular output of the Burpee pottery was jugs, jars, and pans, and he was quite positive that stoneware had never been made in Boscawen.

This statement was corroborated by Mrs. Durgin, whose memory went back many years earlier, since she was then ninety-five years old. She had once been a teacher in a little school that stood on the north corner of the road opposite the pottery. She distinctly remembered watching James Burpee making redware, and among her possessions were three pans of pie-plate size, one with a yellowish glaze, that had come from the Burpee kiln.

No claim for stoneware appears in Coffin's *History of Boscawen and Webster*, published in 1878. Instead, the writer mentions milk pans, cream pots, and jugs, turned on the wheel and left to dry upon long boards set out on the south side of the building. Coffin calls the ware "Queen's-ware"—a term sometimes erroneously applied to any kind of earthenware.

These statements are emphasized because a number of collectors have mistakenly attributed to Boscawen a type of high-fired brown salt-glazed stoneware with incised decoration. This kind of pottery is so far alien to New England manufacture that its foreign origin should be evident to anyone familiar with native products. Moreover, this beautifully finished ware is found all along the New England coast, where it arrived in ships as containers for imported goods. I have seen a jar of the sort that was brought to Gloucester along with other stoneware and Delft from the Low Countries by a sea captain in the Surinam trade. The so-called "Burpee" stoneware is without doubt of German or Flemish origin. In fact, similar jars are made in Belgium even today. It is true that Burpee occasionally incised on his

red clay pieces a decoration bearing a slight resemblance to the more skillfully executed designs on the brown stoneware. A small redware vase with such incised or impressed work, obtained from the Burpee family, may be seen in Fig. 68 *c*.

From the elderly Mrs. Durgin I first learned that her grandfather John Osborne was a potter. Coming to Boscawen from Loudon, he set up his shop and kiln on the main street just south of the cemetery. At the time of his marriage to Mary Carter in 1816, he was working at his trade. He died before the birth of Mrs. Durgin's mother a few years later. His granddaughter said that he left about one thousand dollars' worth of unburned ware. A potter who was engaged to finish it ruined the whole kilnful, and that was the end of the pottery. Mrs. Durgin as a child used to play in the old shop, which was afterwards converted to a hay barn. Two handsome pieces of Osborne's make, both brownish orange in color, were inherited by his granddaughter. One is a small, squatty, handled jar, almost like a straight teapot without a spout. It was used for grated nutmeg. The other is a thin-walled quart ale mug encircled by two slightly raised ridges.

Not far from Boscawen, on the other side of the Merrimac, there was for a time a pottery in Northfield. The sons of Stephen Cross had gone there from Boscawen to establish a number of mills and shops. Among them was Charles C. Cross, a brickmaker, and presumably the redware potter. He obtained his clay from the west bank of the river until washouts carried away the supply and forced him to abandon that part of the enterprise.

In 1840 there were three potteries in West Plymouth, which was then a center of trade in northern New Hampshire. The first was that of Peter Flanders. As previously noted, Peter was a native of Concord and an apprentice of Daniel Clark at Millville. He settled in West Plymouth after his marriage to Diana Heath in 1807. Ezra S. Stearns, writing in 1906, says of his shop that it "is still by the brookside, and there can be found some of the implements which he used, once smoothly worn by the hand of patient toil, but now corroded by the waste and rust of idleness." The brook mentioned runs just west of the old inn that may still be seen in a dilapidated condition on the main road at West Plymouth. The workshop is still standing, but all evidence of the kiln has disappeared. Peter Flanders' son George was his father's assistant. After 1856 he carried on the pottery and ran a farm until his death in 1869.

A second pottery closely allied to the Boscawen industry was operated by William and John H. Gill, brothers of Jeremiah Burpee's second wife. Both were born in Boscawen — William in 1800 and John nine years later. They were the sons of William and Ruth Hazelton Gill. William removed to Plymouth in 1823, and by 1830 the brothers were plying their trade east of the schoolhouse at West Plymouth. At the present time a gasoline station stands on the site. They carried on this business for seventeen years until William returned to Boscawen. John managed the shop alone for some time, but eventually became a farmer. He lived until 1888 and in 1886 was still listed in the Plymouth directory (in *Gazetteer of Grafton County, N. H.*) as a potter and farmer.

The third pottery belonged to Daniel Dolbear Webster, who probably began his potting career about the time of his marriage in 1817. He lived only until 1832. His business was inherited by William Webster, perhaps a brother, whose name appears in the directory above mentioned as "formerly potter," then living on Highland Street. In the year 1886 John H. Webster was both farmer and proprietor of the potworks. Local residents tell me that the later Websters worked in the

Gill pottery near the schoolhouse, the only shop in town within their memory. The Plymouth potteries were, therefore, in existence from about 1807 to 1887. We cannot doubt that they made great quantities of redware, sufficient to supply all the remote villages in northern New Hampshire. The sugar bowls in Fig. 68 *a* and *d* are characteristic examples of their output.

Redware pieces attributed to Rumney are occasionally found. One of these, a miniature jug labeled "Rumney pottery," is in the collection of the New Hampshire Historical Society at Concord. A muffin cup in the writer's possession was bought with a Rumney history. As it has been impossible to find a record of any pottery in the town, it seems probable that these pieces were made at West Plymouth, a few miles from Rumney.

Northwest of Plymouth, on the Connecticut River, the small town of Orford boasted an earthenware business more than a century ago. This was first called to my attention by an aged relative, who owned an Orford jug said to be more than seventy-five years old when given to her in 1910. The existence of this pottery is verified by Haskel & Smith's *Gazetteer*, which notes its presence in Orford in 1840.

There are vague accounts of several potteries in the region around Lake Winnipesaukee. At Gilford, once a part of Gilmanton, Nathaniel Goodhue was running a shop about 1830. Hurd's *History of Belknap County* says that he had carried on the business for many years and that he got his clay from The Weirs. Goodhue advertised it for sale in the *New Hampshire Patriot and State Gazetteer*, March 1, 1833, describing it as a "large pottery for making earthenware and a good kiln on same." He was apparently succeeded by Charles Stark, who, four years later, "contemplating a removal from Gilford," offered for sale a "shop, kiln, and apparatus for the manufacture of brown ware." *

Cornelius Weygandt, in *The White Hills*, has noted a potter named Bennett in Moultonborough and the existence of a pottery in New Durham, near Alton. In *November Rowen*, the same author describes a quart mug tooled with lines and marked "old Cider" that he found in Meredith. He notes its resemblance to pieces from the Gill pottery. The mug could, however, have been made in Meredith. During the excavation of a cellar under the house of H. B. Twombley on Plymouth Street, setting tiles and a cockspur were unearthed. For several years Mr. Twombley did not know the significance of these curious baked clay objects and he was greatly surprised to learn that his house stood directly over a potter's dump. The circumstance was explained by the fact that the house had been moved from another site to its present location. A perusal of Meredith history reveals that Joshua W. Burpee, eldest son of Jeremiah, lived in Meredith for about nine years preceding his death in 1839. It is more than likely that he was responsible for the waste pile.

Another craftsman of the 1830's, Jeremiah Bean, worked in Bristol. He was a native of the town and was twenty-seven years old when he started his potworks on Hemlock Brook. The business was short-lived, as Bean soon removed to Boston, dying there in 1834.

Farther north, at the foot of Mt. Cardigan, in what must then have been a wilderness, Isaac Lowell from Loudon established a pottery in 1818. Its history was verified by Miss Margaret H. Jewell, who visited the site. This earthenware shop was carried on successfully until 1872 by three generations of the family. Elijah C. Lowell, Isaac's son, worked with his father and continued the business after the

* *N. H. Patriot and State Gazetteer*, February 13, 1837; quoted in *Hands That Built New Hampshire* (W.P.A., 1940).

elder Lowell's death in 1865. Elijah lived only five years thereafter. The pottery went to his son Allen, but by that time the demand for redware had waned, and Allen Lowell closed the shop after two years.

The Lowell pottery was on the road from Canaan to Orange. It stood well back on the property now owned by Roy H. Skinner. A large dump pile over the edge of a ravine gives evidence of the great quantities of ware produced in this remote factory. Water for the shop was conducted from a spring near the Lowell house and the road in pipes made of bored logs. These were found by the Skinners when they bought the place in 1917. A superficial examination of this waste pile in 1944 revealed nothing of the earlier output, which is well under the surface, but a great many fragments of jars, bean pots, and flowerpots of the later period. This concern must have had a fairly wide market, as they found it worth while to advertise in the *New England Business Directory* during the fifties and sixties.

In the New Hampshire Historical Society at Concord are three examples of the work of Elijah C. Lowell, made in 1869 and presented to the museum by Miss Jewell. They are a deep porringer, a cup of the same shape, and a small black jug (Fig. 70), all perhaps reminiscent of the articles turned by Lowell in his youth rather than of the wares produced in 1869.

Reference to another pottery near Canaan appears in *The Canaan Reporter*, July 17, 1942. According to the account, it was over the line in Grafton at Razor Hill near a building called the El-Nathan Home. This house was formerly a tavern run by one Flagg. Flagg's great-great-granddaughter is a resident of Canaan, and I paid her a visit in 1944. She was unable to give me any information beyond the fact that the potter dug clay from the hillside back of the tavern and that his name was not known.

Farthest north of New Hampshire potteries was an earthenware shop in North Conway started by Jethro Furber before 1839. Jethro was probably one of the Concord Furbers and connected with the Millville group, for he was in that section in 1827, when he bought fifteen acres of Peter Whittemore. Six acres of this land, which was all on the north side of the Hopkinton road, was the south end of a lot formerly owned by Joseph F. Stickney and adjoined on the east land of Samuel Fletcher. The other nine acres had been part of the dower of Mary Whittemore. Furber and his wife Eliza conveyed the two pieces to Hiram Dow and Samuel L. Baker, both of Concord, July 6, 1839. His pottery in the mountains was still running in 1856, when he advertised in the *New England Business Directory*.

Besides the potteries for the manufacture of household utensils, there was in East Alton near the Wolfeboro line a factory that made nothing but redware tobacco pipes. This establishment was begun in 1864 by one John Taber, who was not a native of the town. It is quite likely that he was the same Taber who was making pipes in Wells, Maine, a few years earlier. Taber bought land of Enos Rollins and put up a sizeable building near Lake Winnipesaukee. The site may be seen on the north bank of a running stream that enters the lake between Camp Kehonka and the Brook and Bridle Inn. Taber brought with him a crew of about thirty workmen. An elderly resident of the village, Mrs. Carrie B. Carpenter, born in 1858, can remember how they were boarded about among the farmers until quarters were built for them. She recalls the construction of the building and incidents about its operation. When she was fourteen years old — that is, after Taber had run the works for eight years — he moved it to South Wolfeboro on Mink Brook. In Wolfeboro it was not the successful enterprise it had

been in Alton and was abandoned after a few years.

One reason why we do not run across many of these pipes locally is that Taber shipped his product out of the state, sending it down the lake by boat and thence to New York and other points by train. There are, however, enough wasters at the pottery site to show clearly what the pipes were like (Fig. 85). All were cast in molds that were a good step beyond the crude ones of the Wells pipe factory. We found three distinct types: the first, cast in several sizes and in a number of slightly different molds, is covered with little nubs to make it look like a corncob pipe; the second, and rarest, displays a claw or talon gripping a plain bowl; the third is the head of a bearded man, who, we were assured by Mrs. Carpenter, was not Zeus, but General Grant. All of these designs appear in the biscuit stage and also with a brown glaze. It is obvious that they were given two firings. The stem in one of the pipes illustrated was obtained from the factory by Mrs. Carpenter when she was a child. It is like all corncob pipe stems.

CHAPTER SEVENTEEN

Redware Potters of Vermont

Pottery manufacture in Vermont was begun somewhat later than in the seacoast states and its development was different. Since the Vermonters had easier access to supplies of New Jersey clay brought up the Hudson to Troy, they turned to stoneware production at the period when the country potters of New Hampshire and Maine were still working with local clay. Many of the Vermont craftsmen were trained in the busy Albany-Troy area, an early seat of stoneware manufacture. Influenced by contact with business on a large scale, the Vermont potteries, especially those in the western part of the state, became the most important producers in New England of molded Rockingham and yellow wares. The simple and unsophisticated redware of the country potter was almost abandoned for these more standardized products. These were undoubtedly considered a vast improvement in their day, as indeed they were for durability and utility. They were, however, the result of mass production, and as such soon strayed far afield from the feeling of the old folk pottery. This trend brought about the great Bennington works, which for a time competed successfully with the Staffordshire potteries in England. Other attempts in the same direction are to be seen in the wares of Burlington and Fairfax.

A number of Vermont potteries that are known to have made redware are the very ones that later became most prosperous as stoneware manufactories. They nevertheless continued to turn out a certain quantity of earthenware in the form of milk pans and jugs as long as there was any demand for it.

Vermont potting history is notable for the fact that it was dominated by a few enterprising families. The Nortons of Bennington were among the earliest in the field and carried on through successive generations for one hundred years. The Fentons, makers of both redware and stoneware, worked in Dorset, Bennington, and St. Johnsbury, while the numerous Farrars were potters in Fairfax, Middlebury, Burlington, and St. Albans. The Nortons and Fentons came from Connecticut; the Farrars from New Ipswich, New Hampshire.

In the earliest Vermont potteries the background of Essex County is dimly descried. The first recorded clayworker in the Green Mountain state came from Amesbury. He

was Charles Bailey, born August 27, 1744. After finishing his training, he spent brief periods in Harvard and North Brookfield, Massachusetts, going thence at some time after 1772 to Hardwick in far northern Vermont. I have been unable to trace his further history. A pottery was still running in Hardwick in 1840, but it may not have been a successor to the Bailey shop.

The next craftsman in point of time was Moses Bradley, who went from Haverhill, Massachusetts, to Chimney Point, Addison County, in 1790. After a residence of seven years, Bradley, with his family, returned eastward to Windsor, Vermont, remaining there until 1800. In June of that year he started a redware shop in a section of West Woodstock later known as Bradley's Flat. The town had already had a potter for a number of years in the person of one Edson, who had left town just before Bradley's arrival. Bradley bought the house previously owned by Col. Joseph Safford; his shop stood where Aaron Whitney lived in the eighties. It is said that this West Woodstock pottery did a thriving business. Moses Bradley ran it until September 20, 1824, when his son John W. took it over and kept it going a few years longer.

In his *History of Woodstock, Vermont*, written in 1889, Henry Swan Dana describes the delight of the school children of Bradley's Flat in watching proceedings at the potshop. He quotes N. Williams in a brief reminiscence that seems to illustrate the influence exerted on the young by the old-time craftsman:

> I have stood silently by him a great many hours and watched him, while from a lump of clay put upon the wheel he would draw up a structure which would turn out to be a vase, a pitcher or a jug. If a vase, the walls were carried up perpendicularly; if a pitcher, when the sides were carried up, he would at some place on the rim put his thumb on the outside and his finger on the inside and bend down the slope, which would be the pitcher's nose; and if a jug, he would put both hands across the upper part of the vessel and contract it, and around the forefinger of his left hand he would bring up the top of the vessel to form the nose of the jug. I admired to watch this handicraft, but the converting of dull colored bars of lead into a brilliant red powder and then a red glazing—a liquid with which the outsides of the pottery were washed—was a mystery which, in my ignorance of chemistry seemed to savor of witchcraft and necromancy.

Mrs. Mary Grace Canfield of Woodstock is authority for the statement that Bradley's shop was later moved to the easterly end of Woodstock village. She also notes a redware pottery in nearby Quechee.

Captain John Norton, who had attained his rank in the Revolutionary War, is said to have built the first kiln in Bennington in 1793. Norton had gone north from Goshen, Connecticut, some eight years earlier, sojourning for a time at Williamstown. John Spargo, in *The Potters and Potteries of Bennington*, says that Norton spent those eight years working the large farm he had purchased about one mile south of the meetinghouse. This land lay on the road from Pownal to Bennington —the main highway from Massachusetts to Canada. The pottery shop was put up a little to the north of Norton's house, on the site later occupied by the Tudor house. In 1823, when the business was assumed by Norton's sons, Luman and John, Luman Norton moved the building onto part of his own land opposite his dwelling house. This second location is known as the Rockwood farm. Remains of kilns have been found in both places.

Before leaving Connecticut, Captain Norton had married Lucretia Buell, daughter of Captain Jonathan Buell of South End, Goshen, and their first son was eleven years of age when the pottery was started. Luman was soon old enough to learn the trade. In

1796 Norman L. Judd, Mrs. Norton's nephew, also came from South End to work as Captain Norton's apprentice. He was then a lad of fifteen. The beginnings of John Norton's enterprise were relatively small and simple. Up to 1830 and perhaps somewhat later, bricks and red earthenware were made in the Norton pottery from clay dug on the Tudor farm.

Several well authenticated examples of the early redware manufactured at Bennington have survived. One, a small lead-glazed jug ornamented with a crudely swashed design in white slip was made for Mrs. Omindia Gerry in 1798, when she was not quite ten years of age. It was the work of Abel Wadsworth, an employee at the Norton pottery, and it was handed on by Mrs. Gerry to one of his descendants. Another specimen, a handled jar, was owned by Mrs. Peter Ostrander, who died in 1827. A milk pan and vases have also been identified as examples from the Norton redware kiln (see Spargo, Plate II).

Before 1815 the Nortons had added the stoneware kiln that was the basis for their subsequent operations. Since their stoneware is marked with the family name, it is familiar to all collectors, while their redware is practically unknown. It must be remembered, however, that large quantities of ware made from local clay were turned out in this pottery for nearly forty years. A redware pie plate that I purchased in Brandon, Vermont, was always known to its former owners as the "Bennington" plate. With it was a Rockingham ware dish of exactly the same shape.

It has already been noted in the story of the Clark family that Peter Clark, son of the major, was, in 1796, a pioneer settler of Brownington, originally part of Barton, Vermont. He took the freeman's oath there in September 1798, six months before the town was organized, and he was one of the first town officers. Deacon Peter's homestead was on the land that was occupied as a farm by Rev. S. R. Hall and his son in 1877. Clark undoubtedly pursued his craft in the new community, for his brother Daniel, while on a visit in July 1809, bought four hundredweight of red lead from him. The exact date of Peter Clark's return to his native Lyndeboro is not recorded, but it was probably before 1813, when another potter had begun to work in the town. This man, Samuel Ward, is said to have run the *first* pottery in Brownington, but the local historian did not know that Peter Clark was a clayworker. Ward's shop was on what was later the Townsend farm.

One of the first settlers of Poultney, Vermont, was an Essex County man who went there in 1800. He is mentioned by Rev. William Bentley in his famous diary under date of June 14, 1814 (IV, 259):

> Mr. Woodman, formerly of Salem, who has four sisters married in Salem, in town from Poultney, Vermont. He could give us no history. He is a potter & is down to purchase materials for glazing his ware. He is in search of manganese in this quarter. He learnt his trade in Braintree, removed to Connecticut, & thence to Poultney on the river which enters at the south end of Lake Champlain. He tells me that his neighbors are chiefly from Connecticut & from his prejudices I am inclined to believe him.

Samuel Woodman was forty-seven when he started his pottery in Poultney. He carried it on until about 1820, when his son John succeeded him. His shop stood where the bank building was later erected. There is no documentary evidence that he made anything more substantial than "brown earthenware," as noted in the local history. His search for manganese for use in glazing corroborates this tradition. John Spargo says that Woodman made stoneware jugs, and he attributes to him a quart mug of stoneware with dark brown Albany slip, which is in the Bennington Museum.

From 1801 to 1835 Jonathan Fenton and

his sons made earthenware along with stoneware in Dorset. Their story has been reserved for the chapter on stoneware, which was their more notable output.

The Farrars, likewise, were known principally as stoneware potters, except for Caleb, who settled in Middlebury in 1812. He was born in New Ipswich, New Hampshire, and was one of the numerous sons of Rev. Stephen Farrar who sought their fortunes in Vermont. He was thirty-two years old when he started in Middlebury the pottery that he ran for so many years. Farrar was its owner until 1850, when he sold it to James Mitchell. After Mitchell's death it was bought by Nahum Parker, who was probably a connection of the Farrars (Caleb had married Sarah Parker). The site of this establishment has been discovered by the local chapter of the Daughters of the American Revolution on Munger Street.

I have read various statements about the types of ware made at Middlebury. At first, and probably throughout Farrar's tenure, it was merely a redware pottery. Tradition says that white crockery was a Middlebury product. If so, I should be inclined to attribute it to the very late years of the factory. A toby jug of Bennington type with light brown glaze in the Bennington Museum is credited to Middlebury. In view of these developments, the Farrar pottery seems to have grown into a commercial works similar to the one at Bennington, where molds superseded the exclusive use of the wheel. Such of the Middlebury examples as I have seen were redware with a glaze varying in tone from rosy to yellow shades. A greenish-yellow glaze is also said to have been a representative color.

A smaller potshop in East Middlebury has not hitherto been noted. It was run by a man named Carpenter, and stood on the north side of the road through East Middlebury opposite a white schoolhouse. A pitcher that was undoubtedly made in this pottery has a yellow-green glaze.

Although St. Johnsbury made much fine stoneware, the town also supported a redware shop. This was started in 1815 by William Hutchinson, either alone or with Ebenezer Hutchinson, who sold his pottery in North Lyndeboro, New Hampshire, in the spring of that year and removed to St. Johnsbury. Ebenezer was the son of Ebenezer Hutchinson and a native of Lyndeboro. He had a brother William, who was presumably the St. Johnsbury man. Their pottery was apparently still running in 1840, when, according to the Haskel & Smith *Gazetteer*, two shops were in operation at St. Johnsbury. Otherwise, nothing further has transpired about them. Richard W. Fenton and his son, who ran the other works, made redware bowls, milk pans, flowerpots, and such utensils in addition to their stoneware output.

If we take the list of Vermont redware potters in chronological order, the next to appear are Justin and Justus Crafts, twin brothers from Whately, Massachusetts. The name of Justin Crafts occurs in the land records of Berlin in 1823 and 1834. These dates do not correspond to those given by the Whately historian James M. Crafts for their stay there. Crafts says that they went to Berlin about 1816 and remained for ten years. In any event, Justin Crafts bought of Robert Johnson Lot 7 in the sixth range on September 29, 1823. This land he held and improved until 1834, when, on January 7, he sold to Wright Cressey his "farm" near the mill and the bridge over Dog River. This location is not in Berlin village, but lies in the westerly section of the town, near Route 12.

In Addison County, not far north of Middlebury, a small pottery was started in New Haven just before 1830. Its owner, Caleb Wright, a native of the town, was born in 1810. He was making and selling redware while still in his teens and he was married at

the age of twenty-one. At that time he purchased the land where he afterwards built his potshop, south of the New Haven schoolhouse on the old Middlebury-Vergennes Turnpike road. His granddaughter was living in 1926 and was able to verify the pottery site. R. M. Maxwell, who wrote a brief account of this industry in the *Antiquarian* (December 1926), was successful in finding two pans and a straight-sided jar from Wright's kiln. The jar is identical with one in my collection (Fig. 72*a*) that was bought with a Middlebury attribution and is a type not commonly seen in eastern New England. Since attributions are uncertain affairs, my jar may have been made in New Haven. Wright may possibly have been an apprentice of Caleb Farrar at Middlebury and would therefore have fashioned his pots in the same manner.

According to John Spargo, there was a pottery in Corinth, and another in Chester is mentioned by C. B. Adams in his *Geology of Vermont* (*First Report*). He says that bricks and earthenware were made there in 1845. The existence of a potworks in Cavendish came to my attention when Mrs. Earle E. Andrews of Winchester, Massachusetts, acquired a redware jar in which was a slip of paper saying, "Probably made by Chris Webber of Cavendish." A visit to Cavendish resulted in arousing only the faintest memories of pottery making in the town. Fragments dug up on the town poor farm led to surmises that a redware shop had once been in operation there, while some of the townspeople spoke of a potter's living on the main road at the east end of the village.

Redware was no doubt made in some of the other stone potteries. Many unrecorded redware kilns, also, must have existed throughout the state, but, if so, their history has been lost in the greater note of Vermont's stoneware industries.

CHAPTER EIGHTEEN

Vermont Stoneware Potteries

All the principal stoneware potteries of Vermont were established in the first decade of the nineteenth century. The matter of priority is a question. Until we know more about the activities of the Farrars, and especially of Isaac Brown Farrar, who was living in Vermont in 1798, it will be impossible to give a definite answer. It seems likely, however, that the art of making stoneware was introduced into the state by Jonathan Fenton when he settled in Dorset after the failure of his Boston venture.

Much has been written about the Fenton family, which has been so thoroughly investigated by John Spargo and others it would seem as if little could be added to the story. Nevertheless, by excavation in the summer of 1938 and by study of the Dorset town records, I am able to contribute a bit more to the account.

Jonathan Fenton was born in Mansfield, a part of Windham, Connecticut, July 18, 1766. By 1793 he was working in New Haven, where, it is said, Jacob Fenton, to whom he was undoubtedly related, was operating a pottery as early as 1792. The birth records of Fenton's children show that he wandered from one place to another for the next few years trying to establish a pottery business. His unsuccessful endeavor to produce stoneware in Boston has already been described. In 1797 he was in Walpole, New Hampshire, and two years later in East Windsor, Connecticut. At some time after the census was taken in 1800, but before November 1801, he arrived in Dorset. Within five years four other of the Fenton children were born there and the family were permanent fixtures in the town.

It has been assumed by other writers that Fenton settled immediately in East Dorset. There is no record, however, of his owning property in that part of the town until 1810, the year when he purchased the land and homestead that he continued to occupy thereafter.

In the meantime, where was Jonathan Fenton living between 1801 and 1810? This question was settled by our discovery of a traditional pottery in Dorset Hollow. It must be explained that the town lies in two parallel valleys, with ranges of hills running north and south on each side and through the center. In a pocket of the middle range a road

leads upward until it approaches an inaccessible barrier of mountain dividing Dorset on the west from East Dorset on the other side. This is the district known as "Dorset Hollow." Zephine Humphrey, in her *Story of Dorset*, notes the presence of a pottery on the Hollow road and also the local tradition that the Fentons lived there before moving to East Dorset. After some investigation, we located the pottery site near the rushing stream that tumbles down the valley. It may be described as being about two hundred feet west of the first bridge as one drives up the Hollow road and about seventy-five feet in from the highway on the left-hand side, at the very top of an overgrown bank that slopes steeply to the river bed. On this spot we found many fragments of redware and stoneware. The latter was well made and finished. A jar that is undoubtedly an example of Fenton's handiwork may be seen in the Barrows House at Dorset. It was found locally, and its rim corresponds exactly to fragments recovered. Its decoration of an incised fish is pleasing and unusual.

On April 10, 1810, Jonathan Fenton bought a lot of land on the "Town Brook" in East Dorset. The evidences of his activities there during the next twenty-five years we found in a garden bordering the stream that runs under the road from East Dorset to Mt. Tabor. The fragments from this site correspond in every particular to those found in Dorset Hollow and leave no doubt that they were fashioned by the same hand.

Once established in this pleasant village, Fenton procedeed to train his sons in the potter's craft. The elder, Richard Lucas, born in 1797, was soon able to help in the shop. Christopher Webber Fenton, nine years younger, grew up in the midst of pots and shards and the burning of kilns. Father and sons worked together until 1827, when Seth Curtis, husband of Jonathan's daughter Melinda, joined them as an actual or a silent partner. On January 20 of that year, Jonathan, Richard, and Curtis purchased from William Ames thirty-five acres of land in common. Two months later Richard bought a one-half interest in the pottery, which, however, he sold the following October to Curtis, together with his share of the Ames land. This transaction may answer Mrs. Humphrey's question as to why Richard Fenton went in 1828 to Bennington to work for Luman Norton so soon after acquiring an interest in his father's business. From 1827 to 1830 the pottery was run by Fenton and Curtis. In 1830 Richard moved back to East Dorset and with his brother Christopher bought for six hundred dollars Curtis's share in the "Potter's Factory, situated near where Jonathan Fenton now resides." For the next three years the brothers apparently had some kind of a partnership of their own. To this period belongs the handsome jug in the Memorial Library at Dorset marked *R & C Fenton/ Dorset, Vt.* This vessel has been attributed to the Dorset Hollow pottery on the strength of the *Dorset* mark. It is obvious, however, that when the Fentons lived in Dorset, the sons were mere children, and, since they never returned there after 1810, the jug must have been made in East Dorset, in spite of the manner of marking.

The Fenton brothers sold their share in the pottery to their father in May 1833. Christopher Webber Fenton was already married to the daughter of Luman Norton in Bennington and at the time called himself a "merchant." Richard died the following year. By two deeds, dated August 26, 1833, and December 25, 1835, Jonathan Fenton conveyed to Job Cleaveland of Hebron, New York, one half of the pottery and two thirds of his remaining land, reserving for himself only the westerly half of his dwelling house and the other half of the potworks. It is not clear whether Cleaveland was a potter, although his purchase of part of the Fenton establish-

ment would seem to indicate that he was. Nor is it known how much longer after 1835 Fenton continued to pursue his trade. He lived to be eighty-two years old. In his last year, 1848, he wrote two long "poems"; one in memory of his son Richard and dedicated to Richard's two little girls, the other in praise of Bennington and its potteries. In the second series of verses he says:

I have fifty-five children and grandchildren
great and small
And not one fool among them all.
I say myself I am no poet
And by reading this you will know it.

By this it appears that Jonathan had a sense of humor. That he was an excellent craftsman is attested by the pieces bearing his mark. As a business man he was not so fortunate. The property for which he paid his sons one thousand dollars in May 1833, he sold in August for six hundred dollars. At the age of sixty-nine he may have found it impossible to run the shop alone and thus have been forced to take this course.

It is unlikely that Bennington stoneware was made before Fenton built his first kiln in Dorset Hollow. As previously noted, John Norton of Bennington began his career as a redware potter, and the exact date when he first fired a stoneware kiln is unknown. The Harwood diary quoted by Spargo shows that in 1810 he was using clay brought from Troy. An entry dated October 23 says: "This morning father sent off 44 bushels of wheat to Troy by three waggons — two of which belong to Capt. Norton. — They carry wheat for father and he brings back a load of clay for them — or at least causes it to be bro't by Ira who went with his team."

Norton's redware was made of local clay, and the only different materials he needed were either white clay for slip decorating or New Jersey clay for stoneware. White clay was not purchased by the wagon load, but by the hundredweight. Such a quantity, therefore, indicates that the clay brought from Troy was the kind used for stoneware by all New England potters. It has been assumed that Norton used Bennington clay entirely, or, at least, that he did up to a certain time. But it would have been impossible to produce good stoneware from Bennington clay, which is not sufficiently refractory to be used alone for that purpose. Neither could Norton have made stoneware from any clay dug around Troy. The only stoneware clay beds in New York State are on Long Island and on Staten Island. It is clear that the clay purchased at Troy was brought up the Hudson River on barges and that Troy was merely a convenient distribution point for potters who needed it. That Norton used an admixture of native clay is probable, however, for the addition of a certain proportion of redware clay reduced expense. This procedure caused the buff color that so often resulted.

Harwood mentions in his diary under date of January 6, 1815, that he had written to Norman Judd, then living in Rome, New York, that Captain Norton and Luman "were making ware of both kinds, stone and clay, very fast." He makes frequent references to the setting of the stoneware kiln, to buying stoneware, and to seeing John Norton throwing salt into the kiln. Thanks to his daily entries the whole history of the Norton pottery up to 1837 is made clear. From him we learn that Captain Norton and his sons dissolved partnership in the spring of 1823, or, rather, Norton gave the business over to Luman and John, while he coördinated his various occupations as farmer, distiller, blacksmith, and storekeeper with theirs as potters. Persons owing the sons for earthenware paid Captain Norton with cider; others indebted to him for goods settled their accounts by services to the pottery. From 1823 to 1827 the firm

was known as *L. Norton & Company*, and this was the first mark used.

Before 1828 Luman Norton became sole owner of the pottery. In that year old Captain Norton died, and John, Jr., moved down to East Bennington on some land that had been his father's. For the next five years Luman Norton ran the business alone in the old building that had been moved to the lot opposite his dwelling house. He made both redware and stoneware and used the mark *L. Norton.* A description of the pottery in the *Bennington Business Directory* for 1831, published in the *Vermont Gazette* of January 11, calls it a "Stone Ware Manufactory" and says that it employed twelve hands. Harwood's notes show that the ware was sent off in wagons to Troy and Berlin, New York, to Lenox Furnace, Massachusetts, to Chesterfield, New Hampshire, to Woodstock, Vermont, and other points. The Norton pottery was already a relatively important concern. The ware was the usual assortment of jugs, preserve and butter pots, crocks, and churns. One interesting item mentioned by Harwood is a six-gallon pot for potting cheese. Among the men who worked for Luman Norton at this time turning ware were Joseph F. Winship, who later was employed for many years at the Risley pottery in Norwich Connecticut. Bliss Sibley was another of the employees.

In 1833 the works was removed to what was later Pottery Street in East Bennington. The new building was much larger and more convenient than the old one built by the Captain, and Luman Norton was able to expand the enterprise. Extra workmen were hired and a greater quantity of ware produced. Luman Norton, who by now had attained the status of judge, left the management more and more to his son Julius, while he withdrew to the counting room. The firm name, however, was L. Norton & Company until the Judge's retirement in the late thirties. Julius then became sole proprietor of the "Bennington Stone Ware Factory."

A bill under the heading "Julius Norton," dated February 11, 1840, charges D. Whittemore, the keeper of a general store in Fitzwilliam, New Hampshire, with the following articles: two- and three-gallon pots; jugs of four sizes; three- and four-gallon churns, butter pots of one-, two-, or four-gallon capacity; cake pots, jars, flowerpots, and fancy pitchers.

Julius Norton advertised these same wares and others in the *State Banner*, February 27, 1841:

BENNINGTON STONE WARE FACTORY

Julius Norton Manufactures and keeps constantly for sale at his factory in Bennington East Village, Vt., a large assortment of STONE WARE, consisting of Butter, Cake, Pickle, Preserve and Oyster Pots, Jugs, Churns, Beer & Blacking Bottles, Jars, Plain and Fancy Pitchers, Ink Stands, Earthen Milkpans, Stove Tubes, Kegs, Mugs, Flower Pots, &c. &c.

Also Patented Firebrick (The best in the world) at $50 per thousand.

Orders from Merchants faithfully executed and ware forwarded on the shortest notice.

Bennington, East Village, Feb. 27, 1841.

It is entirely a matter of conjecture as to whether the inkstands and fancy pitchers mentioned here were anything more than the regular types put out by stoneware potters. The Farrars and others also advertised inkstands. Mr. Spargo shows an illustration of an elaborately molded inkwell with a modeled dog that was handed down in the Norton family and suggests that Julius Norton was selling such stands commercially. It is far more likely that the dog inkwell was a presentation piece and therefore cherished by Norton's descendants. As to the pitchers, no molded or Rockingham pitcher with Norton's mark is known, although he made and marked them with the firm name when he was associated with Fenton. It is possible that

the word "fancy" here refers to the customary blue slip decoration.

The firebrick advertised was the invention of Christopher Webber Fenton, patented by him in 1837. He was living in Bennington at that time, and was undoubtedly connected with the pottery — the business of his wife's family — in some capacity. In his patent he claimed: "The using and applying the aforesaid substances known under the name of 'kaolin' or 'porcelain clay' and fine granular quartz, being a species of white sand or sandstone frequently used in the manufacture of glass, in the manufacturing of fire-bricks, which fire-bricks are capable of resisting an intense heat, and the composing of fire-bricks of these substances in any proportion, be it in equal or unequal parts." This part of the business was conducted in a separate building erected in May 1837 and mentioned by Hiram Harwood as a "Large low building in forwardness for drying newly invented firebricks — erected N. [near] old works." This manufacture was still being carried on in the late fifties.

Late in 1842 or early in January 1843 (see below), Julius Norton formed a partnership with his brother-in-law Christopher Webber Fenton that lasted until November 1847, when it was dissolved by mutual consent. The association involved Norton in a series of ventures in making new types of ware. These ideas almost certainly originated in the fertile brain of Fenton, who eventually carried them to completion, while Norton went back to the stoneware with which he was familiar. In the early days of the partnership, the stoneware business went on as usual. A bill headed "Norton & Fenton" and dated January 20, 1843, itemizes churns, butter pots, and flowerpots. In fact, Norton & Fenton never seem to have advertised any other kind of ware. Before the end of the year, however, an English potter had arrived upon the scene, and experiments in making porcelain were under way. This story and the account of Fenton's subsequent achievements belong to another chapter. In connection with Norton & Fenton it is only necessary to note that their mark appears on several types of large molded pitchers of buff stoneware with plain Rockingham glaze and that these pieces are highly valued as examples of the earliest ware of this kind to be made in New England (Fig. 114).

The stoneware factory was burned to the ground on June 6, 1845, and had to be rebuilt during the summer. A brick structure 114 feet by 92 feet, in the form of a hollow square, was erected and provided with three kilns and all the known improvements of the time. The north wing was reserved for Fenton's experiments in porcelain making; the remainder of the plant was devoted to the manufacture of stoneware. After the dissolution of the partnership, Fenton leased this wing for his own business and worked there until he was able in 1850 to put up a building of his own. The Norton pottery continued in its same routine, following a path from which it did not deviate in the next forty years. As Julius Norton announced in the *Vermont Gazette*, "The business of the late firm is continued by the subscriber at the old stand."

It is not always understood that during the fifties, at least, there were these two distinct potteries in Bennington, and that the Rockingham figures, tobies, and pitchers, and the Parian ware associated with the name of Bennington were produced in Fenton's works in an establishment entirely separate from the one where the familiar gray stoneware was made.

After 1850 Julius Norton and his cousin Edward, son of John Norton, Jr., managed the stoneware factory as J. & E. Norton. The pottery of this period is mentioned in Zadock Thompson's *History of Vermont* as "a stone and earthen ware factory, employing from

12 to 15 hands." A price list dated November 25, 1852, includes jugs, pots, covered jars, and butter pots in half a dozen sizes, besides pots for pudding, bean pots, churns, soap dishes, beer bottles, spittoons, pitchers of four sizes, quart and pint mugs, fountain and common inkstands, water fountains and kegs, flowerpots, plain and fancy, and stove tubes. Undoubtedly some of these objects, such as pitchers, mugs, and soap dishes, were glazed with dark brown Albany slip, while the vessels for storage were the common gray or buff stoneware embellished with birds or flowers in characteristic fashion. Another list, of 1856, presents open and covered cream pots, milk pots, and covered pots for butter, cake, or preserves. This sheet is illustrated with small cuts that leave no doubt in the mind of the customer concerning the gaiety of the decoration that he might expect to find on his kitchen ware.

Two interesting jars of this period, decorated, one with a deer, the other with a house, may be seen in Spargo's *The Potters and Potteries of Bennington*, plate IV. The deer design should be compared with that on the Charlestown jar shown in Fig. 101*b*. The same decorator almost certainly did them both. He was also no doubt responsible for the astounding animals on the water cooler in Fig. 106. A three-gallon preserve jar of this type sold at wholesale for seven dollars a dozen, while the two-gallon size brought five dollars. Stoneware crocks were not the cheap things offered by the redware potters.

The mark *J. & E. Norton & Co.* belongs to the years 1859–1861 and was used after young Luman Preston Norton was admitted to the firm. The style was again changed upon the death of Julius Norton. A large proportion of surviving Bennington stoneware was produced during the next twenty years. The mark *E. & L. P. Norton* is perhaps the one most frequently encountered, and many of the most strikingly decorated pieces were turned out under the management of these two partners. They were so successful in their business that they were able to survive a fire in March 1874, which nearly destroyed their building, tools, and stock. This was a great disaster since they were almost entirely unprotected by insurance. Nevertheless, they rebuilt the works and were again in operation by the end of the summer.

The stoneware of E. & L. P. Norton was widely distributed throughout New England and New York State, and even as far as Canada and New Jersey, by means of peddlers' wagons that sold the pottery to general stores and other traders. As the quality of the output assured its durability and its popularity, the number of pieces still in existence exceeds that from any other manufactory.

Luman Norton died in 1881, and for two years the firm was known simply as E. Norton. C. W. Thatcher acquired a half share in the business in 1883. He was the only person outside the Norton family ever to have an interest in the pottery, and his name does not appear in marks, except as *Co.* Edward Norton died two years after Thatcher's advent, leaving his part ownership to his son Edward Lincoln Norton, of the fourth generation from Captain John. A large part of the business in the remaining years consisted of selling wares from other sources. Dealing thus at wholesale was more profitable than manufacturing stoneware in New England in competition with Ohio concerns. When the Nortons celebrated their one-hundredth anniversary in 1893, only enough pots were being burned to make it possible to say that the pottery had rounded out a century. After the untimely death of young Norton at the age of twenty-nine in the following year, the works were closed.

Those who are interested in the personalities of the craftsmen who devoted their lives to the making of this homely but sturdy ware will find the account of the Nortons in John

Bennington Stone-Ware Pottery.

Bennington, Vt., June 26 1856

Mr [illegible] Whitehall N Y

JULIUS NORTON,
EDWARD NORTON.

Bought of J. & E. NORTON,

MANUFACTURERS OF EVERY DESCRIPTION OF STONE-WARE.

JUGS.	Per Dozen.	$	Cts.
Doz. 4 Gallon,	$8 00		
" 3 "	6 50		
" 2 "	4 50		
" 1½ "	3 75		
" 1 "	3 00		
2 " ½ "	2 00	6	
1 1/3 " ¼ "	1 00	2.66	
1 " 1-8 "	0 75	1	
OPEN CREAM POTS.			
Doz. 6 Gallon,	12 00		
" 5 "	10 00		
" 4 "	8 00		
" 3 "	6 50		
" 2 "	4 50		
" 1½ "	3 75		
" 1 "	3 00		
" ½ "	2 00		
COVERED CREAM POTS.			
Doz. 4 Gallon,	10 00		
" 3 "	8 00		
" 2 "	6 00		
" 1½ "	5 00		
" 1 "	4 00		
CHURNS.			
Doz. 6 Gallon,	12 00		
" 5 "	10 00		
" 4 "	8 00		
" 3 "	7 00		
" 2 "	5 00		
COVERED PRESERVE JARS.			
Doz. 4 Gallon,	8 00		
" 3 "	7 00		
" 2 "	5 00		
" 1½ "	4 25		
" 1 "	3 50		
" ½ "	2 00		
" ¼ "	1 50		
MILK POTS.			
Doz. 2 Gallon,	4 50		
" 1½ "	3 75		
" 1 "	3 00		
PUDDING POTS, Doz. 1 Gallon,	3 00		
" ½ "	2 00		
BEAN POTS, " 1 "	3 00		
" ½ "	2 00	9.66	

BUTTER POTS COVERED.	Per Dozen	$ 9	Cts. 66
Doz. 6 Gallon,	$15 00		
" 5 "	12 00		
" 4 "	10 00		
" 3 "	8 00		
" 2 "	6 00		
" 1½ "	5 00		
" 1 "	4 00		
" ½ "	3 00		
COVERED CAKE POTS.			
Doz. 4 Gallon,	10 00		
" 3 "	8 00		
" 2 "	6 00		
" 1 "	4 00		
PITCHERS.			
Doz. 2 Gallon,	4 50		
" 1½ "	3 75		
" 1 "	3 00		
" ½ "	2 00		
" ¼ "	1 25		
FLOWER POTS.			
Doz. 4 Gallon,	9 00		
" 3 "	7 00		
" 2 "	5 00		
" 1 "	3 00		
" ½ "	2 00		
" ¼ "	1 25		
" 1-8 "	1 00		
STOVE TUBES, Doz 1st size,	6 50		
" 2d "	4 50		
" 3d "	3 00		
CHAMBERS.			
Doz 1st size,	2 50		
" 2d "	2 00		
SPITTOONS, Doz. 1st size,	6 00		
" 2d "	4 00		
Doz. Fountain Ink Stands,	2 00		
Common,	1 00		
Small,	0 50		
Beer Bottles, per doz.	1 00		
Quart Mugs, " "	1 25		
Pint Mugs, " "	0 75		
SOAP DISHES, "	2 00		
WATER KEGS, per gallon.	35 1-2		

Deduct 38⅓ pr cent for cash — $9.66 / 3.54 / 6.12

Rec'd Whitehall June 26/56 Six dollars & Twelve cents in full for above Bill

J & E Norton
pr C. H. Wilcox

Bill of J. & E. Norton, Bennington, Vt., June 26, 1856.

Spargo's book entertaining reading. From the data assembled by him we learn that the men of each generation in the family were educated gentlemen. Captain Norton was a lover of books and music, a churchman, and a patriot. His son Luman was a man of exceptional culture, who entertained his friends and his family by quoting and reading aloud long passages from Homer, Shakespeare, and Milton. He was interested in all public affairs; became a major in the army, and then a judge. Like his father, he enjoyed playing the flute, although he was excelled in this accomplishment by his son Julius, who was the most artistic, as well as the most reserved, member of the Norton family. Each generation of this remarkable family was educated in the old Bennington Academy, where they were inspired with a love for the arts and sciences in a manner that has few parallels today.

The Farrars, as previously noted, came from New Ipswich, New Hampshire. Isaac Brown Farrar, son of Rev. Stephen, was born March 27, 1771. He was in Enosburgh, Vermont, in 1798. Farrar was the first clerk of the town and his daughter the first white child born there. In what year he settled in Fairfax I have not learned. Neither have I been able to discover when he began to make stoneware. That he did do so would appear from a jar in the Brooklyn Museum marked *I. B. Farrar & Sons*, except for the fact that Farrar had a son Isaac Brown, who might have made it. The younger Isaac married his cousin Eveline, daughter of Caleb Farrar of Middlebury; the connection suggests that he followed the family trade. If the elder Brown is indicated by the mark, the jar could hardly have been made before 1815, as the sons would not have been old enough until then. There is some uncertainty as to the names of the other sons. Ebenezer Lawrence and Stephen are recorded, and George W. was probably their brother. The initials J. H., used in 1840, may stand for another of Isaac's boys.

Nothing definite is known about the Farrars and their wares until after the death of "Brown" Farrar in 1838. The only notice of the pottery occurs in the diary of Hiram Harwood of Bennington, who notes that Jason Merrill, a potter, aged twenty-five, with his wife and child, had stopped at Bennington and "intended to go to Fairfax to work for a 'gentleman potter.'" In 1840 George W. and J. H. Farrar were running the Fairfax business. A bill and price list dated August 26 of that year and headed "Vermont Stone Ware" is now in my possession. Itemized therein are handled pots from one to five gallons, costing three to ten dollars a dozen; covered butter pots (crocks), from one to four gallons, four to ten dollars per dozen; churns, from two to five gallons, four to ten dollars per dozen; sweetmeat jars, which were small straight-sided pots with narrow mouths, from one quart to three gallons, at one to seven dollars per dozen; jugs from one quart to four gallons, one to eight dollars per dozen; flowerpots of several sizes (with attached saucers), beer bottles holding three quarts, fountain and common inkstands, and water fountains (coolers), which were sold at twenty-five cents per gallon of capacity.

Ebenezer Lawrence Farrar did business under his own name and also in partnership with C. W. Farrar.* In 1852, and possibly long before, he was in Burlington, where he built a pottery works for the firm of Nichols & Alford. The marks *E. L. Farrar/ Fairfax, Vt.* and *E. L. Farrar* without place name occur. It is recorded that Eben Farrar and his brother Stephen died in the burning of a steamboat on the St. Lawrence River. The other members of the family had left town before 1871.

* Harold G. Rugg, *Antiques* (August 1925). This is probably a misreading for *G.W.*

Paid Aug. 26. 1840 —

VERMONT STONE WARE.

Mr. Elm Carter Jr

Bo't of G. W. & J. H. FARRAR.

		Dolls.	Cts.	
	5 Gall. Stone Pots. per Doz.	10	00	
3	4 " " "	8	"	2.00
6	3 " " "	6	"	3.00
6	2 " " "	4	"	2.00
	1 " " "	3	"	
3	4 Gall. Butter do.	10	"	2.50
	3 " " "	8	"	
	2 " " "	6	"	
	1 " " "	4	"	
	5 Gall. Churns.	10	00	
3	4 " "	8	"	2.00
3	3 " "	6	"	1.50
	2 " "	4	"	
	3 Do. Sweet-meat Jars	7	00	
	2 " "	5	"	
	1 " "	3	33	
	1-2 " "	2	00	
	1-4 " "	1	"	
	4 Do. Jugs	8	00	
	3 " "	6	"	
	2 " "	4	"	2.00
	1 " "	3	"	4.50
24	1-2 " "	2	"	4.00
12	1-4 " "	1	"	1.00
	2 do. Flower Pots.	4	00	
	1 " " "	3	"	
	1-2 " " "	2	"	
	1-4 " " "	1	"	
	3-4 Beer Bottles.	1	00	
	Fountain Inkstands.	1	"	
	Common do.		75	
	Water Fountains 25 Cts per Gall.			24.50

Dis. 12 pr. ct off — — — 3.06

$21.44

Rec'd payment Geo W & J H Farrar

Bill of George W. and J. H. Farrar, Fairfax, Vt., August 26, 1840.

Another Farrar whose given name has not come to light was in partnership with one Stearns in 1851 and 1852. He may have been the son of E. L. Farrar who, with a brother, made earthenware in North Fairfax for a number of years. The marks *A. S. Stearns* and *Farrar & Stearns* are noted by Spargo. He says they made stoneware. Lewis & Cady were also stoneware manufacturers, whose names appear in the *New England Business Directory* of 1856. Mr. Spargo gives the name Bostwick in conjunction with the other two.

That there were three stoneware potteries in Fairfax in 1859 is affirmed by A. J. Coolidge and J. B. Mansfield in their *History and Description of New England*. They were apparently the E. L. Farrar concern, Farrar & Stearns, and Lewis & Cady. A town that has figured so prominently in Vermont's potting history deserves a more detailed account than I am able here to give. Inasmuch as the later Fairfax potters are reputed to have made flint-enameled ware, the subject is one that is worthy of further investigation.

The stoneware of Burlington is almost as widely known as that of Bennington, as it was widely distributed, especially in Vermont and New Hampshire. The Nichols & Alford pottery built by E. L. Farrar got into operation in 1854, with the intention of producing in addition to common stoneware more ornate articles in Bennington style. As an initial demonstration the firm put out a hound-handled pitcher marked *Nichols & Alford/ Manufacturers/ 1854/ Burlington, Vt.* This was given a rather ordinary Rockingham glaze, as were a great many other vessels, both useful and ornamental, that were made by this firm. It has been said that many pitchers, mugs, book flasks, vases, and other objects imitated Bennington forms so closely that even expert collectors are deceived by the similarity. This pottery stood on the south side of Pearl Street between St. Paul's and Church Streets.

In 1856 the company was Nichols & Boynton, but at some time before 1860 it was taken over by H. N. Ballard, whose name appears on a billhead. In 1856 and 1860 the firm O. L. & A. K. Ballard is listed in the *New England Business Directory*. Whether they ran a separate pottery at that time or whether all three Ballards were members of the Ballard & Brothers company whose imprint is found on Rockingham and stoneware is uncertain. Local history records that the brothers enlarged the original Pearl Street works. A cookie jar marked *Ballard & Brothers/ Burlington, Vt.* is illustrated in Fig. 122*a*. It is of buff stoneware with a light brown Rockingham glaze. By the beginning of 1867, O. L. Ballard was out of the concern, either by death or retirement, and A. K. Ballard ran the pottery alone until after 1872, when it passed into the hands of F. Woodworth. In 1867 the Ballards manufactured annually fifteen hundred dollars' worth of ware of all types. Woodworth was later succeeded by H. E. Sulls, who closed the works in 1895.

A bill and price list headed "A. K. Ballard" and dated September 1869 is shown here. The items include straight-sided jugs, molasses jugs with "tunnel tops," covered pots for cream, butter, and cake, preserve jars with covers, tomato or fruit jars, churns and covers, flowerpots, plain pitchers, pudding pots, bean pots, water kegs, beer bottles, stove pipe safes, and chambers, all of stoneware. In Rockingham ware four objects are illustrated: pitchers from one quart to one gallon, fancy flower vases or urns of one-gallon or half-gallon capacity, teapots of three sizes, and spittoons of five sizes. These Rockingham pieces were all molded with relief decoration.

The Fenton family figured in another chapter of Vermont's potting history when Richard Webber Fenton, brother of Jonathan, founded a pottery in St. Johnsbury in 1808. Fenton went to the Vermont town

FAIRFAX STONE WARE POTTERY.

Danville Apl 28 1851

M. N. Bradley & Co

Bought of FARRAR & STEARNS,

Manufacturers and Wholesale and Retail Dealers in STONE WARE, at Fairfax, Vt.

	Doz.	5	gallon	CREAM POTS,	$10,00	
	"	4	"	do do	8,00	
	"	3	"	do do	6,00	
	"	2	"	do do	4,00	
	"	1	"	do do	3,00	
58 ¼	Doz.	4	gallon	COVERED CREAM POTS,	9,00	2 33
31 ⅙	"	3	"	do do do	7,00	1 25
31 ¼	"	2	"	do do do	5,00	1 25
22 ⅙	"	1	"	do do do	3,50	58
	Doz.	6	gallon	BUTTER POTS AND COVERS,	15,00	
	"	5	"	do do do	12,00	
62½ ½	"	4	"	do do do	10,00	5 00
50 ⅓	"	3	"	do do do	8,00	2 67
38 1/12	"	2	"	do do do	6,00	50
¼	"	1	"	do do do	4,00	1 00
	Doz.	4	gallon	CAKE POTS AND COVERS,	10,00	
	"	3	"	do do	8,00	
	"	2	"	do do	6,00	
	"	1	"	do do	4.00	
	Doz.	4	gallon	JUGS,	8,00	
	"	3	"	do	6,00	
25 ¼	"	2	"	do	4,00	1 00
19 ¼	"	1	"	do	3,00	75
12½ ½	"	½	"	do	2,00	1 00
	"	¼	"	do	1,00	
	Doz.	4	gallon	PRESERVE JARS,	8,50	
	"	3	"	do do	7,00	
	"	2	"	do do	4,50	
20 1/12	"	1	"	do do	3,25	27
12½ ¼	"	½	"	do do	2,00	50
	"	¼	"	do do	1,25	
	Doz.	5	gallon	CHURNS,	10,00	
	"	4	"	do	8.00	
	"	3	"	do	6,00	
	"	2	"	do	4,00	
	Doz.	4	gallon	FLOWER POTS,	9,00	
	"	3	"	do do	7,00	
	"	2	"	do do	5,00	
	"	1	"	do do	3,00	
	"	½	"	do do	2,00	
	"	¼	"	do do	1,25	
	"	⅛	"	do do	75	
	Doz.	1	gallon	FANCY PITCHERS,	6,00	
	"	½	"	do do	4,50	
	Doz.	1	gallon	PLAIN PITCHERS,	3,00	
	"	½	"	do do	2,00	
	"	¼	"	do do	1,25	
	Doz.			FANCY SPITTOONS,	4,50	
	Doz.	No. 1		STOVE PIPE SAFES,	4,00	
	"	" 2		do do do	3,00	
				WATER FOUNTAINS, per gallon,	25	

Beer Bottles, Snuff Jars, Ink Stands, and a variety of other Ware.

	18 10
25 prct off	4 52
	13 58

Recd payt S. F. G. Goss Agent

Bill of Farrar & Stearns, Fairfax, Vt., April 28, 1851.

from New Haven, where his brother and Jacob Fenton were working before 1800. Richard Webber's name appears on the St. Johnsbury town records as early as 1804. Local history says that his first kiln was built four years later. The St. Johnsbury pottery made both redware and stoneware, but, as Richard Webber Fenton had been trained as a stoneware potter, it is probable that he had a kiln for that purpose from the start.

After a time Fenton's son, Leander W., helped his father in the pottery and eventually ran the business in his own name. The marks *L. W. Fenton* or *Fenton & Hancock* with the place name are frequently seen on St. Johnsbury stoneware. A jug in my collection (Fig. 107*c*) also bears the date *1852* after the *Fenton & Hancock* mark. This establishes Hancock's entry into the firm as occurring after the death of old General Fenton and before the period when Leander Fenton ran the pottery alone. Hancock was probably Frederick, son of John. His father came to America from England in 1828 and Frederick followed a year later. He served an apprenticeship in the stoneware pottery of Israel Seymour in Troy, New York. In 1839 he went to Bennington, where, with the exception of the year 1840, spent with his father in Louisville, Kentucky, he remained to become an employee in the United States Pottery. Young Hancock married Charlotte Anne Ames, a niece of Christopher Webber Fenton. In 1858 Hancock went to Worcester, Massachusetts, as a partner of Franklin B. Norton.

During the half century from 1808 to 1859 Richard Fenton and his successors made all the usual redware and stoneware articles and some that were unusual. Jugs, jars, bowls, bottles, flowerpots, and milk pans were among the ordinary ware. A stoneware list of the late fifties, when the younger Fenton was running the works, is owned by Mrs. W. W. Husband of St. Johnsbury, a great-granddaughter of Leander W. Fenton. It itemizes:

Jugs, eight sizes, 1 pint to 4 gallons, $.75 to $8.50 per dozen

Pots, six sizes, 2 quarts to 4 gallons, $1.75 to $8.00

Churns, five sizes, 2 gallons to 6 gallons, $4.50 to $12.00

Jars — Covered, seven sizes, 1 quart to 4 gallons, $1.50 to $8.50

Pudding Pots, 2 quarts and 1 gallon, $1.75 and $3.00

Beer Bottles, 1 quart, $1.00

Spittoons, 1st and 2d sizes, $4.00 and $6.00

Butter Pots, eight sizes, 2 quarts to 6 gallons, $3.00 to $15.00

Flower Pots, five sizes, 1 pint to 2 gallons, $1.00 to $4.50

Fancy do., three sizes, 2 quarts to 2 gallons, $3.50 to $7.50

Pitchers, four sizes, 1 quart to 2 gallons, $1.00 to $4.50

Soft Soap Dishes, $1.50

Stove Tubes, 1st, 2d and 3d sizes, $3.00 to $6.50

Chambers, 1st and 2d sizes, $1.50 and $2.00

Butter Boxes, four sizes, 3 gallons to 6 gallons, $6.00 to $12.00

Boston Butter Pots, four sizes, 1 gallon to 4 gallons, $3.25 to $9.25

Bean Pots, 2 quarts and 1 gallon, $2.00 and $3.00

Milk Basins, 1st and 2d sizes, $1.50 and $2.50

Mugs, 1 quart, $1.00

Water Fountains, Per gallon $.25

Do. urn-shaped, ornamented, Per gallon, $1.00

Among the containers last mentioned is one of the handsomest pieces of New England stoneware. It is an urn-shaped water cooler with applied relief decoration and blue slip design, the work of Franklin Wight. A similar piece made at Ashfield and marked with Wight's initials, has been described in connection with the Hastings & Belding pottery. The St. Johnsbury cooler is perhaps the better proportioned of the two. It is marked *L. W. Fenton/ St. Johnsbury, Vt.* As the cobalt design on these pieces bears a close resemblance to painting on fragments found

Burlington, Vt., Sep 7 1869

J. C. Bradley Danville N.H.

Bought of A. K. BALLARD,

MANUFACTURER OF EVERY DESCRIPTION OF

STONE AND ROCKINGHAM WARE.

Billhead showing pottery of A. K. Ballard, Burlington, Vt., September 1869.

at Whately and Ashfield, it may have been done by Eleazer Orcutt, who worked at St. Johnsbury for a time. Another Whately potter, Edward Alonzo Crafts, son of Thomas, was employed at St. Johnsbury in 1851 and for a time thereafter. These craftsmen migrated to northern Vermont after the closing of the Whately and Ashfield potteries.

The "St. Johnsbury Stone Ware Pottery" burned to the ground in November 1859, and the business was never revived. As late as 1914 Edward T. Fairbanks spoke of it as "an old-time landmark with low red buildings west of the river half a mile south of the Centre Village." Its water power was supplied from a nearby brook. Fragments have been recovered by local residents from this site.

Two other concerns may be briefly noted. The firm of Boynton & Farrar was making stoneware and Rockingham in St. Albans in 1860. It seems rather likely that they were the same Boynton and the same Farrar who were in Burlington in the 1850's. I have seen a jar marked *Boynton* in half-inch letters and another marked *J. Boynton*, but cannot ascertain whether the marks were used in Burlington or elsewhere.

Mrs. Mary Grace Canfield of Woodstock, Vermont, has discovered the existence of a stoneware pottery in South Woodstock and has learned that the potter's name was MacKenzie. The remains of his abandoned kiln were torn down by a summer resident some twenty-five or thirty years ago. It had then been unused for years. The photograph of a covered preserve jar with blue decoration marked *Div. No. 288/ South Woodstock, Vt.* appears in Mrs. Canfield's *The Valley of the Kedron*.

Stoneware stamped with the names of firms in Bradford, Brandon, and Wallingford are known. The Brandon mark *Simons & Osgood* I have eliminated, since they were

merely a business house. The Bradford stoneware I have not seen and can say only that there is a tradition that a pottery once existed there. A really noble jug with vertical handles at right angles to the body bears the mark *S. E. Leonard/ Wallingford, Vt.* This is owned by Mrs. Rosamund Niles Moulton, in whose family it descended. From the *Leonard Genealogy*, by Manning Leonard, I have learned that Seth E. Leonard was born in Ware, Massachusetts in 1785. He went to Wallingford in the early nineteenth century. He is called a blacksmith and hotelkeeper, but not a potter. However, his stamp is so similar to the marks of stoneware makers, I am almost inclined to include him among them. The jug resembles the work of some of the early Hartford men.

CHAPTER NINETEEN

Early Maine Potteries

The story of the potting industry in Maine is principally an account of small redware establishments. More than fifty of these are known in nearly as many different towns. Redware was well suited to the needs and tastes of settlements that were still in the pioneer stage in the nineteenth century, and it was in demand long after its manufacture had virtually ceased in Massachusetts. Stoneware was produced in but three places and not until towards the middle of the century. Distance from the clay was a deterrent to the establishment of many potteries of this type.

Maine was a part of Massachusetts until it was admitted to the Union as a separate state in 1820. Previous to 1800, except for the coastal towns, it was largely a wilderness, and several of its earliest potteries were started in new little communities not far from the coast.

One of the first earthenware shops in Maine was in Hallowell. It belonged to Samuel Norcross and his sons, Samuel and Philip, ancestors of mine. Norcross had lived in Newton and Cambridge. Bond's *Watertown* says that he was a brickmaker in Cambridge in 1770, although land records refer to him there only as "yeoman." Before the Revolution he had made an agreement with Dr. Sylvester Gardiner to settle in Gardinerstown, Maine (then Pittston), if Gardiner would give him and each of his sons one hundred acres of land. Since Gardiner was a Tory and his land was confiscated, this contract could not be fulfilled. In 1776, however, Samuel Norcross succeeded in buying his hundred acres from Captain Nathaniel Berry; whereupon, he and his sons were entered on the list of thirty-one petitioners to be incorporated two years later as Gardinerstown. This land was later part of Hallowell, south of Augusta.

The Hallowell pottery was a family enterprise and was assessed for taxes as early as 1784. In 1792 it was run by Samuel, Jr., and Philip Norcross. Their brickyard, earthenware kiln, and lime kiln stood just south of the present railroad crossing at the north end of Water Street. This was a convenient location for them to receive materials brought up the Kennebec by boat and for the operation of their ferry across the river, which they ran for many years. Their brother Josiah was also a potter; he settled in Farmington in the early 1800's. Samuel Norcross's house was on the site where the home of R. H. Gardiner stood in 1852.

One other Hallowell potter is recorded in the person of Edmund Dane, father of a family of ten, who lived on Winthrop Street in a house that was occupied some fifty years ago by Justin E. Smith. Nothing is known

about Dane beyond the melancholy fact that he committed suicide in 1810.

Founded at about the same time, or even antedating the Hallowell pottery, was one in Gorham operated by Hezekiah Smith and Samuel Prentiss. The latter had come from Cambridge after a brief career as a teacher. He was the son of Caleb Prentiss (or Prentice) and grandson of Deacon Henry, whose brickworks were an important industry in the town. The Prentices also owned a potshop in 1760 (see p. 43), but whether it belonged to Deacon Henry is unknown. Samuel was graduated at Harvard in 1771. For a time he taught school in Kennebunk, Maine, going thence to Gorham.* He became the general storekeeper and was soon running a tavern. Hezekiah Smith, born in Eastham on Cape Cod, went to Gorham with his father's family in 1782. The two young men started their pottery and a potash business a short time thereafter. It is said that they did not make a great success of it. Smith remained in the village until 1797, living on land allotted to his father. Prentiss carried on the pottery for a time, but probably not for long. He passed away in 1815. The buildings stood until a fire destroyed them in 1875. Prentiss's home was on the Portland road east of his store, where the J. C. Summerside store was located in 1902. According to the *History of Gorham* by Hugh McLellan, published in 1903, the pottery must have been run by others at a much later date. He says: "The writer can remember when brown earthen tableware, such as cups and saucers, bowls, pitchers, and plates were in use, and an article of sale." Edward Harding of Gorham, who was born about 1850, also remembered a potworks in the town.

Rather more is known about the Porter pottery in Wiscasset, which, it is thought, was started about 1790. Ezra Porter, its founder, was a grandson of Joseph Osborn of Danvers and son of Benjamin Porter, another Danvers potter. His own statement, published in the *Lincoln Intelligencer*, August 1826, declares: "I, Ezra Porter, potter by trade, have worked at the potters' business for about forty years, in Danvers, and Watertown, Mass., in Newcastle and Wiscasset, in the County of Lincoln, in the State of Maine."

According to this, he began his career in 1786 at the age of seventeen. Ezra's pottery in Wicasset has not been located, but that of his son Silas, who succeeded him, was built on the site of the old county poor house in the southern part of the town. This is described as being near Hilton's Cove at Birch Point, on the cross road connecting the state highway with the old road to Jewankee. In this district, near a bed of excellent clay, Silas Porter made a great variety of earthenware, including pipkins, cake molds, money jugs, snuff jars, and the usual assortment of cooking dishes and containers. He also operated a brickyard that was later sold to the New England Brick Company.

Some interesting facts about an early potworks in Alfred have been unearthed by Miss Margaret H. Jewell, who published them in *Old-Time New England* (April 1932). Joshua Emery started the Alfred pottery in 1791. At some time before 1805 he moved to Windham, and later to Gorham, where he ran a gristmill. He was followed in 1805 by Daniel Holmes, whose pottery stood opposite the meetinghouse. Either the shop itself or the business was moved north "to the road in front of Mr. Brook's house," and later, under the ownership of Porter Lambert, it was nearly opposite the courthouse.

The Lambert shop was behind the buildings that composed the Berry Tavern. When the inn was being demolished in 1938, we visited the site, finding numerous fragments, but none of any significance. This tavern was bought in 1832 by General Samuel

* One account says in 1776, but Kennebunk history puts the time at a later date.

Leighton, who, in his diary, facetiously refers to it as his "pot stable." Porter Lambert was working there at least as early as 1825. The following passages from the Leighton diary, now carefully preserved in the Portland Historical Society, are of interest:

Nov. 12 1825 I halld 6 feet more pine wood to P. Lambert & had of him 1 small b. pot 1 pt & 1 qt mug & pt pitcher & wash bowl and pint pot all 20 cents

20th June 1826 I had of Mr. Lambert 6 small pans at 8 cts 6 qt bowles a 8 Cts three large pans at 12½ Cts to be Chd on acct of wood

14th Octr. 1828 — then halld one load of wood, dry pine to Mr. Lambert with two halld yesterday makes 17½ feet and had of him 2 small earthen pots & 3 bread pans at 10 Cts each one qt mug & one do pitcher a 6

17th May 1834 P. Lambert cleared out his ware from his pot house

11th July Benjn Whitten helped me all day about hewing timber and clearing out old bricks from the pot house.

Thus came to a close the Lambert pottery. General Leighton makes a note that Porter Lambert died the morning of August 9, 1839. When Leighton bought the property, Lambert was in business with his son-in-law Albert Webber. The *Executive Documents Relative to the Manufactures in the United States* record that they made annually earthenware of various kinds worth five hundred dollars. They employed two men at seventy-five cents a day and sold all their output in Maine. Albert Webber is remembered by persons now living. After the pottery in Alfred came to an end, he opened a shop at a four corners known as Littlefield's Mills, about two miles from the Alfred town hall. His son Paul carried on the business with his father.

Potteries in Yarmouth were established in the eighteenth century. The first was built at Yarmouth Corner in 1791 by John Thomas, a native of Gloucester, Massachusetts. According to the Yarmouth records, Thomas was buried in 1843 at the age of eighty-eight years, ten months, and twenty-two days. This leaves no question that he was born September 2, 1754. His birth on this date does not appear in the Gloucester Vital Records, although a John Thomas, son of William and Lydia, was baptized there November 27, 1757.

Thomas built his pottery "on the west side of Main Street above the Cumberland road, — a little retired from the street." It is also described as being "on West Main Street, near the property of George H. Welch [1937]." Thomas worked in Yarmouth throughout his lifetime. William and Samuel Thomas continued the enterprise briefly after his death. It was then taken over by Joel Brooks. The buildings were in bad condition after half a century. Brooks tore them down in 1848 and moved his business to North Yarmouth.

A pottery at Yarmouth Corner was operated by Ebenezer Corliss, who had been trained in the Thomas shop. He built this works in 1806 and ran it with George Bruce until 1850. It then passed into the hands of David Cleaves and his son Robert. Cleaves had come from Saco, Maine, and was Corliss's son-in-law, having married Lydia Corliss in 1818. His pottery was the largest in town. Since it ran until 1885, it can be recalled by the older generation. Augustus W. Corliss, quoted by William H. Rowe, has this to say about it:

Uncle David's shop was a favorite resort for the small boys, although at times he made it very lively for them with the hoop used by the potters in carrying their ware from the wheel to the drying board. The boys used to be paid one cent to sit upon the sweep of the clay mill and keep the horse going while the clay was being ground, which took about an hour, — During the burning of the ware it became necessary to keep up the fire for several days and nights,

and it was the custom of the young men to collect there every night and play old sledge, raffle for turkeys, or hustle for coppers.

As in all redware potteries, the firings took place mostly in the autumn and winter, when the ware fashioned during the summer was burned in the large kiln above the pottery. The finished articles were shipped along the Maine coast in small boats as far as Eastport or peddled through the interior from wagons or pungs.

The Cleaves shop occupied the site where the Methodist Church now stands, and the clay pit was on the spot later covered by the Masonic Hall. Ebenezer Corliss's first dwelling house, one of the oldest in town, may still be seen on the north side of Portland Street just above the Cutler house. Cleaves, too, lived for many years in this house next door to the pottery.

A third redware shop was built in North Yarmouth about 1840 by Nathaniel Foster on what was then Gooch's Lane — later the northerly corner of Main and Elm Streets. Foster is known to have been in the earthenware business as early as 1831. He may have come from Exeter, New Hampshire, as he had married Rebecca Swasey of that town. His sons, Benjamin and William, were his assistants. After his death in 1854 they ran the pottery. From notes obtained by Miss Jewell from Benjamin Foster when he was an old man, we learn that the Fosters sold their wares by boat, taking a load "down east" every spring. Thus they disposed of Yarmouth pottery in Freeport, Brunswick, Windham, Gray, and other places. One of their specialties was a small bean pot called a "Quaker," which was rather straight and was glazed part way down the outside. They also made a quart-sized dish called a "Tom pan." In the late period this pottery turned out a great many flowerpots, which they sold to Kendall & Whitney of Portland. Foster confessed to having a great deal of trouble with his red lead. His wares must have been thick and heavy, for he used sixteen pounds of clay to make a two-gallon pot.

Benjamin Foster was always known to his contemporaries as "Berry," and his name so appears in the style "Berry Foster & Brother" in the *Maine Register and Business Directory* of 1855. William Henry Foster died in 1878, but Berry ran the pottery alone until just before 1890. The buildings were torn down a year later. They had covered a large area, extending some one hundred feet down Gooch's Lane. A store now stands on the site of the workshop, while the building next door covers the former location of the clay mill. The Fosters, as well as Cleaves and his son, dug their clay in the hollow between the two villages of Yarmouth Corner and North Yarmouth, where the Masonic Hall was afterwards erected.

Joel Brooks, who succeeded to the Thomas pottery, built a shop of his own on Gooch's Lane (Elm Street) soon after 1850. His buildings stood just back of his house. Brooks and his son John Edward carried on a small business there for nearly thirty years. John Brooks is said to have been not only an expert potter but an ingenious chemist as well. He invented a particular glaze for flowerpots of great beauty and attractiveness. Just what it was has not been told. He constructed a large kiln that was never used, as he became involved in financial difficulties. The business was sold to one Hollohan, who ran it for a time.

The record of these Yarmouth establishments covers almost a century. During that time many changes must have taken place. The examples that have been salvaged were no doubt made in the late period. Since three of the four shops were still running up to 1880 or later, they represent the final stage in New England redware manufacture. Miss Jewell, in *Old-Time New England* (April

1932), shows a mixing bowl with handle and a curious straight-sided baking pot from Yarmouth, both unglazed outside. These pieces and the other Maine examples illustrated with her article may be seen in the museum of the Society for the Preservation of New England Antiquities in Boston. The little jug shown in Fig. 73*b* was made in North Yarmouth. It has a grayish-green glaze dotted with green and incised on the base are the initials *H P B* and the words *Wine Jug.*

The only other eighteenth-century Maine pottery whose establishment has been recorded was operated by Eli Cox and David Flagg in Topsham as early as 1796. It was situated "at the foot of the hill on the south side of Winter Street." At this point a bridge spanned a deep gully formed by the course of a running brook. The potters ground their clay down by this stream. The location is accurately determined by a map of Topsham in 1802 reproduced in the *History of Brunswick, Topsham, and Harpswell*, by G. A. and H. W. Wheeler. Cox's house stood to the west of the pottery, while Flagg lived a short distance to the south.

In 1835 a "Mr." Barker was running a pottery where Mallett's slaughterhouse later stood. It is quite probable that he was related to John Barker 2d, who was a potter in Brunswick across the river in 1823 and for some years thereafter. Indeed he may have been the same person. Barker is said to have been the only man who ever worked at this trade in Brunswick. His shop is mentioned in the Haskel & Smith *Gazetteer* as being in operation in 1840.

CHAPTER TWENTY

The Maine Industry After 1800

The first Maine pottery that started in the nineteenth century was in Portland. It was built by Benjamin Dodge in 1801, a short time after his arrival from his native town of Exeter, New Hampshire. Benjamin was the son of Jabez Dodge, the founder of the Exeter pottery. On the west corner of what was then Main and Green Streets (now Congress Street and Forest Avenue, site of the Congress Square Hotel) he put up a two-story house and shop. This was his home and place of business until a destructive fire in the summer of 1822 leveled his buildings along with many others in the area. The next year Dodge erected a three-story tavern on his corner lot. This establishment he managed in addition to his pottery. His workshop he rebuilt farther down Green Street in the rear of Thomas Osgood's tannery. This location is now that of the post office at the corner of Portland and Brattle Streets. In Dodge's day Portland Street had not been laid out, except as a narrow way called "Potter's Lane."

It would be interesting to see some of the earthenware that Dodge made in the years that immediately followed. Both he and his son seem to have sought expression for an innate feeling of artistry and both alike were oppressed by an overwhelming melancholy that led each of them to die by his own hand. It is said that Dodge began rather early to ornament his more expensive pots and jars, and especially certain water pitchers made to order. In 1825 he commemorated the visit of Lafayette with a pitcher bearing the general's likeness and inscribed on the reverse with the initials of the lady for whom it was created.

Dodge's end came in June 1838, but for some years before that he had been unable to work, and his son Benjamin, then thirty-six years of age, took over the pottery. The younger Benjamin developed a green glaze that was said to be uncommonly good. He kept its proportions a secret, never divulging them to anyone. There is documentary evidence to support this family tradition. In the catalogue of the second exhibition of the Massachusetts Charitable Mechanics' Association, September 23, 1839, appears the following notation:

165. B. Dodge. Portland, Me. One Earthen Ware Flower Pot. Handsome model and good

workmanship; covered with a superior green glaze. The Committee regret that the specimen is confined to this single article, but trust that before long more attention will be paid to this branch of American manufacture. A Diploma.

Upon the death of Benjamin Dodge, Jr., in 1876, the pottery was purchased by Rufus Lamson and Eben Swasey. Rufus Lamson was the elder son of Asa Brown Lamson of Exeter, who has been mentioned in connection with the earthenware business there. He had operated the Osborn pottery in Peabody for a brief period after 1868. The Portland directories from 1877 to 1883 list this firm. By 1882 they had become manufacturers of stoneware. In 1884 Lamson's name is missing, and the style is Swasey, Jones & Company (L. Frank Jones). From 1886 to 1889 the firm name was Swasey, Lamson & Company. In 1890 it was run by Eben and Fred D. Swasey and George A. Young as E. Swasey & Company and was then known as the Portland Pottery Works. By this time we may be sure the output had assumed a wholly commercial character.

There is record of another Portland redware pottery in 1812. We know also that a potter named Robert Hill was in the city and living on Green Street in 1823 and thereafter until 1831 or later. He may have worked for the Dodges.

Two other Maine potteries were founded in the first decade of the century. In 1803, or earlier, Reuben Thorp was at work in Turner Centre. I believe he was the son of Joseph Thorp, who ran a pottery for a short time in Worcester, Massachusetts, in the early 1770's. Joseph had a son Reuben, born there September 19, 1773. The Turner Centre Thorp became a settler in the little town on the Androscoggin in 1802. In December of the next year his name appears on a petition. Nothing is known about his pottery beyond the mere fact of its existence. His house was still standing in 1880.

Up the Kennebec in Skowhegan a pottery was running in 1808. Doubtless at the instigation of John G. Neil, a friend, Samuel Philbrick went from Exeter in that year to settle in the Maine town. Colonel Neil, a native of Newmarket, New Hampshire, had gone to Skowhegan soon after his marriage in 1806, and, according to one account, had built the potshop before Philbrick's arrival. Neil, however, was not himself a potter. He perhaps engaged the skilled craftsman from Exeter to operate the works. The shop was put up on the southeast corner of his own land by the river (now Elm Street). Samuel Philbrick, who had already built his own house, acquired this property from Neil April 4, 1810, paying one hundred and eighty dollars for "one half of an acre together with the Pot-house thereon." After he was established, his younger brother Joseph came from Exeter to join him. They carried on a prosperous business until 1825, when Samuel retired from potting to a position in the new Skowhegan bank. Joseph then moved the pottery to Currier Brook in Bloomfield, a part of Skowhegan. The original pottery lot was sold in 1839 to Aaron Spear, a blacksmith, who built on it a brick house that is still there. Philbrick's house nearby has remained in the same family name for more than one hundred and twenty-five years. The fine Neil mansion was burned in 1938.

The Philbricks got their clay from the river bank and made the usual variety of household utensils. Members of the Philbrick family, questioned by Roland T. Patten, are authority for the statement that the pottery also produced fancy jars ornamented with raised figures made in molds. These were presumably the work of Joseph Philbrick in the Bloomfield period, for his potshop there continued in operation until 1870. Philbrick himself disposed of his earthenware, driving about the country and trading it at farm-

houses and general stores for farm produce or other goods.

A great many redware potteries were started during the next twenty-five years. Some of them were of brief duration, while others, and they were in the majority, found a steady market for their wares over a long period. In the second category was the enterprise of David Webber and his sons in Hebron. Webber was of New Hampshire origin. Going to Hebron in 1811, he bought in December of that year a one-hundred-acre lot on the north bank of the river near the Norway line. In this location he made bricks and turned pots and pans for fifty years. His son, Henry Rust Webber, learned the trade and was associated with his father until 1850. Henry Webber then moved to the Whitehead farm just over the town line in Paris. On this homestead of his wife's family he built a kiln and started a new pottery. Moses A. Webber, his brother, ran the Hebron shop after his father's death. Moses lived until 1900 and carried on the earthenware business to a late date.

A small redware concern in North Bridgton, near the New Hampshire line, served the neighboring communities for a half century or so. It was owned by Richard F. Kitson, who began to work there in 1815. His shop was on the Harrison road by the shore of Long Lake. The site of the Kitson shard pile is known, but is it accessible only during the winter months. In the summer, when the lake is high, it is under water. It is said that Kitson had to haul clay from a pit thirty miles away. This seems unusual, but was perhaps necessitated, not from a lack of *any* clay, but by a dearth of suitable or superior material.

Kitson advertised in business directories from year to year as an earthenware manufacturer. The last date I have noted was 1860, but the pottery was in operation for some years after that. In the 1850's John Hill was master potter there. Several authenticated specimens of his handiwork are in the collection of Edwin Victor Spooner of North Bridgton. These are cylindrical covered spice jars, heavily coated with a brown glaze. They display a bit of incised decoration. By 1890 the pottery had come to a close, and the building was in use by Harris Allen as a carpenter's shop.

A pottery that may have antedated the one at Hebron was established in West Farmington by Josiah Norcross early in the century. He was the son of Samuel Norcross of Hallowell. Born in Newton, Massachusetts, in 1759, he no doubt got his training thereabouts. His son Matthias worked with him and succeeded to his business. In 1840 there were two potteries in the town, both apparently run by the Norcrosses. Matthias Norcross continued to operate the original works until 1868, the year of his death. For a short time Matthias, Jr., tried to keep the pottery going, but without success. Francis Gould Butler, writing in 1885, says that it had been "given up many years ago."

Although the first definite records of a pottery in Windham, a few miles from Gorham, begin in 1825, it is quite likely that there had been some attempt at making earthenware before the coming of John Goodell in that year. When Joshua Emery left Alfred in 1805, he went to Windham, where it is possible that he continued in his same trade. Hezekiah Smith of Gorham also settled in Windham at an even earlier date. Windham's known potting history, however, begins with the arrival of John Goodell from Kennebunk. His first shop was on the east side of the river road near its intersection with Horse Beef Road. Traces of his workshop and the cellar of his house could still be seen in 1916 on the farm of the late John Webb. Later, Goodell bought the farm where Isaiah Staples afterwards lived. He erected there a large barnlike structure with

a workshop at one end and a kiln at the other. The Windham pottery lasted for about twenty-five years, closing when Goodell died.

In the Kennebec valley several redware potters built kilns and shops in the period around 1820. In Winslow, north of Augusta, William Hussey and Ambrose Bruce were at work at this time or before. Their factory stood on the dam at the Hayden millpond. Digging their clay nearby, on the other side of the pond, they turned out ware in great quantity and variety, enough to supply all the region round about. It is related of Hussey that, although his goods were in wide demand, he was too fond of the flowing bowl. After making a batch of ware and taking in the proceeds, he would close the shop and spend his gains in convivial pursuits. Thus the business suffered a gradual decline and eventual collapse.

A few miles west of Augusta, in the town of Winthrop, Thomas Fuller ran a pottery for a number of years. He was the son of John Fuller of Barnstable, Massachusetts, who settled in Winthrop in 1772. At that time there were no other inhabitants between their pioneer home and the New Hampshire line. In 1820 Thomas's pot house stood on the north side of Main Street, where in later years there was a stone blacksmith's shop. His home was on the corner of Main and Bowdoin Streets. In addition to his duties as potter, Fuller carried the mail between Augusta and Portland. While on one of his trips, in March 1828, he died suddenly in Portland, thus bringing the Winthrop pottery to a premature end.

Opposite Bath, near the mouth of the Kennebec, is the town of Woolwich, for many years the seat of one of the best known Maine potteries, that of John Corliss. The story of this enterprise, ably related by Miss Margaret H. Jewell, appears in *Old-Time New England* (April 1932). Miss Jewell's information was largely obtained from Corliss's account book and from the diary of his son Howard. I have been privileged to receive a complete copy of the account book. It is the only such record of an early Maine pottery that I have seen.

At the age of three, John Corliss was taken from his birthplace, Hopkinton, New Hampshire, to North Yarmouth, when his family moved there in the winter of 1802. Growing up among the potters of the town, he developed an aptitude for the craft, and was no doubt apprenticed to his uncle Ebenezer Corliss. When he was twenty-one and old enough to start his own business, he went to Day's Ferry in West Woolwich. This proved to be an excellent location, because there was a suitable bed of clay near at hand and a good market for his wares on both sides of the river. In 1932 the pottery that Corliss built in 1820 was still standing (Fig. 1). It has since been demolished. Running beside it was a small brook which the potter dammed up for the needs of his shop.

During his first years in Woolwich, Corliss boarded here and there, but in 1829 he moved into a home he had built on the slope directly above the pottery and overlooking the river. His mother lived with him there until her death in 1831. A few months later he married Diantha Heald Foster, daughter of the potter Nathaniel Foster of North Yarmouth, Corliss led a long and fruitful life, marrying twice again, and dying in 1892, after a brief sickness, at the age of ninety-three. He had outlived his pottery, which closed in the 1880's, after the demand for almost every form of redware except flowerpots had ceased.

The account book begins in April 1824. It is an illuminating commentary on the life of those days in a small Maine village. Almost all business was conducted by trade and barter, so that very little actual cash exchanged hands. Charge accounts in the book are so

few, it is quite evident that most of Corliss's customers paid on the spot. During the first three months, construction work of some kind was going on at the pottery — perhaps an enlargement or addition to the original shop. The men who labored hauling stone or lumber, shingling, or furnishing hemlock planks, were paid in ware. The name of John Costelow appears at this time. He supplied Corliss with bricks and worked four days "tending masons." The considerable quantities of ware that he took in return would indicate that he sold it. In 1825 Costelow was twice paid for watching the kiln.

Two years later Corliss was running a store or trading post. Customers were charged for an assortment of articles ranging from grain and flour, rum, coffee, cheese, and fish, to rakes, stockings, thread, and "factory" cloth. Values were reckoned in shillings and pence, even when totaled in American dollars and cents. The approximate prices of earthenware made by Corliss in the 1820's appear in the following list:

Small pot	12½	cents
Large pot	17	”
Stew pot	6½	”
Small pan	6½	”
Pudding pan	12½	”
Milk pan	17	”
Flat pan (plate)	12	”
Flat platter	13	”
Flat platter	17	”
Pint jug	07	”
Quart jug	13	”
Two-quart jug	17	”
Gallon jug	25	”
Quart pitcher	10	”
Two-quart pitcher	17	”
Large pitcher		
Mug	10	”
Porringer	09	”
Small bowl	04	”
Two-quart bowl	09	”
Large bowl	20	”
Tumblers	04	”
Tumblers	06	”
Wash bowl	14	”
Chamber	17	”
Wash bowl, pitcher and chamber	39	”
Churn	67	”
Flower pot	17	”
Monkey		

John Corliss's son Howard went into the business with his father. His diary, kept from 1859 to 1868, throws some light on the later transactions in the pottery. He had married and lived near his father. The record shows how both of them sold the earthenware up and down the Kennebec and to villages on the islands at the mouth of the river. A large quantity was disposed of in Bath. They also made fishing leads for sale. In November 1860 they delivered 1,355 of these to the city. Howard Corliss notes that "tea lead" was sometimes used for glazing, but that it caused more trouble than "soft," or red, lead and required a different length of time for burning. October 30, 1863, he made an entry: "conclude to rise on the ware."

At about this time John Corliss put out a printed price list, which, like many such documents, appears to have been a form supplied to potters. It mentions only cream pots, bean pots, flat and deep milk pans, stove pans, bread pans, jugs, flowerpots, glazed or painted, hanging pots, and common unglazed flowerpots. An inventory of articles ready to burn, made by Howard Corliss in 1867, has a slightly wider range:

June	11	large deep pans	300
		with old ones	
	19	large milk pans	500
	25	2nd size deep pans	450
July	1	3rd size deep pans	350
	5	2nd size milk pans	600
	6	small platters	70
	8	Tom pans (a quart pan)	440
Aug.	10	large pots	1450
	14	large pudding pans	250
	21	stove pans	300

	23	2nd size pots	500
	27	large bean pots	200
	29	3rd size pots	250
	31	40 cent flower pots	50
Sept.		2nd size bean pots	500
		covers	150
		600 made before	
		no. 2 flower pots	100
		3	150
		4	200
		5	200
		6	200
		wash bowls	150
		2nd pudding pans	200
		Handle dishes	100
		no. 4 flower pots	100
		pots to hang up	75
		Stew pots	90
		3 sizes	75
		Jugs (some left from year before)	
		gallons	26
		½ gallons	30
		qts.	30
		Unglazed flower pots	
		large size	24
		2nd size	100
		to hang up	16
		3rd pudding pans	150
		large soap pans	200
		Chambers large	24
		Chambers small	12
		unglazed flower smallest	300
Oct.		unglazed flower 3rd size	300
		2nd size soap pans	225
1868			
July		large deep pans	275
		large milk pans	550
		2nd size deep pans	450

It is interesting to note that the demand for common redware cooking pots and pans was still strong at this comparatively late period. A little arithmetic shows that the Corlisses turned out more than seven thousand of these vessels, besides bean pots and stew pots, in about one year. Lighter and more convenient receptacles of tin and other ware were soon generally used, however, and during the next ten years the need for redware gradually became limited to flowerpots. Sometime in the 1880's the pottery came to a close.

A pottery in Buxton, a few miles from Gorham, was founded as early as 1825 by the Bickford family. The father, James, had come from Exeter, New Hampshire, by way of Gorham. Whether he was a potter I have been unable to learn. His son, James, Jr., was born five years after the father's marriage to Betsy Wentworth of Buxton, and was twenty-seven years of age when the pottery started. His much younger brother, Ebenezer Wentworth called "Wentworth," or "Wint," was then only eight years old. In later years these two ran the business together.

The Buxton pottery was situated at a place known as "Haines' meadow," one mile south of Buxton Centre. Residents born in the sixties and seventies can remember the small building there and the two elderly men who worked in it. "Wint," it is said, was a "fat little old man." Neither of the brothers married and they seem to have plied their craft contentedly until nearly 1880. James finally moved to Massachusetts and Wentworth to Parsonsfield, Maine. The building was sold to Moses Bradbury, who moved it across the road. Clarence S. Bradbury tried to reestablish the business, but, after making one kiln of ware that was a failure, he abandoned the attempt. The shop was then moved away and later burned.

The Haines' meadow site is still available and shows plentiful evidence of erstwhile potting activities. Deep holes in the land where clay was dug are now covered by bushes. A pile of bricks marks the site of the kiln. Several pieces of redware made by the Bickfords have come to light. These include a bulbous jug, a small brown tea bowl, a slant-sided pitcher with yellow-green glaze, and a jar splashed with brown. A variety of vases and other types of pitchers are also known, while among the shards are pieces

of common pots and pans, unglazed bean pots, and absolutely plain collarless flower-pots with attached saucers.

In the period after 1825 some twenty other redware potteries and a few stoneware manufactories were carried on in Maine with varying degrees of success. Of several we know only that they are listed in the Haskel & Smith *Gazeteer* as of 1840. Among these are potteries in Berwick, Cornish, Hermon, and Biddeford. It will be recalled that Daniel Goldthwaite of Peabody went to Biddeford for a short time to assist in starting a pottery.

A local history of South Thomaston mentions a potworks there as early as 1828; and this, too, was running in 1840. Two potshops were in operation at this time in Hollis Centre, across the Saco River from Buxton. Twenty years later they were in the hands of John Auld (Allds) and Truxton Kendricks. It is said that the Auld pottery was on the "Cape" road, as one goes north from the town.

The *Maine Register and Business Directory* of 1855 notes several establishments with the owners' names. In Corinth, farthest north of Maine potteries, we find Elden Chase; in Ellsworth, Elisha Jones and one York (possibly Charles E., who had worked at Woolwich). Jones alone appears in another directory the following year. The pottery in Corinth is also noted in Coolidge and Mansfield's *History and Description of New England*, published in 1859.

Three earthenware makers in Monmouth are listed in the 1855 *Register* — John Safford, John M. Safford, and Silas H. Coburn. The Saffords came from Exeter, New Hampshire, where John M., the son, was born in 1811. The younger Safford was running the pottery in 1865 and probably until his death in 1880. Silas H. Coburn was succeeded by Silas M. Coburn. A small greenish-yellow covered jar from the Monmouth pottery is owned by Mrs. Earle E. Andrews. Its cover is plainly marked *John M. Safford/ Stew Pot.* Actually, the piece is not a stew pot. We can only opine that covers were transposed, perhaps at the pottery. George Llewellyn Safford of the third generation was also a potter and was still living in Monmouth in 1895.

Of Orrington on the Penobscot, a short distance below Bangor, it is possible to say a little more. Orrington was the pioneer town of Penobscot County: Bangor and Eddington were the only others there at the time of the 1790 census. Born in this frontier community, George Brooks, son of James, first saw the light of day in 1815. Brooks was well educated for those days at Hampden Academy and Maine Western Seminary at Readfield. For a time he was a teacher and all his life he was interested in matters of education. He served for many years on the town's school committee and was for over thirty years superintendent of the Sunday School.

How or when George Brooks became a potter is not related. His name appears in this capacity in business directories of the fifties and sixties. In 1882 he was a farmer and still a successful manufacturer. At that time he was making earthenware, land tiles, and tobacco pipes. The land tiles were made in quantities to satisfy local demand and for shipments to Boston as well. The manufacture of clay pipes was a new enterprise for Maine, for Brooks's pipes were not the crude redware variety, but were of imported white clay from the very bed used by Glasgow pipe-makers. His other earthenware was doubtless of the conventional kind.

An establishment devoted wholly to the production of redware pipes was in existence in Wells before 1861. At least, the friend who told me about it was born in that year and it was not running during his lifetime, although his father could remember it. I first learned of the pottery when I secured from him one of the pipes he had picked up on the refuse

pile near the ruined buildings when he was a boy. He told me that a man named Taber operated the works. It stood on the road from Wells to Sanford at Taber's Corner, about one-half mile east of the Boston & Maine Railroad tracks. We have tried in vain to locate the exact site of this pottery. The locality has been changed by modern road construction.

The Wells pipes were of a type that may have been made elsewhere. If so, not many have survived. The bowls were designed to accommodate a hollow twig for a stem, and this feature of mine was reconstructed for me by my elderly friend (Fig. 85).

A pipe factory in Alton, New Hampshire, begun in 1864 by John Taber, may have been a second venture by the same potter or his son.

In 1860 John Barker, who may have been the son of the Brunswick John Barker, was running a pottery in Lisbon. Waldoboro, too, had its potter, James H. Stanwood, in the same year. In 1868 he had taken a partner, and the business was conducted under the style of Stanwood & Mayo. This pottery was still flourishing in 1874. It was located on the east side of the Bremen road, south of Kaler's corner, at the present entrance to a gravel pit.

Miss Jewell, in her article on Maine potteries, has noted the presence of a shop in Limington. She has since learned that this works was actually in the town of Standish, at the end of the bridge over the Saco to East Limington. Its owner, one Davis, had another shop in Baldwin. The Standish pottery was discontinued in the 1880's. Miss Jewell also mentions two redware shops in Bangor.

The manufacture of stoneware in Maine was not attempted until after 1830, and then it was begun by men from outside the state. This lag was probably caused by distance from the source of materials and the proximity to a flourishing pottery in Charlestown, Massachusetts.

Martin Crafts of Whately has the distinction of being the first potter to make stoneware in both Maine and New Hampshire. According to the record kept by his brother James M. Crafts, Martin moved to Portland in 1834. He is not listed in the Portland directory of that year, which presumably was published before his arrival. No other directory was printed until 1837. In that issue we find his name and that of his uncle:

> Crafts Martin (& Caleb) stone ware manufacturers, foot of green h. green
> Crafts Caleb at Martin Crafts

Caleb Crafts, brother of Thomas, the noted Whately potter, joined his nephew in the Portland enterprise in this year 1837. The name of Eleazer Orcutt of Whately also appears in the same directory, with a house address on Green Street. Martin remained in Portland until 1839, when he sold out his share in the business and made another move to Nashua, leaving Caleb and perhaps Orcutt to carry on the stoneware pottery. In 1841 Caleb Crafts & Company advertised in the directory as follows:

> STONE WARE MANUFACTORY/ Caleb Crafts & Co./ foot of Green St. near/ Deering Bridge/ Portland./ Have constantly for sale/ a full assortment of/ STONE WARE/ such as Butter Pots, Flower Pots, Jugs, Pitchers, &c./ The above Ware is warranted equal to any manufactured in the United States./ Orders directed to the advertisers will be thankfully received and punctually attended to.

The several marks found on the Crafts jugs and jars leave us in doubt as to the exact organization, if any, of the concern. The mark *M. Crafts & Co./ Portland* must have been used from 1834 to 1839, but when *Orcutt & Crafts/ Portland* was the style is a question, since we do not know when Or-

cutt arrived or departed. And the Crafts of this partnership may have been either Martin or Caleb.

The location of the stoneware pottery was nearly one-half mile north of the present post office on Green Street, now Forest Avenue. Deering Bridge, which used to span a little inlet, has since been torn down and the hollow filled in. Kennebec Street now enters Forest Avenue near that point.

Although the Crafts family did not succeed in establishing a permanent enterprise, they were soon followed by a man who did. It is said that John T. Winslow founded in 1846 the pottery that is still run by his descendants. The Portland directories do not corroborate this date, and it seems likely that it represents the year when Winslow began his career as a potter. In commencing his business he was preceded by a short-lived organization listed in the 1847/48 directory, in which Winslow's name does not appear at all. This was Clough, Calhoun & Company (Levi Clough and William Calhoun), whose stoneware factory was at 105 Green Street. A jug with the mark of this firm, found by Miss Margaret H. Jewell, must be considered a rarity.

The name of John T. Winslow is first seen in the directory of 1850/51, where he is called "stoneware manufacturer — Westbrook Point." The point was at the north end of Deering Bridge in the Westbrook section of Portland, and the Portland Stone Ware Company, run by Winslow's descendants, still has its plant in this same location.

The output of this concern was soon of a far more commercial nature than the homely wares of the country potters. Winslow advertised in 1868 "every description of pottery and stoneware" and also called attention to drain tile and pipes, for which the company had been awarded a silver medal by the Maine Agricultural Society. They also received a silver and bronze medal presented by the New England Agricultural Society in 1872.

A trade card dated 1874 lists under "Stone Ware Goods" jugs, butter pots, cake pots, water jugs, churns, preserve jars, water kegs, bean pots, flowerpots, beer bottles, spittoons, pitchers, cream pots, soap dishes, pudding pots, milk pans, terra cotta, and all kinds of clay goods. Pictures on the card show an ornamental urn called a "Garden Vase," which sold at prices from four dollars to fifty dollars, and a wind guard or safe for a chimney at $1.50. Other products were hanging baskets, clay ventilating flues, fire brick, and plumbing utilities. At this period John T. Winslow was superintendent of the works and J. N. Winslow treasurer. They had an office and yard at 444 Federal Street, Boston, where they did business as the "Boston Drain Pipe Co., Factory at Portland, Me."

One of the finest types of ware turned out by the Portland company was their stoneware with a variegated glaze in tones of blue, brown, and cream yellow, which compares favorably with the flint enamel of Bennington. A "pig" hot-water bottle of the kind is impressed with the firm name in a circular mark. At an earlier period Winslow made use of Albany slip. A foot warmer with foot-shaped depressions on the side is glazed in this dull, dark brown color and stamped *J. T. Winslow/ Portland, Me.* The pitcher in Fig. 123 is similarly glazed and marked, while another in my own collection has a nearly black glaze.

It should be noted that, beginning with Martin and Caleb Crafts and including Swasey, Jones & Company, four stoneware potteries were operated in Portland. With the exception of those in Gardiner and Bangor, they were the only ones in Maine to attempt the manufacture of this kind of ware.

At Gardiner, stoneware was first made in 1837 by Lyman & Clark. It is a known fact that the first member of this partnership was Alanson Potter Lyman, who was later asso-

ciated with Fenton at Bennington, Vermont. He was not a potter and his relation to the business was a purely financial one. Clark was undoubtedly Decius W. Clark, one of the most remarkable of the Bennington potters. He had finished his apprenticeship at Troy only a short time before the Gardiner venture started, but was already an unusually skilled craftsman. Lyman, therefore, was backing an arrangement that promised a high degree of success. That it lasted only four years is no reflection on the ability or acumen of the pair, but was rather the result of the same old difficulty of expense in transporting clay.

Gardiner is on the Kennebec River, just below Hallowell. Its later pottery was in Farmingdale, the northern part of the town, and that, too, may have been the site of the Lyman & Clark enterprise. Occasional pieces from their pottery are seen, and they are obviously from the same hand that fashioned the fine, bulbous Norton & Fenton jugs (Fig. 101). I have seen one of these jugs, beautifully decorated in sepia, which was marked *Lyman & Clark/ Gardiner.* In September 1837, the partners exhibited a specimen of their work at the first annual fair of the Massachusetts Mechanics' Association. The catalogue lists it as "179. Lyman & Clarke, Gardiner, Me. — A Stone Churn; the quality of this article is good, and probably the form is such as would be approved by the practical dairymaid." The partnership was dissolved late in 1841 and the pair returned to Bennington, where Clark went to work for Norton & Fenton.

By 1850 the same or another stoneware factory was in operation in Farmingdale. The United States census of 1850 mentions "1 extensive pottery" in Gardiner. This is also noted in Hanson's *History of Gardiner*, published in 1852, as "a flourishing pottery." It was owned by Francis A. Plaisted, a native of the town, who started the works as a very young man. In the *New England Business Directory* of 1856 the business is listed under the style *F. A. Plaisted & Co.* In 1868 his name appears alone. A resident of Farmingdale, Miss Annie Stilphen, recalls playing with Plaisted's daughter when she was a very small child in 1870, and she has supplied some facts about the pottery gleaned from elderly persons. She says that Plaisted failed and that he went to California "to start all over again," probably after the fire that destroyed his buildings in 1874.

The pottery was rebuilt and the manufacture of stoneware revived. Pierson & Horn are said to have been Plaisted's successors. William Wood and Charles Swift followed them. A man named Billings was also connected with the later operation of the works. Wood and Swift were both Gardiner business men, not potters, and they ran the factory as a commercial venture.

Another name enters the Gardiner picture with the mark *Thompson & Co./ Gardiner*, which I have seen on a stoneware jug; but I have been unable to find out where Thompson fits in. Plaisted used the mark *Plaisted/ Gardiner, Me.* Pieces stamped *Gardiner Stoneware/ Gardiner, Maine* probably belong to the late period of the pottery. All manufacture came to an end in Gardiner in 1887.

The site of Plaisted's pottery was near the intersection of the London Hill road with the highway from Gardiner to Hallowell. It stood on the west side of the main road near Captain Smith's house. Miss Stilphen tells me that in her mother's childhood there was a brickyard at this point.

A notice in the *Maine Register and Business Directory* of 1855 advertises "Ballard & Brothers (Stoneware Manufacturers)" as of Gardiner. This suggests a connection between the Burlington, Vermont, firm and the Gardiner pottery. It is possible that they took orders in Maine to be filled by Plaisted.

A late pottery in Bangor used the mark *Bangor Stoneware Co.*, either with or without the words *Bangor, Maine.* Some pieces have the place name alone. The concern was started in the 1890's by Andrew Pierson (Pehrson), formerly of Gardiner. The pottery stood on Patton Street and was managed by its owner until his death in 1913; then for three years by his son. They made the usual utilities.

CHAPTER TWENTY-ONE

Early Connecticut Redware and the Goshen Group

Connecticut was the only New England state within easy reach of South Amboy clay. For this reason it was able to produce stoneware at a comparatively early date, and approximately two-thirds of its potteries manufactured stone pottery rather than redware. However, since many of them made both types of ware, I have made no division in recounting their histories.

The most striking feature of Connecticut redware is the marked influence from New York, New Jersey, and Pennsylvania. In Connecticut alone of the New England states the notched-edge plates and platters called by collectors "Connecticut" pottery are known to have been made. The stoneware of this state, on the other hand, has no particular characteristic to distinguish it from the work of other New England potters, unless it be the vertical outstanding handles that are occasionally seen on jars. The general similarity is explained by the fact that the first men who worked in the northern states—Jonathan Fenton, Frederick Carpenter, and John Norton—were born in Connecticut and learned their trade either there or in the region near Albany.

Connecticut redware has been more widely known to collectors than the pottery of northern New England, because the gay slip-decorated pie plates and red and black jugs and pitchers were made to a rather late period and have survived in considerable quantity. Since these wares were shipped along the seacoast to Rhode Island and Massachusetts, they are found quite commonly in the neighboring states. Very little of this type of redware dates before 1800.

There are indications that pottery was made in the very first settlements, but tracing craftsmen by means of Connecticut records is difficult, since they do not mention trades and occupations with names. Such information as we have of seventeenth- and eighteenth-century activities is meager indeed in comparison with the copious data to be unearthed in Massachusetts. Edward E. Atwater, in his *History of New Haven Colony*, says: "Few instances occur in the history of colonization, where within ten years from the commencement there was such fulness of equipment for producing at home the requirements of civilized life as at New Haven. The writer has never made a sys-

tematic attempt to collect the names of such trades as are incidentally mentioned; but these are some which he has remembered," etc., and he includes potters. It is indeed unfortunate that the historian neglected to compile such a list of craftsmen, which would be invaluable to students. He tells us just enough to establish the fact that New Haven was the site of the first Connecticut pottery of which we have even a hint.

Greenwich was the location of the earliest recorded Connecticut pottery. The detailed story of Adam States, a stoneware potter who was living in the town in 1750, appears in the chapter on the States family. In the same decade, John Pierce was running a redware pottery in Litchfield. Its owner lived there for more than thirty years and was followed by a group of clay workers in the adjoining town of Goshen, where earthenware was made until 1870. The pots and pans of this area partook of the characteristics of both northern and southern New England, with some distinguishing features of their own.

Norwich had a stoneware kiln before 1770 and a redware pottery in 1771 (probably earlier). Although Norwich in the nineteenth century was better known for its stoneware, the manufacture of both kinds of pottery was carried on there for many years. The Seymours and Goodwins began to make redware in West Hartford in the 1790's — an industry that was carried on by the Goodwins until 1870. The Hoyt pottery at South Norwalk was founded before 1800, and Norwalk continued to be a center for the potting business until 1887. These were the principal pottery groups in Connecticut. Their stories will be found in other chapters. Isolated potteries were also established throughout the state from time to time, and their output was important.

In spite of the general impression that Connecticut was the main source of New England redware, statistics list only a limited number of earthenware shops in the state. Several of them were in Hartford County, where nine potteries flourished in 1810. Of these, five were in the city of Hartford and three of the five were stoneware factories. The locations of the others are still unknown. A great deal of lead-glazed ware is found even today in this area. In 1819 there were five potteries in Hartford and one in East Windsor. Seven potteries existed in the county in 1840, but only one at that time was in Hartford itself.

Scattered across the state were several other redware establishments. The earliest I have noted was in Pomfret in northeastern Connecticut near the Massachusetts line. It was brought to my attention by Mrs. Nina Fletcher Little, who discovered this notice in the *Norwich Packet*:

> Wanted as an apprentice to the potters business, a boy about 14 or 16 years of age. One that suits will meet with advantageous terms by applying to
> Philemon Adams, Pomfret, Conn. June 16, 1785.

This was only a few miles from the well-known pottery in South Woodstock, or Quasset, as it used to be called, that was founded by Thomas Bugbee, Jr., in 1793. Bugbee, who was then thirty-three years old, was apparently untrained in the potter's art, for he employed a "foreign" artisan to oversee the various processes of preparing the clay and glazing the wares. The word "foreign" does not necessarily mean that his master workman came from across the sea, but perhaps only from Massachusetts or a distant part of Connecticut; in those days of limited travel, all outside towns were foreign. So we would not expect Bugbee's output to differ in any respect from the wares made elsewhere in New England. It is said that he produced large quantities of pottery. In six firings during the summer, he burned some five thousand pieces. Of these, two thousand

were milk pans. They were distributed by cart to stores in all the neighboring settlements of Windham County. Bugbee also operated a brickyard. Traces of it still remain near his former homestead in Quasset. He was financially successful and in 1807 was one of the largest taxpayers of the town. The pottery continued until 1843, when its owner died.

There was a potshop in the little town of Canterbury in 1819 and a Mansfield pottery is listed in 1840. Aside from these small redware potteries, all others in Connecticut are included in the Norwalk group, in the establishments of the States family along the coast, in the Goshen and Hartford centers, or among the potters of Norwich and New London.

All previous notices of the potting industry in Litchfield have placed John Pierce, Hervey Brooks, and Jesse Wadhams in the town in 1752. Actually, neither Wadhams nor Brooks was born until more than twenty years after this date, and, at the time of Pierce's death in 1783, Brooks was only four years old, Wadhams but ten. Furthermore, neither of the two worked in Litchfield, but in Goshen.

John Pierce, born in 1730, was the son of John of Wethersfield. In 1751 he married Mary, daughter of Major John Patterson of Farmington. His first child, John, was born there at the Patterson home the following year. Whether John Pierce was working at the time in Farmington I have been unable to ascertain. In any event, it is said, the Pierces arrived in Litchfield in 1752. The scanty accounts of the elder Pierce have been confused with the records of his son John, but the facts are these. Pierce was twice married, taking as his second wife Mary Goodwin, daughter of Thomas. She was four years younger than he, and his already large family continued to grow. He had fifteen children, of whom nine lived. The family attained a degree of distinction in Litchfield. The son John became a paymaster-general in the Revolutionary forces, with the rank of colonel. After his father's death, he assumed the responsibility of the family. He had married a young lady from New York, and, perhaps on this account, he sent his little sister Sarah to a finishing school there. When Sarah came back, she started the famous Litchfield Female Academy in her home town.

The story of Goshen potters has been memorialized by Hervey Brooks in a history of South End, written in 1858. This community, just north of the Litchfield line, was a trading post for craftsmen and peddlers. It was conveniently situated on the New Haven-Albany post road, only a few rods west of the highway from Litchfield to Goshen Centre. It is possible that the potteries of this section were a continuation of the Pierce shop.

Jonathan Kettell (Kettle), son of Jonathan and grandson of James of Danvers, was in Goshen as early as 1776, when he was mentioned as a potter in a Danvers deed. This is the earliest known date for the craft in this village. Kettell probably lived in what Hervey Brooks describes as the "old Kittle place" in the center of the town.

John Norton of Bennington fame was born in Goshen in 1758 and lived there until 1785. He married Lucretia Buell of South End shortly before his departure to Williamstown and thence to Vermont.

The pottery of Jesse Wadhams stood a little more than a mile north of South End. Reverend A. G. Hibbard, in his *History of Goshen*, says that Wadhams "built a house on the west side of the turnpike, about 80 rods south of the south end of Long Swamp. Here he worked at his trade, which was that of a potter. He manufactured the red earthen ware from the common clay. This was between 1790 and 1810." Wadhams was the son of Seth and Anne (Catling) Wadhams. He

was born August 22, 1773, six years before the birth of Hervey Brooks. He probably established his business shortly before his marriage to Polly Hopkins in 1795.

In that year Hervey Brooks, then a lad of sixteen, went to live in South End. The inference is obvious that at first he was Wadhams' apprentice. Hervey was the eldest of twelve children of Joseph Brooks, a native of Durham, and his wife, Amanda Collins, was a Goshen girl. In South End he boarded with Captain Jonathan Buell in the same house where Norton had courted his sweetheart. While the Buells were always considered residents of Goshen, their house had been built by mistake in two townships and stood squarely on the Litchfield line.

Brooks kept accounts from the year 1802 until his death in 1873. From these, together with his history and with the assistance of his grandson John Norton Brooks, who lives in the old family homestead and who owns many products of his ancestor's skill, I am able to present a remarkably complete record of the potter's career.

Just after the accounts begin, on April 24, 1803, Hervey Brooks married Polly Taylor of Granville. Thenceforth, he led a life of almost ceaseless activity. When he was not working for Wadhams, he picked up odd jobs here and there. It is not quite clear whether at this time he had a kiln of his own: he may have done his turning in Wadhams' shop, buying materials to fill his private orders. In any event, a country potter's trade was never sufficient to take all of a man's time, and Hervey was apparently able to turn his hand to any task that came along. He entered bills in his book for haying, chopping and hauling wood, hoeing potatoes, spreading dung, grafting apple trees, picking apples, shingling, splitting nails, driving a horse to the mill, and even butchering a calf. He also seems to have kept up a lively business as a trader. Much of his pottery was sold to peddlers who perhaps paid in kind rather than in cash. Previous to 1801, he must have had a store, for he sold such articles as pins, combs, salt, tea, and rum.

For Jesse Wadhams, Hervey did the usual tasks in a pottery. May 23, 1803, he noted: "half days work at the frame" (turning); May 25 he spent digging clay; in 1809 he presented bills for "turning 8 doz Milkpans @ 9d; to a days work Glazing; to Burning the Kiln one night and day." Most of the entries, however, are itemized accounts of piecework done for Wadhams or long lists of articles made and sold, sometimes at retail and sometimes at wholesale. Often buyers were charged for loading the ware. Already Hervey Brooks' habits of thrift, which must not be judged by present-day practice, were evident. In 1803 he got rid of six cracked milk pans and a warped jug for a little more than four shillings, to Heman Beach, a peddler. The habit of wringing the most out of every deal and of accounting faithfully for every cent was customary in that day. So it is not surprising to find a memorandum when Brooks lent a postage stamp or when a friend borrowed ten cents for the Sunday collection plate.

The last bill entered against Jesse Wadhams is dated June 22, 1810. During the ensuing years, several transactions indicate that other potters were at work in South End. Twice during 1814 Hervey made out a bill to David Vaill to "turning" milk pans or bowls, and he also itemized finished ware. Possibly Vaill was a peddler, not a potter, but there is little doubt about George Holton, to whose account four entries are put down in 1815: "To 2 days work glazing ware." In 1822 and 1825 Isaac Wadhams is billed "To ½ day digging clay — \$.37" and "to 2 quarts sand — \$.06" and "8 lbs. White clay — \$.25." During Jesse Wadhams' lifetime Brooks had sold sand in small quantities to Pitt Buell and a certain Norton. Since common sand was

plentiful enough in South End, they presumably bought a finer material for glazing.

In 1811 Brooks worked for a time in Granville, where he was accustomed to make periodic visits in the home of his wife's father. Three years later this entry occurs: "Wednesday February 2nd 1814 we moved from Granville and arrived at our present place of residence in Goshen February 5th 1814." This marks the time, according to South End history, when Brooks bought the house and land that had previously been owned and occupied by Nathaniel Merrills. He records that he was living there in 1858; the original building, however, had been torn down long before. The house that replaced it was the potter's home until his death. He says:

June 17th 1829. Pulled down my old House. Thursday June 25th finished the cellar wall and underpinning.
Wednesday July 1st raised the new house, (without rum).
Tuesday November 10th 1829, Moved into the new House.

In December 1813, Revellard Dutcher, Jr., came to work with Brooks for a year, his wages to be $109. He is the only person mentioned at any time as assistant. After his departure Brooks must have taken his ten-year-old boy, Isaac, into the pottery. Isaac, however, had no desire to be a potter, nor was he happy in the alternative prospect of selling clocks. Before he was twenty years old he ran away to Georgia. This was in 1823. His father dolefully figured out that Isaac owed him $133 on his apprenticeship, $144.76 for clocks, and $37 on his wagon. The debt was never paid, although it was marked "settled." Several years later, when Isaac was sick and alone in New York, his father made the journey to Staten Island to bring him home. Georgia claimed Isaac eventually, while the younger son, Watts H. (both were named after the famous hymn writer), remained in South End.

Hervey Brooks left a particularly careful record in 1819 of his work and expenses. It throws a helpful light on old-time methods of production and distribution:

An acct of my expenses in & at the Shop for 1819:
March 29th & 30th To Watertown Woodbury & Washington 2 days making contracts for ware &c. Expenses $1.50
2 days splitting wood
3 days into York State making contracts &c. Expenses $3.50
May 20th Myself & Team 3 days to Wethersfield after sand, Expenses 4 dollars
25th Turned 6 doz. Milkpans
26th glazing & Setting 1 day
28th diging Clay 1 day; Drawing 3 loads clay
29th Burning 1 day
31st drawing the kiln & loading ware
June 2nd turned 4 doz. large pots; carried a load of ware to Wasington; carried a load of ware to Mount tom
8½ day at the Shop painting &c.
June 18 Issac with team drawing clay
(Loads to Woodbury, Bethlehem, Holbrook, N. Y.; Kent, Cornwall, Canaan — (Expenses 34 cents))
Aug 22 ½ day painting platters
Aug 26 glazing & painting
Sept. 19 4 doz. Bowls & 3 do. pudg bags
26 — 7 — 8 Sheffield & Salisbury — 40 cents
Nov. 24th 1 day after lead & painting
25th 1 day glazing
Dec. 4th 1 day setting
6th 1 day burning

The account book shows that he must have followed a similar routine in succeeding years. New names appear from time to time. Usually the transactions were connected with the pottery. Once in a while Hervey made a deal in bricks or watched Samuel Buell's brick kiln. From his own land he sold many a load of clay, which he dug and hauled. Sometimes he took in exchange articles that

he peddled along with his pots and pans. Amos Sanford settled an account with "six good new clocks." These doubtless came from the shop of Frederick Sanford, a clockmaker who lived in South End from 1812 to 1829 and whose brother — presumably Amos — worked with him. Another member of the Sanford family, Garwood, must have been a chairmaker: Brooks records buying from him six chairs for $8.50, two rocking chairs at $1.25 and $3.00, and other similar purchases. From 1835 to 1838 he bought seventeen clocks from Richard Ward, who was a clockmaker in Salem Bridge (now Naugatuck), Connecticut, between 1832 and 1840.

The demand for household pottery had appreciably declined before the middle of the century, but Hervey Brooks kept his business alive by turning out, in addition to his more ornamental wares, such things as safes for stove pipes, drain tiles, and flowerpots. These coarser articles constituted his entire later output. Some of his most interesting offhand pieces, however, were made during this period, when he had greater leisure.

Hervey Brooks' wife died in 1858, leaving him alone with his granddaughter Ann. She kept his house, but rather indifferently. After two years she left him, and the old potter was cared for by a housekeeper until his death, February 17, 1873, at the age of ninety-four. In his failing years two touching entries appear in his account book. The first, dated Goshen, October 8, 1862, reads: "Memorandum. It may be remembered that I have made in the course of this summer, a kiln of ware, consisting mainly of Flowerpots and Stove tubes, and have this day finished burning the same. Hervey Brooks." But his potting days were not quite over. Two years later — he was then eighty-five — he wrote: "Goshen, September 23rd, a kiln of ware this summer, consisting of Milkpans, some Pots, Pudding pans and Wash bowls, but mostly of Stove tubes and Flowerpots, and have this day finished burning the same. Hervey Brooks."

The feature of particular interest in the output of the Wadhams and Brooks potteries is the use of white slip for decoration. This material was ordinarily imported from England, the only local source of supply being the bed of kaolin in Moncton, Vermont. Hervey made at least one trip to Troy, New York, to buy white clay for Wadhams. It may have been Moncton slip. In the same year, 1809, he notes time spent "painting" platters. "Painting" was the potters' term for a process accomplished with a slip cup and not with a brush. The red lead for glazing, which cost nine dollars per hundredweight, was purchased in New Haven.

During the period when the two potters worked together, Brooks made numerous entries that show what objects they made. Forms mentioned before 1810 include: half-pint, pint, quart, and gallon jugs, pint and quart bowls, pint and quart mugs, two- and three-quart pitchers, a small cream pot, small, "midling," and large platters, a porringer, pudding pans, milk pans, small and large pots, preserve pots, chamber pots, an earthen jar, a small churn, an inkstand, pudding "bags," and sap pans.

Churns of redware seem unusual and not very practicable. They are almost nonexistent today. A churn cover with a hole and cup for the plunger is among the pieces handed down to Brooks' descendants.

The later items in the account book, entered when Brooks worked alone, are evidence of the gradual change in the type of pottery that was in demand. American redware, even in country districts, was being replaced by pictorial Staffordshire earthenware. It is more than a coincidence that Hervey's first mention of a "puncheon" for a stove pipe occurs in 1829 and that flowerpots are first noted in 1831. While pitchers, dishes,

pudding pans, and churns still found a market, the potter added to his sales by making an occasional washbowl or bed pan, and in one instance he notes a "spitting" dish. Once Brooks sold for seventy-five cents a pot filled with gin. In 1850 he records making a pitcher for "emptyings," in which some of the bread dough was reserved and set away after each baking to create yeast for the next batch. It is rather surprising to read of porringers made in 1855, but Brooks notes the sale of three in that year.

Hervey Brooks' last bill for ware was made out in 1867. His active days were then over. For six years more he kept his household accounts with scrupulous care, but the writing grew ever more feeble; the hand that had worked so long was about to fail.

CHAPTER TWENTY-TWO

The States Family of Greenwich and Stonington

Adam Staats, or States, who established a pottery in Greenwich in 1750, is the first Connecticut potter of whom we have actual record and is besides the first man in Connecticut to manufacture stoneware. Other members of the family, all stoneware potters, appear at an early date in Stonington, Norwich, and New London, and in Westerly, Rhode Island. Their contribution to this branch of ceramics is therefore considerable.

According to family tradition, Adam Staats and his brothers Peter and Matthias came from Holland and settled in South Amboy on Cheesequake Creek. However accurate this story may be, it is true that Adam Staats was in New York City April 17, 1743, when he was a witness at the baptism of Johannes Ryferner in the Reformed Dutch Church. Again, August 28, 1744, his name appears on the church records upon the occasion of his marriage to Elizabeth Gelderner. He was presumably in his early twenties at the time and was therefore born about 1720. The brother Peter, however, was only twelve years old in 1744 — too young to have been a settler. As he later became a stoneware potter, it is probable that he was in Adam's charge as an apprentice. Matthias is said to have worked at a later time as a potter with General James Morgan at Perth Amboy. Adam States' sojourn in South Amboy was brief, for, when his first child Anna was born in 1746, he was living in Pennsylvania. A son Matthias was also born in Pennsylvania, January 28, 1748. Adam is said to have moved to Rye, New York, remaining there for a time. In 1750 or earlier, he was in Greenwich.

The States family were residents of Greenwich until the death of the father in the 1760's. Between 1750 and 1758, two daughters, Mary and Elizabeth, and three sons, William, Adam, and Peter, came to swell the household. Adam, Jr., who settled in Stonington, was the founder of the well-known stoneware pottery in that town.

There seems to be little doubt that Adam States was the Dutch potter of Greenwich to whom Abraham Mead was apprenticed and who figures in a colorful account by Charles Messer Stow entitled "The 'Deacon Potter' of Greenwich," which was published in *The Antiquarian* (March 1930). States is also mentioned by Spargo, but as of Huntington, Long Island — an error that has arisen

because the potter was digging clay there in 1751. A lease from the trustees of the town of Huntington to Adam States in that year shows that he was then actually a resident of "Horse Neck" (the old name for what is now the western part of Greenwich), and local records prove that he never lived in Huntington. The curious document drawn up between the trustees and Adam, October 22, 1751, stipulates that the "Trustees abovesaid hath sold unto the Said adam States above named a Considerable Quantity of white Clay by the Cord for one shilling per Cord. . . said clay lying and being In the East neck in the township of huntington." The agreement was to last for a period of five years, during which time States was to be allowed to carry away as much clay as he wished, provided that it was for his personal use and not to be sold to "any other man," he to pay for each load as he took it. Should States become a resident of Huntington, the privilege would be extended another five years.

The "white clay" was dug from the stoneware clay bank which is part of the same bed that appears in Amboy and Staten Island. It is the only clay in New York State suitable for the purpose of making stoneware. By this fact we are assured that States was indeed a stoneware potter. Later he is said to have brought clay from South Amboy.

The Mead story concerns a young native of Greenwich, born in 1742, who was apprenticed to the "Dutch potter" at an early age. When still a lad, he fired a kiln of stoneware while his master was away and carried the process of burning and salt glazing to completion quite successfully. His teacher, finding him in the act of throwing salt into the kiln, is said to have exclaimed, "He's got it! He's got it!" — an expression of reasonable pride in the boy's cleverness.

States died at some time between 1761, when his name appears in a town record, and 1769. Abraham Mead, it is thought, took over the pottery after this event, and, although there is no record of a transfer of the property, this is no doubt correct. Mead's career was interrupted by the Revolution, but, after performing his duty in the war, he resumed his potting activities. The pottery is located by a historian of 1852, who describes it as being "on the westerly side of Indian Harbor, about where the Held house now stands." Its owner became a prominent citizen of Greenwich. He served as town treasurer for ten years and was very active in the affairs of the Second Congregational Church. In fact, he paid off the church mortgage by shipping out a boatload of pottery and giving the proceeds of its sale for that purpose. There were so many Meads in the town that he was distinguished by the title "Deacon Potter Mead."

Fortunately, seven interesting examples of Mead stoneware have been preserved by Augustus I. Mead, Abraham's great-great-grandson. All but one of these are dated, either 1790 or 1791, and three are marked with initials applied with cobalt slip. These pieces have certain pronounced European characteristics, reflecting the style of work done by Adam States. Two are jars with upward-curving horizontal handles that stand well out from the shoulder. They are decorated with a double-scroll motif combined with a triangle or diamond of dots. More noteworthy is a small handleless jar six and one-half inches in height that is well covered with dots in diamond formation, bands of blue at shoulder and base, and a continuous scroll motif on one side. The date *1791* appears with the letters *I M*, thought to stand for Isaac Mead, the potter's son. A batter jar with spout and vertical handles bears the date *1790* and a series of double-scroll decorations. A miniature jug only four inches tall and a 1791 jar with the initials *H L* (Fig. 87) complete the collection. The example illustrated was presented to the Brooklyn Museum by Mrs.

Luke Vincent Lockwood. It is dark gray in color and neatly potted. Made for Hannah Lewis, this also bears the initials *H L* and the 1791 date. Family tradition says that the pottery closed in 1791 and that these Mead pieces were made to mark its ending. Abraham Mead, however, continued to live in Greenwich until his death in 1827.

The approximate time of Adam States' death is determined by the fact that Elizabeth States was a widow in 1769, when she bound out her young son Adam to his Uncle Peter in Norwich to learn the potter's trade. The article of indenture, preserved by Charles B. Staats of Stonington, reads as follows:

This indenture made & ratified this 26th day of October, in the Tenth year of his Majestes Reighn, A D 1769, by & between Peter States of Norwich, Conn. in the County of New London, of the one part, and Elizabeth States of Great Ake Harbor, widow, of the other part. Witnesseth that I, the said Elizabeth States, do put and bind my son Adam States, her heir and assign, until he shall arrive at the age of Twenty One, he being on this 7th day of June last fourteen years old, to learn the Art and Mistery of the Potter's Trade, during which time he faithfully serve & not absent himself from his Master's service without leave, & I the said Peter States, Promise for myself my heirs & assigns to find Good Sufescent Clothing, Meat, and Trink, Washing, & Lodging, during the said term, I learn the said Adam to read, rite, and civer, & find him one new sute Close when he shall arrive at the age of Twenty One, besides his wearing appreell. In Witness whereof We have herunto set our hands and seal the day and date above.

Peter States (seal)
Elizabeth (her mark) States (seal)
Signed, Sealed and delivered in presence of
Benjamin Brush
William States

Elizabeth's place of residence, quaintly spelled Great "Ake" Harbor, was in reality Great Egg Harbor in New Jersey. After a short time, she married the Benjamin Brush who witnessed the indenture and they settled in the New Jersey town.

Peter States was a resident of Westerly, Rhode Island, and was only a temporary sojourner in Norwich. He remained there, however, until after April 14, 1772. As this period coincides with Leffingwell's introduction of the stoneware industry in Norwich, we may assume that States was the master craftsman who supervised the initiation of the works. In Westerly, Peter lived near the Stonington line on the bank of the Paucatuck River. He was a citizen of the town and member of the train band as early as 1754, and must therefore have gone there soon after learning his trade. His first purchase of land was in 1761. In April 1772 he bought two lots on the river with a mansion house, warehouse, and barn. In the numerous deeds recorded in his name, he is always called yeoman, even during his stay in Norwich, and there is no mention of a pottery. His sons became potters, but both he and they may have worked in Adam States' nearby Stonington shop. Peter States and his wife Abigail (Knowles) States are buried in the Stonington Borough Cemetery. The gravestones indicate that he died September 3, 1802, at the age of seventy, a few months after his wife had passed away. Their sons, Joseph H. and William, and William's two wives are buried in the same lot.

Adam States of Stonington began his career when only thirteen years of age by making a trip to the West Indies as a sailor, in accordance with a custom among the young lads along the coast. He was then trained by his uncle to be a stoneware potter. Almost as soon as he had finished his apprenticeship, Adam married Esther Noyes of Stonington, April 11, 1778. By the generosity of her father James Noyes, who gave the young couple a house, he was enabled to set up in business. The so-called States-Wentworth house is still

standing on the old Post Road, not far from Westerly; it is so built against the southern slope of Hinckley Hill that it has an extra story in front. Here Adam States lived and worked until the end of his life in 1826. He was three times married and had in all fifteen children. Five of them, including Adam, Jr., were Esther's offspring. Shortly after her death, Adam espoused her sister, Mary Noyes Pendelton, who lived but a few months. The third wife, Cynthia Brown, had nine children. Her oldest son, Ichabod Brown States, followed his father's trade.

In the spring of 1946, hoping to discover a sizeable pottery dump, we paid a visit to this site. Although quantities of stoneware shards, setting tiles, and wedges are scattered about the grounds, we were unable to find any one spot where they could be excavated. The land back of the house has been filled in to the level of a retaining wall about six feet high, close to the building. Setting tiles are mortared into this wall, showing that it was built after the pottery days, and perhaps encloses an area where shards lie underneath. Among many pieces of pots and jugs, I picked up in the garden a rather thin pitcher rim decorated with an undulating line of dark blue with interspersed dots. This fragment is so unlike any I have seen in later New England stoneware potteries, its eighteenth-century origin seems assured. A shard with the mark *States* was found, but it was broken in half, leaving doubt as to whether the first part was *A.*, *Adam*, or even *Peter*. It may be noted that there was not a single trace of glazed redware at this site.

Adam States carried on a farm as well as a pottery. By several purchases of land he acquired seventy-five acres in addition to the original property, besides a large share of the Noyes estate that he purchased from his son. One twenty-three acre lot was a piece of woodland that he owned jointly with Shephard Wheeler of Stonington. August 20, 1785, he made a list of his ratable estate, which included "One Head, One Horse, One Cow, One Yoak Four Year Old Oxen, One Two Year old Heffer, Two Swin Pig."

It is said that Erastus Wentworth of Norwich, who married States' daughter Esther, ran the family pottery after Adam's death. I have been unable to confirm this story. Wentworth was still of Norwich in 1832.

Stonington tradition says that Adam States ran the pottery at East Stonington, while his "son" operated the one at Long Point or Stonington Borough. In following the history of this second venture in the land records, there is some confusion, because the signature of Adam, Jr. (3d), is not always written with this distinguishing tag. One Adam or the other was connected with the second pottery. I believe it was Adam, Jr., since he signed a quitclaim deed to the property formerly owned in the name of "Adam."

Previous to 1811 the land and pottery buildings at the point were owned by Dr. Charles Phelps. As he was not a potter, it seems likely that he erected the works for William States, who purchased them, March 4, 1811, from Phelps' son Jonathan after the father had died. William States was the son of Peter and cousin of Adam States. He first appears in Stonington records at the age of twenty-one, when he bought a part interest in a house and land from his brother Joseph, January 21, 1799. Both were then living in Providence. Nothing more is heard of William until January 5, 1810, when James Chesebrough sold him land and a house at the point. States paid seven hundred dollars for the pottery works. It is described in the deed from Jonathan Phelps as "1 house, 1 kiln, 1 work shop, with wharf adjoining which came to him from his father's estate."

During the following summer Adam States, Jr., sold to his father one third of the large estate he had inherited from his grandfather

Noyes and a piece of salt marsh. For these holdings he received twenty-five hundred dollars. He was then of Lyme. In April 1812, Adam States — and I believe it was the son and not the father — bought from William a one-half interest in the pottery and one half of his dwelling house. That this was more than a mere financial arrangement is shown by a trustee's deed of September 20, 1815, releasing a further part of the Phelps estate, which mentions the property as having been deeded to William and "occupied by Adam and William." There was another transfer of Adam's share from him to Ichabod in May 1816, and again from Ichabod back to Adam in March 1819. These were actual sales, but as they were all in the family, they are of little importance. February 21, 1821, however, *Adam, Jr.*, of Stonington disposed of all his interest in the pottery to William States.

The Stonington Point pottery was run and managed by William States until he died in October 1823, and his name appears upon the stoneware made before that time. He was but forty-five years of age and had perhaps suffered a lingering sickness, as he was in debt far beyond the value of his pottery. His widow Honor sold at auction enough of the estate to pay the two thousand dollars that he owed. This included one half of the pottery land and buildings.

The business was then taken over by Joshua Swan, Jr., and Ichabod States, who ran the establishment together as Swan & States. This association continued for eleven years. November 20, 1835, Ichabod sold out to Swan for $1125, and he, in turn, ten days later, disposed of one half of the original land, wharf, and works to Charles P. Williams, who was not a potter. It is possible that Swan continued to make stoneware for a time. If so, no piece with his mark alone has as yet been found. The mark *Swan & States/ Stonington* is seen on the shards at the point and on occasional surviving pieces.

The Stonington pottery site is at the foot of Wall Street (formerly Shinbone Alley) on a little greensward that meets the water in a rocky shore on the east and south. At the southeast corner is the old wharf — Kiln Dock — now partially dismembered by wind and waves. At this pier the *Dolphin*, first centerboard vessel ever made in Connecticut or Rhode Island, used to dock to take on loads of stoneware. This ship was purchased by Adam States from Captain John Aldrich Saunders, who had been using it for general freighting. Saunders took half of his pay in stoneware, which he was able to sell in the Newport market. Still plainly visible is the outline of the building foundation, and pottery fragments greet the eye in every direction. The hurricane of 1938, which carried away most of the houses in Wall Street, uncovered part of the shard pile in a more thorough excavation than we had previously been able to make. Since then other storms have tossed bricks and shards about so they are easily accessible. Many bits of pottery gleam brightly through the clear water lapping the shore.

Perhaps because this site is so extremely clean, Stonington ware always seems more beautiful and pleasant to handle than any other. Browsing through our carton of fragments confirms this sensation. The first thing to attract the attention is that the body of this stoneware is often buff or light red, indicating an admixture of some clay of local origin or from Martha's Vineyard. Such pieces are underfired and more porous than the regular gray ware. Nearly every article is glazed inside with a coating of Albany slip. Pitchers and some crocks are entirely covered with this dark substance. Occasionally a red, light tan, or nearly black color developed from this treatment. A few small bottles and jugs are not glazed on the inside.

The Stonington shapes were simple and decoration sparingly used. Jugs, wide-

mouthed jars, some with a deep rim, crocks, pitchers and bottles, all in various sizes, chamber mugs, inkwells, and a deep plate, are among the things we found there (Fig. 111). Jugs were made with tooled necks and were touched up with swashes of color above and around the handles. One jug of a warm buff is brushed with brown; another of gray hue with chocolate color; a brown jug has very dark blue, while many others display a lighter cobalt coloring.

Jars are gray, buff, or a stained brown of rich tone, and are of two distinct shapes: one without any decorative rim, having straight sides curving in at the base; the other with a rim or collar an inch or more in depth at a slight angle to the body and emphasized by tooled lines. The latter form is typical of early nineteenth-century work and may also be seen in redware. The handles are rolls of clay hugging the body of the vessel near the rim. One fragment is decorated with a tooled band of vertical lines placed just below the collar. Another has an inch-wide band of brown stain near the rim above a nondescript flower in blue. A few shards, which seem to be parts of jars or crocks, show incised floral or conventional motifs filled in with dull or dark blue.

The inkwells are about one inch in height and two and one-half inches in diameter. They have a hole in the center for filling and dipping the pen and a smaller opening on the shoulder to accommodate the pen when it was not in use.

Stonington pitchers are in a category by themselves. The example in Fig. 110*c* holds about one and one-half pints and is marked *W. States*. Its elongated form is suggestive of ewers of the medieval period. Rims and spouts of much larger but similar pitchers are among the fragments. Another vessel has a deep straight neck joined by a narrow band to an outward sloping shoulder. This, too, is probably a pitcher. All are dark brown in color and glazed with Albany slip.

CHAPTER TWENTY-THREE

Potters of New London County

The beginnings of the potting industry in Norwich are surrounded by a certain glamour. Perhaps the charming group of aged buildings ranged along the green in old Norwich Town brings back the feeling of times long gone more forcibly than do the usual relics of the past. Some of these structures were the eighteenth-century shops of "Leffingwell's Row" put up by Christopher Leffingwell to sell the products of his many enterprises. It is said on good authority that as early as 1766 he had built paper and grist-mills, a chocolate mill, and a pottery. They were all in the "Bean Hill" section of the town along the Yantic River.

Documentary proof of the existence of a stoneware pottery in Norwich before 1770 appears in the indenture between Peter States and his nephew Adam quoted in the previous chapter. Peter was in Norwich in 1769 and remained there until after April 14, 1772. As Adam went there to learn the trade, and as both he and his uncle were always stoneware potters, the evidence is clear that a stoneware kiln, probably Leffingwell's, was in operation at that time. The kiln is mentioned in a conveyance of land from Leffingwell to Thomas Williams dated August 9, 1774, which describes the property as "about 14 rods of land lying a little southerly from my Stoneware Kiln in the First Society of Norwich . . . with the privilege of passing and re-passing upon my land from the east end of said lot on 20 feet broad, thence in a direct line by my said Potter's Kiln and Shop, between said Shop and my House that Judah Paddock Spooner Lives in, to the Highway." Leffingwell also ran an earthenware shop in partnership with Williams. It was a new works in 1771, but another may have preceded it. An advertisement in the *New-York Gazette and the Weekly Mercury*, June 10, 1771, reads:

> Wanted at the new earthenware manufactory in Norwich in Connecticut, New-England, two throwers, or wheelmen, for which good encouragement will be given by the proprietors, Christopher Leffingwell, Thomas Williams.
>
> Said Leffingwell will also give good encouragement to one or more young men (paper makers) to work in his mill in said Norwich.

Miss Mary E. Perkins, in *Old Houses of the Antient Town of Norwich*, clarifies the

location of Leffingwell's pottery lot by the history of the houses on and near it. She says: "Christopher Leffingwell gave a house to his son William. He sold it to Epaphras Porter. Back of the Porter house stood a small house — torn down in 1850. A path twenty feet wide led from this house to a lot on the north, where stood Leffingwell's stoneware kiln and shop." In 1944, with the assistance of Mrs. Albert Hunt Chase, an ardent student of Norwich antiquities, we located the Porter house. It has been greatly changed and is now hardly recognizable as an old building. Using it as a starting point, we followed Miss Perkins's directions and discovered the unmistakable remains of Leffingwell's manufacture, both stone- and earthenware. The site is now occupied by gardens and is not available for digging. It lies along the bank of the Yantic River in the area between it and the road leading from Harland's Corner to Norwich Town church, and is less than two city blocks south of the common.

In August 1777 the wares made in the new pottery were advertised in *The Norwich Packet and The Weekly Advertiser*:

To be sold for Cash or Country Produce by the Maker, at his house near Doctor Lathrop's at Norwich; A New Assortment of home made Earthenware consisting of Milk Pans, Chamber Pots, Mugs, etc.

Another notice reads:

To be sold at the Printing Office (for Cash or Country Produce) a Fresh Assortment of Home Made Earthen Ware; consisting of the following articles, viz., Pans, Butter Pots, Pitchers, Jugs, Pudding-Pans, Bowls, Mugs, Platters, Plates, etc.

An advertisement in the same paper, September 21, 1780, mentions quart and pint mugs, and another, April 5, 1781, calls attention to cups and saucers.

It will be seen that this early Connecticut pottery turned out many of the same articles that the Massachusetts men were making. Many of the shards that we found were slip decorated on backgrounds of dark brown, brick red, or tan. Both white and black slips were used. One piece has black lines on light tan; others present a combination of light and dark slips on darker grounds. One fragment is undoubtedly part of a notched-edge pie plate. It alone is not proof that this type of dish was of Norwich manufacture, but, as Leffingwell's workmen were drawn from the New York area rather than from northern New England, we would expect them to make the types of ware that prevailed around New York. There were also among these fragments pieces of turned dishes of milk-pan shape with bold stripings of slip. Another Connecticut type found frequently in and about Norwich and New London is the cylindrical jar of deep red color splashed with black (Fig. 90*b*). Similar jars are attributed to Norwalk and I have seen one of known New Jersey origin. I have never found these in Massachusetts potteries. The splash technique appears on the fragment of a bowl with rim rolled back in a delicate curve. Other quite thin pieces with plain glaze resemble other eighteenth-century workmanship.

The stoneware shards from this site belong to different periods. The earliest is probably the light gray ware with blue lines and decorations, *without* an interior glaze. Albany slip glazing was later introduced and appears on some pieces as a lining color and on others as an exterior coating. Some shards have a strong resemblance to the ancient brown "tiger" ware.

In 1792 Charles Lathrop, Leffingwell's son-in-law, was running the pottery. He advertised in the *Norwich Packet*, July 26:

Charles Lathrop

Wants a large quantity of Ash, Maple, Birch, Poplar, and Butternut Wood, suitable to burn

in a Potter's Kiln, for which he will make good payment.

He manufactures and has on hand Stone Ware, which he will sell at low prices to anyone who will purchase a large or small quantity, and make good and ready payment.

Merchants residing in the Country, or anywhere else, who will favor him with their custom may depend on having their orders (if they will send them) attended to with fidelity.

The need of fuel again impelled Lathrop to insert a notice in the town paper, April 17, 1794: "Wanted at the Pottery of Charles Lathrop, 40 Cords of White Wood, White Ash, Maple and Birch, for which Cash will be given, if brought soon."

Two years later, Lathrop, who was a very young man and obliged to struggle in competition with another pottery, sold the business to Christopher Potts and his son. They wasted no time in making a bid for the trade of their fellow townsmen. September 15, 1796, the *Packet* carried the announcement:

C. Potts & Son

Informs the Public, that they have lately established a Manufactory of Earthen Ware at the Shop formerly improved by Mr. Charles Lathrop, where all kinds of said ware is made and sold, either in large or small quantities and warranted good.

It is thought that Lathrop's successors came to Norwich from New London, where there were many families of the name. They dissolved their copartnership August 15, 1797, and that is the last known about them. Miss Perkins says that the pottery went out of existence before 1816, when the shop, occupied in 1811 by Cary Throop, was no longer standing.

Meanwhile, the successful innovations of the Leffingwell family in pottery manufacture had stimulated other adventurers in the same field. In 1786 Andrew Tracy and a partner named Huntington built a stoneware kiln on the bank of the Yantic where the Saxton Woolen Company is now situated. This site was accidentally discovered in 1910, when a trench for a water main was being dug in the mill yard. Some stoneware ink bottles and various shards were recovered. In 1944 we too found numerous stoneware fragments in the mill grounds, but were informed that the original dump was under the driveway back of the mill building. There was no evidence of a waste pile on the river's edge.

The *Norwich Packet* published the following notice July 5, 1786:

Tracy and Huntington

Have erected the Stoneware Manufactory And have ready for Sale, every article and size usually made in that branch, which they will dispose of by Wholesale at the usual price before the War. They expect to keep a constant supply so as to answer any orders on the shortest notice.

The next year, on May 24, they advertised for "an Apprentice to the Stone Ware Manufactory. An ingenious active Boy, 14 or 15 years old." A similar advertisement appeared in the *Packet*, April 2, 1790. It read: "Wanted two apprentices at the Stone Ware Manufactory, apply to Tracy and Huntington who expect to keep every article of Ware usually made in said branch, on as reasonable terms as they can be had in New York." This evidence of competition with the New York market is interesting.

The Tracy and Huntington company carried on for more than ten years, running a mill, blacksmith's shop, and pottery, but apparently under difficulties. On December 24, 1798, Tracy mortgaged the property to a Boston firm. The conveyance mentions three pieces of land in Norwich. The third is described as "the mill lot, mill house, the privileges and appurtenances, Rents and Profits viz.: My two-thirds part thereof and all my interest in the Blacksmith Shop, forge, trip

hammer and tools, Potter's work, etc." In January 1800 Tracy moved to Luzerne County, Pennsylvania, leaving an agent to look after his affairs in Norwich. The potworks was soon afterwards turned over to one Captain Joseph Hosmer of Salem, Massachusetts, who had taken up the mortgage. Tracy signed a quitclaim deed in June 1801.

As Hosmer was not himself a potter, he must have hired craftsmen to carry on the business. When he died two years later, part of this estate was conveyed to William Cleveland, another Salem man. Cleveland ran the pottery until May 2, 1814, when he sold out to Peleg Armstrong and Erastus Wentworth. This concern is the best known in old Norwich, for its handsome jugs and jars, marked with the firm name, are frequently seen. The indications are that this company used first the Tracy and Huntington pottery on Clinton Avenue, but later erected works on both sides of the Yantic where the main road to Willimantic crosses the river. In this latter location we found many stoneware fragments near the foundations of a building, where, it is said, potting was carried on to a rather late period. The Armstrong and Wentworth business came to an end in June 1834. It had been for sale for several years. The Norwich newspaper, under date of February 12, 1828, printed this notice:

Armstrong & Wentworth A Rare Chance

The subscribers contemplating a removal from this town, now offer their Stone Ware Pottery for sale, consisting of a work shop, store, house and kiln, in complete order, not surpassed by any establishment of the kind in this state.

Also, a dwelling house and lot with a good well of water, and other conveniences.

N. B. — All persons having open accounts with us are requested to call and settle the same immediately unless they prefer settling with an Attorney.

It is interesting to note that Erastus Wentworth, who was born in Norwich November 8, 1788, married Esther States, daughter of the Stonington potter, Adam States. Their marriage took place in the little town on the Sound, where Wentworth later lived in the States homestead. Armstrong had wedded his partner's sister Lucy just before the purchase of the Norwich pottery. A year after her death in 1831, he took as his second wife her sister Mary.

There were numerous other redware potters and potteries in Norwich whose names have long since been forgotten. The district of Bean Hill was always noted for its red earthenware. Two of these artisans are mentioned in an advertisement that appeared in the *Norwich Packet* November 21, 1788:

James Christie

Has just opened and is now selling on the most reasonable terms if ready pay An Assortment of Goods suitable for the present season Among which are the following Articles, viz: Broadcloths, Coatings, Baize, of different colors and qualities with a variety of Hard Ware and Groceries.

He also carries on the Potters Business, at the place where the late Mr. John Young formerly carried it on, and determines to furnish a Good Ware, and on as easy terms for the purchaser, as can be had in Connecticut.

Baking done as usual and the smallest favors gratefully acknowledged.*

Stoneware marked *S. Risley / Norwich* is often found in eastern Connecticut and, indeed, throughout New England. It is the product of forty years of manufacture in a pottery on Cove Street that was founded by Sidney Risley. The old building, bearing an historical tablet to commemorate the pottery, is even now standing on the grounds of the Yantic grain mill. Originally the site was on the shore of Yantic Cove, but the land was filled in when the New London, Willimantic and Palmer Railroad was built.

* It was a custom in Danvers and elsewhere to take pots of beans to the pottery to be baked in the kiln.

Some years ago we went in search of this landmark and of possible fragments. The shards were immediately in evidence, even in the street leading to the entrance of the mill. While we were picking them up, one of the millowners, intrigued by the sight of two middle-aged people scratching about between parked cars, looked us over and then invited us into the mill yard. Mr. Slosburg was kind enough to show us the interior of the Risley building, where we saw still in place the wheel that once conveyed power to the turning wheels. We learned that the foundation of the grain mill was constructed with bricks taken from the old kilns. The yard itself was filled with pottery shards, mostly of rather late type. On another day the gracious owner of the property insisted on my husband's investigating with him the cellar of the pottery in the hope that some remaining articles might be found there. The total result of this expedition into the depths, however, was a drapery of cobwebs and half of a stoneware milk pan — an object we had never before seen in this material.

The story of the Risley pottery begins with the erection of this building on land owned by a Norwich grocer, Elijah A. Bill, and Cushing Eells. The purchase deed, dated September 4, 1835, makes no mention of a pottery on the premises, but, ten years later, when Eells sold his share of the land to Bill, the conveyance speaks of a "building now improved as a pottery." It is thought that Risley came from Hartford, where his brother Albert was a potter for many years, and he may have come at the instigation of Elijah Bill. Bill's interest in the venture appears in the *Norwich Almanac, Directory and Business Advertiser* of 1846, in which he announced that he was "manufacturing extensively Stone Ware of the very best quality, which he offers at wholesale or retail on the very best terms." On April 2, 1856, Risley bought the land and buildings, which he had previously leased from Bill, and in the 1857 directory advertised in his own name.

In 1846 Joseph F. Winship and Orestes Root were working at the pottery. Winship was perhaps the man mentioned by Spargo in *The Potters and Potteries of Bennington* as having been employed by Captain Norton in the 1820's. Previous to his engagement at Risley's factory, Winship had made some attempt at establishing a business for himself. I have seen a jug marked *Winship & Spencer/ Norwich*. There is also a three-gallon pitcher owned by F. H. Norton with the mark, incised by hand, *J. F. Winship/ Norwich*. This, however, could have been made when the potter was working for Risley. Winship remained at the Norwich pottery until 1875 or later. In the years between 1853 and 1861, the names of Root, Thomas Irons, Albert Risley, Richard Quinlan, and John McPherson appear in Risley's account book as employees. A few years later McPherson was conducting a stoneware business in East Haven, Connecticut.

Sidney Risley's son George L. entered the business with his father in 1865 and worked with him during the next ten years. After his father's death in April 1875, he was sole owner of the plant, which he continued to manage until a fatal accident ended the family's connection with the pottery. On the day before Christmas, 1881, George L. Risley went to the works to light a fire under an upright boiler at the rear of the building. A terrific explosion took place, blowing the fifteen-hundred-pound tank through the roof and over a tall elm tree into the mud of the cove one hundred and twenty feet away. Risley was so severely injured that he died that evening.

The business was taken over the next year by Benjamin Cartwright Chace from Somerset, Massachusetts. Thereafter, until its close in 1895, the concern was known as the Norwich Pottery Works. Chace ran it only three

years, selling out to George B. Chamberlain, who was even less successful. The final owner, Otto N. Sudarberg, bought the pottery in 1887. He added a second kiln to the original equipment, besides enlarging the facilities for working and storage. Stories are told about the damage caused by the river's overflowing. In 1889 Sudarberg lost an entire baking of pottery when the waters rose into the kilns, putting out the fires.

Sidney Risley's first output was quite similar to other stoneware of a century ago, but a special interest attaches to his pottery, because he tried to create some wares of a less primitive character. Following the general trend towards mass production by the use of molds, as practiced at Bennington, he turned out some creditable specimens of Rockingham and slip-glazed stoneware. Some unusual examples of these types are in the possession of his grandson George A. Risley, who also owns his grandfather's account book, dating from 1853 to October 1861. This document gives considerable information about the pottery in its heyday.

A circular in the Metropolitan Museum also throws some light on the manufacture at the same period or earlier (it is undated). A reproduction of this bill may be seen in Scott Graham Williamson's *The American Craftsman.* It mentions "jugs, pots, pitchers, and jars of all kinds" from one-quart to four-gallon capacity. The quart sizes were advertised at one dollar per dozen, the four-gallon pieces at eight dollars, with intermediate sizes in proportion. Two-, three-, and four-gallon churns brought from five dollars to nine dollars a dozen. Pots with covers and cake pots were made in several sizes. The bill also notes "Beer, Cider, and Ginger Pop Bottles, Water Kegs, 12 to 15 gallons, Ink Stands and Wash Bowls, Stove Tubes, and Flower Pots of all sizes," and announces, "Articles ordered for the southern and western market, packed in the best manner, and at short notice."

The ledger apprises us of few forms besides those in this list, excepting spittoons and pudding pots, until the year 1855. In April occurs the first mention of molded ware. The first objects made in this fashion were pitchers in quart, two-quart, and gallon sizes. There is no way of ascertaining what they were. There are, however, in collections a number of hexagonal pitchers glazed in dull dark brown Albany slip, with relief motives in each panel, which seem to fit the description. They are marked *S. Risley/ Norwich.* I have seen perhaps half a dozen of this type. A two-quart example in George A. Risley's collection displays a shell design. A larger pitcher owned by the author is illustrated in Fig. 115. These pitchers correspond to vessels of similar form made at Bennington, Jersey City, and elsewhere during the initial period of manufacture by molding.

Risley's Rockingham glaze, in some instances was highly successful. This was perhaps what he called "Agate" in describing half-gallon and gallon jugs. The color is a pale buff lightly smudged with brown — a lighter and brighter tone than the usual Rockingham. A one-quart pitcher of this kind (Fig. 120*b*) is divided into eight panels — the front and back sections decorated with bunches of grapes in relief, the sides with full-blown roses. Around the neck are small clusters of flowers, with bunches of grapes in front. Altogether it is a charming piece. This rare example of Risley Rockingham and another of more primitive type are owned by George A. Risley. The second pitcher (Fig. 120*a*), of nearly one-quart capacity, was obviously the result of an early and not too successful attempt at the Rockingham technique. Its buff body is daubed irregularly with dark brown smudges and the glaze is dull and poor. Its principal interest derives from a relief design of stalks and ears of corn. Both examples are marked *S. Risley/ Norwich.* A two-quart pitcher with the same

mark and ear-of-corn design, owned by Charles B. Gardner of New London, exhibits a glaze as fine as the best Bennington flint enamel.

Risley made cuspidors by two methods: some were turned on the wheel and others cast in molds. Pint and half-pint flasks were probably molded, as were his one-quarter gallon soap dishes. Other articles mentioned in the ledger are half-gallon bean pots and lead pans, a double jug, and half a dozen milk pans (the only entry of this form). Tiny stoneware jugs with stoppers complete were made to be worn as watch charms and were doubtless popular gifts for visitors to the pottery.

A handsome stoneware water cooler owned by Henry R. Armstrong (see *Antiques*, October 1923) is a product of the works after Risley's time. This is indicated by the mark *Norwich Pottery Works/ Norwich, Conn.* and by the stenciled lettering of the stamp. It is nevertheless a notable piece. The front is adorned with a finely modeled eagle in relief, while sprays of grape leaves ornament the sides. It is supplied with a domed cover.

The ledger reveals several facts of interest concerning the operation of the pottery. From it we learn that Risley bought clay and sand from A. T. Pearce. The clay was brought from New Jersey and Long Island. The sand cost about one dollar a ton. We find that Risley sometimes filled orders for jugs for Edmands & Company of Charlestown. He gave them a forty per cent discount and was paid by a "check on Bunker Hill bank." He rarely paid his employees in cash, but rather with such necessities as shoes, shirts, molasses, potatoes, or "mittings." Like all other potters one hundred years ago, Sidney Risley utilized a peddler's cart for the distribution of his wares. His wagon, driven by Alvin T. Davis, George A. Risley's maternal grandfather, presented a unique appearance, with two fine Newfoundland dogs hitched ahead of the horses.

The existence of a stoneware pottery in New London in the early nineteenth century is established by crocks marked *S. T. Bruer/ New London* and by the mention of such a works in the Pease and Niles *Gazetteer* of 1819. Such other information as I have been able to gather has come from land records.

The story begins in April 1800, when Job Taber bought of Thomas Lathrop a lot of land on the road from New London to Norwich. The following year he purchased from Sawney Crosley another lot with a dwelling house. Later records show that Taber built a kiln there and that his pottery was located on Mill Cove in New London near the westerly end of the present traffic bridge over the Thames River. In February 1803 his neighbor to the south, William Hurlbutt, released to Taber his right in the land "adjoining the lot on which the said Taber's Pottery stands." Three months later Job Taber and Stephen Tripp were in bankruptcy and the estate was in the hands of assignees. In a quitclaim deed they turned the property over to Michael Omensetter, who was already living there. Omensetter paid fourteen hundred dollars and secured the use of the land, dwelling house, and pottery. On July 2, 1810, Omensetter bought the estate outright. It was then described as having a frontage of one hundred and eleven feet on Main Street to the west and the same on the cove to the east.

Omensetter was the potter listed by Pease and Niles. He is next mentioned in the records May 13, 1826, when this same lot was sold by John A. Fulton and Nathaniel Saltonstall to Daniel Goodale, Jr., of Hartford for eighteen hundred dollars. The deed notes a dwelling house with a store in part of it, a small store, pottery kiln, and other buildings — "heretofore occupied by Michael Omen-

setter, dec'd., and said premises have lately been occupied by Mr. States."

Goodale got a mortgage on the pottery and may have attempted to operate it. Two years later, June 28, 1828, we find him selling a two-thirds interest to Stephen T. Brewer for two thousand dollars. That Brewer actually made stoneware there we know. He had, however, mortgaged the property to Goodale for the amount of the purchase, a debt that he undertook to pay back in five payments of four hundred dollars each. This he was apparently unable to do, and his attempt at stoneware manufacture was a failure. September 3, 1830, Goodale released the New London pottery to Thomas C. Perkins in a quitclaim deed, and that was the end of this particular venture.

The "Mr. States" who had lived on the premises shortly before the spring of 1826 was William States, son of Adam, Jr., and grandson of Adam of Stonington. With Benjamin B. Knowles he had bought land with buildings thereon at the corner of Mill and Main Streets and a barn nearly opposite. The purchase deed was signed November 9, 1825. At some time between this date and December 30 of the following year, Knowles and States built a stoneware kiln, which is referred to in a mortgage deed from them to Adam States of New London. The land was near the town mill. It was bounded west and north by highways, south by Nicholas Darrow, and east by the cove, and could not have been far from the Omensetter pottery. During the construction of the new traffic bridge, excavations for the piers uncovered the site of a pottery, presumably the States kiln, just south of the old mill and the bridge at the head of the cove. William States died at sea September 8, 1832. With his passing this pottery probably came to a conclusion.

These New London records indicate stoneware manufacture at all times rather than redware. There are, however, numerous cylindrical jars of Connecticut type, as well as other pieces of lead-glazed ware, that have been attributed to New London. Pitkin so ascribed a melon-shaped jar and a large preserve pot. Without further evidence of the existence of a redware pottery, I should be inclined to attribute these pieces to Norwich.

The Brewer stoneware must be considered in the category of comparative rarities, since it was all made in the brief span of two years. It has two marks: one with the alternative spelling of the name—*S. T. Bruer/ New London*; the other with the initials separated by little impressed motives like asterisks—*S * T * Brewer/ New London.* This second mark appears on a gallon jug adorned with an incised blue leaf in the collection of George S. McKearin.

CHAPTER TWENTY-FOUR

Hartford and New Haven Potteries

Hartford County was the meeting place of various influences in pottery manufacture. The early redware makers seem to have been trained in the Massachusetts tradition as well as in the ways of southwestern Connecticut. I have been unable to determine whether notched-edge pie plates were made in the Hartford area. They are still found in the neighboring towns, but may be of Norwalk origin. It was Mr. Pitkin's observation that the Hartford redware potters made principally hollow ware. In this category he probably included the deep dishes of northern New England style, while noting the absence of "Connecticut" plates in his local investigations. The dish illustrated in Fig. 45 is almost a counterpart of one attributed to Major Seymour of Hartford. At the site of the Goodwin pottery I found a similar smooth-edged dish fragment. Hartford stoneware bears some resemblance to New Jersey work, especially in occasional jars with opposing vertical handles. Men from Norwalk and New Haven must have worked at times in the Hartford potteries, bringing with them the craft characteristics of men trained in New Jersey.

In 1818 there were five potteries in Hartford. These must have been the Goodwin and the Seymour shops in West Hartford, the Goodwin & Webster stoneware works on Front Street, the nearby pottery run by Daniel Goodale, and one other.

The first Goodwins and the first Seymours were redware men. The Goodwin pottery was started by Seth of that name before 1800 in the suburb now known as Elmwood. It is thought that he set up in business in 1795, when he was twenty-three years old. His son Thomas O'Hara came into the world the following year. It was he who built in 1821 the house still standing at 1198 New Britain Avenue (Route 6) and now the home of his great-granddaughter, Mrs. W. J. Craig. Thomas O. Goodwin moved into this house at the time of his marriage. He lived until 1880, becoming a prosperous and influential citizen. At one time he owned almost one third of the land between his home and Hartford. Part of this estate was a farm. The present town of Elmwood derives its name from the rows of elm trees that Goodwin set out along its main street.

Seth Goodwin was a redware potter of

the old school; his son was a stoneware maker as well. Jugs bearing the mark *T. O. Goodwin/ Hartford* are not uncommon today. In the later period some very practical earthenware was produced. Mrs. Craig found in the Goodwin yard the redware pipe that conveyed water to the house from the well. Each section was about three and one-half inches in diameter, with a one-inch bore, and was pointed at one end to fit into the next unit. This tile had the peculiarity of being glazed inside.

Seth Goodwin's nephew Harvey, born in 1802, became a potter. His first venture was in Torrington, Connecticut (possibly Goshen), where he lived for four years. Returning to West Hartford, he worked for his uncle until 1832, then started an enterprise of his own. This pottery ran until 1870 under his management and was carried on in its later days by his sons Harvey Burdett and Wilbur Elmore as Goodwin Bros. Their shop stood on the south side of New Britain Avenue just east of the railroad tracks.

For such meager information as I have concerning the original Seymour pottery I am indebted to Albert W. Pitkin's account in his *Early American Folk Pottery*. Pitkin obtained his story from Major Frederick Seymour, grandson of the founder, who occupied the ancestral home until his death in 1903. He says that Nathaniel Seymour built his kiln about 1790 at the southeast corner of Park Street and Quaker Lane in West Hartford. Until 1825 Seymour's output was wholly earthenware made of native clay. His sand for glazing he dug at Rocky Hill nearby. A great deal of ware was produced in this pottery. Four men were employed to turn the vessels in such quantity that a kiln could be fired every week. Mr. Pitkin was informed that the inside diameter of the Seymour kiln was ten feet. The redware was retailed in the usual way — one-gallon dishes selling for one dollar a dozen and two-gallon milk pans at one dollar and a half. A magnificent pitcher made by Nathaniel Seymour is displayed in the Pitkin collection at the Wadsworth Atheneum, Hartford (Fig. 44). It is a strong, heavy piece of redware of bulging form suggestive of much earlier jugs. It has a light tan glaze boldly splotched with brushings of white slip dotted with green.

Like other potters, the Seymours turned to flowerpots when the demand for redware began to wane. It is said they were the principal output after 1830. Although Nathaniel had three sons, they may not all have been potters. His grandson Frederick was his successor. He took over the pottery when he was twenty-one, but ran it only two years. The shop at this time was moved a quarter of a mile up Quaker Lane. In 1842 Seymour went west to Michigan. Seven years later he was in the stoneware business with one Stedman in Ravenna, Ohio. He returned to his native town after the Civil War, but no reference is made to his again operating a pottery in Hartford.

The principal clues to present-day knowledge about the potteries on Front Street in Hartford proper come from the recollections of Albert Risley, published in the *Hartford Evening Post*, May 26, 1883. Risley, who was a brother of Sidney of Norwich, had worked for sixty years in the potworks then operated by Seymour & Bosworth. His story and some further data from land records form the basis of this account.

The first potter whom I can place by actual date in the city is Ashbel Wells. He is mentioned in the Judd Manuscript in the Forbes Library, Northampton, Massachusetts, as a trader dealing in stoneware from 1785 to 1794. In 1787 he sent to the store at Northampton for sale on commission "pots and jugs of several sorts and 2 doz. Chamberpots @ 10/." It was a simple matter to determine that Wells was the owner of a pottery. He

is called "Junior" in all deeds and so appears to have been the son of Ashbel Wells, whose land in 1773 abutted on the dividing line between Hartford and Farmington. On April 13, 1787, Ashbel, Jr., purchased of John H. Lord for $110 a lot of land on the east side of Front Street, measuring sixty feet on the street and two hundred and eighteen feet deep. A mortgage deed ten years later mentions a house, potter's kiln, and well on the premises. Whether Wells actually operated this shop himself there is no means of knowing, because occupations are not specified in Connecticut deeds. It is a safe presumption however, that it was he who made and peddled the stoneware. He owned numerous other pieces of property in Hartford. One lot, purchased in June 1787, lay to the west of the burying ground. In 1792 he bought a dwelling house of Caleb Woodward on the north side of Bachelor Street, which is described as being "34 feet by 26 feet and 2 stories high." During the period up to 1802 these holdings were always heavily mortgaged, and we may judge that Wells was in debt. I was unable to find record of the conclusion of his pottery business.

In the 1790's, also, John Souter, an Englishman, made his appearance in Hartford. He is said to have built an earthenware shop on the northeast corner of Potter and Front Streets. In 1805 he sold it to Peter Cross, a stoneware manufacturer. The name Cross does not occur in the land records, and I believe he was not a native of Hartford. Although he made some excellent stoneware, he was not altogether successful. After a few years he sold his first building to Horace Goodwin and Mack C. Webster and moved to 38 Front Street; but this, too, he abandoned at some time before 1818. Cross's business was taken over by two retired sea captains, George Benton and Levi Stewart, who lived on either side of the pottery. They found a manager in Daniel Goodale, Jr. Although there seems to be no confirmation of the statement, he is said to have come from Whately, Massachusetts. Goodale soon acquired the potworks in his own right. Risley gives the date as 1818, but the land records show that he made the purchase with Absalom Stedman on March 5, 1822. The conveyance specifies land on the east side of Front Street, "on which stand Pottery works now occupied by said Goodale and Stedman." The purchase price was sixteen hundred dollars, which was to be paid back to the former owners, Nathaniel Terry and his wife, in sixteen yearly installments. Goodale bought Stedman out on October 6, 1825, and thereafter ran the works alone. Various other mortgages were placed on the property. Like Cross, Goodale was unable to make a go of the stoneware business. April 19, 1830, he sold the pottery, with the fixtures and apparatus, to Thomas C. Perkins for ten thousand dollars. Goodale received little, if any, of this seemingly huge amount and he even lost his rights in a pottery at New London in the settlement of his affairs. Goodwin and Webster acquired the pottery in the following year for fourteen hundred dollars and ran it in connection with their old shop.

There is a great similarity in the jugs made by Peter Cross and those from the hand of Goodale. The most noteworthy piece by Cross that I have seen is an urnshaped water cooler in the Deerfield Memorial Museum. It has a domed cover and is marked *P. Cross/ Hartford*. Goodale was perhaps something of an artist. He delighted in making presentation pieces with cleverly incised decorations. The jug shown in Fig. 47 was made in the year 1822, when Goodale and Stedman bought the pottery, and is marked with the firm name. It was a gift to L. Watson, whose name is stamped on it in five different places, and who, as the dividers and compass indicate, was apparently a Masonic confrere. A

similar jug, even more elaborate, is owned by George S. McKearin. Made for Captain Stewart, it bears his name as well as Goodale's and is most appropriately set out with a ship under full sail. A Goodale jug in the Brooklyn Museum is adorned with a spread eagle. The incised decoration on all these pieces is colored with cobalt blue.

Goodale's subsequent career is unknown. In 1827 he had bought twelve and one-half acres of land south of the center of Hartford where the crossroad to Wethersfield left the New Haven turnpike. Stedman went to New Haven.

Several other potters worked in Hartford during the first quarter of the century or earlier. Isaac Hanford, a stoneware maker, is placed in the town by Spargo as early as 1796. January 20, 1800, he secured a patent for a new method of making bricks, tiles, and pottery ware in general and of discharging the molds. Jacob Fisher was turning out both redware and stoneware in 1805.

The name of Thompson Harrington is perpetuated by a splendid four-gallon water cooler in the Avery Memorial of the Wadsworth Atheneum (Fig. 46*a* and *b*). One side bears the legend: *Made by T. Harrington/ Hartford/ Conn.*; while the other is marked *Isaiah Gilbert/ West Hartford, Conn.*, for whom the piece was evidently made. The fine form, with vertical handles for lifting, the incised decoration colored with cobalt blue, and the impressed rosettes and tassels make this a truly noble specimen. Long after he had produced this cooler, Harrington was working in Lyons, New York. He was the manager of a pottery there in 1852 and its owner in 1867. A Jacob C. Fisher, associated with him, may have been the former Hartford potter or his son. Stephen T. Brewer was of Hartford in 1828 when he bought the New London pottery of Goodale.

Horace Goodwin, a brother of Seth Goodwin of Elmwood, and Mack C. Webster * ran both the Front Street potteries after 1830. They had acquired numerous pieces of land in the vicinity and had laid the foundations for the first successful manufactory of stoneware in Hartford. Risley says that the old corner pottery was sold and the firm dissolved in 1850. He has confused the two events, for Goodwin was no longer in the firm after 1840, when the style *M. C. Webster & Son* appears in the *Hartford City Directory*, with the address 27 Front Street. The son, Charles T. Webster, after his father's death in 1857, ran the works in partnership with Orson Hart Seymour as Webster & Seymour.

O. H. Seymour was a nephew of Israel T. Seymour of the West Hartford family, who is well known in connection with his potting activities in Troy, New York. Seymour's association with Webster lasted for some ten years. In 1867 the firm was Seymour & Brother at 50 Front Street. The brother was Henry Phelps Seymour, who combined his pottery interests with a position as chief engineer of the fire department. He died in 1871. His brother, two years later, reorganized the business with Stanley B. Bosworth as partner. Seymour & Bosworth were still running in the eighteen-eighties. These Front Street potteries, therefore, have a history of continuous operation, although under different managements, for about ninety years.

In East Hartford a stoneware pottery was at one time conducted under the name E. Frayd & Company.

Richard Pitkin, brother of William and Elisha who built the famous glass works in Manchester, a few miles east of Hartford, made an attempt to establish a stoneware pottery there also. Little is known about it, except that Pitkin ran it with his son-in-law Dudley Woodbridge. As Woodbridge did not marry Elizabeth Pitkin until 1800, the

* Sometimes called "McCloud," but signed his name "Mack C."

pottery must have been a nineteenth-century venture.

The Pitkins were an influential family at the time of the Revolution and they owned large tracts of land between Manchester Centre and Manchester Green, about one mile to the east. Richard Pitkin had his home at the Green, which was then the trading center of the town. The store and tavern and the glass-house were in this vicinity. The pottery stood a short distance northwest of the glass works. Albert Pitkin, in a conversation with Ralph Cone, whose wife was a daughter of Dudley Woodbridge, was told that the family made stoneware, and he obtained from Cone a salt-glazed stoneware jar that had been handed down to Mrs. Cone by her mother as a product of the Pitkin shop. He says, however, that the clay was dug on the Pitkins' land about one-quarter mile east of Aaron Cook, Jr.'s house — a lot known as the "clay-hole piece." This would indicate earthenware manufacture. Although the pottery boasted only one kiln, it is possible that both redware and stoneware were made. Pitkin asserts that jugs, jars, churns, and barrel-shaped stoneware bottles were part of the output. As twelve men were employed, the enterprise must have been organized on a fairly large scale. The history of this pottery would bear further investigation.

There were still other potteries in Hartford County, since seven are recorded in the 1840 census. Only one of these was in the city. Some of them may have produced the Norwalk-type pie plates that are still discovered in the region east of Hartford. The presence of a pottery in East Windsor is suggested by the fact that Jonathan Fenton spent a year or two there and was living in the town when one of his children was born in 1799. He was perhaps working in the employ of another potter or was trying to establish a place of his own.

New Haven had a fairly continuous record of pottery manufacture over a long period. The pioneer potters mentioned by Atwater did not, however, carry on through the eighteenth century. A checklist of inhabitants and professions in 1748 * shows that there were no potters in the town at that date. In the last decade of the century several men who later achieved success as skilled potters elsewhere were living in New Haven and probably working there. Jacob Fenton, afterwards of Burlington, New York, was in the city from 1792 to 1800. His brother Jonathan was there in 1793 and Frederick Carpenter, later of Charlestown, in 1797 and 1799. All were stoneware potters. Carpenter went to New Haven from his home town of Lebanon, Connecticut, and the inference is that he learned his trade with the Fentons. If they did, indeed, operate a pottery, it was closed after Jacob Fenton's departure. In 1811, according to Dwight's *Statistical Account of the Towns in Connecticut*, there was no pottery in New Haven.

It is possible that the Fentons were preceded by Samuel Dennis, who, October 9, 1789, appealed to the General Assembly for financial assistance to enable him to start a works for making superior ware. His petition states:

> That he is acquainted with the potter's business, and is about to erect a stone pottery; there is in this country a plenty of clay which he presumes of the same kind with that from which the queen's-ware of Staffordshire is usually made; and that he wishes to erect a pottery for the purpose of manufacturing the finer kinds of ware usually made in Staffordshire, particularly the queen's-ware.

The petition was not granted and Dennis's fate is unknown. I have ascertained, however, that he was a native of New Haven, born in 1769, and that he died there in 1815.

* Punderson and Barber, *History and Antiquities of New Haven*, 1855.

The next reference to a pottery in this town is in 1825. At that time there was a shop on the shore side of East Water Street near Custom House Square and the head of the wharf. It is also described as being near Olive Street. In 1831 Absalom Stedman, the former partner of Daniel Goodale in Hartford, advertised a stoneware pottery on Water Street. This was no doubt the works above mentioned, founded when Stedman sold out to Goodale in 1825. The notice of his business appears in the *American Advertising Directory*, calling attention to his "Fire Brick and Stone Ware Manufactory." I have seen stoneware marked *Stedman/ New Haven* and *Stedman & Seymour/ New-Haven.* Which of the potting Seymours was in the partnership does not appear, but it will be recalled that Frederick Seymour of Hartford was in the stoneware business with one Stedman in Ravenna, Ohio, in 1849.

Frederic Fairchild Sherman in *Early Connecticut Artists and Craftsmen* mentions J. Duntze as a New Haven potter. He is probably the man who marked a dark brown stoneware jar in the Old Sturbridge Village collection "John Dunes/ keep it for you sake/ September first 1835." Mr. George McKearin has found a cylindrical jar which displays an incised ship with the American flag and the inscription "25000 majority Gnl Jackson," and the identifying mark, incised on the shoulder, *A. Duntze / New Haven.* There is no clue to the history of the Duntze family.

In 1840 the name of James Harrison, a potter, is listed in the New Haven directory. Other names occur in later days. The *New England Business Directory* of 1856 lists "Wm. R. Floyd — Pottery" and in 1865 the name of John McPherson. The latter is probably the man who was working for Risley in Norwich in 1861. A late pottery began in New Haven in 1868. It was started by S. L. Pewtress, who came from Worcester, although born in New York State. This stoneware factory at 71 Chatham Street was still running in 1887. Its management was assumed before 1880 by George Henderson, who ran the works under the style Henderson and O'Halloran for a time before founding his pottery in Dorchester, near Boston. The mark used was *S. L. Pewtress/ New Haven, Ct.*

A New Haven County pottery in Naugatuck was operated by Edwin Benham in 1860.

CHAPTER TWENTY-FIVE

Pots and Dishes of Norwalk

One of the busiest potting centers in Connecticut was Norwalk. No fewer than six redware or stoneware potteries were operated within the limits of the township. The history of these concerns has been written in admirable detail by Andrew L. and Kate Barber Winton and presented in two well illustrated articles in *Old-Time New England* (January and April, 1934). Mr. and Mrs. Winton have so nearly exhausted the possibilities of research, which they have amplified by actual excavations on one site, that little can be added to their findings.

For a complete understanding of the localities mentioned, it must be explained that the present city of Norwalk was formerly made up of two communities. The section originally known as "Old Well" is now South Norwalk and is that part lying near the tracks of the New York, New Haven, and Hartford Railroad. About one mile to the north was Norwalk Borough, while at about the same distance south of Old Well was a settlement called "The Village."

There is a tradition, probably well founded, that a pottery was running in Norwalk before 1700. A descendant of its former owner is responsible for the statement that it was sold when the family moved to Long Island. Albert W. Pitkin was assured that pottery was made in the town at least as early as 1780. This is verified by a passage in Hall's *Ancient Historical Record of Norwalk, Conn.*, written in 1847: "Onesimus, at one time after the town was burnt, went down to get salt hay at Miss Phoebe's meadow, not far from the old potter's shop, sometimes called 'The Village,' below Old Well . . . Onesimus saw some 'Red-Coats' stealing along up a creek, and gave alarm to Miss Phoebe."

The owner of this pottery has not been determined, but the evidence points to the elder Asa Hoyt. He and his son and namesake appear as grantees in eighty-five deeds registered in the Norwalk Land Records. None of these mentions the pottery, nor is there record of its coming to either of them by inheritance. Nevertheless, when, on November 30, 1816, the younger Hoyt mortgaged sixty acres of land in two tracts, the "pottery" was standing on one of them. At this time, Asa was living in New York State, where he had migrated in 1807, five years after his father's death. It is established that he was

a potter. He was born in 1772 and therefore must have worked at his trade in Norwalk for nearly fifteen years. Previous to 1796 he owned another "Potter House" at Old Well, where he had no doubt set up in business for himself after reaching his majority. This he sold, January 1, 1796, to Absalom Day, a potter from New Jersey, who had arrived in Norwalk three years before and had perhaps worked for Hoyt.

After mortgaging the village pottery to Isaac Hicks in 1818, Hoyt signed a quitclaim deed on February 1 of the following year to John, Samuel, and Valentine Hicks, administrators of the Hicks estate. The potshop was advertised for sale by them in the *Norwalk Gazette*, July 19, 1820, and was described as "That valuable property, lately belonging to Mr. Asa Hoyt, lying at the Village, so called, in Norwalk, near a good landing consisting of two Houses, two Barns, a Store, an extensive Pottery and about sixty acres of land, well proportioned for Meadow, Plough, and Pasture Land, and under good improvement." As late as 1825 part of this estate was unsold and was advertised as "that valuable & pleasant situation known by the name of 'The Village' lying about a mile from the Old Well," with "a large Pottery, 2 Kilns for burning Ware" and "a good Wharf." This property was sold in 1827 and resold in 1833, but no further mention is made of the potworks, which were evidently put to other uses.

This earliest pottery stood near a creek on the present grounds of the Nash Engineering Company, the site discovered by Mr. and Mrs. Winton. They found that, in the process of constructing a causeway across the salt marsh to a rocky point, material from the pottery dump had been excavated and used for filling. For about two hundred feet along both sides of the roadway, shards could be recovered by digging in the rubbish. They obtained a great many redware fragments, which determine beyond a doubt the types of vessels made by the Hoyts.

As this early Norwalk earthenware displays some features that differ from the northern tradition, it is worth noting in detail. First, its range of glaze color is far more limited. With few exceptions, the Hoyt fragments are black or plain red, or red with black splashes. With regard to careful turning and finishing and good glazing, their workmanship is excellent. Among black-glazed pieces, the Wintons have identified bottles somewhat flattened on two sides (a typical Connecticut shape), jugs, jars, and chambers, with reeded lines, a three-and-one-half-inch cup, and a small, narrow flowerpot with crimped edge. Plain glazed milk pans and lard pots similar to those made in every pottery were found and an almost complete pitcher, red in color, with black splashes. Parts of curved jars with rolled rims are unlike any known entire specimen. A domeshaped cover, corresponding to the cover of a slant-sided jar in the Winton collection, is a type seldom found in New England, except in southwestern Connecticut. Cylindrical jars, so common in Connecticut at a later period, do not appear in the Hoyt shards. The characteristic jug of this pottery had its handle attached to the shoulder instead of the neck. Also typical of the Hoyt output is the practice of not allowing the glaze to flow all the way to the base. This will be noted especially in Mr. Winton's photograph of the pitcher and bottle. Large unglazed jars designed for use as water coolers were made at the Hoyt pottery, and fragments of their rims and of the openings where the spigot was to be inserted were unearthed.

Most interesting are the parts of slip-decorated plates, which differ from the later Norwalk product in having a dotting of green over the yellow design. This practice has been noted in the work of Daniel Bayley and other eighteenth-century potters of Mas-

sachusetts. It seems to have been discontinued soon after 1800. One fragment of a pan-shaped dish, the usual eighteenth-century type, was discovered on this site. Its color is an olive-green, appearing brown in artificial light, and it is decorated with parallel lines of clear yellow intersected by a single wavy line. It is probable that Asa Hoyt fashioned dishes of this kind in the early days of the pottery, but, after coming in contact with potters who had been trained in the more exuberant style of New Jersey, he began to execute the rather complicated slip trailing that is seen on other shards. These pieces show the use of a triple-quill slip cup, which was manipulated by a turn of the wrist to give a wavy ribbon effect. This was further treated by a slight feathering with a pointed instrument, particularly where straight parallel lines appear in the decoration. Nearly all pieces of this description are dotted with green and are round or oval with notched edges.

Although knowledge of the Day pottery must be derived from documents rather than from shards, there is plentiful evidence of the wares produced over a long period in examples owned by Day's descendants. Absalom Day came to Norwalk from Chatham, New Jersey, where he was born May 15, 1770, and where he had been trained in the potter's craft. In 1793 he leased from Samuel Gibbs for twenty-one years a piece of land on the harbor shore adjoining Asa Hoyt's property, and in the following year he purchased the homestead where he was then living. As mentioned above, he acquired Asa Hoyt's "Potter House" at Old Well in January 1796. These transactions were followed by numerous others by which he added to his holdings in Norwalk.

Soon after his arrival in the town (February 26, 1793), Absalom Day married Betsey Smith. During their early married life both husband and wife worked in the pottery, which was a small shop set off from their house. Absalom turned the ware and Betsey helped him with the burning. He was his own salesman. When a kiln of ware was finished, he loaded it in his small boat and set out on trips along the coast that often lasted several weeks. Once his potshop burned down during his absence, but this calamity was only a temporary setback in his career. Besides being a potter, Day was an itinerant Methodist preacher, and in his later years he ran a large farm. He had a reputation for open-handed generosity and benevolence that no doubt contributed to his success. The Days had eleven children. Two of the sons followed their father's calling. Many of Norwalk's later craftsmen were trained in the Day shop. The following notice in the *Norwalk Gazette* is amusing, not only because it illustrates the customs of the day, but also because Jason Merrills (Merrill) was undoubtedly apprehended: his picture, taken many years later, may be seen in a group photograph of some Norwalk potters published in *Old-Time New England* (July 1934).

One Cent Reward — Runaway from the service of the subscriber on the 7th ult, an indented apprentice to the Potting Business by the name of Jason Merrills, about 17 years of age. Rather large of his age, stocky built, has a large head, large blue eyes, and lightish hair. Had on when he went away a blue surtout coat, a blue undercoat, blue mixt satinett pantaloons, and is supposed to have had some other clothes with him. Whoever will return said apprentice shall be entitled to the above reward and no charges. All persons are forbid harboring or trusting said apprentice on penalty of the law,

Absalom Day

Norwalk, March 10, 1824.

When Absalom Day was sixty-one years old (December 9, 1831), he deeded to his sons, Noah S. and George, land "with brick building lately erected and standing thereon" with "privilege of a driftway in the old path"

and the use of Absalom's well. The sons were now starting in business for themselves. The next year they advertised for "Three or four apprentices to the Earthen and Yellow Ware business to whom good encouragment will be given." This venture was not wholly successful. George withdrew from it and quitclaimed his share to Noah March 26, 1834, and he in turn, on April 5, deeded the property "with a brick building standing thereon used as a pottery & a slip-house & kiln house" back to Absalom Day. On May 17, 1834, the father leased the pottery to William Taylor, stipulating that the premises might "be used for the purpose of making and burning ware of any description the said Taylor may choose to make," and that "said Taylor is to have the use of the Tools now used for making ware in said buildings and is to leave the same in good repair."

An advertisement in the *Norwalk Gazette*, November 26, 1833, shows that Taylor was already associated with one of the Days in the manufacture of "fire proof earthen ware." This notice reads:

Day, Venables & Taylor, Fire Proof Earthenware manufacturers, Norwalk, Conn. — The subscribers recommend the above with confidence and particularly such articles as are for baking by fire. The ware has been known in the market over two years. In 1831 they received the premium from the New York Institute at their annual fair. Since then they have made extensive improvements in the pottery. The article may be seen in the rear of the old red ware factory at Old Well, near the steam boat landing, or at 38 Peck Slip, New York. All orders punctually attended to and the ware carefully packed for transportation. Articles will be made to pattern and that of an inferior quality, one-third less in price.
Norwalk Sept 10.

Nothing is known of the fate of this concern. Absalom Day, however, was still carrying on his old business until December 31, 1841, when he conveyed to his son Noah S. one-half an acre of land with "the potter's shop and other buildings thereon standing." This lot abutted on the land "where George Day now lives." Noah S. Day owned this pottery until 1849. In the meantime, his father having died in May 1843, he formed a partnership with his cousin Asa E. Smith. The old shop was perhaps abandoned at that time. It was sold, October 16, 1849, to Russell W. Norton and Alonzo Isbell and was then described as one acre with "Pottery building, Clay house, Kiln House and Store House and other buildings . . . together with the Steam Engine, Lathes, and main shafting." In 1852 the plant became the property of The Russell & Erwin Manufacturing Company of New Britain and was used for the production of "mineral" knobs. The pottery was finally destroyed by fire.

The Day pottery stood on the west side of North Water Street, South Norwalk, just south of the present railroad embankment. Day's house was on the southwest corner of Water and Washington Streets, while his son George lived on the northwest corner of the land adjoining the pottery. Factories and business establishments now cover the site of this once flourishing enterprise.

Photographs of pitchers, jugs, and other pieces owned by the Misses Day, great-granddaughters of Absalom, show that lead-glazed redware and buff ware with a less lustrous glaze (probably Albany slip) were the regular products of the Day potteries. The decorated ware is molded in the form of pie plates and rectangular platters or deep trays, all with notched edges. The slip trailings are done with a single-quill cup and are of the simplest variety, such as a few zigzag lines or scrolls. A few plates have lettering. One in the Day collection has the legend in script: *A penny up the Cast.*

The Smith pottery of Norwalk Borough was in reality an offspring of the Day fac-

tory, although it was for some fifteen years its contemporary. Asa E. Smith, the nephew of Absalom Day's wife, was apprenticed to Day in 1812, when he was fourteen years old. Thus, he too was trained in the ways of the New Jersey potters. The first intimation that he had started a business of his own appears in the *Gazette*, November 1, 1825. His advertisement reads:

Stone Ware Factory/ The subscriber informs the public that he has established a Manufactory of/ Stoneware/ in Norwalk at the foot of Mill Hill a few rods east of the Bridge, where he will be able to supply Orders in that line to any extent. He has now on hand an extensive assortment of Ware which as to quality and beauty cannot be surpassed by the Ware made at any other Factory in the country. It will be sold reasonably both at Wholesale and Retail. Merchants in the country can have their orders met to their complete satisfaction upon the shortest notice.

Asa E. Smith

Norwalk Oct. 31, 1825.

This establishment is shown in a "South View of the Borough of Norwalk" from John Warner Barber's *Connecticut Historical Collections*, published in 1836. It was on the shore of the long inlet from the sea that makes up in to Norwalk Borough. Here Asa Smith had his own wharfing facilities, where the clay from South Amboy and Long Island could be conveniently dumped and where the pottery could be shipped to many points along the coast. Much of it was sent to New York to a distributing agency at 38 Peck Slip.

Until 1837 Smith was the sole proprietor of his pottery. January 18 of that year he announced in the *Gazette* that he had taken a partner:

Notice Co-Partnership/ Noah Selleck having this day associated with him Mr. Asa E. Smith, the business of Stone Ware Manufacturing, at the Manufactory at Norwalk, will be continued under the firm of/ Selleck & Smith/

N. B. All persons having demands upon Noah Selleck, or being indebted to him, are requested to call at the Factory as above or at 38 Peck Slip, N. York, for the settlement of the same.

Norwalk Jan. 11, 1837

This association lasted but six years. Selleck does not appear to have been a potter, as he was engaged in running two steam packets to New York, besides keeping a store "west of the Bridge," and his connection with the business could have brought little change. The following notice of the conclusion of the partnership reveals that Asa's cousin, Noah S. Day, was entering the concern in Selleck's place:

Dissolution. The firm of Selleck & Smith is this day dissolved by mutual consent. The business of the firm will be settled by either of the subscribers who are hereby authorized to use the name of the firm in liquidation.

Noah Selleck
Asa E. Smith

Norwalk Feb. 1st, 1843

The business of the above firm will be continued by the subscribers under the firm name of Smith & Day.

Asa E. Smith
Noah S. Day

This association was not a successful one, for Noah S. Day had no capacity for business and he incurred so many debts of a personal nature that his unfortunate partner was arrested and even imprisoned for a day in New York City on his account. After this unhappy experience, Smith continued the business alone until his son Theodore was old enough to become his partner. At the age of sixteen Theodore was managing the agency at Peck Slip. His advent into the firm spelled greater prosperity. The sons Asa and Howard Hobart also joined the family enterprise in due time. For about twenty years the Smiths worked together as A. E. Smith &

Sons. The father retired in the early sixties, devoting himself to various local and business activities. The pottery went on as A. E. Smith's Sons. In 1874 a corporation known as A. E. Smith's Sons Pottery Company was formed. This lasted until 1887, ending in financial collapse. Young Wilfred Smith, son of Theodore, took the business over for a year and then sold out to the Norwalk Pottery Company, which still was managed by a Smith—"young Asa," of another generation. The actual manufacture of pottery at Norwalk was soon discontinued, although merchandise made elsewhere was sold until 1901. Wilfred Smith, after 1888, ran the agency at 38 Peck Slip, New York, selling stoneware from Ohio and from a factory of his own in South Amboy.

As the Smith pottery was in operation over such a long period, its products are varied. Up to 1850, according to information obtained from Wilfred Smith by Mr. and Mrs. Winton, slip-decorated ware was made. The great majority of "Connecticut" pie plates emanated from this pottery. Some are embellished with names or legends, such as "Oysters and Clams," "Good and Cheap," or "Mary's Dish," and numbers of them are labeled "Mince Pie," "Apple Pie," "Curren Pie," and so forth. The handwriting on all is so similar it has been attributed to one person—a workman named Chichester. Triple wavy or straight-line decoration is also commonly seen on the Smith redware. These pie plates have finely toothed rims, not cut by hand, but notched with a cogglewheel.

During the Smith & Day partnership the company received an award at the seventeenth annual fair of the American Institute in New York City, October 18, 1844. This was a diploma for "superior earthen spittoons."

A great deal of utilitarian redware was made in the early years at the pottery. I have

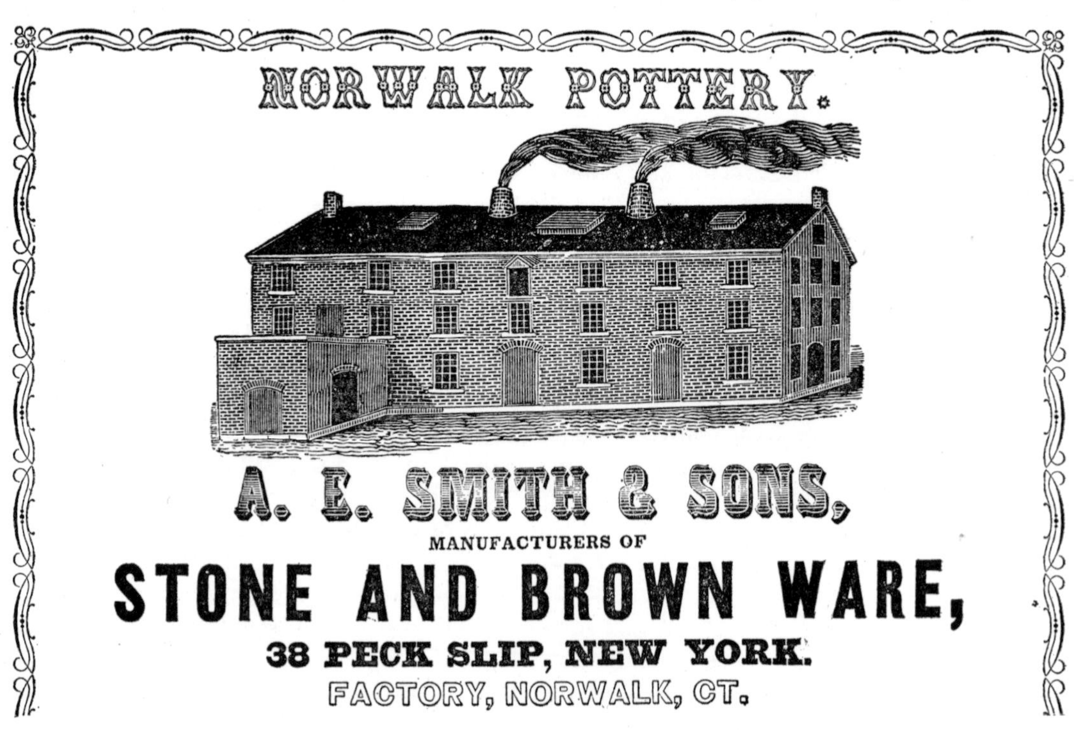

Billhead showing Norwalk Pottery, *ca.* 1860.

a price list headed "Norwalk Pottery/ A. E. Smith & Sons/ Manufacturers of/ Stone and Brown Ware," which itemizes in various sizes baking dishes, round and square, chambers, cups, wash bowls, pots, preserve pots, covered jars, milk pans, flat pans, yellow glazed or red glazed, pudding pans, butter coolers, cake molds, jugs, bottles, mugs, pitchers, pipkins, tea and coffee pots, money jugs, toy cups and dishes, bed pans, roach traps, and flowerpots — all of "brown earthenware." The color of the clay used by the Smiths was indeed a dark reddish brown, quite different from the orange shades of northern New England. It came from Elizabethport, New Jersey, and from a brickyard on the northern shore of Long Island.

The stoneware containers on this sheet are presented with illustrations of "bellied" pots (open-mouthed jars with handles), jugs, pitchers, churns, straight and bellied jars (the latter rimmed for lids), straight butter pots with covers (crocks), and barrel-shaped water kegs. Other items are oyster jars, milk pans, cake pots, beer and pop bottles, chambers, spittoons, and stove tubes. Jar lids and pot covers, as well as wooden covers for churns, were provided at extra cost. Spittoons, teapots, pitchers, and preserve jars of Rockingham ware are also advertised in this list, but the Wintons ascertained that such ware was merely sold, not made, at the Smith pottery.

A later price sheet published by A. E. Smith's Sons mentions bean bakers, stove tubes, and chimney tops in earthenware, while teapots and coffee pots are omitted. Tomato jars, molasses jugs, and butter pots are among the stoneware articles. This second price list, which is reproduced in *Old-Time New England* (April 1934), includes some twenty-five objects of yellow and Rockingham ware sold by the Smiths. It is interesting to note that the prices were "adopted by Convention at New-York, April 20th, 1864." They are fully twenty-five per cent lower than those of the earlier sheet.

With one or two exceptions, the forms are the same that we find in all stoneware potteries. Milk pans of stoneware are perhaps unusual outside of Connecticut. Oyster jars differed from preserve jars in having a sharp rather than a rounded shoulder. Tomato jars, or "corkers" were the forerunners of the modern preserve jar. They had narrow necks for the insertion of cork stoppers. The molasses jugs were a squatty type with a lip. Other stoneware articles made at Norwalk are birdhouses, jewelers' dipping baskets, and a variety of miniature teapots, pitchers, crocks, jugs, and pipkins for children's toys.

The Smith stoneware after 1843 was marked with the firm name, followed by *Manufacturers/ Norwalk, Con.*, within an oval. Examples may be dated by these marks: *Smith & Day*, 1843–1846 or 1847; *A. E. Smith & Son*, 1848; *A. E. Smith & Sons*, 1849–1865; *A. E. Smith's Sons*, 1865–1874; *A. E. Smith's Sons Pottery Co.*, 1874–1887.

In the late seventies the Norwalk pottery turned to the manufacture of unglazed redware vases and other decorative forms for home embellishment. This was in line with what other redware potteries were doing at the time, and for a while it was a lucrative part of the business. A price list of these ornamental wares is discussed in Chapter XXVIII.

The Smith pottery in the seventies and eighties was probably the largest in New England. At that time fifty men were employed and two ships plied constantly from Norwalk to New York and New Jersey for loads of clay, to Virginia for pine wood, or to New York with finished ware. A great deal of stoneware, especially jugs for the whalers, was sent to New London, New Bedford, and Sag Harbor. Like other New England industries, this productive business was obliged to succumb to competition, first from

New York, and then from Ohio, where potteries were nearer the sources of fuel and clay.

According to Barber's *Connecticut Historical Collections*, there were three potteries at Old Well and one at Norwalk Borough in 1838. The borough pottery was that of Asa Smith and one of the Old Well potteries was the Day shop. The other two were an earthenware manufactory near the Day pottery run by James Quintard and his associates and the Gregory works on Half Mile Isle.

The Quintard business began previous to 1825. The *Gazette* on May 10 of that year, contains a notice of the dissolution of partnership between Quintard and Henry Chichester. It reads:

> The connexion in the Earthen Ware Manufacturing business between Henry Chichester and James Quintard, Jr. under the firm name of *Chichester & Quintard*, is by mutual consent, this day disolved. All persons endebted are requested to make immediate payment
>
> Henry Chichester
> James Quintard, Jr.
>
> Norwalk May 2, 1825
>
> This business will hereafter be carried on by the subscribers under the firm name of Quintard, Merrill & Co.
>
> James Quintard, Jr.
> Marvin Merrill
> Henry Chichester, Jr.

Several other changes in the firm occurred. At some time before 1834 Merrill left the business and, on August 19, 1834, the other two partners separated. As James Quintard announced in the *Gazette* his intention of continuing the pottery in his own name, he was undoubtedly one of the three potters of Old Well in 1838. Nothing definite is known of his further history. His daughter, Mrs. Mary E. Burritt, born about 1847, is authority for the statement that Quintard made domestic utensils, redware knobs, and sugar cones. Large redware coat buttons are also said to have been among his products.

Old Well's third pottery was owned by John Betts Gregory and was situated on a small island offshore near the present Shorehaven Golf Club. Gregory learned his trade under the tutelage of Absalom Day. He spent his early years at Huntington, Long Island, and at a pottery in Clinton, Oneida County, New York, which he established. In 1831 he returned to Norwalk and bought Half Mile Isle. He paid the former owner, Samuel Hanford, but $325 for this tract of farm land. Gregory proceeded to make his home on it. He moved the oaken frame of the old house that had belonged to his father Abraham Gregory from its site near the old burying ground on the way to the "Ballast" to the eastern end of the island, where he reërected it as part of a new dwelling. According to Selleck, Norwalk's historian, he built "a kiln for the burning of earthen and stoneware" the following year. The masonry work was done by George Raymond and one Lewis of Norwalk. Gregory carried on his business there until 1840, two years before his death. His widow, later known as "Grandmother Gregory," survived him until 1883. She remained on Half Mile Isle, where she was a familiar figure around the little home her husband had built.

The business of making knobs and buttons was conducted by several persons in Norwalk. L. D. Wheeler, in partnership with Dr. Asa Hill, turned out buttons of plastic clay. At first these were formed in clay molds, but afterwards were pressed in dies. They were of mixed color and of two bodies: one a redware covered with a light brown glaze, the other a white body with mottled glaze. Some were made with four holes for the thread, while others were fitted with metal shanks. This button manufacture was discontinued before 1853. In the following

year Enoch Wood, a descendant of the old English potting family and formerly a mold maker at Bennington, came to Norwalk to work in Wheeler's pottery. He married his employer's daughter and three years later, with her brother, bought out the pottery. From 1853 until 1865, when the enterprise came to an end with the burning of the buildings, the Wheelers and Wood devoted themselves to the production of so-called "mineral" knobs for doors, furniture, and shutters. These were composed of variegated red, white, and black clays, coated with an ordinary Rockingham glaze. The location of the Wheeler pottery is not mentioned by any writer. It is possible that it was operated in the old buildings of the Day pottery, which, as noted above, were sold in 1852 and used thereafter for the manufacture of mineral knobs. Although the Bennington works produced some door and curtain knobs with their well-known mottled glazes, the Norwalk knobs seem to be the only ones of mixed clays made in New England. The button manufacture also was confined to the Quintard and Wheeler output. Specimens of Norwalk buttons and knobs may be seen in the Pitkin collection in the Wadsworth Atheneum at Hartford.

One or two other potteries in southwestern Connecticut have been recorded. In Bridgeport stoneware was being manufactured as early as 1814 and as late as 1840 or thereafter. Louis F. Middlebrook, in a brief article in the *Antiquarian* (April 1928), illustrates an ink bottle made at Bridgeport, with a note that inkwells were sold there at four shillings per dozen.

A pottery in Stamford, whose proprietors were Wardwell & Gibson, is listed in the *New England Business Directory* of 1860. It was probably a redware shop. A nineteenth-century pottery in Danbury, run by C. S. Andrews, has been noted by Frederic Fairchild Sherman in *Early Connecticut Artists and Craftsmen.*

CHAPTER TWENTY-SIX

Rhode Island

There is but little evidence that the potter's trade flourished to any extent in Rhode Island. The names of only four redware makers are known. Of these, two were brothers. They, with a third craftsman, stemmed from the Danvers area and tradition. None of them worked for more than ten or twelve years.

A variety of factors may explain the lack of potters in this state. First, it is possible that the clay was not of the best quality. A second explanation is that Rhode Island was always supplied with earthenware from other localities. The Berkley and Somerset men, sailing in their sloops down Mt. Hope Bay, captured a large part of the Rhode Island market, while the potters from Connecticut and Pennsylvania, trading along the Sound, got the rest.

In Rhode Island and in the towns along Cape Cod notched-edge plates and platters similar to known examples from Norwalk, New Jersey, and Pennsylvania are still found locally. It is certain that the men from Danvers and their successors in Somerset never made pieces in this style. On the other hand, slip-decorated deep dishes like those made by Daniel Bayley of Newburyport and by many other Massachusetts potters are also to be found in Rhode Island. This state, therefore, was the meeting place of two traditions, while itself producing almost nothing.

The first potter in this section of New England has been noted in the chapter on men of the seventeenth century. John Wilkins worked in Boston from 1670 to 1680 and then migrated to Bristol, Rhode Island, as a pioneer settler of the town. Recorded deeds leave us in no doubt that for a time, at least, Wilkins continued in his trade at the new settlement. The documents reveal that he met with no great success. In 1785, on March 4, he and his wife mortgaged all their Bristol possessions to four Boston merchants. These lands included "all that their farme tract or parcel of Land containing 100 acres (in Bristol) distant from sd. town about a mile and a halph"; their lot of twenty-four acres on Poppasquash Neck, and one acre, one and one-half miles from Bristol, all of which were then "in tenure and occupation" of Wilkins. The large farm tract stood between the country road to Swansea and the Swansea River and was bounded on the north by land of William Ingraham and south by William Brenton. This was the Wilkins homestead and presumably the location of the pottery. On August 6, 1686, the town of Bristol gave Wilkins permission "to keep an Ordinary, or Publick House of Entertain-

ment." He is mentioned in this connection in 1689 in the diary of Samuel Sewall. As late as 1689 Wilkins was still called "potter." In the following year he sold his original holdings at Mt. Hope to Israel Wardell and thereafter, in other transfers of land, he is designated "yeoman."

John Wilkins' daughter Abigail married Benjamin Ellery, one of Newport's most prominent merchants and ancestor of William Ellery who signed the Declaration of Independence. The Ellerys lived in high style, with several Negro servants. Their silver plate and the family portraits, attributed to Smibert, are still in existence. Wilkins died at some time before 1711, when Mrs. Wilkins, then a widow, passed away at Abigail's house in Newport.

A pottery in East Greenwich was brought to public attention by Charles D. Cook in an article in *Antiques* (January 1931). He discovered that Isaac and Samuel Upton, whom I have mentioned in the chapter on Quaker potters, were the founders and owners of the establishment. Although he noted the Danvers connection of the brothers, Mr. Cook did not know that they were the nephews of Joseph and Paul Osborn. There are some errors in his published account. Isaac, the eldest son of Edward and Eleanor (Osborn) Upton, was born October 6, 1736, while his parents were living in Hampton Falls, New Hampshire. From about 1745 to 1768 they were in Berkley, and Samuel, their seventh child, arrived April 3, 1748, during their residence there.

Dr. D. H. Greene, in his *History of East Greenwich, R. I.*, says that the Uptons came to East Greenwich from Nantucket just before the Revolution and that they built their workshop and kiln on a lot at the corner of King and Marlborough Streets (occupied in 1877 by the house of John Weeden). He says they obtained their clay from Gould's Mount at Quidnessett. Shortly after the war, Greene goes on, "Mr. Upton returned to Nantucket, and no earthen ware has been made here since." Mr. Cook failed to find any reference to the Uptons' residence in Nantucket. If they actually lived there at any time, their stay must have been temporary. Deeds prove that they bought the land on King Street December 9, 1771, and that they owned it jointly. In 1783, Isaac, who was then living in Berkley, sold his share in the house and pottery to Samuel, who, however, soon afterwards moved to Stanford, Dutchess County, New York. Isaac has a further claim upon our interest by the fact that he married Phebe Peirce, sister of our friend Preserved, the trader. In later life Isaac was himself a sea captain, although he ended his days in South Adams, Massachusetts.

The pieces of pottery shown in photographs to illustrate Mr. Cook's article are typical Danvers forms. Those found in the vicinity of East Greenwich without a definite Upton history may, however, as well have been made by any one of the Uptons' many cousins in Berkley or Somerset, whose products were sold along the Rhode Island coast by Preserved Peirce. Greene's account describes the coarse red earthenware from this pottery as if it were a substitute for china made principally during the Revolution. A glance at the accounts of John Parker of Charlestown will show at once that the very same articles were produced by our country potters long before hostilities began.

Rhode Island's fourth potter was Joseph Wilson, a brother of the first Robert Wilson, who followed the trade in South Danvers, or Peabody, Massachusetts. He was the ninth child in the family and was born not long before the advent of his brother's son Robert 3d. Perhaps the prospects were not very good in a family already blessed with so many potters. Soon after his marriage he was living in Dedham, where he and his wife Elizabeth

and his two children, Joseph and Elizabeth, were baptized April 29, 1764. It is probable that he worked there with Daniel Felton, another Danvers potter, somewhat younger than Wilson, who went to the town at about the same time. Wilson is mentioned as of Dedham in a deed dated March 23, 1764, by which he sold his common rights in Salem inherited from his father.

The potter next appears in North Providence (Pawtucket) in the year 1767. An advertisement bearing the date June 22 of that year was inserted in the *Newport Mercury*, as follows:

> Joseph Wilson — potter At the North End of Providence Informs the Public, that he can Supply them with Earthen Ware at a cheap Rate, made in the best Manner and glazed in the Same Way as Practised in Philadelphia — All persons in this Town may be regularly supplied by Means of the Boats which constantly pass between this Place and Providence.

This advertisement gives excellent proof that Pennsylvania pottery was known and used in Rhode Island. Wilson, a newcomer, had to compete with the products of "foreign" potters. His reference to glazing probably does not indicate any change from the traditional techniques of his training, but was rather an assurance that his ware was fully as good as the Pennsylvania earthenware which Newport citizens had been buying (see Fig. 26).

Joseph Wilson remained in Pawtucket only three years. On April 10, 1770, he purchased from John Matthewson for thirty pounds a house lot in Providence. This is described as "a certain tract of Land, bounded north on Weybosset Street, so called,* on which it measures 44 feet, and holding its breadth it extends back about 77 feet, more or less, to the lot of Thomas Green and others called the Sugar House Lot, east, bounded on Joshua Spooner's Lot and partly on a Jogg in the Sugar House." A few months later he bought a one-eighth interest in the sugar house lot and building. Wilson put up a dwelling and pottery shop on his land and remained there for ten years. He seems to have been in financial difficulties during the whole period and in 1780 is called "yeoman." He disposed of his sugar house investment in 1773 and all his other property March 16, 1780.

In his article, "An Early Rhode Island Pottery," Charles D. Cook shows a handled jug or jar with cover, which he attributes to Joseph Wilson on the ground that it was found in Pawtucket. Knowing as we now do how widely pottery was distributed by various means, we cannot feel that this is a sure attribution. The domed cover is a feature that does not appear in the Danvers tradition familiar to Wilson, but is typical of southwestern Connecticut and the New York and Pennsylvania regions. The shape of the pot, too, is of early eighteenth- or even seventeenth-century character. The only Rhode Island potter who could have made it was John Wilkins.

The Providence area has been a fertile hunting ground for pottery enthusiasts, and many handsome specimens have been found thereabouts. It is quite possible that some of them were made by Joseph Wilson and that he is thereby proved to be more of an artist than a business man.

Wilson is twice mentioned in the Inferior Court Records of Suffolk County, Massachusetts, when suits were brought against him. The first, dated April 23, 1782, was instigated by John Thomas, potter, of Newburyport. In this case the plaintiff defaulted. Wilson was then of Providence. The second, in 1784, was brought by "Thomas Seward, Esq.,

* "Weybosset Street" is an error and should read "Westminster Street," as it appears in Wilson's other conveyances and in a surveyor's plan of Providence.

of Boston vs. Joseph Wilson of Providence now resident at Boston, Potter." Seward won six pounds and costs.

Further investigation may show that in addition to these small redware potteries, there was also a stoneware kiln at the home of Peter States in Westerly and that he and his sons made an attempt to establish stoneware manufacture in Providence. The main facts about States will be found in Chapter XXII. It will be noted that he was in Westerly in 1754, when he was only twenty-two years of age. At that time there was no pottery in Stonington or elsewhere nearby, as far as we know. While he may have supported himself by farming or in some similar occupation for the next fifteen years, it seems rather unlikely. For in 1769 he was a practicing potter. After two and one-half years in Norwich, he settled down again in Westerly. Then, if not before, he may have built a kiln near the Paucatuck River. His sons, Joseph H., born in 1764, and William, fourteen years later, learned the trade, either with Peter or with Adam States.

In a deed dated January 23, 1796, Peter conveyed to "Joseph States of Westerly, Potter" a small piece of land east of the river and by another transaction of the same date twenty-one acres of land and two fifths of a dwelling house in Stonington. The documents describe him as "of Westerly, yeoman, but now residing in Providence." The following March, when the father deeded to his son two lots of land and a dwelling house in Westerly, both Peter and Joseph were in Providence and were called potters. Joseph paid nine hundred dollars for the Westerly house and three hundred and forty dollars for his share in the Stonington dwelling. He made both of them over to his younger brother January 8 and January 21, 1799, for two hundred and fifty dollars. The Westerly deed speaks of "Joseph States of Providence, Stone Potter" and "Wm. States of Prov., Stone Potter." Thus, for three years this family was living in Providence and apparently supporting themselves by their trade. I have been unable to find any record in Providence of their sojourn in the vicinity, but it seems likely that the father tried to establish his sons in an independent business to compete with the flourishing works at Stonington. Their pottery may have been the one noted in the *Providence Directory* of 1854 by a writer under the nom de plume "Octogenarian," who says he can remember back as far as "1790 and earlier." He states: ". . . and very near the cove, was a pottery, for the manufacture of earthen ware."

CHAPTER TWENTY-SEVEN

Bennington and Kindred Developments

The artisans of the potter's wheel began to be supplanted before the mid-years of the last century by less skilled workmen who could execute with little training the new techniques for mass production. As early as 1830 the Hendersons at Jersey City had molded ornamental figures for application on turned ware. This method, reminiscent of Wedgwood, was soon abandoned for the use of molds in which entire vessels could be cast. In the 1840's numerous potteries in New Jersey, Ohio, and elsewhere adopted these mechanical short cuts, thereby establishing a real ceramic industry modeled upon Staffordshire in place of the minor efforts of individual craftsmen. This was the course taken by every kind of manufacture in the American democracy. The greatest number of things for the greatest number of people was the desideratum. Glassmaking, in the pressing process developed at Sandwich, Cambridge, Jersey City, and Pittsburgh, had already undergone the change in the thirties. The day of the artisan who created an object from start to finish was declining. In his place were employed designers, technicians, and laborers to carry the various processes through to completion.

The result in the ceramic field was improvement and standardization in bodies and glazes and an efflorescence of ornamental design not always in the best taste. At first the wares created by the influx of English potters who manned these industries were almost wholly copies of English models. Molds may have been brought here by British designers, although such a proceeding would hardly have been necessary when it was so easy to take a plaster cast from Staffordshire pieces already in this country. Tobies, pitchers, vases, and figures were all of Staffordshire inspiration, if not exact copies, and their only distinctive features were some characteristic American glazes.

The one place in New England where this type of mass production got under way to any extent was Bennington, Vermont. The famous works there was the brain child of Christopher Webber Fenton, a son of Jonathan, who was connected with the Nortons' stoneware pottery as early as 1837, when he patented a firebrick made by them. He was a

volatile and aggressive person, better able to initiate and create than to organize. Norton, his brother-in-law, was his opposite in every respect.

In 1840 Julius Norton advertised "fancy" pitchers. Whether these were the first attempts at Bennington Rockingham we cannot tell, because no pitchers of the type with the Norton mark alone have been found. Norton and Fenton became partners before January 20, 1843, a date established by a bill headed "Norton & Fenton," which is owned by F. H. Norton.* The hexagonal stoneware pitchers with dark brown glaze marked *Norton & Fenton/ Bennington, Vt.* in a circle or oval or *Norton & Fenton/ East Bennington, Vt.* in two lines belong, therefore, to the period between 1843 and 1847.

The term "Rockingham" as applied to the glaze of the first period, means merely a plain dark brown glaze, not unlike the brown lead glaze on redware. Indeed, the potters of West Sterling, as previously noted, advertised brown-glazed redware under this designation. The word originated in Swinton, England, where teapots of a similar color were produced in the works of the Marquis of Rockingham. The Norton & Fenton pitchers are of buff stoneware, are hexagonal in form, occur in three sizes, and are decorated with relief ornament of floral or conventional type on body and neck. They are rather more pleasing than the hound-handled pitchers that followed them. The glaze, although not perfectly clear, is often of a rich mahogany color. Occasional specimens have a light yellow-brown tone.

During the four years of his association with Norton, Christopher Webber Fenton, ambitious to make Bennington the Staffordshire of America, experimented with new clays and new techniques. Towards the end of 1843, John Harrison, who had been employed at the Copeland works in England, came to Bennington to help bring the project to fruition. It is said that one of his first pieces was a Parian figure of a baby modeled as a gift for Mrs. Julius Norton upon the occasion of the birth of her first child in November 1843. This story acquires the character of a legend when we learn that John Mountford did not cast his first Parian figure at the Copeland works until December 25, 1845. In any event, Harrison must have taught Fenton all he knew about the art of porcelain manufacture, and it is a remarkable fact that this son of a stoneware potter should have acquired so large a store of knowledge of the bodies and glazes in the brief period, interrupted by the fire of 1845, of his partnership.

Norton was always a stoneware man, and he may well have been a little frightened at the dubious ventures of his brother-in-law. On June 25, 1847, the partnership was dissolved. Fenton continued in his attempts at making a more decorative line of ware, and he was permitted to lease the north wing of Norton's pottery for the furtherance of his experiments. He enlisted the aid of Henry D. Hall, son of a former governor of Vermont, who became a silent partner for a few months.

During the years 1847 and 1848 Fenton made common white and yellow crockeries, mottled Rockingham ware, and Parian porcelain. At this time he used the mark *Fenton's Works:/ Bennington,/ Vermont* impressed on a raised ornamental panel or lozenge. An octagonal water cooler in the Wadsworth Atheneum at Hartford, Connecticut, is so marked, and several types of Parian pitchers bear the same label.

In 1848 Fenton was a member of the drygoods firm of Lyman, Fenton, & Park. He evidently persuaded his partners to help him finance the pottery. A modest advertisement under their names appeared in the *Vermont Gazette*, November 22, saying that they were

* Spargo surmised that the partnership began in the latter part of 1844.

"manufacturers of every description of Rockingham, White Flint and White Earthen, Crockery Ware — East Bennington, Vt." No mention was made of Parian ware.

Calvin Park withdrew from this connection late in 1849, leaving Fenton and Alanson Potter Lyman in charge of the business. Fenton's patent for coloring a glaze, dated November 27, 1849, was taken out at this time. In this invention Fenton devised a means of sprinkling metallic oxides directly on the ware, which had first been burned and then dipped in plain glaze. Both the Rockingham and flint enamel glazes made by Fenton contained powdered flint and were extremely hard and durable. The flint enamel ware was distinctive by reason of the varied effects that resulted when tones of blue, yellow, or orange were blended with what would otherwise have been an ordinary mottled brown Rockingham. Fenton used this minor invention to call attention to his new wares. He adopted an oval impressed mark reading *Lyman, Fenton & Co./ Fentons/ Enamel/ Patented/ 1849/ Bennington, Vt.*, which was applied indiscriminately to mottled Rockingham and the more colorful flint enamel wares. He continued the use of this stamp long after Lyman had withdrawn from the business.

While Lyman was a member of the firm, a new factory, soon to be known as the United States Pottery, was built not far from the old Norton works on the site where the Bennington Graded School stands today. Under the direction of Decius W. Clark, who had formerly worked as a stoneware potter with Norton and who was a practical genius in every branch of the potter's art, new buildings and three large double kilns were constructed at a cost of some fifteen thousand dollars. The first kiln of ware burned in this plant was drawn November 15, 1850.

Lyman's connection with the enterprise ended before 1852. The interest of Oliver A. Gager, a New York merchant in the china trade, was then secured, and he became the active backer of the new pottery. An incorporation as the United States Pottery Company was effected June 11, 1853, in the names of Jason H. Archer, Henry Willard, Christopher Webber Fenton, Samuel H. Johnson, and Oliver A. Gager. Gager was the nominal head of the concern and was designated "manufacturer" of the Bennington wares displayed at the New York Exhibition of 1853.

An excellent account of the Bennington exhibit at New York is to be found in the *General Report of the British Commissioners on the New York Industrial Exhibition*, in the section written by George Wallis, entitled *Report on Porcelain and Ceramic Manufacture*. He says:

> Messrs. O. A. Gager and Company, Bennington, in the State of Vermont, manufacture a ware known as "Fenton's patent flint enamelled ware." This is produced from a very white clay found near Charleston, South Carolina, and the beds of which this firm has secured the rights of working for twenty-one years. It takes a beautiful glaze, and presents a remarkably clear and transparent appearance. It is chiefly used in the manufacture of the mottled-brown ware, but presents a white fracture, as the mottled surface is simply in the glaze. Of this kind of ware, even at the present rate of production, $1500 worth per week is manufactured, for which a ready market is found. This ware is got up in imitation of a much commoner article usually manufactured of yellow clay.

His statement that flint enamel ware was made of white clay may be a surprise to many collectors, although Edwin Atlee Barber also noted its white fracture. I verified these assertions when I accidentally broke one piece. I found that the body was indeed white and not yellow, although I should describe it as ivory or cream white. This fine body establishes the superiority of the Rockingham-type glazed wares produced by Fenton.

Although the new flint enamel wares were

featured in the Bennington booth at New York, and Parian ware is not even mentioned in the catalogue, examples of Parian were nevertheless on display. This porcelain, already made popular by Copeland and Minton, was primarily intended as an imitation of Parian marble for figure work. At Bennington the ware sometimes approached this ideal, but more often, especially in vases, it had the appearance of a biscuit porcelain. The question of whether it is not a true Parian unless it realizes the texture of marble may best be decided by those who have analyzed its composition. Parian is defined as "a biscuit porcelain containing feldspar." Its texture depends somewhat on the quantity of feldspar incorporated in it. The amount varied at Bennington. The use of native materials must also have made the composition uncertain. The earliest pieces, like the Fenton's Works pitchers, are dotted with impurities; the figure work is fairly good; the vases are often rough and brittle. But all may be called Parian without fear of inaccuracy, just as they were called Parian in their day.

Wallis has this to say of the Parian ware:

> A parian ware, of good colour and surface, is also manufactured by this firm, from materials obtained near the manufactory, in the State of Vermont. It is composed of flint, quartz, feldspar, and clay obtained from the Green Mountain district and the adjacent rivers. This ware is unglazed, and will not stand the test of hot water. It presents, however, a valuable and useful material for certain productions not as yet manufactured in the United States, especially in the more ornamental articles for which parian is so largely used in England.

Although this last sentence seems to imply that ornamental Parian ware was not being made commercially in 1853, there is ample evidence that it was. A bill of sale dated July 1853, lists Parian pitchers in four sizes, from four dollars to twelve dollars per dozen wholesale, and the following figures in "Parian marble":

Adoration	per doz.	$75.00
Cupid	"	30.00
Indian Queen	"	24.00
Hope	"	12.00
Good Night	"	12.00
Grey Hound	"	12.00
Swan	"	12.00
Sailor Boy and Dog	"	4.00
Mustard Cup	"	4.00
Sheep	"	4.00
Bird Nests	"	3.00

Parian doorplates and doorknobs also appear in this list. This bill is headed "Fenton's Patent Flint Enamel Ware/ Manufactured in Bennington, Vermont/ Architectural Work Made to Order/ General Agency for the United States — 35 Tremont Row/ Boston." It contains the most complete list of Bennington wares known. Some of the articles are without doubt common Rockingham, others of the finest quality of flint enamel. Heading the list are "Grecian temples" at one hundred dollars per dozen. These were perhaps designed for stoves and may have resembled the monumental structure still standing at the entrance of Fenton's former home on Pleasant Street in Bennington. This affair is ten feet in height and is said to have been modeled by Daniel Greatbach. It is composed of four sections: the base, of lava or "scroddled" ware in imitation of marble; the next of flint enamel ware, upon which is a life-sized bust of Fenton surrounded by eight Corinthian columns in Rockingham; and the whole crowned by a Parian figure of a woman presenting a Bible to a young child. Its appearance, when displayed at the New York Exhibition, is sketched in the cut from *Gleason's Pictorial* reproduced herewith. This picture also shows many other objects mentioned in the price list.

The articles mentioned on this sheet (prices are omitted) are water urns, soda fountain

Exhibition of Bennington ware at the Crystal Palace, New York, from a wood cut in *Gleason's Pictorial*, October 22, 1853

domes, coffee urns, stove urns, slop jars, foot baths, ewers, wash basins, chambers, bed pans, bread bowls, soap boxes, brush boxes, spittoons in five sizes, pitchers in seven sizes from one-half pint to six quarts, molasses pitchers, coffee pots in three sizes, teapots in five sizes, sugar bowls, creamers, pipkins, cake pans, oval bakers in six sizes, nappies from six inches to eleven inches, pie plates eight inches to eleven inches, lift cake pans, Turk's-head cake pans, milk pans, butter, soup, and pickle plates, flower vases and pots, preserve jars in four sizes, round preserve jars, plug basins, goblets, flange mugs, tumblers, tobies, candlesticks and low candlesticks, each in three sizes, fancy bottles, book bottles, one pint, two quarts, and four quarts, pocket flasks, wafer boxes, shovel plates, picture frames, lamp bases and pedestals, eight inches, nine inches, and thirteen inches in height, sign letters, doorplates, Parian or enameled, number plates with figures, curtain pins, furniture knobs, and doorknobs, enameled. A briefer list, under the heading "Fancy Articles," contains those objects for which all Bennington collectors yearn: dogs with baskets, at $18 per dozen; lions, $18; lions on base, $24; cow creamers, $4.50; Swiss ladies, $3.50; stags and does, $24; cows reclining, $24.

In addition to common white crockery, yellow earthenware, the flint-glazed wares, and Parian porcelain, Fenton developed a semi-porcelain or stone china largely used for gold-band tea sets and fruit compotes; a so-called "granite" ware, which was a hard crockery suitable for toilet sets; and lava or scroddled ware. These utilitarian ceramics cannot for the most part be identified except when they occasionally appear in some characteristic Bennington shape. The granite ware can sometimes be distinguished when in the form of a "St. Nicholas" water pitcher. These ovoid pitchers were made for the St. Nicholas Hotel in New York, which opened in 1854. They were usually decorated in blue, green, and gold, and were lettered with the name and address of the person or company for whom they were made and sometimes with the name of the pottery as well. Imported pitchers of the same type were soon on the market. Bennington examples may be differentiated by the strut or brace between the handle and the body of the vessel.

Lava or "scroddled" ware was a revival of the agate ware made by Whieldon in England. The scroddled effect was obtained by wedging together different colored clays until the mass was variegated as in a marble cake. Slices cut from the bat of clay could be utilized for turning or molding and exhibited the same striations throughout and not only upon the surface. The colors in Bennington lava ware are two tones of brown running through a cream-colored body. Only a small quantity of this type of ware was produced at Bennington, usually in the form of toilet sets and cuspidors, although occasional tulip vases and cow creamers have been found. After the Civil War, Enoch Wood, an English potter who had been employed at Bennington before 1853, made scroddled ware in quantity at his pottery in Perth Amboy, New Jersey. His products are so similar to the Bennington lava ware that it is difficult to make attributions of such pieces.

It is amazing that such a variety of objects and so many kinds of bodies and glazes should have been developed in the short space of ten years, for the Bennington venture died in 1858 after little more than a decade. It is said that overproduction combined with poor methods of marketing the wares were contributing causes to the failure of the works. Fenton's pottery was sold just as in the old days of peddling redware, by sending it out to country stores on wagons. But it was one thing to load a cart with pots and pans and another to pack safely the delicate

Parian figures and vases, the cow creamers, and all the other elaborations of Fenton's fancy. The cost of packing, the loss by breakage, and the great number of employees necessary for this kind of distribution soon ate up the profits. Although the company raised new capital in 1855, its finances became so involved in the winter of 1857–1858 that it was obliged to close in the following May. During that winter one hundred and fifty men were employed at the United States Pottery. Most of them were unpaid throughout the winter, but, as soon as Fenton was able to collect money that was due him, he settled all their claims. His failure, whatever the cause, was an honorable one.

Much has been written by Mr. Spargo and others in the way of discussion about the United States Pottery and its output. In the short space allotted here for this important enterprise, I may perhaps add a few useful thoughts.

The most significant development at Bennington was the creation of Parian figures — the first biscuit figures produced in America. They are naïve, almost childish, in character. They are not the work of artists, but are a bit too smug for mere primitives. There is something overpious about them — the praying children and the lambs on Bibles — which, nevertheless, is quite Victorian. Several of them, like the little girl tying her shoe, the kneeling children, and the greyhound, repose on cushions with tassels at the corners. The figure of Red Riding Hood illustrated by Spargo (Pl. XIX, *The Potters and Potteries of Bennington*), I have seen with the Minton mark, and there is some doubt of its Bennington ancestry. Some of the figures are coated with a very slight or "smear" glaze.

The Parian vases, which frequently appear with a pitted blue background, are never marked and can with difficulty be distinguished from similar objects made in England. The blue coloring was applied as a slip directly to the molds in which vases or other pieces were cast, thus being incorporated with the porcelain body when burned. Bennington vases are overornate in the style of the period, but were probably more effective against a black marble mantelpiece than in the home of today. Bunches of grapes, made by hand and applied, are often incongruous with the conception of the design as a whole, but were evidently considered a pleasing addition. The stippled or pitted appearance of the backgrounds on these vases is reminiscent of the groundwork on lacy glass and was accomplished in the same laborious manner in the mold making: each individual dot was placed separately by hand. The affinity between the glass and Parian designs is also noteworthy.

Pitchers of Parian appear in plain unglazed white, in white with a smear glaze, which gives a slight gloss or luster, very rarely with full glaze, and in white with blue or tan backgrounds. Two types, at least, were made in the 1840's — one, the rare pitcher copied from a design by Alcock known as "Love and War"; the other, the more common rose pattern. Both are marked *Fenton's Works, Bennington, Vermont* on a raised lozenge. The rose pitchers are, however, frequently unmarked. Still a third very rare pitcher with the Fenton mark displays a beautiful snowdrop or lily against a plain smooth ground. The flower follows in its arrangement the lines of the pitcher, thus bringing out its form according to the best canons of decoration. The conception, although not original, is the finest produced at the Bennington works.

During the United States Pottery period two marks appear on pitchers and other pieces. The earlier is in the form of a ribbon impressed *U. S. P.* with numerals denoting both the size and the pattern. A raised medallion mark with the words *United States Pottery Co./ Bennington, Vt.* was also used.

Both marks were cut in the mold. The pitchers were almost without exception copies or adaptations of the work of Alcock and other English potters. As Fenton's ideal was the approximation of English work, and as nearly all the potters who designed his better wares came from the British Isles, this lack of originality is not to be wondered at. Familiar are the daisy design, which was cast in three variations of mold, the oak leaf and acorn, the pond lily, the palm tree, and the "Niagara Falls" pattern, which, singularly enough, is an attempt to represent cliffs and a cataract within the bounds of a pitcher's surface. The latter, though crude, has the merit of being an American conception. Various other floral designs appear on syrup pitchers and tea sets.

Collectors have probably paid more attention to Rockingham and flint-enameled wares than to any other pottery from Bennington. The glaze colorings are endlessly varied and often really beautiful. It is generally accepted that Daniel Greatbach, who began his career in this country at Jersey City, and who went to Bennington early in 1852, was the modeler of most of the amusing tobies, coachman bottles, and other animal figures made at Bennington. Nevertheless, the price list I have quoted was in circulation in May of that year. If Greatbach really created all the items set forth therein, he was a rapid worker! Perhaps he arrived at Bennington with his molds in hand. Whoever was responsible for them, they have delighted more people than all the Parian pitchers, or even figures, ever will.

The handsome large stag and doe and the recumbent cow represent the epitome of Bennington potting and are rare indeed. Bennington's lions, too, are now in the category of museum pieces. Whether with or without a base, whether marked or unmarked, they are among the finest achievements in American ceramics. This is equally true of the dogs with baskets in their mouths — baskets of fruit and flowers, often beautifully touched with color. At least one pair of these animals was made in Parian porcelain. It must be emphasized that dogs in a sitting position were never made at Bennington.

Tobies are of four types. The one most frequently encountered is identified by its vine-leaf handle. It depicts the usual toper with mug in hand. Another, the bust of a man in cloak and cocked hat, is called the Benjamin Franklin toby and has a peculiar handle in the shape of a leg in a riding boot. Rarer than either of these is the "Duke of Wellington" or "Major Stark" toby, which is an exact copy of an earlier Staffordshire jug that was produced in color. The authenticity of the Rockingham type has been established by the finding of fragments in the *biscuit* stage at the site of the Bennington works. A fourth toby is a jolly little man with a broad-brimmed hat that forms a cover for what was either a tobacco jar or a match holder. This one has no handle. With the exception of the Wellington jug, the tobies often bear the oval 1849 patent mark.

At least three styles of bar bottles may be found. Two represent coachmen in long coats. One of these was designed to be fitted with a cork stopper in the tall hat; the other is so made that the hat itself is the stopper. The third bottle, less well known, is in the shape of a man astride a barrel.

Book-shaped bottles are attributed to the invention of Greatbach. They have a twist of humor in the titles impressed on the back. Such legends as *Ladies' Companion*, *Departed Spirits*, and *Hermit's Companion* are facetiously suggestive of their purpose.

Cow creamers are as attractive as anything in American pottery of the period. They were intended for actual use. The cream was poured into the animal through a hole in the back fitted with a tiny cover, the beast was lifted by its tail, and the liquid ran out

through its mouth. Although all manner of cows with all kinds of glazes have been made by potters through the years, the Bennington bovine has its points of difference. It may be recognized by the distinct marking of its eyes and nostrils, the folds in the skin below the neck, and its faintly perceptible, but not prominent, ribs. It is a rather plump and stocky animal. These cows, for some unknown reason, were never marked.

Also unmarked, but easily identifiable, are the hound-handled pitchers attributed to Greatbach. They are similar in many respects to the dog pitchers that he made at Jersey City, for the general conception is the same: a stag hunt on one side, a boar hunt on the other, a border of grapes and leaves around the neck. The Bennington hound is a highly conventionalized canine. Its nose, long and flat like a duck's bill, rests just inside the rim of the pitcher, with the head arched in such a way that one may put a finger between the head and the paws. On the under side of its body is a pronounced ridge, which is characteristic, and a collar in the form of a chain instead of a plain band is further help to identification. The hound-handled pitchers appear with mottled Rockingham glaze only and never in flint enamel.

It would take far more space that I have here to describe in detail the many articles in the price list. I can only refer the reader to Spargo's exhaustive book on the subject. Its many illustrations furnish a safe standard of comparison for those who are attracted to these wares. Like lacy glass, they were vastly popular in their day and, while they followed English styles too closely to be a true American development, they still are marked by our native sense of humor.

While Bennington was capturing the market with these alluring novelties, ambitious potters elsewhere must have viewed its expansion with alarm. There were a few attempts at imitation. At Burlington, Nichols & Alford put out a Rockingham hound-handled pitcher in 1854, and they are credited with numerous other products in the Bennington manner. At Norwich, Connecticut, Sidney Risley attempted cast wares with Rockingham glaze in a small way. J. T. Winslow of Portland, at a later time, put out foot warmers and other articles glazed with a handsome blending of brown, blue, and cream color in the flint-enamel style.

Only one other concern in New England, however, actually succeeded in operating on a large scale with the idea of competing with the English market. This was a pottery in East Boston started in 1854 by Frederick H. Mear, an Englishman. Mear had previously been engaged in the manufacture of yellow and Rockingham wares in partnership with James Salt and John Hancock at East Liverpool, Ohio, in a works founded by them in 1841. There are conflicting accounts about Mear and his East Boston pottery; these may be more easily understood when it is known that the business was owned continuously by William F. Homer, a Boston merchant, from the beginning to 1876. Mear superintended the factory and acted as Homer's agent. The pottery buildings were at 146 Condor Street near the Chelsea bridge.

In the *Boston Directory* of 1854/55 Homer first advertised the Boston Earthen Ware Manufacturing Company, as he called it, with a picture of the works, saying that "wares made at this Factory are for sale by Wm. F. Homer & Co./ 15 & 17 Union Street./ Boston/ Samples at Office, 15 Union Street, where Orders are received, or at the Works, on Condor Street, East Boston/ Frederick Mear, Agent."

During the first year twenty-nine men were employed and twenty-nine thousand dollars' worth of ware was manufactured. It is strange that almost none of the early output has come to light, as some of it was

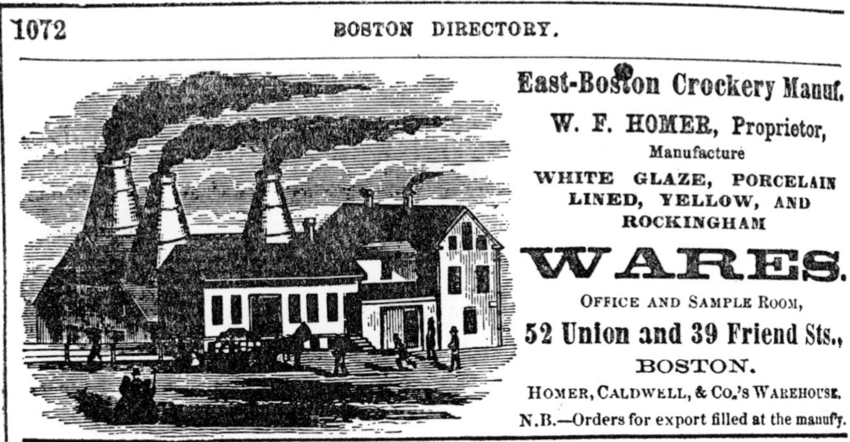

Advertisement of East Boston Crockery Co., *Boston Directory*, 1869.

marked. Dr. Burton N. Gates discovered a Rockingham pudding dish with the impressed label *Boston Earthen Ware Manufacturing Co.*, and I recently found the cuspidor with similar mark shown in Fig. 112, but I believe these are the only known examples of Mear's pottery.

In June 1857 Mear had left his position, and the pottery was leased by J. H. Lord & Company, who were still managing it in 1869. The name was changed to the East Boston Crockery Manufactory. In 1862 Homer, Caldwell & Company* advertised as "Importers and Manufacturers of China and Parian Ware,/ White Granite and Iron-Stone/ and/ Flint and Yellow Stoneware/ Plumbers' Basins, etc." Statistics show that rather less ware was produced in 1865 than in 1855, although twenty-five men were still employed. From 1865 to 1871 James Robertson, who later was to become noted in connection with the Chelsea Keramic Art Works, was superintendent at this East Boston pottery. During this time there was little change in the type of output. The following advertisement, appearing in 1869, indicates the character of the products: "East-Boston Crockery Manuf./ W. F. Homer, Proprietor,/ Manufacture/ White Glaze, Porcelain/ Lined, Yellow, and/ Rockingham/wares. . ."

In 1876 Thomas Gray and Lyman W. Clark, son of Decius W. Clark of Bennington, bought the pottery at East Boston and changed the name to the New England Pottery Company. Clark had had much useful experience in preparing clays and glazes while at Bennington, then for a short time at Kaolin, South Carolina, and later at Peoria, Illinois. The first wares made under his direction at East Boston were of a utilitarian

* The name is Caswell in the 1862 directory.

nature. From the company's advertisements we learn that white granite and common crockery, table and toilet ware were the sole output. In 1881 they were also producing "stone porcelain" ware. The same announcement appeared year after year until 1893, when chocolate pots, jugs, cuspidors, vases, etc. are mentioned.

Some Parian ware of Bennington type was made at East Boston. Noteworthy is a daisy pattern pitcher in the Bennington museum. It has a stippled buff ground and bears the mark *L. W. Clark* and the monogram *N.E. P. Co.* on the base. Vases are also said to have been produced.

We are indebted to Edwin Atlee Barber, who knew Lyman W. Clark personally, for a description of the New England Pottery wares and marks. He shows that the products were more ornate than the advertisements indicate. From 1886 to 1895, Thomas H. Copeland, of the famous English potting family, modeled most of the pieces. J. W. Phillips originated many of the designs used in the printing processes. Doulton and Royal Worcester wares were the sources of inspiration. Barber illustrates four pieces. A handled cracker jar in the Royal Worcester style is embellished with cornflowers on an ivory body, contrasted with borders at neck and base in robin's-egg blue ornamented with gold. A semiporcelain vase designed in 1889 by a Mr. Bands of the Royal Worcester Works is decorated with berry and leaf sprays upon which a bird is perched. This was an ambitious effort, of excellent form, twenty inches in height. A chocolate pot has a ground color of mazarine blue contrasting with a cameo-style decoration in raised white enamel. A bird and insect on a hawthorn spray constitute the design. On the shoulder the white body of the ware is picked out with gold filigree work relieved by reserves of maroon. The shape of this piece and the suitability of its short spout are beyond criticism.

The New England Pottery Company used at least seven marks. From 1878 to 1883 their ironstone china was stamped with the arms of Massachusetts over the initials *N.E.P. Co.* and under the words *Ironstone China*. During the next three years this ware exhibited a mark of diamond shape containing the company's monogram, the words *Stone China*, and the initials *G* and *C*. After 1886 an angular shield with the firm monogram was used on stone and granite ware. Cream ware had a black-printed circular mark resembling a dahlia or daisy, with *N E P* as a monogram and again the initials *G* and *C*.

In 1886 the company put out a cream-colored earthenware which they called *Rieti* ware. For two years it bore an underglaze printed mark composed of an arm and hand holding a dagger over the word *Rieti*. From 1888 to 1889 an underglaze mark in black in the form of a shell with the word *Rieti* was adopted on colored bodies of this type. After 1889 both Rieti and other decorated wares were marked in red over the glaze with a conventional design using the company's initials.

An example of Rieti with the shell mark is shown in Fig. 127. It is cream ware, shaped by pressing in a mold, and is decorated by hand in rose, green, and gold.

The New England Pottery continued until 1914. Examples of its output may be seen in the museum of the Society for the Preservation of New England Antiquities in Boston.

CHAPTER TWENTY-EIGHT

The Art Potteries

No other single event in the past century has had so great an influence on American appreciation of art as the Centennial Exhibition of 1876. At those displays the everyday citizen was for the first time enabled to study classic forms and the art of the Orient. Among others, potters were greatly inspired by what they saw there. Some of them, like Hugh Robertson of Chelsea and Maria Longworth Nichols of Rookwood fame, went home so fired with enthusiasm that they devoted their lives to the creation of beautiful glazes and decorations. Others, possessed of less originality, turned to imitation of the world's art as a means of salvation for their redware potteries, which were fast going under in competition with more practical wares.

Victorian ideas of decoration — the application of unrelated design to all sorts of forms — were then prevalent. It was the age of the home decorator. Even before the Centennial, the redware potters, in response to the demand for shapes for domestic embellishment, had been turning out copies of Oriental and classic forms. The clays were refined to produce a smooth terra cotta. In the *North Shore* for 1872 we read:

> The Beverly Pottery at the request of Boston Ladies began to copy beautiful forms of ancient vases to order.
>
> To meet the constantly increasing demand, the manufacture was carried on on a more extensive plan.

At Chelsea the Robertsons, too, were making a fine terra cotta as early as 1870.

The best exemplification of this development in redware potting appears in a catalogue entitled *Ancient Pottery*, published at some time after the Centennial by the Hews pottery at Cambridge. This catalogue, listing undecorated clay forms only, specifies that when orders were given in quantity books of designs for home decoration would be included. One hundred and fifty-one different shapes, many in several sizes, are illustrated in the catalogue. Of these, twenty were exact copies of vessels found by Dr. Schliemann in his excavations at Troy; seven were modeled from pieces supposed to be of Phoenician origin found by Louis Palma de Cesnola in ancient tombs on the Island of Cyprus; eight were copied from Etruscan pottery in the Peabody Museum at Harvard College. A "whistling jar" or water bottle duplicated a prehistoric burial vessel found at Ancon,

Peru, also in the Peabody Museum. There were, besides, replicas of Roman, Greek, Carthaginian, Assyrian, Egyptian, Spanish, German, early English, Japanese and Chinese, and American Indian pottery.

Among the numerous objects fashioned in these divurgent styles were card receivers shaped like Greek *tazzi*; saucer candlesticks with handles, some having extinguishers; barrel and cylinder match safes that sold for eight and ten cents each; tobacco jars with match stands, seven and one-half inches high and costing one dollar each; cigar holders of plain cylindrical form, three and one-half inches in height, at twenty cents each; tripod ash bowls, two inches in height; five-inch beehive match safes at fifty cents; an egg match box at one dollar; a cylindrical puff box with domed cover; umbrella stands that sold for two and three dollars; and innumerable vases inspired by the art of many countries.

The foregoing objects were made for definite purposes, but many curious vessels, such as copies of ancient Greek and Roman lamps, the whistling jars, and a duplication of the Portland vase had no utilitarian value. Mugs and jugs designed from medieval pieces, cremation jars and lachrymatory vases, were of little use, especially when bedecked, as they sometimes were, with colored pictures and decalcomanias, or painted by amateur lady artists.

One extremely popular article was the plaque, which provided a perfect surface for painting. This shape was made with a slight flange at the back, perforated with holes for a cord, so that it might be hung on the wall. Very similar were the discs of milk-white glass turned out at glasshouses of the period for the identical purpose.

The Hews catalogue concludes with directions for getting to the pottery. It says: "Take steam cars from Fitchburg Rail Road to Cambridge Station, or horse cars from Bowdoin Square (North Ave. or Arlington cars, which leave Square every 15 minutes) to Walden Street." The works was said to be in operation from seven in the morning until six at night. No doubt many artistically inclined ladies trailed their skirts out Walden Street to make their own selection from these fascinating wares.

A list that is almost the duplicate of the one published by Hews, but headed "The A. E. Smith's Sons Pottery Co. / Price List" is owned by the Society for the Preservation of New England Antiquities. Its sources of inspiration, including the Cesnola and Schliemann collections and other pottery of ancient origin, are identical with those noted above. Modern conceptions, such as barrel match safes, tobacco jars, cigar holders, card receivers, and beehive match safes, are of the same dimensions and are listed at the same prices as in the Hews catalogue. A descendant of the Smiths tells of her ancestor studying the ceramic displays in museums in order to create these objects. If that be true, Hews must have copied all his unglazed art ware from Norwalk pieces. This seems hardly credible. It presents a puzzle for which there is no logical explanation, except that there must have been some interchange of designs between the two potteries.

This trend towards bric-a-brac may be observed at other redware potteries that were running in the seventies and eighties. At Exeter, at Merrimacport, at Keene, and at Concord, terra-cotta vases, ewers, and knickknacks were substituted for the heavy kitchenware of the early manufacture. Surviving examples from the Clark pottery in Concord are vases of simple and useful shape, a candlestick, a covered jar, a feeding cup resembling an ancient lamp, and numerous pieces decorated at the pottery by John Farmer Clark. A mug and pitcher, unglazed, are encircled by bands of motifs in black, while a well-modeled vase has similar ornamentation in dull gold. These

pieces were suggested by a design book of classic forms, but the decoration was original. They are a good step beyond the incongruities of the amateur artist.

Out of all the growing interest in pottery for purely decorative purposes grew one development that was a true expression of creative art. This was the Chelsea Keramic Art Works at Chelsea, Massachusetts. Whatever note it has achieved it owes to the personality of Hugh C. Robertson, whose untiring efforts brought to the public the beauty of colored glazes.

The Robertson family came to this country from Scotland by way of England in 1853, settling in Roundabout (Sayreville), New Jersey, where the boys were taught the potter's trade. Hugh also spent some time at the Jersey City Pottery. After a time they moved to East Boston. Robertson got employment there at the East Boston Crockery Manufactory, becoming its manager in 1865. This position he held for six years.

Meantime, in 1866, the eldest son, Alexander, started a pottery for himself in an old varnish shop. The location at the corner of Willow and Marginal Streets on the Lynn marshes was near a supply of good red clay on the bank of Snake River near Powder Horn Hill. His intention was to produce brown wares such as were made in England and lava ware of German type. Hugh joined Alexander in the business the following year, and they set about making all kinds of red clay flowerpots and vases. These were either unglazed or were given a coat of dark green paint in the prevailing style and were not remarkable in any way. An advertisement of their wares calls attention to fancy and common flowerpots, ferneries, hyacinth boxes, match boxes, and crocus pots.

After James Robertson ended his connection with the East Boston pottery, he and his son George W., who had been his assistant there, joined the brothers in their Chelsea venture. During the next twelve years the Chelsea Keramic Art Works, as it was called, introduced a great variety of interesting and wholly new decorative wares. For the first time handsome glazes appeared on articles that were made, not experimentally, but in a commercial enterprise. James Robertson died in 1881, and Alexander departed for California four years later, while George had already found other work with the Low Art Tile Company. Hugh, the most artistic and ambitious of the family, was therefore left to run the pottery alone. He devoted his time to ardent experiments with glazes, which wrecked his health as well as the business. By 1889, when he had succeeded in creating some of his long-sought-for colorings, the pottery had to be closed for lack of funds. By this time, however, he had attracted the attention of a group of Boston art lovers, who came to his rescue. They raised capital to enable him to continue, and the works was reopened in 1891 as the Chelsea Pottery, U. S., with Robertson as superintendent. Among the persons who thus aided Robertson were A. Wadsworth Longfellow, the architect who built Robertson's later pottery in Dedham, and Joseph Lindon Smith, the artist, who originated many of the decorative designs used there.

Hugh Robertson's son William was by this time an expert potter. In the new organization he took charge of the firing. The concern was once more on its feet and in a short time was making the crackle ware for which it became famous at Dedham. New difficulties arose, however, resulting from the situation of the pottery building in a damp place; the foundations of the kiln were being undermined by water. For this reason the plant was removed to Dedham in 1895. It was later conducted there by William Robertson's son J. Milton, and then by his son, the eleventh generation of the family to be a potter.

The earliest ware of the Chelsea Keramic

Art Works was a red bisque or terra cotta, which was either perfectly plain in classic forms or else was decorated by painting in direct imitation of the old Greek vases. Such forms as the amphora, lekythos, oinochoe, stamnos, and krater, were adopted. The figure designs usually appeared in the red bisque against the black painted ground, although the colors were occasionally reversed and the figures painted in black. This kind of decoration was the work of John G. Low, a young Chelsea artist, who a year or two later was to establish the tile works for which he became noted. The finished pieces were subjected to a polishing process that completed the resemblance to the original works of art. So fine and smooth was this ware that it was also suitable for incised design in the manner of engraving on silver. A few vases of this body were ornamented with sculptured design in relief. These were from the hand of Franz Xavier Dengler, a talented young man, whose career was cut short by death when he was but twenty-five years of age. Although the creations of this period were adjudged good enough for exhibition in the Museum of Fine Arts in Boston, they did not meet with public favor, and the Robertsons set about finding new types of ware.

In 1876 Hugh Robertson visited the Centennial Exhibition. He was so much impressed by the Korean and Chinese porcelains that he returned to Chelsea eager to imitate their glazes, especially the glowing "dragon's-blood" red of the Ming wares. It was a number of years before Robertson could devote himself to this ambition. In the meantime, from 1876 to 1884, the Art Works produced a variety of colored glazes and devised original methods of decoration. In 1877 the term *Chelsea faïence* was used to designate pieces of buff body painted under the glaze with blue and white slips in the Limoges manner. This clay-upon-clay method was also known as the *Bourg-la-Reine* of Chelsea. At the same time other buff faïence was given a glaze of light or dark brown or olive green and ornamented in unusual ways. A great many pieces were hammered by hand as in metal work or were embellished with flower or leaf designs sprigged on or boldly sculptured and applied. These creations were executed by Josephine Day, Robertson's sister-in-law and pupil, and were never duplicated. Some of the hammered vases were cut intaglio and the designs filled in with white clay, affording a pleasing contrast to the buff body when seen through the transparent glaze.

A *dry glaze*, one of the best invented at Chelsea, was obtained by reducing the heat of the kiln when ware with high glaze was being burned, the lowering of the temperature producing a dull, satiny surface. The little vase Fig. 130*c*, is an example of this type. It has a dark brown body that appears without glaze around the neck and base. The middle section is a softly-glowing gray-brown like polished bronze.

At this period Hugh Robertson modeled a number of plaques that were either engraved or carved in high relief under the glaze. He drew upon literary sources for his inspiration, using Dorés illustrations of La Fontaine's fables, scenes from Dickens, or actual portraits of literary celebrities, such as Longfellow, Holmes, Byron, and Dickens. These were of stoneware glazed in quiet tones of blue or gray. A bisque plaque modeled by Robertson with a simple design of cupids is in the Brooklyn Museum; it is an interesting memento of the potter, as samples of his many glazes are on the back.

A most unusual and original flowerpot is shown in Fig. 128. It has a rather ordinary brown glaze, but its pattern of flowers and grasses is almost identical with those made from impressions of real leaves and flowers by John G. Low in his Art Tile Works. Suggestive of his later work, it is obviously one of his creations.

Many of the Chelsea vases found in shops today have a mottled coloring of brown and blue. These were often cast in molds. One of the commonest forms is a flattened round flower holder on feet.

After the death of his father and the withdrawal of his brother from the firm, Robertson launched upon his long-cherished enterprise. He devoted the remainder of his life to discovering the secrets of various glaze colors and especially to the reproduction of the famous oxblood red. It may seem strange today, when every process of the kind has been reduced to a chemical formula, that a man should have to sacrifice so much time and strength in order to obtain a color. But so it was. Robertson did not rest, night or day. Over and over he tried this combination and that, sleeping fitfully beside the kiln that he might regulate its temperature to a nicety. In this way he spent some four years. The business of the pottery naturally declined, but Robertson, nearly penniless, kept on until he had wrested his desired secrets from the materials of the earth.

The best of his dragon's-blood red is a pure rich color, glowing with a golden luster that catches the light in changing hues. Only three hundred pieces of this description were completed. Others, of beautiful color, but lacking the luster, are desirable additions to any pottery collections. The body of the successful specimens is a gray-white stoneware, impervious to water or changes of temperature. Th experimental pieces sometimes have a hard white body, sometimes a paste of buff earthenware. These vases were severely simple, in forms that always expressed the Oriental influence. In the course of his attempts to produce red, Robertson also obtained a deep sea green, an apple green, mustard yellow, greenish blue, maroon and rich purple. At least two collectors, Augustus V. Peabody and William G. A. Turner of Malden, Massachusetts, acquired examples of Robertson's experimental ware as it came from the kiln. Their cabinets, filled with beautiful vases in all these many colors and combinations of color, were a delight to the eye, and were, indeed, one of the first sources of ceramic inspiration to me.

As early as 1886 Hugh Robertson had succeeded in copying the Japanese crackle ware. His first specimens had a smoky gray tone, even where the blue decoration was applied. The example in Fig. 130*b*, marked *CPUS* and made, therefore, between 1891 and 1895, has strong black lines of crackle and deep blue floral design. In Dedham the crackle ware composed almost the entire output of the Robertson pottery. Plates, bowls, mugs, cups and saucers, and many other forms were produced in quantity and held their popularity year after year. The painted designs, although drawn from natural forms, were highly conventionalized and were most often applied as a band of pattern around the vessels. Such motifs as the rabbit (the most common), the lion, swan, crab, tulip, magnolia, iris, water lily, grape, and dolphin were utilized. The popular rabbit border was designed by Joseph Lindon Smith, the lion by Denman Ross. Of the other patterns, many were originated or adapted by Charles E. Mills, who had a noteworthy influence on this pottery.

The crackle bowl in Fig. 131 was made by Hugh Robertson as a gift for Mr. Turner and was acquired by the present owner with a letter from the potter explaining the significance of the design. It was suggested, he said, by the wheels and bands of the power apparatus in the pottery.

The only other type of ware made to any extent at Dedham was a so-called "volcanic" ware. First created in the late nineties, this was a high-fired stoneware with glazes of two tones, one running down over the other or blending with it. A little vase made during th experiments to perfect this ware is signed *Dedham Pottery HCR*. The volcanic ware

was rather heavy and ungainly and lacked the refinement of the earlier Chelsea faïence.

There are many marks on Chelsea pottery. The first is said to have been the firm name *A. W. & H. C. Robertson*. From 1872 to 1884 or later the impressed letters *CKAW* in a diamond appeared on the ware for sale. Sometimes the words *Chelsea Keramic/Art Works/ Robertson & Sons* were used and sometimes both marks together. The small vase in imitation of bronze (Fig. 130*c*) has the *CKAW* mark on a raised diamond-shaped lozenge. From 1891 to 1895 an impressed four-leafed clover with the initials *CPUS* on its leaflets was the regular stamp. The same initials, incised by hand, appear on experimental pieces. An outlined rabbit facing front was the mark in 1895. This was changed to a rabbit facing right under the words Dedham Pottery, all in a square, in 1896, and was kept thereafter. Hugh Robertson's monogram, his private mark, was scratched on his individual creations.

The Dedham pottery continued in operation until a short time before the second World War. It is perhaps too soon to appraise the work of Hugh Robertson and his family. The one almost certain factor that will bring lasting fame to them is that Hugh Robertson worked out the formulas for colored glazes at a time when the ordinary citizen was still thinking of pottery in terms of brown Rockingham or Albany-slip-glazed stoneware. His experiments were paralleled by the development of an almost unlimited palette in glassmaking. The glassmakers, however, organized as an industry, were able to publicize their creations, which became vastly popular, while Robertson, an artist, could not do this. In any event, the public was not ready for the severity and purity of form that characterized most of his early vases. Not until now have we come to a realization of his high place in our ceramic history.

A contemporaneous project in Chelsea was the Art Tile Works of John G. Low, which produced the first successful decorative tiles to be made in America. John Gardner Low was the son of John Low, a civil engineer, and he came from five generations of the name in the town. He was born January 10, 1835. When still a boy he showed a decided talent for drawing and painting and at the age of twenty-six he had completed a course of several years' art study in Paris under such famous teachers as Couture and Troyon. In 1862 he returned to America with high hopes of becoming a landscape painter, but the necessity for earning a living led him to an expression of his genuine artistic impulses through commercial channels.

In the early 1870's Low was working at the Robertsons' pottery, where he became absorbed in the study of ceramics and began some experiments on his own account. Just why he turned toward the development of tiles is not recorded. In 1877 John and his father formed a partnership and immediately set about building the tile works at 948 Broadway, on the corner of Stockton Street. Some time was consumed in securing and installing necessary apparatus and machinery, for this was no small craftsman's shop, but a factory designed for production on a large scale. Not until May 1, 1879, according to Low, did the first successful firing take place. Within five months Low tiles were awarded a silver medal at the Cincinnati Industrial Exposition.

Low's tiles have designs in relief. In making them, two processes were used: one for *dust* tiles, the other for *wet* or *plastic* tiles. The wet process was not fundamentally different from that employed by any potter in modeling. Damp or plastic clay was pressed into molds with a wetted sponge and allowed to remain until, by drying, it had shrunk enough to be easily removed. The molded tiles were then placed carefully on their backs

on blocks of plaster covered with cloth and left for twenty-four hours. They were then ready for the artist who improved the relief by undercutting. A three- or four-weeks period in the drying room followed before they could be fired. In burning, the tiles, separated by sand, were stood on edge in saggers or boxes of fire clay. The first or biscuit firing took from forty-eight to sixty hours at intense heat; the glaze firing, twenty-eight to thirty-two hours at a low temperature. The glazed tiles were burned in shallow boxes known as *hillers*, which were sealed with fire clay against the action of gases from the kiln.

The dust process was known in England long before the time of John G. Low. In fact, it was patented by Richard Prosser in 1840 and was used for making buttons. The Mintons, Maw, and others, had also made use of the dust process. In preparing the clay for dust tiles, it was reduced to a powder, and allowed to retain just enough water to make it workable, but not wet. Low pressed this clay into dies by machine presses, thereby obviating the difficulties of warping, twisting, and shrinkage that had made relief work in wet tiles a failure up to that time.

By a novel method, wholly original with himself, Low ornamented his tiles with natural objects, such as grasses, leaves, or bits of fabric (Fig. 132*c*). He accomplished this by pressing a bat of clay into a box the shape of the tile, arranging the decorative motifs on its unfinished surface, and then forcing them into the clay under the weight of a screw press. The leaves were thus broken or destroyed, but the impression remained intaglio. The surface was then covered with a sheet of Japanese paper and then with clay to form a twin tile. After they were again subjected to pressure, the tiles could be removed and separated. The paper was peeled away, and a pair of tiles, one intaglio and one in relief, had been formed. After devising this ingenious scheme, Low, by the same method, made a "die" tile of paraffin, which he coated with plumbago to form a durable mold in which hundreds of tiles could be pressed. Dies for relief tiles were also made by engraving, the designs being later elaborated by undercutting.

By these methods rapid duplication was assured, and the Low Art Tile Works, in consequence, became mass producers of these extremely decorative ceramics. Low's creations were soon in great demand for architectual purposes, such as panels, dadoes, mantel and hearth facings, and soda fountains. The company also found a market for a number of smaller objects. Paper weights, clock cases, candlesticks, bonbon boxes, and small ewers and flower holders bearing their mark were made.

In addition to regular tiles and other related objects, Low produced what he called "plastic" sketches. These were, in fact, sketches in very low relief made by an artist using clay instead of oils or water colors as a medium. I believe that all the plastic sketches sold by the Low company were conceived and executed by Arthur Osborne, a young artist who joined the concern a few months after its organization and who was still working for the Lows in 1893. He was the designer of the majority of all tiles made at Chelsea, and one has only to examine a Low catalogue to realize the fertility of his imagination. His conceptions ranged over every field of classic and Oriental art and included naturalistic motifs in endless variety, mythological heads and portraits, and an infinity of conventional designs. In his plastic sketches he created numerous genre subjects and farm scenes, groups of animals, figures of monks, and allegorical presentations of beautiful women or delightful *putti*. These reliefs, all marked with the monogram *AO* of the artist, as were some of the regular tiles, were comparatively large, some running to eighteen inches in length. The only examples of Os-

borne sketches I have seen are the one illustrated in Fig. 133 and another owned by Mr. E. Stanley Wires. It is high time that recognition should be given this really fine artist, who so often sought his inspiration in the American scene. Like many persons of imagination, he was lost in the midst of big business. It is significant that a de luxe portfolio of his designs in photogravure is entitled *Plastic Sketches by John G. Low* and makes no mention of the man whose signature appears in the corner of each one.

Only a little over a year after the first tile came from the kiln, Low was invited to exhibit his product at Crewe, England, near Stoke-on-Trent, where a gold medal worth ten pounds was offered for the best collection of English or American tiles. Low won this award in competition with the foremost English potters. In December of the same year, 1880, he received a bronze medal from the American Institute in New York, and in October 1881 a silver medal at St. Louis. Other awards followed. So much interest was displayed in these unusual creations that Low planned an exhibition in London, more dignified and better organized than his first, which had been assembled hastily overnight from stock on hand. The show opened June 15, 1882. It was a display of both tiles and plastic sketches arranged like an art exhibit in the rooms of the Fine Arts Society in New Bond Street. The salon was given a good deal of favorable attention by the newspaper critics, who hailed the plastic sketches as "a new phase in art, somewhere between sculpture and painting," and the tiles as the first ceramic ware of a high order that America had produced.

The Lows now settled down to a long period of production. New designs were put out from year to year, and the business was a success. In 1883 John Low the father retired, and John G. Low's son, John F. Low, became his assistant.

The best source of information concerning the regular output of the tile works is an illustrated catalogue published in 1884. This may be seen at the Massachusetts Institute of Technology. From it we learn that nearly all the individual tiles we now see — most of them about six inches square — were parts of compositions or repeats. The greater number were intended for mantel facings whose corner tiles were used interchangeably with different floral or conventional designs at top and sides. The upper panel of several units frequently formed an artistic composition of great merit. In creating these mantel sets, Arthur Osborne did not go far afield to find his material. Such familiar flowers as the apple blossom, daisy, buttercup, wild rose, narcissus, Japanese quince, poppy, and blackberry he used in the most ingenious way. For more pretentious designs he employed Renaissance, Elizabethan, Jacobean, Queen Anne, and other period motifs. Mantelpiece facings were made at all prices, from $4.60 for a simple "swag" set to $500 for "The Revel." The latter was an elaborate Grecian composition, with cupids, graceful maidens, and youths bearing garlands. Copyrighted in 1881, it was intended for a fireplace about ten feet wide.

The catalogue shows many small conventional tiles of the kind intended for dadoes or for allover areas on walls or ceilings. It also illustrates the small round reliefs of classic profiles that were inserted in box or inkwell covers. There is, too, a series of portrait busts of Washington, Lincoln, Grant, and Cleveland, each measuring six by four and one-quarter inches. Circular examples with designs well fitted to the shape were made for teapot rests. A few tiles were undercut to extremely high relief. They could be used without difficulty on wall surfaces, but depart so far from true tile technique as to be something quite different.

The collecting of Low tiles is simplified

by the fact that nearly all of them are marked and some are dated. The earliest are those made with real leaves and grasses in Low's naturalistic style. I have seen these with two marks: the first, *J. & J. G. Low/ Chelsea, Mass.* in rectangles and *Pat'd/ Feb. 18/ 1879* in a circle; the second, *J. & J. G. Low* over crossed keys and *Patent Art Tile Works/ Chelsea, Mass.* The firm name *J. & J. G. Low*, with or without the company style, appears with the dates 1881, 1883, or 1884. I have never seen a tile dated 1882. In 1885, the mark, used in several ways, was *J. G. & J. F. Low.*

The Hampshire Pottery of J. S. Taft & Company at Keene, New Hampshire, began in 1871 (see p. 117). At first only redware was produced, then stoneware. Highly glazed ware of majolica type, in which the colors are mixed with the glazes, was the first innovation. Tones of green, brown, yellow, or blue were applied over a hard white body, which was sometimes cast in molds to give relief figuration. This type of ware was first made after Thomas Stanley, an English potter, came to the works as superintendent in 1879. It is often seen in the form of mugs with dark green glaze that shades to red, over a border of fine relief below the rim. Many pitchers and tea sets of unusual form were made with brown glaze. An article on the Hampshire Pottery by Miss Florence Morse, written for the Historical Society of Cheshire County, also notes a majolica ear of corn pattern and numerous vases in brown and orange or with green and white stripes. She says that marmalade dishes in the shape and color of an orange were a specialty. A tea set in so-called "Nantucket" pattern was copied from a piece obtained by James Taft on the island. There was also a "Monadnock" pattern, of dark green hue.

In 1883 a new kiln for burning decorative pottery was added and an artist, Wallace L. King, put in charge. Under his direction a number of new wares and glazes were introduced. Perhaps the most characteristic type of the following decade was a ware of opaque white body with an ivory mat glaze resembling that of Royal Worcester ware. It was, in fact, called the "Royal Worcester finish." According to Dr. Barber, this pottery was fashioned into baskets, jugs, cracker jars, cuspidors, brush-and-comb trays, bonbon boxes, rose bowls, tea sets, and umbrella stands. It was frequently embellished with transfer-printed designs in black. Executed from copper plates prepared in Boston from photographs, these were often local views intended to be sold as souvenirs. A noteworthy example is the "Witch" jug, made as a commemorative piece for Daniel Low of Salem, a dealer in china and silver. Of graceful ewer shape, it displays appropriate witch figures and the inscription *Salem — 1892.* Handle, foot, and rim are gilded. The date of this jug seems to leave no question that the Hampshire Pottery was the first in the country to produce commercially a dull, or mat, glaze. According to William Watts Taylor, a mat glaze was experimentally developed at Rookwood as early as 1896, but was not put on the market before that time. The Grueby works of South Boston, which is generally given the credit of first introducing mat finishes, did not begin operations until 1897.

The ivory ware was usually faintly tinted with pink in a manner comparable to that of the delicate shading on glass in the eighties. It was made with great care and, since it had to be fired a number of times, must have been rather expensive. The plain biscuit body came from the kiln at the first burning. This was tinted and the process repeated. The printed or hand-painted decoration was then added and the ware burned a third time. A glaze firing and a final one when gilt was added completed the sequence.

The Hampshire Pottery also produced

plain white ware. Some of it was made in shapes suitable either for home decorating or to be painted at the factory. A large plaque signed by King shows a Dutch landscape with windmills in sepia. In 1904 Cadmon Robertson came to the pottery and soon was placed in entire charge of its manufacture. A chemist, he was born in Chesterfield, New Hampshire, getting an education there and in Keene, besides studying under a private tutor. While at the Hampshire Pottery, he devised no fewer than nine hundred formulas and was responsible for its great variety of mat glazes in green, old blue, peacock blue, gray, bronze, brown, and yellow. These dull colors were used principally for vases, bowls, and flower holders, although such things as candlesticks, clocks and lamps were produced. Glass lamp shades to match the pottery bases were supplied by a Connecticut firm. Miss Morse notes a shade decorated with evergreen trees, which no doubt harmonized with the popular green hue of the lamp. Mat glazes were employed until the pottery closed in 1917. More pleasing to the touch than Grueby ware, they present a smooth satiny finish.

Wallace L. King retired from the works in 1908; Robertson died six years later. Without the artist who not only designed wares, but also decorated some of them with his own brush, and the chemist who had made such successful innovations, Taft must have been at a loss to carry on the pottery. He did, in fact, sell it in 1916. The new owner, George N. Morton, had been connected with the Grueby works. By the purchase he acquired the main building, kiln shed, engine and boiler house, and storage building. Included were all the machinery, equipment, and stock, as well as the process records and the formulas developed by Cadmon Robertson. The pottery ran for only one year under Morton's management and was then sold for other purposes. In 1945 it became a garage.

Several different marks appear on Keene pottery. I have noted the following: *J. S. Taft & Co/ Keene, N. H.*, on a majolica jug and also on a yellow-glazed vase; *Hampshire Pottery/ Keene, N. H.*, on green mat glaze; *J. S. T. & Co./ Keene, N. H.*, impressed, with *Hampshire, Keene, N. H.* printed in red, on a green mat-glazed jug; and *Hampshire Pottery* in script, impressed, with initials *N. B.* written in blue, also on green mat glaze. Barber also records a three-line mark composed of the firm name in script between the words *Hampshire* and *Pottery*, printed in red over the glaze on art ware of opaque white body.

A peculiar ware of unique type was made for many years at Cottage City on Martha's Vineyard. W. F. Willard began about 1879 in his Gay Head Pottery to make unburnt vases from the famous colored clays found on the cliffs at the western end of the island. The brilliant red, blue, slate-color, and buff of these deposits appears in the finished ware as striations or whorls. The effect was obtained by mixing the various clays before turning. When a piece was partly dried, it was shaved to smoothness and allowed to harden in the sun. It would not, of course, hold water, and had no value except as a memento of a visit to the Vineyard. A few articles of red clay were burned. Unfortunately, the bright coloring disappeared in the firing — a fact that explains Willard's reason for baking his vases in the sun. The impressed mark *Gay Head* will be found on the side (not the base) of each piece.

The name of W. J. Walley has been mentioned briefly in connection with West Sterling. He bought the old Wachuset Pottery there before 1890 and continued to operate it alone until his death in 1917. Born in England August 3, 1852, Walley had come to Canada, working for a time in a glasshouse, and then going to Ohio. During the seven-

ties, he was employed at the Norton pottery in Worcester. At West Sterling he continued the flowerpot business in a small way, and also made "art" ware with fancy glazes. Many of his pieces were finished in the green mat glaze so much favored forty years ago. Others were of various shades of blue or of an unglazed terra cotta. Some examples owned by Mrs. Elizabeth Davis of West Sterling show that he was an extremely able modeler and designer, who created vases, candlesticks, and other objects well suited for their intended uses. Walley was accustomed to incise his ware with his initials, thus making identification simple.

The Grueby Faience & Tile Company was organized in June 1897 by William H. Grueby, William H. Graves, and George Prentiss Kendrick. It was located on the corner of East First and K Streets, South Boston, and had an office at 2A Park Street in the city. As a great deal of architectural work was done, this pottery was run on a large scale, employing one hundred hands. It continued until 1907.

Grueby tiles are well known, but less familiar are the fine vases, usually fashioned in suggested leaf forms, and other objects of imaginative character. All Grueby wares were made of a hard semiporcelain body and were finished with a mat glaze. William Grueby originated this glaze at South Boston, and his name has become the generic one for the type. Kendrick was responsible for the shapes.

The Grueby wares have never been surpassed by any in this country for artistic quality. No molds were used, and every piece was an original creation. Young women graduates of the Museum of Fine Arts School, the Massachusetts Normal Art School, and the Cowles Art School were engaged to design and execute the decorations. W. Ellsworth Gray, in an article in *Brush and Pencil* quoted W. P. Jervis, says of Grueby ware:

> Many competent critics regard this ware as the highest achievement of the potter's art in this country. It has a distinct individuality in character and tone. It is not the product of imitation, not mere decorated china, not clay vessels trucked out with designs borrowed from workers in other forms of art. It is simple and chaste, relying for its effect in a perfectly legitimate way on the superb finish of its surface, on the subdued richness of its colors, and on the idea embodied in its designs. In this regard it is practically unique among American fictile products.

Although many Grueby tiles were of a strictly utilitarian nature, others were so beautifully modeled and colored that they are works of art in themselves. Many of them show landscapes with trees painted with colored enamels laid thickly on the surface. Yellow, blue, purple, and green were used. Decorative objects were treated in the same manner. Jervis describes a lamp that has yellow pond lilies on a green ground and a vase ornamented with narcissi whose pale yellow blossoms and light green leaves appear in contrast to a dark green background. The Grueby company also produced a fine crackle ware in lustreless ivory-white enamel similar to old Korean ware and thought by ceramic experts to be quite its equal.

A number of impressed marks have been recorded. *Grueby*, or *Grueby/ Boston/ Mass.*, is probably the most common. The stamp *Grueby Pottery/ Boston, U. S. A.* appears in straight lines or in a circle with a small flower in the center. The mark *Grueby Faience Co./ Boston, U. S. A.* is seen in the same circular arrangement.

A pottery in New Milford, Connecticut, which ran well into the twentieth century, was organized as a stock company in 1886 and called the New Milford Pottery Company. Its first products were ordinary white ware and semiopaque china. The white ware was marked with a square enclosing the let-

tering *N. M. P. Co.* or the initials *L & S* in a circle. The latter stood for Lang & Schafer, the New York agents for whom the china was made.

The name of the works was after a time changed to the Wannopee Pottery Company — a style that was still in use in 1904. During this period "Duchess" ware, characterized by mottled glazes, and porcelain were produced. A letter *W* in a sunburst was the mark on Duchess ware, while a sunburst with the word *Porcelain*, the letter *W* in the center, and *W. P. Co.* below appears on porcelain.

The Park Lane Pottery, as it was also called, under the same management of A. H. Noble, brought out a ware with metallic glaze resembling copper. An accidental discovery, made while Noble was trying for a different result, it was given the name "Scarabronze," and an Egyptian scarab with a monogram *P L P* was used as a mark (sometimes on a paper label). Scarabronze is said to have had a smooth and pleasing texture. The shapes were inspired by the pottery of ancient Egypt. To heighten the Oriental effect Egyptian figures and characters were sometimes painted on the surface with liquid slips in which metallic colors had been mixed.

The company also producd, about 1895, some semiporcelain pitchers with a smear or dull glaze slightly resembling Parian ware. One was designed with relief medallions of Beethoven and Mozart, another with busts marked *Napoleon.* These were white except for a band of brown leaves in relief at the top and another of greenish yellow at the base. They were modeled by Victor Gallimore of Trenton, New Jersey, and, according to Barber, were rather "cheap affairs."

CHAPTER TWENTY-NINE

Redware Forms

POTS

Judging by excavated fragments, the vessel made in greatest quantity by our early potters was the common pot. It was straight-sided, rounding in towards the base, was unglazed outside, and usually had a plain rim but no cover. Pots of this type were made in small, medium, and large sizes, and served many useful purposes in the household. They were convenient receptacles for soft soap,

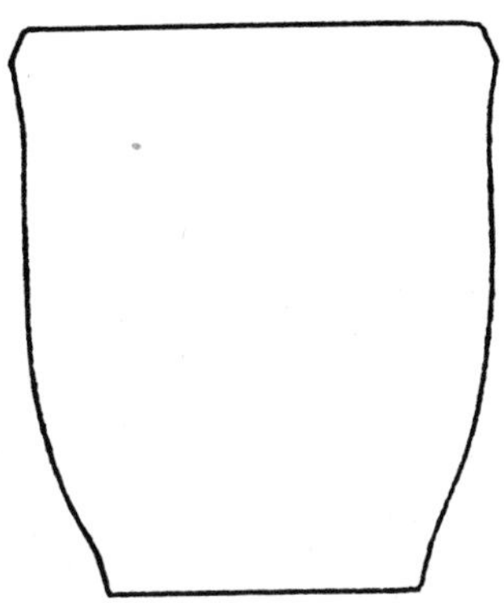

dye, or lard, or for baking beans, pudding, and other foods. There is no observable change in the pot shape from 1685 to 1885.

Pots of perfectly cylindrical form, but otherwise similar, were made in Essex County in the nineteenth century and were used for the same purposes. Pudding pots with sides slanting in like a flowerpot were an extremely common form, produced without variation in style during the whole era of earthenware manufacture.

The earliest mention of a bean pot as such that I have found occurs in William Jackson's "Lynn Earthenware" advertisement in 1811. Beanpots as we now know them were

not devised until the 1840's. The first ones, unglazed outside, appeared both with and without handles. They were soon replaced by stoneware pots of the same shape.

The stew pot with a cover in pint and quart sizes is also listed by William Jackson and is found throughout New England. What its exact shape was I have not discovered, but I believe it was the straight-sided glazed pot with a lip and handle.

Rounded pots with covers, with or without pouring lips, are a nineteenth-century form once common in Massachusetts and New Hampshire. The smaller sizes, it is said, were used for herb tea or similar brews; some of

the larger ones were pots for "emptyings," the handful of dough reserved from each baking to ferment and provide leaven for the

next batch. Herb pots are often prettily glazed, as they no doubt came to the table.

PANS

Pans, platters, and plates, all shallow receptacles with sloping sides, were fashioned in a series of sizes from small affairs no larger than a saucer to milk pans eighteen and one-half inches in diameter. The milk pans were sold in small and large sizes; the platters, identical in form, were small, large, or "great" — the latter perhaps nearly as large as the milk pans; plates were made in numerous sizes. Platters and plates were usually decorated. Today we would call them pans rather than plates or platters, but I have established

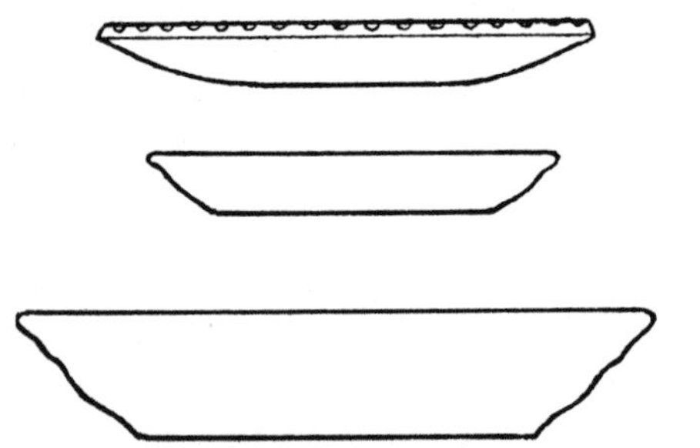

the fact the objects listed by potters as platters were actually deep dishes and were so called within the memory of persons now living. These northern New England forms were turned entirely on the wheel. In southern Connecticut, molds were used as early as 1800. The shallow pie plates with notched edges were more quickly shaped over a mold turned on the wheel. Oblong platters with square or rounded ends somewhat like modern ones, but much deeper, were also formed on molds.

Pudding and bread pans, mentioned in Parker's 1750 book, were round dishes with high sides, usually rather larger than our baking dishes of today. "Bake" pans are also noted at a later period. Vessels of this kind, like modern kitchen utensils, were turned

out in a variety of shapes and sizes. In the Bayley pottery we found some small enough to be called custard cups. All were glazed on the interior only.

JUGS

Jugs of redware were, I believe, not so common in the eighteenth century as in the years that followed. They are mentioned only once in John Parker's account book; Preserved Peirce had but few to sell; and we found only one jug and parts of two others among the bushels of fragments recovered at Newburyport. It is probable that more serviceable jugs of imported stoneware were generally used. They assuredly were in the seventeenth century. At the Kettle pottery we found no bit of the familiar jug shape, but rather pot-bellied vessels with straight necks and wide mouths (possibly mugs).

In New England there are two types of handle attachment on jugs. The more common is the handle from neck to body, but a handle from shoulder to body also appears. It is difficult to date jugs, but I believe the type of handle attachment is not an indication of period. The earliest jugs are of a slender ovoid form; those with an extreme bulge

are probably of nineteenth century origin, corresponding to the bulging stoneware jugs of known date.

Lips may be an indication of period, as they are on flasks. I have found one jug with wide mouth opening that I think is very early — possibly the work of Joseph Gardner of Gloucester (Fig. 13*b*). Others have reeded necks, and some a rounded lip. Occasionally a plain straight neck is seen (Fig. 65*b*). These differences characterize the work of different potting groups.

BOWLS

The bowls of the early potters were made in half-pint, pint, and quart sizes. They were glazed inside and outside and were as thin as the potters could turn them. There is no doubt that they were intended for table use. In shape they were the duplicates of fine English earthenware. The smallest size was used as a drinking vessel for a "dish" of tea or coffee, as the familiar expression goes, and were not equipped with saucers. A print made in the reign of Queen Anne, alluded to in Chapter VIII, shows some gentlemen in a coffee house drinking out of such bowls, while the maid at the counter has numbers of them out ready for serving.

In nineteenth-century potteries large bowls were made for use in the kitchen. The one illustrated in Fig. 41*a* is of gallon capacity. There is some question whether the "basons" listed by John Parker and Peirce were not rather mixing bowls, as the word *basin* is still used in that sense in England. They were, however, such inexpensive articles, selling

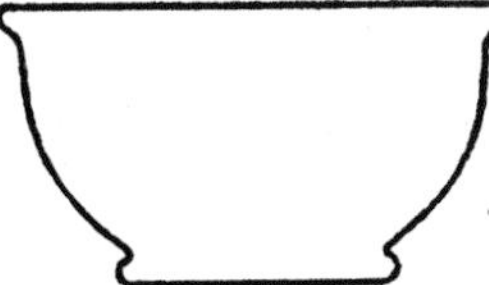

for three or four pence apiece — less than the cost of small bowls — it seems improbable that they were large objects.

PITCHERS

Pitchers of different sizes, including "little" pitchers, or creamers, were made as early as 1750 and doubtless much earlier. The seventeenth-century shape as illustrated in Dutch paintings before 1660 was that of the large pitcher in Fig. 9. This piece was found in Haverhill, Massachusetts. Its body and glaze are so like other Essex County ware, it may indeed be the work of one of the seventeenth-century men in that area — perhaps William Vinson himself. In the Kettle dump (1685–1710) we found vessels with a shorter neck and rounded body that could have been either pitchers or mugs. These bulbous shapes were the standard forms before and somewhat after 1700.

Pitchers of the second half of the eighteenth and early nineteenth centuries were as simple as possible. A mere pull of the thumb was all that changed them from a handled jar to a pouring vessel. But they did pour well. This form was made throughout New England. Other types appear in the later period. Covered pitchers, used in much the same way as the emptyings and herb tea pots, had a narrow flaring collar with slightly more prominent lip above a more bulging body.

In Connecticut is found a distinct type that reflects Dutch and German influence. An elongated neck slanting inward to a rounded

body and almost at an angle to it is the characteristic feature. It is also marked by a handle describing a wide curve, whereas the

pitchers of northern New England have rather long handles set at a slight curve from the body. Handles on all early pitchers are conveniently shaped and placed for lifting.

Small low pitchers that were little more than a mug with a pouring lip were made at Danvers. The example in Fig. 71*c*, although it came from Vermont, corresponds in its two tooled lines and yellowish coloring with a fragment dug on the site of the Southwick pottery. A similar pitcher may be seen at the Peabody Historical Society.

MUGS

The Kettle mug or jug previously mentioned (unless it had a lip) resembles the form of seventeenth-century drinking pots made in England and Germany. Further light on the work of our earliest men would undoubtedly show that they turned bulging mugs. Straight-sided mugs were in vogue as early as 1700, and probably before; they became the regular style by 1720. The form continued to be made for about one hundred years. The early examples are sometimes plain and sometimes elaborated with bands of tooled ridges around the body or, at least, invariably around the base. Later pieces have no tooling. These ale mugs appear in half-pint, pint, and quart sizes. The splendid example in Fig. 28 holds two and one-half pints. They were often extremely thin and their height was about twice their diameter.

An eighteenth-century type, like the glass can of the same period, was the mug of curved or barrel shape swelling towards the base. The Fitchburg mug in Fig. 56 has a tiny beading around the very thin rim — a feature of the earliest work.

Nineteenth-century mugs are comparatively clumsy. They are wider and lower in proportion to their size and have little to recommend them. A barrel type with lines suggesting barrel hoops was made until a late period.

PORRINGERS

Early porringers were shallow and were provided with a loop handle at right angles to the body (Fig. 23). They are mentioned

in potters' accounts from 1750 in Charlestown to 1855 in Goshen, Connecticut. They were a convenient dish for any kind of food — soup, stew, or porridge — that had to be eaten with a spoon. Benjamin Franklin, in his autobiography, writes of using porringers in his early married life: "We kept no idle servants, our table was plain and simple, our furniture of the cheapest. For instance, my breakfast was a long time bread and milk (no tea), and I ate it out of a twopenny earthen porringer, with a pewter spoon." "The Independent Beggar" (Fig. 72), a portrait by Waldo in the Boston Athenaeum, painted in 1819, demonstrates the use of the porringer.

By 1820 this vessel was deeper, like a huge cup, but with the rim rolling a bit outwards.

I have sometimes had difficulty in persuading people that this form should be called a porringer, but I think there is no question of its

name, for it is mentioned in potters' lists throughout New England, and the same form prevailed in Pennsylvania. The early lists specify small and large porringers. In the course of time, it is true, they were called "large and small cups," like the pieces made by Elijah Lowell in 1869 (Fig. 70), but they are the descendants of the original porringer.

JARS

The word *jar* does not appear in any early potter's list that I have seen. Undoubtedly the vessels that we call jars were simply termed "pots." Nevertheless, the word connotes something to modern ears that the expression *pot* does not. I refer to those containers, covered or uncovered, with an allover glaze, that were used not so much for cooking as for the storage of food.

Some of the handsomest pieces of redware are of this type. Frequently the potters expended considerable effort to make them attractive. Generally speaking, they are found in two forms, cylindrical or ovoid. A rather

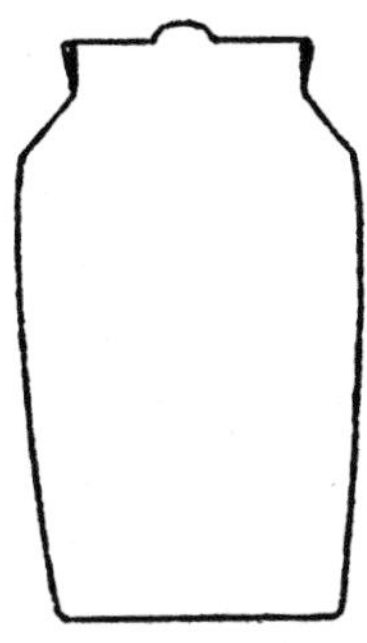

early and thin type of cylindrical jar has a straight reeded collar and a cover with flattish knob that rests inside the rim. Later examples are likely to have slightly concave collars and sometimes, as at Middlebury and Newbury, Vermont, ear handles. It is known that early Staffordshire butter pots were cylindrical. This fact may give a clue to the purpose of our American pieces. Smaller sizes were called "spice jars." These sometimes have numbers painted with white slip or incised on both body and cover to insure the matching of the correctly fitting lid. The jar of this kind in Fig. 57*c* has a single handle — a rather rare feature. The straight-sided glazed jar was a favorite form in southwestern Connecticut. It has an angular shoulder and sometimes its lip flares out at an angle,

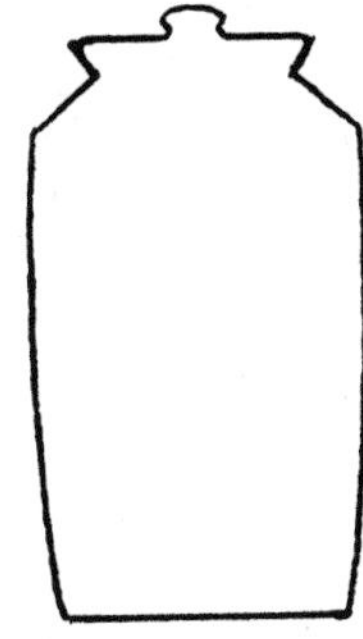

but never so sharply as in examples from New Jersey. The cover fits inside the rim. Other cylindrical jars, unusually tall and slender, have neatly formed rims that roll outwards, leaving no ledge for a cover. They were designed for preserves and could be sealed by paper tied over the mouth and made airtight by coating with wax or a similar substance. Little jars of this type were utilized as containers for salves or medicine.

The ovoid jar, with or without handles, covered or without cover, is the most beau-

tiful shape made by our New England potters. The commonest type has ear handles and a cover. It was made throughout New England. The handleless jar often has a beauty

of form that is not surpassed in the finest wares of the Orient. Its gently swelling curves give it perfect proportion. Some of these jars have narrow rolled rims. It is quite possible that they were intended for flower vases. Rather small ovoid jars with covers are also attractive specimens of the potter's art.

A type of large jar made principally, I believe, in southwestern Connecticut, has a bulbous body, a straight or flaring collar from one to two inches in depth, and ear handles. It is exactly like the large jars of Huntington, Long Island, or from New Jersey. The deep

collars, both on redware and on stoneware, are indication of manufacture in the first quarter of the nineteenth century.

An unusual curved jar made at Chesham (Pottersville), New Hampshire, is illustrated in Fig. *66a*. Its spread towards the base is a feature that does not seem to have been repeated outside of southern New Hampshire.

BOTTLES

While bottles and flasks were not among the articles in a redware potter's regular output, they were nevertheless made to some extent, especially in Connecticut. The most common type is the bottle with round base and slightly flattened sides. This is almost invariably red splashed with black. Cylindrical bottles with angular shoulders (Fig. 52*c*) are also a Connecticut product.

A rare early flask in my collection is enlivened with a brushing of light slip dotted with green. This came to light in Rhode Island. A plainer example with brownish mottled glaze was found in New Hampshire. These are the counterparts in shape of early glass flasks.

An earthen bottle whose form was obviously inspired by the Keene three-mold glass decanters is another New Hampshire type rarely encountered.

TOILET ARTICLES

Country people depended upon the redware potter to supply them with toilet necessities as well as with kitchen utensils. Long before Staffordshire pitchers and wash basins came into general use, common redware sets were made. As noted before, the "basons" mentioned in eighteenth-century accounts may or may not have been vessels for toilet use, but were perhaps mixing bowls. Nevertheless, wash basins of redware were among the things made by Daniel Bayley before 1795.

The lowly chamber mug was a staple article with all potters from the beginning, and they probably produced the greater number used in colonial days. The eighteenth-century examples are somewhat deeper in proportion to the diameter than are those made in the 1800's. Shards of these vessels may be instantly distinguished from parts of jars by their flat rims at right angles to the body.

Various utensils for the sick room were

turned out as occasion demanded. Hervey Brooks mentions a "spitting dish." This was a receptacle for the unfortunate victim of tuberculosis. It was merely a very large cup

and is not to be confused with a child's chamber mug, which has a flat rim, while the expectoration cup has a simple straight rim. Vessels of the same shape were also produced in Staffordshire wares.

Bed pans, perfectly round, as the limitations of the potter's wheel determined, were among the sick-room necessities. Hot-water bottles were useful both for the sick and the well; the usual shape is cylindrical with one side flattened to keep the bottle from rolling. The opening for filling is on the rounded surface. One end is always smaller than the

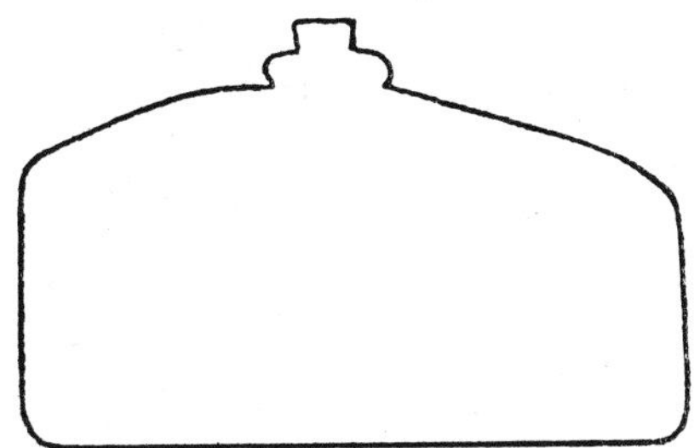

other — a peculiarity caused by the difficulty of closing in the end of what was in reality a turned cylinder. The irregular form of these containers has led to the appellation "pig bottle."

Shaving mugs of several styles were made by redware potters. The most primitive type was nothing more than an ale mug with a small cup for the soap and brush attached to the inside of the rim. A later type has a partition through the center and is more conveniently shallow in form.

Cuspidors of the plainest kind were another object commonly made in redware.

SOME OTHER COMMON FORMS

Large objects of redware may usually be given a comparatively early date, as they were not made to any extent after the first third of the last century, when stronger and more suitable stoneware containers came into general use. Crocks for butter or preserves may occasionally be found, but most of them have gone the way of all perishable things. Except that some Connecticut examples have domed covers, they are little different from stoneware crocks.

Churns were a regular early redware product. They were provided with covers such as we see on stoneware churns, with a collared hole for the dasher.

In Chesham (Pottersville), New Hampshire, was made a container that I have never seen elsewhere. It was a slender and very deep glazed pot for storing cream after it had been skimmed from the pans. A slight narrowing below the rim gave hold for a string

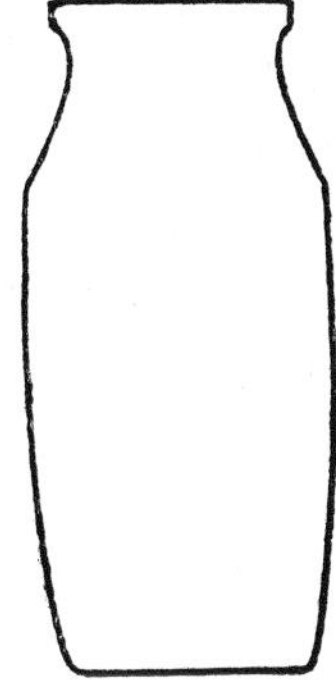

by which the vessel could be suspended in a spring or in the cold running stream which, oddly enough, is often found in the cellars of old houses in that part of the country. The example illustrated (Fig. *76d*) has lost all its glaze. I have, however, seen a perfect specimen of about the same diameter, but considerably taller, that was completely

glazed and was ornamented with a band of incised decoration.

Although potters' lists do not mention them, strainers of various shapes are not uncommon. A rare and early strainer from Sandown, New Hampshire is perhaps unique (Fig. 75). The usual type is deep and has legs. An example from the Hews pottery in Weston is about as wide as it is deep. A taller one was found not many miles from the Somerset potteries. From an elderly relative I have learned that utensils like these were commonly used in her girlhood as colanders. All are glazed inside, but unglazed without.

In a number of redware potteries pipkins were made. These were small cooking pots glazed on the inside only and furnished with a straight hollow handle projecting from the body. They were a survival of an early type of utensil.

Wasters in the Daniel Bayley dump prove that teapots were produced in the eighteenth century. A black teapot fragment showing the strainer in the nose also appeared in Joseph Bayley's Rowley site, where he worked from 1720 to 1735. It seems to have the same glaze and body as his other fragments and was perhaps an early effort at copying the new teapots from England. These eighteenth-century pots are round with slightly domed covers that rest over the rims and little thin handles like those of a porringer.

The globular black teapot has persisted in almost the identical form to the present day. In the 1820's, when Crafts at Whately was making them commercially, he turned the rounded bodies, but cast the handles, noses, and covers in molds. He then found it possible to make the whole pot by casting in oval or rectangular molds. This development is not characteristic of early American potting, which as a rule was governed by the limitations of the wheel.

Sugar bowls, salts, and cups with handles are other forms suggested by the more elegant ceramics from England, although in this country they were always fashioned in the simplest, most direct way. Tumblers or beakers were made in the eighteenth century and were advertised in Maine as late as 1820. These could hardly have been needed except in places where glass was neither cheap nor plentiful.

Table ware showing foreign influence was made in comparatively small quantity. As traditional ware we should consider only the pots, jugs, pans, and plates, bowls, pitchers, mugs, and porringers, and the various kitchen and dairy utensils. These formed the bulk of every potter's output. If today we find a piece now and then that expresses some whimsey on the part of its maker — a miniature, perhaps — we are indeed fortunate to preserve it in our collections.

APPENDICES

I. Documents

PAPERS IN THE MASSACHUSETTS ARCHIVES RELATING TO THE PARKERS OF CHARLESTOWN

PETITION OF ISAAC PARKER, SEPTEMBER 1742 (MASS. ARCHIVES, LIX, 332–333)

To His Excellency William Shirley Esqr Captain General and Governour in Cheif in and over His Majestys Province of the Massachusetts Bay To the Honble His Majestys Council and House of Representatives for the sd Province in General Court assembled at Boston Sept 1742

Humbly Shews Isaac Parker of Charlestown Potter

That he has for several years last past, with great charge and Expence, been Endeavouring to discover the Art of making Stone Ware and has now found out the same, and clay suitable to carry on the sd Business in this Government and your petr is desirous to follow the sd Trade and hath accordingly one James Deusha a Person (who understands the sd Business well, having Served his apprenticeship to it in Philadelphia) to assist him in carrying on the sd Business and will assist him therein — And your Petr would suggest to your Excellency and Honours That there are large quantities of said Ware imported into this Province every year from New York, Philadelphia, & Virginia, for which, as your petr is informed, returns are mostly made in Silver and Gold by the Gentn who receive them here, and therefore he humbly conceives it would be of advantage to this Government to have the sd Trade carried on; and your petr would immediately set up and carry on the sd Business was he able to advance the mony for setting up the sd Business; But in regard he is not

Your petr humbly prays your Excellency and Honours will be pleased to lend him one hundred and twenty five pounds of the last emission for that purpose without interest for a number of years he giving good Security for the paying the mony at the time which shall be assigned by your Excellency and Honours, and that if your Excellency & Honrs shall think it reasonable that your petr shall have the sole privilege of making said ware in this Province for any certain term of years that you in your wisdom shall think fit

And your petr (as in Duty bound) shall ever pray &c

Isaac Parker

ORDER GRANTING A LOAN OF £ 125 TO ISAAC PARKER, SEPTEMBER 10, 1742 (MASS. ARCHIVES, LIX, 333; ACTS AND RESOLVES OF THE PROV. OF MASS. BAY, XIII, 165)

Ordered that the Petitioner be allowed to receive out of the Appropriation for Premiums now in the Province Treasury, for his encouragement in making Stone Ware, the sum of One hundred and twenty five Pounds, he giving Land Security to the value of Two Hundred Pounds for the payment of 375 ounces of Silver into the said Treasury in lieu thereof with lawful Interest of the same, at or before the last Day of December 1746; provided nevertheless that if the money be improved for the purposes aforesaid no Interest shall be taken; Provided also that if he pay in the Bills within the time limited therefor, they shall be received in full discharge

of his mortgage instead of the Silver; Provided further that the repayment of the whole sum be made within one year from this time, in case the Petitioner does not proceed in the work aforesaid; the Security to be to the satisfaction of the Treasurer.

PETITION OF GRACE PARKER AND THOMAS SYMMES, DECEMBER 1, 1742

A Petition of Grace Parker and Thomas Symmes, both of Charlestown, Shewing that whereas this Court were pleased to give encouragement to Isaac Parker late husband to the said Grace to carry on the manufacture of Stone Ware, the said Isaac died soon after, the said Grace in partnership with the other Petitioner has undertaken that business, her husband having been at great expence in his lifetime in providing materials for it; And therefore Praying that the Petitioners may have leave to bring in a Bill for granting them the sole privilege of making the said Stone Ware for the term of Fifteen Years.

In the House of Represent^{ves},

Read and Ordered that the prayer of the Petition be granted and the Petitioners are allowed to bring in a Bill accordingly.

In Council; Read and Concur'd.

PETITION OF GRACE PARKER, OCTOBER 1747 (MASS. ARCHIVES, LIX, 347–349)

To His Excellency William Shirley Esqr Capt. General & Governour in Chief in and over His Majesty's Province of the Massachusetts Bay in New England, the Honble his Majesty's Council & House of Representatives in General Court assembled, this twentieth Day of October AD 1747. Humbly sheweth

Grace Parker of Charlestown relict Widow of Isaac Parker late of the same Town Potter Deceased;

That to encourage the said Isaac to undertake & carry on the trade or mistery of making Stoneware, your Excellency and Honours were pleased (in September A.D. 1742) to allow him to receive out of the publick Treasury, one hundred and twenty-five Pounds, upon his giving Security to repay the same by the last of December 1746, & in case the said money should be improv'd for the purpose aforesaid, then to be repayed without Interest: That the said Isaac receiv'd the aforesaid Sum out of the Treasury, & gave Security accordingly, but died soon after; whereupon your Petitioner (in Partnership with Mr Thomas Symmes), having obtained from the Great and General Court the Sole Privilege of making that kind of ware for a time limitted, engaged in that Business & carryed on the same 'till the Commencement of the War — which has oblig'd them for a time to desist therefrom — on account of the Risque and Expence of transporting their Clay from afar, the Freight whereof only would cost them more than the ware when manufactured could be sold for:

Your Petitioner would further humbly represent that when she & her Partner first engaged in this work, being aprehensive that the great Expense that would unavoidably attend the purchasing and transporting their materials form New York & Pennsylvania would eat out & consume most (if not all) the Profit likely to arise by the Sale of the ware, they made divers Tryals with Clay procured nearer at hand & with less expense, which tho' to appearance as promising as the other for the purpose of making this kind of ware —, yet by repeated and expensive tryals was found (by reason of some latent Quality in it) to be unfit to be used in this art; by means of which fruitless & unsuccessful experiments, and the loss of their kiln (wch was Spoilt thro' the Badness of the Clay) together with the prime Cost of preparing & providing the Buildings, Furniture & materials necessary for prosecuting that Business, they sank (in the first year) double the money which was lent them by the Province & this without Success or Fruit, beside the loss of their Time & Labour, and the maintenance of the Operator & his Family in the meanwhile: This notwithstanding your Petr & Partner being loth to give over their pursuit of that which in time might prove of publick Benefit (more especially if continued to carry on that Business with Clay brought from New York & Pennsylvania, & therewith made that kind of ware in good Perfection, tho' with small (or no) advantage to themselves, untill their further Proceeding therein was rendred impracticable by reason of the

War as beforementioned, nor are they yet altogether discouraged, altho' the Purchase of Clay & Wood is likely to be so expensive (even when the War is over), that any advantage they may ever receive by it is very uncertain & precarious:

However, as your Petitioner & her sd Partner have been great Loosers on the whole hitherto, and as their misfortunes & Disappointment abovementioned (altho' no other than what have usually attended such as have enterprized things new & uncommon, how beneficial soever thay may in time have prov'd to the Publick, or gainfull to the after-undertakers, Yet) have so straitened your Petitioner that as she could [not] without the utmost difficulty repay the money receiv'd on Loan from the Province within the time limitted therefor, So she cannot but humbly hope that your Excellency & Honours will be pleased to allow her to make Payment thereof (in any of the Bills of Publick Credit of this Province) by five several annual Payments, each one hundred pounds old tenor, or otherwise relieve your Petitioner as to your Excellency & Honours in your Wisdom and Goodness shall seem meet.

And, as in Duty bound, shall ever pray, &c

Grace Parker

ORDER GRANTING GRACE PARKER AN EXTENSION OF TIME TO MAKE PAYMENT (MASS. ARCHIVES, LIX, 349; ACTS AND RESOLVES, XIV, 331)

In the House of Reptes March 10 1747

Read and Ordered that the Prayer of the Petr be so far granted as that the time for the replacing the Sum mentioned of one hundred twenty five pounds in the Treasury; be further lengthened out to the last of December 1751 The said Grace giving Security to the Province Treasurer for the due performance thereof. And in the mean time she have the liberty of paying in the same by three several annual payments, or sooner, if she finds it for her advantage, and without Interest; provided the money be improved for the purpose, on which it was first granted.

In Council Decembr 28, 1749

The foregoing Petition being read, it was thereupon ordered — that the same be Revived; and that the Petitioner be allow'd to pay into the Publick Treasury the beforementioned one hundred & twenty five Pounds in time & manner as set forth in the abovewritten Vote of both Houses, she giving Security as therein directed.

PETITION OF JOHN AND DANIEL PARKER, DECEMBER 1755

To his Honour Spencer Phipps Esqr Lieut Governour & commander in chief of the province aforesaid, The Honble his majesty's council and House of Representatives in General court assembled December 1755

The Petition of John Parker & Daniel Parker in behalf of themselves, and the rest of the Heirs of Isaac Parker late of Charlestown potter, deceased Humbly Shew,

That whereas your Petrs said Father was contriving for several years before his Death to introduce the manufacture of Stone Ware into this province, to which he was encouraged by many gentlemen who knew his design, concluding it would be of great advantage if it could be effected, and in order to get some Insight in the affair, he took a journey to New York, but was disappointed, the Tradepe — [people?] there keeping the Business so private, this disappointment did not discourage him from pursuing so good a design, for he sent to Philadelphia for a man that knew that Art, and one came, but so poor that he and his Family were supported at your Petrs father's charge; He went with this man to the Vineyard for clay and upon his return Petitioned the General Court then being for a Sum of money to enable him to carry on his Scheme, which they lent him for a number of years, to the amount of £500 old tenor, but before anything was brought to perfection he dyed and your Petrs mother after his Decease, not knowing what method to take, advised with many persons thereon, and upon the whole was prevail'd upon to proceed, whereupon she erected a Kiln of the Vineyard Clay, made a large quantity of Ware & Burnt a Kiln, which was all spoiled; the workman imputed this to the Newness of the work which shrank from the Heat, & fell to pieces; The Kiln was repair'd and a second parcel of Ware made which likewise miscarried, this the workman said

was for want of proper wood to heat the Kiln: Your Petrs mother made a third attempt but met with no better success thus all her cost & labour was lost, but having got some New York clay she made a small Kiln & burnt good Ware, encouraged by this Success she sent her man to Philadelphia for Clay which cost between three hundred or four hundred pounds, which answered very well, but the charge of getting it from such a distant place was so great (a sloop load landed at home amounting to between eight or nine hundred pounds), there could be no profit from the Ware, and there being no clay to be found in these parts after searching therefor in many places Your Petrs Mother was obliged to give over, and the workman went home, and not only a considerable part of her own small Estate was sunk, but also the whole of the money borrowed of the Province, and the Period for the money's being paid into the Treasury being come, she sued to the General Court for a longer time which was Granted her, but by reason of disappointments she met with, such as a Son & Kinsman being disabled from working in the Common Potters Business by weakness they had contracted whilst they wer employed in making the Stone Ware, and the loss of another Son in the Cape Breton Expedition, who left a widow and child to be supported in a great measure by the Petrs Mother she was obliged to Sell part of her Estate to raise the £200 she has already paid into the Treasury, and tho' she was then in hopes she should have been able to pay in the remaining £300 old tenor yet by reason of her having had the Small Pox in her Family, and almost a total Stop put to her Business she found it impossible to do it, having lost at least Two Thousand pounds old tenor by the abovementioned Scheme laid at first for the good of this Province — That the Petrs said mother is now dead, and there are a number of Minors Orphans, who are Interested in the little remaining part of the said Deceaseds Estate, whose chief dependance for a support are upon their Shares therein.

The Petitioners therefore humbly pray Your Honour & Honours would be pleased to take the premisses into your wise and compassionate consideration, that payment of the remaining sum Borrowed as aforesaid, for the use aforesaid, may be remitted them, or otherwise relive the Petrs in the premisses as to Your Honour & Honours shall seem just, And they as in duty bound will ever pray &c

Daniel Parker for himselfe & others
the Petitioners

[The payments were remitted by the General Court March 9, 1756.]

II. Check List of New England Potters

Note: Birth and death dates are given in this list as the best indications of the period when a potter worked. Where they are not available, a working date, if known, is given. If place names have been changed, I have generally used the modern term. Such changes have occurred in all the great centers of the trade. It may be well to remember that Somerset was incorporated from Swansea in 1790; that Peabody was set off from Danvers in 1868 (I have designated the town as South Danvers, for few potters lived there after it became Peabody); and Chesham, N. H. is of such recent origin that the old name Pottersville is preferable.

Aborn, Samuel	South Danvers, Mass.
Adams, Philemon, 1785	Pomfret, Conn.
Alford, ——, *c.*1854	Burlington, Vt.
Allds (Auld), John, *c.*1840	Hollis Centre, Me.
Allman, John, 1769	Boston, Mass.
Andrews, C. S., 19th cent.	Danbury, Conn.
Annis, Abraham, b. March 4, 1708, Newbury; d. 1767, Haverhill	Newbury and Haverhill, Mass.
Applegate, Asher, 1850, 1860	Taunton, Mass.
Archer, Thomas, b. July 2, 1671, Salem; d. *c.* 1703, Salem	Salem, Mass.
Armstrong, Peleg, b. April 14, 1785, Norwich	Norwich, Conn.
Atkins, Robert, 1726	Boston, Mass.
Badger, Stephen, b. Feb. 18, 1696/97, Charlestown; d. June 1774, Natick, Mass.	Charlestown, Mass.
Bailey, Charles, b. Aug. 27, 1744, Amesbury, Mass.; d. May 15, 1835	Brookfield, Mass., and Hardwick, Vt.
Baker, Ebenezer, b. Nov. 19, 1743, Dorchester	Dorchester, Mass.
Ballard, A. K., *c.*1855–1870	Burlington, Vt.
Ballard, John, d. 1801, Danvers	Danvers, Mass.
Ballard, H. N., 1855, 1860	Burlington, Vt.
Ballard, O. L., *c.*1855–1870	Burlington, Vt.
Barker, John, 1860	Lisbon, Me.
Barker, John 2d., 1823	Brunswick, Me.
Barker, ——, 1835 (perhaps same)	Topsham, Me.
Bates, William, first half 19th cent.	Bennington, Vt.
Bayley, Daniel (s. Joseph), b. June 27, 1729, Rowley, Mass.; d. before March 23, 1792, Newburyport	Newburyport, Mass.

Bayley, Daniel (s. Daniel), b. July 15, 1755, Newburyport; d. Feb. 22, 1799, Newburyport	Newburyport, Mass.
Bayley, Joseph, b. Oct. 17, 1701, Rowley; d. before June 8, 1761, Newburyport	Rowley and Newbury (Newburyport), Mass.
Bayley, Nathaniel (s. Daniel), b. June 16, 1771, Newburyport; d. May 5, 1849, Newburyport	Newburyport, Mass.
Bayley, William (s. Daniel), b. May 9, 1766, Newburyport; d. May 27, 1799, Newburyport	Newburyport, Mass.
Bean, Jeremiah, b. March 9, 1803, Bristol; d. Jan. 28, 1834, Boston, Mass.	Bristol, N. H.
Belding, David, b. March 7, 1813, Whately; d. Sept. 10, 1854, Ashfield	Whately and Ashfield, Mass.
Benham, Edwin, 1860	Naugatuck, Conn.
Benner, John Henry, 1765–1795	Abington, Mass.
Bennetts, ——	Moultonborough, N. H.
Benton, George, 1815	Hartford, Conn.
Bickford, James, Jr., b. 1798, Buxton	Buxton, Me.
Bickford, Wentworth, b. 1817, d. 1890	Buxton, Me.
Bodge, Amos P., after 1866	Beverly, Mass.
Bodge, Benjamin, bapt. Jan. 18, 1746/47, Haverhill, Mass.	Amesbury, Mass.
Bodge, John (s. Benjamin), b. Oct. 30, 1772, Haverhill, Mass.	Wayne and Fayette, Me.
Bodge, Moulton (s. John), *c.*1832	Fayette, Me.
Bodge, Samuel, b. April 21, 1719, Charlestown; d. Jan. 15, 1755, Charlestown	Charlestown, Mass.
Bodge, Samuel (s. Samuel), b. March 8, 1743, Charlestown; d. April 10, 1806, Charlestown	Charlestown, Mass.
Bodwell, William, 1829	Concord, N. H.
Bostwick, ——, 1856	Fairfax, Vt.
Bosworth, Stanley B., 1873	Hartford, Conn.
Bowers, Ed.(?), 1862	Norwalk, Conn.
Boyce, Enoch (s. Enoch), b. Jan. 15, 1814, Berkley; d. May 12, 1876, Berkley	Berkley, Mass.
Boyce, Enoch (s. William), b. July 17, 1773, Berkley; d. April 7, 1859, Berkley	Berkley, Mass.
Boyce, John (s. John), b. 1817, Berkley; d. 1893, Berkley	Berkley, Mass.
Boyce, John (s. William), b. *c.*1760, Berkley; d. July 12, 1839, Berkley	Berkley, Mass.
Boyce, William, b. 1727/28, Salem; d. before 1799, Berkley	Salem and Berkley, Mass.
Boyden, George Washington, 1854	Ashfield, Mass.
Boynton, J., *c.*1856	Burlington, Vt.
Boynton, ——, 1860 (perhaps same)	St. Albans, Vt.

CHECK LIST OF POTTERS

Bradford, Noah, b. May 28, 1761, Kingston; d. Dec. 20, 1841, Kingston	Kingston and Barnstable, Mass.
Bradford, Stephen, b. Dec. 23, 1771, Kingston; d. April 22, 1837, Kingston	Kingston, Mass.
Bradford, Stephen, Jr. (s. Stephen), b. June 4, 1807, Kingston	Kingston, Mass.
Bradley, John W. (s. Moses), 1824	Woodstock, Vt.
Bradley, Moses, 1790, 1824	Chimney Point and Woodstock, Vt.
Bresnan, Jeremiah, 1862	Norwalk, Conn.
Bresnan, John, 1862	Norwalk, Conn.
Brewer, Stephen T., 1828	New London, Conn.
Brooks, George, b. June 21, 1815, Orrington	Orrington, Me.
Brooks, Hervey, b. Oct. 26, 1779, Goshen; d. Feb. 17, 1873, Goshen	Goshen, Conn.
Brooks, Joel, *c.*1851–1880	North Yarmouth, Me.
Brooks, John Edward (s. Joel), 1855	North Yarmouth, Me.
Brown, George	Somerset, Mass.
Bruce, Ambrose, *c.*1820	Winslow, Me.
Bruce, George, *c.*1806	North Yarmouth and Yarmouth Corner, Me.
Bruitan, ——, 1814–1818	East Cambridge, Mass.
Bugbee, David, *c.*1780	Brimfield, Mass.
Bugbee, Thomas, b. Sept. 19, 1761; d. 1843, South Woodstock	South Woodstock, Conn.
Bullard, Joseph O., 1870, 1895	Cambridgeport, Mass.
Burn (Bourne), James	Westford, Mass.
Burnham, ——, 1872	Lawrence, Mass.
Burpee, James G. (s. Jeremiah), b. June 3, 1830, Boscawen; d. Aug. 6, 1876, Boscawen	Boscawen, N. H.
Burpee, Jeremiah, b. 1781, Boscawen; d. Nov. 16, 1862, Boscawen	Boscawen, N. H.
Butterfield, William, b. 1808; d. Feb. 14, 1841, Salem	Salem, Mass.
Cadwell, Orson S., Jr., 1856	Hartford, Conn.
Cady, ——, 1856	Fairfax, Vt.
Calhoun, William, 1847	Portland, Me.
Carpenter, Frederick, b. Nov. 13, 1771, Lebanon, Conn.; d. June 20, 1827, Charlestown	Boston and Charlestown, Mass.
Carpenter, ——	East Middlebury, Vt.
Chace, Asa, b. Aug. 4, 1744, Freetown, Mass.; d. July 19, 1812, Somerset	Somerset, Mass.
Chace, Benjamin Cartwright (s. Benjamin)	Somerset, Mass., and Norwich, Conn.
Chace, Benjamin G. (s. Clark), b. Feb. 24, 1812, Somerset	Somerset, Mass.
Chace, Clark (s. Asa), b. Nov. 16, 1780, Somerset; d. June 8, 1836, Somerset	Somerset, Mass.
Chace, Clark (s. Clark), b. Feb. 8, 1814, Somerset	Somerset, Mass.
Chace, Enoch Boyce, b. Jan. 14, 1794, Somerset; d. Sept. 14, 1825, Berkley	Somerset and Berkley, Mass.

Chace, Joseph (s. Asa) b. Feb. 20, 1785, Somerset; d. after 1815, Somerset	Somerset, Mass.
Chace, Leonard (s. Clark)	Somerset, Mass.
Chace, Lloyd (s. Stephen IV)	Somerset, Mass.
Chace, Marcus P.(M.?) 1850, 1857	Taunton, Mass.
Chace, Stephen (s. Asa), b. May 23, 1769, Somerset; d. after 1815, Somerset	Somerset, Mass.
Chace, Stephen II (s. Stephen), d. after 1824, Somerset	Somerset, Mass.
Chace, Stephen III (s. Stephen II), d. before June 6, 1843, Somerset	Somerset, Mass.
Chamberlain, George B., 1885	Norwich, Conn.
Chamlet (Chamblet, Champlet), Curtis, b. before 1700	Boston, Mass.
Champnoine, Curtice, d. after April 26, 1738	Boston, Mass.
Chase, Elden, 1855	Corinth, Me.
Chase, James, b. April 9, 1779, Haverhill, Mass.; d. Dec. 31, 1849, Merrimacport	Merrimacport, Mass.
Chase, Phineas (s. James), b. April 5, 1820, Merrimacport; d. 1863, Merrimacport	Merrimacport, Mass.
Chase, Richard, 1856	Merrimacport, Mass.
Chichester, Henry, before 1825	South Norwalk, Conn.
Chichester, Henry (s. Henry), 1825, 1834	South Norwalk, Conn.
Chichester, —— (perhaps same), 1862.	South Norwalk, Conn.
Christie, James, after 1788	Norwich, Conn.
Clapp, Job, 1840	Medford, Mass.
Clark, Benjamin (s. Peter I), b. Feb. 26, 1770, Braintree, Mass.; d. Aug. 11, 1844, Lyndeboro	Concord and Lyndeboro, N. H.
Clark, Benjamin (s. William), b. Sept. 23, 1808, Lyndeboro; d. May 28, 1879, Lyndeboro	Lyndeboro, N. H.
Clark, Daniel (s. Daniel I), b. March 26, 1793, Concord; d. 1863, Concord	Concord, N. H.
Clark, Daniel (s. Peter I), b. March 14, 1768, Braintree, Mass.; d. Aug. 11, 1828, Concord	Concord, N. H.
Clark, Decius W., 1841, 1858; b. 1815, Burlington, Vt.; d. April 1, 1887, Croton, N. Y.	Bennington, Vt.
Clark, John Farmer (s. Daniel II), b. Sept. 19, 1823, Concord; d. 1885, Concord	Concord, N. H.
Clark, Peter I, b. Feb. 4, 1743, Braintree; d. Oct. 14, 1826, Lyndeboro	Braintree, Mass., and Lyndeboro, N. H.
Clark, Peter (s. Daniel I), b. Aug. 11, 1794, Concord; d. Oct. 18, 1855, Concord	Concord, N. H.
Clark, Peter (s. Peter I), b. Sept. 27, 1764, Braintree, Mass.; d. Feb. 3, 1851, Lyndeboro	Lyndeboro, N. H., and Brownington, Vt.
Clark, Peter (s. William), b. Oct. 12, 1797, Lyndeboro; d. Sept. 5, 1879, Lyndeboro	Lyndeboro, N. H.

Clark, William (s. Peter I), b. May 18, 1766, Braintree, Mass.; d. Nov. 11, 1855, Lyndeboro	Lyndeboro, N. H.
Clark, ——, 1861	Pottersville (Dublin), N. H.
Cleaveland, Benjamin, 1856	Somerset, Mass.
Cleaveland, Job, 1833–	East Dorset, Vt.
Cleaves, David, b. Sept. 1, 1794, Saco, Me.; d. Feb. 13, 1860, North Yarmouth	North Yarmouth, Me.
Cleaves, Robert C. (s. David), 1875–1885	North Yarmouth, Me.
Cleveland, William, 1805–1814	Norwich, Conn.
Clough, Levi, 1847	Portland, Me.
Coburn, Silas H. (M?), 1865	Monmouth, Me.
Collier, Charles, 1841–1850	Charlestown, Mass.
Collins, Samuel B.	Somerset, Mass.
Cook, Henry, b. Dec. 28, 1762, Danvers	South Danvers, Mass.
Cook, Samuel	South Danvers, Mass.
Cook, Samuel, Jr. (s. Samuel)	South Danvers, Mass.
Cook, Samuel (s. Samuel, Jr.)	South Danvers, Mass.
Coolidge, Henry, 1869–1881	West Sterling, Mass.
Corliss, Ebenezer, b. 1764.	Yarmouth, Me.
Corliss, Howard (s. John), b. *c.*1833, West Woolwich	West Woolwich, Me.
Corliss, John, b. Feb. 1799, Hopkinton, N. H.; d. Nov. 6, 1892, West Woolwich	West Woolwich, Me.
Cornell, Elijah, b. Oct. 17, 1771, Swansea; d. March 27, 1862, Albion, Mich.	Swansea (Somerset), Mass., and New York State
Cox, Eli, 1798	Topsham, Me.
Crafts, Caleb, b. July 29, 1800, Whately; d. Jan. Jan. 1, 1854, Whately	Portland, Me., Nashua, N. H., and Whately, Mass.
Crafts, Edward Alonzo (s. Caleb), b. Jan. 28, 1830, Whately; d. 1872, Chicago	Whately, Mass., and St. Johnsbury, Vt.
Crafts, James M. (s. Thomas), b. Feb. 26, 1817, Whately; d. after 1899, Whately	Whately, Mass., and Nashua, N. H.
Crafts, Justin, b. 1791, Whately; d. 1850, Sycamore, Ill.	Whately, Mass., and Berlin, Vt.
Crafts, Justus, b. 1791, Whately; d. Dec. 13, 1869, Whately	Whately, Mass., and Berlin, Vt.
Crafts, Martin (s. Thomas), b. April 4, 1807, Whately; d. March 21, 1885, Newark, N. J.	Whately, Mass., Portland, Me., and Nashua, N. H.
Crafts, Ralph Erskine (s. Rufus), b. Jan. 26, 1812, Whately; d. after 1869, Whately	Whately, Mass.
Crafts, Rufus, b. March 8, 1787, Whately; d. 1843, Whately	Whately, Mass.
Crafts, Thomas, b. Sept. 10, 1781, Whately; d. Oct. 7, 1861, Whately	Whately, Mass.
Crafts, Thomas Spencer (s. Thomas), b. April 21, 1825	Whately, Mass.
Cross, Peter, 1805–*c.*1815	Hartford, Conn.
Curtis, Seth, 1827	East Dorset, Vt.
Cutler, Philip, 1714–1733; d. 1733, Boston	Charlestown and Boston, Mass.

Dakin, Samuel, b. Nov. 1770, Mason, N. H.	Jaffrey, N. H.
Dalton, R. C., 1866	Taunton, Mass.
Dane, Edmund, before 1810	Hallowell, Me.
Davis, ——, before 1880	Baldwin and Standish, Me.
Davis, Jacob, b. Feb. 26, 1662, Gloucester; d. Feb. 1, 1717/18, Gloucester	Gloucester and Ipswich, Mass.
Day, Absalom, b. May 15, 1770, Chatham, N. J.; d. May 6, 1843, Norwalk	South Norwalk, Conn.
Day, George (s. Absalom), 1832–1847	Norwalk, Conn.
Day, Noah S. (s. Absalom), 1832–1847	Norwalk, Conn.
Deibel, George, 1866–	Peabody, Mass.
Dennis, Samuel, 1789	New Haven, Conn.
Dimond, Israel, early 19th cent.	Warner, N. H.
Dimond, Timothy K., 1827	Warner, N. H.
Dodge, Benjamin (s. Jabez), b. May 1, 1774, Exeter; d. June 1, 1838, Portland	Exeter, N. H., and Portland, Me.
Dodge, Benjamin (s. Benjamin), b. Dec. 18, 1802, Portland; d. 1876, Portland	Portland, Me.
Dodge, Jabez (Jabesh), b. Jan. 15, 1746/47, Beverly, Mass.; d. April 11, 1806, Exeter	Exeter, N. H.
Dodge, Jabez (s. Joseph), b. 1804, Portsmouth	Portsmouth, N. H.
Dodge, John (s. Jabez), b. Nov. 30, 1791, Exeter; d. Jan. 31, 1865, Exeter	Exeter, N. H.
Dodge, Joseph (s. Jabez), b. May 9, 1776, Exeter	Portsmouth, N. H.
Dodge, Samuel (s. Jabez), b. Feb. 26, 1783, Exeter	Exeter, N. H.
Donovan, John, b. 1851, Exeter, N. H.; d. 1932, Peabody	Peabody, Mass.
Dow, David, b. Sept. 19, 1802 (prob.); d. Nov. 13, 1874 (prob.)	North Weare, N. H.
Drake, Elisha, b. *c.*1750, d. after 1823	North Brookfield, Mass.
Drinker, Edward (s. Philip), b. 1612, Exeter, England; d. Dec. 1700, Boston	Charlestown and Boston, Mass.
Drinker, Philip, b. 1596, Exeter, England; d. June 23, 1647, Charlestown	Charlestown, Mass.
Duce, Thomas, 1847	Portland, Me.
Duché, James (s. Anthony) b. *c.*1715, Philadelphia; d. Dec. 1749, Philadelphia	Charlestown, Mass.
Dunbar, Peter, b. July 18, 1822, Taunton	Taunton, Mass.
Duntze, J.	New Haven, Conn.
Dutcher, Revellard, Jr., 1814	Goshen, Conn.
Edes, Daniel, b. April 26, 1708, Charlestown; d. Nov. 1764, Charlestown	Charlestown, Mass.
Edes, Daniel (s. Daniel), bapt. Sept. 1, 1734	Charlestown, Lexington, and Watertown, Mass., and Exeter, N. H.
Edmands, Barnabas, b. March 1, 1778, Charlestown; d. Jan. 13, 1872, Charlestown	Charlestown, Mass.
Edmands, Benjamin, b. July 18, 1782	Charlestown, Mass.

Edmands, Edward Townshend (s. Barnabas), b. Feb. 1, 1813, Charlestown	Charlestown, Mass.
Edmands, Thomas Russell Burroughs (s. Barnabas), b. Jan. 24, 1820, Charlestown	Charlestown, Mass.
Edmands, William Burroughs (s. Barnabas), b. March 21, 1811	Charlestown, Mass.
Edson, ——, before 1800	Woodstock, Vt.
Emery, Joshua, 1791	Alfred, Me.
Farrar, Caleb, b. June 1780, New Ipswich, N. H.; d. June 1849, Middlebury	Middlebury, Vt.
Farrar, Charles Adelbert, b. April 24, 1844, Troy	Troy, N. H.
Farrar, C. W., 1856	Fairfax, Vt.
Farrar, Daniel W., b. March 25, 1755, Lincoln, Mass.; d. Nov. 13, 1837, Troy	Troy, N. H.
Farrar, George W., 1840	Fairfax, Vt.
Farrar, Ebenezer Lawrence (s. Isaac Brown), 1854	Burlington and Fairfax, Vt.
Farrar, Isaac Brown, b. March 27, 1771, New Ipswich, N. H.; d. 1838, Fairfax	Fairfax, Vt.
Farrar, J. H., 1840	Fairfax, Vt.
Farrar, ——, 1860	St. Albans, Vt.
Farrar, ——, 1852	North Fairfax, Vt.
Felton, Daniel, bapt. March 11, 1743, Danvers; d. Dec. 1828	Dedham (Needham), Mass.
Felton, Jedediah, b. 1768, Danvers	South Danvers, Mass., and Mason, N. H.
Felton, ——, (prob. Jedediah), b. Danvers, Mass.	Pottersville, N. H.
Fenno, Enoch, before 1798 — (prob. 1847)	Milton (Mattapan), Mass.
Fenton, Christopher Webber (s. Jonathan), b. Jan. 30, 1806, Dorset; d. June 7, 1865, Joliet, Ill.	East Dorset and Bennington, Vt.
Fenton, Jacob, before 1800	New Haven, Conn.
Fenton, Jonathan, b. July 18, 1766, Windham, Conn.; d. 1848, Dorset	Boston, Mass., Dorset and East Dorset, Vt.
Fenton, Leander W. (s. Richard W.)	St. Johnsbury, Vt.
Fenton, Richard Lucas (s. Jonathan), b. Jan. 22, 1797, Walpole, N. H.; d. July 25, 1834, East Dorset	East Dorset and Bennington, Vt.
Fenton, Richard Webber, b. Sept. 4, 1771	St. Johnsbury, Vt.
Fisher, J. C., 1805	Hartford, Conn.
Fitch, Josiah, d. June 9, 1865	Pottersville and Lowellville, N. H.
Flagg, David, 1796	Topsham, Me.
Flanders, George (s. Peter), b. May 20, 1808, Plymouth; d. Oct. 24, 1869, Plymouth	West Plymouth, N. H.
Flanders, Peter, b. June 19, 1784, Concord; d. Aug. 23, 1856, Plymouth	Concord and West Plymouth, N. H.
Flanders, Richard, b. April 23, 1788, Concord; d. March 16, 1833, Concord	Concord, N. H.

Name	Place
Floyd, William R., 1856	East Haven, Conn.
Foster, Benjamin (s. Nathaniel), 1855, 1878	North Yarmouth, Me.
Foster, Nathaniel, d. 1854.	North Yarmouth, Me.
Foster, William Henry (s. Nathaniel), 1856	North Yarmouth, Me.
Frayd, E.	East Hartford, Conn.
French, Jonathan B., 1813–1821	Jaffrey and Troy, N.H.
Frothingham, Benjamin, b. Dec. 26, 1679, Charlestown; d. Mar. 14, 1752, Charlestown	Charlestown, Mass.
Fuller, Thomas, *c.*1820	Winthrop, Me.
Furber, Jethro, b. Oct. 19, 1800, Newington, N. H.; d. Sept. 24, 1876, North Conway	Concord and North Conway, N. H.
Furber, Nathaniel, b. *c.*1775, Concord, N. H.	Pottersville, N. H.
Gardner, Israel, bapt. July 22, 1744, Danvers; d. Apr. 1771, Danvers	South Danvers, Mass.
Gardner, Joseph; b. Oct. 23, 1672, Gloucester; d. after 1749, Gloucester	Gloucester, Mass.
Gibbs, Ebenezer, *c.*1780–1794; b. (prob.) Chatham, N. J.	Northampton, Mass.
Gibson, ——, 1860	Stamford, Conn.
Gill, John Hazelton, b. Sept. 16, 1809, Boscawen, N. H.; d. July 30, 1888, Plymouth	West Plymouth, N. H.
Gill, William, b. Jan. 4, 1800, Boscawen; d. Sept. 12, 1853, Penacook, N. H.	Boscawen and Plymouth, N. H.
Gleason, Eben, c.1823–1828	Bennington, Vt.
Goddard, Charles	North Orange, Mass.
Goddard, John	North Orange, Mass.
Goddard, Solomon, Sr., b. Apr. 30, 1768, Troy	Troy, N. H.
Goddard, Solomon, b. May 2, 1796; d. Jan. 8, 1854, Troy	Troy, N. H.
Goldthwaite, Daniel (s. John), b. Jan. 27, 1802, Danvers	South Danvers, Mass.
Goldthwaite, John, b. Nov. 27, 1771, Danvers; d. Sept. 1851, Danvers	South Danvers, Mass.
Goldthwaite, Samuel (s. Thomas); bapt. Feb. 21, 1762, Danvers	South Danvers, Mass.
Goldthwaite, Thomas, b. 1738, Voluntown (Petersham), Mass.; d. before 1780, Springfield	South Danvers and Springfield, Mass.
Goldthwaite, William, b. *c.*1743; d. March 29, 1808, Danvers	South Danvers, Mass.
Goodale, Daniel, Jr., 1818–1830	Hartford, Conn.
Goodale, Enoch, bapt. Nov. 9, 1725, Salem, d. after 1807, Salem	Salem, Mass.
Goodell, John, d. 1850, Windham	Windham, Me.
Goodhue, Nathaniel, before 1823	Gilford, N. H.
Goodwin, Harvey, b. 1802, New Hartford; d. after 1870, Elmwood	Elmwood (West Hartford), Conn.

Goodwin, Harvey Burdett (s. Harvey), after 1870	Elmwood, Conn.
Goodwin, Horace H., b. New Hartford; d. 1850, Elmwood	Hartford, Conn.
Goodwin, Seth, b. Aug. 12, 1772, New Hartford; d. Oct. 3, 1828, Elmwood	Elmwood, Conn.
Goodwin, Thomas O'Hara (s. Seth), b. Nov. 22, 1796, Elmwood; d. July 6, 1880, Elmwood	Elmwood, Conn.
Goodwin, Wilbur Elmore (s. Harvey), after 1870	Elmwood, Conn.
Graves, Quartus, b. Jan. 23, 1797, Whately	Whately, Mass.
Gray, Joseph, 1854	Somerset, Mass.
Gray,——, *c.*1770	Great Barrington, Mass.
Greatbach, Daniel, 1852–1858	Bennington, Vt.
Greenwood, Daniel, b. Feb. 14, 1794, Dublin; d. May 19, 1833, Dublin	Pottersville (Dublin), N. H.
Greenwood, Edwin (s. William), b. after 1813, Marlborough, N. H.	Pottersville and Keene, N. H., and West Sterling, Mass.
Greenwood, William, b. Sept. 1, 1791; d. Dec. 8, 1841, Marlborough	Pottersville (Marlborough), N. H.
Gregory, John Betts, d. July 22, 1842, Norwalk	South Norwalk, Conn.
Guinette, George, after 1870	Cambridge, Mass.
Hall, David, b. July 7, 1711, Dorchester, d. after 1760, Dorchester	Dorchester, Mass.
Hall, Jonathan, b. Oct. 12, 1706, Charlestown, Mass.; d. Dec. 25, 1753, Medford	Medford, Mass.
Hall, Jonathan (s. Jonathan), b. Oct. 16, 1733, Medford; d. (prob.) 1776, Northampton	Medford and Roxbury, Mass.
Hall, Joseph, Jr., b. July 3, 1701, Dorchester; d. March 27, 1762, Dorchester	Dorchester, Mass.
Hall, Pelatiah, b. Dec. 28, 1704, Dorchester; d. after 1777	Dorchester, Mass.
Hancock, Frederick (s. John), b. 1817, Hanley, Staffordshire, England; d. after 1893	Bennington, Vt., and Worcester, Mass.
Hancock, ——, 1852 (perhaps same)	St. Johnsbury, Vt.
Hanford, Isaac, 1796, 1800	Hartford, Conn.
Harrington, Thompson, 1825	Hartford, Conn.
Harris, John, bapt. June 1, 1718, Charlestown; d. Nov. 1, 1780, Charlestown	Charlestown, Mass.
Harrison, James, 1840	New Haven, Conn.
Hart, Peter, 18th cent.	Petersham, Mass.
Hart, ——, 1861	Pottersville (Dublin), N. H.
Hastings, Wellington, b. Nov. 6, 1812	Ashfield, Mass.
Hathaway, Charles E., 1880, 1895	Somerset, Mass.
Hatstat, George, 18th cent.	Petersham, Mass.
Hayward, Ezekiel, bapt. July 4, 1703, Beverly; d. before Dec. 10, 1744, Salem	Beverly, Mass.

Hayward, Jonathan, bapt. May 6, 1673, Beverly	Beverly, Mass.
Hazeltine, Joseph, d. after 1880, Concord	Concord, N. H.
Herrick, Robert Annabel, b. Jan. 23, 1814, Wenham	Beverly, Mass.
Hews, Abraham, b. 1741, Watertown (?); d. May 17, 1818, Weston	Weston, Mass.
Hews, Abraham (s. Abraham I), b. May 30, 1766, Weston; d. July 15, 1854, Weston	Weston, Mass.
Hews, Abraham, Jr. (s. Abraham II), b. Feb. 13, 1797, Weston; d. April 7, 1868, Boston	Weston, Mass.
Hews, Albert Horatio (s. Horatio), b. Jan. 13, 1844, Weston	Cambridge, Mass.
Hews, Horatio (s. Abraham II), b. Jan. 9, 1810, Weston; d. Jan. 5, 1891, Cambridge	Weston and Cambridge, Mass.
Hill, John, 1853	North Bridgton, Me.
Hill, Robert, 1823, 1831	Portland, Me.
Holmes, Daniel, 1805	Alfred, Me.
Holton, George, 1815	Goshen, Conn.
Hosmer, Joseph, d. 1803, Norwich	Norwich, Conn.
Hoyt, Asa, b. 1772	South Norwalk, Conn.
Huntington, ——, 1786	Norwich, Conn.
Hussey, William, *c.*1820	Winslow, Me.
Hutchinson, Ebenezer, before 1815	Lyndeboro, N. H.
Hutchinson, William, 1815	St. Johnsbury, Vt.
Ingalls, James, b. *c.* 1710, Charlestown; d. before 1752, Charlestown	Charlestown, Mass.
Irons, Thomas, 1853, 1861	Norwich, Conn.
Jackson, William, 1812–1816	Saugus, Mass.
Jacobs, George, b. April 12, 1812, Danvers	South Danvers, Mass.
Johnson, ——, 1872	Lawrence, Mass.
Jones, Elisha, 1855	Ellsworth, Me.
Jones, L. Frank, 1884	Portland, Me.
Judd, Norman L., b. 1782, Goshen, Conn.	Bennington and Burlington, Vt.
Kendall, Loammi, 1836, 1870	Chelsea, Mass.
Kendrick, ——, 1856	Merrimacport, Mass.
Kendricks, Truxton, 1860	Hollis Centre, Me.
Kenney, Thomas	Somerset, Mass.
Kent, Clement (s. Stephen), d. before Jan. 25, 1774, Newburyport	Newburyport, Mass.
Kent, Stephen, d. March 1747/48, Newbury	Newbury (Newburyport), Mass.
Kettell, John, b. before 1662, Charlestown; d. March 17, 1690/91, Charlestown	Charlestown, Mass.
Kettell, Richard, b. Dec. 8, 1693, Charlestown; d. after 1757, Charlestown	Charlestown, Mass.
Kettell, Samuel, b. Nov. 19, 1642, Charlestown; d. Dec. 20, 1694, Charlestown	Charlestown, Mass.

Potter	Place
Kettell, William, b. Feb. 3, 1680/81, Charlestown; d. Feb. 19, 1718/19, Charlestown	Charlestown, Mass.
Kettle (Kettell), James, b. March 20, 1664/65, Gloucester, Mass.; d. Nov. 24, 1712, Charlestown	Danvers and Charlestown, Mass.
Kettle (Kettell), James, Jr. (s. James), b. Dec. 27, 1691, Danvers; d. April 3, 1737, Charlestown	Danvers and Charlestown, Mass.
Kettle (Kettell), Jonathan, b. 1701, Beverly, Mass.; d. before July 4, 1763, Danvers	South Danvers, Mass.
Kettle (Kettell), Jonathan (s. Jonathan), b. Oct. 2, 1749, Charlestown, Mass.; d. May 6, 1848, Newburyport, Mass.	Goshen, Conn.
Kidder, Isaiah, b. Feb. 3, 1770, New Ipswich; d. April 28, 1811, New Ipswich	New Ipswich, N. H.
Kidder, Josiah, b. July 27, 1771, New Ipswich; d. Oct. 27, 1848, Hampden, Me.	New Ipswich, N. H.
Kitson, Richard F., 1815–after 1860	North Bridgton, Me.
Knowles, Benjamin B., 1825	New London, Conn.
Lambert, Porter, 1825, 1832	Alfred, Me.
Lamson, Asa Brown, b. 1818, Exeter	Exeter, N. H.
Lamson, Frank Hudson (s. Asa B.), b. 1859	Exeter, N. H.
Lamson, Rufus (s. Asa B.), b. 1844, Exeter	Exeter N. H., Peabody, Mass., and Portland, Me.
Larkin, Joseph, b. Sept. 11, 1726, Charlestown; d. after 1773, Charlestown	Charlestown, Mass.
Lathrop, Charles, b. Jan. 11, 1770, Norwich	Norwich, Conn.
Lawrence, Charles A. (né Solares), d. 1906, Beverly	Peabody and Beverly, Mass.
Leavitt, Samuel, 1872	Exeter, N. H.
Lee, Ed., 1862	Norwalk, Conn.
Leffingwell, Christopher, b. June 13, 1734, Norwich; d. Nov. 27, 1810, Norwich	Norwich, Conn.
Leigh, Benjamin, 1769	Boston, Mass.
Letts, Alfred W., 1857	Taunton, Mass.
Levins, Thomas, 1850	Taunton, Mass.
Lewis, ——, 1856	Fairfax, Vt.
Libby, Nathaniel, b. *c.*1710, Portsmouth; d. before Jan. 1752, Exeter	Portsmouth and Exeter, N. H.
Lord, Nathaniel, b. June 4, 1701, Charlestown; d. July 12, 1729, Charlestown	Charlestown, Mass.
Low, John F. (s. John G.)	Chelsea, Mass.
Low, John G., 1877	Chelsea, Mass.
Lowell, George Allen (s. Elijah C.), b. 1856, Orange	Orange, N. H.
Lowell, Elijah C. (s. Isaac), b. 1823, Orange; d. 1873, Orange	Orange, N. H.

Lowell, Isaac, b. Oct. 28, 1797, Loudon, N. H.; d. Nov. 26, 1865, Orange	Orange, N. H.
Lundy, Sandford P., 1842	Charlestown, Mass.
Lyman, Alanson Potter, b. Dec. 4, 1806, Woodford, Vt.; d. 1883, Bennington	Bennington, Vt., and Gardiner, Me.
MacKenzie, ——,	South Woodstock, Vt.
Mann, ——, 1852	Merrimacport, Mass.
Manning, Daniel, b. Feb. 5, 1715, Cambridge, Mass.; d. before 1739/40, Charlestown	Charlestown, Mass.
Manning, Daniel (s. William), b. *c.*1744, Charlestown; d. *c.*1777, Charlestown	Charlestown, Mass.
Manning, William, b. Oct. 24, 1712, Cambridge, Mass.; d. Nov. 8, 1776, Medford, Mass.	Charlestown, Mass.
Marble, Abijah	North Orange, Mass.
Marble, Jonathan, b. Feb. 28, 1730/31, Salem, Mass.; d. May 27, 1815, Danvers	South Danvers, Mass.
Marshall, Samuel, d. Dec. 1749, Portsmouth	Portsmouth, N. H.
Matthias, Joseph, 1862	Norwalk, Conn.
Mayo, Barney, 1860, 1874	Waldoboro, Me.
McPherson, John, 1853, 1865	Norwich and New Haven, Conn.
McVey, John, *c.*1870	Cambridge, Mass.
Mead, Abraham, b. Dec. 14, 1742, Greenwich; d. Dec. 27, 1827, Greenwich	Greenwich, Conn.
Mear, Frederick, b. 1822, Burslem, England	East Boston, Mass.
Merrill, Jason, b. 1807	Fairfax, Vt., and Norwich, Conn.
Merrill, Marvin, 1825, 1834	Norwalk, Conn.
Metcalf, Chauncey, 1834	Marlborough, N. H.
Mitchell, James, 1850	Middlebury, Vt.
Moore, James, d. Sept. 1, 1829	Brimfield, Mass.
Morrison, Ebenezer, b. May 15, 1741, Newburyport; d. April 4, 1803, Newburyport	Newburyport, Mass.
Moulton, Henry, b. March 1, 1698, Hampton; d. before Aug. 1762, Sandown	Hampton and Sandown, N. H.
Nash, Jonathan, 1775, 1784	Worcester, Mass.
Neil, John, 1730	Scituate, Mass.
Neil, John G., b. Sept. 13, 1775, Newmarket, N. H.; d. July 13, 1859, Skowhegan	Skowhegan, Me.
Newell, Eliphalet, b. Jan. 8, 1704/05, Charlestown; d. Dec. 12, 1752, Charlestown	Charlestown, Mass.
Newell, James (s. Eliphalet), b. Feb. 29, 1731/32, Charlestown; d. after 1778	Charlestown, Mass.
Newhall, Nathaniel, before 1788	Charlestown, Mass.
Nichols, ——, 1854	Burlington, Vt.
Norcross, Josiah, b. Feb. 16, 1759, Newton, Mass.	Farmington, Me.
Norcross, Matthias (s. Josiah), 1840	Farmington, Me.
Norcross, Matthias, Jr. (s. Matthias)	Farmington, Me.

Norcross, Philip (s. Samuel), b. March 16, 1754, Newton, Mass.	Hallowell, Me.
Norcross, Samuel, b. Oct. 18, 1729, Newton, Mass.; d. Dec. 2, 1800, Hallowell	Hallowell, Me.
Norton, Edward (s. John, Jr.), b. Aug. 23, 1815, Bennington; d. Aug. 3, 1885, Bennington	Bennington, Vt.
Norton, Franklin B. (s. John, Jr.), b. Bennington, Vt.	Worcester, Mass.
Norton, John, b. Nov. 29, 1758, Goshen; d. Aug. 24, 1828, Bennington	Goshen, Conn., and Bennington, Vt.
Norton, John (s. John), before 1823	Bennington, Vt.
Norton, Julius (s. Luman), b. Sept. 23, 1809, Bennington; d. Oct. 5, 1861, Bennington	Bennington, Vt.
Norton, Luman (s. John), b. Feb. 9, 1785, Williamstown, Mass.; d. 1853, Bennington	Bennington, Vt.
Norton, Luman Preston (s. Julius), 1859, 1881	Bennington, Vt.
Norton, Norman (s. John), b. 1806	Bennington, Vt.
Omensetter, Michael, d. before 1825, New London	New London, Conn.
Orcutt, Eleazer (s. Stephen), b. Dec. 7, 1796, Whately	Whately and Ashfield, Mass., and St. Johnsbury, Vt.
Orcutt, Stephen, 1796	Whately, Mass.
Orcutt, Walter (s. Stephen), b. May 7, 1799, Whately; d. March 1, 1854, Conway, Mass.	Whately and Ashfield, Mass.
Osborn, Aaron (s. Joseph), b. Nov. 15, 1752 (prob.), Danvers; d. before Jan. 11, 1804, Danvers	South Danvers, Mass.
Osborn, Abel (s. Joseph), b. Nov. 9, 1746, Danvers; d. Feb. 12, 1784, Danvers	South Danvers, Mass.
Osborn, Amos (s. Amos), b. Nov. 22, 1807, Danvers	South Danvers, Mass.
Osborn, Amos (s. Joseph, Jr.), b. April 2, 1773, Danvers; d. June 21, 1836, Danvers	South Danvers, Mass.
Osborn, Benjamin	South Danvers, Mass.
Osborn, Caleb, b. May 1, 1760 (prob.), Danvers; d. May 4, 1827, Danvers	South Danvers, Mass.
Osborn, Daniel, Jr. (s. Joseph), b. Sept. 10, 1768, Danvers; d. Feb. 11, 1826, Danvers	South Danvers, Mass.
Osborn, David, b. Feb. 24, 1775, Danvers; d. Aug. 1820, Danvers	South Danvers, Mass.
Osborn, Elijah, b. 1801, Loudon	Loudon and Gonic, N. H.
Osborn, George (s. Jonathan), b. 1792, Danvers	South Danvers, Mass.
Osborn, Green (s. Elijah)	Loudon, N. H.
Osborn, Henry (s. John III), b. July 4, 1789, Danvers	South Danvers, Mass.
Osborn, Henry M. (s. Henry), b. May 12, 1829	South Danvers, Mass.
Osborn, Israel (s. Joseph), bapt. May 27, 1739, Danvers; d. before Nov. 1790, Danvers	South Danvers, Mass.

Osborn, Jacob, 1856	Dover, N. H.
Osborn, Jacob, 1785	Loudon, N. H.
Osborn, James, b. July 20, 1738, Danvers; d. Aug. 31, 1810, Danvers	South Danvers, Mass.
Osborn, James (s. Elijah), *c.*1850–1885	Gonic, N. H.
Osborn, James, Jr. (s. James), b. June 22, 1766, Danvers; d. Oct. 9, 1833, Danvers	South Danvers, Mass.
Osborn, John (s. Jacob), d. 1820, Boscawen	Loudon and Boscawen, N. H.
Osborn, John, b. Nov. 22, 1765, Danvers	South Danvers, Mass., and Exeter, N. H.
Osborn, John, Jr., b. May 11, 1768, Danvers; d. before Dec. 7, 1819, Danvers	South Danvers, Mass.
Osborn, John (s. Elijah), *c.*1850–1875	Gonic, N. H.
Osborn, John III (s. Joseph, Jr.), b. April 2 (or Nov. 22), 1765, Danvers; d. Nov. 3, 1845, Danvers	South Danvers, Mass.
Osborn, John Procter (s. Aaron), b. Feb. 26, 1775, Danvers	South Danvers, Mass.
Osborn, Jonathan (s. Joseph, Jr.), b. Aug. 30, 1763, Danvers; d. July 29, 1833, Danvers	South Danvers, Mass.
Osborn, Joseph, b. Oct. 26, 1702, Danvers; d. before Dec. 4, 1780, Danvers	South Danvers, Mass.
Osborn, Joseph, Jr. (s. Joseph), b. Aug. 26, 1726 (prob.), Danvers; d. July 9, 1804, Danvers	South Danvers, Mass.
Osborn, Joseph III (s. Joseph, Jr.), b. Jan. 5, 1757, Danvers	South Danvers, Mass., and Exeter, N. H.
Osborn, Kendall (s. John III), b. July 22, 1796, Danvers	South Danvers, Mass.
Osborn, Miles (s. John III), b. March 6, 1795, Danvers	South Danvers, Mass.
Osborn, Paul, 1740, 1760; b. *c.*1704, Danvers	South Danvers and Berkley, Mass.
Osborn, Philip (s. Amos), b. July 19, 1800, Danvers; d. Sept. 29, 1837, Danvers	South Danvers, Mass.
Osborn, Richard, 1845, 1868	Charlestown, Mass.
Osborn, Richard (s. Jonathan), b. 1788, Danvers	South Danvers, Mass.
Osborn, Richard Sprague (s. James, Jr.), 1849, 1865	South Danvers, Mass.
Osborn, Samuel	South Danvers, Mass.
Osborn, Stephen (s. James), b. June 2, 1774, Danvers; d. before Oct. 11, 1855, Danvers	South Danvers, Mass.
Osborn, Sylvester (s. Joseph), b. Nov. 10, 1758, Danvers; d. Oct. 2, 1845, Danvers	South Danvers, Mass.
Osborn, William Sumner (s. Richard), b. Jan. 4, 1819/20, Danvers	South Danvers, Mass.
Osborne, Oliver	Exeter, N. H.
Osborne, William A. (s. James), 1875, 1885	Gonic, N. H.
Paige, Moses B., 1872	Peabody, Mass.
Parker, Benjamin, 1849	West Barnstable, Mass.
Parker, Daniel, 1831	West Barnstable, Mass.

Parker, Grace (w. Isaac), b. June 17, 1697, Charlestown; d. Dec. 1754, Charlestown	Charlestown, Mass.
Parker, Isaac, bapt. Oct. 4, 1692, Charlestown; d. Nov. 7, 1742, Charlestown	Charlestown, Mass.
Parker, John (s. Isaac), b. July 18, 1725, Charlestown; d. Sept. 8, 1765, Charlestown	Charlestown, Mass.
Parker, Nahum, after 1850	Middlebury, Vt.
Pearson, Joseph, 1859	Cambridgeport, Mass.
Pecker, William, b. Oct. 10, 1758, Haverhill; d. Nov. 22, 1820, Merrimacport	Merrimacport, Mass.
Penny, Jonathan, b. Feb. 15, 1742, Charlestown; d. July 19, 1789, Charlestown	Charlestown, Mass.
Perkins, Wesley, 1845, 1853	Hartford, Conn.
Perry, Sanford S., *c.*1820	Whately, Mass.
Philbrick, Samuel, b. 1759	Exeter, N. H.
Philbrick, Joseph (s. Samuel), b. Jan. 8, 1797, Exeter, N. H.; d. Oct. 13, 1874	Skowhegan (Bloomfield), Me.
Philbrick, Samuel (s. Samuel), b. 1783, Exeter, N. H.; d. before 1855, Skowhegan	Skowhegan, Me.
Philbrick, William, b. May 24, 1803, Exeter	Exeter, N. H.
Pierce, John, b. Dec. 22, 1703, Charlestown	Charlestown and Boston, Mass.
Pierce, John, b. *c.*1730, Wethersfield, Conn.; d. Oct. 1, 1783, Litchfield	Litchfield, Conn.
Pierce, Jonathan, b. July 2, 1737 (prob.), Wethersfield, Conn.	Whately (North Hatfield), Mass.
Pitkin, Richard, b. Oct. 24, 1759, E. Hartford; d. May 7, 1822, E. Hartford	East Hartford (Manchester), Conn.
Plaisted, Francis A., b. Jan. 2, 1829, Farmingdale; d. after 1874	Gardiner (Farmingdale), Me.
Plympton, Nathaniel, 1859, 1865	East Boston, Mass.
Porter, Benjamin (s. Benjamin), b. *c.*1720, Danvers; d. June 9, 1794, Danvers	Danvers, Mass.
Porter, Benjamin III, bapt. Oct. 22, 1738, Danvers; d. before Sept. 17, 1805, Wiscasset	Danvers, Mass., and Wiscasset, Me.
Porter, Ezra (s. Benjamin III), b. 1769, Danvers; d. 1847, Wiscasset	Newcastle and Wiscasset, Me.
Porter, Silas (s. Ezra)	Wiscasset, Me.
Potter, John, bapt. Feb. 24, 1681, Charlestown; d. Dec. 16, 1696, Charlestown	Charlestown, Mass.
Potts, Christopher, 1796	Norwich, Conn.
Powers, Battery, bapt. Oct. 31, 1736, Charlestown; d. Dec. 1807, Boston	Charlestown, Mass.
Prentice, ——, 1760	Cambridge, Mass.
Prentiss, Samuel, b. May 26, 1753, Cambridge, Mass.; d. Jan. 10, 1815, Gorham	Gorham, Me.
Pride, John, d. 1647, Salem	Salem, Mass.
Procter, Joseph, b. Aug. 31, 1743, Danvers; d. Jan. 29, 1805, Gloucester	Gloucester, Mass.
Proctor, Nathan (s. Nathan S.)	South Danvers, Mass.

Proctor, Nathan Stephen (s. Stephen), b. Dec. 3, 1818, Danvers	South Danvers, Mass.
Proctor, Stephen, 1818	South Danvers, Mass.
Purinton, Clark (s. Daniel), b. *c.*1730, Danvers; d. after 1786, Somerset	Somerset, Mass.
Purinton, Clark, Jr. (s. Clark), d. 1817, Somerset	Somerset, Mass.
Purinton, Daniel, d. May 23, 1764, Danvers	South Danvers, Mass.
Purington, David P. (s. Samuel), 1856	Somerset, Mass.
Purington, Dexter H., 1856	Somerset, Mass.
Purinton, George (s. Clark, Jr.), 1835	Somerset, Mass.
Purington, George S., 1856	Somerset, Mass.
Purington, Samuel S., 1856	Somerset, Mass.
Quintard, James Jr., 1825, 1834	Norwalk, Conn.
Rawlings (Rollins), James, bapt. Nov. 12, 1734, Marblehead, Mass.	Danvers, Mass.
Reed, Joseph Whittemore, b. Sept. 26, 1809, Danvers	Peabody, Mass.
Rich, Edwin A., b. Nov. 15, 1855, Northfield, Vt.	Peabody and Beverly, Mass.
Richardson, ——, 1769	Boston, Mass.
Richardson, Ruel, d. 1814, Mason	Mason, N. H.
Risley, Albert, 1845, 1880	Hartford, Conn.
Risley, George (s. Sidney L.), d. Dec. 24, 1881, Norwich	Norwich, Conn.
Risley, Sidney L., c.1836–1875; d. 1875–Norwich	Norwich, Conn.
Risley, William D., 1875	Norwich, Conn.
Robertson, Alexander W. (s. James), 1866, 1884	Chelsea, Mass.
Robertson, Hugh C. (s. James), b. July 4, 1844, Durham, England; d. May 26, 1908, Chelsea	Chelsea, Mass.
Robertson, James, d. May 22, 1880	East Boston and Chelsea, Mass.
Root, Orestes, 1846, 1861	Norwich, Conn.
Rose (Ross), Seth, 1755–1765	Concord, Mass.
Runey, James, 1856	Somerville, Mass.
Runey, John, bapt. Oct. 1, 1758, Charlestown; d. 1829, Somerville, Mass.	Charlestown, Mass.
Runey, John, Jr. (s. John), b. *c.*1785, Charlestown, Mass.	Somerville, Mass.
Runey, John (s. John, Jr.), 1842, 1865	Somerville, Mass.
Russell, Eben, b. Nov. 27, 1797, Dublin	Pottersville, N. H.
Russell, Osgood N. (s. Eben), b. Aug. 12, 1827, Marlborough, N. H.	Pottersville, N. H.
Sables, John, 1840	Medford, Mass.
Sables, Thomas, b. Sept. 17, 1805	Medford, Mass.
Safford, George Llewellyn (s. John M.), b. Nov. 30, 1847, Monmouth; d. after 1895, Monmouth	Monmouth, Me.
Safford, John, 1855	Monmouth, Me.

Safford, John M. (s. John), b. May 26, 1811, Exeter, N. H.; d. Aug. 19, 1880, Monmouth	Monmouth, Me.
Sanders, John, 1817	Conn.
Sargeant, ——, 1854	Marlborough, N. H.
Sargent, Smith, 1825	Merrimacport, Mass.
Scott, Alexander F., 1880, 1895	Cambridgeport, Mass.
Seaver, John (s. William), b. March 4, 1771, Dorchester, Mass.	Taunton, Mass.
Seaver, William, b. May 8, 1743/44, Dorchester; d. July 28, 1815, Taunton	Dorchester and Taunton, Mass.
Seaver, William, Jr. (s. William), b. March 26, 1779, Taunton	Taunton, Mass.
Seymour, Frederick, b. March 12, 1819	West Hartford, Conn.
Seymour, Nathaniel, b. Aug. 23, 1763, W. Hartford; d. Feb. 26, 1849, W. Hartford	West Hartford, Conn.
Seymour, Orson Hart, b. Sept. 1, 1807, New Britain, Conn.; d. Dec. 1, 1883, Hartford	Hartford, Conn.
Seymour, Phelps, b. Aug. 2, 1818, New Britain, Conn.; d. Dec. 6, 1871, Hartford	Hartford, Conn.
Shaw, Joseph, b. Sept. 27, 1760, Danvers; d. Feb. 4, 1840, Danvers	South Danvers, Mass.
Shove, Asa (s. Edward), b. March 26, 1741, Berkley; d. Oct. 26, 1826, Berkley	Berkley, Mass.
Shove, Azariah, b. Oct. 13, 1749, Berkley; d. July 16, 1814, Berkley	Berkley, Mass.
Shove, Edward, b. Dec. 21, 1716, Berkley; d. July 22, 1778, Berkley	Berkley, Mass.
Shove, George, b. Nov. 1738, Berkley; d. before 1793, Berkley	Berkley, Mass.
Shove, Nathaniel, b. May 9, 1723, Berkley; d. before May 24, 1774, Swansea	Swansea, Mass.
Shove, Samuel (s. Edward), b. Jan. 29, 1740, Berkley; d. 1763, Berkley	Berkley, Mass.
Shove, Theophilus, Jr., b. Nov. 21, 1741, Swansea; d. before Dec. 1803, Somerset	Somerset, Mass.
Sibley, Bliss, before 1823	Bennington, Vt.
Sibley, David, before 1823	Bennington, Vt.
Silsby, C. M., 1878	Troy, N. H.
Simmons, Peleg, b. Aug. 2, 1818, Kingston	Kingston, Mass.
Smiley, Francis, before 1818	Charlestown, Mass.
Smith, Aaron, b. 1791, Pottersville; d. 1840, Pottersville	Pottersville, N. H.
Smith, Aaron (s. Aaron), b. 1822, Pottersville	Pottersville, N. H.
Smith, Asa (s. Asa E.), 1850, 1887	Norwalk, Conn.
Smith, Asa E., b. Oct. 1, 1798; d. Jan. 3, 1880, Norwalk	Norwalk, Conn.
Smith, H. E., *c.*1890	Burlington, Vt.
Smith, Hezekiah, 1782	Gorham, Me.
Smith, Howard Hobart (s. Asa E.), 1850, 1887	Norwalk, Conn.

Smith, James, 1866	West Sterling, Mass.
Smith, Theodore E. (s. Asa E.), 1848–1887	Norwalk, Conn.
Smith, Wilfred (s. Theodore), 1887	Norwalk, Conn.
Snow, Marcus L., 1866, 1881	West Sterling, Mass.
Souter, John, before 1805	Hartford, Conn.
Southwick, Daniel, *c.*1800	South Danvers, Mass.
Southwick, George, d. April 19, 1775, Lexington	South Danvers, Mass.
Southwick, James Chapman (s. William), b. 1793, Danvers; d. 1841, Danvers	South Danvers, Mass.
Southwick, Jedediah Kilbourn (s. William), b. 1783, Danvers; d. April 11, 1843, Pottersville	South Danvers, Mass., and Pottersville, N. H.
Southwick, Jedediah Kilbourn (s. Jedediah Kilbourn), after 1843	Pottersville, N. H.
Southwick, John	South Danvers, Mass.
Southwick, John (poss. same), b. Sept. 18, 1788, Danvers; d. after 1841, Danvers	South Danvers, Mass., and Lyndeboro, N. H.
Southwick, Joseph, b. 1723, Danvers; d. Aug. 1786, Danvers	South Danvers, Mass.
Southwick, Nathaniel	South Danvers, Mass.
Southwick, Orlando (s. William, Jr.), b. Jan. 21, 1819, Danvers	South Danvers, Mass.
Southwick, Samuel	South Danvers, Mass.
Southwick, William, b. 1715, Danvers; d. Aug. 21, 1785, Danvers	South Danvers, Mass.
Southwick, William (s. William), b. May 17, 1754, Danvers; d. Sept. 11, 1828, Danvers	South Danvers, Mass.
Southwick, William, Jr. (s. William II), b. July 30, 1787, Danvers; d. Jan. 15, 1826, Danvers	South Danvers, Mass.
Standish, Alexander, b. Oct. 28, 1809, Halifax, Mass.	Taunton, Mass.
Stanley, Robert, b. Nov. 27, 1720, Charlestown	Charlestown, Mass.
Stanwood, James H., 1860	Waldoboro, Me.
Stark, Charles, 1837	Gilford, N. H.
Staats (States), Adam, b. Holland; d. before 1769, Greenwich	Greenwich, Conn.
States, Adam (s. Adam I), b. June 8, 1756, Greenwich, Conn.; d. March 1, 1826, Stonington	Stonington, Conn.
States, Adam, Jr. (s. Adam II), b. May 7, 1779, Stonington; d. Jan. 12, 1864, buried Stonington	Stonington, Conn.
States, Joseph H. (s. Peter), b. 1767, Westerly	Westerly and Providence, R. I.
States, Peter, b. 1732, Holland; d. Sept. 3, 1802, buried Stonington, Conn.	Norwich, Conn., and Westerly, R. I.
States, William (s. Adam, Jr.), b. 1803, Stonington, Conn.; d. Sept. 8, 1832, buried Stonington	New London, Conn.
States, William (s. Peter), b. 1778, Westerly, R. I.; d. Oct. 17, 1823, Stonington	Providence, R. I., and Stonington, Conn.

Stearns, A. S., 1852	Fairfax, Vt.
Stedman, Absalom, 1822, 1831	Hartford and New Haven, Conn.
Steinbrecher, Jacob, 1875	Peabody, Mass.
Stevens, Benjamin, *c.*1870	Peabody, Mass.
Stevens, Samuel, 1815, 1837	North Brookfield, Mass.
Stewart, Levi, 1815	Hartford, Conn.
Stone, Edmund, b. Nov. 4, 1770, Danvers	South Danvers, Mass.
Stone, Robert, b. Sept. 17, 1755, Danvers; d. Aug. 10, 1811, Danvers	South Danvers, Mass.
Stone, Samuel, *c.*1800	South Danvers, Mass.
Stone, Samuel, Jr. (s. Samuel), *c.*1800	South Danvers, Mass.
Suderberg, Otto N., 1890	Norwich, Conn.
Sullivan, ——, before 1890	Andover (Ballardvale), Mass.
Swan, Joshua, Jr., b. Feb. 20, 1798, Stonington	Stonington, Conn.
Swasey, Eben, 1877, 1890	Portland, Me.
Swasey, Fred D., 1890	Portland, Me.
Swift, Charles, *c.*1875	Gardiner (Farmingdale), Me.
Swift, Heman, Jr., b. Aug. 20, 1796, Whately; d. Nov. 30, 1848, Whately	Whately, Masss.
Swinnerton, Ebenezer, b. Oct. 30, 1730, Danvers; d. Nov. 12, 1795, Lynnfield	Danvers (Lynnfield), Mass.
Symmes, Thomas, b. Jan. 11, 1702, Boxford, Mass.; d. July 11, 1754, Charlestown	Charlestown, Mass.
Symonds, David, 1751, 1766	Boston, Mass.
Symonds, John	Salem, Mass.
Symonds, Nathaniel, b. Sept. 1, 1723, Salem; d. Dec. 11, 1792, Salem	Salem, Mass.
Symonds, Nathaniel (s. Nathaniel), b. Aug. 18, 1754, Salem; d. Nov. 1803, Salem	Salem, Mass.
Symonds, Nathaniel (s. William), b. May 3, 1780, Salem; d. Feb. 6, 1848, Salem	Salem, Mass.
Symonds, William (s. Nathaniel), bapt. Jan. 14, 1749/50, Salem; d. July 26, 1830, Salem	Salem, Mass.
Synan, Patrick, 1893	Somerset, Mass.
Synan, William, 1893	Somerset, Mass.
Taft, J. S., 1871–1916	Keene, N. H.
Taber, ——, before 1860	Wells, Me.
Taber, Job, d. 1803	New London, Conn.
Taber, John, 1865	East Alton and South Wolfeboro, N. H.
Tarbell, Jonathan, Jr., bapt. July 19, 1772, Danvers	South Danvers, Mass.
Tarbell, William, bapt. March 31, 1754, Danvers; d. June 9, 1815, Beverly	Beverly, Mass.
Tarbell, William (s. William, b. Nov. 22, 1793, Beverly; d. before Jan. 5, 1819, Beverly	Beverly, Mass.
Taylor, William, *c.*1833	Norwalk, Conn.
Tewksbury, Henry, b. June 8, 1819, Danvers	South Danvers, Mass.
Thayer, S., 1825	Bennington, Vt.

Potter	Place
Thomas, John, b. Sept. 2, 1754, Gloucester, Mass.; d. July 24, 1843, Yarmouth	North Yarmouth, Me.
Thomas, John, 1777, 1787	Newburyport, Mass.
Thomas, Samuel (s. John), 1843	North Yarmouth, Me.
Thomas, William (s. John), 1843	North Yarmouth, Me.
Thompson, ——	Gardiner, Me.
Thorp, Joseph, bapt. Sept. 15, 1745, Dedham, Mass.	Charlestown and Worcester, Mass.
Thorp, Reuben (prob. s. Joseph), b. Sept. 19, 1773, Worcester, Mass.	Turner Centre, Me.
Thurston, David, *c.*1795	Pottersville, N. H.
Tolman, Henry, b. 1783, d. March 6, 1851, West Sterling	Troy, N. H., and West Sterling, Mass.
Tolman, Henry (s. Henry), 1849, 1861	West Sterling, Mass.
Tracy, Andrew, 1786–1800; b. March 17, 1749/50	Norwich, Conn.
Trask, Amos (s. Joseph), b. Oct. 23, 1803, Danvers	South Danvers, Mass.
Trask, John, *c.*1800	South Danvers, Mass.
Trask, Joseph, b. March 28, 1768, Danvers; d. May 26, 1813, Danvers	South Danvers, Mass.
Tuttle, ——, 1862	Norwalk, Conn.
Twiss, Peter, d. July 14, 1832, Lynnfield, Mass.	South Danvers, Mass.
Upton, Isaac, b. Oct. 6, 1736, Hampton Falls, N. H.	East Greenwich, R. I.
Upton, Samuel, b. April 3, 1748, Berkley, Mass.	East Greenwich, R. I.
Van Loon, Staats, 1854	Ashfield, Mass.
Venables, ——, *c.*1833	Norwalk, Conn.
Vincent (Vinson), William, b. *c.*1610, England; d. Sept. 17, 1690, Gloucester	Salem and Gloucester, Mass.
Wade, Samuel, b. April 2, 1715, Charlestown; d. Jan. 8, 1788, Malden, Mass.	Charlestown, Mass.
Wadhams, Isaac, *c.*1815	Goshen, Conn.
Wadhams, Jesse, b. Aug. 22, 1773, Goshen; d. 1810, Goshen	Goshen, Conn.
Wadsworth, Abel, 1798	Bennington, Vt.
Wait, Lemuel, b. May 1, 1776, Whately; d. Oct. 21, 1843	Whately, Mass.
Wait, Luke, b. May 9, 1785, Whately; d. March 10, 1853	Whately, Mass.
Wait, Obediah, b. Jan. 8, 1783, Whately; d. Dec. 10, 1853	Whately, Mass.
Walley, William J., b. Aug. 3, 1852, England; d. April 27, 1918, West Sterling	Worcester and West Sterling, Mass.
Walton, Timothy, b. May 27, 1798, Danvers (Lynnfield), Mass.	South Danvers, Mass.

Ward, Samuel, after 1813	Brownington, Vt.
Wardwell, ——, 1860	Stamford, Conn.
Weaver, Constant, 1821	Troy, N. H.
Webb, Jotham, d. April 19, 1775, Lexington, Mass.	South Danvers, Mass.
Webber, Albert, 1832	Alfred, Me.
Webber, Paul, *c.*1835	Alfred, Me.
Webber, Chris	Cavendish, Vt.
Webber, David, d. Aug. 15, 1861, Hebron	Oxford (Hebron), Me.
Webber, Henry Rust (s. David), b. Nov. 26, 1808, Oxford (Hebron); d. March 4, 1870, Paris	Hebron and Paris, Me.
Webber, John, b. July 1, 1703, Charlestown; d. June 7, 1734, Charlestown	Charlestown, Mass.
Webber, Moses A. (s. David), b. July 25, 1827, Oxford (Hebron); d. Feb. 21, 1900, Hebron	Oxford (Hebron), Me.
Webster, Charles T. (s. McCloud), d. 1857, Hartford	Hartford, Conn.
Webster, Daniel Dolbear, b. 1796; d. March 16, 1832, Plymouth	Plymouth, N. H.
Webster, Henry, 1840	Hartford, Conn.
Webster, McCloud (Mack. C.), d. 1850, Hartford	Hartford, Conn.
Webster, William (s. Daniel Dolbear), after 1847	Plymouth, N. H.
Welch, William, 1785	Northampton, Mass.
Wells, Ashbel, 1785, 1794	Hartford, Conn.
Wells, David Dwight, b. Oct. 1, 1822, Whately; d. April 17, 1870	Whately, Mass.
Wells, Isaac N., b. Dec. 21, 1830, Whately; d. July 17, 1860, Whately	Whately, Mass.
Wentworth, Erastus, b. Nov. 8, 1788, Norwich; d. June 14, 1873	Norwich, Conn.
West, John, d. before May 7, 1781, Bradford	Haverhill (Bradford), Mass.
Weston, ——, before 1890	Andover(Ballardvale), Mass.
Wheeler, L. D., 1850	Norwalk, Conn.
Whittemore, Daniel (s. Joseph), b. Sept. 2, 1767, Danvers; d. July 14, 1825, Danvers	South Danvers, Mass.
Whittemore, Joseph, b. Dec. 19, 1744, Danvers; d. June 21, 1821, Danvers	South Danvers, Mass.
Whittemore, Nathaniel	South Danvers, Mass.
Whittemore, Samuel, d. Oct. 26, 1826, Concord	Lyndeboro and Concord, N. H.
Wickwire, F., before 1823	Bennington, Vt.
Wight, Abner S. (s. John), b. July 28, 1822, Marlborough; d. after 1890	Marlborough, N. H., and West Sterling, Mass.
Wight, Franklin (s. John), b. March 11, 1814, Marlborough; d. after 1890	Marlborough, N. H., Ashfield, Mass., and St. Johnsbury, Vt.

Wight, John, b. Jan. 24, 1791; d. Sept. 19, 1874, Charlestown, Mass.	Jaffrey and Marlborough, N. H.
Wilkins, John, 1670, 1689	Boston, Mass., and Bristol, R. I.
Willard, L., before 1890	Andover (Ballardvale), Mass.
Willard, W. F., 1879, 1893	Gay Head, Martha's Vineyard, Mass.
Williams, Thomas, 1771	Norwich, Conn.
Wilson, Isaac III (Jr.), b. Jan. 8, 1758, Danvers; d. Jan. 13, 1809, Danvers	South Danvers, Mass.
Wilson, Job (s. Robert, Jr.), bapt. Jan. 10, 1762, Danvers; d. Feb. 24, 1791, Danvers	South Danvers, Mass.
Wilson, John (s. Robert I), b. Nov. 22, 1791, Danvers	South Danvers, Mass.
Wilson, Joseph, b. *c.*1735, Danvers	Danvers and Dedham, Mass., and Providence, R. I.
Wilson, Robert I, d. before July 10, 1782, Danvers	South Danvers, Mass.
Wilson, Robert, Jr. (s. Robert I), b. *c.*1745, Danvers; d. Jan. 4, 1797, Danvers	South Danvers, Mass.
Wilson, Robert III (s. Robert, Jr.), b. Sept. 5, 1776, Danvers; d. Nov. 9, 1803, Danvers	South Danvers, Mass.
Winship, Joseph F., 1846, 1875	Norwich, Conn.
Winslow, John T., 1847, 1857	Portland, Me.
Wood, Enoch, 1853, 1865	Bennington, Vt., and Norwalk, Conn.
Wood, L. M.	Canaan (prob. Grafton), N. H.
Wood, William, *c.*1875	Gardiner (Farmingdale), Me.
Woodbridge, Dudley, b. April 20, 1782, Manchester; d. Oct. 13, 1844, Manchester	Manchester, Conn.
Woodman, John (s. Samuel), after 1820	Poultney, Vt.
Woodman, Samuel, bapt. Dec. 2, 1753, Salem, Mass.	Poultney, Vt.
Woodworth, F. W., 1870	Burlington, Vt.
Worthen, C. F., 1868	Peabody, Mass.
Wright, Caleb, b. 1810, New Haven	New Haven, Vt.
Wright, Franklin T., 1849, 1867	Taunton, Mass.
Wyer, Edward, b. March 1, 1733/34, Charlestown	Charlestown, Mass.
Wyman, George E., 1866	Taunton, Mass.
Wyman, ——, before 1845	Concord, Mass.
York, Charles E.	Woolwich, Me.
York, ——, 1856 (perhaps same)	Ellsworth, Me.
Young, George A., 1890	Portland, Me.
Young, John, before 1788	Norwich, Conn.

III. Bibliography

GENERAL

Adams, C. B., *Annual Reports on the Geology of Vermont* (First Report), Goodrich, Burlington, Vt., 1845.

Belknap, Henry W., *Artists and Craftsmen of Essex County, Massachusetts*, The Essex Institute, Salem, Mass., 1927.

—— *Trades and Tradesmen of Essex County*, The Essex Institute, Salem, Mass., 1929.

Coolidge, A. J., and J. B. Mansfield, *History and Description of New England* (Gazetteer), 2 vols., Austin J. Coolidge, Boston, 1859.

Cornell, Alonzo B., *Biography of Ezra Cornell, Founder of Cornell University*, A. S. Barnes Co., New York, 1884.

Diary of William Bentley, The Essex Institute, Salem, Mass., 1914.

Documents Relative to the Manufactures in the United States, 2 vols., printed by order of the House of Representatives, Washington, 1833.

Dow, George Francis, ed., *Records and Files of the Quarterly Courts of Essex County, 1636–1683*, 8 vols., The Essex Institute, Salem, Mass., 1911–1921.

Dwight, Timothy, "Statistical Account of the Towns and Parishes in the State of Connecticut," in *Connecticut Academy of Arts and Sciences*, I, 1–83, New Haven, 1811.

Haskel, Daniel, and J. Calvin Smith, *Descriptive and Statistical Gazetteer of the United States of America*, Sherwin & Smith, New York, 1843.

Municipal Records, 39 vols., Boston, 1876–1909.

Pease, John Chauncey, and John M. Niles, *A Gazetteer of the States of Connecticut and Rhode Island*, William S. Marsh, Hartford, 1819.

Prime, Alfred Coxe, *Arts and Crafts in Philadelphia, Maryland, and North Carolina*, New York Historical Society, New York, 1938.

Probate Records of Essex County, Massachusetts, 1635–1681, 3 vols., The Essex Institute, Salem, Mass., 1916.

The Procter Gathering, in commemoration of the one hundredth anniversary of the wedding day of their progenitors, Joseph Procter and Elizabeth Epes, Procter Bros., printers, Gloucester, 1868.

Ries, Heinrich, "Clays of New York," in *Bulletin of New York State Museum*, vol. 7, no. 35 (June 1900).

—— *History of the Clay-Working Industry in the United States*, Wiley, New York, 1909.

Sherman, Frederic Fairchild, *Early Connecticut Artists and Craftsmen*, privately printed, New York, 1925.

Smith, Albert W., *Ezra Cornell, A Character Study*, William A. Church Co., Ithaca, N. Y., 1934.

Statistics of the Condition and Products of Certain Branches of Industry in Massachusetts, state publication, Boston, 1846.

Statistical Information Relating to Certain Branches of Industry in Massachusetts, state publication, Boston, 1856, 1866.

Thompson, Zadock, *Geography and Geology of Vermont*, the author, Burlington, 1848.

Weston, William Bradford, *Hon. Seth Sprague of Duxbury, Plymouth County, Massachusetts*, Boston, 1915.

Weygandt, Cornelius, *The White Hills; mountain New Hampshire, Winnepesaukee to Washington*, H. Holt, New York, 1934.

AMERICAN POTTERY

Barber, Edwin Atlee, *Catalogue of American Potteries and Porcelains*, Pennsylvania Museum, Philadelphia, 1893.

—— *Lead Glazed Pottery*, Pennsylvania Museum, Philadelphia, 1907.

—— *Marks of American Potters*, Patterson & White Co., Philadelphia, 1904.

—— *Salt Glazed Stoneware*, Pennsylvania Museum, Philadelphia, 1906.

—— *The Ceramic Collector's Glossary*, Printed for the Walpole Society, New York, 1914.

—— *The Pottery and Porcelain of the United States*, G. P. Putnam's Sons, New York, 1893; second edition, 1901.

—— *The Tulip Ware of the Pennsylvania German Potters*, Pennsylvania Museum, Philadelphia, 1903.

Clement, Arthur W., *Notes on American Ceramics, 1607–1943*, Brooklyn Museum, Brooklyn, N. Y., 1944.

Earle, Alice Morse, *China Collecting in America*, Scribner's, New York, 1892.

Hews, A. B., publ., *Catalogue of "Antique" Pottery.*

Hough, Walter, *An Early West Virginia Pottery*, *Annual Report of the Smithsonian Institution*, Washington, 1899.

James, Arthur E., *The Potters and Potteries of Chester County, Pennsylvania*, Chester County Historical Society, 1945.

Jervis, W. P., *The Encyclopedia of Ceramics*, Blanchard, New York, 1902.

Low, John G., and John F. Low, *Illustrated Catalogue of Art Tiles*, Chelsea, 1884.

—— *Plastic Sketches (Tiles)*, C. A. Wellington & Co., Boston, 1882.

—— *Plastic Sketches (Tiles)*, Lee & Shepard, Boston, 1887.

Pitkin, Albert Hastings, *Early American Folk Pottery*, Hartford, 1918.

Prime, William C., *Pottery and Porcelain of All Times and Nations*, Harper, New York, 1878.

Ramsay, John, *American Potters and Pottery*, Hale, Cushman & Flint, Boston, 1939.

Rice, A. H., and John Baer Stroudt, *The Shenandoah Pottery*, Shenandoah Publishing Co., Strasburg, Va., 1929.

Spargo, John, *Early American Pottery and China*, Century, New York, 1926.

—— *The Potters and Potteries of Bennington*, Houghton Mifflin, Boston, 1926.

Taylor, William Watts, *The Rookwood Pottery*, reprinted from the *Forensic Quarterly*, September 1910, University Press, Sewanee, Tennessee.

Williamson, Scott Graham, *The American Craftsman*, Crown Publishers, New York, 1940.

Wallis, George, *Report on Porcelain and Ceramic Manufacture* in *General Report of the British Commissioners on the N. Y. Industrial Exhibition*, T. Harrison, London, 1854.

Young, Jennie J., *The Ceramic Art*, Harper, New York, 1878.

ENGLISH POTTERY

Aiken, A., *Lecture on Pottery before Royal Institution, London*, in *Franklin Institute Journal*, vol. XI, no. 3 (March 1833).

A Guide to the English Pottery and Porcelain, British Museum, London, 1923.

Hayden, Arthur, *Chats on English Earthenware*, T. Fisher Unwin, London, 1909; third edition, 1919.

Hodgkin, J. E. and E., *Examples of Early English Earthenware, Named, Dated, and Inscribed*, Cassell, London, 1891.

Honey, W. B., *English Pottery and Porcelain*, A. & C. Black, London, 1933.

Rackham, Bernard, and Herbert Read, *English Pottery*, Ernest Benn, London, 1924.

Rhead, G. Wooliscroft and Frederick A., *Staffordshire Pots and Potters*, Hutchinson & Co., London, 1906.

Solon, L. M., *The Art of the Old English Potter*, D. Appleton, New York, 1886.

HISTORICAL AND GENEALOGICAL

Connecticut

Atwater, Edward E., ed., *History of the City of New Haven, to the Present Time*, W. W. Munsell, New York, 1887.

—— *History of the Colony of New Haven*, The Journal Publishing Co., Meriden, Conn., 1902.

Brooks, Hervey, *A History of South End, Goshen, Connecticut* (written in 1858), John Norton Brooks, Goshen, 1935.

Caulkins, Frances Mainwaring, *History of Norwich, Connecticut*, published by the author, 1874.

Dwight, Timothy, *A Statistical Account of New-Haven, 1811*, New Haven, 1874.

Hibbard, Rev. A. G., *History of the Town of Goshen, Connecticut*, Press of the Case, Lockwood & Brainard Co., Hartford, Conn., 1897.

Perkins, Mary E., *Old Houses of the Antient Town of Norwich*, Norwich, 1895.

Staats, Harold, *The Staats Family*, privately printed, 1921.

States, James Noyes, comp., *The States Family*, New Haven, Conn., 1913.

Wheeler, Grace D., *Homes of Our Ancestors in Stonington, Conn.*, Newcomb & Gauss, Salem, Mass., 1903.

—— *Old Homes in Stonington*, The Mystic Standard, Mystic, Conn., 1930.

Wheeler, Richard Anson, *History of the Town of Stonington, Connecticut, from 1649 to 1900*, Press of the Day Publishing Co., New London, Conn., 1900.

Maine

Butler, Francis Gould, *A History of Farmington, Franklin County, Maine*, Knowlton, McLeary & Co., 1885.

Chase, Mrs. Fannie (Scott), *Wiscasset in Pownalborough*, The Southworth-Anthoensen Press, Portland, 1941.

Clayton, W. W., *History of Cumberland Co., Maine*, Everts & Peck, Philadelphia, 1880.

Cochrane, Harry H., *History of Monmouth and Wales*, 2 vols., Banner Co., East Winthrop, 1894.

Dole, Samuel Thomas, *Windham in the Past*, Merrill & Webber Co., Auburn, Me., 1916.

French, W. R., *History of Turner, Maine*, Hoyt, Fogg & Donham, Portland, 1887.

History of Penobscot County, Maine, Williams, Chase & Co., Cleveland, 1882.

History of the town of Wayne, Kennebec County, Maine, from its settlement to 1898, Maine Farmer Publishing Co., Augusta, 1898.

King, Marquis Fayette, *Annals of Oxford, Maine*, privately published, Portland, 1903.

Kingsbury, Henry D., and Simeon L. Deyo, eds., *Illustrated History of Kennebec County, Maine*, Blake, New York, 1892.

McLellan, Hugh, *History of Gorham, Me.*, Smith & Sale, Portland, 1903.

North, James W., *The History of Augusta*, Clapp & North, Augusta, 1870.

Parsons, Dr. Usher, "Historical Sketch of Alfred," in *Atlas of York Co., Maine*, Sanford, Everts & Company, Philadelphia, 1872.

Rowe, William Hutchinson, *Ancient North Yarmouth & Yarmouth, Maine, 1636–1936*, Yarmouth, Me., 1937.

Wheeler, George Augustus, and Henry Warren Wheeler, *History of Brunswick, Topsham, and Harpswell, Maine*, A. Mudge & Son, Boston, 1878.

Massachusetts

Babson, John J., *A History of the Town of Gloucester*, Procter Bros., Gloucester, 1866.

Bond, Henry, *Genealogies of Early Settlers of Watertown, Waltham, and Weston*, New England Genealogic Historical Society, 1860.

Brooks, Charles, *History of the Town of Medford*, Rand, Avery & Co., Boston, 1886.

Caller, James M., and Mrs. M. A. Ober, *Genealogy of the Descendants of Lawrence and Cassandra Southwick of Salem, Mass.*, J. H. Coate & Co., printers, Salem, Mass., 1881.

Coffin, Joshua, *A Sketch of the History of Newbury, Newburyport, and West Newbury*, Samuel G. Drake, Boston, 1845.

Crafts, James M., *History of the Town of Whately, Mass.*, printed for the town, D. L. Crandall, Orange, Mass., 1899.

Deane, Samuel, *History of Scituate, Massachusetts*, James Loring, Boston, 1831.

Emery, Samuel Hopkins, *History of Taunton, Massachusetts*, Mason & Co., Syracuse, 1893.

Field, D. D., *A History of the County of Berkshire, Massachusetts*, printed by S. W. Bush, Pittsfield, 1829.

Hart, William A., *History of the Town of Somerset: Shawomet Purchase 1677, Incorporated 1790*, Somerset, 1940.

Hobart, Benjamin, *History of the Town of Abington*, T. H. Carter & Son, Boston, 1866.

Hodgman, Rev. Edwin R., *History of the Town of Westford*, Westford Town History Association, Lowell, Mass., 1883.

Hunnewell, James F., *Century of Town Life in Charlestown*, Little, Brown, Boston, 1888.

Hurd, D. Hamilton, ed., *History of Bristol County, Massachusetts*, J. W. Lewis, Philadelphia, 1883.

—— *History of Essex County, Massachusetts*, 2 vols., J. W. Lewis, Philadelphia, 1888.

—— *History of Middlesex County, Massachusetts*, 3 vols., J. W. Lewis, Philadelphia, 1890.

—— *History of Worcester County, Massachusetts*,, 2 vols., J. W. Lewis, Philadelphia, 1889.

Hyde, Rev. Charles M., *Historical Celebration of the Town of Brimfield*, published by the town, Clark W. Bryan Co., Springfield, 1879.

Judd, Sylvester, *History of Hadley*, H. R. Huntting, Springfield, 1905.

Leland, Gus, "Descendants of Anthony Duché," in *Our Ancestors*, October 1882.

Our Country and Its People (Bristol County, Massachusetts), Fall River News and Taunton Gazette, ed., 1899.

Pattee, William S., *A History of Old Braintree and Quincy*, Green & Prescott, Quincy, 1878.

Pemberton, Thomas, "A Topographical and Historical Description of Boston, 1794," in *Massachusetts Historical Society Collections*, III (1810), 241–304.

Perley, Sidney, *The History of Salem, Massachusetts*, 3 vols., privately printed, 1924.

Pringle, James R., *History of Gloucester, Mass.*, Gloucester, 1892.

Shattuck, Lemuel, *A History of the Town of Concord*, Russell Odiorne & Co., Concord, 1835.

Sumner, William H., *A History of East Boston*, W. H. Piper & Co., Boston, 1869.

Taylor, Charles J., *History of Great Barrington (Berkshire) Massachusetts* (extension, Part II, George Edwin MacLean), published by the town, 1928.

Temple, J. H., *History of North Brookfield, Massachusetts*, published by the town, 1887.

Teele, A. K., ed., *The History of Milton, Massachusetts*, published by the town, 1887.

Trayser, Donald G., *Barnstable*, F. B. & F. P. Goss, Hyannis, Mass., 1939.

Waters, Thomas Franklin, *Ipswich in the Massachusetts Bay Colony*, 2 vols., The Ipswich Historical Society, Ipswich, Mass., 1905.

Winsor, Justin, ed., *The Memorial History of Boston*, 4 vols., Ticknor & Co., Boston, 1880.

Wright, O. O., comp., *History of Swansea, Mass., 1667–1917*, Fall River, 1917.

Wyman, Thomas Bellows, *The Genealogies and Estates of Charlestown*, David Clapp & Son, Boston, 1879.

New Hampshire

Annett, Albert, and Alice E. Lehtinen, *History of Jaffrey, New Hampshire*, 2 vols., published by the town, Transcript Printing Co., Peterborough, 1937.

Bemis, Charles A., *History of the Town of Marlborough*, George H. Ellis, Boston, 1881.

Bill, Charles H., *History of the Town of Exeter, N. H.* (J. E. Farwell & Co., printers, Boston) Exeter, 1888.

Bouton, Nathaniel, *The History of Concord*, Benning W. Sanborn, Concord, N. H., 1856.

Caverly, A. M., *Historical Sketch of the Town of Troy, New Hampshire*, Sentinel Printing Co., Keene, N. H., 1859.

Child, Hamilton, *Gazetteer of Grafton County, N. H., 1709–1886* (Part I of *County Gazetteer and Directory*), Syracuse Journal Co., Syracuse, 1886.

Cochrane, Rev. W. R., and George K. Wood, *History of Francestown, N. H.*, published by the town, Nashua, N. H., 1895.

Coffin, Charles C., *The History of Boscawen and Webster*, Republican Press Association, Concord, 1878.

Cross, Lucy R. H., *History of Northfield, New Hampshire*, Rumford Printing Co., Concord, N. H., 1905.

Donovan, D., and Jacob A. Woodward, *The History of the Town of Lyndeborough, New Hampshire*, 2 vols., published by the town, The Tufts College Press, 1906.

Dow, Joseph, *History of the Town of Hampton, New Hampshire*. 2 vols., Salem Press Publishing and Printing Co., Salem, Mass., 1893.

Griffin, S. G., *A History of the Town of Keene*, Sentinel Printing Co., Keene, N. H., 1904.

BIBLIOGRAPHY

Harriman, Walter, *The History of Warner, New Hampshire*, The Republican Press Association, Concord, N. H., 1879.

Kidder, Frederick, *The History of New Ipswich*, Gould and Lincoln, Boston, 1852.

Leonard, Levi W., *The History of Dublin, N. H.*, John Wilson and Son, Boston, 1855.

Little, William, *The History of Weare, New Hampshire*, published by the town, S. W. Huse & Co., Lowell, Mass., 1888.

Musgrove, Richard W., *History of the Town of Bristol, Grafton County, New Hampshire*, 2 vols., R. W. Musgrove, Bristol, 1904.

Rice, Franklin Pierce, ed., *Memorials of Meredith, New Hampshire*, Massachusetts Record Society, Worcester, 1891.

Stearns, Ezra S., *History of Plymouth, New Hampshire*, 2 vols., published by the town, University Press, Cambridge, Mass., 1906.

Writers' Program of W. P. A. in the State of New Hampshire, *Hands That Built New Hampshire*, Stephen Daye Press, Brattleboro, Vt., 1940.

Rhode Island

Greene, D. H., *History of East Greenwich, R. I.*, J. A. & R. A. Reid, Providence, 1877.

Munro, Wilfred H., *History of Bristol, R. I.*, J. A. & R. A. Reid, Providence, 1880.

Vermont

Canfield, Mary Grace, *The Valley of the Kedron: the story of the South Parish, Woodstock, Vermont*, Kedron Associates, South Woodstock, Vt., 1940.

Dana, Henry Swan, *History of Woodstock, Vermont*, Houghton Mifflin, Boston and New York, 1889.

Fairbanks, Edward T., *The Town of St. Johnsbury, Vt.*, The Cowles Press, St. Johnsbury, 1914.

Humphrey, Zephine, and Elizabeth Sykes Lee, *The Story of Dorset*, Tuttle Co., Rutland, Vt., 1924.

Joslin, J., B. Frisbee, and F. Ruggles, *History of Poultney, Vt.*, published by the authors, Poultney, Vt., 1875.

Thompson, Zadock, *History of Vermont, Natural, Civil, and Statistical*, published for the author by Chauncey Goodrich, Burlington, 1842.

MAGAZINE ARTICLES

Armstrong, Henry R., "The Norwich Pottery Works," *Antiques*, IV, 170–173 (October 1923).

Bradford, Emma F., "A Search for Local Pottery" (Orange, Mass.), *The Chronicle of the Early American Industries Association*, vol. I, no. 20 (November 1936).

Burbank, Leonard F., "Lyndeboro Pottery," *Antiques*, XIII, 124–126 (February 1928).

Chandler, L. Reginald, "The Methods of Early American Potters," *Antiques*, V, 174–178 (April 1924).

Cook, Charles D., "An Early Rhode Island Pottery" (East Greenwich), *Antiques*, XIX, 37–38 (January 1931).

Coolidge, Edwin H., "The Pottery Business in Sterling, Mass.," *Old-Time New England*, vol. XXIII, no. 1, pp. 17–21 (July 1932).

Dyer, Walter A., "Early Pottery of New England," *Antiques*, I, 19–22 (January 1922).

Flint, William W., "The Millville Pottery, Concord, N. H.," *Old-Time New England*, vol. XVII, no. 3, pp. 99–106 (January 1927).

Gates, Burton N., "Boston Earthenware: Frederick Mear, Potter," *Antiques*, V, 310–311 (June 1924).

"Glaze Mill Stones from Hervey Brooks Pottery, South End, Goshen, Connecticut," *The Chronicle of Early American Industries*, vol. III, no. 5 (September 1945).

Jewell, Margaret H., "Notes on Maine Potteries," *Old-Time New England*, vol. XXII, no. 4, pp. 184–187 (April 1932).

—— "The Corliss Pottery at Woolwich, Maine," *Old-Time New England*, vol. XXII, no. 4, pp. 180–183 (April 1932).

Norton, F. H., "The Crafts Pottery in Nashua, New Hampshire," *Antiques*, XIX, 304–305 (April 1931).

—— "The Exeter Pottery Works," *Antiques*, XXII, 22–25 (July 1932).

Norton, F. H., and V. J. Duplin, Jr., "The Osborne Pottery at Gonic, New Hampshire," *Antiques*, XIX, 123–124 (February 1931).

Notes on Whately and Burlington, *Antiques*, VIII, 76–78 (August 1925).

Old Times in North Yarmouth, Me., A Magazine, Yarmouth, Me., 1877–1884.

Peterson, Charles E., "Some Recent Discoveries at Jamestown, Virginia," *Antiques*, XXIX, 192–194 (May 1936).

"Potter and Potter's Wheel" (pictorial demonstration), *Antiques*, XIX, 23–25 (January 1931).

Ramsay, John, "Early American Pottery," *Antiques*, XX, 224–229 (October 1931).

Sammis, Mrs. Irving S., "The Pottery at Huntington, Long Island," *Antiques*, III, 161–165 (April 1923).

Sim, Robert J., and Arthur W. Clement, "The Cheesequake Potteries," *Antiques*, XIV, 122–125 (March 1944).

Spargo, John, "Burlington Pottery," *Antiques*, VI, 254 (November 1924).

—— "The Fentons — Pioneer American Potters," *Antiques*, IV, 166–169 (October 1923).

Stow, Charles Messer, "The 'Deacon Potter' of Greenwich," *The Antiquarian*, vol. XIV, no. 9, p. 46 (March 1930).

Swan, Mabel M., "The Dedham Pottery," *Antiques*, X, 116–121 (August 1926).

Watkins, Lura Woodside, "A Check List of New England Stoneware Potters," *Antiques*, XLII, 80–83 (August 1942).

—— "Beans and Bean Pots," *Antiques*, XLVI, 276–277 (November 1944).

—— "Early New England Redware Potters," *The Chronicle of Early American Industries*, III, no. 2 (December 1944).

—— "Low's Art Tiles," *Antiques*, XLV, 250–252 (May 1944).

—— "The Bayleys: Essex County Potters," *Antiques*, Part I, XXXIV, 253–255 (November 1938); Part II, vol. XXXV, pp. 22–27 (January 1939).

—— "The Brooks Pottery at Goshen, Connecticut," *Antiques*, XXXVII, 29–31 (January 1940).

—— "The Potters of Whately, Massachusetts," *American Collector*, Part I, vol. VII, no. 6, p. 6; Part II, vol. VII, no. 7, p. 10 (July and August 1938).

—— "The Stoneware of South Ashfield, Massachusetts," *Antiques*, XXVI, 94–97 (September 1934).

Wheeler, Robert G., "The Potters of Albany," *Antiques*, XLVI, 345–347 (December 1944).

Winton, Andrew L., and Kate Barber Winton, "Norwalk Potteries," *Old-Time New England*, Part I, vol. XXIV, no. 3, pp. 75–92 (January 1934); Part II, vol. XXIV, no. 4, pp. 111–128 (April 1934).

Wood, Ruth Howe, "Memories of the Fentons," *Antiques*, VIII, 150–154 (September 1925).

MANUSCRIPTS

Brooks, Hervey, Goshen, Conn., Account Book, 1804–1870. Owned by John Norton Brooks, Torrington, Conn.

Corliss, John, West Woolwich, Maine, Account Book, 1824–1832. In Portland Historical Society, Portland, Maine.

Judd, Sylvester, Manuscripts. In Forbes Library, Northampton, Mass.

—— Accounts of Ebenezer Hunt, Northampton, Mass. In Judd Mss., Prices and Account Books, p. 105.

Leighton, Samuel, Alfred, Maine, Diary. In Portland Historical Society, Portland, Maine.

Parker, John, Charlestown, Mass., Account Book, 1747–1759. In Library of Harvard School of Business Administration.

Peirce, Preserved, Swansea, Mass., Accounts, 1783. Owned by Lura Woodside Watkins.

Procter, Joseph, Gloucester, Mass., Account Book, 1783–1806. In Essex Institute, Salem, Mass.

Risley, Sidney, Norwich, Conn., Account Book, 1852–1861. Owned by George A. Risley, Norwich, Conn.

Seaver, William, Taunton, Mass., Account Book, *c.*1785–1814. In Old Colony Historical Society, Taunton, Mass.

Illustrations

ILLUSTRATIONS IN THE TEXT

Petition concerning a new bridge over the town dock, Charlestown, Mass., with signature of Thomas Symmes 27

Signature of Daniel Bayley of Newburyport, Mass., on a deed dated May 15, 1789 51

Bill of Orcutt, Guilford & Co., Ashfield, Mass., August 9, 1848 107

Bill of J. & E. Norton, Bennington, Vt., June 26, 1856 147

Bill of George W. and J. H. Farrar, Fairfax, Vt., August 26, 1840 149

Bill of Farrar & Stearns, Fairfax, Vt., April 28, 1851 151

Billhead showing pottery of A. K. Ballard, Burlington, Vt., September 1869 153

Billhead showing Norwalk Pottery, *ca.* 1860 203

Exhibition of Bennington ware, Crystal Palace, New York, from wood cut in *Gleason's Pictorial*, October 22, 1853 215

Advertisement of East Boston Crockery Co., *Boston Directory*, 1869 220

ILLUSTRATIONS IN THE PLATE SECTION

1. Potters' workshops, West Woolwich, Maine, and Ashfield, Mass.

2. Pug mill, Exeter, N. H.

3. Edwin A. Rich turning ware, Peabody, Mass., 1906.

4. Glaze mill used by Hervey Brooks, Goshen, Conn.

5. Kiln, Lawrence pottery, Beverly, Mass.

6. Redware cockspurs for stacking ware in kiln.

7. Redware setting tiles for stacking ware.

8. Stoneware wedges and tiles for stacking ware.

9. Pitcher of 17th- or early 18th-century type, probably Essex County, Mass.

10. Pots and tiles from site of Kettle pottery, Danvers, Mass., 1687–1710.

11. Shards from Kettle pottery, Danvers, Mass.

12. Redware jug, perhaps *ca.* 1700.

13. Early red earthenware.

14. Jar with combed decoration, Salem area, early period.

15. Early crock with combed decoration, Essex County.

16. Vase with combed bands, probably by Peter Clark, Braintree, Mass., *ca.* 1770.

17. Shards from pottery of Joseph Bayley, Rowley, Mass., *ca.* 1722–1735.

18. Ale mugs from site of Daniel Bayley pottery, Newburyport, Mass., 1764–1799.

19. Bowls from Bayley pottery, Newburyport.

20. Parts of slip-decorated plates and pans, Bayley pottery, Newburyport.

21. Shards from Bayley pottery, Newburyport.

22. Slip-decorated pan with initials *W B*, Bayley pottery, Newburyport.

23. Slip-decorated porringer, Bayley pottery, Newburyport.

24. Fragments of slip-decorated chamber mugs, Bayley pottery, Newburyport.

25. Slip-decorated chamber mug, Bayley pottery, Newburyport.

26. Slip-decorated dish, dated *1764*, Dedham, Mass., probably by Joseph Wilson.

27. 18th-century shards from Purinton pottery, Somerset, Mass.

28. Slip-decorated mug, *ca.* 1750.
29. Redware washbowl coated with light slip, 18th century.
30. Teapot by John Henry Benner, Abington, Mass., 1765–1796.
31. Pitcher by John Henry Benner.
32. Massachusetts redware.
33. Slip-decorated plate, 18th-century pan shape, probably Massachusetts.
34. Slip-decorated plates, 18th-century pan shape, probably Massachusetts.
35. Slip-decorated platter and jar, 18th century.
36. Red earthenware of 18th-century type.
37. Early Massachusetts pieces.
38. Redware covered pitchers and jar.
39. Redware from Osborn and Southwick potteries, South Danvers, Mass.
40. Examples from Pecker pottery, Merrimacport, Mass.
41. Kitchen vessels.
42. Covered jar, probably southeastern Massachusetts.
43. Jar with yellow and green glaze, attributed to Seymour pottery, Hartford, Conn.
44. Pitcher by Nathaniel Seymour, Hartford, Conn., *ca.* 1800.
45. Pan-shaped plate, type made by Frederick Seymour, Hartford, Conn.
46. Workshop and house of Hervey Brooks, Goshen, Conn.
47. Slip-decorated plates by Hervey Brooks, Goshen, Conn., late period.
48. Red earthenware from Connecticut.
49. Connecticut-type covered jar, early 19th century.
50. Redware jar, probably Connecticut.
51. Slip-decorated pie plates from Norwalk, Conn.
52. Connecticut redware.
53. Connecticut redware.
54. Slip-decorated tray, Connecticut and Long Island type.
55. Slip-decorated pan, initialed *D M A* and dated *1830*, probably Exeter, N. H.
56. Mugs from various sources.
57. Pitcher, bowl, and spice jar, Essex County, Mass.
58. Covered herb or stew pots.
59. Molds and Bradford, Massachusetts, mugs.
60. Pans and jar with simple manganese decoration.
61. Portrait of Thomas Crafts, of Whately, Mass., 1802–1861.
62. Farm and pottery of Thomas Crafts, Whately, Mass.
63. Black-glazed teapot from Crafts pottery with New Hampshire cups.
64. Fragments of black-glazed teapots from Crafts pottery, Whately, Mass.
65. Pieces made at Hews pottery, Weston, Mass.
66. Red earthenware from Chesham, N. H.
67. Incised redware plate, dated *1808*, Concord, N. H.
68. Types of redware from Plymouth and Boscawen, N. H.
69. Pieces made by the Clarks, Lyndeboro and Concord, N. H.
70. Porringers made by Elijah C. Lowell, Orange, N. H.
71. Examples of Vermont redware.
72. "The Independent Beggar," by S. L. Waldo.
73. Red earthenware from Maine.
74. Sickroom necessities.
75. Redware colanders.
76. Kitchen utensils, Massachusetts and New Hampshire.
77. Glazed flowerpots with attached saucers.
78. Flowerpots of stoneware and green-glazed redware.
79. Flowerpots, implements, and molds excavated at West Sterling, Mass.
80. Shards from West Sterling, Mass.
81. Redware grayhounds with Rockingham glaze, West Sterling, Mass.
82. Miniature redware pieces.
83. Miniature redware and stoneware pieces.
84. Small objects of red earthenware.
85. Earthenware pipes excavated at Alton, N. H., and Wells, Maine.
86. Crude stoneware pot, perhaps Charlestown, Mass., 1742–1745.

ILLUSTRATIONS

87. Stoneware pot, dated *1791*, by Abraham Mead, Greenwich, Conn.

88. Taunton pot, probaby from Seaver pottery, 1790–1800.

89. Boston stoneware, *ca.* 1800.

90. Stoneware jar, marked *Boston*, incised and signed by Marshall Timson.

91. Boston jug with incised decoration.

92. Stoneware jug marked *Boston 1804*.

93. *Boston 1804* jars and Charlestown pitcher.

94. Charlestown pot with incised decoration, 1812–1825.

95. Charlestown jar with impressed motives, 1812–1825.

96. Water cooler with incised and stamped decoration, by T. Harrington, Hartford, Conn.

97. Presentation jug, dated *1822*, by Goodale & Stedman, Hartford, Conn.

98. Gemel bottle, New Haven, Conn.

99. Stoneware pot by Smith & Day, Norwalk, Conn.

100. Handled jug, Wallingford, Vt.

101. Mid-19th-century stoneware.

102. Water cooler with applied relief decoration, Ashfield, Mass.

103. Water cooler with applied relief decoration, by Franklin Wight, Ashfield, Mass.

104. Miniature churn by Wight, Ashfield, Mass.

105. Display of Ashfield stoneware.

106. Twelve-gallon water cooler, elaborately decorated with blue slip, Bennington, Vt.

107. Examples of stoneware from Vermont.

108. Stoneware cider pitcher, Somerset, Mass.

109. Stoneware grotesque jug.

110. Connecticut pottery types.

111. Stoneware shards from States pottery, Stonington Point, Conn.

112. Stoneware shards from Crafts pottery, Whately, Mass.

113. Stoneware shards from Ballardvale, Mass.

114. Pitchers with Rockingham glaze, Norton & Fenton, Bennington, Vt.

115. Slip-glazed cider pitcher, Sidney Risley, Norwich, Conn.

116. Rockingham and flint enamel wares, Bennington, Vt.

117. Rockingham and flint enamel tobies and tile, Bennington, Vt.

118. Flint-enameled doe, Bennington, Vt.

119. Bennington hound-handled pitcher.

120. Rockingham pitchers, Sidney Risley, Norwich, Conn.

121. Hound-handled pitcher, dated *1854*, Burlington, Vt.

122. Examples of Rockingham ware.

123. Slip-glazed pitcher, J. T. Winslow, Portland, Maine.

124. Parian porcelain, Bennington, Vt.

125. Parian figures, Bennington, Vt.

126. Display of pottery, A. H. Hews & Co., Cambridge, Mass., 1878.

127. *Rieti* pitcher, New England Pottery Co., East Boston, Mass.

128. Vases and tile from Robertson pottery, Chelsea, Mass.

129. Trial pieces by Hugh C. Robertson, Chelsea, Mass.

130. Vases from Robertson pottery, Chelsea, Mass.

131. Crackle ware bowl by Hugh C. Robertson, Chelsea, Mass.

132. Tiles, Low Art Tile Works, Chelsea, Mass.

133. Plastic sketch by Arthur Osborne, Chelsea, Mass.

134. Ivory ware tea set, Hampshire pottery, Keene, N. H.

135. Examples from Newburyport and Gay Head, Mass., and Keene, N. H.

136. Grueby pieces and vase by W. J. Walley, West Sterling, Mass.

INDEX

Index

(See also check list of Potters, pp. 249 ff)

Abington, Mass., 45–46; shards, 46
Adams, Joseph, 33
Adams, Philemon, 172
"Agate" ware, 189
Aikins, A., quoted, 9–10
Albany, N. Y., 82, 102, 171
Alcock, 217, 218
Alfred, Me., 156–157, 162
Allman, John, 40–41
Allston, Mass., 89
Alstead, N. H., 117
Alton, N. H., 167
American Institute, N. Y., 203, 229
Amesbury, Mass., 69–70, 92, 136
Amherst, N. H., 122, 125
Anabaptists, 19
Andover, Mass., 90
Andrews, Mrs. Earle E., 10, 140, 166
Annis, Abraham, 59, 67
Antimony, 98, 99, 100
Apprentice, 16, 20, 59–60, 126, 127, 132, 138, 174, 179; advertisement for, 41, 172, 186, 201; runaway, 200; system, 2, 3; woman, 32
Apprenticeship, indenture of: Goldsmith, John, 16; Morrison, Ebenezer, 59–60; States, Adam, 180
Armstrong & Wentworth, 187
Armstrong, Henry R., 190
Armstrong, Peleg, 187
Ashfield, Mass., 12, 102, 105–109, 115, 152, 153; forms, 109; industries, 105; marks, 106, 108, 109; presentation pieces, 109; shards, 108; water cooler by Wight, 12, 109, Fig. 103; workshop, Fig. 1
Assonet Neck, Mass., 63, 75, 76, 79
Astbury ware, 56, 128
Attleboro, Mass., 89
Atwater, Edward E., quoted, 14, 171

Badger, Stephen, 20, 25
Badger, Rev. Stephen, 25
Bailey, Charles, 92, 137
Baker, Ebenezer, 42, 81
Baldwin, Me., 167
Ballard & Brothers, 150, 169
Ballard, A. K., 150, 151; cut showing pottery of, 153
Ballard, H. N., 150
Ballard, O. L., 150
Ballardvale, Mass., 90; shards, 90, Fig. 113
Bangor, Me., 166, 167, 168, 170
Barber, Edwin Atlee, 213, 221, 230
Barker, John, II, 159, 167
Barker, "Mr.," 159
Barnstable, Mass., 33, 45, 87
Bath, Me., 163, 164
Bayley, Daniel, 9, 49 ff, 121, 199, 207, 239, 241; deed signed by, 51; inventory of, 50; publications of, 50
Bayley, Daniel, Jr., 53; inventory of, 53
Bayley, Joseph, 49, 52, 55, 58, 59, 78, 241; inventory of, 49
Bayley, Nathaniel, 53
Bayley, William, 53, 57
Bean Hill (Norwich, Conn.), 184, 187
Beekman, Dukes Co., N. Y., 76
Belding, David, 104, 106–109
Benner, John Henry, 45–46; teapot by, 46, Fig. 30
Bennington Battle Monument and Historical Association, 120
Bennington Museum, 138, 139, 221
Bennington, Vt., 89, 100, 120, 136–138, 142–148, 150, 152, 168, 169, 189, 206, 211–218; exhibition at N. Y., 1853, 215; flint enamel ware, 213, 214, 218; granite ware, 216; lava ware, 214, 216; marks, 144, 146, 212, 213, 217; Norton pottery, cut of Fig. 147; Parian ware, 212, 214–218, Figs. 124, 125; Rockingham ware, 212–216, 218, 219, forms, 216; scroddled ware, 214, 216; stoneware, forms, 144–146, jars, decorated, 146, water cooler, decorated, 146, Fig. 106; white wares, 213, 216
Bentley, William, Rev., diary, quoted, 17, 93, 138
Benton, George, 194
Berkley, Mass., 63, 75–77, 207, 208
Berlin, Vt., 103, 139
Berwick, Me., 166
Beverly, Mass., 18–19, 21, 22, 64, 71–72; Lawrence kiln after fire, Fig. 5; ware made at, 72, 222
Bickford, James, Jr., 165
Bickford, Wentworth, 165
Biddeford, Me., 63, 166
Bill, Elijah A., 188
Biscuit, 135, 214, 217
Bloomfield, Me., 161
Bodge, Amos P., 64, 72
Bodge, Benjamin, 69–70
Bodge, John, 70
Bodge, Samuel, 30, 32, 70
Bodge, Samuel, II, 43
Book bottles, 150, 218
"Bourg-la-Reine," 225
Boscawen, N. H., 130–132; forms, 131, 132; shards, 131; stoneware attributed to, 131
Boston Athenaeum, 237
Boston Earthen Ware Manufacturing Co., 219–220
Boston, 1804, 11, 83
Boston, Mass., 11, 14, 15, 16, 19–20, 26, 33, 34, 39–41, 82–84, 109, 113, 125, 141, 207, 210, 232; marks, 83; stoneware pots, Figs. 89, 93
Boston Porcelain and Glass Co., 41, 73
Boston Pottery Co., 90
Boyce, Enoch, 76
Boyce, Enoch, II, 76–77
Boyce, John, 76
Boyce, John, II, 76–77
Boyce, William, 75–77
Boyd, George, 33
Boyden, George W., 108
Boynton & Farrar, 153
Boynton, J., 153
Bradford, Elfleda, J., Miss, 47
Bradford, Emma Fitts, Mrs., 94
Bradford, John, 46
Bradford, Mass., 67
Bradford, Noah, 46, 47
Bradford, Stephen, 46
Bradford, Stephen, Jr., 46
Bradford, Vt., 153, 154
Bradley, Moses, 137
Braintree, Mass., 46, 81, 120, 122, 138
Brass, 7, 30, 74
Brewer, Stephen T., 190, 191, 195
Brewster, Deborah, 33
Brickmaker, 15, 24, 42, 43, 116, 131, 132, 155
Brickmaking, 15; Boscawen, N. H., 131; Boston, 15; Cambridge, 43, 155, 156; Charlestown, 15; Medford, Mass., 15, 42; Plymouth, Mass., 15; Salem, Mass., 15; Scituate, Mass., 15; Concord, N. H., 125
Bricks, 15, 81, 140, 195; kiln, 9, 44, 52; laws regulating size of, 15
Brickyards: Gardiner, Me., 169; Hallowell, Me., 155; Kingston, Mass., 46; Medford, Mass., 42; Scituate, Mass., 15; Taunton, Mass., 86; Whately, Mass., 101; Wiscasset, Me., 156; Woodstock, Conn., 173
Bridgeport, Conn., 206
Brimfield, Mass., 93
Bristol, N. H., 133
Bristol, England, 8
Bristol, R. I., 14, 20, 207
Brooklyn Museum, 148, 179, 195, 225
Brooks, George, 166
Brooks, Hervey, 10, 173–177, 240; account book of, 174–177; plates by, Fig. 47; shop and home of, Fig. 46
Brooks, Isaac, 175
Brooks, Joel, 157, 158
Brooks, John E., 158

INDEX

Brooks, John Norton, 6, 174
Brouwer, Adriaen, "Pancake Turner," 7
Brownington, Vt., 121, 122, 126, 138
Bruce, Ambrose, 163
Bruce, George, 157
Bruitan, 41
Brunswick, Me., 158, 159
Bugbee, Thomas, Jr., 172
Bullard, Joseph O., 89
Burlington, N. Y., 83, 196
Burlington, Vt., 136, 148, 150, 153, 169, 219; Ballard pottery, cut of, 153; hound-handled pitcher, 150, 219, Fig. 121; Rockingham ware, 150; stoneware forms, 150
Burn (Bourne), James, 45
Burnap, James, 117
Burpee, James G., 131
Burpee, Jeremiah, 131, 132, 133; vase by, 132, Fig. 68c
Burpee, Joshua, 131, 133
Burroughs, William, 84
Butterfield, William, 67
Buttons, 205–206, 228; dust process, 228; redware, 205; variegated, 205
Buxton, Me., 165–166; shards, 165–166

Cambridge, Mass., 28, 29, 34, 156, 222–223; Hews pottery: catalogue, 222–223; display of pottery, 1878, Fig. 126; terra-cotta forms, 222–223
Cambridgeport, Mass., 89
Canaan, N. H., 134
Canfield, Mary Grace, Mrs., 137, 153
Canterbury, Conn., 173
Cape Ann, Mass., 33
Carpenter, Mrs. Carrie B., 134, 135
Carpenter, Frederick, 83–84, 171, 196
Casco Bay, Me., 26, 33
Cavendish, Vt., 140
Centennial Exhibition, 1876, 222, 225
Chace, Asa, 77, 78, 87, 88
Chace, Benjamin Cartwright, 188
Chace, Benjamin G., 87
Chace, Clark, 77
Chace, Clark, Jr., 87
Chace, Leonard, 87, 88
Chamlet, Curtis, 39
Charlestown, Mass., 11, 14, 15, 16, 19, 20, 22, 24–38, 39, 42, 45, 70, 81, 83–86, 87, 89, 94, 167, 190, 245–248; claims for loss after fire, 28, 29; marks, 85; stoneware jars, 11, 84, 85, 109, 146, Figs. 94, 95; Swing bridge, 24, 27, 28, 29, 37
"Charlestown ware," 24, 45, 111
Chase, Mrs. Albert Hunt, 185
Chase, James, 70–71; inventory of, 71
Chase, Phineas, 71
Chatham, N. J., 98, 200
Chelsea Keramic Art Works, 220, 224–227; marks, 230; types of decoration, 225; vases, Figs. 128, 130
Chelsea, Mass., 85–86, 222, 224–230
Chesham, N. H., see Pottersville
Chester, Vt., 140
Chichester, Henry, 205
Chicopee, Mass., 101
Chimney Point, Vt., 137
Chimney safes, 112, 168
Chimney tops, 93, 204
Christie, James, 187
Cincinnati Industrial Exposition, 227
Clapp, Job, 86
Clark, Annie, Miss, 122
Clark, Arthur Estes, 124
Clark, Benjamin, 121, 122, 125, 126
Clark, Daniel, 121–219, 132, 138; diary of, 121–129; houses built by, 124; jug dated 1792 by, Fig. 69c
Clark, Daniel, II, 121–129; keg dated 1839 by, Fig. 69b
Clark, Decius W., 169, 213, 220; jug dated 1837 by, Fig. 101a
Clark, John Farmer, 128, 223; feeding cup by, 128, 223, Fig. 74c
Clark, Lyman W., 220–221
Clark, Peter, 46, 120–122; diary of, 120; jar attributed to, 122, Fig. 16
Clark, Peter, II, 121–122, 125, 126, 138
Clark, William, 121, 122
Clay, 5, 6–7, 15, 35–38, 41, 60, 63, 67, 119, 120, 122, 123, 179, 246–248; Bennington, 143, 214; glacial, 5; impurities in, 6, 7; Glasgow, 166; local, sources of, 18, 24, 42, 46, 63, 64, 71, 72, 93, 95, 98, 100, 103, 113, 120, 124, 126, 129, 131, 133, 138, 158, 161, 162, 163, 196, 224; Martha's Vineyard, 10, 35, 36, 88, 182, 247; Moncton, 115; New Jersey, 5, 10, 82, 83, 84, 88, 108, 113, 118, 136, 143, 171, 179, 190, 202; New York, 36, 84, 143, 246; Pennsylvania, 5, 246; Philadelphia, 37, 248; pipe, 8; porcelain, 145; preparation of, 5; South Carolina, 213; stoneware, 5, 10, 35–38, 82, 155, 246, 248, admixture of red clay to, 81, 82, 108, 143, expense of transporting, 37, 38, 82, 246, 248, variegated, 206, 231, white, 82, 98, 99, 100, 115, 120, 143, 166, 174, 179, 213
Clay mill, 5, 28, 29, 59, 60, 64, 71, 99, 100, 101, 111, 157
Cleaves, David, 157–158
Cleveland, William, 187
Cliftondale, Mass., see Saugus
Clinton, Oneida Co., N. Y., 205
Clockmaker, 176
Clocks, 175, 176
Clough, Calhoun & Co., 168
Coachman bottles, 218
Cockspurs, 9, 56, 133
Coffee house, 56
Collier, Charles, 84, 85; fifteen-gallon pitcher by, 84
Collins, Samuel B., 79
Concord, Mass., 44; shards, 44
Concord, N. H., 121–129, 133, 134, 223; forms, 128, 129; incised plate made at, 128, Fig. 67
Cook, Charles D., 208, 209
Coolidge, Henry, 95
Copeland, 212, 214
Copeland, Thomas H., 221
Copper, 7, 50, 74
Corinth, Me., 166
Corinth, Vt., 140
Corliss, Augustus W., quoted, 157–158
Corliss, Ebenezer, 157, 158, 163
Corliss, Howard, 163–165; diary of, 163–165
Corliss, John, 163–165; account book of, 163, 164
Cornell, Elijah, 78–79
Cornell, Ezra, 79
Cornell University, 79
Cornish, Me., 166
Corwin, George, 14, 16
Cottage City, Mass., 231
Cow creamers, 216, 218–219
Cox, Eli, 159
Crackle ware, 226, 232
Crafts, Caleb, 102, 103, 118, 167–168
Crafts, Edward A., 103, 153
Crafts, Elbridge Gerry, 103, 104
Crafts, James M., 102, 103, 118, 119, 139, 167
Crafts, Justin, 103, 139
Crafts, Justus, 103, 104, 139
Crafts, Martin, 103, 118, 119, 167–168
Crafts, Ralph E., 102, 103
Crafts, Rufus, 102
Crafts, T., & Co., 104, 119
Crafts, Thomas, 10, 102–106, 118, 119, 153, 167; house and pottery of, Fig. 62; portrait of, Fig. 61
Crafts, Thomas Spencer, 103
Craig, Mrs. W. J., 192, 193
Cranch, Judge, 45
Cranch, Richard, 45
Creamware, 52, 221
Crockery, 113, 115, 139, 212, 213, 216, 221
Crockery Ware Corporation, 115
Cross, Peter, 194; water cooler by, 194
Crucible, first American, 82
Curtis, Seth, 142
Cutler, Chester T., 21
Cutler, Philip, 25, 39

Dakin, Samuel, 115
Danbury, Conn., 206
Danvers, Mass., 7, 8, 18, 21–23, 43, 46, 62–66, 75, 81, 113, 120, 156, 173, 187, 207, 208, 209, 237; shards, Kettle pottery, 22, 23, Figs. 10, 11
Davis, Elizabeth, Mrs., 232
Davis, Jacob, 18
Day, Absalom, 199–202
Day, George, 200–201
Day, Josephine, 225
Day, Noah S., 200–202
Day, Venables & Taylor, 201
Dedham, Mass., 43, 66, 208–209, 224, 226, 227; Robertson pottery, 226–227, designs, 226, forms, 226, marks, 226, 227
Deerfield Memorial Museum, 101, 104, 105, 194
Delft ware, 14, 34, 52, 131
Dengler, Franz Xavier, 225
Dennis, Samuel, 196
Dennisons, Knesseth, 91
Derry, N. H., 113
DeRuyter, N. Y., 79; shards, 79
Dighton, Mass., 63, 65, 75
Dighton Rock, 75
Dimond, Israel, 127
Dimond, Timothy K., 127
Dodge, Benjamin, 111, 160; Lafayette pitcher by, 160
Dodge, Benjamin, II, 160, 161; glazed flowerpot by, 160–161
Dodge, Jabez, 111, 112, 160
Dodge, Joseph, 111
Dodge, Samuel, 111, 112
Dogs, pottery: Bennington, 216, 218; Parian, 218; redware, Fig. 81; stoneware, 109
Dolphin, The, 182
Donovan, John, 64, 65, 71, 93, 112, 113
Doolittle, "View of the Town of Concord," 44
Dorchester, Mass., 41–42, 81, 91, 197

INDEX

Dorset Hollow, Vt., 141–142, 143; shards, 142
Dover, N. H., 63, 130
Dow, George Francis, 42
Drake, Arthur H., 92
Drake, Elisha, 92
Drake, Francis H., 92, 93
Drinker, Edward, 16, 19, 20, 39
Drinker, Philip, 16
Dublin Earthen Ware Manufactory, 114
Dublin, N. H., 95, 113–115
Duché, Andrew, 35
Duché, Anthony, 35
Duché, James, 35–38, 245–247
Duntze, A., incised jar by, 197
Duntze, J., 197
Durgin, Mrs., 130, 132
"Duchess" ware, 233
Duxbury, Mass., 33, 45
Dyer Memorial Library, 45

Earthenware: Bristol, 8; in early inventories, 13–14; English, 8, 14; fireproof, 201; Whieldon type, 40
Earthenware forms, early, 13, 14, 17, 22
East Alton, N. H., 134–135; shards, 135; tobacco pipes, Fig. 85
East Boston Crockery Manufactory, 220, 224
East Boston, Mass., 90–91, 219–221, 224; forms, 221; marks, 220, 221
East Brookfield, Mass., 92–93
East Cambridge, Mass., 41
East Dorset, Vt., 141–143; shards, 142
East Greenwich, R. I., 75, 208
Eastham, Mass., 156
East Hartford, Conn., 195
East Haven, Conn., 188
East Kingston, N. H., 8
East Liverpool, Ohio, 219
East Middlebury, Vt., 139
Eastport, Me., 158
East Windsor, Conn., 141, 172, 196
Edes, Daniel, 28, 30, 43
Edes, Daniel, II, 28, 111
Edison Institute of Technology, 111
Edmands & Co., 85, 190
Edmands & Hooper, 85
Edmands, Barnabas, 84–85
Edmands, Benjamin, 85
Edmands, Edward T., 85
Edmands, Thomas R. B., 85
Edmands, William B., 85
Edson, 137
Elizabethport, N. J., 204
Ellsworth, Me., 166
Elmwood, Conn., 192–193
Emery, Joshua, 156, 162
Emery, Sarah Ann, quoted, 60
Epping, N. H., 131
Epps, Benjamin, 122, 125
Epsom, N. H., 125
Essex County probate records, 13, 14
Essex Institute, 66
Exeter, N. H., 9, 64, 111–113, 158, 160, 161, 165, 166, 223; forms, 112; pug mill, Fig. 2

Faïence, Chelsea, 225, 227
Fairbanks, Edward T., quoted, 153
Fairfax, Vt., 113, 136, 148–150; bills of ware, 149, 151; forms, 148; marks, 148, 150
Farmingdale, Me., 169
Farmington, Me., 155, 162
Farrar & Stearns, 150
Farrar, Caleb, 139, 140, 148
Farrar, Charles Adelbert, 116
Farrar, Daniel W., 116
Farrar, Ebenezer L., 148, 150
Farrar, George W., 148, 149
Farrar, Isaac Brown, 113, 141, 148
Farrar, J. H., 148, 149
Farrar, Stephen, 148
Felton, Daniel, 43, 209
Fayette, Me., 70
Feldspar, 214
Felton, Jedediah, 113
Fenno, Enoch, 42
Fenton & Hancock, 152
Fenton, Christopher Webber, 83, 142, 145, 152, 211–219
Fenton, Jacob, 83, 141, 152, 196
Fenton, Jonathan, 83, 113, 138–139, 141–143, 150, 171, 196, 211; jar by, 142
Fenton, Leander W., 89, 152
Fenton, Richard L., 83, 89, 142, 143
Fenton, Richard Webber, 139, 150, 152
Fenton's Works, 212, 214, 217
Figures, 211; biscuit, 217; flint enamel, 216, 218, Fig. 118; Parian, 212, 214, 217, Fig. 125; redware, Fig. 81; Rockingham, 216, 218
Firebrick, 85, 86, 88, 90, 145, 168, 197, 211–212; patented by C. W. Fenton, 144–145
Fitchburg, Mass., 94, 237; mug made at, Fig. 36
Flagg, David, 159
Flagg, Mary, 33
Flanders, Peter, 126–128, 132
Flanders, Richard, 126–127
Flint enamel ware, 168, 190, 213, 214–219
Flint, ground, 10
Flint, William W., 124, 126
Flowerpots: attached saucers, with, 97, 112, 114, 148, 166; closed saucer pot, 118; decorated, 118; fancy, 152; glazed, 158, fancy, 96, 114, green, 47, 79, 160–161; hand-turned, 97, 113; hanging, 97, 118, 165; impressed decoration, 225, Fig. 128; mass production of, 43; molded, 96–97, Figs. 79, 80; painted, 93, 97, 116, 224; redware, 72, 73, 129, 134, 139, 164, 176, 204; Rockingham, Bennington, 216; Rockingham glaze, with, 96; ruffled-edge, 97; scalloped, 114; stoneware, 119, 144, 145, 146, 148, 150, 152, 167, 168, 189; Taunton, 1780's, 82; urn-shaped, 85
Forbes Library, Northampton, Mass., 193
Ford, Henry, 111
Folk art, potting as a, 1–3
Foster, Benjamin, 158
Foster, Nathaniel, 158, 163
Foster, William H., 158
Francestown, N. H., 122; shards, 122
Franklin, Benjamin, 237
Frayd, E., & Co., 195
Freeman house, Gloucester, Mass., 18
Freeman, Joshua, 33
Freetown, Mass., 76
French, Jonathan, 115, 116
Frothingham, Benjamin, 20, 25
Fuller, Thomas, 163
Furber, Jethro, 134
Furber, Nathaniel, 113

Gager, Oliver A., 213
Galena, 6
Gallimore, Victor, 233
Garden seat, 89, 97
Gardiner, Me., 168–170; marks, 169
Gardner, Charles B., 190
Gardner, Joseph, 18, 49, 52, 236
Gardner's Island, 88
Gates, Dr. Burton N., 220
Gay Head, Mass., 82, 88, 231
Gay Head Pottery, 231
General Court (Massachusetts), 15, 16, 26, 35, 36, 38, 40, 41, 245–248
Germantown, Mass., 45; shards, 45
Gibbs, Ebenezer, 98, 100
Gilford, N. H., 133
Gill, John H., 132
Gill, William, 132
Gilmanton, N. H., 122, 125, 133
Glass: flint, 99; ground, 6; pounded, 100
Glaze: black, 7, Peabody, 65, Whately, 104; clear, 7, 8; green, 7, 47, 54, 71, 79, 160, 161; "dragon's-blood" red, 225, 226; dry, 225; flint-enamel, 213, 219; lead, 6, 7, 23, composition of, at Exeter, 111, dangers of, 80; manganese, 7, 96; mat, 230, 231, 232; oxblood red, 226; Rockingham: Bennington, 145, 212, 213, 219, Burlington, 150, Norwalk, 206, Norwich, 189, 219, W. Sterling, 96; salt, 11, 80, 91, 108; "smear," 217, 233; tin-enamel, 8, 65; variegated, 168
Glaze mill, 5, 6, 69, 100, 111; Goshen, Conn., 6, Fig. 4
Gloucester, Mass., 14, 17, 18, 22, 49, 52, 61, 157, 236; shards, Bayley pottery, 52, 58, Davis pottery, 18
Goddard, Charles, 95
Goddard, John, 95, 116
Goddard, Solomon, 95, 116
Goldsmith, 24, 34
Goldsmith, John, 16, 20
Goldthwaite, Daniel, 67, 166
Goldthwaite, Samuel, 66
Goldthwaite, Thomas, 66, 94
Goldthwaite, William, 66
Gonic, N. H., 9, 63, 130
Goodale & Stedman, presentation jug by, 194, Fig. 97
Goodale, Daniel, Jr., 190, 191, 192, 194, 195, 197; presentation jugs by, 194, 195
Goodale, Enoch, 67
Goodell, John, 162–163
Goodhue, Nathaniel, 133
Goodrich, Dorothy M. A., pan made for, Fig. 55
Goodwin & Webster, 192, 194, 195
Goodwin Bros., 193
Goodwin, Harvey, 193
Goodwin, Horace H., 194, 195
Goodwin, Seth, 192–193
Goodwin, Thomas O., 192, 195
Gorham, Me., 43, 156, 162, 165
Goshen, Conn., 10, 100, 137, 138, 172, 173–177; forms, 176, 177; glaze mill, Fig. 4; workshop, Fig. 46
Grafton, N. H., 134
Gould, Thomas, 19
Grant, General, 135

INDEX

Granite ware, 220, 221
Granville, Conn., 174, 175
Gray, Daniel, 33
Gray, Thomas, 220
Gray, W. Ellsworth, quoted, 232
Greatbach, Daniel, 214, 218, 219
Great Barrington, Mass., 100
Greene, D. H., Dr., quoted, 208
Greenwich, Conn., 172, 178–180; jars by Abraham Mead, 179, Fig. 87
Greenwood, Edwin, 114–115
Greenwood, William, 114
Gregory, John Betts, 205
Griffith, Benjamin, 33
Grueby, William H., 232
Grueby Faience & Tile Co., see South Boston
Guilford, John L., 106–108

Hall, David, 41–42
Hall, Jonathan, 42
Hall, Jonathan, II, 42, 97, 98
Hall, Joseph, Jr., 41–42
Hall, Pelatiah, 41–42
Hallowell, Me., 155–156, 162
Hampshire Pottery, 117, 230, 231; tea set made at, Fig. 134. See also Keene, N. H.
Hampton, N. H., 110, 113
Hancock, Frederick, 89, 152
Hancock, John, 152, 219
Hanford, Isaac, 195
Hanson, Fernald L., 77
Hanson, Louise, Miss, 78
Hardwick, Vt., 137
Harrington, Thompson, 195; water cooler by, 195, Fig. 96
Harris, John, 28–29, 30, 32, 38, 94
Harris, Josiah, 26, 29, 30, 32, 34
Harrison, John, 212
Harrison Gray Otis House, 128
Hart & Clark, 114
Hartford, Conn., 172, 188, 192–197; marks, 193–195
Hart, William A., 79
Harvard School of Business Administration, 29
Harvard, Mass., 92, 137
Harwich, Mass., 33, 45
Harwood, Hiram, diary of, 143, 144, 145, 148
Hastings & Belding, 106, 109
Hastings, Wellington, 106, 109
Hatfield, Mass., 97
Hathaway, Charles E., 79, 88, 89
Hathaway, William, 89
Haverhill, Mass., 59, 67, 70, 137, 236
Hawthorne, Nathaniel, 105
Hayward, Jonathan, 18–19, 49, 63
Hazeltine, Joseph, 127
Hebron, Me., 162
Henderson and O'Halloran, 91, 197
Henderson, C. W., 91
Henderson, Ethel Hill, 91
Henderson, George H., 91, 197
Hermon, Me., 166
Hews, Abraham, 43–44
Hews, Abraham, II, 43
Hews, Abraham, Jr., III, 43
Hews, Albert H., 43
Hibbard, Rev. A. G., quoted, 173
Higginson, Rev. Francis, quoted, 15
Hillers, 228
Hingham, Mass., 120, 122
Historical Society of Cheshire Co., 230
Hollis Centre, Me., 166
Holmes, Daniel, 156
Holton, George, 174
Homer, William F., 219
Hommel, Rudolph P., 35
Hosmer, Joseph, 187
Hound-handled pitchers: Bennington, Vt, 212, 219, Fig. 119; Burlington, Vt., 150, 219, Fig. 121; Jersey City, 219
Hoxie, Edna M., Miss, 75
Hoyt, Asa, 198–200
Hubbard, Howard G., 105
Hunt, Ebenezer, account book of, 98–100
Huntington, L. I., 178–179, 205, 239
Husband, W. W., Mrs., 152
Hussey, William, 163
Hutchinson, Ebenezer, 123, 139
Hutchinson, William, 123, 139
Hyannis, Mass., 47

Indians, Gay Head, 82, 88
Ingalls, James, 28, 37–38
Ingell, Jonathan W., 86
Ingell, William H., 86
Ipswich, Mass., 14, 18
Ironstone, 220, 221
Ivory ware, 230

Jackfield ware, 56, 104
Jackson, William, 72–73, 234
Jaffrey, N. H., 115–116
Jersey City, N. J., 189, 211, 218, 219, 224
Jewell, Margaret H., 133, 134, 156, 158, 163, 167, 168
Judd, Norman L., 138, 143
Judd, Sylvester, manuscript notes of, 97–100, 193

Kaolin, 118, 145, 176
Keene, N. H., 72, 93, 115, 117–118, 223, 230–231; forms: Hampshire Pottery, 230, redware, 118, stoneware, 118; marks, Hampshire Pottery, 231
Kendall, Loammi, 85–86
Kent, Clement, 59
Kent, Stephen, 59
Kettell, John, 20
Kettell, Jonathan, 22, 62, 63, 64, 173
Kettell, Jonathan, II, 173
Kettell, Richard, 20, 25, 26
Kettell, Samuel, 20, 22, 25
Kettell, William, 20, 21, 25, 32
Kettle, James, 18, 20, 21–23, 25, 26, 62, 66, 173
Kettle (Kettell), James, Jr., 22, 25
Kidder, Isaiah, 113
Kidder, Josiah, 113
Killingworth, Conn., 15, 33
Kiln: brick, 15, 87, 175; drawing, 31, 32, 120, 175; early Salem, 17; law regulating erection of, 26; setting, 9, 23, 31, 143; stacking, 9, 56, 112; temperature of, 7, 9, 11; wood for, 79, 84, 90, 115, 185, 186, 204
Kilns, redware: Beverly, Mass., Fig. 5; Exeter, N. H., described, 9; Gonic, N. H., described, 9; Hartford, Conn., Seymour, 193; Peabody, Mass., Paige, 63–64; Salem, Mass., Vinson, 17; Somerset, Mass., 79; Whately, Mass., J. M. Crafts, 103
Kilns, stoneware: Ballardvale, Mass., 90; Bennington, Vt., 143; Charlestown, Mass., 36, 246, 247; Dorchester, Mass., described, 91; Norwich, Conn., 184; Somerset, Mass., 79, 88
King, Mrs. Perley, 65
King, Wallace L., 230, 231
Kingsbury, J. D., quoted, 67
Kingston, Mass., 14, 46–47; shards, Bradford pottery, 46–47, Howland house, 14
Kitson, Richard F., 162
Knobs, 205; Bennington, 206, 214, 216; "mineral," 201, 206; redware, 205
Knowles, Benjamin B., 191

Lambert, Porter, 156–157
Lamson, Asa Brown, 112, 161
Lamson, Frank H., 111, 112
Lamson, Rufus, 64, 112, 161
Lang & Schafer, 233
Larkin, Joseph, 29, 30–32
Lathrop, Charles, 185–186
Lawrence, Charles A., 64, 72
Lead, 6, 74, 77, 98, 99, 102, 117, 125; bar, 67, 99, 125; calcining, 99, 100; New Orleans, 116; red, 6, 125, 158, 164, 176; "tea," 164
Lead mill, 60, 71
Lead ore, 125
Lead poisoning, 80, 127
Lead works, Salem, 66
Lear, Tobias, 33
Leavitt, Samuel, 112
Lebanon, Conn., 83, 196
Lebanon, N. H., 121
Lee, Mass., 100
Leffingwell, Christopher, 184–185
Leigh & Allman, petition of, 40–41
Leigh, Benjamin, 40–41
Leighton, Samuel, Gen., diary of, 156, 157
Leonard, Seth E., 154
Lewes, James, 33
Lewis & Cady, 150
Lexington, Mass., 43
Libby, Nathaniel, 111
Limington, Me., 167
Linley, Richard, 93
Lisbon, Me., 167
Litchfield, Conn., 101, 172, 173
Litharge, 6, 98, 100, 125
Little, Mrs. Nina Fletcher, 172
Littlefield's Mills, Me., 157
Liverpool ware, 80
Livesley, Mrs. Fred B., 47
Lockwood, Mrs. Luke Vincent, 180
Longfellow, A. Wadsworth, 224
Long Island, 143, 190, 202, 204
Lord, Nathaniel, 26
Loudon, N. H., 63, 130–133
Low Art Tile Co., 224, 225, 227–230; catalogue, 228–229; exhibition in London, 229. See also Tiles
Low, John F., 229–230
Low, John G., 225, 227–230
Lowell, Elijah C., 133–134, 238; porringers by, 134, 238, Fig. 70
Lowell, Isaac, 134
Lyman, Alanson Potter, 168–169, 213
Lyman & Clark, 169
Lyman, Fenton & Co., 213
Lyndeboro, N. H., 120–126, 138, 139; shards, 121
Lynn, Mass., 64, 72, 73; forms, 73
Lyons, N. Y., 195

INDEX

Mackdugle, Ann, 32
Majolica, 230, 231
Malden, Mass., 33, 120, 226
Malin, Joseph, 33
Manchester, Conn., 195–196; forms, 196
Manganese, 7, 60, 74, 77, 99, 138
Mann, Daniel, 33
Manning, Daniel, 28
Manning, Daniel, II, 28
Manning, William, 28
Mansfield, Conn., 141, 173
Marlboro' Earthen Ware Factory, 114
Marlborough, N. H., 93, 113
Marshall, Mrs. Eleanor, 33
Marshall, Samuel, 33, 110, 111
Martha's Vineyard, Mass., 10, 35, 81, 82, 88, 182, 231
Mason, N. H., 113
Massachusetts Charitable Mechanics' Association, 84, 85, 160, 169
Massachusetts Institute of Technology, 52, 111, 229
Massachusetts State Archives, documents in, 34, 245–248
Mattapan, Mass., 42
Maxwell, R. M., 140
McKearin, George S., 104, 191, 195, 197
McLellan, Hugh, quoted, 156
McPherson, John, 188, 197
Mead, Abraham, 178–180; pot dated 1791 by, 179, Fig. 87
Mead, Augustus I., 179
Mear, Frederick, 219–220
Mechanics' Fair, 84, 85
Medford, Mass., 15, 42, 86
Meredith, N. H., 131, 133; shards, 133
Merrill, Jason, 148, 200
Merrimacport, Mass., 69–71, 223; ware made at, 71
Metropolitan Museum, 189
Middlebury, Vt., 136, 139, 140, 148
Milford, Mass., 33
Mill stones, 5, 28, 29, 44, 50, 67, 99, 100, 125
Mills, Charles E., 226
Milton, Mass., 42
Millville, N. H., 123–129
Minor, Clement, 33
Minton, 214, 217, 228
Mitchell, James, 139
Molds, 5, 10, 93, 96, 135, 139, 189, 190, 195, 205, 211, 218, 221, 226, 227, 228, 230, 235, 241
Moncton, Vt., 115, 176
Monmouth, Me., 10, 166
Moore, James, 93
Morgan, Gen. James, 178
Morrison, Ebenezer, 53, 59, 60
Morse, Florence, 230, 231
Moulton, Henry, 110
Moulton, Mrs. Rosamond Niles, 154
Moultonborough, N. H., 133
Mount Desert, Me., 69
Mountford, John, 212
Muffler, 50
Museum of Fine Arts, Boston, 225, 232

Nantucket, Mass., 208
Nash Engineering Co., 199
Nash, Jonathan, 94
Nashua, N. H., 103, 118, 167; forms, 118; marks, 118
Naugatuck, Conn., 176, 197
Needham, Mass., 43
New Bedford, Mass., 204
Newbury, Mass., 49, 52, 59
Newburyport, Mass., 7, 8, 48–61, 67, 113, 207, 235; excavations at, 48, 53–58; forms, 54–58; pan marked W B, Fig. 22; porringer, slip-decorated, Fig. 23; shards, Bayley pottery, 53–58, Figs. 20, 21, 24, Morrison pottery, 60
Newcastle, Me., 63, 156
New Durham, N. H., 133
New England Glass Co., 41
New England Pottery Co., 220–221
Newhall, Daniel, 33
Newhall, Nathaniel, 29
New Hampshire Antiquarian Society, 127
New Hampshire Historical Society, 123, 128, 133, 134
New Hampton, N. H., 125
New Haven, Conn., 15, 83, 152, 172, 176, 192, 195, 196–197
New Haven, Vt., 139–140
New Ipswich, N. H., 113, 136, 139, 148
New Jersey, 199, 200, 204, 207, 211
New London, Conn., 82, 173, 178, 185, 186, 190–191, 194, 195, 204
Newmarket, N. H., 69
New Milford, Conn., 232–233; marks, 233
Newport, N. H., 125
Newport, R. I., 182, 209
Newton, Mass., 43, 155, 162
New York (city), 15, 35, 36, 82, 89, 104, 178, 185, 201, 202, 203, 204, 213, 245
New York (state), 62, 76, 79, 95, 102, 108, 143, 146, 171, 175, 198
New York Exhibition of 1853, 213–214
Nichols & Alford, 150, 219
Nichols & Boynton, 150
Nichols, Maria Longworth, 222
Noble, A. H., 233
Norcross, Josiah, 155, 162
Norcross, Matthias, 162
Norcross, Philip, 155
Norcross, Samuel, 155, 162
Norcross, Samuel, II, 155
Northampton, Mass., 97–100, 105; forms, 100
North Bridgton, Me., 162
North Brookfield, Mass., 92, 137
North Conway, N. H., 134
Northfield, N. H., 132
North Orange Historical Society, 94
North Providence, R. I., 209
North Weare, N. H., 123
Northwood, N. H., 125
North Yarmouth, Me., 157–159, 163
Norton & Fenton, 145, 169, 212; pitchers by, 212, Fig. 114
Norton, E. & L. P., 146
Norton, Edward, 146
Norton Emery Wheel Co., 89
Norton, Frank B., 89, 152
Norton, Frederick H., 9, 52, 96, 111, 114, 119, 130, 188, 212
Norton, J. & E., Co., 146; bill of ware, 147
Norton, John, 100, 137–138, 143–144, 148, 171, 173; slip-decorated jug by, 138
Norton, John, II, 137, 143–144
Norton, Julius, 144–148, 212
Norton, L., & Co., 144
Norton, Luman, 137, 142, 143–144
Norton, Luman Preston, 146
Norwalk Borough, Conn., 198, 201, 202, 205
Norwalk, Conn., 105, 185, 192, 198–206, 207, 223; Day pottery, 200–201; Gregory pottery, 205; Half Mile Isle, 205; Hoyt pottery: forms, 199, shards, 199–200; Old Well, 198–201, 205; Quintard pottery, 205; Smith pottery, 201–205, catalogue, 223, cut of pottery, 203, forms, redware, 204, stoneware, 204, terra cotta, 223, marks, 204; The Village, 198, 199
Norwich, Conn., 15, 33, 85, 144, 172, 178, 180, 181, 184–190, 193, 219; forms, Leffingwell pottery, 185, Risley pottery, 189; shards, Armstrong & Wentworth, 187, Leffingwell, 185, Risley, 188, Tracy & Huntington, 186; water cooler made at, 190

Ocher, red, 11
Old Colony Historical Society, 82
Oldroyd, James, 90
Old Sturbridge Village, Mass., 10, 197
Omensetter, Michael, 190–191
Orange, Mass., 94–95, 116; pieces made at, 94
Orange, N. H., 133–134; shards, 134
Orcutt & Crafts, 167
Orcutt & Wait, 101
Orcutt, Belding & Co., 106
Orcutt, Eleazer, 102, 106, 152, 167
Orcutt, Guilford & Co., 106, 108; bill of ware, 107
Orcutt, Stephen, 101, 102, 106
Orcutt, Walter, 102, 106
Orcutt, Walter, & Co., 106
Orford, N. H., 133
Orrington, Me., 166
Osborn, Aaron, 63
Osborn, Abel, 63
Osborn, Amos, 63
Osborn, Amos, II, 64
Osborn, Caleb, 63
Osborn, Daniel, Jr., 63
Osborn, Elijah, 130
Osborn, Mrs. Eliza S., quoted, 63
Osborn, Green, 130
Osborn, Israel, 63
Osborn, James L., 130
Osborn, John, III, 63
Osborn, John C., 130
Osborn, John Procter, 63
Osborn, Jonathan, 63
Osborn, Joseph, 62, 63, 75, 156, 208
Osborn, Joseph, II, 63
Osborn, Joseph, III, 63
Osborn, Kendall, 63
Osborn, Miles, 64
Osborn, Paul, 63, 75, 76, 208
Osborn, Philip, 63
Osborn family, 62–65, 130; influence of, 62; pieces by, Fig. 39
Osborne, Arthur, 228–229; plastic sketch by, 229, Fig. 133
Osborne, John, 130, 132
Osborne, William A., 130

Paige, Moses B., 64
Paige Pottery, 63–65, 72, 112
Parian ware, 145, 212, 214, 216–218, 220, 221; figures, 212, 217; pitchers, 214, 217–218; vases, 217, 221
Paris, Me., 162

INDEX

Parker, Benjamin, 47, 87
Parker, Daniel, 34, 38, 247, 248
Parker, Daniel, Jr., 47
Parker, Grace, 28, 34–38, 81, 246–248
Parker, Isaac, 25, 29, 30, 34–36, 245–247
Parker, John, 30–33, 38, 111, 208, 247; account book of, 30–33, 38, 45, 208, 235
Park Lane Pottery, 233
Pawtucket, R. I., 209
Peabody, Augustus V., 226
Peabody Historical Society, 66
Peabody, Mass., 64–65, 112, 113, 161, 166; shards, Southwick pottery, 65
Pecker, William, 70, 71; pieces by, Fig. 40
Peddlers' carts, 2, 79, 94, 105, 106, 113, 125, 126, 146, 158, 173, 190, 216
Peirce, Preserved, 74, 76, 208, 235; account book of, 74–75
Pemberton, Thomas, quoted, 83
Pennell, Warren, 21
Penney, Jonathan, 28
Perkins, Mary E., quoted, 184, 185, 186
Perry, Sanford S., 102
Perth Amboy, N. J., 83, 108, 178, 216
Petersham, Mass., 66, 95
Pewter, 2, 14, 30, 34, 50, 74
Pewterer, 24, 50
Pewtress, S. L., 197
Philadelphia, 35, 37, 104, 209, 245, 248
Philadelphia Museum, 7
Plaistow, N. H., 71
Philbrick, Joseph, 112, 161
Philbrick, Samuel, 112, 161
Philbrick, Samuel, II, 112
Philbrick, William, 112
Pie plate, Connecticut, 5, 78, 171, 192, 196, 203
Pierce, John (Charlestown), 26
Pierce, John (Litchfield), 101, 172, 173
Pierce, Jonathan, 101
Pierson & Horn, 169
Pierson (Pehrson), Andrew, 170
Pipe, drain, 72, 85, 103, 168; water, 103, 105, 118, 193
Pipe stems, 93, 135, 167
Pipes, tobacco: East Alton, N. H., 134–135; Orrington, Me., 166; Shirley, Mass., 93; Wells, Me., 134, 166, 167; Wolfeboro, N. H., 134–135
Pitkin, Albert H., 106, 108, 109, 191, 192, 193, 196, 198
Pitkin, Richard, 195–196
Pitman, Thomas, 72
Pittsfield, N. H., 130
Plaisted, Francis A., 169
Plaques, 223, 225, 231
Plaster of Paris, 96
Plastic sketches, 228, 229
Plates: "Green Colour," 41; notched-edge, 8, 78, 171, 185, 192, 200, 201, 207, 235; tortoise-shell, 41
Platters, notched-edge, 8, 171, 201, 207
Plymouth, Mass., 14; shards, Jabez Howland house, 14
Plymouth, N. H., 126, 130, 132, 133
Pomfret, Conn., 172
Poole, John W., II, 115
Porcelain, 41, 145, 212, 214, 225, 233
Porter, Benjamin, III, 156
Porter, Ezra, 43, 156
Porter, Silas, 156
Portland Historical Society, 157
Portland, Me., 47, 102, 103, 106, 111, 118, 119, 160–161, 167–168, 219; Crafts pottery: forms, 167, marks, 167; Winslow pottery: forms, 168, glaze, variegated, 168, pitcher, slip-glazed, Fig. 123
Portsmouth, N. H., 33, 110, 111, 113, 125
"Pot-baker," 16
Potters: Delft, 8; Dutch, 7, 8, 11, 178, 179; Flemish, 37; folk, 58; German, 11, 37; Italian, 65, 91; New Jersey, 10, 100, 199, 202; New York, 10, 35; Pennsylvania, 37; Pennsylvania-German, 12; Philadelphia, 10; pioneer, 1–3, 14, 15; women, 32–33
Pottersville, Mass., see Somerset
Pottersville, N. H., 113–115, 239; forms, 114, 239, 240; pieces made at, Fig. 66
Pottery, decoration of, 7, 8; applied relief, 12, 109, 152, 190, 211; combing, 122; feathering, 200; impressed motives, 85, 195; incising, 7, 11, 56, 83, 84, 91, 128, 132, 142, 162, 183, 194, 195, 197; marbling, 79; "painting," 14, 32, 69, 82, 175, 176; spattering, 7; splashing, 7, 185, 199; sponging, 8, 58; tooling, 7, 55, 58, 78, 183. See also Slip decoration
Pottery, distribution of, 15, 17, 30, 33, 45, 68, 69, 79, 82, 104, 106, 113, 116, 125–126, 130, 135, 144, 146, 158, 161–162, 164, 171, 173, 175, 200, 204, 216–217
Pottery, manufacture of, 5–12; burning, 7, 9–10, 11, 79, 91, 123, 157, 158, 174, 228; glazing, lead, 6, 7, salt, 11, 80, 113, 143, slip, 10, 11, 91; Revolution, at time of, 80–81; "throwing," 2; turning, 2, 64, 137, 174
Potts, Christopher, 186
Poultney, Vt., 138
Powers & Edmands, 85
Powers, Battery, 29
Prentiss, Henry, 43, 156
Prentiss, Samuel, 43, 156
Pride, John, 17
Procter, Joseph, 68–69; account book of, 68, 69; houses built by, 68–69; mills of, 68, 69; pitcher, "green painted," by, 69; shipping interests, 68, 69
Providence, R. I., 61, 65, 89, 181, 209–210
Pug mill, 5, 10, Fig. 2
Purington, George S., 79
Purington, Samuel S., 79
Purinton, Clark, 65, 75–78, 87, 88
Purinton, Clark, Jr., 77, 78
Purinton, Daniel, 65, 66, 76, 78

Quakers, 63, 65, 75, 76, 77, 208
Quartz, 145
Quasset, Conn., see South Woodstock
Queechee, Vt., 137
Quincy, Mass., 45
Quintard, James, Jr., 205, 206

Rackham and Read, quoted, 3
Rand, Edward, 50, 53
Rand, Thomas, 33
Ravenna, Ohio, 193, 197
"Red and yellow" ware, 32
Redware: aesthetic qualities of, 1, 4; described, 1, 2; marking of, 3, 10; scarcity of early, 2; tin-enameled, 65; use of, 2, 54–56, 234–241
Redware forms, 234–241
"Bag," pudding, 175, 176
Baker, bean, 204
Bank, 93
Basin, 32, 74, 236, 239
Beaker, 54, 56
Boiler, pudding, 73, 96, 114, 115
Bottle, 199, 204, 239; hot water, 240; "pig," 240
Bowl, 8, 22, 31, 32, 54, 55, 56, 58, 73, 74, 78, 82, 114, 115, 157, 164, 175, 176, 185, 236; kneading, 96; milk, 96; mixing, 159, 236; tea, 55, 165, 235
Box, butter, 73
Cake mold, 156, 204
Churn, 74, 176, 240
Cooler, 73; blancmange, 96; butter, 204; water, 6, 55, 199
Creamer, 75, 128
Crock, 93, 96
Cup, 32, 55, 56, 82, 134, 156, 185, 199, 204, 238, 241; feeding, 128; muffin, 133; toy, 204
Cuspidor, 96, 112, 118, 240
Dish, 22, 54, 56, 57, 58, 73, 200; baking, round, 23, 71, 204, square, 54, 204; handled, 165; pudding, 100; soap, hard, 96, soft, 96; "spitting," 177, 240; toy, 204
Flowerpot, see Flowerpots
Flask, 239
Gallipot, 32, 73, 82
Inkstand, 176
Jar, 8, 22, 23, 58, 94, 132, 142, 165, 176, 185, 191, 199, 209, 238; preserve, 238; snuff, 156; spice, 162, 238
"Jeger," 32
Jug, 10, 23, 32, 54, 55, 58, 70, 73, 74, 96, 100, 112, 128, 129, 134, 164, 165, 176, 185, 199, 204, 235–236; blacking, 73; doctor's, 69; essence spruce, 73; miniature, 133; money, 156, 204
Keg, 128, 144
"Monkey," 164
Mug, 7, 31, 32, 44, 54, 55, 58, 67, 69, 73, 74, 78, 82, 94, 157, 164, 176, 185, 204, 237; ale, 55, 132, 133, 144, 237; campaign, 128; chamber, 57, 239; shaving, 96, 114, 115, 240
Pail, milk, 82
Pan, 23, 32, 44, 57, 94, 140, 157, 185, 235; bake, 73, 96, 114, 235; bed, 73, 177, 204, 240; bread, 32, 54, 73, 74, 82, 114, 129, 157, 164, 235; flat, 114, 129, 164, 204; milk, 9, 10, 18, 23, 31, 32, 54, 58, 73, 74, 82, 96, 100, 112, 114, 129, 138, 164, 165, 173, 175, 176, 185, 193, 199, 204, 235; pie, 73; pudding, 31, 32, 54, 73, 82, 96, 100, 112, 129, 164, 165, 176, 185, 204, 235; sap, 176; seed, 96; soap, 165; stool, 73; stove, 164; "Tom," 158, 164
Pipkin, 96, 156, 204, 241

INDEX

Pitcher, 9, 31, 32, 54, 55, 56, 69, 73, 74, 93, 96, 100, 115, 129, 139, 156, 164, 165, 176, 185, 199, 204, 236–237; cream, 56; emptyings, 177; stew, 114; toy, 96; water, 160
Plate, 9, 31, 32, 73, 74, 77, 78, 82, 104, 114, 185, 199, 235; pie, 5, 8, 114, 131, 138, 235
Platter, 5, 31, 32, 54, 57, 73, 74, 82, 100, 105, 129, 164, 175, 176, 185, 235; flat, 164
Porringer, 8, 31, 32, 54, 56, 57, 74, 75, 82, 100, 134, 164, 176, 177, 237
Pot, 9, 17, 31, 32, 44, 58, 74, 100, 114, 129, 157, 165, 175, 176, 204, 234–235; baking, 159; bean, 71, 73, 93, 96, 112, 114, 128, 129, 158, 164, 165, 166, 234; butter, 73, 114, 115, 185, 238; cake, 73, 96; chamber, 8, 31, 32, 54, 56, 73, 74, 82, 100, 114, 129, 164, 165, 176, 185, 199, 204; coffee, 204; corroding, 66; cream, 96, 131, 164, 176, 240; drinking, 23, 237; dye, 63; herb, 64, 73, 234, 235; lard, 10, 22, 54, 55, 73, 96, 112, 114, 131, 199; medicine, 73; mustard, 128; pickle, 73; preserve, 73, 96, 114, 176, 191, 204; pudding, 54, 73, 112, 234; "Quaker," 158; stew, 10, 73, 127, 164, 165, 166, 234; tamarind, 73
Roach trap, 204
Salt, 73, 94, 241
Saucer, 55, 156, 185
Spittoon, 203
Strainer, 110, 241
Sugar bowl, 56, 73, 128, 133, 241
Sugar cone, 205
"Sugar drips," 30, 32
Teapot, 54, 56, 58, 102, 104, 204, 241
Tub, butter, 73
Tumbler, 56, 73, 164, 241
Urn, flower, 73
Vase, 72, 138, 204
Washbowl, 8, 54, 58, 73, 96, 114, 157, 164, 165, 176, 177, 204
Reed, Joseph Whittemore, 64, 72
Rhead and Rhead, 57
Rich, Edwin A., 65, 72, 90; photograph of, Fig. 3
Richardson, Mr., 40
Richardson, Ruel, 113
Riding chair, 59, 65
"Rieti" ware, 221, Fig. 127
Risley, Albert, 188, 193
Risley, George A., 189
Risley, George L., 188
Risley, Sidney L., 85, 187–190, 193, 219; account book of, 189–190; Rockingham pitchers by, 189, 190, Fig. 120
Robertson, Alexander W., 224
Robertson, Cadmon, 231
Robertson, George W., 224
Robertson, Hugh C., 222, 224–227; experiments with glazes, 224, 226; presentation bowl by, 226, Fig. 131; trial pieces by, Fig. 129
Robertson, James, 224
Robertson, J. Milton, 224
Robertson, William, 224
Robinson, Mrs. Joseph N., 120
Rochester, N. H., 113, 130
Rockingham ware, 88, 90, 96, 136, 138, 150, 153, 189, 190, 204, 212, 213, 214, 218–220, 227
Rockingham ware forms:
Baker, oval, 216
Basin, wash, 216
Bottle, 216
Box, brush, 216; soap, 216; wafer, 216
Bowl, bread, 216
Candlestick, 216
Chamber, 216
Cooler, blancmange, 96; water, 212
Creamer, 216
Curtain pin, 216
Dish, 220; fluted cake, 96; soap, 96
Doorknob, 216
Doorplate, 216
Ewer, 216
Flask, book, 150; pocket, 216
Foot bath, 216
Foot warmer, 96
Furniture knob, 216
Goblet, 216
Jar, cookie, 150, Fig. 122a; preserve, 204, 216; slop, 216
Lamp base, 216
Lamp pedestal, 216
Mug, 150; flange, 216
Nappie, 96, 216
Number plate, 216
Pan, bed, 216; cake, 216; lift cake, 216; Turk's-head cake, 216; milk, 216
Picture frame, 216
Pipkin, 216
Pitcher, 96, 144, 145, 150, 204, 216; molasses, 216
Plate, 216; butter, 216; pie, 216; pickle, 216; soup, 216
Pot, cake, 96; coffee, 216
Shovel plate, 216
Sugar bowl, 216
Spittoon, 96, 150, 204
Teapot, 118, 150, 204, 216
Toby, 139, 145, 216
Tumbler, 216
Urn, 150; coffee, 216; stove, 216; water, 214
Vase, 150, 216
Rockport, Mass., 69
Rome, N. Y., 143
Rockwood, 222, 230
Rose, Seth, 44
Ross, Denman, 226
Roundabout, N. J., 224
Rowley, Mass., 49, 55, 58, 78; forms, 58; shards, 58, 241, Fig. 17
Roxbury, Mass., 33, 42, 97
Royal Worcester ware, 221, 230
Rumney, N. H., 133
Runey, James, 29
Russell, Eben, 114
Russell, Osgood N., 114
Rye, N. Y., 178

Sables, John, 86
Sables, T. & Co., 86
Sables, Thomas, 86
Safford, John, 166
Safford, John M., 166; marked stew pot by, 10, 166
Sagger, 9, 228
Sag Harbor, 204
St. Albans, Vt., 136, 153
St. Johnsbury, Vt., 12, 89, 115, 123, 136, 139, 150, 152–153; forms, 152; shards, 153; water cooler by Wight, 12, 109, 152
"St. Nicholas" pitcher, 216
St. Paul's Church, 50, 53, 59
St. Paul's School, 124, 129
Salem, Mass., 14, 16–17, 21, 22, 66–67, 102, 125, 138, 187
Salem Village, 21, 22, 25
Salisbury, Mass., 65, 78, 125
Salt glaze, English, 37, 52
Salt, James, 219
Sam Adams, The, 82
Sandown, N. H., 110, 241
Sanford, Amos, 176
Sanford, Frederick, 176
Saugus, Mass., 72–73
"Scarabronze," 233
Scott, Alexander F., 89
Scroddled ware, 214, 216
Seaver, William, 42, 81, 82; account book of, 81, 82; early pot by, Fig. 88
Selleck & Smith, 202
Selleck, Noah, 202
Semiporcelain, 216, 221, 233
Sewall, Samuel, diary of, 208
Seymour & Bosworth, 193, 195
Seymour, Maj. Frederick, 192, 193, 197
Seymour, Israel, 152, 195
Seymour, Nathaniel, 193; pitcher by, 193, Fig. 44
Shakers, 93
Sheffield, Lord, quoted, 81
Sheldon, Isaac, 98
Shirley, Mass., 93
Shop, potter's, 2, Fig. 1
Shove, Asa, 75, 76
Shove, Azariah, 75, 76
Shove, Edward, 75, 76
Shove, George, 75, 76, 77
Shove, Nathaniel, 75, 76
Shove, Samuel, 75
Shove, Theophilus, Jr., 76
Silsby, C. M., & Co., 116
Simmons, George W., 90
Skinner Museum, 105
Skinner, Roy H., 134
Skowhegan, Me., 112, 161
Slave, Negro, 20, 26, 34
Slip: Albany, 10, 11, 20, 23, 108, 138, 146, 168, 182, 183, 185, 189, 201, 227; white, 7, 8, 57, 138, 176
Slip decoration, 7–9, 11, 12, 56–58, 60, 69; Abington, Mass., 46; Bennington, Vt., Norton, 138; brushing, 11; Charlestown, Mass., 32; Danvers, Mass., 22, 23; De Ruyter, N. Y., 79; Dorset, Vt., 8; dotting with green, 8, 57, 73, 193, 199, 200; Gloucester, Mass., Bayley, 58, Procter, 69; inscriptions, 8, 57, 201, 203; Newburyport, Mass., Bayley, 56–58, Morrison, 60; Norwalk, Conn., 199–200, 201, 203; Norwich, Conn., 185; Orange, Mass., 94; period of, 7, 11, 12; process of, 8; Rowley, Mass., 58; Somerset, Mass., Purinton, 78; Taunton, Mass., 82; Weston, Mass., 43, 44; Whately, Mass., 104, 105
Slippers, redware, 93
Smith, Asa, 202–205
Smith, Asa E., 202–205
Smith, Hezekiah, 156, 162
Smith, Howard H., 202–205

INDEX

Smith, James, 92, 195
Smith, Joseph Lindon, 224, 226
Smith, Theodore E., 202–205
Smith, Wilfred, 203
Snow, Marcus L., 95
Society for the Preservation of New England Antiquities, 159, 221, 223
Somerset, Mass., 75–79, 86–89, 188, 207; shards, Collins pottery, 79, Purinton pottery, 78, Fig. 27, Somerset pottery, 78
Somerset Potters' Works, 79, 87, 88
Somerville, Mass., 29
Souter, John, 194
South Amboy, N. J., 171, 178, 179, 202, 203
South Ashfield, Mass., see Ashfield
South Ashfield Public Library, 109
South Boston, 230–232; Grueby Pottery: decoration, 232, marks, 232, tiles, 232, ware, 231, 232
Southbridge, Mass., 93
South End, see Goshen, Conn.
South Hadley, Mass., 97, 98, 105
South Norwalk, Conn., 172, 198, 201
South Thomaston, Me., 166
Southwick, James C., 65; jug by, Fig. 39e
Southwick, Jedediah Kilbourn, 65, 114
Southwick, Joseph, 65
Southwick, William, 65, 114
Southwick, William, II, 65
Southwick, William, Jr. (III), 65
South Woodstock, Conn., 172
South Woodstock, Vt., 153
Spargo, John, 109, 123, 137, 138, 140, 141, 144, 146, 148, 150, 178, 188, 212, 217, 219
Spooner, Edwin V., 162
Sprague, Seth, quoted, 45
Springfield, Mass., 94, 99
Staats, Adam, see States
Staats, Charles B., 180
Staffordshire, 8, 13, 104, 136, 176, 196, 211, 212, 238, 239, 240
Stamford, Conn., 206
Standish, Alexander, 86, 87
Standish, Elias E., 86
Standish, Me., 167
Standly, Robert, 29, 30, 32
Stanley, Thomas, 230
Stark, Maj. Caleb, 124, 125
Stark, Charles, 133
Starkey & Howard, 117, 118
Staten Island, N. Y., 143, 179
States, Adam, 172, 178, 179
States, Adam, II, 178, 180–182, 184, 187, 191, 210
States, Adam, Jr. (III), 181, 182, 191
States, Elizabeth, 178, 180
States, Ichabod, 181, 182
States, Joseph H., 180, 210
States, Matthias, 178
States, Peter, 178, 180, 184, 210
States, William, 180–183, 210
States, William, III, 191
States-Wentworth house, 180, 181
Stearns, Ezra S., quoted, 132
Stedman, Absalom, 194, 195, 197
Stedman & Seymour, 197
Steinbrecher, Jacob, 64
Stevens, Benjamin, 64, 72
Stevens, Samuel, 92
Stewart, Levi, 194, 195
"Stick" heels, 82
Stilphen, Annie, 169
Stilts, 9, 52
Stone, Heman, 33
Stone, M. T., quoted, 116
Stone porcelain ware, 221
Stoneware: "blue and white," 37; decorative design on, 11, 12, 85, 86, 89, 90, 142, 146, 179, 194, 195; described, 10; English, manufacture of, 10, 37; Flemish, 13, 131; flint, 220; German, 13, 14, 131; introduction of, 35–38, 80–81, 178, 245–248; marking of, 81; New York, 35; Philadelphia, 35; Provincial period in, 35–38, 80, 81, 178, 245–248; slip-glazed, 189; staining of, 11, 84, 183; Virginia, 35; yellow, 220
Stoneware forms:
Bank, 109
Basin, milk, 152
Basket, dip, 91; jeweler's, 89, 204
Birdhouse, 204
Bottle, 13, 182, 183, 196; cider, 189; beer, 119, 144, 146, 148, 150, 152, 168, 189, 204; blacking, 144; hot water, 168; ink, 186, 206; pop, 189, 204
Bowl, 11, 108, 109
Box, butter, 119, 152
Churn, 109, 118, 119, 144, 145, 146, 148, 150, 152, 168, 169, 189, 204; miniature, 109
"Corker," 204
Crock, 109, 183; butter, 109, 148; miniature, 204; sixty-gallon, 88
Cuspidor, 190
Dish, soap, 146, 152, 168, 189
Foot warmer, 168, 219
Fountain, water, 146, 148, 152
Gallipot, 13
Inkstand, 82, 144, 146, 148, 189
Inkwell, 183, 206
Jar, 12, 37, 91, 131, 142, 144, 148, 179, 183, 189, 197, 204; covered, 146, 152; fruit, 150; ice, 119; oyster, 204; pickle, 109; preserve, 109, 118, 150, 153, 168; snuff, 88; sweetmeat, 148; tomato, 85, 150, 204; water, 84
Jelly mold, 108
Jug, 12, 82, 118, 119, 138, 142, 144, 146, 148, 150, 152, 167, 168, 182, 183, 189, 193, 204; batter, 11; double, 190; "Holland," 13; miniature, 179, 190, 204; molasses, 109, 118, 150, 204; water, 119, 168
Keg, 118, 119, 146, 168, 189, 204
Measure, 11
Mug, 138, 146, 152
Pan, lead, 190; milk, 82, 168, 188; pudding, 119, 190, 204
Pipkin, miniature, 204
Pitcher, 11, 118, 119, 144, 145, 150, 152, 167, 168, 182, 183, 189, 204; cider, 109; miniature, 204
Plate, deep, 183
Pot, 82, 144, 146, 148, 152, 189, 193, 204; bean, 89, 109, 118, 119, 146, 150, 152, 168, 190; butter, 37, 82, 91, 118, 119, 144, 145, 146, 148, 150, 152, 167, 168, 204; cake, 118, 144, 146, 150, 168, 189, 204; chamber, 37, 82, 150, 183, 193, 204; cheese, 144; cream, 119, 146, 150; drinking, 13; milk, 146; oyster, 144; pickle, 119, 144; preserve, 119, 144, 146; pudding, 146, 150, 168, 189
Sand shaker, 109
Spittoon, 118, 119, 146, 152, 168, 189, 204
Teapot, miniature, 204
Washbowl, 189
Water cooler, 12, 109, 146, 152, 190, 195
Stonington, Conn., 15, 33, 179, 180–183, 187, 210; forms, 183; marks, 181–183; shards, East Stonington, 181, Long Point, 182, 183, **Fig. 111**
Stovepipe safe, 150
Stove tube, 10, 114, 115, 144, 146, 176, 204
Stow, Charles Messer, 59, 178
Strickland, Sidney L., 14
Suderberg, Otto N., 189
Swan & States, 182
Swan, Joshua, Jr., 182
Swansea, Mass., 76–79
Swasey, Eben, 161
Swasey, Jones & Co., 168
Symmes, Thomas, 25, 26, 28, 30, 36–38, 246; signature of, 27
Symonds, David, 39–41
Symonds, John, 67
Symonds, Nathaniel, 66–67
Symonds, Nathaniel, Jr., 67
Symonds, Nathaniel, II, 67
Symonds, William, 67
Synan, Patrick, 88–89
Synan, William, 88–89

Taber, 167
Taber, Job, 190
Taber, John, 134, 135, 167
Taft, J. S., 117, 118, 230, 231
Tarbell, William, 71–72
Tarbell, William, II, 72
"Taunton Great River," 77, 82
Taunton, Mass., 42, 47, 75, 81–82, 86–87; forms, 82; marks, 86, 87
Taylor, William, 201
Taylor, William Watts, 230
Terra cotta, 72, 168, 222, 223, 225, 232
Thacher, Rev. Peter, 42
Thatcher, C. W., 146
Thomas, John (Newburyport), 60–61, 209
Thomas, John (Yarmouth, Me.), 157
Thompson & Co., 169
Thompson, Zadock, quoted, 145
Thoreau, Henry, quoted, 44
Thorp, Joseph, 94, 161
Thorp, Reuben, 94, 161
Throwers, 184
Thurston, David, 113
"Tiger" ware, 11, 185
Tile factory, 112
Tilers, 15, 16
Tiles, 15, 16, 23, 81, 195, 227–230; drain, 102, 118, 168, 176; dust, 227; Grueby, 232; land, 166; law regulating use of, 16; Low's Art, 227–230, Fig. 132, catalogue, 228–229, designs, 228–229, exhibition in England, 229, marks, 230, portraits on, 229; manufacture of, 15, 227–228; ornamentation of, 228, 229, 232; plastic, 227; relief, 227–229; roofing, 15, 16, 23; setting, 9, 11, 121, 133, 181; wet, 227, 228
Timson, Marshall, pot decorated by, 83, Fig. 90

INDEX

Tobies, 139, 211, 218
Tolman, Henry, 95, 116
Tolman, Henry, Jr., 95
Topsham, Me., 159
Torrington, Conn., 193
Towle, Edward, jar marked, 10
Tracy and Huntington, 186, 187
Tracy, Andrew, 186
Troy, N. H., 95, 115–117, 169
Troy, N. Y., 102, 106, 136, 143, 144, 152, 176, 195
Tub mill, 125
Tufts, James, 42
Turnbull, Alice, 109
Turner Centre, Me., 94, 161
Turner, William G. A., 226
Twombley, H. B., 133

United States Pottery, 213–219
Upton, Isaac, 75–76, 208
Upton, Samuel, 75–76, 208
Utensils, potter's: brush, 8, 12, 57, 176; cogglewheel, 47, 203; comb, 7; quill, 8, 57, 200, 201; rib, 23; sieve, horsehair, 6, 112; slip cup, 12, 176, 200

Van Loon, Staats, 108, 109; stoneware dog by, 109
Vinson (Vincent), William, 16, 22, 236
Virginia, redware shipped to, 69; stoneware from, 204, 245
Volcanic ware, 226–227
Voluntown, Mass., see Petersham

Wachusett Pottery, 95–97, 231
Wadhams, Jesse, 173–174, 176
Wadsworth, Abel, 138
Wadsworth Atheneum, 109, 193, 195, 206, 212
Wait, Luke, 101–102
Wait, Obediah, 101–102
Walden Pond, 44
Waldo, "The Independent Beggar," 237, Fig. 72
Waldoboro, Me., 167
Walley, William J., 89, 231–232
Wallingford, Vt., 153, 154
Wallis, George, quoted, 213, 214
Walpole, N. H., 83, 141
Wannopee Pottery Co., 233
Ward, Richard, 176
Ward, Samuel, 138
Warner, N. H., 125, 127
Warren, The, 77
Washington, George, 12, 109, 229
Watertown, Mass., 43, 156
Webber, Albert, 157
Webber, David, 162
Webber, Henry Rust, 162
Webber, John, 25–26
Webber, Moses A., 162
Webster & Seymour, 195
Webster, Charles T., 195
Webster, Daniel Dolbear, 132
Webster, John H., 132
Webster, Mack C., 194, 195
Webster, William, 132
Wedging table, 111
Wells, Ashbel, Jr., 193–194
Wells, Crafts & Wells, 103
Wells, Me., 134, 135, 166–167; tobacco pipe made at, Fig. 85
Wentworth, Erastus, 181, 187
West Amesbury, Mass., see Merrimacport
West Barnstable, Mass., 47
Westchester Landing, N. Y., 79
Westerly, R. I., 178, 180, 181, 210
Westford, Mass., 44
West Hartford, Conn., 172, 192–193, 195
West, John, 67
Westmoreland, N. H., 117
Weston & Willard, 90
Weston, Mass., 8, 43, 44, 241; pieces made at, 44, Fig. 65; shards, 43–44
West Plymouth, N. H., 132–133
West Sterling, Mass., 89, 93, 95–97, 114, 115, 116, 118, 212, 231–232; forms, 96, 97; shards, 96, 97, Figs. 79, 80
West Woolwich, Me., 163–165; forms, 164–165; workshop, Fig. 1
Wethersfield, Conn., 101, 172
Weygandt, Cornelius, 133
Whately, Mass., 8, 10, 100, 101–106, 118, 119, 139, 152, 167, 194, 241; industries of, 101; marks, 101, 103, 104; pitcher, grotesque, made at, 103; shards, 104, 105, Fig. 112
Wheel, potter's, 5, 6, 10, 69, 77, 88, 111
Wheeler, Allen T., 44
Wheeler, L. D., 205–206
White ware, 88, 115, 213, 232
Whiting, Dr. William, 100
Whittemore, Daniel, 64
Whittemore, Joseph, 64, 113
Whittemore, Samuel, 122–123, 126
Wight, Abner S., 93, 95, 109, 114, 115, 118
Wight, Franklin, 108, 109, 152; churn, miniature, by, 109, Fig. 104; water cooler, Ashfield, by, 12, 109, 152, Fig. 103, St. Johnsbury, by, 12, 109, 152
Wight, John, 95, 109, 114–116, 118
Wight, Marcellus, 93, 95
Wilkins, John, 19–20, 207–208, 209
Willard & Sullivan, 90
Willard, L., & Sons, 90
Willard, W. F., 231
Williams, Joseph, 33
Williams, N., quoted, 137
Williams, Thomas, 184
Williamson, Scott Graham, 189
Williamstown, Mass., 100, 137
Wilson, Isaac, III, 66
Wilson, Job, 65–66
Wilson, Joseph, 61, 65, 208–210; dish dated 1764 by, Fig. 26
Wilson, Robert, Jr., 65, 208
Wilson, Robert, III, 65–66
Windham, Conn., 141
Windham, Me., 156, 158, 162–163
Winn, Frank, 71
Windsor, Vt., 137
Winship, Joseph F., 144, 188
Winslow, John T., 168, 219
Winslow, Me., 163
Winthrop, Me., 64, 163
Winton, A. L. and K. B., 198, 199, 203, 204
Wires, E. Stanley, 16, 229
Wiscasset, Me., 63, 156; forms, 156
"Witch" jug, 230
Wolfeboro, N. H., 134–135
Wood, Enoch, 206, 216
Woodbridge, Dudley, 195, 196
Wooden ware, 2, 14, 45, 49, 74, 117
Woodman, Samuel, 138
Woodstock, Conn., 92, 93. See also South Woodstock
Woodstock, Vt., 137, 144, 153
Woodworth, F., 150
Worcester, Mass., 89, 94, 152, 161, 232
Worthen, C. F., 64, 89
Wrentham, Mass., 33, 45
Wright, Caleb, 139–140
Wright, Franklin T., 87
Wyman, 44

Yarmouth Corner, Me., 157–158
Yarmouth, Me., 157–159
Yellow ware, 72, 88, 90, 136, 201, 204, 212, 216, 219

ILLUSTRATIONS

Note: The glaze on the red earthenware in these illustrations is without exception a lead glaze. Unless otherwise noted, it is a clear glaze. White slip on redware assumes a yellow color after it is burned. Although it looks yellow, I have described it in all instances as "light" slip. As body color under *clear* glaze varies greatly, from the nature of the clay and accidents of firing, I have noted colors as they appear. All pieces illustrated, except as noted, are from the collection of the author.

1. (*a*) Typical potter's workshop: Pottery of John Corliss, Jr., West Woolwich, Maine; built *ca.* 1820.

(*b*) Old Ashfield pottery.

2. Pug mill turned by a horse at pottery of Asa B. Lamson, Exeter, N.H.

3. Edward A. Rich working at the wheel in the Paige pottery, Peabody, Mass., August 1906.

5. (*a*) Kiln of Lawrence pottery, Beverly, Mass., after fire of May 14, 1883; Charles A. Lawrence, third from right. (*b*) Sign from Lawrence pottery.

4. (*a*) and (*b*) Glaze mill used by Hervey Brooks, Goshen, Conn. 1814–1864. (Courtesy John Norton Brooks)

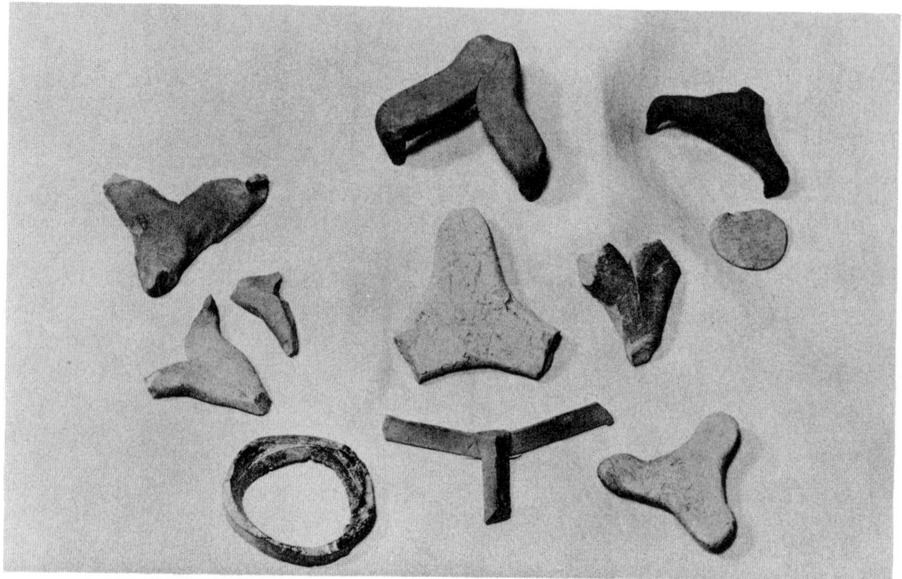

6. Red earthenware cockspurs or stilts for stacking ware in kiln. Top: West Sterling, Mass., and Dorset, Vt. Middle: (*a*) Peter Clark, Lyndeboro, N.H.; (*b*) Ebenezer Morrison, Newburyport, Mass.; (*c*) Thomas Crafts, Whately, Mass. Bottom: (*a*) and (*b*) Teapot factory of Thomas Crafts, Whately; (*c*) Buxton, Maine.

7. Red earthenware setting tiles for stacking ware in kiln. Top: Corliss pottery, West Woolwich, Maine. Middle: (*a*) and (*c*) Peter Clark, Francestown, N.H. (*b*) Jonathan Fenton, Dorset, Vt. Bottom: West Sterling, Mass.

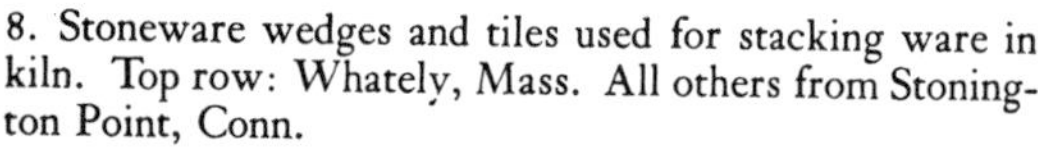

8. Stoneware wedges and tiles used for stacking ware in kiln. Top row: Whately, Mass. All others from Stonington Point, Conn.

9. Red earthenware pitcher. Orange-red. Probably Essex County, Mass., 17th or early 18th century. Perhaps William Vinson of Gloucester. Ht. 11 in.

10. Red earthenware excavated by author on site of James Kettle's pottery, Danvers, Mass. 1687–1710. Background: Unglazed pots, probably part of kiln; roof tile, 7 x 10 in. Foreground: Parts of pots and drinking mugs or pitchers with dull dark brown glaze.

12. Red earthenware jug. Olive green with orange mottling. Tooled wavy line around neck. Early form, perhaps *ca.* 1700. Ht. 8½ in.

11. Shards from the site of James Kettle's pottery, Danvers, Mass. 1687–1710. Upper left: Fragment of plate adhering to kiln brick; black glaze with light slip decoration. Upper right: Section of 15-inch pan; light slip trailing dotted with green on tan ground. Lower rows: Parts of plates and bowls with rolled rims.

14. Red earthenware handled jar. Orange coloring. Tooled lines enclosing combed wavy lines. Salem area, probably very early. Rim broken off during use as churn. Ht. 15½ in.

13. Early red earthenware. (*a*) Jug; greenish-gray glaze, dotted with bright green; ht. 6 in. (*b*) Jug; crackled greenish-gray glaze, showing red body; found in East Gloucester, Mass.; perhaps Joseph Gardner, fl. 1693–1749; ht. 8½ in. (*c*) Herb pot; dull green glaze with markings of bright green; ht. 3¾ in.

16. Red earthenware vase. Yellow glaze brushed with dark brown. Bands of straight and wavy lines. Corresponds in dimensions and decoration to vases made by Peter Clark of Braintree, Mass., and Lyndeboro, N. H.; probably Braintree, *ca.* 1770. Ht. 6¼ in.

15. Red earthenware crock. Natural red color. Decorated with bands of straight and wavy lines. Found in Salem. Early Essex County type. Ht. 8¾ in.

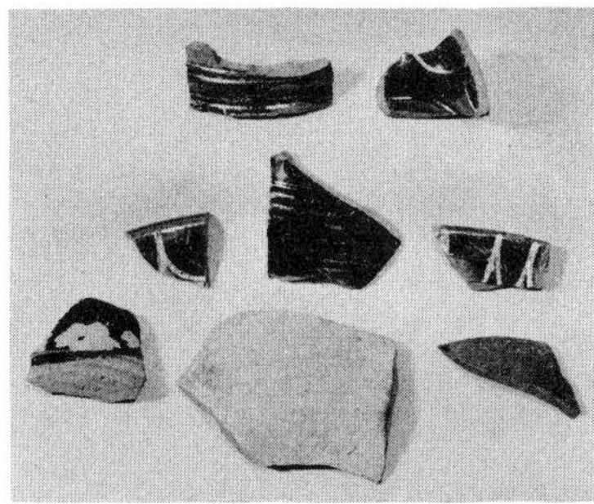

17. Red earthenware shards from pottery of Joseph Bayley, Rowley, Mass. *ca.* 1722–1735. Top: (*a*) Base of black-glazed mug; (*b*) Interior of bowl; loopings of light slip on black glaze. Middle: (*a*) and (*c*) Brown glazed rims of bowl and plate; loopings of light slip; (*b*) Side wall of mug showing band of tooled ridges. Bottom: Mug and milk-pan fragments.

18. Red earthenware ale mugs excavated by author on site of Daniel Bayley pottery, Newburyport, Mass. 1764–1799. (*a*) and (*d*) Brown glaze. (*b*) Black glaze. (*c*) Brown glaze spattered with darker brown. Ht. *ca.* 6¼ in.

19. Red earthenware bowls from site of Daniel Bayley pottery, Newburyport, Mass. 1764–1799. Brown glazes spattered with darker brown.

20. Red earthenware shards from site of Daniel Bayley pottery, Newburyport, Mass. 1764–1799. Top: Teapot, jar rim, cup rim with band of light slip, pitcher bases, glazed base of pot. Middle: Jar, pitcher base, jug, teapot cover, porringer handle. Bottom: Crock, washbowl (cf. Fig. 29), unglazed jar.

21. Parts of red earthenware plates and pans with slip decoration from site of Daniel Bayley pottery, Newburyport, Mass. 1764–1799. Bottom row, middle: diam. 7¾ in.

23. Red earthenware porringer from site of Daniel Bayley pottery, Newburyport, Mass. 1764–1799. Red with decoration of light slip. Ht. 2⅞ in.; diam. 5¾ in.

25. Red earthenware chamber mug from site of Daniel Bayley pottery, Newburyport, Mass. 1764–1799. Slip decoration applied with a brush on yellow-green ground.

22. Red earthenware pan from site of Daniel Bayley pottery, Newburyport, Mass. 1764–1799. Blurred yellow and green glaze. Lines of light slip and initials *W B* dotted with green. Diam. 13¼ in.

24. Fragments of red earthenware chamber mugs with slip decoration from site of Daniel Bayley pottery, Newburyport, Mass. 1764–1799. Bottom row: (*a*) lettered *Betwixt* . . . in light slip dotted with green; (*b*) lettered . . . *ry Ba* . . . (probably Mary Bayley).

26. Red earthenware deep dish. Brown ground. Decoration of straight and wavy lines in light and dark brown slips. Date *1764* in center. Attributed to a Dedham potter, probably Joseph Wilson, Dedham. 1764–1767. Diam. 11⅜ in. (Courtesy Mrs. Arthur M. Greenwood)

27. Red earthenware shards from site of Purinton pottery, Somerset, Mass. 18th century. (*a*) Rim of bowl; dripped brown glaze; cf. Fig. 37. (*b*) Tooled band from wall of black-glazed mug. (*c*) Light slip on tan ground; cf. Fig. 35.

28. Red earthenware mug. Decoration of light slip on orange-red ground. Bands of tooled ridges. Probably southeastern Massachusetts, *ca.* 1750.

29. Red earthenware wash basin. Coated with white slip which appears yellow under a clear glaze. Sponged with dark brown. Ht. 3½ in.; diam. 12½ in. Cf. center fragment, bottom row, Fig. 20.

30. Red earthenware teapot. Brown glaze. John Henry Benner, Abington, Mass. 1765–1796. Ht. 3⅝ in. (Courtesy Dyer Memorial Library)

31. Red earthenware cream pitcher. Orange-red with brown glaze flowing down neck and handle. John Henry Benner, Abington, Mass. 1765–1796. Ht. 4¼ in. (Courtesy Historical Society of Old Abington)

32. Early red earthenware. (*a*) Half-pint ale mug; brown glaze; ht. 3¾ in. (*b*) Mustard pot; variegated ground with green, yellow, and brown tones; brushings of light slip; Newburyport area; ht. 3½ in. (*c*) Flask; brushings of light slip dotted with green on red ground; probably southeastern Massachusetts; ht. 6½ in.

33. Red earthenware plate. 18th-century pan shape. Probably southeastern Massachusetts. Diam. 9 in.

34. Red earthenware plates. 18th-century pan shape. Probably southeastern Massachusetts. (*a*) Decoration of light slip dotted with green on brownish-red ground; diam. 8¾ in. (*b*) Decoration of light slip on light red ground; diam. 7⅜ in. (*c*) Decoration of light slip brushed with green on red ground; diam. 8¾ in.

35. (*a*) Red earthenware small platter; 18th-century pan shape; trailings of light slip on tan ground; probably southeastern Massachusetts; diam. 12 in. (*b*) Red earthenware covered jar; olive-green glaze on cover and shoulder flowing over ground of mottled green and yellow; ht. 8¼ in.

36. Red earthenware of 18th-century type. (*a*) Mug; brown glaze dotted with darker brown; decorated with tooled lines; ht. 5¼ in. (*b*) Mug; black glaze; torn attached label reads: ". . . clay dug and made in Fitchburg . . . given to T. Marshall by his cousin Jon . . ."; ht. 4¾ in. (*c*) Bowl; olive-brown glaze with wavy line of dark slip; diam. 6 in.

37. Early red earthenware pieces. (*a*) Bowl; red brown; dark brown glaze dripping from rim in fine lines; probably southeastern Massachusetts (cf. Fig. 27); diam. 7¼ in. (*b*) Jug; green glaze streaked and spotted with darker green; found in ground at Siasconset, Mass.; ht. 5½ in. (*c*) Jug; reddish ground; dark brown glaze dripping from rim and handle; ht. 4 in. (*d*) Shaving mug; ale-mug form with attached interior cup for brush; orange-red with brown glaze dripping from rim; bands of tooled lines at rim and base; ht. 5 in.

38. Red earthenware covered pitchers and jar. (*a*) Greenish glaze with brown and orange spots; fine reeding around lip; early 19th century; ht. 7½ in.

39. Red earthenware from South Danvers (Peabody), Mass. (*a*) Mug found in old chimney of Joseph Osborn's house; rough black glaze; evidently a waster. (*b*) Miniature jug; red with brushings of dark brown; series of circular slices around shoulder and base; made for Abraham C. Osborn at Richard Osborn's pottery in 1828; ht. 2¾ in. (*c*) Lipped bowl; orange-red with brushings of dark brown; Osborn pottery, Central Street. (*d*) Pitcher; orange-red with brown streaks; bought at pottery of Richard Osborn in 1856. (*e*) Jug; mottled dark green shading to red at base; made by James Chapman Southwick, Lowell Street, before 1841; ht. 8 in.

40. Red earthenware from Pecker pottery, Merrimacport, Mass. 1784–1820. (*a*) Pitcher; light orange-red ground brushed with dark brown; ht. 5¾ in. (*b*) Two-quart jug; mottled orange-red ground brushed with dark brown; formerly owned by Mr. Frank Winn, great-grandson of William Pecker; ht. 9¼ in. (*c*) Quart jug; light ground with red mottling and brushings of dark brown; ht. 7 in.

42. Red earthenware covered jar. Mottled greenish-yellow ground. Dark brown glaze on cover and over shoulder. Probably southeastern Massachusetts. Ht. 6 in.

41. Red earthenware kitchen vessels. (*a*) Mixing bowl; natural red; attributed to Portland, Maine; ht. 5 in.; diam. 10¾ in. (*b*) Gallon jug; orange-red brushed with dark brown; perhaps from Merrimacport, Mass.; ht. 11 in. (*c*) Mixing bowl; olive-brown mottled with orange; diam. 9¾ in. (*d*) Pitcher; orange-brown brushed with dark brown; probably 18th century; ht. 8½ in.

43. Red earthenware jar. Yellow glaze with decorative markings of bright green. Attributed to Seymour pottery, Hartford, Conn. Early 19th century. Ht. 8½ in. (Courtesy Mrs. Nina Fletcher Little)

44. Red earthenware pitcher. Brushings of light slip dotted with green on brown ground. Nathaniel Seymour, Hartford, Conn., *ca.* 1800. Ht. 12½ in. (Courtesy Wadsworth Atheneum)

46. Workshop and house of Hervey Brooks, Goshen, Conn. Shop used 1814–1864. House built 1829.

45. Red earthenware pan-shaped plate. Tan ground with light slip decoration. Type made in Seymour pottery, Hartford, Conn., 19th century. Diam. 9½ in. Fragment of similar plate from Goshen, Conn.

47. Red earthenware plates made by Hervey Brooks, at Goshen, Conn., 19th century. (Courtesy John Norton Brooks)

48. Red earthenware from Connecticut. (*a*) Deep red brushed with black; attributed to Norwalk; ht. 7½ in. (*b*) Covered crock; orange-red brushed with dark brown; ht. 11¾ in. (*c*) Pitcher; bright red brushed with dark brown; Hartford area; ht. 6½ in. (*d*) Pitcher; deep red brushed with dark brown; Hartford area; ht. 8½ in.

49. Red earthenware covered jar. Natural red color brushed with dark brown. Embellished with tooled ridges and wavy lines and row of beading. Southwestern Connecticut type, early 19th century. Ht. 11 in.

50. Red earthenware jar. Brown glaze with streakings of dark brown. Probably Connecticut. Ht. 9¼ in.

51. Red earthenware pie plates from Norwalk, Conn., *ca.* 1800–1850. (*a*) Shallow rounded form with tooled notched edge; word *Cus* . . . in light slip on dark red ground; diam. 10¾ in. (*b*) Shallow rounded form with tooled notched edge; light slip decoration on dark red ground; diam. 10 in. (*c*) Shallow rounded form with tooled notched edge; light slip decoration on dark red ground; diam. 11 in.

52. Red earthenware from Connecticut. (*a*) Flask; red brushed with dark brown; ht. 8 in. (*b*) Pitcher; brown brushed with black; southwestern Connecticut type; ht. 5 in. (*c*) Bottle; orange brushed with dark brown; ht. 7½ in. (*d*) Covered jar; dark greenish brown; Connecticut or Massachusetts; ht. 4½ in. (*e*) Covered spice jar; brown glaze; numerals *19* appear in light slip on cover and on body; ht. 6½ in.

53. Red earthenware from Connecticut. (*a*) Herb pot; deep red brushed with black; ht. 3½ in. (*b*) Bean pot; deep red brushed with black; ht. 6½ in. (*c*) Porringer; deep red brushed with black; ht. 2¾ in.

55. Red earthenware deep pan. Lines of light slip and single wavy line of dark brown on tan ground. Initials *D M A* and date *1830*. Made as a christening present for Dorothy Melissa Ann Goodrich, of East Kingston, N.H. Probably Exeter, N.H. Diam. 13½ in.

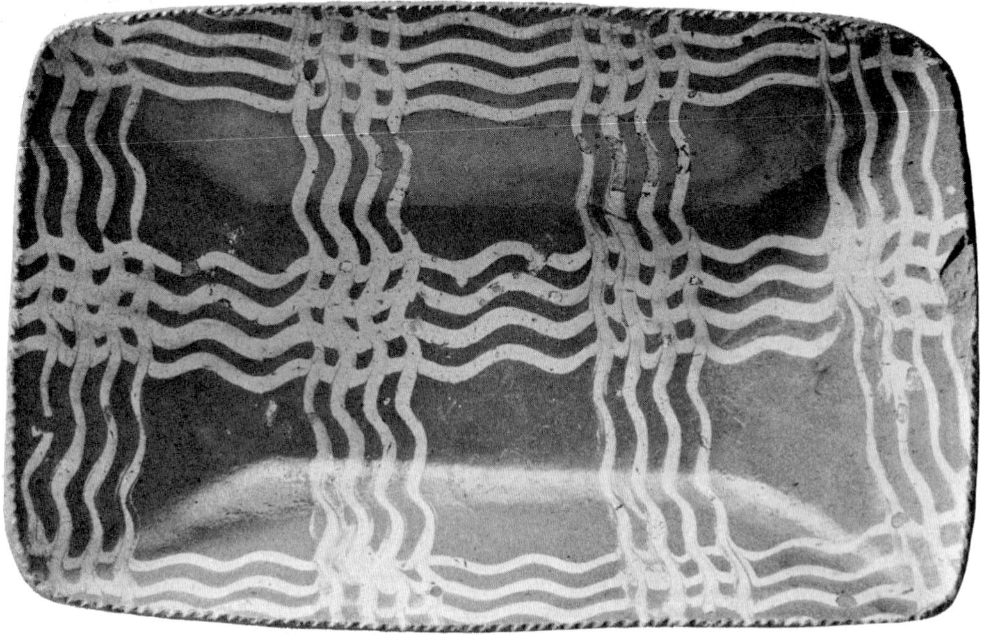

54. Red earthenware tray. Bands of wavy lines in light slip on orange-red ground. A type found on Cape Cod, but possibly made on Long Island or elsewhere. L. 18½ in.

56. Red earthenware mugs. (*a*) Mottled brown glaze; ht. 6¼ in. (*b*) Brilliant orange brushed with black; ht. 4½ in. (*c*) Buff glaze marked with dark brown; Essex County, Mass.; ht. 3½ in. (*d*) Brilliant black glaze; ht. 5¾ in.

57. Red earthenware from Essex County, Mass. (*a*) Pitcher; tan ground brushed with green and light slips; Beverly, after 1866. (*b*) Bowl; greenish ground mottled with orange; diam. 7¾ in. (*c*) Spice jar; light brown glaze with dark brown markings; incised number *60* on cover and base; ht. 6½ in.

58. Red earthenware covered herb or stew pots. (*a*) Greenish brown mottled with orange; Essex County, Mass.; ht. 6¾ in. (*b*) Mottled green and orange; Plymouth, N.H. area; ht. 7¾ in. (*c*) Speckled orange; Essex County, Mass.; ht. 5¼ in.

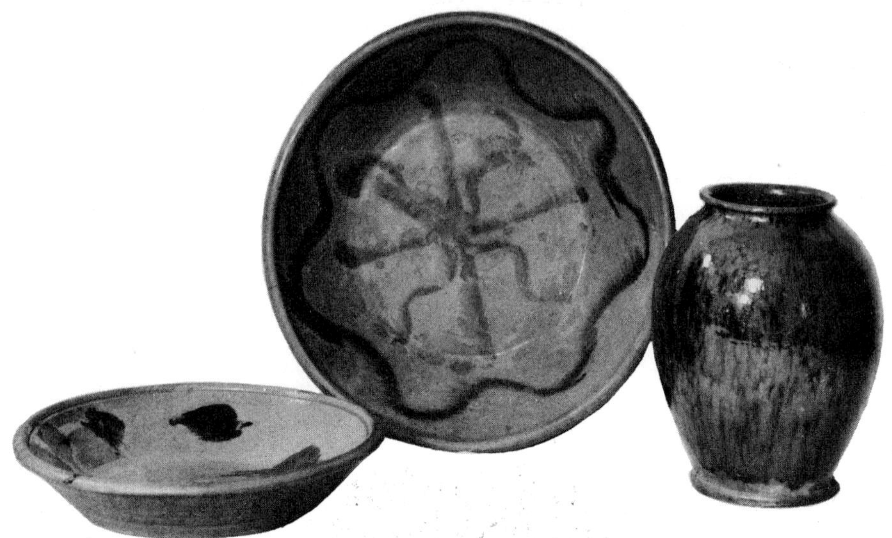

60. Red earthenware pans and jar. (*a*) Red ground brushed with dark brown; probably Connecticut; diam. 10¼ in. (*b*) Brown ground trailed with lines of dark brown; found in southwestern New Hampshire; diam. 12½ in. (*c*) Brown glaze streaked with darker brown; probably Connecticut; ht. 8 in.

59. Red earthenware molds and mugs. (*a*) Jelly mold; mottled brown glaze in imitation of Rockingham ware; diam. 7¼ in. (*b*) Three-pint mug; natural red color; probably Bradford, Mass., early 19th century; ht. 6 in. (*c*) Mug; olive-brown; Bradford, Mass., early 19th century; ht. 4⅛ in. (*d*) Angel-cake mold; variegated greenish-orange coloring; diam. 8 in.

61. Portrait of Thomas Crafts, potter in Whately, Mass., 1802–1861. (Courtesy Miss Mary Persis Crafts)

62. Farm and pottery of Thomas Crafts, Whately, Mass. Workshop in right end of barn. Built 1806.

63. Red earthenware with black glaze. (*a*) Teapot; waster from pottery of Thomas Crafts, Whately, Mass., *ca.* 1825; ht. 6 in. (*b*) Cup; New Hampshire; diam. 3½ in. (*c*) Bowl; 18th-century type; diam. 4¼ in.

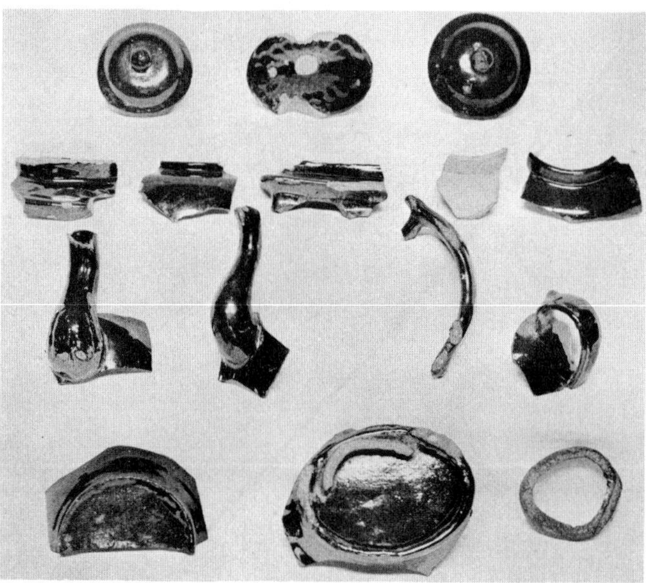

64. Fragments of black-glazed red earthenware teapots excavated by the author on site of Thomas Crafts pottery, Whately, Mass. Manufacture begun 1821. Top row: Covers of round and oval teapots. Second row: Rims of round and oblong teapots. Third row: Noses and handles. Bottom row: Bases and setting ring.

65. Red earthenware from Hews pottery, Weston, Mass. (*a*) Custard cup; light glaze speckled with red and brushed with dark brown; ht. 3 in. (*b*) Jug; variegated greenish-yellow coloring; ht. 8½ in. (*c*) Baking cup; brown glaze on handle and interior; ht. 2 in. (*d*) Vase; orange-red; ht. 5½ in.

66. Red earthenware from Chesham, N.H. (*a*) Covered jar; green glaze with darker green on cover and shoulder; ht. 7 in. (*b*) Bottle in imitation of glass form; black glaze; ht. 6½ in. (*c*) Covered jar; mottled green glaze with darker green flowing down from rim; ht. 11 in. (*d*) Half-pint jug; black glaze; ht. 4 in.

67. Red earthenware plate. Dark brown glaze. Tooled wavy line border. Incised inscription on back: *Concord September th 12 1807*. Perhaps made by Peter Flanders, who started his pottery in Millville, in autumn of 1807. Diam. 12 in. (Courtesy New Hampshire Historical Society)

69. Red earthenware from New Hampshire made by the Clarks. (*a*) Mug; rough brown glaze; incised, *The Hayes and Wheeler Mug/H C S;* made for H. C. Sturtevant at Concord, 1876. (*b*) Miniature keg; yellowish-brown glaze; incised date *1839* on base; Daniel Clark, 2d., Concord. (*c*) Jug; inscribed, *Made by Daniel Clark in Lyndeborough during the year 1792.* (Courtesy New Hampshire Historical Society)

70. Red earthenware from Lowell pottery, Orange, N.H. (*a*) Porringer; made by Elijah O. Lowell, *ca.* 1869; diam. 6 in. (*b*) Cup; made by Elijah O. Lowell, *ca.* 1869; diam. 4 in. (Courtesy New Hampshire Historical Society)

68. Red earthenware from New Hampshire. (*a*) Sugar bowl; orange-red; decorated with tooled wavy lines; type made by Gills at Plymouth and probably also at Boscawen; ht. 3⅛ in. (*b*) Flask; mottled olive-brown glaze; ht. 6 in. (*c*) Vase; brown glaze; decoration of tooled scallops and wavy line; Burpee pottery, Boscawen; ht. 3 in. (*d*) Sugar bowl; natural red color; decoration of tooled scallops and beaded lines; Plymouth and Boscawen type; ht. 4 in.

71. "The Independent Beggar," painting by S. L. Waldo, showing use of porringer. (Courtesy Boston Athenaeum)

72. Red earthenware from Vermont. (*a*) Jar; mottled red, smearings of greenish yellow at rim; attributed to Middlebury (perhaps New Haven); ht. 7 in. (*b*) Covered jar; brownish-gray glaze with spatterings of dark brown; ht. 4¾ in. (*c*) Pitcher; tan glaze brushed with dark brown; bands of tooled ridges; ht. 3¾ in. (*d*) Jug; yellowish glaze; attributed to Middlebury; ht. 7¼ in.

73. Red earthenware from Maine. (*a*) Milk pan; light tan overlaid with area of opaque greenish glaze; diam. 13¾ in. (*b*) Jug; olive glaze dotted with green; incised initials *H P B* and words *Wine jug* on base; ht. 5¾ in. (*c*) Jug; reddish to yellow-green coloring; tooled line indenting body peculiar to work of Matthias Norcross, Farmington; ht. 7¼ in.

74. Sickroom necessities of red earthenware. (*a*) Hot-water bottle; glaze variegated from orange to green and brown; L. 11 in. (*b*) Bed pan; glaze covering entire piece, dark green and orange; overall L. 12 in. (*c*) Feeding cup; brown glaze; John Farmer Clark, Concord, N.H.; L. 7½ in. (*d*) Spitting cup; light glaze speckled and brushed with dark green; ht. 3¾ in.

75. Red earthenware colanders. (*a*) Brown glaze on interior; stands on three feet; southeastern Massachusetts; ht. 8½ in. (*b*) Tan glaze on interior; owned at early period in Sandown, N.H.; perhaps Henry Moulton, Sandown. 1736–1762; diam. 11¼ in. (*c*) Brown glaze on interior; four small feet; Hews pottery, Weston, Mass.; ht. 6½ in.

76. Kitchen utensils of red earthenware. (*a*) Pudding or bean pot; brown glaze on interior; ht. 8½ in. (*b*) Pudding dish; brown glaze on interior; Chase pottery, Merrimacport, Mass.; diam. 12½ in. (*c*) Muffin cups; brown and greenish glazes; ht. *ca.* 2¼ in. (*d*) Cream pot; originally brown glazed; Chesham, N. H.; ht. 10 in.

77. Red earthenware flowerpots with attached saucers. (*a*) Streaked dark brown glaze; attributed to Alfred, Maine; ht. 4 in. (*b*) Dark brown glaze; ht. 9½ in. (*c*) Dark brown glaze; ht. 3¾ in. (*d*) Dark brown glaze; Paige pottery, Peabody, Mass.; ht. 4 in.

78. Flowerpots with attached saucers. (*a*) Stoneware; red-brown Albany slip glaze; molded decoration; found in Alfred, Maine; ht. 4½ in. (*b*) Red earthenware; dull green glaze; Massachusetts; ht. 6¼ in. (*c*) Stoneware; light brown Rockingham glaze streaked with dark brown; found in Alfred, Maine; possibly Portland; ht. 4½ in.

79. Turned flowerpots, wooden implements, and plaster-of-Paris molds excavated by the author on site of pottery at West Sterling, Mass., mid-19th century.

80. Redware from West Sterling pottery. Mid-19th century. Top: Cuspidor, molded flowerpot and unglazed hanging pots, black-glazed hanging pots, one painted. Bottom: Unglazed hanging pots, saucers, and part of log garden seat.

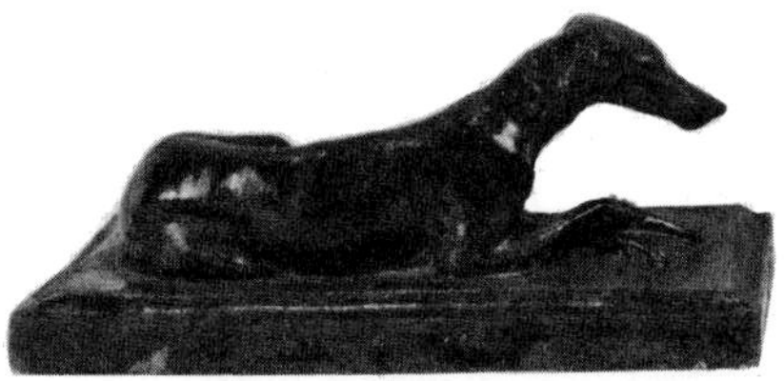
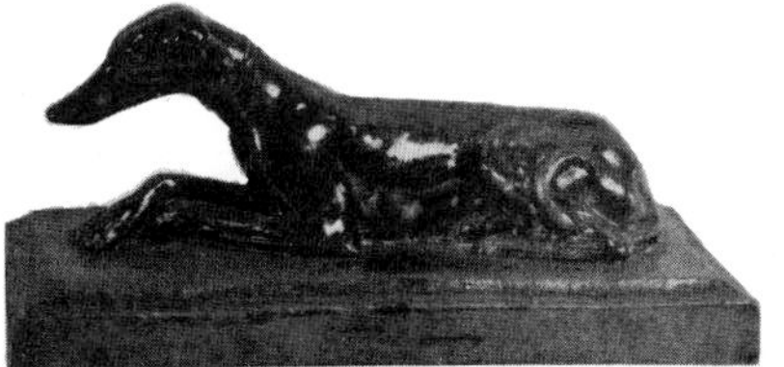

81. Pair of red earthenware grayhounds, West Sterling, Mass. Dull dark brown glaze. L. 5⅞ in. (Courtesy George S. McKearin)

82. Miniature pieces of red earthenware. (*a*) Chamber mug; red; ht. 1¾ in. (*b*) Bean pot; brown glaze on interior, cover, and handle; ht. 2⅞ in. (*c*) Pitcher; brown glaze; probably Connecticut; ht. 2½ in. (*d*) Bowl; brown glaze; diam. 2 in. (*e*) Shaving mug; orange-red; New Hampshire; ht. 2½ in. (*f*) Porringer; red; ht. 1¾ in.

83. Miniature pieces. (*a*) Red earthenware jar; black glaze; New Hampshire; ht. 2¾ in. (*b*) Red earthenware pudding pan; black glaze; Massachusetts; ht. 1½ in. (*c*) Red earthenware pitcher; red brushed with black; Massachusetts; ht. 2¼ in. (*d*) Stoneware jar; salt glazed; ht. 2½ in.

84. Small red earthenware pieces. (*a*) Salve jar; black glaze; ht. 3 in. (*b*) Jug; orange-red with dribblings of light slip; ht. 3 in. (*c*) Salt; mottled olive and orange; ht. 1¾ in. (*d*) Salve jar; brown glaze with darker brown markings; ht. 4 in. (*e*) Inkwell; black glaze; ht. 2 in. (*f*) Jug; orange-brown; incised initials *W K* on center of base, initials *J. A. H.* and date *185–* near edge of base; ht. 4 in. (*g*) Salve jar; greenish yellow; ht. 2¾ in.

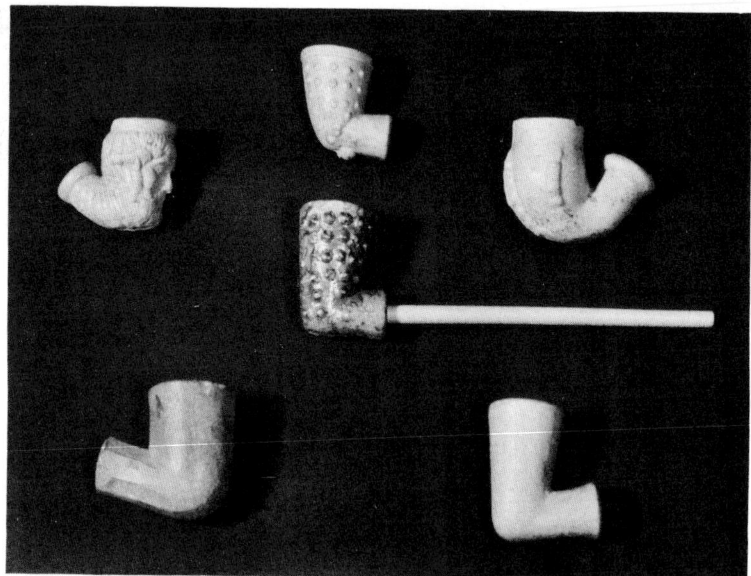

85. Earthenware pipes. Top row: Excavated by the author on site of John Taber pottery, East Alton, N.H. 1864–1872: (*a*) General Grant; reddish-buff biscuit after first firing; ht. 1¼ in.; (*b*) imitation of corn cob; biscuit; (*c*) eagle claw; biscuit; ht. 1½ in. Center: Excavated at East Alton; brown glaze, after second firing; fitted with an original stem; ht. 1¾ in. Bottom row: (*a*) Red earthenware from site of Taber pottery in Wells, Maine; mid-19th century; ht. 1¾ in.; (*b*) red earthenware; source unknown; ht. 1⅞ in.

86. Stoneware pot. Exterior salt glazed; interior unglazed. Warped in burning. Cobalt-blue swashes around handles almost black. Condition and form with vertical handles suggest Charlestown origin in pottery of Grace Parker, *ca.* 1742–1745. Ht. 8½ in.

87. Stoneware pot. Dark gray body. Salt glazed. Initials *H L* and date *1791* in dark blue slip. Abraham Mead, Greenwich, Conn. Ht. 6¼ in. (Courtesy Brooklyn Museum)

88. Stoneware pot. Light gray body. Salt glazed. Marked *Taunton/Pot*. Probably William Seaver, Taunton, Mass. 1790–1800. Ht. 11¾ in. (Courtesy Currier Gallery of Art)

89. Boston stoneware. (*a*) Three-gallon jug; stained brown at lip and base and salt glazed; decorated with band of tooled lines; marked *Boston, ca.* 1800; ht. 15½ in. (*b*) Gallon jug; salt glazed; decorated with tooled lines and with sprays touched with deep blue; probably Boston; ht. 10½ in. (*c*) Pot; salt glazed; impressed bird touched with dark blue on each side; marked *Boston;* ht. 12¼ in.

90. Stoneware pot. Stained rich brown and salt glazed. Tooled and incised decoration. Marked *Boston* and, below Boston mark, in script: *Lydia Osborn*; reverse, in script: *Marshall Timson*. Ht. 10½ in.

91. Stoneware two-quart jug. Upper and lower surface dipped in stain, leaving buff body showing between. Salt glazed. Incised floral spray. Marked *Boston*. Ht. 9 in.

92. Stoneware jug. Rich brown color, dipped in deep brown at base. Salt glazed. Impressed swag and tassel and mark *Boston/1804*, touched with dark blue. Ht. 14½ in.

93. Salt-glazed stoneware from Boston area. (*a*) Covered jar; decorated with tooled lines and impressed swag and tassels touched with dark blue, a motif used by "Boston 1804" in Fig. 92; ht. 9¼ in. (*b*) Jar; bands of swags and tassels touched with blue; probably "Boston 1804"; ht. 5½ in. (*c*) Pitcher; bands of tooled lines; marked *Charlestown*. 1812–1825.

94. Stoneware pot. Salt glazed. Interior coated with dark brown Albany slip. Incised decoration. Marked *Charlestown. ca.* 1812–1825. Ht. 15½ in.

95. Stoneware pot. Salt glazed. Stained brown at rim and base. Decorated with tooled lines and three crosses impressed. Marked *Charlestown. ca.* 1812–1825. Ht. 14 in.

96. Salt-glazed stoneware water cooler. (*a*) Obverse: decoration of incised floral sprays touched with blue and stamped rosettes; marked *Made by T. Harrington/ Hartford/Conn.* (*b*) Reverse: stamped rosettes and tassels; marked *Isaiah Gilbert/West Hartfor./Conn.* Ht. 20½ in. (Courtesy Wadsworth Atheneum)

97. Stoneware three-gallon jug. Salt glazed. Decorated with incised Masonic emblems, bird, and date *1822*. Stamped *L. Watson* in five places. Marked *Goodale & Stedman/ Hartford*. Ht. 17 in.

98. Stoneware gemel bottle. Salt glazed. Tan body with incised birds and stamped words *New Haven*, *ca.* 1830. Ht. 8 in. Owned by New York Historical Society. (Courtesy Index of American Design)

99. Stoneware pot. Salt glazed. Decorated with floral spray in cobalt-blue slip. Marked *Smith & Day/Manufacturers. Norwalk Conn.* 1843–1846. Ht. 9 in. Privately owned. (Courtesy Index of American Design)

100. Stoneware four-gallon jug. Salt glazed. Incised bird touched with dark blue slip on tan body. Marked *S. E. Leonard/ Wallingford, Vt.* Early 19th century. (Courtesy Mrs. Rosamond Niles Moulton)

102. Stoneware four-gallon water cooler. Salt glazed. Dark gray body decorated with cobalt-blue slip and relief figure of Washington. Marked *Hastings & Belding/Ashfield, Mass.* 1850–1854. Ht. 13¾ in.

101. Mid-19th-century stoneware. (*a*) Three-gallon jug; salt glazed; dated *1837* in cobalt-blue slip; probably made by Decius Clark in opening year of pottery at Gardiner, Maine; marked *Lyman & Clark/Gardiner;* ht. 15 in. (*b*) Pot; salt glazed; cobalt-blue slip decoration; marked *Edmands & Co.;* Charlestown, Mass., after 1850; ht. 10¼ in. (*c*) Two-gallon jug; buff body; salt glazed; cobalt-blue slip decoration; marked *Norton & Fenton/Bennington, Vt.;* probably made by Decius Clark. 1841–1845; ht. 13 in.

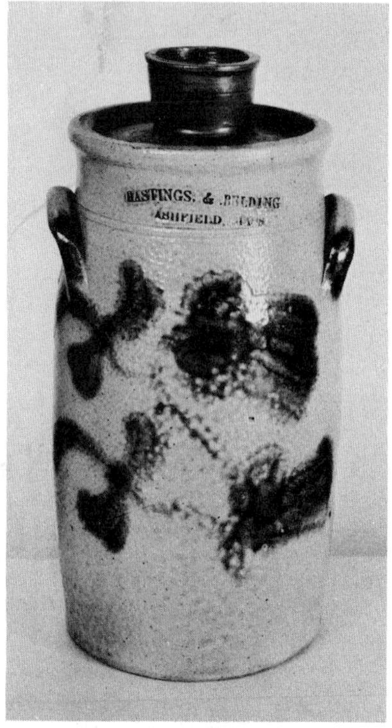

104. Miniature stoneware churn. Salt glazed. Cobalt-blue slip decoration. Marked *Hastings & Belding/Ashfield, Mass.*; reverse: *August, 1852.* Ht. 8⅛ in. (Courtesy Wadsworth Atheneum)

103. Stoneware four-gallon water cooler. Salt glazed. Decorated with floral sprays in cobalt-blue slip and relief figure of Diana. Touches of blue on handle, rim, etc. Marked *Hastings & Belding/Ashfield, Mass.* Ht. 16¾ in. (Courtesy Wadsworth Atheneum)

105. Examples of stoneware from South Ashfield, Mass., displayed in exhibition of local handcrafts at Ashfield House, September 1933.

106. (*a*) and (*b*) Stoneware twelve-gallon water cooler. Salt glazed. Elaborately decorated in cobalt-blue slip with figures of deer, a lion, an eagle, houses, and trees. The three spigot openings and the tooled lines are colored blue. Marked *J. & E. Norton/Bennington, Vt.* 1850–1861. Ht. 24 in.

106. (*a*) and (*b*) Stoneware twelve-gallon water cooler. Salt glazed. Elaborately decorated in cobalt-blue slip with figures of deer, a lion, an eagle, houses, and trees. The three spigot openings and the tooled lines are colored blue. Marked *J. & E. Norton/Bennington, Vt.* 1850–1861. Ht. 24 in.

108. Stoneware two-gallon pitcher. Salt glazed, with lining of dark brown Albany slip. Cobalt-blue slip decoration. Marked *L. & B. G. Chace/Somerset, Mass.* Ht. 12 in.

107. Salt-glazed stoneware from Vermont. (*a*) Two-gallon crock; cobalt-blue slip decoration; marked *Fenton & Hancock/St. Johnsbury, Vt.;* ht. 10½ in. (*b*) Six-gallon crock; cobalt-blue slip decoration; marked *A. K. Ballard/ Burlington, Vt.;* ht. 13½ in. (*c*) Two-gallon jug; cobalt-blue slip decoration; marked *Fenton & Hancock/St. Johnsbury, Vt./1852;* ht. 14½ in.

109. Stoneware grotesque jug. Light greenish-tan glaze. Found in Portsmouth, N.H. Ht. 7¼ in.

110. Connecticut pottery types. (*a*) Stoneware pitcher; salt glazed; cobalt-blue slip decoration; type found in Hartford area; ht. 6¾ in. (*b*) Red earthenware covered jar; deep red brushed with brown; type found in Norwich area; ht. 8½ in. (*c*) Stoneware pitcher; glazed with dark brown Albany slip; marked *W. States;* Stonington Point, 1811–1823; ht. 7½ in.

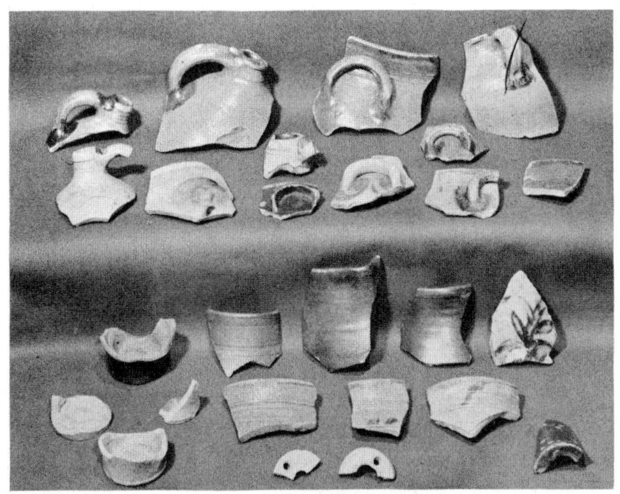

111. Stoneware shards from site of States pottery, Stonington Point, Conn. 1811–1835. Upper rows: Parts of jugs and pots. Lower left: Bases of bottles and small jugs. Lower right: Rims of pitchers glazed with Albany slip, jar rims, and inkwells.

112. Stoneware shards from site of Crafts pottery, Whately, Mass. 1833–*ca.*1860. Upper rows: Parts of jugs, bottles, flasks, butter crock, and crock cover. Lower rows: Walls of crocks and pots, showing blue slip decoration; large fragment marked *Wells, Crafts & Wells.*

113. Stoneware shards from site of Willard pottery, Ballardvale, Mass.; 1880's. Cobalt-blue freehand and stenciled decoration. An example of the continued use of traditional ornamentation in a very late pottery.

115. Molded stoneware cider pitcher. Buff body. Almost black Albany slip glaze. Marked on base *S. Risley/Norwich. ca.* 1840–1850. Ht. 10¼ in.

114. Molded stoneware pitchers from Bennington, Vt. (*a*) Buff body; red-brown Rockingham glaze; marked *Norton & Fenton/Bennington, Vt.* in circular arrangement on base; ht. 10¼ in. (*b*) Buff body; red-brown Rockingham glaze; same mark; ht. 7¾ in. (*c*) Buff body; yellowish-brown glaze; marked *Norton & Fenton/East Bennington, Vt.* in two lines; ht. 10¼ in.

116. Rockingham and flint-enamel wares from pottery of Christopher Webber Fenton, Bennington, Vt. (*a*) Candlestick; cream body; mottled brown and green flint-enamel glaze; ht. 9½ in. (*b*) Candlestick; cream body; mottled brown and blue flint-enamel glaze; ht. 6¼ in. (*c*) Cow creamer; buff body; mottled brown glaze; ht. 5¾ in. (*d*) Book bottle; buff body; mottled brown and green flint-enamel glaze; "Ladies Companion"; ht. 7¾ in.

117. Rockingham and flint-enamel wares from Fenton pottery of Bennington, Vt. (*a*) Toby jug; cream body; mottled dark brown glaze; circular mark: *Lyman Fenton & Co./Fenton's Enamel Patented 1849/Bennington, Vt.;* ht. 6½ in. (*b*) Tile for fireplace utensils; cream body; mottled brown glaze; same mark; L. 8¾ in. (*c*) Tobacco jar; cream body; brown and green flint-enamel glaze. (*d*) Duke of Marlborough toby; cream body; mottled brown glaze; ht. 6 in.

118. Figure of doe. Cream body. Flint-enamel glaze in olive and orange coloring. Circular mark: *Lyman Fenton & Co./Fenton's Enamel Patented 1849/Bennington, Vt.* L. 11½ in. (Courtesy Wadsworth Atheneum)

120. Molded Rockingham pitchers from Risley pottery, Norwich, Conn., *ca.* 1850. (*a*) Buff body; crude mottled brown glaze; ht. 6¼ in. (*b*) Buff body; excellent glaze lightly smudged with brown; ht. 5¼ in. Both marked *S. Risley/Norwich.* (Courtesy George A. Risley)

119. Hound-handled pitcher. Cream body with mottled brown Rockingham glaze. Christopher Webber Fenton, Bennington, Vt., *ca.* 1855. Ht. 10 in.

121. Stoneware hound-handled pitcher. Brown Rockingham glaze. Hunting scenes in molded relief. Marked *Nichols & Alford/Manufacturers/Burlington, Vt./1854.* Ht. 8¼ in. (Courtesy Wadsworth Atheneum)

123. Stoneware pitcher. Buff body. Dark brown Albany slip glaze. Marked *J. T. Winslow/Portland, Me.* Ht. 10 in. (Courtesy Frederick H. Norton)

122. Molded pieces of the mid-19th century. (*a*) Stoneware cookie jar; plain brown Rockingham glaze; marked *Ballard & Brothers/Burlington, Vt.*, 1860's; ht. 10½ in. (*b*) Buff earthenware cuspidor; mottled Rockingham glaze; marked *Boston Earthenware Manufg. Co.*, 1850's; diam. 8½ in. (*c*) Buff stoneware foot warmer; variegated Rockingham glaze; 1850's; ht. 9½ in.

125. Parian porcelain figurines from United States Pottery, Bennington, Vt. (*a*) Lamb on Bible; wool carefully modeled by hand; thickness of Bible reduced; l. 3⅜ in. (*b*) Girl tying shoe; ht. 3¾ in. (*c*) Girl tying shoe; smear glaze; ht. 4¾ in. (*d*) Kneeling child; ht. 3⅛ in. (*e*) Lamb on Bible; cast in mold; l. 3⅜ in.

124. Parian porcelain from United States Pottery, Bennington, Vt. (*a*) Pitcher; unglazed; ht. 5⅜ in. (*b*) Water pitcher; high glaze; ht. 10 in. (*c*) Vase simulating ear of corn; smear glaze; ht. 4¾ in. (*d*) Syrup jug; unglazed; ribbon mark in relief, *U. S. P. No. 11.*; ht. 5⅜ in.

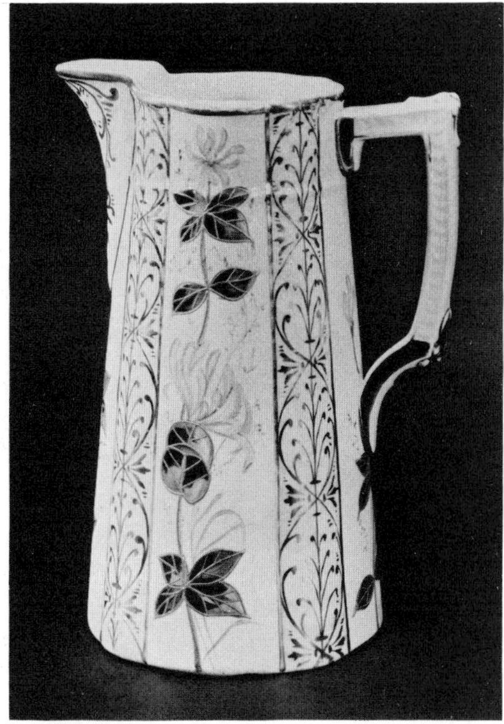

127. Earthenware pitcher. Cream body. Pressed in mold. Panels of chrysanthemums painted in rose, green, and gold, flanked by bands of gold line decoration. Marked *Rieti* in shell. New England Pottery Co., East Boston, Mass., 1888.

126. (*a*) and (*b*) Display of pottery made by A. H. Hews & Co., Cambridge, Mass., at 13th exhibition of Massachusetts Charitable Mechanic Association, 1878.

128. Vases and tile from Robertson pottery, Chelsea, Mass. (*a*) Red earthenware; olive glaze; impressed natural grass design (cf. Fig. 132); marked *C K A W;* 1875; ht. 6 in. (*b*) Unglazed red earthenware; *ca.* 1870; ht. 4¼ in. (*c*) Yellow glaze; marked *Chelsea Keramic/Art Works/Robertson & Sons;* diam. 5½ in.

129. Trial pieces made by Hugh C. Robertson at Chelsea, Mass., *ca.* 1885. (*a*) White stoneware; oxblood red glaze; ht. 4½ in. (*b*) Brown stoneware; green glaze; ht. 5¾ in. (*c*) White stoneware; oxblood red glaze; ht. 7½ in. (*d*) Buff earthenware; mottled light red glaze; ht. 4¼ in.

130. Vases from Robertson pottery, Chelsea, Mass. (*a*) Buff earthenware; gray-blue glaze mottled with brown and gray; marked *C K A W; ca.* 1880; ht. 4 in. (*b*) White stoneware; crackle glaze; floral motif in cobalt blue; marked *C P U S;* 1891–1895. (*c*) Brown stoneware; metallic gray glaze around center of body; marked *C K A W* on raised diamond-shaped lozenge; *ca.* 1880; ht. 5 in. (*d*) White stoneware; light green glaze; marked *C K A W; ca.* 1880; ht. 4½ in. (*e*) Brown stoneware; dark red-brown glaze; scratched initials *L * W.;* ht. 3¼ in. (*f*) Red earthenware; greenish-blue glaze mottled with brown; marked *Robertson & Sons/Chelsea Keramic/Art Works/C K A W; ca.* 1880; ht. 4 in.

131. Rose bowl. Grayish-white stoneware. Crackle glaze. Design in cobalt blue representing wheels and belts of pottery machinery. Presentation piece made for W. G. A. Turner by Hugh C. Robertson, at Chelsea, Mass., *ca.* 1895. Ht. 5¼ in. (Courtesy Mrs. Marjorie Cutting Mason)

132. Tiles from the Low Art Tile Works, Chelsea, Mass. (*a*) White body; olive-green glaze; design of impressed natural grasses; marked *J. & J. G. Low/Chelsea, Mass.* in rectangles, *Pat'd/Feb. 18, 1879* in circle; diam. 6 in. (*b*) White body; light brown glaze; marked *J. & J. G. Low/1881;* diam. 6 in. (*c*) White body; olive-green glaze; impressed naturalistic design; marked *J. & J. G. Low* over crossed keys, *Patent Art Tile Works/Chelsea, Mass.;* diam. 6 in.

133. Plastic sketch by Arthur Osborne. White body. Yellow-green glaze. Signed *A O.* Low Art Tile Company, Chelsea, Mass., *ca.* 1882. Ht. 11 in.

134. Earthenware tea set. Cream body. Ivory mat glaze tinted with rose. Gilded handles and rims. Marked *Hampshire Pottery* in block letters; *J. S. Taft* in script. Ht. of teapot 5¼ in. Keene, N.H., *ca.* 1890.

135. Examples from late potteries. (*a*) Red earthenware vase; green mat glaze; impressed mark *Merrimac* over a sturgeon; Newburyport, Mass., 20th century; ht. 3½ in. (*b*) Vase of sun-baked earthenware; striations formed by use of varicolored clays; impressed mark *Gay Head Clay* on side; Gay Head Pottery, Martha's Vineyard, Mass., late 19th century; ht. 5¾ in. (*c*) White stoneware mug; green majolica glaze shading to red at lip; marked *J. S. T. & Co./Keene, N.H.;* late 19th century; ht. 4 in. (*d*) White stoneware vase; green mat glaze; impressed mark *Hampshire Pottery, N.H.; ca.* 1916; ht. 4¾ in.

136. Examples from late potteries. (*a*) Stoneware vase, hand-modeled; green mat glaze; marked *Grueby Pottery/Boston, U. S. A.*, South Boston; 1897–1907. (*b*) Tile; mat glaze, blue, green, and brown; marked *Grueby/Boston;* 1897–1907; diam. 8 in. (*c*) Red earthenware vase; green mat glaze; marked *W J W;* William J. Walley, West Sterling, Mass., 1900–1917; ht. 7 in.

EARLY NEW ENGLAND POTTERS AND THEIR WARES